CONCEPTS OF DATABASE MANAGEMENT

CONCEPTS OF DATABASE MANAGEMENT

Tenth Edition

Lisa Friedrichsen | Lisa Ruffolo | Ellen F. Monk
Joy L. Starks | Philip J. Pratt | Mary Z. Last

Australia • Brazil • Canada • Mexico • Singapore • United Kingdom • United States

Concepts of Database Management,
Tenth Edition
Lisa Friedrichsen, Lisa Ruffolo,
Ellen F. Monk, Joy L. Starks, Philip J. Pratt,
Mary Z. Last

SVP, Higher Education Product Management:
Erin Joyner

VP, Product Management: Mike Schenk

Product Director: Lauren Murphy

Product Team Manager: Kristin McNary

Product Manager: Jaymie Falconi

Product Assistant: Thomas C. Benedetto

Director, Learning Design: Rebecca von Gillern

Senior Manager, Learning Design: Leigh Hefferon

Learning Designer: Emily Pope

Vice President, Marketing – Science, Technology,
& Math: Jason Sakos

Senior Marketing Director: Michele McTighe

Marketing Manager: Cassie Cloutier

Product Specialist: Mackenzie Paine

Director, Content Creation: Juliet Steiner

Senior Manager, Content Creation: Patty Stephan

Senior Content Manager: Anne Orgren

Director, Digital Production Services:
Krista Kellman

Digital Delivery Lead: Dan Swanson

Developmental Editor: Lisa Ruffolo

Production Service/Composition:
Lumina Datamatics, Inc.

Design Director: Jack Pendleton

Designer: Lizz Anderson

Cover Designer: Lizz Anderson

Cover image: iStockPhoto.com/Viorika

For product information and technology assistance, contact us at
Cengage Customer & Sales Support, 1-800-354-9706 or support.cengage.com.

For permission to use material from this text or product, submit all requests online at **www.copyright.com**.

Library of Congress Control Number: 2019958007

Student Edition ISBN: 978-0-357-42208-3

Loose-leaf Edition ISBN: 978-0-357-42209-0

Cengage
200 Pier 4 Boulevard
Boston, MA 02210
USA

Cengage is a leading provider of customized learning solutions with employees residing in nearly 40 different countries and sales in more than 125 countries around the world. Find your local representative at **www.cengage.com**.

To learn more about Cengage platforms and services, register or access your online learning solution, or purchase materials for your course, visit **www.cengage.com**.

Notice to the Reader

Printed in the United States of America
Print Number: 02   Print Year: 2022

BRIEF CONTENTS

CONTENTS

Contents

Module 3

The Relational Model: SQL

Module 4

The Relational Model: Advanced Topics

Contents

Module 5

Module 6

Module 7

Contents

Module 8

Database Industry Careers

Module 9

Database Industry Trends

Contents

Appendix C

FAQ Reference

Appendix D

Introduction To MySQL

Appendix E

A Systems Analysis Approach to Information-Level Requirements

Glossary

Index

ABOUT THIS BOOK

This book is intended for anyone who is interested in the database industry. As a textbook, it is appropriate for business and computer science students in an introductory database concepts course. Traditional database concepts such as data normalization, table relationships, and SQL are thoroughly covered. Emerging database concepts and trends are explained using realistic, current, and practical examples. Anyone who is currently managing or using an existing database will find the book helpful, given that it describes database best practices and how to create and leverage the benefits of a healthy database. Anyone wanting to enter the database industry will enjoy the book given that both traditional and new careers in the field are carefully explored.

This book assumes that students have some familiarity with computers such as solid Microsoft Office and file and folder management skills. Students do not need to have a background in programming, only a desire and curiosity to learn about how to harness the power of databases.

CHANGES TO THE TENTH EDITION

The Tenth Edition includes the following new features and content:

- Full-color screen shots using Access 2019.
- Extensive coverage of the relational model, including hands-on exercises that guide students through the data normalization process, how to build relationships, how to query a database using a QBE tool, and how to write SQL (Structured Query Language) to create, update, and select data from a relational database.
- Hands-on exercises for creating and using Microsoft Access data macros to accomplish the similar functionality to SQL triggers.
- A new module on careers for those interested in database administration, data analysis, data science, and other related careers in the database industry.
- General information about current trends in database management systems, including the management of "big data," object-oriented database management systems, NoSQL systems, data-driven web apps, and popular software application stacks.
- A new case study, JC Consulting, a web development and data consulting company, used to illustrate skills within each module.
- An updated end-of-module case study, Pitt Fitness.
- Updated exercises for Sports Physical Therapy, the second end-of-module case study.
- New critical-thinking questions and exercises that reinforce problem-solving and analytical skills.
- New data files if using MySQL with the database cases.
- An updated appendix to guide users through the installation of MySQL.

MINDTAP FEATURES

- Integration with SAM and SAM projects, Cengage's leading-edge, hands-on skills assessment management system. These activities provide auto-grading and feedback of students' mastery of Microsoft Access.
- Module quiz evaluates students' understanding of foundational database concepts in each module.
- Quick Lesson concept videos dig deeper into database concepts and innovations to improve students' comprehension.
- Candid Career videos highlight database and data-focused career paths to inform students of various careers and ways to apply their database skills.

ORGANIZATION OF THE TEXTBOOK AND KEY FEATURES

Updated Case Studies

Module 1 covers essential database terminology and examines the benefits of and key factors for a healthy relational database system. It also introduces the JC Consulting, Pitt Fitness, and Sports Physical Therapy case studies and databases that are used throughout the textbook and end-of-module exercises.

Detailed Coverage of the Relational Model, Query-By-Example (QBE), and SQL

Module 2 includes in-depth, hands-on exercises to select and summarize data from a relational database using Access's QBE (Query By Example), Query Design View. Module 2 also covers relational algebra, foundational information for SQL. Module 3 is an in-depth look at selecting and summarizing data with SQL. Module 4 covers advanced topics for the relational model such as indexes, data integrity, security, inner and outer joins, triggers, and data macros.

Normalization Coverage

Module 5 dives into the data normalization process, taking a new list of nonnormalized data from first to second to third (Boyce-Codd normal form) to fourth normal form using hands-on exercises. The module describes the update anomalies associated with lower normal forms. Access queries and tools are used to take the data through the normalization process. Access is used to create new, normalized tables, data is analyzed and updated, fields and data types are properly defined, primary and foreign key fields are created, and lookup tables are created.

Database Design

Module 6 continues the process of building a healthy relational database by focusing on table relationships, again using hands-on exercises to illustrate the concepts. Database Design Language (DBDL), E-R diagrams, and entity-relationship models are all used to document and implement one-to-many relationships between the tables of data that were properly normalized in Module 5.

Functions Provided by a Database Management System

Module 7 covers traditional database management processes and concerns such as the data recovery processes, security issues, data integrity and concurrency issues, data replication, and database documentation features.

Careers in the Database Industry

Module 8 explores the jobs and careers in the database industry starting with the traditional career of a database administrator (DBA), as well as the emerging areas of data analysts and data scientists. Valuable educational credentials and industry certifications are identified.

Trends

Module 9 compares and contrasts historical mainframe database management systems with current data management trends such as distributed database management systems, client/server systems, data warehouses, object-oriented database management systems, web access to databases, XML, and JSON.

TEACHING TOOLS

When this book is used in an academic setting, instructors may obtain the following teaching tools from Cengage Learning through their sales representative or by visiting www.cengage.com:

- **Instructor's Manual.** The Instructor's Manual includes suggestions and strategies for using this text. It includes many ideas for classroom activities and graded projects.

  For instructors who want to use an Access text as a companion to the Tenth Edition, consider *Microsoft Access 2019: Comprehensive* by Friedrichsen, also published by Cengage.

- **Data and Solution Files.** Data and solution files are available at *www.cengage.com*. Data files consist of copies of the JC Consulting, Pitt Fitness, and Sports Physical Therapy databases that are usable in Access 2010, Access 2013, Access 2016, Access 2019, and script files to create the tables and data in these databases in other systems, such MySQL.
- **PowerPoint Presentations.** Microsoft PowerPoint slides are included for each module as a teaching aid for classroom presentations, to make available to students on a network for module review, or to be printed for classroom distribution. Instructors can add their own slides for additional topics they introduce to the class. The presentations are available at www.cengagebrain.com.

Cengage Learning Testing Powered by Cognero is a flexible, online system that allows you to:

- author, edit, and manage test bank content from multiple Cengage Learning solutions
- create multiple test versions in an instant
- deliver tests from your LMS, your classroom, or wherever you want

GENERAL NOTES TO THE STUDENT

Within each major section, special questions or "Your Turn" exercises have been embedded. Sometimes the purpose of these exercises is to ensure that you understand crucial material before you proceed. In other cases, the questions are designed to stretch your understanding into real world application of the concepts. Read the question or exercise, try to answer the question or complete the exercise on your own, and then compare your work against the answer that is provided.

You also will find complementary SAM projects in MindTap, which allow you to apply the concepts learned in a meaningful hands-on project. These critical thinking exercises help you solidify the process and well as solve the problem.

The end-of-module material consists of a summary, a list of key terms, review questions, and exercises for the JC Consulting, Pitt Fitness, and Sports Physical Therapy databases. The summary briefly describes the material covered in the module. The review questions require you to recall and apply the important material in the module. Review questions and exercises include critical-thinking questions to challenge your problem-solving and analytical skills.

ACKNOWLEDGMENTS

We would like to acknowledge all of the talented professionals who made contributions during the creation of this book. We also want to thank those professors and students who use this book to teach and learn. Stay curious!

INTRODUCTION TO DATABASE MANAGEMENT

LEARNING OBJECTIVES

- Examine JC Consulting (JCC), the company used for many of the examples throughout the text
- Define basic database terminology
- Describe database management systems (DBMSs)
- Explain the advantages and key factors for a healthy relational database system
- Prepare for a career in database administration
- Review Pitt Fitness, a company used in a case that appears at the end of each module
- Review Sports Physical Therapy, a company used in another case that appears at the end of each module

INTRODUCTION

In this module, you will examine the requirements of JC Consulting (JCC), a company that will be used in many of the examples in this text. You will learn how JCC initially stored its data, what problems employees encountered with that storage method, and why management decided to employ a database management system (DBMS). You will also study the basic terminology and concepts of relational databases, database management systems, and big data. You will learn the advantages and key factors of a properly designed relational database. Finally, you will examine the database requirements for Pitt Fitness and Sports Physical Therapy, the companies featured in the cases that appear at the end of each module.

JC CONSULTING COMPANY BACKGROUND

JC Consulting (JCC) is a digital development and consulting business. The founder, Jacqueline Cabrero, started the business in the mid-1990s when the Internet became publicly available. Jacqueline grew the business from a sole proprietorship that built static webpages for small businesses to a firm with more than 20 employees. JCC's services range from building websites and web apps to back-end database conversions and programming.

Initially, Jacqueline kept track of her clients and project bids in a spreadsheet. As the company grew, she used a homegrown project estimator program to bid new projects. Jacqueline has now determined that the company's recent growth means it is no longer feasible to use those programs to maintain its data.

What led JCC to this decision? One of the company's spreadsheets, shown in Figure 1-1, displays project estimates, and illustrates JCC's problems with the spreadsheet approach. For each estimate, the spreadsheet displays the number and name of the client, the project estimate number and date, the task ID, a description of the task, and a quoted price for that task. Tri-Lakes Realtors received two different project estimates (ProjectIDs 1 and 31). In the first project estimate, Tri-Lakes Realtors needed general help to establish online goals. In the second estimate, the agency needed help with relational database design and data conversion. The result was seven lines in the spreadsheet, two project estimate numbers, and several task IDs.

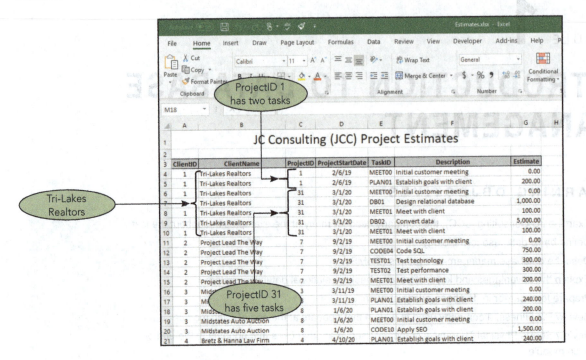

FIGURE 1-1 Project estimates spreadsheet

Data redundancy is one problem that employees have with the project estimates spreadsheet. Data redundancy, sometimes shortened to **redundancy**, is the duplication of data, or the storing of the same data in more than one place. In the project estimates spreadsheet, redundancy occurs in the ClientName column because the name of a client is listed for each line item in each project estimate. Redundancy also occurs in other columns, such as in the ProjectID column when a project has more than one task, or in the TaskID and Description columns when two projects contain the same tasks.

Q & A 1-1

Question: What problems does redundancy cause?

Answer: Redundant data yields a higher frequency of data errors and inconsistencies, which in turn leads to poorer decision making. For example, if you entered "Tri-Lakes Realtors" and "Tri Lakes Realtors" on separate rows in the ClientName column, you would be unsure about the correct version of this client's name. Summarized data about this client would not be complete or correct given the client would be misinterpreted as two different companies because of the two different spellings.

When you need to change data, redundancy also makes your changes more cumbersome and time-consuming. For example, to change a client's name, you would need to update it in each row where it appears. Even if you use a global find-and-replace feature, multiple changes require more editing time than updating the client name in one location.

Finally, while storage space is relatively inexpensive, redundancy wastes space because you're storing the same data in multiple places. This extra space results in larger spreadsheets that require more space in memory and storage. Larger-than-necessary files also take longer to save and open.

Difficulty accessing related data is another problem that employees at JCC encounter with their spreadsheets. For example, if you want to see a client's address, you must open and search another spreadsheet that contains this data because the client's address is not currently stored in the project estimates spreadsheet.

Spreadsheets also have limited security features to protect data from being accessed by unauthorized users. In addition, a spreadsheet's data-sharing features prevent multiple employees from updating data in one spreadsheet at the same time. Finally, if JCC estimates continue to increase at their planned rate, spreadsheets have inherent size limitations that will eventually force the company to split the project estimates into multiple spreadsheets. Splitting the project estimates into more than one spreadsheet would create further redundancy, data organization, and reporting problems. For these reasons, JCC decided to replace the estimating spreadsheet with a **database**, a collection of data organized in a manner that allows access, retrieval, and use of that data.

After making the decision, management has determined that JCC must maintain the following information about its employees, clients, tasks, and project estimates:

- For employees: Employee ID, last name, first name, hire date, title, and salary
- For clients: Client ID, name, address, and government status
- For projects: Project ID, start date, task IDs, task descriptions, costs, project notes, and task notes

Figure 1-2 shows a sample project estimate.

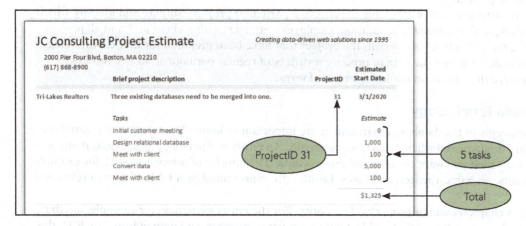

FIGURE 1-2 Sample project estimate

- The top of the estimate contains the company name, JC Consulting, the words "Project Estimate," and company contact information.
- The body of the estimate contains the name of the client for which the project estimate has been created, a brief description of the project, the project ID, an estimated project start date, and one or more line items. Each line item contains a task description and the estimated price for that task.
- The bottom of the estimate contains the total estimated price for the project.

Internally, JCC also must store the following items for each client's estimate:

- For each project estimate, JCC must store the client's address as well as the employee assigned as the project leader for the project.
- For each task line item, JCC not only stores the project ID but also the task ID, the estimated completion date for that task, and task notes. If the task is considered complex or risky, a factor is applied to increase the estimate. The task description and task category (coding, meeting, planning, and so forth) are also stored for each task.
- The overall project estimate total is not stored. Instead, the total is calculated whenever a project estimate is printed or displayed on the screen.

The problem facing JCC is common to many businesses and individuals that need to store and retrieve data in an efficient and organized way. JCC is interested in several areas of information such as employees, clients, estimates, and tasks. A school is interested in students, faculty, and classes; a real estate agency is interested in clients, houses, and agents; a distributor is interested in customers, orders, and inventory; and a car dealership is interested in clients, vehicles, and manufacturers.

The difficult question is not how to manage single categories or lists of information, but how to manage the lists of data and the relationships between the lists. For example, besides being interested in client and project estimate information, JCC also wants to know which clients have received more than one project estimate. The company wants to know which employees are assigned as the lead to which projects and which tasks are most commonly added to which projects.

4

Likewise, a school is not only interested in students and classes but also which students are enrolled in which classes. A real estate agency is not only interested in their lists of agents and homes for sale; they also want to know which agents are listing or selling the most homes. A distributor wants to know which customers are ordering specific inventory items, and a car dealership not only wants to know about their customer base and car inventory but also which customers are buying multiple cars over time.

SELECTING A DATABASE SOLUTION

After studying the alternatives to using spreadsheet software, JCC decided to switch to a relational database system. A **relational database** is a structure that contains data about many categories of information as well as the relationships between those categories. The JCC database, for example, will contain information about employees, clients, project estimates, and tasks. It also will provide facts that relate employees to the projects they manage, clients to their project estimates, and the project estimates to the tasks that are contained within each project.

With a relational database, JCC will be able to retrieve a particular project estimate and identify which client and tasks belong to that estimate. In addition, employees can start with a client and find all project estimates, including the individual tasks within the project that have been prepared for that client. Using a relational database, JCC can use the data to produce a variety of regular periodic or ad hoc reports to summarize and analyze the data in an endless number of ways.

Defining Database Terminology

Some terms and concepts in the database environment are important to know. The terms *entity*, *attribute*, and *relationship* are fundamental when discussing databases. An **entity** is a person, place, event, item, or other transaction for which you want to store and process data. The entities of interest to JCC, for example, are employees, clients, project estimates, and tasks. Entities are represented by a **table** of data in relational database systems.

An **attribute** is a characteristic or property of an entity. For the entity *employee*, for example, attributes might include such characteristics as first and last name, employee number, and date of hire. For JCC, the attributes of interest for the *client* entity include client name, street, city, state, zip code, and whether the client is a government body. An attribute is also called a **field** or **column** in many database systems.

Figure 1-3 shows two entities, Clients and Projects, along with the attributes for each entity. The Clients entity has seven attributes: ClientID, ClientName, Street, City, State, Zip, and Government (whether the client is any type of government institution). Attributes are similar to columns in a spreadsheet. The Projects entity (which represents project estimates) has five attributes: ProjectID, ProjectStartDate, ClientID, EmployeeID, and ProjectNotes. Entity (table) names and attribute (field) names should be easy to understand, concise, indicative of their content, and contain no spaces or other special characters.

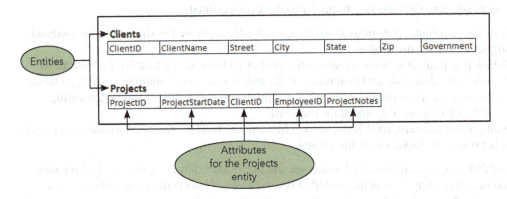

FIGURE 1-3 Entities and attributes

A **relationship** is an association between entities. For example, there is an association between clients and projects. A client is *related to* all of its projects, and a project is *related to* its client.

This relationship is called a **one-to-many relationship** because each client may be associated with *many* projects, but each project is associated with only *one* client. In this type of relationship, the word *many* is used differently from everyday English because it does not always indicate a large number. In this context, the term *many* means that a client can be associated with *any* number of projects. That is, a given client can be associated with zero, one, or more projects.

A one-to-many relationship often is represented visually as shown in Figure 1-4. In such a diagram, entities and attributes are represented in precisely the same way as they are shown in Figure 1-3. A line connecting the entities represents the relationship. The *one* entity of the relationship (in this case, Clients) does not have an arrow on its end of the line, and the *many* entity in the relationship (in this case, Projects) is indicated by a single-headed arrow.

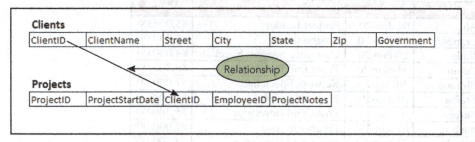

FIGURE 1-4   One-to-many relationship

Q & A 1-2

Question: What happens when the relationship between two entities is best defined as "many-to-many" because one record in one entity relates to many records in the other entity and vice versa? For example, at a college, one student may be related to many classes, and one class is also related to many students.

Answer: A **many-to-many relationship** cannot be directly created in a relational database. To accommodate this relationship between two tables, a third table must be inserted, which is used on the "many" side of two one-to-many relationships with the original two tables. In this case, an Enrollments table could be added between the Students and Classes tables. One student may enroll in many classes. One class may have many enrollments. Two tables that are on the "one" side of a one-to-many relationship with the same table have, by definition, a many-to-many relationship with each other.

STORING DATA

A spreadsheet that is used to store data, often called a **data file**, typically stores data as one large table. Data stored this way is also referred to as a **flat file** because lists in a spreadsheet have no relationships with other lists. A relational database, however, not only stores information about multiple entities in multiple tables but also identifies the relationships between those tables.

For example, in addition to storing information about projects and clients, the JCC database will hold information relating clients to the various project estimates that were created for that client, which employee is assigned as the project leader for that particular project, and more. A relational database can store information about multiple types of entities, the attributes of those entities, and the relationships among the entities.

How does a relational database handle these entities, attributes, and relationships among entities? Entities and attributes are fairly straightforward. Each entity has its own table. The JCC database, for example, will have one table for employees, one table for clients, one table for the project estimates, and so on. The attributes of an entity become the columns in the table. Within each table, a **row** of data corresponds to one record. A **record** is a group of fields (attributes) that describe one item in the table (entity).

What about relationships between entities? At JCC, there is a one-to-many relationship between clients and projects. But how is this relationship established in a relational database system? It is handled by using a common field in the two tables to tie the related records from each table together. Consider Figure 1-4. The ClientID column in the Clients table and the ClientID column in the Projects table are used to build the relationship between clients and projects. Given a particular ClientID, you can use these columns to determine all the projects that have been estimated for that client; given a ProjectID, you can use the ClientID columns to find the client for which that project estimate was created.

How will JCC store its data via tables in a database? Figure 1-5 shows sample data for JCC.

Employees

EmployeeID	LastName	FirstName	HireDate	Title	Salary
19	Kohn	Ali	01-Jan-20	Project Leader	$5,000.00
22	Kaplan	Franco	01-Feb-20	Programmer	$5,500.00
35	Prohm	Nada	29-Feb-20	Customer Support Specialist	$4,000.00
47	Alvarez	Benito	31-Mar-20	Front End Developer	$5,200.00
51	Shields	Simone	30-Apr-20	Network Specialist	$7,000.00
52	Novak	Stefan	01-Jan-19	Project Leader	$8,000.00
53	Anad	Sergei	01-Jan-19	Front End Developer	$5,300.00
54	Allen	Sasha	01-Jan-19	Programmer	$7,000.00
55	Winter	Wendy	31-Dec-20	Front End Developer	$4,300.00
56	Reddy	Kamal	01-Sep-19	Programmer	$6,200.00
57	Yang	Tam	30-Apr-21	Front End Developer	$5,000.00
58	Young	Solomon	01-Jan-19	Programmer	$5,500.00
59	Santana	Carmen	01-Jan-19	Front End Developer	$4,800.00
60	Lu	Chang	01-Mar-19	Database Developer	$7,900.00
61	Smirnov	Tovah	01-Oct-19	Programmer	$6,000.00
62	Turner	Jake	31-Mar-21	Database Developer	$7,800.00
63	Geller	Nathan	01-Jan-19	Project Leader	$8,100.00
64	Lopez	Miguel	01-Jan-19	Programmer	$6,200.00
65	Garcia	Hector	01-Apr-23	UI Designer	$7,000.00
66	Roth	Elena	31-Oct-20	Network Specialist	$7,000.00
67	Horvat	Nigel	30-Apr-24	UI Designer	$6,300.00

Clients

ClientID	ClientName	Street	Zip	Government
1	Tri-Lakes Realtors	135 E Jefferson St	02447	FALSE
2	Project Lead The Way	762 Saratoga Blvd	02446	TRUE
3	Midstates Auto Auction	9787 S Campbell Ln	01355	FALSE
4	Bretz & Hanna Law Firm	8101 N Olive Dr	01431	FALSE
5	Aspire Associates	5673 South Ave	01431	FALSE
6	Bounteous	9898 Ohio Ave	02770	FALSE
7	Netsmart Solutions	4091 Brentwood Ln	01354	FALSE
8	Loren Group	9565 Ridge Rd	02466	FALSE
9	Associated Grocers	231 Tecumsa Rd	02532	FALSE
10	Jobot Developers	1368 E 1000 St	02330	FALSE
11	Harper State Bank	1865 Forrest Dr	01571	FALSE
12	MarketPoint Sales	826 Hosta St	01983	FALSE
13	SecureCom Wireless	5280 Industrial Dr	01852	FALSE
14	The HELPCard	840 Boonville Ave	02466	TRUE
15	Jillian Henry & Associates	815 E California St	02113	FALSE
16	Pediatric Group	4940 W Farm Rd	02113	FALSE
17	SkyFactor	1736 Sunshine Dr	02726	FALSE
18	NuCamp	2500 E Kearny St	01431	FALSE
19	Wu Electric	5520 S Michigan	02447	FALSE
20	Juxly Engineering	4238 Rumsfield Rd	02148	FALSE
21	Carta Training	2445 N Airport Dr	02446	FALSE

FIGURE 1-5 Sample data for JCC *(continued)*

Projects

ProjectID	ProjectStartDate	ClientID	EmployeeID	ProjectNotes
1	06-Feb-19	1	52	Client wants digital solutions to help rebrand company name to emphasize commercial real estate.
2	07-Feb-19	2	63	Client needs help converting, organizing, and managing various sources/formats of donor and donation data.
3	11-Mar-19	3	52	Client wants to establish SEO goals.
4	10-Apr-20	4	52	Client wants to set up an internal server as well as help with a domain name.
7	02-Sep-19	2	63	Client has used the database for several months and now needs new report
8	06-Jan-20	3	52	Develop and implement website SEO strategy.
9	10-Feb-20	6	63	Needs help to manage and organize internal data.
10	31-Mar-21	7	19	Develop new website content.
11	30-Apr-20	9	19	Client needs internal database to manage personnel.
13	30-Nov-20	10	64	Client needs subcontracting help installing a new database for a WordPress site.
14	09-Dec-20	15	19	Client needs new functionality for current JavaScript application.
15	21-Dec-20	14	19	Client needs new functionality for current Ruby/Rails application.
16	04-Jan-21	11	52	Client needs help with server security.
17	15-Feb-21	12	52	Current online sales solution is unreliable.
18	14-Apr-21	6	63	Client needs internal database to manage inventory.
19	04-Jun-21	13	52	Client needs new functionality for current C# / ASP.NET application.
20	30-Jul-21	1	63	Client needs full website reskin.
21	31-Aug-21	16	19	Client needs help with data analytics.
22	30-Sep-21	20	19	Client needs an online reference database
23	12-Nov-21	18	63	Client needs new blog and current pages updated to include responsive web design principles for mobile devices.

ProjectLineItems

ProjectLineItemID	ProjectID	TaskID	TaskDate	Quantity	Factor	ProjectLineItemNotes
1	1	MEET00	06-Feb-19	1	1.00	
2	1	PLAN01	06-Feb-19	1	1.00	
4	2	MEET00	07-Feb-19	1	1.00	
5	2	PLAN01	07-Feb-19	1	1.00	
6	2	DB01	15-Mar-19	1	1.30	Data is stored in multiple spreadsheets.
7	2	DB02	15-Apr-19	20	1.30	Data is not consistent between spreadsheets.
8	3	MEET00	11-Mar-19	1	1.00	
9	3	PLAN01	11-Mar-19	1	1.20	Owner is difficult to pin down.
10	4	MEET00	10-Apr-20	1	1.00	
11	4	PLAN01	10-Apr-20	1	1.20	Two principal attorneys must agree.
12	4	SERV01	11-May-20	1	1.00	
13	4	SERV02	10-Jun-20	1	1.30	Security is a paramount issue.
17	11	MEET00	30-Apr-20	1	1.00	
18	11	PLAN01	30-Apr-20	1	1.00	
19	9	MEET00	10-Feb-20	1	1.00	
20	9	PLAN01	10-Feb-20	1	1.00	
25	9	PLAN10	17-Feb-20	1	1.00	
26	18	MEET00	14-Apr-21	1	1.00	
27	20	MEET00	30-Jul-21	1	1.00	
28	20	PLAN01	30-Jul-21	1	1.00	
29	20	PLAN02	30-Jul-21	1	1.00	

FIGURE 1-5 Sample data for JCC *(continued)*

TaskMasterList

TaskID	Description	CategoryID	Per	Estimate
CODE01	Code PHP	Coding	Hour	$150.00
CODE02	Code C# in ASP.NET	Coding	Hour	$150.00
CODE03	Code Ruby on Rails	Coding	Hour	$150.00
CODE04	Code SQL	Coding	Hour	$150.00
CODE05	Code HTML	Coding	Hour	$100.00
CODE06	Code CSS	Coding	Hour	$100.00
CODE07	Code JavaScript	Coding	Hour	$125.00
CODE08	Perform analytics	Coding	Hour	$100.00
CODE09	Select technology stack	Coding	Hour	$200.00
CODE10	Apply SEO	Coding	Hour	$125.00
CODE12	Create prototype	Coding	Hour	$150.00
CODE13	Code WordPress	Coding	Hour	$100.00
CODE14	Code Python	Coding	Hour	$150.00
CODE15	Create shopping cart	Coding	Hour	$125.00
CODE16	Code other	Coding	Hour	$150.00
DB01	Design relational database	Database	Project	$1,000.00
DB02	Convert data	Database	Hour	$125.00
DB03	Install MySQL database	Database	Project	$500.00
DB04	Install SQL Server database	Database	Project	$500.00
DB05	Install Access database	Database	Project	$400.00
MEET00	Initial customer meeting	Meeting	Project	$0.00

FIGURE 1-5 Sample data for JCC *(continued)*

In the Employees table, each employee has a unique EmployeeID number in the first column. The name of the employee with the EmployeeID value of 19 in the first record is Ali Kohn. His hire date was 01-Jan-20, his title is Project Leader, and his monthly salary is $5,000.00.

The Clients table contains one record for each client, which is uniquely identified by a ClientID number in the first column. The client name, street, zip, and whether the client is a governmental entity are also stored for each record.

In the Projects table, a unique ProjectID number for each project is positioned in the first column. The project start date and project notes are also recorded in fields named ProjectStartDate and ProjectNotes. The ClientID field contains a number that connects the Projects table with the Clients table. In the first record for ProjectID 1, the ClientID value is also 1, which connects with Tri-Lakes Realtors in the Clients table. The EmployeeID value of 52 connects with Stefan Novak in the Employees table.

In the table named ProjectLineItems, each record represents one task for each project. The ProjectID value connects each record to a specific project in the Projects table. Note that the first two records contain a ProjectID value of 1 connecting them with the first project in the Projects table, which in turn connects them with the Tri-Lakes Realtors record in the Clients table. The TaskID column connects each line item with a record in the TaskMasterList table that further describes that task. The ProjectLineItems table also contains fields named TaskDate, Quantity, Factor, and ProjectLineItemNotes, which further describe each task for that project. The Quantity field is used to identify the estimated hours for the hourly tasks. The Factor field is a multiplier that represents additional risk or complexity. For example, 1.1 = 10% increase in perceived complexity or risk for that task. Both the Quantity and Factor fields are used to calculate the price for that task.

The TaskMasterList table uniquely identifies the different tasks that may appear on a project estimate with the TaskID field, and further describes each task with the Description, CategoryID, Per (per hour or per project), and Estimate fields. The Estimate field contains the dollar amount for that task. It is multiplied by the Quantity and Factor fields in the ProjectLineItems table to calculate the total estimated cost for that line item.

The table named ProjectLineItems might seem strange at first glance. Why do you need a separate table for the project line items? Couldn't the project line items be included in the Projects table? The Projects table *could* be structured as shown in Figure 1-6. Notice that this table contains the same projects and line items as those shown in Figure 1-5, with the same fields and data. However, the TaskID, TaskDate, Quantity, Factor, and ProjectLineItemNotes fields contain multiple entries.

ProjectID	ProjectStartDate	ClientID	EmployeeID	ProjectNotes	TaskID	TaskDate	Quantity	Factor	ProjectLineItemNotes
1	06-Feb-19	1	52	Client wants digital solutions to emphasize commercial real estate.	MEET00	06-Feb-19	1	1.00	
					PLAN01	06-Feb-19	1	1.00	
2	07-Feb-19	10	63	Client needs help converting, organizing, and managing donor and donation data.	MEET00	07-Feb-19	1	1.00	
					PLAN01	07-Feb-19	1	1.00	
					DB01	15-Mar-19	1	1.30	Data is stored in multiple spreadsheets.
					DB02	15-Apr-19	20	1.30	Data is not consistent between spreadsheets.
					CODE04	15-May-19	4	1.00	Code SQL to code 4 queries.
					TEST01	03-Jun-19	8	1.00	
					TEST02	03-Jun-19	8	1.00	
					MEET01	03-Jun-19	2	1.00	
					SUPP03	03-Jun-19	8	1.00	
3	11-Mar-19	3	52	Client wants to establish SEO goals.	MEET00	11-Mar-19	1	1.00	
					PLAN01	11-Mar-19	1	1.20	Owner is difficult to pin down.
4	10-Apr-20	4	52	Client wants to set up an internal server as well as help with a domain name.	MEET00	10-Apr-20	1	1.00	
					PLAN01	10-Apr-20	1	1.20	Two principal attorneys must agree.
					SERV01	11-May-20	1	1.00	
					SERV02	10-Jun-20	1	1.30	Security is a paramount issue.
					TEST01	15-Jun-20	16	1.00	
					TEST02	15-Jun-20	16	1.00	
					SUPP03	15-Jun-20	4	1.00	

FIGURE 1-6 Alternative Projects table structure

Q & A 1-3

Question: How is the information in Figure 1-5 represented in Figure 1-6?

Answer: Examine the ProjectLineItems table shown in Figure 1-5 and note the first two records are connected with ProjectID 1 in the Projects table. In Figure 1-6, the entire project estimate for ProjectID 1 is entered in one record. Two task IDs and the other fields that describe the two tasks for that project are entered together in the fields that describe the tasks.

Q & A 1-4

Question: Why does ProjectID 2 have such a large row in Figure 1-6?

Answer: Figure 1-6 shows one row (record) for each project (as opposed to one row for each task). Given that the estimate for ProjectID 2 has nine different tasks, ProjectID 2 requires nine different entries in each of the columns (fields) that describe the tasks for that project.

Figure 1-5 shows a single entry in each field of the ProjectLineItems table. In Figure 1-6, the fields that describe tasks contain multiple entries such as the TaskID, TaskDate, Quantity, Factor, and ProjectLineItemNotes. For example, ProjectID 1 consists of two tasks, and therefore two entries are placed in the TaskID, TaskDate, Quantity, and Factor fields because those fields describe the two tasks for that project. Other projects contain many more tasks and would have many more entries in those fields.

In general, tables that contain more than one piece of information per attribute (column or field) create several problems that can be eliminated with a proper relational database design. The following are some warning signs that your entities, attributes, and relationships are not properly designed:

- You need to enter more than one value in a particular field (see Figure 1-6).
- You are asked to enter two or more pieces of information in a field. For example, using one field to enter both first and last names means you cannot quickly and easily search, sort, and filter on either part of a person's name.
- You are asked to enter both values and units of measure in the same field. Entering numbers and text in the same field generally prevents you from calculating on the numeric part of the data.
- You find yourself adding new columns to handle multiple values for the same type of data. For example, to track employee salaries over time, you wouldn't want to create additional attributes in the Employees table with names such as Salary1, Salary2, and Salary3. A better approach would be to create a Salaries table and relate it to the Employees table. One employee record

would be related to many records in the Salaries table. When an employee earned a salary increase, you would add a new record in the Salaries table for that employee with the new salary value as well as the new salary effective date.

In the tables shown in Figure 1-5, each field is named concisely yet clearly. Each field contains one and only one piece of information, and fields have been created to properly relate the tables in one-to-many relationships. To test your understanding of the JCC data, use the data shown in Figure 1-5 to answer the following questions.

- **Question:** What is the client name for ClientID 10?
  Answer: Jobot Developers

- **Question:** What ProjectIDs and ProjectNotes are connected with ClientID 10?
  Answer: ClientID 10, Jobot Developers, is connected with ProjectID 13, "Client needs subcontracting help installing a new database for a WordPress site."

- **Question:** What are all the TaskIDs that appear for ProjectID 1?
  Answer: MEET00 and PLAN01

- **Question:** What fields are needed to calculate a line item cost estimate for a task such as CODE04 (Code SQL) that requires several hours of effort?
  Answer: The line item cost value is not physically stored in the tables, but calculated using three fields: the Quantity and Factor fields in the ProjectLineItems table are multiplied by the Estimate field in the TaskMasterList table.

- **Question:** What is the Per field?
  Answer: The Per field in the TaskMasterList table identifies the unit of measure for each task. If the task is an hourly task, the value is Hour. If the task is completed once per project, the value is Project.

- **Question:** How is the Per field used in the calculation for the line item cost estimate?
  Answer: The Per field is not directly used in the line item cost estimate. (See the previous question and answer about calculating a line item cost estimate for a task.) If the value in the Per field is Project, the Quantity field value is always 1, indicating that the task happens only once per project. If the value in the Per field is Hour, the Quantity field represents the number of hours estimated for that task.

- **Question:** What is the Factor field?
  Answer: The Factor field is used to increase the cost estimate for a line item based on perceived complexity or risk. By default, the Factor field is 1, but an entry of 1.1 would increase the total line item cost by 10%.

- **Question:** How could you reduce redundancy in the City, State, and Zip fields of the Clients table?
  Answer: You could separate those fields into their own table, perhaps called Zips, and relate the Zips table to the Clients table using a common Zip field. One record in the Zips table would then be related to many records in the Clients table. Doing this would eliminate redundant City and State values in the Clients table.

- **Question:** How could you ensure consistency in the CategoryID field of the TaskMasterList table?
  Answer: You could separate that field into its own table, perhaps called Categories, which stores the individual CategoryID values, one per record such as Coding, Database, and Meeting. One record in the Categories table would be related to many records in the TaskMasterList table. Doing this would prevent the user from entering inconsistent CategoryID values in the TaskMasterList table.

Many database administrators and computer science professionals use a visual way to represent and analyze a database called an **entity-relationship (E-R) diagram** (sometimes referred to as an **ERD**). In an E-R diagram, rectangles represent entities and display their attributes; lines represent relationships between connected entities. The E-R diagram for the JCC database appears in Figure 1-7.

Each of the five entities in the JCC database appears as a rectangle in the E-R diagram shown in Figure 1-7. The name of each entity appears at the top of the rectangle. The attributes (fields or columns) for each entity appear within the rectangle. Because the Clients and Projects entities have a one-to-many relationship, a line connects these two entities; similarly, a line connects the Employees and Projects

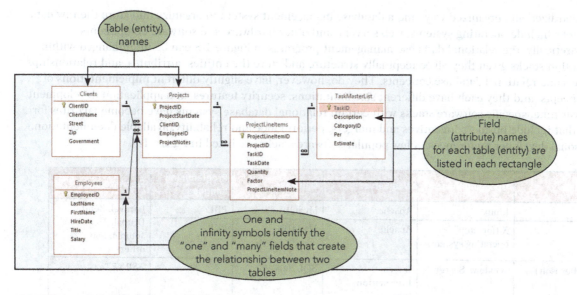

FIGURE 1-7 E-R diagram for the JCC database

entities, the Projects and ProjectLineItems entities, and the TaskMasterList and ProjectLineItems entities. The number 1 indicates the "one" part of the one-to-many relationship between two entities. The infinity symbol (∞) at the end of a line indicates the "many" part of the one-to-many relationship between two entities. Some E-R diagrams represent the relationship lines in a different way. You will learn more about E-R diagrams in module 6.

IDENTIFYING DATABASE MANAGEMENT SYSTEMS

A **database management system (DBMS)** is a program through which users interact with the data stored in a database. Access works well for JC Consulting because only a handful of trusted users will be simultaneously using the application and they are all located in the same building. Fortunately, the relational database design concepts by which you determine and create entities (tables), attributes (fields), and relationships are similar between all relational database management systems, but Access is mostly limited to those situations where a small number of simultaneous trusted users are located in the same physical area.

If the requirements for your relational database application exceed these basic requirements, other relational database management systems that can handle a larger number of users and data, which have more security and application development features, and which can be used across wide area intranets or even the Internet are available as described in Figure 1-8.

Name	Company	Website
Oracle	Oracle Corporation	oracle.com/database/
MySQL	Oracle/Open source	mysql.com/
SQL Server	Microsoft	microsoft.com/en-us/sql-server/default.aspx
PostgreSQL	Open source	postgresql.org/
Db2	IBM	ibm.com/products/db2-database
SQLite	Open source	sqlite.org
MariaDB	Open source	mariadb.org/
Access	Microsoft	products.office.com/en-us/access

FIGURE 1-8 Popular relational database management system software

A **software stack** (also called a solution stack or technology stack) groups several software components that are commonly used to build a new application. A software stack often includes a programming language such as C#, Java, PHP, Ruby, or Python; a framework that provides tools to help write code and applications in a standardized and organized way; and a database management system to organize and store the raw data. Some stacks include operating systems, web servers, and other hardware and software components.

Theoretically, the relational database management programs in Figure 1-8 can be interchanged within most solution stacks given they all conceptually structure and store the entities, attributes, and relationships using the same relational database concepts. They do, however, have slightly different implementations of these concepts, and they each have different size limitations, security features, and application development tools. Over time, specific software stacks with certain relational database systems have become favorites for reasons that include business incentives and mergers, performance and reliability, available documentation, and personal developer preferences. A few popular software stacks are listed in Figure 1-9.

Stack Name	Operating System	Web Server	Database	Programming Language	Framework(s)
LAMP	Linux	Apache	MySQL	PHP	Laravel, Zend, Drupal, Joomla, and others
XAMP	X (for "any" operating system)	Apache	MariaDB	PHP	
WINS (Microsoft)	Windows Server	Internet Information Services	SQL Server	C#	ASP.NET
Ruby on Rails			SQLite or PostgreSQL	Ruby	Rails

FIGURE 1-9 Popular software stacks

Q & A 1-5

Question: Which DBMS should JC Consulting use to create and maintain its database?

Answer: Because JCC's relational database needs fit within the size and location constraints of Microsoft Access, and because Access has excellent built-in application development tools such as query, form, and report generation features, the company should elect to use Access as their initial DBMS. As JCC grows, they can export and migrate their data to other relational database management systems that are designed for larger sets of data, better performance, higher integration with other software stacks, and additional security features.

The **database design** phase is the process of creating the entities, attributes, and relationships between the tables of data shown in Figure 1-5. When that is completed, the database developer creates **forms**, screen objects used to maintain and view data from a database. Employees then use these forms to find, enter, and edit data.

The form that employees use to enter the tasks that may appear on each project estimate is shown in Figure 1-10. Employees can use this form to enter a new task; to view, change, or delete an existing task; or to print the information for a task. Using the form development tools provided by Access, you can create the form without having programming knowledge.

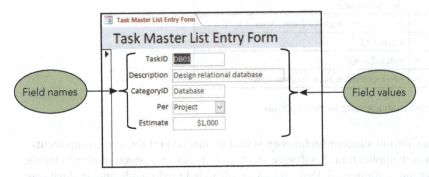

FIGURE 1-10 Task Master List Entry Form

A more complicated form for entering the information needed for each project estimate is shown in Figure 1-11. This form displays data about each project using data from the Clients, Projects, and ProjectLineItems tables.

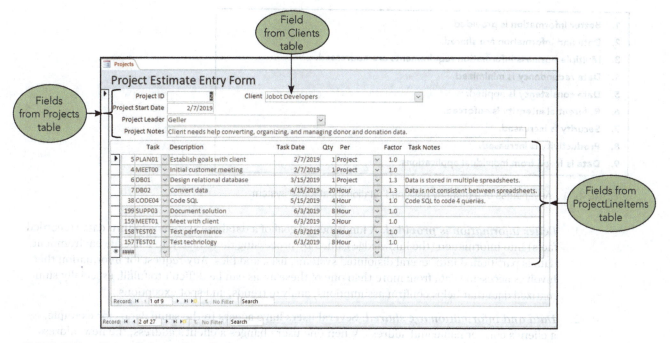

FIGURE 1-11   Project Estimate Entry Form

JCC can create the **reports** it needs using the report generation tools provided by Access. The Project Estimates report, which lists the client, project notes, project ID, project start date, and task information for each project, is shown in Figure 1-12.

Project Estimates

Client	Project Notes			ProjectID	Start Date
Associated Grocers	Client needs internal database to manage personnel.			11	4/30/2020
	Tasks	**Per**	**Quantity**	**Factor**	**Estimate**
	Initial customer meeting	Project	1	1.0	0
	Establish goals with client	Project	1	1.0	200
	Install SQL Server database	Project	1	1.0	500
	Code SQL	Hour	40	1.0	6,000
	Document solution	Hour	8	1.0	800
	Create maintenance agreement	Project	4	1.0	600
	Monthly maintenance	Month	12	1.0	1,200
					$1,200
Bounteous	Needs help to manage and organize internal data.			9	2/10/2020
	Tasks	**Per**	**Quantity**	**Factor**	**Estimate**
	Initial customer meeting	Project	1	1.0	0

FIGURE 1-12   Project Estimates report

ADVANTAGES OF A PROPERLY DESIGNED RELATIONAL DATABASE

The relational database approach to organizing and managing data offers several clear advantages over alternative data management methods. These advantages are listed in Figure 1-13.

1. Better information is provided.
2. Data and information are shared.
3. Multiple business information requirements are addressed.
4. Data redundancy is minimized.
5. Data consistency is applied.
6. Referential integrity is enforced.
7. Security is increased.
8. Productivity is increased.
9. Data is freed from individual applications.

FIGURE 1-13 Advantages of a properly designed relational database system

1. *Better information is provided.* A fundamental goal of a database system is to turn data (recorded facts) into information (the knowledge gained by processing those facts). In a flat-file environment, data is partitioned into several disjointed systems, lists, and files. Any request for information that involves accessing data from more than one of these areas can be difficult to fulfill, especially summarized data that helps confirm assumptions, analyze trends, and spot exceptions.

2. *Data and information are shared.* Several users have access to the same data—for example, a client's correct name and address. When one user changes a client's address, the new address immediately becomes available to all users.

3. *Multiple business information requirements are addressed.* For the database approach to function adequately within an organization, a person or group should be in charge of the database, especially if the database will serve many users. This person or group is often called the **database administrator** or **database administration (DBA)**. By keeping the overall needs of the organization in mind, a DBA can structure the database to benefit the entire organization, not just a single group.

4. *Data redundancy is minimized.* With database processing, data that formerly was kept in separate file-oriented systems is integrated into a single database, so multiple copies of the same data are minimized. Minimizing data redundancy makes the process of updating data simpler and less error prone.

5. *Data consistency is applied.* Using a relational database, attribute values (field values) are entered consistently, which helps users correctly find, filter, and analyze the data. For example, a properly organized relational database will not allow a user to enter a State field value in different ways (TX versus Texas).

6. *Referential integrity is enforced.* **Referential integrity** is a relational database concept that sets rules called **integrity constraints** on table relationships primarily to prevent the creation of orphan records. **Orphan records** are records in an entity (table) on the "many" side of a relationship that do not have a matching record with the entity (table) on the "one" side of a relationship.

   For example, a project estimate cannot be created for a client that doesn't yet exist in the database because that would create a project for an unknown client. Also, a client cannot be deleted from the database if it has related projects as that would also create projects with unknown clients. A database has **integrity** when the data in it satisfies all established integrity constraints.

7. *Security is increased.* A secure DBMS will have features such as the assignment of user IDs, groups, passwords, and permissions that allow access to certain areas of the database. A secure DBMS will also provide for data **encryption**, which protects the data as it moves through a network. Other processes that some DBMS systems provide to ensure data security are methods to prevent and recover from data corruption, protections from unauthorized access and malware attacks, and automatic rollbacks and backups to provide reliable starting points in the event of a security breach.

8. ***Productivity is increased.*** With a DBMS, the programmers who are writing programs that use data from the database do not have to engage in mundane data manipulation activities, such as adding new data and deleting existing data, thus making the programmers more productive. These features increase the productivity of programmers as well as nonprogrammers, who may be able to get the results they seek from the data in a database without waiting for a program to be written for them. Accurate, reliable data and reports improve the productivity as well as the effectiveness of all analysts, managers, and employees who use the information.

9. ***Data is freed from individual applications.*** A good DBMS provides **data independence**, a quality that allows you to change the structure of a database without requiring major changes to the programs that access the database. Without data independence, programmers often need to expend effort to update programs to match the new database structure. The presence of many programs in the system can make this effort so prohibitively difficult that management might decide to avoid changing the database, even though the change might improve the database's performance or add valuable data.

Q & A 1-6

Question: What is data security?

Answer: **Data security** is protection of data from threats and includes preventing unauthorized access to the database, encrypting data as it travels through a network, protecting against data corruption, and protecting against all other electronic and physical attacks to the data.

Key Factors for a Healthy Relational Database

While the advantages of a relational database are compelling, they are predicated on the relational database being healthy. Figure 1-14 identifies some of the key factors for developing and maintaining a healthy relational database system.

```
1.  Design.
2.  Security.
3.  Talent.
```

FIGURE 1-14   Key factors for a healthy relational database system

1. ***Design.*** If the database is not designed properly, meaning that if the entities, attributes, and relationships are not correctly identified and created, it is difficult to enter, edit, find, and analyze data. Improperly designed relational databases mean that queries and reports may be incomplete, inconsistent, or inaccurate, which undermines high-quality decisions.

    In addition, entity (table) and attribute (field) names should be as short as possible, yet long enough to be clear and descriptive. Naming conventions should be established and applied so that all developers can easily read and maintain the relational database system. Poor naming conventions or lack of programming standards and disciplines creates unnecessary confusion and costly programming mistakes.

2. ***Security.*** When several users are sharing the same database, a security breach to the database has a dramatic impact on the business. Security and backup processes and protocols need to be established. A business must commit to hiring experienced talent and modern tools and resources to protect any data that is vital to the operation of the company.

3. ***Talent.*** The process of creating, maintaining, and securing a healthy relational database requires a high level of talent and experience. A business must commit to either hiring or training individuals that can successfully manage these important responsibilities.

BIG DATA

Companies have access to more and different kinds of data than ever before. The term **big data** describes the large volume of data produced by every digital process, system, sensor, mobile device, and even social media exchange. To extract meaningful information from big data, companies need optimal processing power, analytics capabilities, and up-to-date technical skills.

Big data may be structured, unstructured, or a combination of both. **Structured data** is traditional in its retrieval and storage DBMS, similar to the data in the JCC database in this module. **Unstructured data** is not organized or easily interpreted by traditional databases or data models. Unstructured data may involve **metadata**—descriptive data stored with input sources.

Q & A 1-7

Question: What are other examples of unstructured data?

Answer: Twitter tweets, Facebook photographs, blog postings, and other web-based media are good examples of unstructured data.

Unstructured data is often stored in nonrelational database systems. The term **NoSQL** refers to a database management system such as MongoDB that uses a document model made up of collections and documents to store data.

Insights derived from big data enable companies to make better decisions about trends, customer engagement, threats, and new revenue streams. Big data is a source for ongoing discovery and analysis, and the demand for information from big data will require new approaches to database management, architecture, tools, and practices.

PREPARING FOR A CAREER IN DATABASE ADMINISTRATION AND DATA ANALYSIS

Database administrators (DBAs) manage and maintain database management systems and software. Their responsibilities range from managing the physical aspects of the database such as installing, maintaining, and testing hardware and software to designing and improving the database to provide efficient and effective access to the information. Most DBAs for large companies have college degrees and certifications from software vendors.

Data analysts use tools and algorithms to mine a database for answers, information, trends, and insights. An **algorithm** is a set of rules, calculations, and assumptions used to solve a problem. For example, a data analyst might apply an algorithm that includes historical information about product sales and advertising to project future sales. Data analysts in one company might be called business analysts, operations research analysts, management analysts, statisticians, or data scientists in another depending on their focus and responsibilities. Data analysts generally have a college degree and command a healthy annual salary.

Q & A 1-8

Question: What are typical salaries for a database administrator and data analyst?

Answer: According to the US Department of Labor, Bureau of Labor Statistics, the median annual salary for database administrators was over $90,000 per year in 2018, and job growth outlook was faster than average. (See https://www.bls.gov/ooh/computer-and-information-technology/database-administrators.htm.) The US Department of Labor also reports that Management Analysts have faster than average job opportunity growth and command a median annual salary of over $80,000. (See https://www.bls.gov/ooh/business-and-financial/management-analysts.htm.)

INTRODUCTION TO THE PITT FITNESS DATABASE CASE

Pitt Fitness is a chain of three fitness centers that offer classes to the residents of Pittsburgh, Pennsylvania. The centers design the classes for all ages and do not charge a monthly fee. The owners of Pitt Fitness have found that their clients enjoy the concept of paying per class, resulting in a lively revenue stream with this model.

The managers at Pitt Fitness use a database management system to record their customers, instructors, classes, and class reservations. Figure 1-15 displays the instructors that work at Pitt Fitness. Each instructor is

Instructors

InstructorID	InstructorLastName	InstructorFirstName	InstructorStreetAddress	InstructorCity	InstructorState	InstructorZipCode	InstructorEmailAddress	InstructorPhoneNumber
JV01	Varlano	Juan	15A Penn Ave	Pittsburgh	PA	15219	JuanVarlano@cengage.com	412-998-6534
LL01	Lane	Luke	2661 Butler St	Pittsburgh	PA	15201	LukeCLane@cengage.com	561-868-5257
MA01	Nguyen	Michael	2367 Barn Way	Pittsburgh	PA	15219	MichaelNguyen@cengage.com	951-790-6275
MD01	D'Angelo	Maria	245D Wylie Ave	Pittsburgh	PA	15219	MariaDAngelo@cengage.com	724-887-2835
MK01	Kobinski	Megan	9087 Monanca Pl	Pittsburgh	PA	15219	MeganKobinski@cengage.com	878-653-7364
MS01	Said	Memo	45 Webster Ave	Pittsburgh	PA	15219	MemoSaid@cengage.com	412-764-9834
NT01	Tahan	Neda	4588 Penn Ave	Pittsburgh	PA	15219	NedaTahan@cengage.com	417-359-2241
RS01	Stein	Raymond	3254 Forward Ave	Pittsburgh	PA	15217	RaymondStein@cengage.com	269-345-0803
RS02	Sisto	Robert	2836 Maryland Ave	Pittsburgh	PA	15232	RobertJSisto@cengage.com	646-373-8125
VP01	Pegues	Vicki	3700 Murray Ave	Pittsburgh	PA	15217	VickiJPegues@cengage.com	678-597-0247

FIGURE 1-15 Instructor data for Pitt Fitness

identified by a unique InstructorID, which contains two letters and two numbers. Other information about the instructors are their full name, street address, email address, and telephone number.

Figure 1-16 shows some of the classes that Pitt Fitness offers. Each class has a ClassID, which is a unique identification number. Other class information includes class name, center and room identification, length of time, maximum size, category, day of the week and time, plus a brief description.

Classes

ClassID	ClassName	Room	Location	LengthOfTime	MaxSize	TypeOfClass	Day	Time	Description
1	Combination	159B	Shadyside	60	40	Combo	Saturday	9:00	Cardio, strength, flexibility
2	Yogalates	342	Downtown	60	25	Core	Monday	6:00	Yoga and Pilates fundamentals
3	Barbell Power	Main	Oakland	60	25	Strength	Tuesday	8:00	Barbell program
4	Intense Cycle	163	Shadyside	30	25	Cardio	Saturday	10:00	Sprint
5	Zumba	159B	Shadyside	60	25	Cardio	Saturday	10:00	Zumba dance
6	Low Impact Aerobics	Main	Oakland	60	25	Cardio	Tuesday	11:00	Low impact aerobics
7	Yoga	342	Downtown	60	25	Core	Tuesday	7:00	Traditional yoga
8	Yoga Balance	Main	Oakland	60	25	Core	Thursday	8:00	Balance yoga
9	Barre	Main	Oakland	60	25	Core	Thursday	9:00	Pilates yoga and aerobics
10	Barre Limited	342	Downtown	30	25	Core	Wednesday	17:30	Barre brief
11	Maturity Endurance and Strength	Main	Oakland	60	25	Strength	Friday	10:30	Cardio, strength, flexibility for older adults
12	Maturity Classics	159B	Shadyside	60	25	Strength	Wednesday	7:00	Strength and movement for older adults
13	Agility for Seniors	Main	Oakland	60	25	Core	Friday	9:30	Agility for older adults
14	HIIT	315	Downtown	30	25	Cardio	Thursday	18:00	High intensity interval drills
15	Bootcamp	159B	Shadyside	30	25	Cardio	Saturday	11:00	Weight training and cardio
16	Cycle	320	Downtown	60	25	Cardio	Friday	6:30	Sprints and climbs
17	Cycle and Strength	163	Shadyside	60	25	Cardio	Sunday	12:30	Cycle and strength
18	Aquasize	Pool	Oakland	60	25	Cardio	Tuesday	14:00	Low impact cardio water exercise
19	Aqua Strength and Cardio	125P	Shadyside	60	25	Cardio	Wednesday	6:00	Strength and cardio in the water
20	Aqua Calm	Pool	Oakland	45	25	Strength	Tuesday	13:00	Low impact water exercise
21	Combination	159B	Shadyside	60	40	Combo	Sunday	9:00	Cardio, strength, flexibility
22	Yogalates	342	Downtown	60	25	Core	Tuesday	6:00	Yoga and Pilates fundamentals
23	Barbell Power	Main	Oakland	60	25	Strength	Wednesday	8:00	Barbell program
24	Intense Cycle	163	Shadyside	30	25	Cardio	Sunday	10:00	Sprint
25	Zumba	159B	Shadyside	60	25	Cardio	Sunday	10:00	Zumba dance
26	Low Impact Aerobics	Main	Oakland	60	25	Cardio	Wednesday	11:00	Low impact aerobics
27	Yoga	342	Downtown	60	25	Core	Wednesday	6:00	Traditional yoga
28	Yoga Balance	Main	Oakland	60	25	Core	Friday	8:00	Balance yoga
29	Barre	Main	Oakland	60	25	Core	Friday	9:00	Pilates yoga and aerobics
30	Barre Limited	342	Downtown	30	25	Core	Thursday	17:30	Barre brief
31	Maturity Endurance and Strength	Main	Oakland	60	25	Strength	Saturday	10:30	Cardio, strength, flexibility for older adults
32	Maturity Classics	159B	Shadyside	60	25	Strength	Thursday	7:00	Strength and movement for older adults
33	Agility for Seniors	Main	Oakland	60	25	Core	Saturday	9:30	Agility for older adults
34	HIIT	315	Downtown	30	25	Cardio	Friday	18:00	High intensity interval drills
35	Bootcamp	159B	Shadyside	30	25	Cardio	Sunday	11:00	Weight training and cardio
36	Cycle	320	Downtown	60	25	Cardio	Saturday	6:30	Sprints and climbs
37	Cycle and Strength	163	Shadyside	60	25	Cardio	Monday	12:30	Cycle and strength
38	Aquasize	Pool	Oakland	60	25	Cardio	Wednesday	14:00	Low impact cardio water exercise
39	Aqua Strength and Cardio	125P	Shadyside	60	25	Cardio	Thursday	6:00	Strength and cardio in the water
40	Aqua Calm	Pool	Oakland	45	25	Strength	Wednesday	13:00	Low impact water exercise

FIGURE 1-16 Class data for Pitt Fitness

Figure 1-17 shows customer data for Pitt Fitness. Each customer is identified by a unique customer number. In addition, management stores each customer's last name, first name, street address, city, state, zip code, email address, phone number, and birth date.

Figure 1-18 shows reservations data for Pitt Fitness. Each reservation is identified by a unique number that uses the last two digits of the current year followed by a five-digit number that is incremented

Customers

CustomerID	LastName	FirstName	StreetAddress	City	State	ZipCode	EmailAddress	PhoneNumber	BirthDate
101	Aboud	Nour	4898 Negley Ave	Pittsburgh	PA	15232	NourAboud@cengage.com	412-255-5443	02-23-1998
102	Waldron	Tony	766 Myrtle Way	Pittsburgh	PA	15232	TonyLWaldron@cengage.com	617-825-9347	08-23-1989
103	Arian	Farah	998 Forward Ave	Pittsburgh	PA	15217	FarahArian@cengage.com	878-243-9786	10-21-2000
104	Cane	James	4310 Elmer St	Pittsburgh	PA	15232	JamesJCane@cengage.com	610-555-9951	02-01-1967
105	Brescia	Keith	1595 Holden St	Pittsburgh	PA	15232	KeithWBrescia@cengage.com	724-943-0945	06-11-1948
106	Conner	Don	3004 Alder St	Pittsburgh	PA	15232	DonSConner@cengage.com	412-281-0129	05-18-1957
107	Feldman	Terrance	2158 Semple St	Pittsburgh	PA	15213	TerranceLFeldman@cengage.com	559-673-4340	12-09-1987
108	Gregor	Alice	392 Murray Ave	Pittsburgh	PA	15217	AliceRGregor@cengage.com	770-832-4718	02-16-1957
109	Miller	Roland	2542 York Way	Pittsburgh	PA	15213	RolandJMiller@cengage.com	412-266-5419	04-20-1984
110	Sanchez	Ramiro	4983 McKee Pl	Pittsburgh	PA	15213	RamiroSanchez@cengage.com	878-576-5221	04-01-1953
111	Barry	Juan	4534 Urie Way	Pittsburgh	PA	15213	JuanRBarry@cengage.com	210-444-4773	01-03-1958
112	Smith	Sharon	1937 Bates St	Pittsburgh	PA	15213	SharonMSmith@cengage.com	878-268-2455	10-16-1944
113	Hatcher	Charles	3218 Louisa St	Pittsburgh	PA	15213	CharlesMHatcher@cengage.com	561-550-8190	12-27-1976
114	Spencer	Glenn	2764 Oakland Ave	Pittsburgh	PA	15213	GlennJSpencer@cengage.com	878-688-4980	05-07-1934
115	Hearn	James	1252 Pier St	Pittsburgh	PA	15213	JamesJHearn@cengage.com	231-640-8302	02-15-1996
116	Cornett	Albert	3545 Ermine Way	Pittsburgh	PA	15213	AlbertACornett@cengage.com	724-975-6688	09-29-1947
117	Devito	Sylvia	3281 Fiber Way	Pittsburgh	PA	15213	SylviaKDevito@cengage.com	256-486-5999	05-27-1949
118	Hill	Jess	3161 Argyle Way	Pittsburgh	PA	15213	JessAHill@cengage.com	480-854-3611	01-04-1938
119	Benavides	Philip	1465 Butler St	Pittsburgh	PA	15201	PhilipCBenavides@cengage.com	412-868-4146	10-13-1994
120	Patterson	Margo	3291 Mahon St	Pittsburgh	PA	15219	MargoFPatterson@cengage.com	412-290-1510	09-19-1960
121	Thorn	Debbie	4434 Watt St	Pittsburgh	PA	15219	DebbieLThorn@cengage.com	412-323-5436	06-01-1968
122	Shaffer	Gene	2041 Wylie Ave	Pittsburgh	PA	15219	GeneKShaffer@cengage.com	281-817-7573	06-10-2002
123	Brough	Pablo	1812 Penn Ave	Pittsburgh	PA	15224	PabloRBrough@cengage.com	909-577-5726	08-30-1975
124	Agnew	Betty	201 Barn Way	Pittsburgh	PA	15219	BettyBAgnew@cengage.com	878-263-7528	11-23-1985
125	McCauley	Raymond	3254 Memory Lane	Pittsburgh	PA	15219	RaymondCMcCauley@cengage.com	878-345-0803	03-10-1986
126	Sisto	Robert	2836 Bedford Ave	Pittsburgh	PA	15219	RobertJSisto@cengage.com	646-373-8125	11-25-1966
127	Lara	Tamara	4588 Monaca Pl	Pittsburgh	PA	15219	TamaraRLara@cengage.com	417-359-2241	08-31-1984
128	Allen	Michael	2367 Cliff St	Pittsburgh	PA	15219	MichaelHAllen@cengage.com	412-790-6275	08-14-1966
129	Pegues	Vicki	3700 Penn Ave	Pittsburgh	PA	15219	VickiJPegues@cengage.com	412-597-0247	12-14-1994
130	Choi	Min Jee	2661 Webster Ave	Pittsburgh	PA	15219	MinJeeChoi@cengage.com	412-868-5257	04-05-2001

FIGURE 1-17   Customer data for Pitt Fitness

Reservations

ReservationID	ClassID	ClassDate	ClassPrice	OtherFees	CustomerID
2100001	39	01-07-2021	$9.00		102
2100002	24	01-03-2021	$11.00	$5.00	102
2100003	10	01-06-2021	$9.00		103
2100004	9	01-07-2021	$9.00		104
2100005	7	01-05-2021	$9.00		106
2100006	1	01-02-2021	$9.00		106
2100007	2	01-04-2021	$9.00		107
2100008	3	01-05-2021	$9.00		108
2100009	5	01-02-2021	$9.00		109
2100010	8	01-07-2021	$9.00		111
2100011	4	01-02-2021	$9.00		111
2100012	9	01-07-2021	$9.00		113
2100013	10	01-06-2021	$9.00		113
2100014	14	01-07-2021	$9.00		120
2100015	15	01-02-2021	$9.00		121
2100016	17	01-03-2021	$11.00	$5.00	122
2100017	18	01-05-2021	$10.00		123
2100018	35	01-03-3021	$9.00		124
2100019	36	01-02-2021	$11.00	$5.00	119
2100020	2	01-04-2021	$9.00		120
2100021	9	01-07-2021	$9.00		121
2100022	6	01-05-2021	$9.00		122
2100023	4	01-02-2021	$11.00	$5.00	123
2100024	21	01-03-2021	$9.00		124
2100025	24	01-03-2021	$11.00	$5.00	125
2100026	26	01-06-2021	$9.00		126
2100027	15	01-02-2021	$9.00		127
2100028	25	01-03-2021	$9.00		127
2100029	29	01-08-2021	$9.00		129
2100030	27	01-06-2021	$9.00		130
2100031	31	01-02-2021	$9.00		101
2100032	32	01-07-2021	$9.00		105
2100033	33	01-02-2021	$9.00		110
2100034	40	01-06-2021	$10.00		112
2100035	20	01-05-2021	$10.00		114
2100036	11	01-08-2021	$9.00		115
2100037	12	01-06-2021	$9.00		116
2100038	13	01-08-2021	$9.00		117
2100039	31	01-02-2021	$9.00		118

FIGURE 1-18   Reservation data for Pitt Fitness

sequentially as each reservation is received. The table also stores the identification number of the class, the date of the class, the price of the class, and any other fees associated with the class. Finally, the customer's unique identification number is included.

The table named ClassInstructors shown in Figure 1-19 is used to relate classes and instructors. It includes the class number and the instructor number. The class number in the ClassInstructors table matches a class number in the Classes table, and the instructor number in the ClassInstructors table matches an instructor number in the Instructors table. Note that some classes use more than one instructor.

ClassInstructors

ClassID	InstructorID
1	RS02
2	RS01
3	VP01
4	MS01
5	MK01
6	MK01
7	RS01
8	LL01
9	LL01
10	LL01
11	MA01
11	MD01
12	MA01
12	MD01
13	MA01
13	MD01
14	RS01
15	RS02
16	MS01
17	MS01
18	NT01
19	NT01
20	JV01

ClassInstructors (continued)

ClassID	InstructorID
21	MD01
22	RS01
23	RS01
24	MS01
25	MK01
26	NT01
27	LL01
28	RS01
29	VP01
30	VP01
31	MA01
31	MD01
32	MA01
32	MD01
33	MA01
33	MD01
34	RS02
35	RS02
36	MS01
37	MS01
38	JV01
39	JV01
40	NT01

FIGURE 1-19 Table used to relate classes and instructors

Q & A 1-9

Question: To check your understanding of the Pitt Fitness data, which classes does InstructorID NT01, Neda Tahan, teach?

Answer: To determine what instructor teaches which classes, look at the ClassInstructors table, shown in Figure 1-19, and find out which classes the InstructorID NT01 teaches. In that table, you can scan the InstructorID column and see that InstructorID NT01 teaches classes with ClassIDs 18, 19, 26, and 40. Using those numbers, look up those classes in the Classes table, shown in Figure 1-16. These classes are Aquasize, Aqua Strength and Cardio, Low Impact Aerobics, and Aqua Calm.

To check your understanding of the relationship between instructors, classes, and class instructors, answer the following questions.

- **Question:** What instructor teaches Barbell Power on Wednesday in Oakland?
  Answer: First look at the Classes table, shown in Figure 1-16, to determine the ClassID of that specific class. The Wednesday Barbell Power class has a ClassID of 23. Refer to the ClassInstructors table, shown in Figure 1-19, to find that InstructorID RS01 teaches the class with ClassID 23. Finally, in the Instructors table, shown Figure 1-15, look for InstructorID RS01 to find that Raymond Stein teaches Barbell Power, ClassID 23, on Wednesday in Oakland.

- **Question:** Customer Philip Benavides cannot remember his class reservation. Which class did he sign up for?
  Answer: First look at the Customers table, shown Figure 1-17, and find out that customer Philip Benavides is CustomerID 119. In the Reservations table, shown in Figure 1-18, read that

CustomerID 119 signed up for ClassID 36 under reservation number 2100019. In the Classes table, shown in Figure 1-16, look up ClassID 36 to find that the class Philip Benavides signed up for is Cycle.

- **Question:** Which classes does Michael Nguyen teach? What are those classes called?
  Answer: First look up the instructor, Michael Nguyen, in the Instructors table, shown in Figure 1-15. Reading that Michael Nguyen has InstructorID MA01, you can use the ClassInstructors table, shown in Figure 1-19, to look up which classes Michael Nguyen teaches. The ClassInstructors table shows that Instructor MA01 teaches classes with ClassIDs 11, 12, 13, 31, 32, and 33. Finally, use the Classes table, shown in Figure 1-16, to look up the names of those classes: Maturity Endurance and Strength, Maturity Classics, and Agility for Seniors.

The E-R diagram for the Pitt Fitness database appears in Figure 1-20.

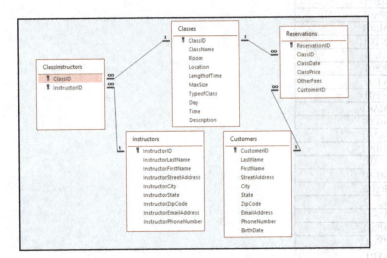

FIGURE 1-20 E-R diagram for the Pitt Fitness database

INTRODUCTION TO THE SPORTS PHYSICAL THERAPY DATABASE CASE

Sports Physical Therapy provides evaluation, treatment, and rehabilitation of all types of acute and chronic injuries for both athletes and non-athletes. The highly skilled, certified therapists use their background of biomechanics, sport mechanics, and clinical experience to provide one-on-one comprehensive rehabilitation for all types of injuries. The company stores information about their patients, therapists, therapies, and sessions.

In the Patient table shown in Figure 1-21, Sports Physical Therapy stores information about its patients. Each patient is identified by a unique, four-digit patient number. The patient's name and address, as well as the balance due on their bill, also are stored in the table.

Patient

PatientNum	LastName	FirstName	Address	City	State	ZipCode	Balance
1010	Koehler	Robbie	119 West Bay Dr.	San Vista	TX	72510	$1,535.15
1011	King	Joseph	941 Treemont	Oak Hills	TX	74081	$212.80
1012	Houghland	Susan	7841 Lake Side Dr.	Munster	TX	72380	$1,955.40
1013	Falls	Tierra	44 Applewood Ave.	Palm Rivers	TX	72511	$1,000.35
1014	Odepaul	Ben	546 WCR 150 South	Munster	TX	74093	$525.00
1015	Venable	Isaiah	37 High School Road	Waterville	TX	74183	$432.30
1016	Waggoner	Brianna	2691 Westgrove St.	Delbert	TX	72381	$714.25
1017	Short	Tobey	1928 10th Ave.	Munster	TX	72512	$967.60
1018	Baptist	Joseph	300 Erin Dr.	Waterville	TX	76658	$1,846.75
1019	Culling	Latisha	4238 East 71st St.	San Vista	TX	74071	$1,988.50
1020	Marino	Andre	919 Horton Ave.	Georgetown	TX	72379	$688.95
1021	Wilson	Tammy	424 October Blvd.	Waterville	TX	76658	$2,015.30

FIGURE 1-21 Patient data for Sports Physical Therapy

Sports Physical Therapy records information about each of its therapy sessions. The fields of data are stored in the Session table shown in Figure 1-22. A session record will have a unique number, the session date, the patient number, and the length of the session, as well as the therapist number and therapy code.

Session

SessionNum	SessionDate	PatientNum	LengthOfSession	TherapistID	TherapyCode
27	10/10/2021	1011	45	JR085	92507
28	10/11/2021	1016	30	AS648	97010
29	10/11/2021	1014	60	SW124	97014
30	10/12/2021	1013	30	BM273	97033
31	10/15/2021	1016	90	AS648	98960
32	10/16/2021	1018	15	JR085	97035
33	10/17/2021	1017	60	SN852	97039
34	10/17/2021	1015	45	BM273	97112
35	10/18/2021	1010	30	SW124	97113
36	10/18/2021	1019	75	SN852	97116
37	10/19/2021	1020	30	BM273	97124
38	10/19/2021	1021	60	AS648	97535

FIGURE 1-22   Session data for Sports Physical Therapy

To check your understanding of the relationship between patients and sessions, which patient had therapy on October 15, 2021? What therapy code was listed for the session belonging to Isaiah Venable? What session number(s) is (are) listed for Tierra Falls?

Answer: The Session table (Figure 1-22) lists PatientNum 1016 as having therapy on October 15, 2021. When you look that patient up in the Patient table (Figure 1-21), you see that it is Brianna Waggoner. To find the therapy code for Isaiah Venable, you must start with the Patient table, look up his number, 1015, and then examine the Session table. Patient number 1015 had the therapy coded as 97112. Finally, Tierra Falls is patient number 1013 (Patient table). Looking up her session number in the Session table, it is 30.

Sports Physical Therapy stores information about the therapists who work in their office, as shown in the Therapist table in Figure 1-23. Each therapist is identified by a unique ID number that consists of two uppercase letters followed by a three-digit number. For each therapist, the table also includes the last name, first name, street, city, state, and zip code.

Therapist

TherapistID	LastName	FirstName	Street	City	State	ZipCode
AS648	Shields	Anthony	5222 Eagle Court	Palm Rivers	TX	72511
BM273	McClain	Bridgette	385 West Mill St.	Waterville	TX	76658
JR085	Risk	Jonathan	1010 650 North	Palm Rivers	TX	72511
SN852	Nair	Saritha	25 North Elm St.	Livewood	TX	72512
SW124	Wilder	Steven	7354 Rockville Road	San Vista	TX	72510

FIGURE 1-23   Therapist data for Sports Physical Therapy

To check your understanding of the relationship between therapists and sessions, which therapist worked with patient 1021? How many patients did Bridgette McClain work with? What were the therapy codes (TherapyCode) for those sessions?

Answer: To determine which therapist worked with patient 1021, first examine the Session table (Figure 1-22). Find patient 1021; look across the table to see the TherapistID, AS648. Then look up the TherapistID in the Therapist table (Figure 1-23) to find the name, Anthony Shields.

To determine the number of patients that Bridgette McClain worked with, look up her TherapistID number in the Therapist table (Figure 1-23). You will see that it is BM273. Then look at the Session table (Figure 1-22). In the TherapistID column, count the number of times you see BM273—it should be three. Finally, look at the TherapyCode column for each of those three sessions. You should identify therapies 97033, 97112, and 97124.

In the Therapies table, each kind of therapy is identified by a unique number, which corresponds to the medical physical therapy code sent to insurance companies for reimbursement. The TherapyCode, a description, and the billable unit of time, if any, are included in the table. Time-based therapies are billed in groups of minutes (listed in the table). Service-based therapies are billed per service (no time is listed in the table). Figure 1-24 displays data for therapies.

Therapies

TherapyCode	Description	UnitOfTime
90901	Biofeedback training by any modality	
92240	Shoulder strapping	
92507	Treatment of speech	15
92530	Knee strapping	
92540	Ankle and/or foot strapping	
95831	Extremity or trunk muscle testing	
97010	Hot or cold pack application	
97012	Mechanical traction	
97014	Electrical stimulation	
97016	Vasopneumatic devices	
97018	Paraffin bath	
97022	Whirlpool	
97026	Infrared	
97032	Electrical stimulation	15
97033	Iontophoresis	15
97035	Ultrasound	15
97039	Unlisted modality	15
97110	Therapeutic exercises to develop strength and endurance, range of motion, and flexibility	15
97112	Neuromuscular re-education of movement, balance, coordination, etc.	15
97113	Aquatic therapy with therapeutic exercises	15
97116	Gait training	15
97124	Massage	15
97139	Unlisted therapeutic procedure	
97140	Manual therapy techniques	15
97150	Group therapeutic procedure	15
97530	Dynamic activities to improve functional performance, direct (one-on-one) with the patient	15
97535	Self-care/home management training	15
97750	Physical performance test or measurement	15
97799	Unlisted physical medicine/rehabilitation service or procedure	
98941	CMT of the spine	
98960	Education and training for patient self-management	30

FIGURE 1-24   Therapies data for Sports Physical Therapy

Q & A 1-10

Question: To check your understanding of the relationship between therapies and the other tables, answer the following questions: Did any patient have a hot or cold pack application? Which therapist(s) helped a patient with gait training? How many minutes did Jonathan Risk work with his patient on speech therapy, and how many units will be billed to insurance?

Answer: To determine if any patient had an application for a hot or cold pack, look through the descriptions in the Therapies table (Figure 1-24). Note that the TherapyCode code for the procedure is 97010. Look up that number in the Sessions table (Figure 1-22). You will see that it corresponds with SessionNum 28, so the answer is yes.

(continued)

Q & A 1-10 (continued)

To look up which therapist did gait training, begin with the Therapies table (Figure 1-24). You will see that gait training is the description for therapy 97116. Move to the Sessions table (Figure 1-22) and look for 97116. You will find that session 36 lists that TherapyCode. Find the TherapistID column in the Sessions table that aligns with session 36. The TherapistID is SN852. Finally, move to the Therapist table (Figure 1-23) and look up therapist SN852. It is Saritha Nair.

The final question is a bit more difficult. How many minutes did Jonathan Risk work with his patient on speech therapy, and how many units will be billed to insurance? Looking in the Therapies table (Figure 1-24), the only description related to speech therapy is TherapyCode 92507, Treatment of Speech. Note that it is billable in 15-minute units. (You may want to write down the TherapyCode and the billable units.)

The Therapist table (Figure 1-23) will reveal that Jonathan Risk has a TherapistID number of JR085. (Again, make a note of that.)

Finally, you can use these pieces of information in the Sessions table (Figure 1-23). Look up TherapyCode 92507. Look across the row to verify that therapist JR085 performed the work. Now look at the LengthOfSession field. You will see that it was 45 minutes. With a billable unit of 15 minutes, Sports Physical Therapy will bill the insurance for three units (45 divided by 15 equals 3).

The E-R diagram for the Sports Physical Therapy database appears in Figure 1-25.

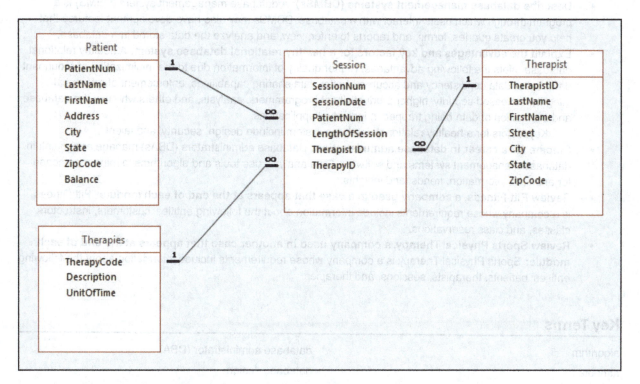

FIGURE 1-25   E-R diagram for the Sports Physical Therapy database

Summary

- **Examine JC Consulting (JCC), the company used for many of the examples throughout the text:** JC Consulting (JCC) is a digital development and consulting business that has been tracking business data in a spreadsheet but is now developing a relational database to maintain information about the following entities: employees, clients, project estimates, project line items, and tasks.

  The problems associated with a flat file or disorganized approach to data management include increased data redundancy, which lowers the quality of data and information, difficulties accessing related data, disorganized and limited data security options, and inadequate data sharing capabilities.

- **Define basic database terminology:** An entity is a person, place, event, item, or other transaction for which you want to store and process data. The data for each entity is stored in its own table. An attribute or field is a characteristic or property of an individual entity. Attributes are created as columns in a table. Individual entities are stored as records or rows in a table. A relationship is an association between entities.

  A one-to-many relationship between two entities exists when each occurrence of the first entity is related to zero, one, or many occurrences of the second entity. Each occurrence of the second entity is related to only one occurrence of the first entity.

  A relational database is a structure that can store information about multiple entities, the attributes of the entities, and the relationships among the entities.

  An entity-relationship (E-R) diagram represents a database visually by using a rectangle for each entity that includes the entity's name above the rectangle and the entity's attributes (fields) inside the rectangle. A line is used to connect two entities that have a relationship with an infinity symbol at the end of the line to indicate the "many" part of a one-to-many relationship.

- **Describe database management systems (DBMSs):** A database management system (DBMS) is a program through which users interact with a database. DBMSs may also have development features that help you create queries, forms, and reports to enter, view, and analyze the data stored in a database.

- **Explain the advantages and key factors for a healthy relational database system:** A healthy relational database offers the following advantages: Higher quality of information due to the minimization of redundant data, better data consistency and accuracy, better data sharing capabilities, enforcement of referential integrity, increased security, higher productivity of programmers, analysts, and others who use the database, and elimination of data being trapped in individual applications.

  Key factors for a healthy relational database system include design, security, and talent.

- **Prepare for a career in database administration:** Database administrators (DBAs) manage and maintain database management systems and software. Data analysts use tools and algorithms to mine a database for answers, information, trends, and insights.

- **Review Pitt Fitness, a company used in a case that appears at the end of each module:** Pitt Fitness is a company whose requirements include information about the following entities: customers, instructors, classes, and class reservations.

- **Review Sports Physical Therapy, a company used in another case that appears at the end of each module:** Sports Physical Therapy is a company whose requirements include information about the following entities: patients, therapists, sessions, and therapies.

Key Terms

algorithm	database administrator (DBA)
attribute	database design
big data	database management system (DBMS)
column	encryption
data analyst	entity
data file	entity-relationship (E-R) diagram
data independence	field
data redundancy	flat file
data security	form
database	integrity
database administration (DBA)	integrity constraint

many-to-many relationship	relational database
metadata	relationship
NoSQL	report
one-to-many relationship	row
orphan record	software stack
record	structured data
redundancy	table
referential integrity	unstructured data

Module Review Questions

Problems

1. _____ is the duplication of data or the storing of the same data in more than one place.
   a. Data security
   b. Data inconsistency
   c. Data independence
   d. Data redundancy

2. Which of the following is *not* a problem associated with redundancy?
   a. prevents orphan records
   b. makes updating data more cumbersome and time-consuming
   c. can lead to inconsistencies
   d. results in more frequent data errors

3. A(n) _____ is a person, place, object, event, or idea for which you want to store and process data.
   a. attribute
   b. entity
   c. relationship
   d. flat file

4. A(n) _____ is a characteristic or property of an entity.
   a. metadata
   b. database
   c. flat file
   d. attribute

5. A(n) _____ exists between two entities when each row in the first entity may match many rows in the second entity, and each row in the second entity matches only one row in the first entity.
   a. record
   b. many-to-many relationship
   c. one-to-many relationship
   d. attribute

6. A(n) _____ is a structure that contains data about many categories of information as well as the relationships between those categories.
   a. table
   b. data file
   c. relational database
   d. software stack

7. Which of the following describes how to create a one-to-many relationship in a database system?
   a. Insert a new table between two existing tables.
   b. Use a common field in the two tables to tie the related records from each table together.
   c. Create an entity-relationship (E-R) diagram.
   d. Include multiple entries in a single field.

8. In a(n) _____, rectangles represent entities and display their attributes; lines represent relationships between connected entities.
   a. entity-relationship (E-R) diagram
   b. unstructured data file
   c. spreadsheet
   d. software stack

9. Which of the following defines a DBMS?
   a. a collection of data that corresponds to one record
   b. a file used to store data about a single entity
   c. the person or group in charge of a database
   d. a program through which users interact with the data stored in a database

10. Which of the following describes database design?
    a. collecting the large volume of data produced by digital processes and devices
    b. creating a file used to store data about a single entity
    c. creating the entities, attributes, and relationships between tables of data
    d. converting the data in a database to a format indecipherable to normal programs

11. Which of the following allows you to get more information from the same amount of data?
    a. creating a healthy relational database
    b. entering the same information more than once
    c. using a flat file system
    d. encrypting the data
    e. designing professional forms

12. A(n) _____ is the person in charge of an organization's database.
    a. database management server (DBMS)
    b. database administrator (DBA)
    c. organization administrator (OBA)
    d. big data administrator (BDA)

Critical Thinking Questions

1. Explain how redundant data often leads to poorer decision making.

2. An attribute is a characteristic or property of an entity. If *person* is an entity, would the same attributes be used to describe a person in different databases that store medical, student, and fitness club data? Why or why not?

JC Consulting Case Exercises

Answer each of the following questions using the JCC data shown in Figure 1-5. No computer work is required.

Problems

1. Which employee has a salary value of $8,100?
   a. Nathan Geller
   b. Nigel Horvat
   c. Hector Garcia
   d. Nada Prohm

2. What client is *not* a government entity?
   a. Project Lead The Way
   b. Aspire Associates
   c. The HELPCard
   d. All are government entities.

3. Which projects had an estimated start date prior to 1/1/2020?
   a. ProjectIDs 1, 2, 3, and 7
   b. ProjectIDs 8, 16, and 24
   c. ProjectIDs 8–30
   d. ProjectID 1, 9, and 17

4. List ProjectLineItemID values that are related to ProjectID 3.
   a. ProjectLineItemIDs 1 and 2
   b. ProjectLineItemIDs 8 and 9
   c. ProjectLineItemIDs 39, 40, and 41
   d. ProjectLineItemID 4

5. List the name of the client related to ProjectID 3.
   a. SecureCom Wireless
   b. Loren Group
   c. Midstates Auto Auction
   d. Project Lead The Way

6. Which of the following tasks is *not* priced by the project?
   a. TaskID DB01 Design relational database
   b. Task ID DB04 Install SQL Server database
   c. Task ID MEET00 Initial customer meeting
   d. Task ID CODE04 Code SQL

7. For the record with a ProjectLineItemID value of 7, why does the Quantity field contain 20?
   a. It represents an estimate of 20 hours.
   b. It represents an estimate of 20 minutes.
   c. It represents an estimate of 20 projects.
   d. It represents the project ID.

8. For the record with a ProjectLineItemID value of 7, why does the Factor field contain 1.3?
   a. It represents an estimated increase of 1.3% due to risk or complexity for that task.
   b. It represents an estimated increase of 30% due to risk or complexity for that task.
   c. It represents an estimate of 1.3 hours for that task.
   d. It represents an additional 1.3 hours to add to the task.

9. What is the cost for an initial meeting with a client, TaskID MEET00?
   a. $100
   b. $150
   c. $0 (no charge)
   d. $1

10. What is the cost for creating a shopping cart, TaskID CODE15?
    a. $150/hour
    b. $125/project
    c. $100/month
    d. $125/hour

Critical Thinking Questions

1. JCC needs to be able to contact clients when problems arise concerning an estimate. What other attributes could JCC include in the Clients table to assist in contacting clients?
2. JCC wants the database to include data on all its employees, not just those who may be involved in projects. What additional entities would the DBA need to include in the database to store this data? What attributes?
3. What kinds of unstructured data or big data might JCC want to gather in the future?

Pitt Fitness Case Exercises

Answer each of the following questions using the Pitt Fitness data shown in Figures 1-15 through 1-19. No computer work is required.

Problems

1. Which instructor lives on Webster Avenue?
   a. Vicki Pegues
   b. Neda Tahan
   c. Memo Said
   d. Luke Lane

2. Who is the oldest customer?
    a. Glenn Spencer
    b. Jess Hill
    c. Gene Shaffer
    d. Nour Aboud

3. What class did Terrance Feldman reserve?
    a. Barre
    b. Barbell Power
    c. Yoga Balance
    d. Yogalates

4. In what location and room is ClassID 9, Barre, held?
    a. Shadyside, 159B
    b. Oakland, Main
    c. Shadyside, Main
    d. Oakland, 159B

5. What time does ClassID 24, Intense Cycle, begin?
    a. 2 pm
    b. 1 pm
    c. 12 pm
    d. 10 am

6. How long is the ClassID 15, Bootcamp?
    a. 60 minutes
    b. 45 minutes
    c. 30 minutes
    d. 90 minutes

7. Who teaches ClassID 21, Combination?
    a. Maria D'Angelo
    b. Robert Sisto
    c. Michael Nguyen
    d. Megan Kobinski

8. What customer has reservation 2100014?
    a. Debbie Thorn
    b. Tamara Lara
    c. Sylvia Devito
    d. Margo Patterson

9. When was customer Ramiro Sanchez born?
    a. 10/21/2000
    b. 4/20/1984
    c. 2/16/1957
    d. 4/1/1953

10. How many classes are offered on Mondays?
    a. 2
    b. 3
    c. 0
    d. 5

11. Which facility does *not* have the three senior classes: Maturity, Endurance, and Strength, Maturity Classics, and Agility for Seniors?
    a. Shadyside
    b. Downtown
    c. Oakland
    d. All of the facilities have the three senior classes

12. How many classes are offered at the Downtown location at 6:00 pm?
    a. 1
    b. 2
    c. 3
    d. 4

13. What two classes did Charles Hatcher sign up for?
    a. Aquasize, Aqua Strength and Cardio
    b. Barre, Barre Limited
    c. Cycle, Cycle and Strength
    d. HIIT, Bootcamp

14. Where does Juan Varlano teach his classes?
    a. Oakland and Downtown
    b. Oakland only
    c. Oakland and Shadyside
    d. Shadyside and Downtown

15. Which class holds the largest number of participants?
    a. Yoga
    b. Cycle
    c. Barbell Power
    d. Combination

Critical Thinking Questions

1. A few of the classes have data in a field called "OtherFees." These are rentals of bicycle shoes for the cycle classes. Should that fee be combined with the ClassPrice field? What if a participant has their own bike shoes?

2. Currently, the class price and other fees reside in the Registration table. If Pitt Fitness practices dynamic pricing (the management changes the prices as the classes fill up like the airlines do), should they put the class price in the Classes table? Why or why not?

Sports Physical Therapy Case Exercises

Answer each of the following questions using the Sports Physical Therapy data shown in Figures 1-21 through 1-24. No computer work is required.

Problems

1. What therapist lives in Palm Rivers?
   a. Steven Wilder
   b. Bridgette McClain
   c. Saritha Nair
   d. Jonathan Risk

2. What patient lives in Palm Rivers?
   a. Tierra Falls
   b. Ben Odepaul
   c. Susan Houghland
   d. Andre Marino

3. Which patient has the highest balance?
   a. Joseph King
   b. Robbie Koehler
   c. Latisha Culling
   d. Tammy Wilson

4. Which therapy takes the longest time?
   a. Massage
   b. Education and training for patient self-management
   c. Ultrasound
   d. Electrical stimulation

5. What treatment is Ben Odepaul having?
   a. Paraffin bath
   b. Knee strapping
   c. Electrical stimulation
   d. Hot or cold pack application

6. Who is having self-care/home management therapy?
   a. Tammy Wilson
   b. Tobey Short
   c. Brianna Waggoner
   d. Isaiah Venable

7. What therapist is performing unlisted modality on 10/17/2021?
   a. Steven Wilder
   b. Bridgette McClain
   c. Saritha Nair
   d. No therapist has that session

8. Which patient is undergoing aquatic therapy with therapeutic exercises? What is the length of the session? Who is the therapist in charge?
   a. Tierra Falls, 15 minutes, Bridgette McClain
   b. Tierra Falls, 30 minutes, Jonathan Risk
   c. Tierra Falls, 30 minutes, Bridgette McClain
   d. Robbie Koehler, 30 minutes, Steven Wilder

9. What patient is therapist Saritha Nair seeing on 10/18/2021?
   a. Susan Houghland
   b. Isaiah Venable
   c. Tierra Falls
   d. Latisha Culling

Critical Thinking Questions

1. The Sports Physical Therapy database does not include a field for the hours that the therapist is working. For example, doing any sort of treatment requires set up and break down of equipment, reading patients' charts, etc. In which table would you put the hours worked? What might be a better way to record when therapists begin their work and end their work?

2. What table might the database need to help determine the balance field in the Patient table? Would you want to record when a bill is paid and the amount? How would the insurance part of the bill be recorded?

MODULE **2**

THE RELATIONAL MODEL: INTRODUCTION, QBE, AND RELATIONAL ALGEBRA

LEARNING OBJECTIVES

- Describe the relational database model
- Explain Query-By-Example (QBE)
- Use criteria in QBE
- Create calculated fields in QBE
- Summarize data by applying aggregate functions in QBE
- Sort data in QBE
- Join tables in QBE
- Update data using action queries in QBE
- Apply relational algebra

INTRODUCTION

The database management approach implemented by most systems is the relational model. In this module, you will study the relational database model and examine a visual interface that helps you retrieve data from relational databases, called **Query-By-Example** (**QBE**). Finally, you will learn about relational algebra, which provides the fundamental concepts upon which the manipulation of data in a relational database is rooted.

EXAMINING RELATIONAL DATABASES

A relational database is a collection of tables like the ones you viewed for JC Consulting (JCC) in Module 1. These tables also appear in Figure 2-1. Formally, these tables are called **relations**.

How does a relational database handle entities, attributes of entities, and relationships between entities? Each entity is stored in its own table. For example, the JCC database has a table for employees, for clients, and so on as shown in Figure 2-1. The attributes of an entity become the fields or columns in the table. The table for employees, for example, has a column for the employee ID, a column for the employee's first name, the employee's last name, and so on.

Employees

EmployeeID	LastName	FirstName	HireDate	Title	Salary
19	Kohn	Ali	01-Jan-20	Project Leader	$5,000.00
22	Kaplan	Franco	01-Feb-20	Programmer	$5,500.00
35	Prohm	Nada	29-Feb-20	Customer Support Specialist	$4,000.00
47	Alvarez	Benito	31-Mar-20	Front End Developer	$5,200.00
51	Shields	Simone	30-Apr-20	Network Specialist	$7,000.00
52	Novak	Stefan	01-Jan-19	Project Leader	$8,000.00
53	Anad	Sergei	01-Jan-19	Front End Developer	$5,300.00
54	Allen	Sasha	01-Jan-19	Programmer	$7,000.00
55	Winter	Wendy	31-Dec-20	Front End Developer	$4,300.00
56	Reddy	Kamal	01-Sep-19	Programmer	$6,200.00
57	Yang	Tam	30-Apr-21	Front End Developer	$5,000.00
58	Young	Solomon	01-Jan-19	Programmer	$5,500.00
59	Santana	Carmen	01-Jan-19	Front End Developer	$4,800.00
60	Lu	Chang	01-Mar-19	Database Developer	$7,900.00
61	Smirnov	Tovah	01-Oct-19	Programmer	$6,000.00
62	Turner	Jake	31-Mar-21	Database Developer	$7,800.00
63	Geller	Nathan	01-Jan-19	Project Leader	$8,100.00
64	Lopez	Miguel	01-Jan-19	Programmer	$6,200.00
65	Garcia	Hector	01-Apr-23	UI Designer	$7,000.00
66	Roth	Elena	31-Oct-20	Network Specialist	$7,000.00
67	Horvat	Nigel	30-Apr-24	UI Designer	$6,300.00

Clients

ClientID	ClientName	Street	Zip	Government
1	Tri-Lakes Realtors	135 E Jefferson St	02447	FALSE
2	Project Lead The Way	762 Saratoga Blvd	02446	TRUE
3	Midstates Auto Auction	9787 S Campbell Ln	01355	FALSE
4	Bretz & Hanna Law Firm	8101 N Olive Dr	01431	FALSE
5	Aspire Associates	5673 South Ave	01431	FALSE
6	Bounteous	9898 Ohio Ave	02770	FALSE
7	Netsmart Solutions	4091 Brentwood Ln	01354	FALSE
8	Loren Group	9565 Ridge Rd	02466	FALSE
9	Associated Grocers	231 Tecumsa Rd	02532	FALSE
10	Jobot Developers	1368 E 1000 St	02330	FALSE
11	Harper State Bank	1865 Forrest Dr	01571	FALSE
12	MarketPoint Sales	826 Hosta St	01983	FALSE
13	SecureCom Wireless	5280 Industrial Dr	01852	FALSE
14	The HELPCard	840 Boonville Ave	02466	TRUE
15	Jillian Henry & Associates	815 E California St	02113	FALSE
16	Pediatric Group	4940 W Farm Rd	02113	FALSE
17	SkyFactor	1736 Sunshine Dr	02726	FALSE
18	NuCamp	2500 E Kearny St	01431	FALSE
19	Wu Electric	5520 S Michigan	02447	FALSE
20	Juxly Engineering	4238 Rumsfield Rd	02148	FALSE
21	Carta Training	2445 N Airport Dr	02446	FALSE

FIGURE 2-1 JC Consulting data *(continued)*

Projects

ProjectID	ProjectStartDate	ClientID	EmployeeID	ProjectNotes
1	06-Feb-19	1	52	Client wants digital solutions to emphasize commercial real estate.
2	07-Feb-19	10	63	Client needs help converting, organizing, and managing donor and donation data.
3	11-Mar-19	3	52	Client wants to establish SEO goals.
4	10-Apr-20	4	52	Client wants to set up an internal server as well as help with a domain name.
7	02-Sep-19	2	63	Client has used the database for several months and now needs new reports.
8	06-Jan-20	3	52	Develop and implement website SEO strategy.
9	10-Feb-20	6	63	Needs help to manage and organize internal data.
10	31-Mar-21	7	19	Develop new website content.
11	30-Apr-20	9	19	Client needs internal database to manage personnel.
13	30-Nov-20	10	64	Client needs subcontracting help installing a new database for a WordPress site.
14	09-Dec-20	15	19	Client needs new functionality for current JavaScript application.
15	21-Dec-20	14	19	Client needs new functionality for current Ruby/Rails application.
16	04-Jan-21	11	52	Client needs help with server security.
17	15-Feb-21	12	52	Current online sales solution is unreliable.
18	14-Apr-21	6	63	Client needs internal database to manage inventory.
19	04-Jun-21	13	52	Client needs new functionality for current C# / ASP.NET application.
20	30-Jul-21	22	63	Client needs full website reskin.
21	31-Aug-21	16	19	Client needs help with data analytics.
22	30-Sep-21	20	19	Client needs an online reference database
23	12-Nov-21	18	63	Client needs to include responsive web design principles for mobile devices.
24	14-Jan-22	17	63	Client wants an audit on current website performance.

ProjectLineItems

ProjectLineItemID	ProjectID	TaskID	TaskDate	Quantity	Factor	ProjectLineItemNotes
1	1	MEET00	06-Feb-19	1	1.00	
2	1	PLAN01	06-Feb-19	1	1.00	
4	2	MEET00	07-Feb-19	1	1.00	
5	2	PLAN01	07-Feb-19	1	1.00	
6	2	DB01	15-Mar-19	1	1.30	Data is stored in multiple spreadsheets.
7	2	DB02	15-Apr-19	20	1.30	Data is not consistent between spreadsheets.
8	3	MEET00	11-Mar-19	1	1.00	
9	3	PLAN01	11-Mar-19	1	1.20	Owner is difficult to pin down.
10	4	MEET00	10-Apr-20	1	1.00	
11	4	PLAN01	10-Apr-20	1	1.20	Two principal attorneys must agree.
12	4	SERV01	11-May-20	1	1.00	
13	4	SERV02	10-Jun-20	1	1.30	Security is a paramount issue.
17	11	MEET00	30-Apr-20	1	1.00	
18	11	PLAN01	30-Apr-20	1	1.00	
19	9	MEET00	10-Feb-20	1	1.00	
20	9	PLAN01	10-Feb-20	1	1.00	
25	9	PLAN10	17-Feb-20	1	1.00	
26	18	MEET00	14-Apr-21	1	1.00	
27	20	MEET00	30-Jul-21	1	1.00	
28	20	PLAN01	30-Jul-21	1	1.00	
29	20	PLAN02	30-Jul-21	1	1.00	

FIGURE 2-1 JC Consulting data *(continued)*

TaskMasterList

TaskID	Description	CategoryID	Per	Estimate
CODE01	Code PHP	Coding	Hour	$150.00
CODE02	Code C# in ASP.NET	Coding	Hour	$150.00
CODE03	Code Ruby on Rails	Coding	Hour	$150.00
CODE04	Code SQL	Coding	Hour	$150.00
CODE05	Code HTML	Coding	Hour	$100.00
CODE06	Code CSS	Coding	Hour	$100.00
CODE07	Code JavaScript	Coding	Hour	$125.00
CODE08	Perform analytics	Coding	Hour	$100.00
CODE09	Select technology stack	Coding	Hour	$200.00
CODE10	Apply SEO	Coding	Hour	$125.00
CODE12	Create prototype	Coding	Hour	$150.00
CODE13	Code WordPress	Coding	Hour	$100.00
CODE14	Code Python	Coding	Hour	$150.00
CODE15	Create shopping cart	Coding	Hour	$125.00
CODE16	Code Other	Coding	Hour	$150.00
DB01	Design relational database	Database	Project	$1,000.00
DB02	Convert data	Database	Hour	$125.00
DB03	Install MySQL database	Database	Project	$500.00
DB04	Install SQL Server database	Database	Project	$500.00
DB05	Install Access Database	Database	Project	$400.00
MEET00	Initial customer meeting	Meeting	Project	$0.00

FIGURE 2-1   JC Consulting data *(continued)*

What about relationships? At JC Consulting, there is a one-to-many relationship between clients and projects. (Each client may be related to *many* project estimates created for that client.) How is this relationship implemented in a relational database? The answer is through common columns in the two tables. Consider Figure 2-1 again. The ClientID columns in the Clients and Projects tables implement the relationship between clients and projects. For any client, you can use these columns to determine all the projects that were created for that client. If the Projects table did not include the ClientID value, you could not identify which client that particular project estimate belonged to.

A relation is a two-dimensional table. In Figure 2-1, you might see certain patterns or restrictions that you can place on relations. Each column in a table should have a short but descriptive unique name, and all entries in each column should be consistent with this column name. (For example, in the Salary column, all entries should be for the same length of time, one month.) Each row should contain information for a new item in that entity and should not be repeated. In addition, the order in which columns and rows appear in a table should be immaterial. Rows in a table (relation) are often called **records** or **tuples**. Columns in a table (relation) are often called **fields** or **attributes**. A **relation** is a two-dimensional table (rows and columns) in which the following are true:

1. The entries in the table are single-valued; that is, each intersection of the row and column in the table contains only one value.

2. Each column has a distinct name (technically called the attribute name).

3. All values in a column are values of the same attribute (that is, all entries must match the column name).

4. The order of the columns is not important.

5. Each row is distinct.

6. The order of rows is immaterial.

Later in this text, you will encounter structures in which some of the entries contain **repeating groups** and, thus, are not single-valued. Such a structure is called an **unnormalized relation**. (This jargon is a little strange in that an unnormalized relation is not really a relation at all.) The table shown in Figure 2-2 is an example of an unnormalized relation.

ProjectID	ProjectStartDate	ClientID	EmployeeID	ProjectNotes	TaskID	TaskDate	Quantity	Factor	ProjectLineItemNotes
1	06-Feb-19	1	52	Client wants digital solutions to emphasize commercial real estate.	MEET00 PLAN01	06-Feb-19 06-Feb-19	1 1	1.00 1.00	
2	07-Feb-19	10	63	Client needs help converting, organizing, and managing donor and donation data.	MEET00 PLAN01 DB01 DB02 CODE04 TEST01 TEST02 MEET01 SUPP03	07-Feb-19 07-Feb-19 15-Mar-19 15-Apr-19 15-May-19 03-Jun-19 03-Jun-19 03-Jun-19 03-Jun-19	1 1 1 20 4 8 8 2 8	1.00 1.00 1.30 1.30 1.00 1.00 1.00 1.00 1.00	Data is stored in multiple spreadsheets. Data is not consistent between spreadsheets. Code SQL to code 4 queries.
3	11-Mar-19	3	52	Client wants to establish SEO goals.	MEET00 PLAN01	11-Mar-19 11-Mar-19	1 1	1.00 1.20	Owner is difficult to pin down.
4	10-Apr-20	4	52	Client wants to set up an internal server as well as help with a domain name.	MEET00 PLAN01 SERV01 SERV02 TEST01 TEST02 SUPP03	10-Apr-20 10-Apr-20 11-May-20 10-Jun-20 15-Jun-20 15-Jun-20 15-Jun-20	1 1 1 1 16 16 4	1.00 1.20 1.00 1.30 1.00 1.00 1.00	Two principal attorneys must agree. Security is a paramount issue.

FIGURE 2-2 Structure of an unnormalized relation

Relational Database Shorthand

A commonly accepted shorthand representation shows the structure of a relational database. You write the name of the table and then, within parentheses, list all the columns in the table. In addition, each table should appear on its own line. Using this method, you would write the JC Consulting database as follows:

```
Employees (EmployeeID, LastName, FirstName, HireDate, Title, Salary)
Clients (ClientID, ClientName, Street, Zip, Government)
Projects (ProjectID, ProjectStartDate, ClientID, EmployeeID, ProjectNotes)
ProjectLineItems (ProjectLineItemID, ProjectID, TaskID, TaskDate,
    Quantity, Factor, ProjectLineItemNotes)
TaskMasterList (TaskID, Description, CategoryID, Per, Estimate)
```

The JC Consulting database contains some duplicate column names. For example, the ClientID column appears in *both* the Clients table *and* the Projects table. In some situations, a reference to the column might be confused. For example, if you write ClientID, how would the computer or another user know which table you intend to use? That could be a problem. When a database has duplicate column names, you need a way to indicate the column to which you are referring. One common approach to this problem is to write both the table name and the column name, separated by a period. You would write the ClientID column in the Clients table as Clients.ClientID. You would write ClientID column in the Projects table as Projects.ClientID. Technically, when you combine a column name with a table name, you say that you **qualify** the column names. It *always* is acceptable to qualify column names, even when there is no possibility of confusion. If confusion may arise, however, it is *essential* to qualify column names.

The **primary key** of a table (relation) is the column or columns that uniquely identify a given row in that table. In the Clients table, the ClientID number uniquely identifies a given row (Figure 2-1). For example, ClientID 6 occurs in only one row of the Clients table. Because each row contains a unique number, the ClientID is the primary key for the Clients table. The primary key provides an important way of distinguishing one row in a table from another and cannot be blank or null. (*Note:* If more than one column is necessary to make the row unique, it is called a **composite primary key**.)

Primary keys usually are represented by underlining the column or columns that comprises the primary key for each table in the database. The complete representation for the JC Consulting database is as follows:

Employees (<u>EmployeeID</u>, LastName, FirstName, HireDate, Title, Salary)

Clients (<u>ClientID</u>, ClientName, Street, Zip, Government)

Projects (<u>ProjectID</u>, ProjectStartDate, ClientID, EmployeeID, ProjectNotes)

ProjectLineItems (<u>ProjectLineItemID</u>, ProjectID, TaskID, TaskDate, Quantity, Factor, ProjectLineItemNotes)

TaskMasterList (<u>TaskID</u>, Description, CategoryID, Per, Estimate)

Q & A 2-1

Question: Why is it customary to list the primary key field as the first field in a table?

Answer: While it isn't necessary to identify the primary key field as the first field in a table, it's customary to do so because the value in the primary key field uniquely identifies each record in the table.

The term **foreign key** refers to the field used to connect a table on the "many" side of a one-to-many relationship. In the previous example, the ClientID field is a primary key in the Clients table and a foreign key in the Projects table. The primary key in the Projects table is ProjectID. You will learn more about foreign keys in a future module.

CREATING SIMPLE QUERIES AND USING QUERY-BY-EXAMPLE

When you ask Access or any other DBMS a question about the data in a database, the question is called a query. A **query** is a question structured in a way that the DBMS can recognize and process. In this section, you will investigate **Query-By-Example (QBE)**, a visual **GUI (graphical user interface)** approach to writing queries. For example, using a QBE system, users ask their questions by dragging column names to a grid as opposed to writing commands from a keyboard. Microsoft Access provides a QBE approach to building queries using **Query Design View**.

In Access, Query Design View has two panes. The upper portion of the window contains a field list for each table used in the query, as shown in Figure 2-3. The lower pane contains the **design grid**, the area in which you specify the fields to include in the query results, a sort order for the query results, any criteria, and other instructions.

To create a new, simple query in Access, perform the following steps:

- Click the Create tab on the ribbon.
- Click the Query Design button (Create tab | Queries group) to create a query using Query Design View. Access displays the Show Table dialog box and a new tab on the ribbon named Query Tools Design.
- Click the table in the Show Table dialog box that you want to use in the query.
- Click the Add button (Show Table dialog box) to add the table to the query.
- When you finish adding the tables needed for the query, click the Close button (Show Table dialog box) to close the Show Table dialog box.

A field list for the table or tables you selected appear in the Query Design View window as shown in Figure 2-3. You can resize the field list by dragging any of its borders. You create the query by adding fields and other information to the design grid in the lower portion of the window.

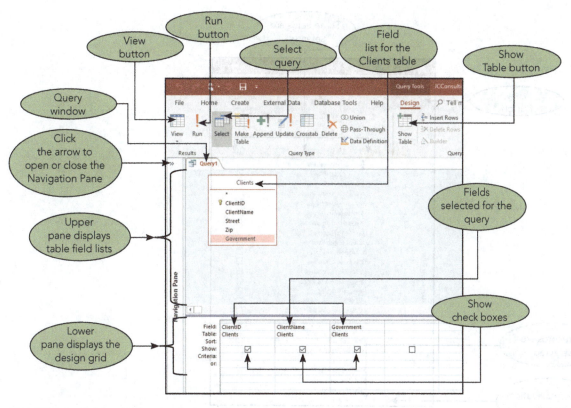

FIGURE 2-3 Fields added to the design grid

Selecting Fields and Running the Query

Suppose you need to list the ClientID, ClientName, and Government field values for each record in the Clients table.

To select a field in an Access query, perform the following steps:

- Add the field list for the desired table, such as the Clients table, to Query Design View.
- Double-click the field in the field list to place it in the next available column in the design grid, or drag it from the field list to the desired column in the design grid. In this case, you would double-click ClientID, then ClientName, and then Government in the Clients field list.
- The checkmarks in the Show check boxes indicate the fields that will appear in the query results. To omit a field from the query results, clear the checkmark from the field's Show check box or remove the field from the design grid.
- Click the Run button (Query Tools Design tab | Results group) to run or execute the query and display the query results in Query Datasheet View, as shown in Figure 2-4. If the query is a **select query**, a query that selects fields and records from the database, clicking the View button (Query Tools Design tab | Results group) also runs the query to select and display the fields and records that the query has identified. A select query is also sometimes called a **simple query**.

Note that the View button's appearance changes when you run a query. For a select query, clicking the View button in Query Datasheet View switches to Query Design View and vice versa.

As shown in Figure 2-4, the record navigation buttons indicate the current record number as well as the total number of records selected in the query.

To add or remove a table from a query, perform the following steps:

- If you add the wrong table to a query, you can remove it in Query Design View by right-clicking the field list title bar, and then clicking Remove Table on the shortcut menu.
- You can add a new table to a query by clicking the Show Table button (Query Tools Design tab | Query Setup group). Access displays the Show Table dialog box, in which you can select and add the desired table.

38

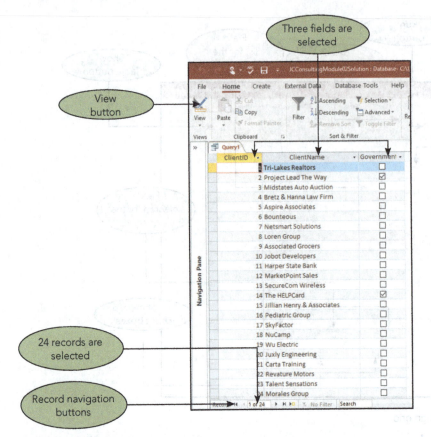

FIGURE 2-4 Clients table query results

The two query views you will use in this module are **Datasheet View** to see the results and **Design View** to change the design. It's common to build a select query in incremental steps, switching multiple times between Query Design View, where you build the query, and Query Datasheet View, where you see the selected records, as the query is developed. The View button (Home tab | Views group in Query Datasheet View and Query Tools Design tab | Results group) changes icons to help you quickly flip between these two views.

Running a query in Access does not create a copy of the data, but rather, simply selects the current information from underlying tables where the data is physically stored. If new records are added or existing data is changed, those updates are automatically presented in the results of the query the next time it is run.

You can add and delete records as well as modify data in Datasheet View of a select query. Because a query does not store any data, changes you make to data in the Datasheet View of a select query are actually being stored in an underlying table. The changes are immediately reflected in the current query as well as any other query that selects or otherwise uses that data. The ability to store data in only one location, the tables, yet allow you to select, view, and analyze it in multiple queries is a powerful feature of all modern relational database systems.

Saving and Using Queries

To save a query, perform the following steps:

- Click the Save button (Quick Access Toolbar).
- Enter a name for the saved query in the Save As dialog box.
- Click the OK button (Save As dialog box). As the data in your database changes over time, the query will always select the most current, accurate data.

After you create and save a query, you can use it in a variety of ways:

- To view the results of a saved select query that is not currently open, run it (which is the same as opening it in Query Datasheet View) by double-clicking the query in the Navigation Pane.
- To change the design of a query that is already open, return to Design View by clicking the View button (Home tab | Views group), and then make the desired changes.

- To change the design of a query that is not currently open, right-click the query in the Navigation Pane, and then click Design View on the shortcut menu to open the query in Design View.
- To print the records selected in Query Datasheet View, click the File tab, click Print, and then click Quick Print.
- To print the query without first opening it, select the query in the Navigation Pane, click the File tab, click Print, and then click Quick Print.
- To save the query with a different name, right-click it in the Navigation Pane, click Rename on the shortcut menu, enter the new name, and then press the Enter key. A query must be closed in order to rename it.

YOUR TURN 2-1

Create a query to list the task IDs, categories, and task descriptions in the TaskMasterList table.

To display the TaskID, CategoryID, and Description fields for all records in the TaskMasterList table, perform the following steps:

- Begin a new query using the TaskMasterList table.
- Double-click the TaskID field in the TaskMasterList field list to add it to the first column of the query grid.
- Double-click the CategoryID field in the TaskMasterList field list to add it to the first column of the query grid.
- Double-click the Description field in the TaskMasterList field list to add it to the second column of the query grid. The query design is shown in Figure 2-5.

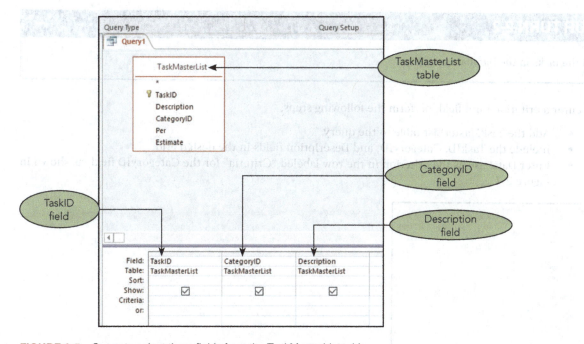

FIGURE 2-5 Query to select three fields from the TaskMasterList table

- Click the Run button (Query Tools Design tab | Results group) to display the query results, shown in Figure 2-6.

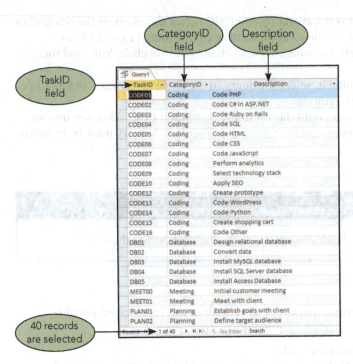

FIGURE 2-6   TaskMasterList table query results

USING SIMPLE CRITERIA

When the records you want must satisfy a condition, you enter that condition in the appropriate column in the query design grid. Conditions also are called **criteria**. (A single condition is called a **criterion**.) The following example illustrates the use of a criterion to select data.

YOUR TURN 2-2

Find the tasks in the Database category.

To enter a criterion for a field, perform the following steps:

- Add the TaskMasterList table to the query.
- Include the TaskID, CategoryID, and Description fields in the design grid.
- Enter Database as the criterion in the row labeled "Criteria" for the CategoryID field, as shown in Figure 2-7.

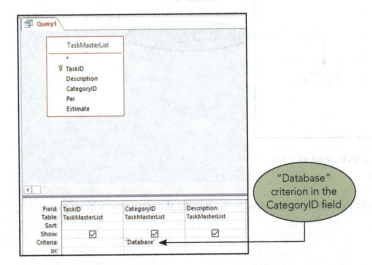

FIGURE 2-7   Query to find the tasks in the Database category

When you enter a criterion for text (string) fields, Access automatically adds quotation marks around the criterion when you run the query or when you move the insertion point to another box in the design grid. Typing the quotation marks is optional. (Some database management systems use single quotation marks to identify string criteria.)

According to Figure 2-6, TaskID, Description, and CategoryID all contain text. Figure 2-1 shows the other fields in the TaskMasterList table: Per and Estimate. The Per field also contains text and the Estimate field contains numbers.

The query results shown in Figure 2-8 display those records where Database is the entry in the CategoryID field. In Access, textual criteria are not case sensitive, so "Database", "database", or "DATABASE" used as a criterion would all select the same records, but entering your criterion using the same case as the data often makes it easier to read.

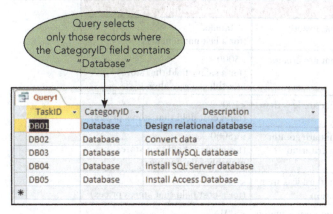

FIGURE 2-8   Database tasks query results

Parameter Queries

If you plan to use a query repeatedly, but with different criteria, you might want to save it as a parameter query. In Access, a **parameter query** allows you to enter criteria when you *run* the query, as opposed to placing it in the design grid. For example, if you want to search for a different CategoryID each time you run a query, you can type a prompt in the Criteria row of the design grid for the CategoryID field versus a specific criterion such as "Database". As you run the query, Access displays a prompt that allows you to enter the desired category. Prompts must be enclosed in square brackets. For example, if you type [Enter a category] in the Criteria cell of the design grid for the CategoryID field, Access displays a dialog box when you run the query, allowing you to enter the desired category. A parameter query is easy for novice users to supply information in saved queries.

To enter parameter criteria for a field, perform the following steps:

- Add the table to the query.
- Include the field or fields in the design grid.
- Enter the prompt in [square brackets] in the row labeled "Criteria" for the desired field, as shown in Figure 2-9.

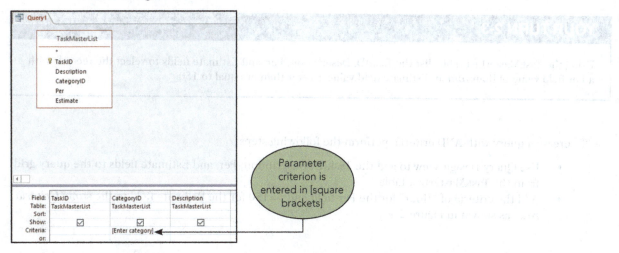

FIGURE 2-9   Parameter criterion

Comparison Operators

A **comparison operator**, also called a **relational operator**, can be used in criteria to compare two values in a test that returns true or false. The comparison operators are = (equal to), > (greater than), < (less than), >= (greater than or equal to), <= (less than or equal to), and <> (not equal to). They are commonly used to compare numeric and data values, and are summarized in Figure 2-10. When you enter criteria without an operator, the = (equal to) operator is assumed. You will learn about other types of **operators** as you work through the examples in this text. For example, the familiar math operators of + (add), − (subtract), * (multiply), and / (divide) are commonly across all languages.

Operator	Name	Description	Example Criterion
=	Equal to	Select all records that exactly match this criterion	="Tanaka" (for a last name field)
>	Greater than	Select all records that are greater than the criterion	>5000 (for a salary field that stores monthly salary values)
<	Less than	Select all records that are less than the criterion	<100 (for a cost field that stores prices)
>=	Greater than or equal to	Select all records that are greater than or equal to the criterion	>=5000 (for a salary field that stores monthly salary values)
<=	Less than or equal to	Select all records that are less than or equal to the criterion	<=100 (for a cost field that stores prices)
<>	Not equal to	Select all records that do not match the criterion	<>"MA" (for a state field)

FIGURE 2-10   Comparison operators

USING COMPOUND CRITERIA

You also can combine more than one criterion to create **compound criteria**, or **compound conditions**. If you use **AND criteria**, *each* criterion must be true for a record to be selected. If you use **OR criteria**, *only one* of the criterion must be true for a record to be selected. You may add as many AND or OR criteria as desired to create the combination needed for the query. The key is to remember that *all* AND criteria must be true and only *one* OR criterion must be true for the record to be selected.

In QBE, to create an AND criterion, place the conditions on the *same Criteria row* in the design grid (see Figure 2-11). To create an OR criterion, place the conditions on *different Criteria rows* in the design grid (see Figure 2-13).

YOUR TURN 2-3

Using the TaskMasterList table, list the TaskID, Description, Per, and Estimate fields to select the records with a Per field value of Hour *and* an Estimate field value greater than or equal to 150.

To create a query with AND criteria, perform the following steps:

- Use Query Design View to add the TaskID, Description, Per, and Estimate fields to the query grid from the TaskMasterList table.
- Add the criteria of "Hour" for the Per field and >=150 for the Estimate field to the *same Criteria row*, as shown in Figure 2-11.

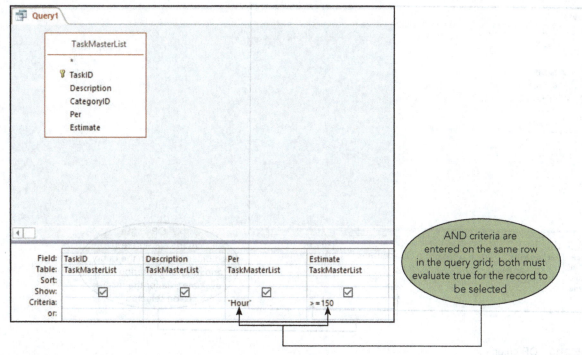

FIGURE 2-11   AND criteria

The query results appear in Figure 2-12.

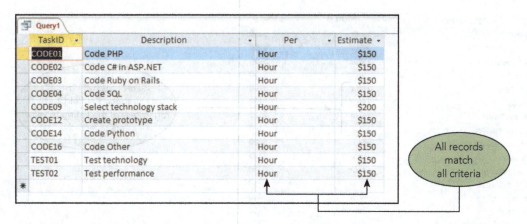

FIGURE 2-12   AND criteria query results

YOUR TURN 2-4

Using the TaskMasterList table, list the TaskID, Description, Per, and Estimate fields to select the records with a Per field value of Hour *or* an Estimate field value greater than or equal to 150.

To create a query with OR criteria, perform the following steps:

- Use Query Design View to add the TaskID, Description, Per, and Estimate fields to the query grid from the TaskMasterList table.
- Add the criteria of "Hour" for the Per field and >=150 for the Estimate field *using different Criteria rows*, as shown in Figure 2-13.

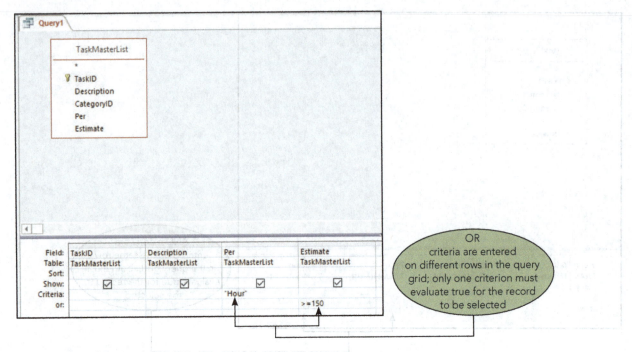

FIGURE 2-13   OR criteria

The query results appear in Figure 2-14.

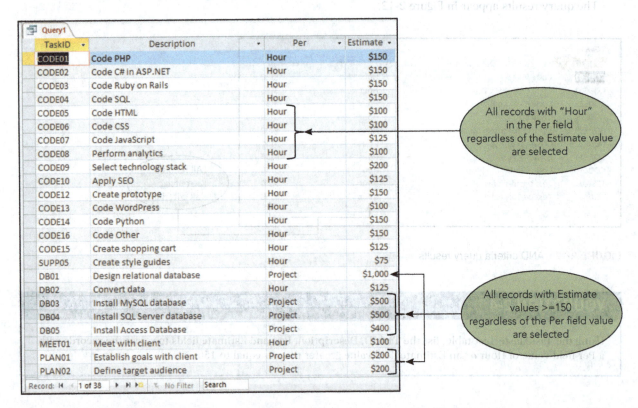

FIGURE 2-14   OR criteria query results

Given that a record is selected if it is true for only *one* OR criterion, queries with OR criteria always have the potential to select more records than using the same criteria in an AND query. In Access, this means that for each row of criteria that you add (or for each OR criterion you add), you potentially increase the number of records that are selected by that query.

Using the TaskMasterList table, suppose you need to list the TaskID, Description, Per, and Estimate values for all records that contain "Hour" in the Per field and have Estimate values between 100 and 150.

This example requires you to query a single field for a range of values to find all records that contain an Estimate value between 100 and 150. When you ask this kind of question, you are looking for all values that are greater than or equal to 100 as well as less than or equal to 150. The answer to this question requires using a compound criterion in the same field.

To place two criteria in the same field, perform the following steps:

- Use Query Design View to add the TaskID, Description, Per, and Estimate fields to the query grid from the TaskMasterList table.
- Add the criterion of "Hour" for the Per field and >=100 and <=150 for the Estimate field *using the same Criteria rows*, as shown in Figure 2-15.

Query criteria are not case sensitive, so AND does not need to be in all capital letters.

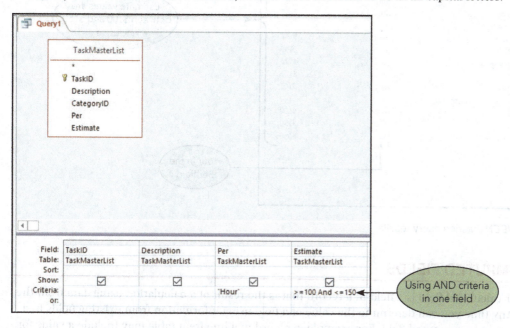

FIGURE 2-15 Query uses AND condition for a single field to select a range of values

An alternate compound condition that tests for a range of values is the **BETWEEN operator**. The BETWEEN operator is inclusive, which means it includes the lower number, the higher number, and all numbers in between, as shown in Figure 2-16.

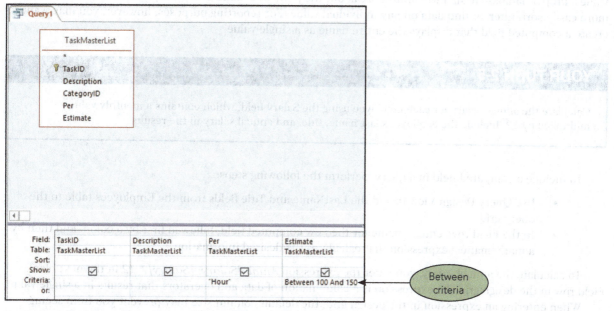

FIGURE 2-16 Alternative criterion to query for a range of values

The criteria in Figures 2-15 and 2-16 select the same records, as shown in Figure 2-17.

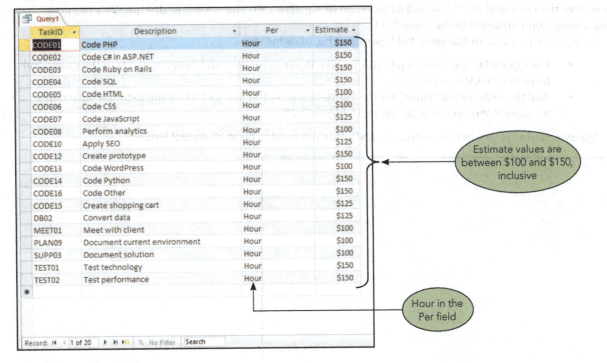

FIGURE 2-17 BETWEEN criterion query results

CREATING COMPUTED FIELDS

A **computed field** or **calculated field** is a field in a record that is the result of a calculation using data from the rest of the record. Any time you can determine the value of a field using information from existing fields in a record, you should create a computed field. For example, a record in a line item table may include a value for a discount or a tax. By calculating the discount or tax from other data in the record, you can be confident that the discount or tax values are calculated correctly as compared to asking a user to enter the discount or tax values, a process that is both error prone and unproductive.

You can also create computed fields from existing fields that contain text. For example, you may want to combine the values in a FirstName field with the values in a LastName field to create a field that contains both values. Proper database design will always break out the parts of a name into multiple fields so that you can more easily sort, filter, or find data on any individual value. For reporting purposes, however, you may want to create a computed field that displays the entire name as a single value.

YOUR TURN 2-5

Calculate the annual salary for each employee using the Salary field, which contains a monthly value multiplied by 12. Include the employee's last name, title, and annual salary in the results.

To include a computed field in a query, perform the following steps:

- Use Query Design View to add the LastName and Title fields from the Employees table to the query grid.
- In the Field row, enter a name for the new computed field, followed first by a colon, and then by a mathematical expression that calculates the desired information.

To calculate the annual salary, you enter the expression *AnnualSalary: [Salary] * 12* in the next blank Field row in the design grid. An **expression** is a combination of data and operators that results in a single value. When entering an expression in the design grid, the default column size may prevent you from seeing the complete expression. To address this, you can either widen the column by dragging its right edge, or right-click the column in the Field cell, and then click Zoom on the shortcut menu to use the Zoom dialog box to enter the expression. Both techniques are shown in Figure 2-18.

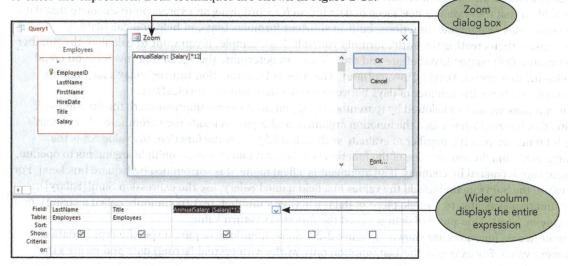

FIGURE 2-18   Using the Zoom dialog box

Q & A 2-2

Question: When I run the calculated field query, Access asks me for a parameter value. What should I do?

Answer: An unexpected parameter prompt generally means that you have spelled a field name incorrectly when creating a new calculated field expression. Double-check your calculated field.

In Access, when you use a field name in an expression, it is enclosed in [square brackets]. When you are entering the expression, you do not need to include the [square brackets] for field names that do not contain spaces. However, field names that have spaces *require* this syntax, so it's a good habit to include the square brackets around field names any time you are using them in an expression.

If you open the Zoom dialog box to create a computed field, close the dialog box by clicking OK, and then click the Run button (Query Tools Design tab | Results group) to display the query results as shown in Figure 2-19.

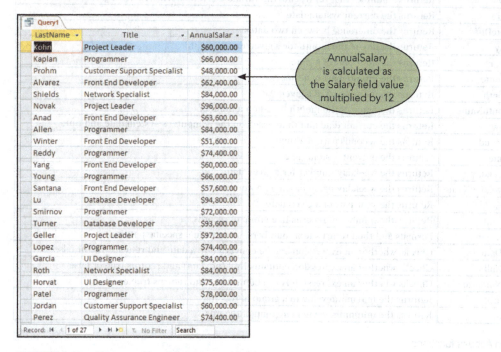

FIGURE 2-19   Query results with computed field

You also can use addition (+), subtraction (–), and division (/) in your expressions. You can include parentheses to indicate which computations Access should perform first. The main thing to understand about computed fields is that they create a new piece of data for *each* record using an expression to calculate that data.

Expressions may also include **functions**, built-in shortcut formulas that can help you calculate information faster than creating the entire formula yourself. For example, if you want to calculate the number of days between a field named InvoiceDate and today's date to determine the age of that invoice, you could use the following expression: Date()–[InvoiceDate]. The Access Date function returns today's date and the entire expression returns the number of days between today's date and the InvoiceDate.

Function names are always followed by (parentheses). If you need to pass information to the function so it can operate, that information is called the function **argument** and is passed inside the parentheses. For example, to use the Int function, pass it a number to evaluate such as Int(5.5). Int is the function, the value 5.5 is the function argument, and the return value of the function is 5. When a function uses multiple arguments to operate, the arguments are separated by commas. If an argument is a field name, it is surrounded by [square brackets]. For example, to use the Sum function to add the values in a field named Salary, use the expression Sum([Salary]).

Every function evaluates to a single piece of data, whether a number, text (commonly called a **string**), or a **Boolean** (true or false). That piece of data is called the function's **return value**.

Common Access functions are shown in Figure 2-20. Some functions require a specific type of data as their argument value. For example, the Len function only works with textual (string) data and returns the

Data Type for the Function Argument	Function	Description and Return Value
Text (String)	LCase	Converts and then returns a string to all lowercase characters
	Left	Returns the number of characters in a string (starting from left)
	Len	Returns the length of a string
	Right	Returns the number of characters from a string (starting from right)
	Trim	Removes both leading and trailing spaces from text (a string) and returns the string
	UCase	Converts and then returns a string to all uppercase characters
Numeric	Avg	Returns the average value of a numeric field for a group of records
	Int	Returns the integer part of a number
	Rnd	Returns a random number between 0 and 1
	Round	Rounds and then returns a number to a specified number of decimal places
	Sqr	Returns the square root of a number
	StDev	Returns a number that represents the standard deviation of a numeric field for a group of records
	Sum	Adds then returns the sum of a numeric field for a group of records
	Var	Returns a number that represents the variance of a numeric field for a group of records
	Date	Returns the current system date
Date	DateDiff	Returns the difference between two dates
	Day	Returns the day of the month for a given date
	Hour	Returns the hour part of a time
	Minute	Returns the minute part of a time
	Month	Returns the month part of a given date
	MonthName	Returns the name of the month based on a number
	Now	Returns the current date and time based on the computer's system date and time
	Second	Returns the seconds part of a time
	Time	Returns the current system time
	Weekday	Returns the weekday number for a given date
	WeekdayName	Returns the weekday name based on a number
	Year	Returns the year part of a given date
	Count	Returns the number of records in a group of records
General	Format	Formats and then returns text, numbers, or dates in a specific pattern
	IsDate	Checks whether an expression can be converted to a date and returns true or false
	IsNull	Checks whether an expression contains Null (no data) and returns true or false
	IsNumeric	Checks whether an expression is a valid number and returns true or false
	Max	Returns the maximum value in a group of records
	Min	Returns the minimum value in a group of records

FIGURE 2-20 Common Access functions

number of characters in the string. The Month function only works with a date argument and returns a number that represents the number of the month in a given date (January is 1, February is 2, and so forth). Other functions such as Count, Format, Max, and Min may be used with different types of data including text, numbers, and dates.

SUMMARIZING WITH AGGREGATE FUNCTIONS AND GROUPING

Some of the functions listed in Figure 2-20 are **aggregate functions**, which make calculations on groups of records. Aggregate functions use a single field name as their only argument such as Sum([Salary]) or Count([LastName]). The following are common aggregate functions:

- Avg: Returns the average value of a numeric field in a group of records
- Count: Returns the number of records in a group
- Max: Returns the maximum field value in a group of records
- Min: Returns the minimum field value in a group of records
- Sum: Returns the summed total of a numeric field in a group of records

Before creating a query with an aggregate function, you should decide how you want to **group** the records together. QBE programs use grouping to create groups of records that share some common characteristic. Without a **grouping field**, *all* records are summarized for the calculation.

Secondly, decide which field contains the information you want to use for the calculation. Many of the aggregate functions such as Avg, Sum, StDev, and Var only make sense when applied to a field that contains numbers. Others such as Count, Max, and Min can be applied to any type of data.

To use aggregate functions in an Access query, perform the following steps.

- Determine how you want to group the records.
- Determine which field or fields you want to use for the aggregate calculations.
- In Query Design View, add the tables containing the fields you want to use in the query, and then add those fields to the query grid.
- Click the Totals button (Query Tools Design tab | Show/Hide group). Access displays the Total row (see Figure 2-21) with Group By as the default value for each field.
- Change the Group By value to the appropriate aggregate function for the desired computation, and then run the query.

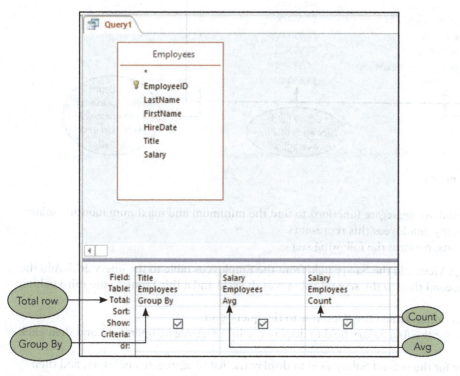

FIGURE 2-21 Query to group, average, and count records

You can add criteria to the query grid to further refine which records are selected for the query. If you remove the Group By field altogether, all records are grouped for the calculation.

YOUR TURN 2-6

What is the average salary value for each job title? Also include the total number of employees that share the same title.

To determine the average salary value as well as how many employees share the same job title, perform the following steps:

- In Query Design View, add the Title and Salary fields from the Employees table to the query grid. Add the Salary field a second time to the third column of the grid.
- Click the Totals button to add the Total row to the query grid.
- Click Group By for the first Salary field to display the list of aggregate operators, and then click Avg.
- Click Group By for the second Salary field to display the list of aggregate operators, and then click Count as shown in Figure 2-21.
- Run the query.

The query results appear in Figure 2-22. Access creates new default names for the columns with calculations, AvgOfSalary and CountOfSalary. You could rename those fields in Query Design View using *newfieldname:fieldname* syntax if desired such as *AverageSalary:Salary* or *Count:Salary*. It doesn't matter which field you count if all fields have a value, given the Count function returns the number of records in the group.

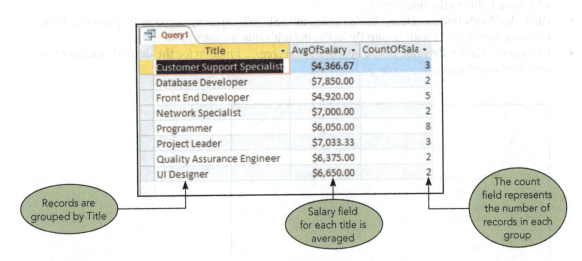

FIGURE 2-22 Grouped query results

You also group records and use aggregate functions to find the minimum and maximum monthly salary for all employees and how many employees this represents.

To make these calculations, perform the following steps:

- In Query Design View, add the Salary field from the Employees table to the query grid. Add the Salary field a second time to the second column of the grid and a third time to the third column of the grid.
- Click the Totals button to add the Total row to the query grid.
- Click Group By for the first Salary field to display the list of aggregate operators, and then click Min.
- Click Group By for the second Salary field to display the list of aggregate operators, and then click Max.

- Click Group By for the third Salary field to display the list of aggregate operators, and then click Count as shown in Figure 2-23.
- Run the query.

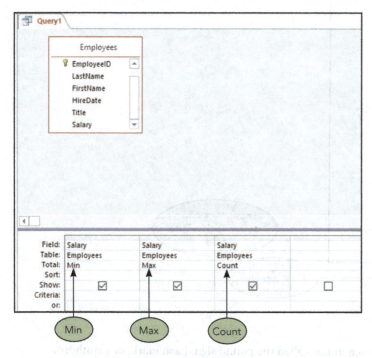

FIGURE 2-23   Query to calculate the minimum, maximum, and count of Salary

The query results appear in Figure 2-24.

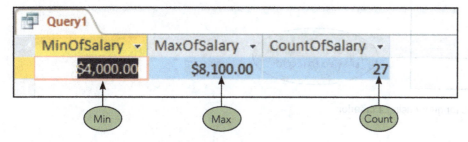

FIGURE 2-24   Grouped and summarized query results

You can also add criteria to the query grid for queries that group and summarize data using the WHERE keyword.

Suppose you need to know the total monthly salary for all employees that were hired prior to 1/1/2020. Perform the following steps:

- In Query Design View, add the Salary field from the Employees table to the query grid. Add the HireDate field to the second column.
- Click the Totals button to add the Total row to the query grid.
- Click Group By for the Salary field to display the list of aggregate operators, and then click Sum.
- Click Group By for the HireDate field to display the list of aggregate operators, and then click Where.
- Click the Criteria cell for the HireDate field and enter <#1/1/2020# as shown in Figure 2-25.
- Remove the checkmark from the Show check box for the HireDate field. You can't both Sum the Salary field and show all of the dates prior to 1/1/2020 in Query Datasheet View, so the HireDate field is not displayed.
- Run the query.

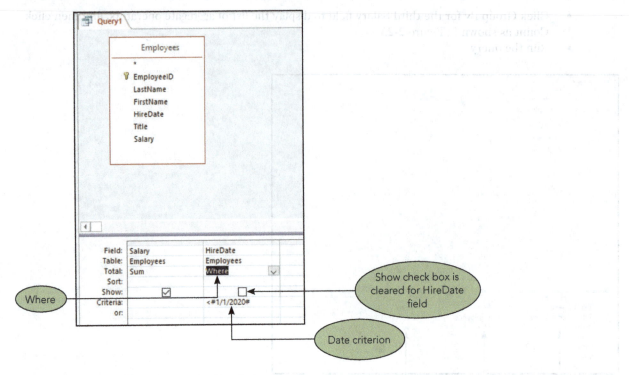

FIGURE 2-25   Query to group records with criteria

Date criteria is surrounded by # symbols (sometimes called the pound sign, hash mark, or octothorpe symbol) similarly to how text criteria is surrounded by "quotation marks". Access automatically adds the # symbols around date criteria if you do not enter those symbols yourself. The query results appear in Figure 2-26.

FIGURE 2-26   Grouped results for query using a criterion

SORTING RECORDS

Specifying a **sort** order to determine the order of the records that are selected for a query can make the information easier to read. For example, you might want to see employees listed based on their hire date, clients listed alphabetically by client name, or tasks listed alphabetically by task name within a category.

The field on which records are sorted is called the **sort key**; you can sort records using as many fields as desired. The first field used in the sort order determines the order of the records until two records have the same value in the first sort field. At that point, the second sort field takes over to determine the order of the records that have the same value in the first sort order, and so forth. To sort in Access, you specify the sort order (ascending or descending) in the Sort row of the design grid for the sort fields. Sort orders are evaluated left to right, so the leftmost sort order is the first sort order, and so forth.

YOUR TURN 2-7

List the task ID, description, and category ID for each task in the TaskMasterList table. Sort the records in ascending order by description.

To sort the records alphabetically using the Description field, perform the following steps:

- In Query Design View, add the TaskID, Description, and CategoryID fields from the TaskMasterList table to the query grid in that order.
- Select the Ascending sort order in the Sort row for the Description column, as shown in Figure 2-27.
- You can click the Totals button (Query Tools Design tab | Show/Hide group) to turn off the total in the grid.

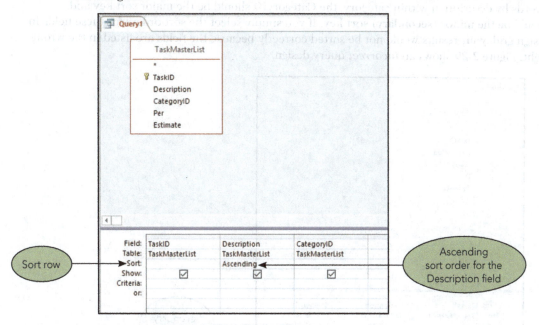

FIGURE 2-27   Query to sort records

The query results appear in Figure 2-28 with the task descriptions listed in alphabetical order.

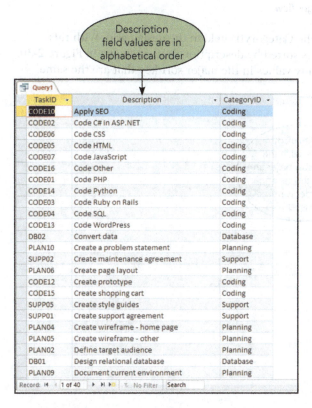

FIGURE 2-28   Query results with one sort key

Sorting on Multiple Keys

You can specify more than one sort key in a query. The leftmost sort order in the design grid is the **major (primary) sort key**. Each additional sort key determines the order of the records when the previous sort field's values are the same.

For example, suppose you need to list the TaskID, Description, and CategoryID for each task in the TaskMasterList table, and sort the records in ascending order by task description within their category.

To sort records by description within category, the CategoryID should be the major sort key and Description should be the **minor (secondary) sort key**. If you simply select the sort orders for these fields in the current design grid, your results would not be sorted correctly because the fields are listed in the wrong order left to right. Figure 2-29 shows an *incorrect* query design.

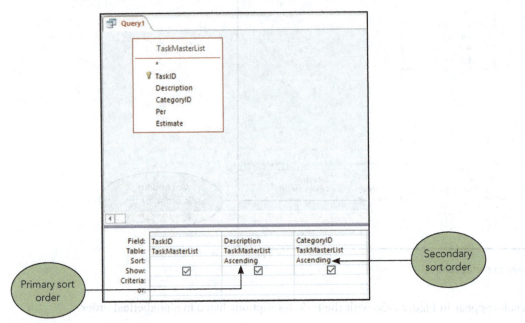

FIGURE 2-29   Sort orders work from left to right in Query Design View

In Figure 2-29, the Description field is to the left of the CategoryID field in the design grid. With this order, Description becomes the major sort key; the data is sorted by description first, as shown in Figure 2-30. The minor sort key is not needed given there are never any values in the major sort key that are the same.

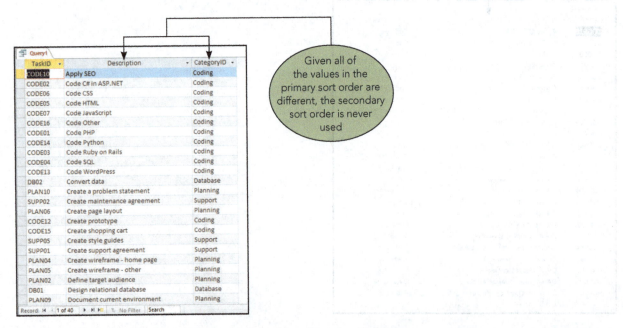

FIGURE 2-30   Results of query with incorrect design for sorting on multiple keys

To correct this problem, the CategoryID field needs to move to the left of the Description field in the design grid. To move a field in the design grid, perform the following steps:

- Point to the top of the column.
- When the pointer changes to a down arrow, click to select the column.
- Drag the column to the new location.

Moving a column changes the output order, however, which you may not want to do. If the original order is important, you can include the secondary sort field twice—once before the primary sort field for sort order purposes, and once after for display purposes. You then can sort by the first occurrence of the field but hide it from the output, as shown in Figure 2-31. Notice the first occurrence contains the Ascending sort order but displays no checkmark in the Show check box. The second occurrence will be displayed, but it has no sort order selected.

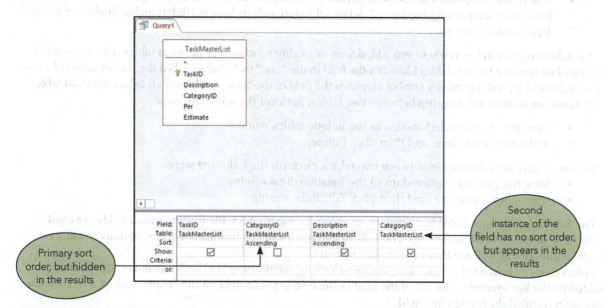

FIGURE 2-31   Query design to sort by CategoryID then by Description, but display CategoryID after Description

In Figure 2-31, the CategoryID field is the major sort key, and the Description is the secondary, or minor, sort key given their left-to-right positions. The second CategoryID field in the design grid will display the category values in the query results in the desired position, as shown in Figure 2-32.

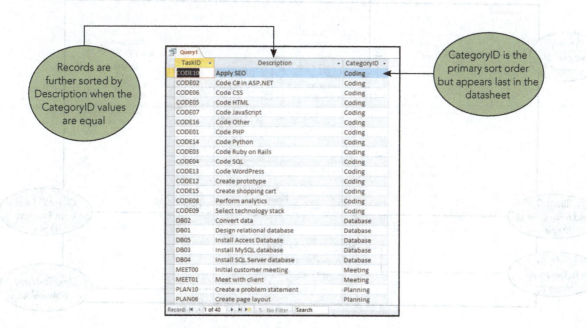

FIGURE 2-32   Results of query with multiple sort keys

JOINING TABLES

So far, the queries used in the examples have displayed records from a single table. In many cases, however, you will need to create queries to select data from more than one table at the same time. To do so, it is necessary to **join** the tables based on a common field. You can join two tables in the upper pane of Query Design View, but it is more productive to join the tables ahead of time, in the Relationships window, so that they are automatically joined for every query that uses them.

To view the existing relationships in a database, perform the following steps:

- Click the Database Tools tab on the ribbon.
- Click the Relationships button (Database Tools tab | Relationships group).
- The relationships for the database appear in the Relationships window, but to be sure that none have been temporarily hidden, click the All Relationships button (Relationship Tools Design tab | Relationships group).

The Relationships window is where you add, delete, or modify relationships between tables. The one symbol on the **join line** between the two tables identifies the field in the "one" table (often called the **parent table**) of a one-to-many relationship, and the infinity symbol identifies the field in the "many" table (often called the **child table**).

To delete an existing relationship between two tables, perform the following steps:

- View the existing relationships in the Relationships window.
- Right-click a join line, and then click Delete.

To edit an existing relationship between two tables, perform the following steps:
- View the existing relationships in the Relationships window.
- Right-click a join line, and then click Edit Relationship.

The Edit Relationships dialog box appears, as shown in Figure 2-33, identifying which fields are used in each table to create the relationship. The Edit Relationships dialog box also provides options to enforce referential integrity as well as other relationship options.

Notice that the field on the "one" side of a one-to-many relationship is always a **primary key field** as indicated by the **key symbol** to the left of the field in the field list. The field on the "many" side of a one-to-many relationship is called the **foreign key field**.

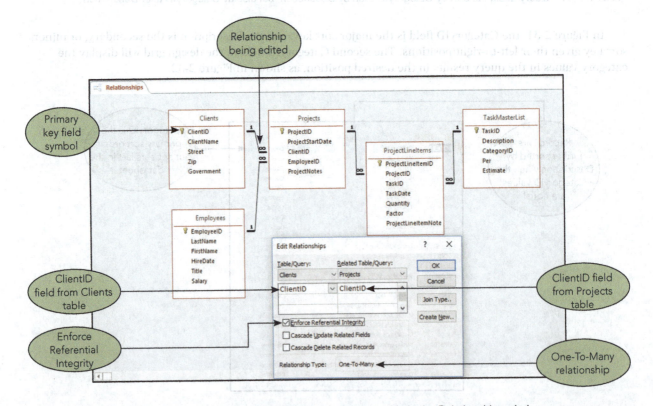

FIGURE 2-33 Editing the relationship between the Clients and Projects table in the Relationships window

Recall from Module 1 that **referential integrity** is a set of rules applied to the relationship that prevents the creation of orphan records. An **orphan record** is a record in the "many" (child) table that has no match in the "one" (parent) table. In the relationship shown in Figure 2-33, referential integrity prevents orphan records from being created in the Projects table. In other words, you cannot enter a record in the Projects table with a ClientID value that doesn't already exist in the Clients table. You also cannot delete a record in the Clients table that has existing related records in the Projects table. When referential integrity is enforced on a one-to-many relationship, the link line displays "one" and "infinity" symbols to identify the "one" (parent) table and "many" (child) table.

To create a new existing relationship between two tables in the Relationships window, perform the following steps:

- View the existing relationships in the Relationships window.
- Drag the field used to create the relationship from the table on the "one" side of the relationship (which is always a primary key field) to the field used to create the relationship in the table on the "many" side of the relationship (which is never a primary key field. Rather, it is called the foreign key field).

    Technically, it doesn't matter if you drag from the primary key field to the foreign key field or vice versa to make the relationship, but logically, it makes more sense to drag from the "one" (parent) table that contains the primary key field to the "many" (child) table that contains the foreign key field.
- The Edit Relationships dialog box opens, in which you can further modify the relationship by choosing options such as the Enforce Referential Integrity check box.
- Click OK in the Edit Relationships dialog box to complete the new relationship.

Note that creating relationships in the Relationships window requires that the table on the "one" side of the relationship have a primary key field, given the primary key field *always* becomes the linking field on the "one" side of a one-to-many relationship. If you do not see a key symbol to the left of a field in the field list, you first need to establish a primary key field in that table before it can participate on the "one" (parent) side of a one-to-many relationship.

To establish a primary key field for a table in the Relationships window, perform the following steps:

- Right-click the field list that represents the table for which you want to establish a primary key field.
- Click Table Design on the shortcut menu.
- Click the field that you want to establish as the primary key field.
- Click the Primary Key button (Table Tools Design tab | Tools group).

In order to serve as a primary key field, a field must contain unique information in each record. If several records are entered into a table before the primary key field is established for the table, you may have to find and correct any duplicate entries in the field before it can be established as the primary key field, a process that is sometimes referred to as **scrubbing** the data. Some tables have natural primary key fields such as an employee ID or number, a student number, product ID, or an invoice number. Others, however, do not have an obvious candidate for the primary key field. In that case, an AutoNumber field, which automatically increments to the next integer value for each new record entered into the table, often serves as the primary key field for that table.

If table relationships have not been established in the Relationships window, you can still join tables in the upper pane of Query Design View. While not as productive as setting up the relationships ahead of time in the Relationships window, and also more computing-intensive, you may occasionally need to establish a specific relationship for a specific query in Query Design View.

To join two tables in Query Design View, perform the following steps:

- Drag the field used to create the relationship from the table on the "one" side of the relationship to the field used to create the relationship in the table on the "many" side of the relationship.

    Technically, it doesn't matter which field you start with to make the relationship, but logically, it makes more sense to drag from the "one" (parent) table to the "many" (child) table.

When you create a relationship between two tables in Query Design View, Access draws a join line between matching fields in the two tables, indicating that the tables are related. (If no relationships have been established in the Relationships window, Query Design View will try to automatically join two tables that have corresponding fields with the same field name if the field is a primary key field in one of the tables.)

A relationship created in Query Design View will not allow you to enforce referential integrity. A join line between two tables that does not have referential integrity is displayed as a thin line without the "one" and "infinity" symbols. Although the symbols are not displayed on the join line, the relationship is still a one-to-many relationship. Without enforcing referential integrity, however, orphan records may be easily created in the table on the "many" side of the relationship. More information on enforcing referential integrity as well as the other options in the Edit Relationships dialog box are covered in Module 4.

Once the tables are properly related in Query Design View, you can select fields from either or both tables for the query.

YOUR TURN 2-8

List each client ID and name, along with their related project IDs and project notes.

You cannot create this query using a single table—the client name is in the Clients table and the project information is in the Projects table. To select the fields needed for this query, perform the following steps:

- In Query Design view, use the Show Table dialog box to add the Clients and Projects tables.

  A join line appears, indicating how the tables are related. Given the join line has the "one" and "infinity" symbols, you know that the relationship was previously created in the Relationships window and that referential integrity was enforced.

- Add the ClientID and ClientName fields from the Clients table to the design grid, and then add the ProjectID and ProjectNotes fields from the Projects table as shown in Figure 2-34.

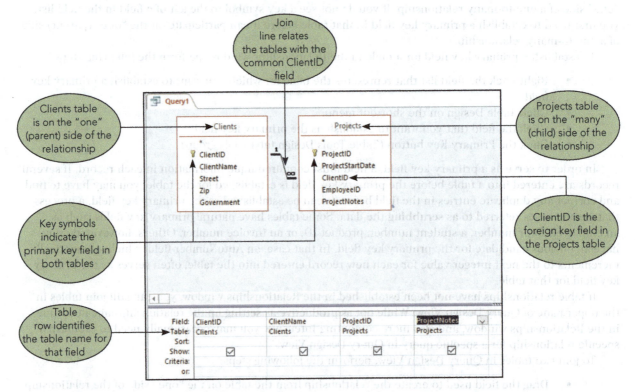

FIGURE 2-34 Query Design View with related tables

The Table row in the design grid indicates the table from which each field is selected. The query results appear in Figure 2-35. Notice that some clients are listed more than once. Those clients have more than one related record in the Projects table. Their ClientID value is listed more than once in the ClientID field of the Projects table, which links each record in the Projects table to the corresponding client in the Clients table.

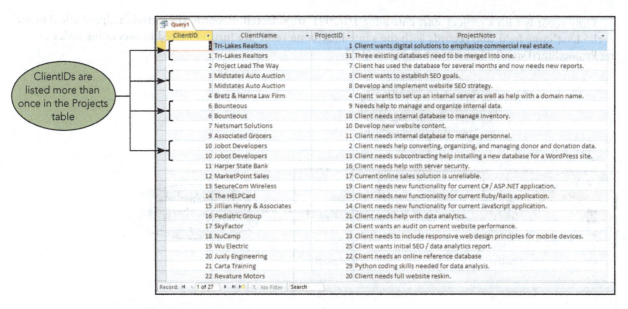

FIGURE 2-35   Results of query with related tables

For each project, suppose you need to list the project ID, project start date, employee ID, and last name for the employee assigned to that project. You must also select only those projects that start after 1/1/2021, and sort the records by the project start date within each employee's last name.

You cannot create this query using a single table—the client name is in the Clients table and the employee information is in the Employees table. To select the fields needed for this query, perform the following steps:

- In Query Design view, use the Show Table dialog box to add the Employees and Projects tables.
  A join line appears, indicating how the tables are related. Given the join line has the "one" and "infinity" symbols, you know that the relationship was previously created in the Relationships window and that referential integrity was enforced.
- Add the EmployeeID and LastName fields from the Employees table to the design grid, and then add the ProjectID and ProjectStartDate fields from the Projects table.
- Add an Ascending sort order to the LastName and ProjectStartDate fields.
- Add >#1/1/2021# to the Criteria row for the ProjectStartDate field as shown in Figure 2-36.

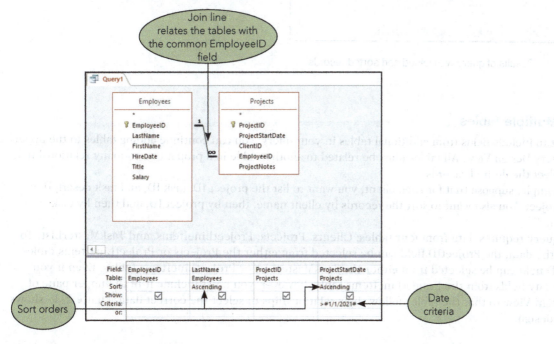

FIGURE 2-36   Query to sort joined records

Only records with a project start date after 1/1/2021 are selected. Records are sorted in alphabetical order on the LastName field, and records with the same LastName value are further sorted in ascending order on the ProjectStartDate field, as shown in Figure 2-37.

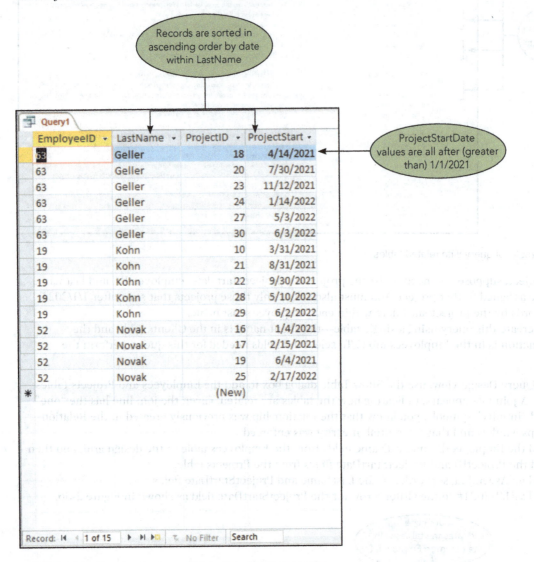

FIGURE 2-37 Results of query with joined and sorted records

Joining Multiple Tables

If you want to include fields from additional tables in your query, you can continue adding tables to the upper pane of Query Design View. All tables must be related to another table in a proper one-to-many relationship in order to select the desired records.

For example, suppose that for each client, you want to list the project ID, task ID, and task description for each project. You also want to sort the records by client name, then by project ID, and then by task description.

This query requires data from four tables: Clients, Projects, ProjectLineItems, and TaskMasterList. To only view the data, the ProjectID field can be selected from either the Projects or ProjectLineItems tables. The TaskID field can be selected from either the TaskMasterList or ProjectLineItems tables. Even if you do not use any fields from the ProjectLineItems table, however, you must include it in the upper pane of Query Design View so that the tables follow their relationships to select the correct data. Figure 2-38 shows the query design.

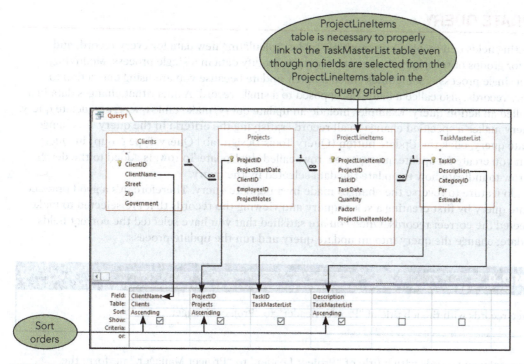

FIGURE 2-38   Query with four related tables and three sort orders

The query results appear in Figure 2-39.

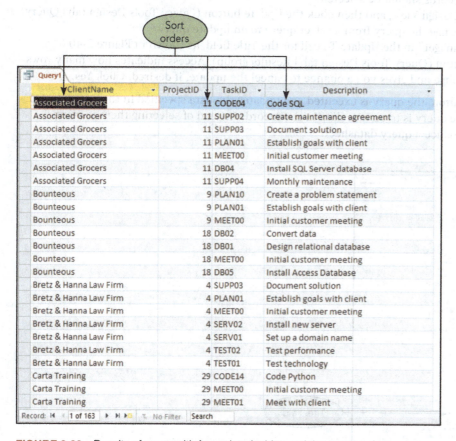

FIGURE 2-39   Results of query with four related tables and three sort orders

USING AN UPDATE QUERY

In addition to selecting fields and records from multiple tables, calculating new data for every record, and summarizing data for groups of records, you can use a query to modify data in a single process. Modifying several records in a single process is sometimes called a **batch update** because you are using one action to update data in many records, also called a batch, as opposed to a single record. A query that changes data in a batch process is called an **action query**. Examples include an update query, make table query, and delete query.

An **update query** makes a specified change to all records satisfying the criteria in the query. To change a query to an update query, click the Update button (Query Tools Design tab | Query Type group) in Query Design View. When you create an update query, a new row, called the Update To row, is added to the design grid. You use this row to indicate how to update the data selected by the query.

There is no undo feature to reverse the changes made by an update query. Therefore, it's a good practice to build your update query by first creating a select query and viewing the records that are selected to make sure you have selected the correct records. Once you are satisfied that you have selected the correct fields and records to update, change the query into an update query and run the update process.

YOUR TURN 2-9

Change employee records with the job title of "Project Leader" to "Project Manager."

To update the employee records with a title of "Project Leader" to "Project Manager," perform the following steps:

- In Query Design View, add the Employees field list and drag the Title field to the query grid.
- Enter "Project Leader" in the Criteria cell, and then run the query to check the records that are selected. Three records should be selected.
- Return to Query Design View, and then click the Update button (Query Tools Design tab | Query Type group) to change the query from a select query to an update query.
- Enter "Project Manager" in the Update To cell for the Title field, as shown in Figure 2-40.
- Click the Run button (Query Tools Design tab | Results group). Access indicates how many rows the query will change and gives you a chance to cancel the update, if desired. Click Yes.

When you click the Yes button, the query is executed and updates the data specified in the query design. Because the result of an update query is to change data in the records instead of selecting them to view, running the query does not produce a query datasheet.

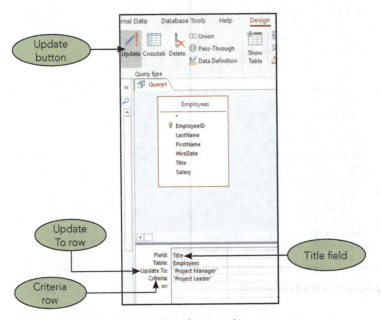

FIGURE 2-40 Query Design View for an update query

USING A DELETE QUERY

A **delete query** permanently deletes all the records satisfying the criteria entered in the query. For example, you might want to delete all the tasks associated with a certain project in ProjectLineItems table if the project has changed significantly and you want to start over with new tasks to create the project estimate.

YOUR TURN 2-10

Delete all ProjectLineItems records for the project with a project ID of 20.

To delete all ProjectLineItems records for the project with a project ID of 20, perform the following steps:

- In Query Design View, add the ProjectLineItems field list to the upper pane and drag the ProjectID field to the query grid.
- Enter 20 in the Criteria cell for the ProjectID field, click the Select button (Query Tools Design tab | Query Type group), and then run the query to check the records that are selected. Thirteen records should be selected.
- Return to Query Design View, and then click the Delete button (Query Tools Design tab | Query Type group) to change the query from a select query to a delete query.
  A new row, the Delete row, is added to the design grid as shown in Figure 2-41.
- Click the Run button. Access indicates how many rows will be deleted and gives you a chance to cancel the deletions, if desired. Click Yes.

Running a delete query permanently deletes the records and cannot be undone.

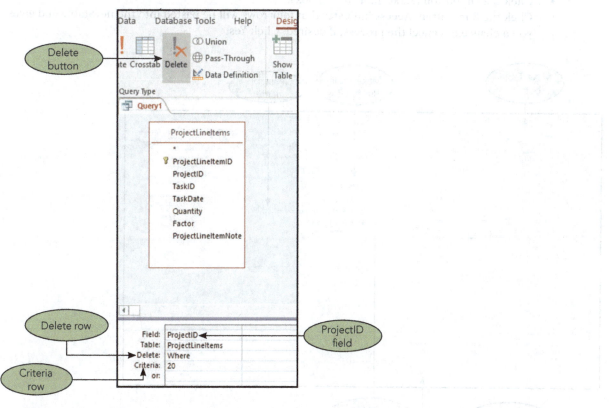

FIGURE 2-41   Query Design View for a delete query

If you run a delete query with no criteria, *all* records are selected. Running a delete query in that situation would delete all records from the table with fields in the query grid. Be careful!

USING A MAKE-TABLE QUERY

A **make-table query** creates a new table in the current or another database with the records selected by the query. The new table is a *copy* of the selected data, so make-table queries are only needed for specific reasons such as preparing data to be used by programs outside of the database or creating archived copies of data to capture information as of a particular point in time.

YOUR TURN 2-11

Create a new table containing the client name, as well as the project IDs and project start dates prior to 1/1/2020. Name the table ClientProjectsPriorTo2020.

To create a query that creates a new table with the ClientName, ProjectID, and ProjectStartDate fields prior to 1/1/2020, perform the following steps:

- In Query Design View, add the Clients and Projects field lists to the upper pane.
- Drag the ClientName field from the Clients table, and the ProjectID and ProjectStartDate fields from the Projects table to the grid.
- Enter <1/1/2020 in the Criteria cell for the ProjectStartDate field, click the Select button (Query Tools Design tab | Query Type group), and then run the query to check the records that are selected. Four records should be selected.
- Return to Query Design View, and then click the Make Table button (Query Tools Design tab | Query Type group) to change the query from a select query to a make-table query. The Make Table dialog box opens as shown in Figure 2-42.
- Enter the new table's name, ClientProjectsPriorTo2020 (Make Table dialog box).
- Click the OK button (Make Table dialog box).
- Click the Run button. Access indicates that four rows will be pasted into the new table and gives you a chance to cancel the process, if desired. Click Yes.

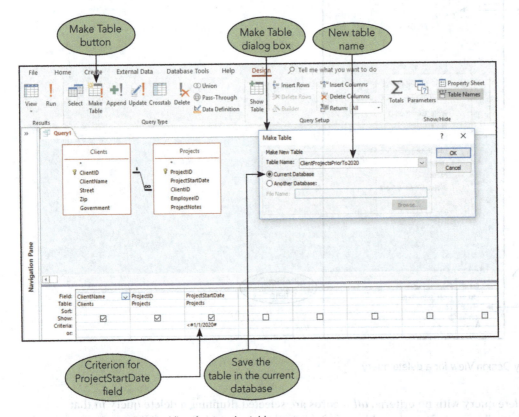

FIGURE 2-42 Query Design View for a make-table query

After running the make-table query, the records are added to a new table named ClientProjectsPriorTo2020 in the current database. Figure 2-43 shows the new table created by the make-table query. In the figure, the columns in the table have been resized by dragging the right edge of the column heading. You can also specify sort orders within the make-table query if you want to order the records in a specific way in the new table.

ClientProjectsPriorTo2020		
ClientName	ProjectID	ProjectStartDate
Tri-Lakes Realtors	1	2/6/2019
Jobot Developers	2	2/7/2019
Midstates Auto Auction	3	3/11/2019
Project Lead The Way	7	9/2/2019
*	(New)	

FIGURE 2-43 ClientProjectsPriorTo2020 table created by the make-table query

OPTIMIZING QUERIES

A **query optimizer** is a DBMS component that analyzes a query and attempts to determine the most efficient way to execute it. Generally, the query optimizer is a process that occurs behind the scenes without direct access to those who use the database.

In addition to using a query optimizer, you can use other techniques to increase the speed of your queries. The larger the database and the more simultaneous users, the more important these techniques become.

- Establish as many relationships in the Relationships window as possible.
- Enforce referential integrity on as many relationships as possible.
- In Query Design View, double-click fields to add them to the query grid and use list arrows to choose query options whenever possible to avoid typing errors.
- Include only the minimum number of fields necessary, especially if the query also groups records or uses aggregate functions.
- Delete any field lists that are not needed for the query or do not supply needed relationships between tables.
- Include meaningful criteria to select only those records needed for the question at hand.

Q & A 2-3

Question: If your database is performing well, why is it still important to concern yourself with techniques that improve the performance of queries?

Answer: Over time, the number of users, processes, and programs that rely on a successful database often grows dramatically, which in turn has a substantial impact on overall performance. Taking the time to write efficient queries while your application is small and performing well generally yields tremendous benefits down the road. Not taking the time to write efficient queries while your application is still performing well often creates unnecessary rework, user frustration, and erosion of confidence in your database later.

EXAMINING RELATIONAL ALGEBRA

Relational algebra is a query language that takes instances of relations as input and yields instances of relations as output. Given the popularity of QBE approaches to relational database queries, relational algebra is rarely directly used with modern database management systems today. Still, relational algebra provides the foundation for **SQL**, **Structured Query Language**, which is vitally important to programmers seeking to select, enter, update, and delete data stored in relational databases.

Figure 2-44 lists some of the common commands and operators used with relational algebra.

Commands/Operators	Purpose
SELECT	Chooses a subset of rows that satisfies a condition
PROJECT	Reorders, selects, or deletes attributes during a query
JOIN	Compounds similar rows from two tables into single longer rows, as every row of the first table is joined to every row of the second table
UNION	Includes all rows from two tables, eliminating duplicates
INTERSECTION	Displays only rows that are common to two tables
SUBTRACT	Includes rows from one table that do not exist in another table (also called SET DIFFERENT, DIFFERENCE, or MINUS operation)
PRODUCT	Creates a table that has all the attributes of two tables including all rows from both tables (also referred to as the CARTESIAN PRODUCT)
RENAME	Assigns a name to the results of queries for future reference

FIGURE 2-44 Relational algebra operators

As in the following examples, each command ends with a GIVING clause, followed by a table name. This clause requests that the result of the command be placed in a temporary table with the specified name.

Selection

In relational algebra, the **SELECT** command retrieves certain rows from an existing table (based on some user-specified criteria) and saves them as a new table. The SELECT command includes the word *WHERE* followed by a condition. The rows retrieved are the rows in which the condition is satisfied.

YOUR TURN 2-12

List all information about ClientID 19 from the Clients table.

```
SELECT Clients WHERE ClientID=19
GIVING Answer
```

This command creates a new table named Answer that contains only one row in which the ClientID value is 19, because that is the only row in which the condition is true. All the columns from the Clients table are included in the new Answer table.

To list all information from the Clients table about all clients with a Zip value of 02113, you would use the following command:

```
SELECT Clients WHERE Zip='02113'
GIVING Answer
```

This command creates a new table named Answer that contains all the columns from the Clients table, but only those rows in which the Zip field value is '02113'. Note that a Zip field should be created as a text (string or character) field given the numbers do not represent quantities and should not be used in mathematical calculations. If the Zip field was created as a Number field, entries such as 02113 would be shortened to 2113 because leading zeros are insignificant to numbers, and are therefore deleted from the entry. As a text field, all characters are treated as significant pieces of information and saved with the entry.

Projection

In relational algebra, the **PROJECT** command takes a vertical subset of a table; that is, it causes only certain columns to be included in the new table. The PROJECT command includes the word *OVER* followed by a list of the columns to be included.

```
PROJECT Clients OVER (ClientID, ClientName) GIVING Answer
```

This command creates a new table named Answer that contains the ClientID and ClientName columns for all the rows in the Clients table.

Suppose you want to list the client ID and name of all clients with a Zip field value of 02447.

This example requires a two-step process. You first use a SELECT command to create a new table (named Temp) that contains only those clients with a Zip field value of 02447. Next, you project the new table to restrict the result to only the indicated columns.

```
SELECT Clients WHERE Zip='02447'

GIVING Temp

PROJECT Temp OVER (ClientID, ClientName)

GIVING Answer
```

Joining

The **JOIN** command is a core operation of relational algebra because it allows you to extract data from more than one table. In the most common form of the join, two tables are combined based on the values in matching columns, creating a new table containing the columns in both tables. Rows in this new table are the **concatenation** (combination) of a row from the first table and a row from the second table that match on the common column (often called the **join column**). In other words, two tables are joined *on* the join column.

For example, suppose you want to join the two tables shown in Figure 2-45 on the ClientID field (the join column), creating a new table named Temp.

Clients

ClientID	ClientName	Street	Zip	Government
1	Tri-Lakes Realtors	135 E Jefferson St	02447	FALSE
2	Project Lead The Way	762 Saratoga Blvd	02446	TRUE
3	Midstates Auto Auction	9787 S Campbell Ln	01355	FALSE
4	Bretz & Hanna Law Firm	8101 N Olive Dr	01431	FALSE
5	Aspire Associates	5673 South Ave	01431	FALSE
6	Bounteous	9898 Ohio Ave	02770	FALSE
7	Netsmart Solutions	4091 Brentwood Ln	01354	FALSE
8	Loren Group	9565 Ridge Rd	02466	FALSE
9	Associated Grocers	231 Tecumsa Rd	02532	FALSE
10	Jobot Developers	1368 E 1000 St	02330	FALSE
11	Harper State Bank	1865 Forrest Dr	01571	FALSE
12	MarketPoint Sales	826 Hosta St	01983	FALSE
13	SecureCom Wireless	5280 Industrial Dr	01852	FALSE
14	The HELPCard	840 Boonville Ave	02466	TRUE
15	Jillian Henry & Associates	815 E California St	02113	FALSE
16	Pediatric Group	4940 W Farm Rd	02113	FALSE
17	SkyFactor	1736 Sunshine Dr	02726	FALSE
18	NuCamp	2500 E Kearny St	01431	FALSE
19	Wu Electric	5520 S Michigan	02447	FALSE
20	Juxly Engineering	4238 Rumsfield Rd	02148	FALSE
21	Carta Training	2445 N Airport Dr	02446	FALSE

FIGURE 2-45 Clients and Projects tables *(continued)*

Projects

ProjectID	ProjectStartDate	ClientID	EmployeeID	ProjectNotes
1	06-Feb-19	1	52	Client wants digital solutions to emphasize commercial real estate.
2	07-Feb-19	10	63	Client needs help converting, organizing, and managing donor and donation data.
3	11-Mar-19	3	52	Client wants to establish SEO goals.
4	10-Apr-20	4	52	Client wants to set up an internal server as well as help with a domain name.
7	02-Sep-19	2	63	Client has used the database for several months and now needs new reports.
8	06-Jan-20	3	52	Develop and implement website SEO strategy.
9	10-Feb-20	6	63	Needs help to manage and organize internal data.
10	31-Mar-21	7	19	Develop new website content.
11	30-Apr-20	9	19	Client needs internal database to manage personnel.
13	30-Nov-20	10	64	Client needs subcontracting help installing a new database for a WordPress site.
14	09-Dec-20	15	19	Client needs new functionality for current JavaScript application.
15	21-Dec-20	14	19	Client needs new functionality for current Ruby/Rails application.
16	04-Jan-21	11	52	Client needs help with server security.
17	15-Feb-21	12	52	Current online sales solution is unreliable.
18	14-Apr-21	6	63	Client needs internal database to manage inventory.
19	04-Jun-21	13	52	Client needs new functionality for current C# / ASP.NET application.
20	30-Jul-21	22	63	Client needs full website reskin.
21	31-Aug-21	16	19	Client needs help with data analytics.
22	30-Sep-21	20	19	Client needs an online reference database
23	12-Nov-21	18	63	Client needs to include responsive web design principles for mobile devices.
24	14-Jan-22	17	63	Client wants an audit on current website performance.

FIGURE 2-45   Clients and Projects tables (*continued*)

The result of joining the Clients and Projects tables creates the table shown in Figure 2-46. The column that joins the tables (ClientID) appears only once. Other than that, all columns from both tables appear in the result.

If a row in one table does not match any row in the other table, that row will not appear in the result of the join.

You can restrict the output from the join to include only certain columns by using the PROJECT command. For example, to list the ClientID, ClientName, ProjectID, and ProjectNotes for each client, use the following command:

```
JOIN Clients Projects
WHERE Clients.ClientID=Projects.ClientID
GIVING Temp
PROJECT Temp OVER (ClientID, ClientName, ProjectID, ProjectNotes)
GIVING Answer
```

In the WHERE clause of the JOIN command, the matching fields are both named ClientID—the field in the Projects table named ClientID is supposed to match the field in the Clients table named ClientID. Because two fields are named ClientID, you must qualify the field names. Just as in QBE, the ClientID field in the Projects table is written as Projects.ClientID and the ClientID field in the Clients table is written as Clients. ClientID.

In this example, the JOIN command joins the Clients and Projects tables to create a new table, named Temp. The PROJECT command creates a new table named Answer that contains all the rows from the Temp table, but only the ClientID, ClientName, ProjectID, and ProjectNotes columns.

ClientID	ClientName	Street	Zip	Government	ProjectID	ProjectStartDate	EmployeeID	ProjectNotes
1	Tri-Lakes Realtors	135 E Jefferson St	02447	FALSE	1	06-Feb-19	52	Client wants digital solutions to emphasize commercial real estate.
1	Tri-Lakes Realtors	135 E Jefferson St	02447	FALSE	31	01-Mar-20	19	Three existing databases need to be merged into one.
2	Project Lead The Way	762 Saratoga Blvd	02446	TRUE	7	02-Sep-19	63	Client has used the database for several months and now needs new reports.
3	Midstates Auto Auction	9787 S Campbell Ln	01355	FALSE	3	11-Mar-19	52	Client wants to establish SEO goals.
3	Midstates Auto Auction	9787 S Campbell Ln	01355	FALSE	8	06-Jan-20	52	Develop and implement website SEO strategy.
4	Bretz & Hanna Law Firm	8101 N Olive Dr	01431	FALSE	4	10-Apr-20	52	Client wants to set up an internal server as well as help with a domain name.
6	Bounteous	9898 Ohio Ave	02770	FALSE	9	10-Feb-20	63	Needs help to manage and organize internal data.
6	Bounteous	9898 Ohio Ave	02770	FALSE	18	14-Apr-21	63	Client needs internal database to manage inventory.
7	Netsmart Solutions	4091 Brentwood Ln	01354	FALSE	10	31-Mar-21	19	Develop new website content.
9	Associated Grocers	231 Tecumsa Rd	02532	FALSE	11	30-Apr-20	19	Client needs internal database to manage personnel.
10	Jobot Developers	1368 E 1000 St	02330	FALSE	2	07-Feb-19	63	Client needs help converting, organizing, and managing donor and donation data.
10	Jobot Developers	1368 E 1000 St	02330	FALSE	13	30-Nov-20	64	Client needs subcontracting help installing a new database for a WordPress site.
11	Harper State Bank	1865 Forrest Dr	01571	FALSE	16	04-Jan-21	52	Client needs help with server security.
12	MarketPoint Sales	826 Hosta St	01983	FALSE	17	15-Feb-21	52	Current online sales solution is unreliable.
13	SecureCom Wireless	5280 Industrial Dr	01852	FALSE	19	04-Jun-21	52	Client needs new functionality for current C# / ASP.NET application.

FIGURE 2-46   Table produced by joining the Clients and Projects tables

The type of join used in the preceding example is called a **natural join**. Although this type of join is the most common, there is another possibility. The other type of join, the **outer join**, is similar to the natural join, except that it also includes records from each original table that are not common in both tables. In a natural join, these unmatched records do not appear in the new table. In the outer join, unmatched records are included and the values of the fields are vacant, or **null**, for the records that do not have data common in both tables. Performing an outer join for the preceding example would produce a table with all client records even if they did not have any related projects.

Union

The **union** of tables A and B is a table containing all rows that are in either table A or table B or in both table A and table B. The union operation is performed by the **UNION** command in relational algebra; however, there is a restriction on the operation. It does not make sense, for example, to talk about the union of the Clients table and the Projects table because the tables do not contain the same columns. The two tables *must* have the same structure for a union to be appropriate; the formal term is *union compatible*. Two tables are **union compatible** when they have the same number of columns and when their corresponding columns represent the same type of data. For example, if the first column in table A contains ClientIDs, the first column in table B must also contain ClientIDs.

For example, suppose you need to list the employee ID and last name of those employees that are related to projects *or* have a title of Programmer or both.

You can create a table containing the employee ID and last and name of all employees that are related to projects by joining the Employees table and the Projects table (Temp1 in the following example) and then projecting the result over EmployeeID and LastName (Temp2). You can also create a table containing the EmployeeID and LastName of all employees with a Title value of Programmer by selecting them from the Employees table (Temp3) and then projecting the result (Temp4). The two tables ultimately created by this process (Temp2 and Temp4) have the same structure. They each have two fields: EmployeeID and LastName. Because these two tables are union compatible, it is appropriate to take the union of these two tables. This process is accomplished in relational algebra using the following code:

```
JOIN Employees, Projects
WHERE Employees.EmployeeID=Projects.EmployeeID
GIVING Temp1
PROJECT Temp1 OVER EmployeeID, LastName
GIVING Temp2
SELECT Employees WHERE Title='Programmer'
GIVING Temp3
PROJECT Temp3 OVER EmployeeID, LastName
GIVING Temp4
UNION Temp2 WITH Temp4 GIVING Answer
```

Intersection

The **intersection** of two tables is a table containing all rows that are *common* in both table A and table B. As you would expect, using the intersection operation also requires that the two tables have the same columns (also called union compatible) for the intersection to work. Compared to the UNION command, you replace the UNION command with the **INTERSECT** command.

For example, suppose you want to list the employee ID and last name of employees that are related to projects *and* that have a title of Project Leader.

In this example, you need to join the Employees and Projects tables first to find which employees are related to projects. You then need to find the employees that have a title of Project Leader. Finally, you need to determine which records are common to both tables. The code to accomplish this is as follows:

```
JOIN Employees, Projects
WHERE Employees.EmployeeID=Projects.EmployeeID
GIVING Temp1
PROJECT Temp1 OVER EmployeeID, LastName
GIVING Temp2
SELECT Employees WHERE Title='Project Leader'
GIVING Temp3
PROJECT Temp3 OVER EmployeeID, LastName
GIVING Temp4
INTERSECT Temp2 WITH Temp4 GIVING Answer
```

Difference

The **difference** of two tables A and B (referred to as "A minus B") is the set of all rows in table A that are not in table B. As with intersection, the two tables must have the same columns, or be union compatible, for the difference to work. The difference operation is performed by the **SUBTRACT** command in relational algebra.

Suppose you want to list the employee ID and last name of those employees that are related to projects but that do *not* have a title of Project Leader.

This process is virtually identical to the one in the union and intersection examples, but in this case, you subtract one table from the other instead of taking their union or intersection. This process is accomplished in relational algebra using the following commands:

```
JOIN Employees, Projects
WHERE Employees.EmployeeID=Projects.EmployeeID
GIVING Temp1
PROJECT Temp1 OVER EmployeeID, LastName
GIVING Temp2
SELECT Employees WHERE Title='Project Leader'
GIVING Temp3
PROJECT Temp3 OVER EmployeeID, LastName
GIVING Temp4
SUBTRACT Temp4 FROM Temp2 GIVING Answer
```

Product

The **product** of two tables (mathematically known as the **Cartesian product**) is the table obtained by combining every row in the first table with every row in the second table. If the first table has *m* rows and the second table has *n* rows, the product would have *m times n* rows. When creating a query in Query Design View, if you include two tables that are not joined directly or by intermediary table(s), the query completes a Cartesian join, and the resulting datasheet shows the number of records in the first table multiplied (joined to) each record of the second table. In some instances, Cartesian joins can be used to produce intentional results, but more often they are the result of tables not being properly joined in Query Design View.

Division

The **division** process also is used infrequently. It is best illustrated by considering the division of a table with two columns by a table with a single column. Consider the first two tables shown in Figure 2-47. The first table contains two columns: ProjectID and TaskID. The second table contains only a single column, TaskID.

ProjectID	TaskID
15	CODE03
15	MEET00
15	MEET01
15	PLAN01
15	TEST01
15	TEST02
16	MEET00
16	MEET01
16	SERV02
16	SUPP01
16	SUPP04
17	MEET00
17	MEET01
17	SUPP01
17	SUPP04
17	TEST01
17	TEST02
17	TEST03

TaskID
TEST01
TEST02

ProjectID
15
17

FIGURE 2-47 Dividing one table by another

The quotient (the result of the division) is a new table with a single column named ProjectID (the column from the first table that is *not* in the second). The rows in this new table contain those ProjectIDs from the first table that have TaskIDs that "match" *all* the TaskIDs in the second table. Figure 2-47 shows the table that results from dividing the first table by the second.

Summary

- **Describe the relational database model**: A relation is a two-dimensional table in which the entries are single-valued, each field has a distinct name, all the values in a field share the same attribute (the one identified by the field name); the order of fields does not affect queries. Each row is distinct, and the order of rows also is immaterial.

  A relational database is a collection of relations.

  An unnormalized relation is a structure in which a field may have multiple values.

  A field name is qualified by preceding it with the table name and a period (for example, Clients. ClientID).

  A table's primary key is the field or fields that uniquely identify a given row within the table.

- **Explain Query-By-Example (QBE)**: QBE is a visual tool for selecting and changing data in relational databases. The QBE tool in Access is Query Design View, which shows field lists in the upper pane and the specific fields, criteria, and sort orders for the query in the lower pane.

- **Use criteria in QBE**: Criteria are conditions added to a query that limit the number of records that are selected.

  To add criteria in an Access query, enter the condition in the Criteria cell in the design grid for the appropriate field in Query Design View.

  To create AND criteria where *all* conditions must evaluate true for a record to be selected in an Access query, place both criteria in the *same* Criteria row of the design grid.

  To create OR criteria where only *one* condition must evaluate true for a record to be selected in an Access query, place the criteria on *separate* Criteria rows of the design grid.

  An Access select query selects and displays data from underlying tables in the database in Datasheet View, where you can add and delete records or modify data.

  Select queries automatically show up-to-date data each time they are run (executed). which happens when you click the Run button or otherwise open the query to display Datasheet View.

- **Create calculated fields in QBE**: To create a calculated field in Access, enter an appropriate expression in the desired column of the design grid.

  Calculated fields are also called computed fields.

  An expression is a combination of data, field names, and operators that result in a single value. An expression may also include a function, a built-in formula provided by Access that returns a single value.

  A function name is always followed by (parentheses). If a function needs information in order to process, the information is called the function's argument(s) and is passed to the function within the function's parentheses.

  If a function argument is a field name, it is surrounded by [square brackets].

  To give a calculated field a specific name, insert the desired name followed by a colon before the expression.

- **Summarize data by applying aggregate functions in QBE**: Aggregate functions are used to summarize data for a group of records.

  The grouping field(s) determines how records are grouped together. If there is no grouping field, *all* records are grouped together.

  To use aggregate functions to perform calculations in Access, include the appropriate function in the Total row for the desired field in the design grid.

  Given the information presented Datasheet View of a query that uses an aggregate function represents a group of records, you cannot enter or delete records or modify field data in the results.

- **Sort data in QBE**: To sort query results in Access, select Ascending or Descending in the Sort row for the field or fields that are sort keys.

  When sorting a query using more than one field, the leftmost sort key in the design grid is the major sort key (also called the primary sort key) and the sort key to its right is the minor sort key (also called the secondary sort key).

- **Join tables in QBE**: To join, delete, or modify table relationships in Access, use the Relationships window.

  When field lists are added to Query Design View, and if the tables have been previously joined in the Relationships window, they are automatically joined in Query Design View.

  When field lists are added to Query Design View, and if the tables have *not* been previously joined in the Relationships window, you can join them for that query. That practice, however, is less productive and more process intensive than joining the tables in the Relationships window.

When joining two tables, the primary key field in the table on the "one" (parent) side of the one-to-many relationship is always used in the relationship.

A field named the foreign key field is used in the table on the "many" (child) side of the one-to-many relationship. The foreign key field is never the primary key field in a one-to-many relationship.

- **Update data using action queries in QBE**: Queries that update data in a batch process are called action queries.

  To update values to all records that satisfy certain criteria, use an update query.

  To delete all records that satisfy certain criteria, use a delete query.

  To save the results of a query as a table (which makes a *copy* of the data), use a make-table query.

- **Apply relational algebra**: Relational algebra is a theoretical method of manipulating relational databases and is the foundation for SQL, Structured Query Language.

  The SELECT command in relational algebra selects only certain rows from a table.

  The PROJECT command in relational algebra selects only certain columns from a table.

  The JOIN command in relational algebra combines data from two or more tables based on common columns.

  The UNION command in relational algebra creates a table that with the all of the rows from two tables. For a union operation to work the tables must be union compatible. Two tables are union compatible when they have the same number of columns and their corresponding columns represent the same type of data.

  The INTERSECT command in relational algebra creates a table with the common rows from two tables. For an intersection operation to make sense, the tables must be union compatible.

  The SUBTRACT command in relational algebra, also called the difference, creates a table with rows which are present in one table but not in the other. For a subtract operation to make sense, the tables must be union compatible.

  The PRODUCT of two tables (mathematically called the Cartesian product) is the table obtained by combining every row in the first table with every row in the second table.

  The DIVISION process in relational algebra divides one table by another table.

Key Terms

action query	Design View
aggregate function	difference
AND criteria	division
argument	expression
attribute	field
batch update	foreign key
BETWEEN operator	foreign key field
Boolean	function
calculated field	GUI (graphical user interface)
Cartesian product	group
child table	grouping field
comparison operator	INTERSECT
composite primary key	intersection
compound condition	join
compound criterion	JOIN
computed field	join column
concatenation	join line
criteria	key symbol
criterion	major sort key
Datasheet View	make-table query
delete query	minor sort key
design grid	natural join

null	relational database
operator	relational operator
OR criteria	repeating group
orphan record	return value
outer join	scrub
parameter query	secondary sort key
parent table	SELECT
primary key	select query
primary key field	simple query
primary sort key	sort
product	sort key
PROJECT	SQL
qualify	string
query	Structured Query Language
Query-By-Example (QBE)	SUBTRACT
Query Design View	tuple
query optimizer	union
record	UNION
referential integrity	union compatible
relation	unnormalized relation
relational algebra	update query

Module Review Questions

Problems

1. Which of the following is *not* a characteristic of a healthy relation?
   a. Each column has a distinct name (technically called the attribute name).
   b. Each intersection of a row and column in a table may contain more than one value.
   c. All values in a column are values of the same attribute (that is, all entries must match the column name).
   d. The order of the rows and columns is not important.

2. Which of the following sentences explains how entities, attributes, and records work together?
   a. A record contains a single attribute with many entities.
   b. An entity can have only one attribute in a record.
   c. A record contains all related entities and all of their attributes.
   d. A record is all of the attribute values for one item in an entity.

3. The _____ contains values that uniquely identify each record in a table and serves as the linking field in the table on the "one" (parent) side of a one-to-many relationship.
   a. primary key field
   b. foreign key field
   c. calculated field
   d. natural field

4. What is the purpose of the foreign key field?
   a. It is the linking field in the table on the "one" (parent) side of a one-to-many relationship.
   b. It establishes the order of the records in a table.
   c. It is the field in the table on the "many" (child) side of a one-to-many relationship.
   d. It links two tables that do not have a common field.

5. In the query design grid in Access Query Design View, you place AND criteria on _____, and you place OR criteria on _____.
   a. the same row, different rows
   b. different rows, the same row
   c. the Total row, the next blank Field row
   d. the AND row, the OR row

6. With _____, only one criterion must evaluate true in order for a record to be selected and with _____, all criteria must be evaluate true in order for a record to be selected.
   a. parameter criteria, double criteria
   b. function criteria, IF criteria
   c. simple criteria, complex criteria
   d. OR criteria, AND criteria

7. Which of the following is an example of a computed field?
   a. MonthlyRate = [AnnualRate] / 12
   b. MonthlyRate: Annual Rate / 12
   c. MonthlyRate: [AnnualRate] / 12
   d. MonthlyRate: "AnnualRate" / 12

8. Which of the following describes an Access aggregate function?
   a. An aggregate function performs a calculation that provides new information for each record.
   b. An aggregate function determines all rows that are in table A but not in table B.
   c. An aggregate function sums, averages, or counts, for example, the records in a group.
   d. An aggregate function makes a specified change to all records satisfying the criteria in a query.

9. How do you sort data in Access Query Design View?
   a. Use the Sort row and specify the sort fields in a left-to-right order.
   b. Enter the sort order on the Criteria row of the query design grid.
   c. Select a grouping field, and then use the Sort row to select a sort order.
   d. In the Sort row, select "major sort key" or "minor sort key" for each field you want to sort.

10. What does it mean to enforce referential integrity on a one-to-many relationship?
    a. You may not set a primary key in the "many" table.
    b. You may not create orphan records by entering a phony foreign key field value in the "many" table.
    c. You may not delete records in the "one" table that have no related records in the "many" table.
    d. You may not create new records in the "one" table.

11. Which of the following types of queries does *not* change data in Access?
    a. update
    b. delete
    c. select
    d. make-table

12. _____ forms the foundational knowledge for SQL, Structured Query Language, which is the most popular way developers select, edit, and add data to a relational database.
    a. Query algebra
    b. Referential integrity
    c. Entity diagramming
    d. Relational algebra

Critical Thinking Questions

1. Using the data for the JC Consulting database shown in Figure 2-1, identify the one-to-many relationships as well as the primary key fields and foreign key fields for each of the five tables.

2. Using the data for the JC Consulting database shown in Figure 2-1 and your answers from the previous question, which tables would need to be involved if you wanted to create a query that showed the EmployeeID and LastName fields from the Employees table as well as all TaskID and Description fields from the TaskMasterList table that were related to that employee?

JC Consulting Case Exercises: QBE

In the following exercises, you will use the data in the JC Consulting database shown in Figure 2-1. (If you use a computer to complete these exercises, use a copy of the JC Consulting database so you will still have the original database for future modules.) In each step, if using Access, use Query Design View to obtain the desired results.

Problems

1. Select the LastName, ProjectID, and ClientName fields for all records for the employee with the last name of Novak. Which of the following ProjectID values is *not* associated with Novak?
   a. 1
   b. 17
   c. 26
   d. 4

2. Select the ProjectID, ProjectStartDate, ClientName, and Government fields for all records where the Government field value is True. Which of the following clients are included in the results?
   a. Project Lead The Way and The HELPCard
   b. Tri-Lakes Realtors and Midstates Auto Auction
   c. Bretz & Hanna Law Firm and Bounteous
   d. Harper State Bank and MarketPoint Sales

3. Select the ProjectID, ProjectStartDate, ClientName, TaskID, and Description fields for TaskID TEST01 and a ProjectStartDate after 1/1/2020. Sort the records in ascending order by ProjectStartDate. What are the ProjectStartDate and ClientName values in the first record of the results?
   a. 1/6/2020, Midstates Auto Auction
   b. 2/7/2019 Jobot Developers
   c. 4/10/2020, Bretz & Hanna Law Firm
   d. 1/14/2022, SkyFactor

4. Select the ProjectID, ClientName, TaskID, and Description fields for TaskIDs TEST01 or TEST02. Sort the records in ascending order by ProjectID and then by TaskID. What are the ProjectID and TaskID values of the first two records in the results?
   a. 2, TEST01 and 4, TEST01
   b. 2, TEST01 and 2, TEST02
   c. 4, TEST01 and 22, TEST01
   d. 17, TEST01 and 17, TEST02

5. Select the EmployeeID, LastName, HireDate, and Salary fields for employees hired on or before 1/1/2020. Create a calculated field named Bonus that is calculated as 50 percent of their monthly salary, which is stored in the Salary field. What is the bonus amount for Lopez?
   a. 2500
   b. 12,400
   c. 6200
   d. 3100

6. Find the total, average, and count of the Salary field for all employees grouped by title. Sort the records in ascending order by title. What is the average of the salaries for the first title in the results?
   a. $6,650.00
   b. $6,000.00
   c. $6,375.00
   d. $4,366.67

7. Select the records in the TaskMasterList table with a CategoryID field value of Database and then create an update query to update their Estimate field values by 10 percent. How many records are updated and what is the highest updated Estimate field value?
   a. 5 and $1,100
   b. 5 and $1,000
   c. 40 and $1,100
   d. 40 and $1,000

8. Delete all of the records in the ProjectLineItems table with a ProjectID field value of 11. How many records were deleted?
   a. 1
   b. 0
   c. 7
   d. 145

9. Make a table with the ClientName, ProjectID, ProjectStartDate, and TaskID fields for all projects with a TaskID field value of MEET00. Sort the records in ascending order by the ProjectStartDate field. Twenty-four records should be selected. Name the table InitialMeetings. What is the ClientName value of the first record in the InitialMeetings table?
   a. Bounteous
   b. Tri-Lakes Realtors
   c. Morales Group
   d. Jobot Developers

Critical Thinking Questions

1. Select the ClientName, ProjectStartDate, and TaskID fields for all records that have a project start date in the year 2020 and have a task ID of MEET00 or MEET01. Sort the records by client name then task ID.

2. An employee of JC Consulting created the query shown in Figure 2-48. He wants to list the client name, project ID, and task description for each task assigned to the projects for that client. Will this query be successful? If not, what needs to change in order for this query to work correctly?

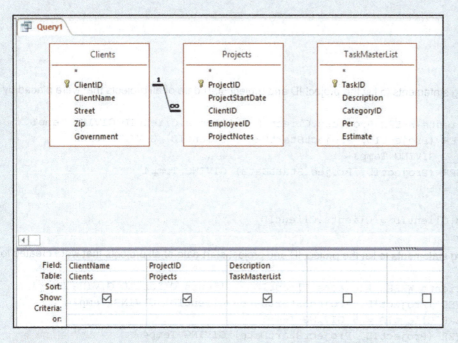

FIGURE 2-48   Query to select the client name, project ID, and description

JC Consulting Case Exercises: Relational Algebra

In the following exercises, you will use the data in the JC Consulting database shown in Figure 2-1. In each step, indicate how to use relational algebra to obtain the desired results.

Problems

1. Complete the following statement to list the employee ID, first name, and last name of all employees.
   _____EMPLOYEES OVER (EmployeeID, LastName, FirstName) GIVING Answer
   a. PROJECT
   b. JOIN
   c. INTERSECTION
   d. SELECT

2. Complete the following statement to list all information from the TaskMasterList table for task ID CODE05.

   ```
   SELECT TaskMasterList WHERE _____ GIVING Answer
   ```
   a. `TaskID = CODE05`
   b. `TaskID = 'CODE05'`
   c. `CODE05 = 'TaskID'`
   d. `(TaskID, CODE05)`

3. Complete the following statements to list the project ID, project start date, client ID, and client name for each project.

   ```
   JOIN Projects Clients WHERE _____ GIVING Temp1
   PROJECT Temp1 OVER (ProjectID, ProjectStartDate, ClientID, ClientName) GIVING
   Answer
   ```
   a. `ClientID.Projects = ClientID.Clients`
   b. `Projects.ProjectID = Clients.ProjectID`
   c. `Projects.ClientID = Clients.ClientID`
   d. `Projects.ProjectID = Clients.ClientID`

4. Complete the following statements to list the project ID, project start date, client ID, and client name for each project created for the employee with the last name of Winter.

   ```
   _____ Projects Clients WHERE Projects.ClientID = Clients.ClientID GIVING Temp1
   JOIN Temp1 Clients WHERE Temp1.EmployeeID = Employees.EmployeeID GIVING Temp2
   SELECT Temp2 WHERE Employees.LastName = 'Winter' GIVING Temp3
   PROJECT Temp3 OVER (ProjectID, ProjectStartDate, ClientID, ClientName) GIVING
   Answer
   ```
   a. `SELECT`
   b. `PROJECT`
   c. `UNION`
   d. `JOIN`

5. Complete the following statements to list the project ID and project start date of all projects that were placed by client ID 5.

   ```
   JOIN Projects Clients WHERE Projects.ClientID = Clients.ClientID GIVING Temp1
   PROJECT Temp1 OVER (ProjectID, ProjectStartDate, ClientID) GIVING Temp2
   SELECT Temp2 _____ GIVING Temp3
   PROJECT Temp3 OVER (ProjectID, ProjectStartDate) GIVING Temp4
   ```
   a. `WHERE ClientID = 5`
   b. `OVER ClientID = 5`
   c. `WHERE Projects.ClientID = Clients.ClientID`
   d. `AND ClientID = 5`

6. Complete the following statements to list the project ID and project start date of all projects that were created for client ID 5 or 6.

   ```
   JOIN Projects Clients WHERE Projects.ClientID = Clients.ClientID GIVING Temp1
   PROJECT Temp1 OVER (ProjectID, ProjectStartDate, ClientID) GIVING Temp2
   SELECT Temp2 WHERE ClientID = 5 GIVING Temp3
   PROJECT Temp3 OVER (ProjectID, ProjectStartDate) GIVING Temp4
   SELECT Temp2 WHERE ClientID = 6 GIVING Temp5
   PROJECT Temp5 OVER (ProjectID, ProjectStartDate) GIVING Temp6
   _____ Temp5 WITH Temp6 GIVING Answer
   ```
   a. `JOIN`
   b. `UNION`
   c. `OR`
   d. `INTERSECTION`

7. Complete the following statements to list the project ID and project start date of all projects with a project start date of 3/1/2020 but *not* for client ID 7.

   ```
   SELECT Projects WHERE ProjectStartDate ='3/1/2020' GIVING Temp1
   PROJECT Temp1 OVER (ProjectID, ProjectStartDate) GIVING Temp2
   SELECT Temp2 WHERE ClientID = 7 GIVING Temp3
   ```

```
PROJECT Temp3 OVER (ProjectID, ProjectStartDate) GIVING Temp4
_____ Temp4 FROM Temp2 GIVING Answer
```
a. UNION
b. PRODUCT
c. SUBTRACT
d. DELETE

Pitt Fitness Case Exercises

The owner of Pitt Fitness knows that the power of the company's database is in running queries to find out important information for making good business decisions. In the following exercises, you use the data in the Pitt Fitness database shown in Figures 1-15 through 1-19 in Module 1. When you use Microsoft Access to respond to these exercises, make a copy of the original database to create the queries. In each step, use QBE to obtain the desired results.

Problems

1. Which customer lives on Negley Avenue?
   a. Gregor
   b. Aboud
   c. Agnew
   d. Sanchez

2. How many customers were born from 2001 onward?
   a. 5
   b. 3
   c. 10
   d. 2

3. Which instructors live in zip code 15217?
   a. Juan Varlano, Michael Nguyen
   b. Robert Sisto, Neda Tahan
   c. Vicki Pegues, Raymond Stein
   d. No instructors live in this zip code.

4. Which classes (by name) have the highest number of reservations?
   a. Intense Cycle, Barre
   b. Combination, Bootcamp
   c. Yoga
   d. Aqua Calm, Yoga Balance

5. How many customers have registered for a class on Wednesdays?
   a. 10
   b. 7
   c. 6
   d. 5

6. What are the three most popular class names on Saturday?
   a. Cycle, Combination, Agility for Seniors
   b. Zumba, Cycle, Combination
   c. Bootcamp, Zumba, Cycle
   d. Maturity Endurance and Strength, Intense Cycle, Bootcamp

7. How many classes did Pablo Brough sign up for?
   a. 5
   b. 2
   c. 1
   d. 0

8. How many customers have signed up for a class on January 8, 2021?
   a. 0
   b. 1
   c. 3
   d. 10

9. Which customers prefer the 45-minute class length?
   a. Glenn Spencer, Sharon Smith
   b. Debby Thorn, Juan Barry
   c. Tamara Lara, Albert Cornett
   d. Min Jee Choi, Ramiro Sanchez

10. Which instructor teaches the most classes?
    a. Raymond Stein
    b. Memo Said
    c. Michael Nguyen
    d. Maria D'Angelo

11. Which instructor teaches Zumba?
    a. Neda Tahan
    b. Juan Varlano
    c. Megan Kobinski
    d. Robert Sisto

12. Of all reservations for classes containing the word Cycle, which customer does not owe another fee besides the class price? (*Note*: this field is called "OtherFees.") Create a calculated field to total both costs.
    a. Gene Shaffer
    b. Philip Benavides
    c. Tony Waldron
    d. Juan Barry

13. According to the reservations so far, how much money will the Combination classes generate?
    a. $9
    b. $18
    c. $36
    d. $0

14. Instructor Michael Nguyen is injured and has to cancel his class on Wednesday. Delete that record and count how many classes he has left to teach.
    a. 6
    b. 2
    c. 5
    d. 10

15. Which instructor will customer Margo Patterson get for her HIIT class?
    a. Raymond Stein
    b. Vicki Pegues
    c. Megan Kobinski
    d. Neda Tahan

16. How many classes are offered on Tuesday at 6 am and last 45 minutes?
    a. 3
    b. 2
    c. 1
    d. 0

17. Which day of the week has the most classes?
    a. Monday
    b. Tuesday
    c. Wednesday
    d. Thursday

Critical Thinking Questions

1. Suppose you want to list information on all the classes that Pitt Fitness offers, including the day of the week, time, location, and length of class. To do this, you could create a query. What table(s) should you add to the query? If you use only the Classes table instead of all the tables together, does it make a difference to the output? What if someone had never reserved a specific class?

2. The owner of Pitt Fitness is considering whether to consolidate his clubs and offer classes in only one location to ensure profitability. To explore his question, what query or queries would you create to answer this business strategy question?

Sports Physical Therapy Case Exercises

In the following exercises, you use data in the Sports Physical Therapy database shown in Figures 1-21 through 1-24 in Module 1. When you use Microsoft Access to answer these questions, make a copy of the original database to create the queries to answer these questions. In each step, use QBE to obtain the desired results.

Problems

1. Which patient has the highest balance?
   a. Latisha Culling
   b. Andre Marino
   c. Tammy Wilson
   d. Isaiah Venable

2. How many patients and therapists live in Georgetown, TX?
   a. One patient and one therapist
   b. Three therapists
   c. Two patients
   d. No one lives in Georgetown, TX.

3. Which patient has a therapy session on October 12, 2021?
   a. Robbie Koehler
   b. Tobey Short
   c. Ben Odepaul
   d. Tierra Falls

4. Which therapist has a session on October 12, 2021?
   a. Saritha Nair
   b. Anthony Shields
   c. Bridgette McClain
   d. Jonathan Risk

5. Which patient has booked the most therapies?
   a. Brianna Waggoner
   b. Tammy Wilson
   c. Andre Marino
   d. Joseph Baptist

6. Who are the busiest therapists?
   a. Wilder, Shields
   b. Risk, Nair
   c. McClain, Shields
   d. Wilder, Nair

7. Which patients live in the same town as their therapist?
   a. Culling, Marino
   b. Venable, Koehler
   c. King, Falls
   d. Baptist, Short

8. How many patients are receiving ultrasound therapy?
   a. 1
   b. 2
   c. 3
   d. 0

9. Which therapist has the longest single session?
   a. Bridgette McClain
   b. Saritha Nair
   c. Steven Wilder
   d. Anthony Shields

10. Create a calculated field that figures the amount each therapist earns assuming they charge $100 per hour and the length of the session is the correct amount of time each therapy takes. How much money does Saritha Nair earn?
    a. $100
    b. $150
    c. $300
    d. $225

11. Which therapist works with a patient's speech?
    a. Jonathan Risk
    b. Anthony Shields
    c. Saritha Nair
    d. Steven Wilder

12. How many therapies refer to pain in their description?
    a. 3
    b. 1
    c. 4
    d. 0

13. How many therapies have a designated 15-minute unit of time?
    a. 5
    b. 10
    c. 15
    d. 30

14. Which patient has the longest single session?
    a. Latisha Culling
    b. Brianna Waggoner
    c. Joseph Baptist
    d. Robbie Koehler

15. Which therapists are scheduled for October 11, 2021?
    a. McClain, Shields
    b. Risk, Shields
    c. Nair, Shields
    d. Wilder, Shields

16. Which therapist works the least, in terms of hours in sessions?
    a. Jonathan Risk
    b. Steven Wilder
    c. Bridgette McClain
    d. Anthony Shields

17. A surcharge is being placed on any patient whose balance is greater than $1,000. That surcharge is 5 percent addition to a patient's current balance. Create an update query to perform the calculation. What is the highest balance now?
    a. $1,939.09
    b. $2,053.17
    c. $2,116.07
    d. $2,087.93

Critical Thinking Questions

1. If you want to find out which therapist is meeting a particular patient on a specific day, what tables do you need for your query? If you also want to know the description of the therapy, does that change your query design? If so, how?

2. If you made a mistake on the update query in question 17 to add a 5 percent surcharge to accounts with balances greater than $1,000, how would you undo the change?

MODULE **3**

THE RELATIONAL MODEL: SQL

LEARNING OBJECTIVES

- Examine Structured Query Language (SQL)
- Create tables and fields with SQL
- Select data using criteria in SQL
- Select data using AND, OR, BETWEEN, and NOT operators
- Create computed fields in SQL
- Use wildcards and the LIKE and IN operators
- Apply built-in SQL aggregate functions
- Group records in SQL
- Use subqueries in SQL
- Join tables using SQL
- Perform union operations in SQL
- Use SQL to update, insert, and delete records
- Prepare for a database career by acquiring SQL skills

INTRODUCTION

In this module, you will examine **SQL (Structured Query Language)**, a standard language for managing, selecting, updating, and analyzing data in a relational database management system. Using SQL, you enter commands to manipulate the database structure or to select the desired data. In this module, you will learn how to use SQL to do the same tasks that you completed in Module 2 using Query Design View, the graphical QBE tool provided by Access. You will also use SQL to create a new table.

SQL was developed under the name SEQUEL as the data manipulation language for IBM's prototype relational DBMS, System R, in the mid-1970s. In the 1980s, it was renamed SQL and is now pronounced as "S-Q-L" ("ess-cue-ell"). SQL is a standard of the **American National Standards Institute (ANSI)** as well as the **International Organization for Standardization (ISO)**, but different RDBMs provide different versions of SQL that result in small variations in features and **syntax**, the rules by which statements must be written. The SQL version used in the following examples works with Microsoft Access. Although SQL between RDBMs is not identical, the core commands are the same.

Some of the SQL **keywords**, also known as **reserved words**, that are used to initiate SQL commands and identify field data types in Microsoft Access SQL are different from those in ANSI SQL. The article at docs. microsoft.com/en-us/office/client-developer/access/desktop-database-reference/comparison-of-microsoft-access-sql-and-ansi-sql provides a comparison of Microsoft Access SQL and ANSI SQL.

You will begin studying SQL by using it to create a table. The part of SQL that is used for creating and altering database objects is called the **data-definition language** (DDL). It includes commands to create and modify tables, create indexes, and create table relationships.

You will also use SQL's SELECT statement to select fields and records from existing tables using a **WHERE clause** with criteria to limit the specific records that are selected. You will also use the WHERE clause to link tables together to select fields and records from multiple related tables. You will use SQL to create calculated fields and the ORDER BY clause to sort records. You will learn how to create subqueries. You will also use SQL's aggregate functions to analyze, group, and summarize groups of data. You will use SQL's UNION operator to combine two different sets of data into one view. Finally, you will use SQL to update, delete, and insert data.

GETTING STARTED WITH SQL

The examples in this module were created in Access 2019; however, you can use any recent version of Access to execute the SQL commands as shown. You may also use any other relational database management system to practice SQL. Some of the examples in this module change the data in the sample database, so if you are going to work through all of the exercises with the sample JCConsulting database, be sure to make a copy of it before you start, as the examples in future modules do not contain the updates to the data demonstrated in this module.

Opening an SQL Query Window in Access

To open an SQL query window in Access and execute SQL commands shown in the figures in this book, perform the following steps:

- Open the JCConsulting database in Access.
- Click Create on the ribbon.
- Click the Query Design button (Create tab | Queries group).
- When Access displays the Show Table dialog box, click the Close button without adding a table.
- Click the View button (Query Tools Design tab | Results group) that displays SQL View, or click the View button arrow and then click SQL View.
- The Query1 tab displays SQL view, ready for you to type your SQL commands (Figure 3-1).

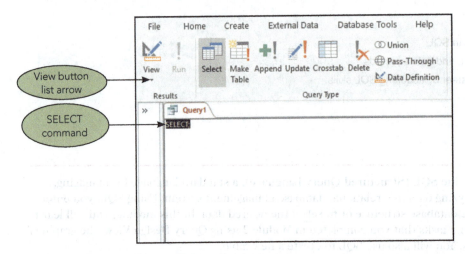

FIGURE 3-1 Access SQL query window

Q & A 3-1

Question: What default command appears in the SQL query window?

Answer: Access automatically places the SELECT SQL keyword in the query window, followed by a semicolon (;). Given a majority of SQL statements select fields and records from existing tables, Access anticipates that you want to build a select query, which starts with the SELECT SQL keyword. You can complete the SELECT statement to select the fields and records you desire, or delete it altogether to enter a different command. In most versions of SQL, the entire command ends with a semicolon (;). In Access, the semicolon is optional but is included as the last character in each example.

The default font face for SQL View is a proportional font, giving each character as much space as needed for the width of that character. Many code editors display code in a **monospaced** font face, which gives each character the same horizontal width on the screen so that each character lines up the same way as shown in textbook examples. Monospaced fonts make it easier to transpose, read, and debug code. They also help differentiate similar but different characters such as a lowercase L and the number 1. The SQL View default font size of 8 points is relatively small, and the default font is not a monospaced font, so you may want to change the default font size of the SQL statements in SQL View to 12 points and the default font to Courier New to match the figures in this book.

Changing the Font and Font Size in SQL View

To change the font size of the SQL statements in SQL View, perform the following steps:

- If an existing SQL query window is open from the previous exercise, close it.
- Click the File tab on the ribbon.
- Click Options on the File menu.
- Click the Object Designers button on the left side of the Access Options dialog box.
- In the Query design area, click the Font list arrow, and then click Courier New.
- In the Query design area, click the Size list arrow, and then click 12 as shown in Figure 3-2.
- Click OK to close the Access Options dialog box.

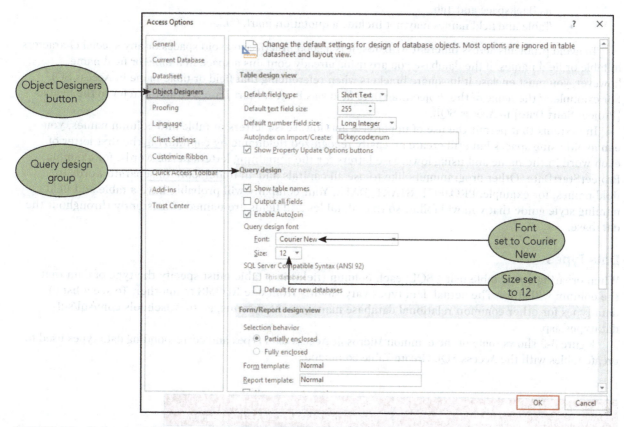

FIGURE 3-2 Setting the default font and font size for SQL View

As you type in SQL View, you correct typing errors just as you would correct errors in a document. Use the arrow keys to move the insertion point as well as the Backspace or Delete keys to delete characters. After completing the SQL statements, you run SQL commands by clicking the Run button (Query Tools Design tab | Results group). To return to SQL View, click the View button arrow (Home tab | Views group), and then click SQL View.

CREATING A TABLE

While the tables for the JCConsulting database (and the databases at the end of the module) have already been developed, you may need to learn how to create a new table to enhance the database at a later time. The SQL **CREATE TABLE** command creates a new table.

Naming Conventions

The rules for naming tables and columns vary slightly from one relational database management system to another. Restrictions placed on field and tables names by Access are as follows and further described on the Access support page. (Visit support.office.com, and then search for "Access guidelines for naming fields, controls, and objects.")

Restrictions on field and table names in Access:

- Table and field names should not include any SQL or Access reserved words.
- Table and field names may not exceed 64 characters.
- Table and field names may include any combination of letters, numbers, spaces, and special characters except for a period (.), an exclamation point (!), an accent grave (`), and square brackets ([ ]).
- Table and field names may not start with a space.
- Table and field names may not include control characters (ASCII values 0 through 31). **ASCII** is the **American Standard Code for Information Interchange**, which is a standardized way to represent characters in numeric form. Characters 0 through 31 are nonprinting characters such as Backspace and Tab.
- Table and field names may not include a quotation mark (").

To avoid problems across different RDBMSs, it is a good practice to avoid spaces or any special characters in table or field names. If the database you are using already contains a space in a table or field name, however, you must enclose it in square brackets when referencing that field or table name in Access SQL. For example, if the name of the ProjectStartDate field was Project Start Date, you would refer to the field as [Project Start Date] in Access SQL.

In systems that permit the use of uppercase and lowercase letters in table and column names, you can avoid using spaces but still create an easily recognized fieldname by capitalizing the first letter of each word in the name and using lowercase letters for the remaining letters in the words, for example, ProjectStartDate. Other programmers like to use all capitals and an underscore to separate words in field names, for example, PROJECT_START_DATE. Your company will probably have a table and field naming style guide that you will follow so that all tables and fields are named consistently throughout the database.

Data Types

When creating a new table using SQL, each column (field) in a table must specify the type of data that the column will store. The actual data types vary slightly from one RDBMS to another. To see a list of data types for other common relational database management systems, go to w3schools.com/sql/sql_datatypes.asp.

Figure 3-3 shows some of the common Microsoft Access data types and corresponding data types used to create tables with the Access SQL Create Table command.

Microsoft Access Data Type (shown in Table Design View)	Microsoft Access SQL Data Type (used in the CREATE TABLE statement)
AutoNumber	COUNTER or AUTOINCREMENT
Currency	CURRENCY
Date/Time	DATETIME
Long Text	LONGTEXT
Number (FieldSize= Single)	SINGLE
Number (FieldSize= Double)	DOUBLE
Number (FieldSize= Byte)	**BYTE**
Number (FieldSize= Integer)	SHORT
Number (FieldSize= Long Integer)	LONG
Short Text	TEXT or VARCHAR
Yes/No	YESNO

FIGURE 3-3 Microsoft Access and Microsoft Access SQL data types

The following Access SQL `CREATE TABLE` command creates a table named Clients with five fields. This table has been created already in the Access JCConsulting database, so you do not have to enter this command. Study the command for understanding.

```
CREATE TABLE Clients (
    ClientID AUTOINCREMENT,
    ClientName TEXT(35),
    Street TEXT(25),
    Zip TEXT(5),
    Government YESNO
    )
;
```

This command creates a new table named `Clients` with five fields. `ClientID` is an **AUTOINCREMENT** field, which means that its values automatically increment by 1 as new records are added. This data type is known as an **AutoNumber** field in Access Table Design View. `ClientName`, `Street`, and `Zip` all store textual data with the given character size limitations shown in parentheses. Government is created with an SQL YESNO data type, also known as a **Boolean** field. Boolean fields may store only Yes or No values, which can also be thought of as On or Off or True or False.

SQL syntax, the rules by which the statements are written, include the following steps:

- The `CREATE TABLE` SQL keywords, also called reserved words, are used to start a command that creates a new table in the current database.
- The new table name follows the `CREATE TABLE` keywords.
- The fields to create in the new table follow the table name and the entire list of new fields is surrounded by (parentheses).
- The fields to create are identified by a field name followed by its Access SQL data type, followed by a comma. Field names are not case sensitive, but for readability, strive to write your SQL statements using the same case as the actual field name in your database.
- If the new field is a `TEXT` data type (which can also be created using the **CHAR** or VARCHAR Access SQL keywords), you may specify a length for the new field with a number in (parentheses) after `TEXT`. If no length is specified, the new field is given the default Access Short Text length of 255 characters.
- You may break SQL statements into multiple lines and use indentation for readability. Often, SQL is written using a new field name or SQL keyword to begin each line.
- SQL is not case sensitive, but it is customary to write SQL keywords in uppercase for readability.
- SQL statements also use parentheses to set the order of operations and clarify expressions.
- SQL statements generally end with a semicolon ; (but the semicolon is optional in Access SQL).
- The final parenthesis and semicolon may be placed at the end of the last line or on their own lines for readability.

The Projects table has also been created in the Access database for JC Consulting, so you do not have to enter this command, but study it for understanding.

```
CREATE TABLE Projects (
    ProjectID AUTOINCREMENT,
    ProjectStartDate DATETIME,
    ClientID LONG,
    EmployeeID TEXT,
    ProjectNotes LONGTEXT
    )
;
```

The Projects table has five fields. `ProjectID` is created with the `AUTOINCREMENT` data type, meaning that it will automatically increment by 1 as new records are added. `ProjectStartDate` will store dates, `ClientID` is a long integer field and will serve as the foreign key field to connect in a one-to-many relationship with the Clients table. In this relationship, the Clients table is on the "one" side (the parent table) and the Projects table is on the "many" side (the child table) given one client may be linked to many projects. `EmployeeID` is text field with the default field size, and `ProjectNotes` is created with the `LONGTEXT` data type, which means that it can store more than 255 characters of data.

Q & A 3-2

How would you create a new table named Zips with two `TEXT` fields named City and Zip? The City field should be 25 characters long and the Zip field should be 5 characters long.

To create a new table named Zips with the two text fields specified, you would perform the following steps:

- Open SQL View and enter the Access SQL command as shown in Figure 3-4 to create a new table.

```
Query1

CREATE TABLE Zips (
    City TEXT(25),
    Zip TEXT(5)
)
;
```

FIGURE 3-4 Access SQL to create a table

- Click the Run button (Query Tools Design tab | Results group) to create the Zips table. If you examined the Zips table in Access Table Design View, you would notice that both fields have a Short Text data type even though they were created with the Access SQL `TEXT` data type. The City field's Size property would be set to 25 and the Zip field's Size property would be set to 5.

SELECTING DATA

When using SQL to select data, the basic form of an SQL retrieval command is **SELECT-FROM-WHERE**. After the word `SELECT`, you list the fields you want to display in the query results. This portion of the command is called the **SELECT clause**. The fields will appear in the query results in the order in which they are listed in the `SELECT` clause. After the word `FROM`, you list the table or tables that contain the selected fields. This portion of the command is called the **FROM clause**. After the word `WHERE`, you list any conditions or criteria that you want to apply, such as indicating that the ProjectStartDate must be after a certain date. This portion of the command is called the **WHERE clause**. If you want to retrieve *all* of the records for the selected fields, omit the `WHERE` clause.

YOUR TURN 3-1

Using the JCConsulting database, select the ClientID and ClientName for all clients from the Clients table.

Figure 3-5 shows the query to select the `ClientID` and `ClientName` for all records in the `Clients` table using SQL View in Access. (Because you want to list all clients, you do not need to use the `WHERE` clause for this statement.)

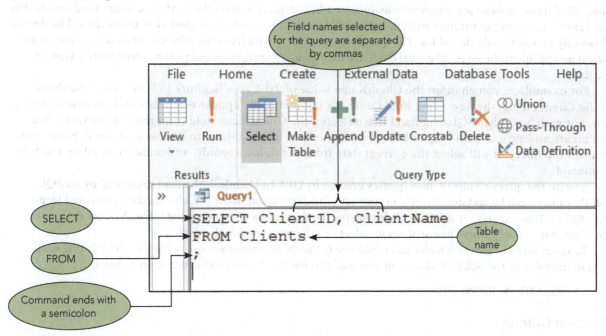

FIGURE 3-5   Access SQL to select two fields from the Clients table

The results of running the query shown in Figure 3-5 appear in Figure 3-6. To return to SQL View in Access, click the View button arrow (Home tab | Views group) and then click SQL View.

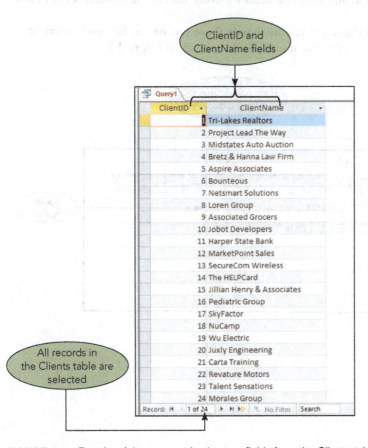

FIGURE 3-6   Results of the query selecting two fields from the Clients table

Running an SQL SELECT command does not create a copy of the data, but rather, simply selects the information from existing tables. In Access, an SQL SELECT command also displays the data in Query Datasheet View. If existing records were edited or if new records were added to the Clients table at a later time, all of those updates are automatically included in the query results the next time query is executed! For this reason, the result of running an SQL command is sometimes called a **logical view** of the data. The data is *physically* stored in only the tables. The query merely *selects* data from the tables to present in a particular logical arrangement. In some relational database management systems, a query is referred to as a **view** of the data.

For example, if you changed the ClientName value of Tri-Lakes Realtors to White River Realtors in the Clients table, the new name would not only automatically appear when this SQL command was run, but with any other SQL command that selected the ClientName field from the Clients table. You can create and save as many SQL SELECT commands as query objects in Access as desired. Every time you run the query, it will select the current data from the fields, records, and tables defined by the SQL command.

As with the query results of most queries created by QBE in Module 2, the data presented by an SQL SELECT query can be updated directly in the view. But remember, when you change data presented by an SQL SELECT query, you are actually modifying the data stored by the underlying table. A query does not store any data. It only stores instructions to select or otherwise modify the data.

To select all the fields in a table, you could use the same approach shown in Figure 3-5 by listing each field in the table in the SELECT clause, or you can also use the * (asterisk) symbol, for example:

```
SELECT * FROM Clients;
```

Numeric Criteria

Recall that queries use criteria or conditions to limit or search for specific rows or records of data. Numeric criteria can be specified in the WHERE clause using digits. Do not enter commas, dollar signs, or spaces within numeric criteria. For example, for a Currency field, $1,000 would be entered as 1000 if used as a criterion in SQL View.

Suppose you need to select the Description and Estimate fields for every task in the TaskMasterList table with an Estimate value greater than $100.

You can use the WHERE clause to restrict the query results to only those records in the TaskMasterList table with an Estimate field value greater than $100. The query design appears in Figure 3-7.

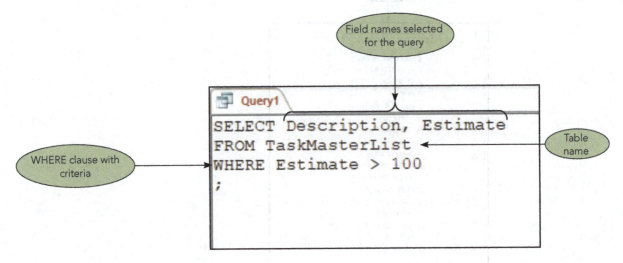

FIGURE 3-7 SQL with numeric criteria

The query results appear in Figure 3-8.

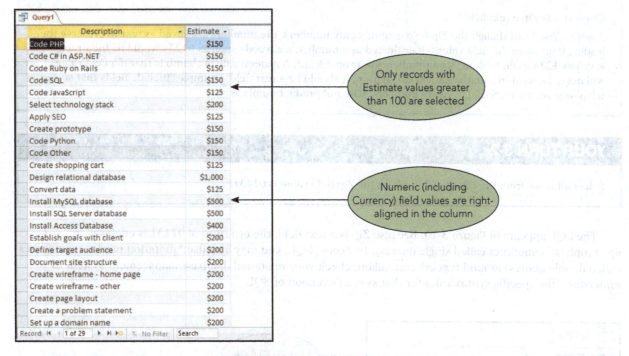

FIGURE 3-8   Results of query with numeric criteria

The WHERE clause shown in Figure 3-7 includes a simple condition. A **simple condition** includes the field name, a comparison operator, and either another field name or a value, such as Estimate > 100. Spaces around the operator are optional, but are encouraged for readability.

Figure 3-9 lists the comparison operators that you can use in SQL commands. Notice that there are two versions of the "not equal to" operator: < > and != that are used in different versions of SQL. Access SQL uses the < > version of the "not equal to" operator.

Comparison Operator	Meaning
=	Equal to
<	Less than
>	Greater than
<=	Less than or equal to
>=	Greater than or equal to
<>	Not equal to in some versions of SQL. including Access
!=	Not equal to in some versions of SQL

FIGURE 3-9   Comparison operators used in SQL commands

Text Criteria

You also can limit the selected records with text criteria. When a query uses a WHERE clause with a text field, such as ClientName, Description, or Zip, the criterion is surrounded with apostrophes.

Q & A 3-3

Question: Is Zip a text field?

Answer: Yes. Even though the Zip field contains only numbers, the numbers are saved as text to preserve the leading 0 on some Zip field values. If evaluated as a number, a zip code such as 01234 would be incorrectly saved as 1234 given leading 0s on numbers are insignificant. A general rule of thumb is that if a field value will never be used in a mathematical calculation, it should be a text field. Examples include fields that store telephone numbers, Social Security numbers, IDs, and product numbers.

YOUR TURN 3-2

Select all fields from the Clients table where the Zip field value is 01431.

The SQL appears in Figure 3-10. Because Zip is a text field, the criterion of 01431 is enclosed in apostrophes (sometimes called single quotes). In Access SQL, you may also use "quotation marks" (sometimes called double quotes) around text criteria. Again, check your relational database management system to understand the specific syntax rules for that system's version of SQL.

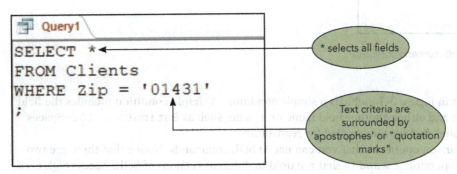

FIGURE 3-10 SQL with text criteria

Running the SQL selects the information shown in Figure 3-11. Three records from the Clients table are selected where the Zip field value is equal to 01431.

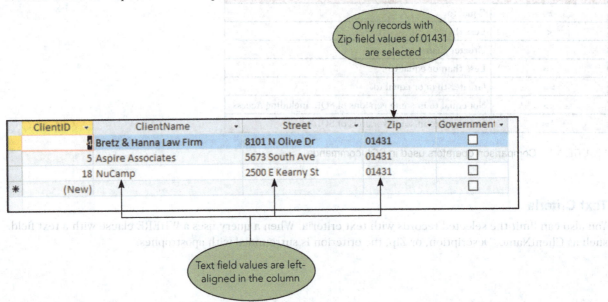

FIGURE 3-11 Results of query with text criteria

Date Criteria

When you want to use the date in a criterion or condition, the syntax often varies slightly from one implementation of SQL to another. In Access, you place number signs (also sometimes called pound signs, hash tags, and octothorpes) around the date (for example, #11/15/2021#). In other programs, you might enter the day of the month, a hyphen, the three-character abbreviation for the month, a hyphen, and the year, all enclosed in apostrophes (for example, '15-NOV-2018').

YOUR TURN 3-3

Select all fields from the Projects table with a ProjectStartDate field value of greater than or equal to 1/1/2021.

The SQL appears in Figure 3-12.

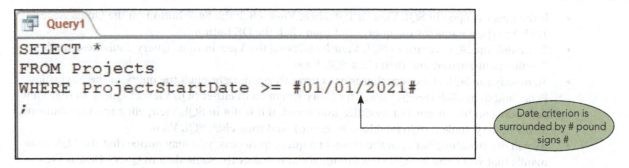

FIGURE 3-12 SQL with date criterion

You do not have to use two digits for the month and day in the date criterion. Also, you do not have to use four digits for the year. In other words, in Access SQL, the criterion of #01/01/2021#, #1/1/2021#, and #1/1/21# are equivalent. Your relational database management system and your company's SQL style guide will determine how you will enter date criteria to make it consistent across all developers. Running the query selects the data shown in Figure 3-13.

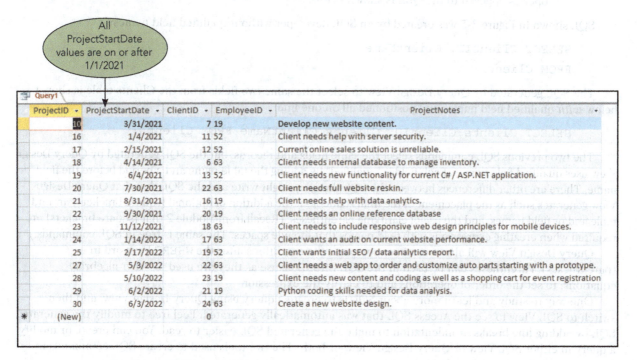

FIGURE 3-13 Results of query with date criterion

Comparing Two Fields

If you want to select records based on a comparison between two fields in the same record, you use the comparative operators (such as <, >, and =) in the WHERE clause. For example, if you wanted to select all fields for the records in a Products table where your price for a product exceeded that of a competitor's price, and if both of those values were stored using the field names of Price and CompetitorPrice, the SQL would look like this:

```
SELECT *
FROM Products
WHERE Price > CompetitorPrice
;
```

Saving SQL Queries

Saving SQL queries in Access is similar to saving the queries you created using Access's implementation of QBE, Query Design View in Module 2. To save a query, you would perform the following steps:

- If the query is open in SQL View or Datasheet View, click the Save button on the Quick Access Toolbar, type a name for the query, and then click the OK button.
- To modify the SQL, return to SQL View by clicking the View button (Query Tools Design tab | Results group) arrow, and then click SQL View.
- To modify the SQL of a query that is not currently open, right-click the query in the Navigation Pane, and then click Design View. The query will open in either SQL View or Query Design View depending on how it was last modified and saved. If it is not in SQL View, click the View button arrow (Query Tools Design tab | Results group), and then click SQL View.
- As you are switching between the views of a query in Access, you may notice that the SQL commands that you write in SQL View are mirrored to select the same data in Query Design View. The opposite is also true. As you build a query using the Access QBE of Query Design View, SQL is being written for you in SQL View. Note, however, that the SQL automatically generated by Query Design View will use **qualified field names**, which identify field names adding the table name followed by a period followed by the field name.
- In other words, a query, whether it is created with the QBE Query Design View or with SQL View saves the same thing: SQL commands. As an SQL coder, you will probably write your code in a shorter, cleaner, more readable style than the QBE. An example of SQL written by an SQL developer as opposed to the QBE is shown below:

SQL shown in Figure 3-5 was created by an SQL developer without qualified field names:

```
SELECT ClientID, ClientName
FROM Clients;
```

The SQL generated by Query Design View to select the same two fields from the Clients table is shown below *with* qualified field names and positioned all on one line:

```
SELECT Clients.ClientID, Clients.ClientName FROM Clients;
```

The two previous SQL commands select the same fields and records, but the SQL generated by Query Design View uses qualified field names. Each field is "qualified" by adding the table name and a period before the field name. There are other differences between the SQL that you might write and the SQL that that Query Design View generates such as the placement of the final semicolon, the addition of optional [square brackets] around table and/or field names, and the use of clarifying parentheses. (Recall from Module 2 that [square brackets] are required when creating expressions with field names that include spaces. The same is true in SQL commands.)

Query Design View will also sometimes surround the conditions after the WHERE keyword in (parentheses). Parentheses can be used in the SQL WHERE clause as they are used in other algebraic equations: to set the order of operations and to clarify the expression.

One way to study and learn more about SQL is to create a query using Query Design View, and then switch to SQL View to see the Access SQL that was automatically generated. Feel free to modify the generated SQL by adding line breaks or indentation to make the generated SQL easier to read. You can create or modify a query in either SQL View or Query Design View, or both. The two tools used to create SQL commands in Access mirror the changes made in the other.

USING COMPOUND CONDITIONS: AND CRITERIA

A **compound condition** is formed by connecting two or more criteria with one or both of the following operators: **AND** and **OR**. A lesser used **BETWEEN operator** allows you to specify a range of values for the criteria.

When you connect conditions using the **AND operator**, all the conditions must be true for a particular record to be selected.

YOUR TURN 3-4

List all of the fields in the Employees table where the Title field contains Programmer and the Salary field (a monthly value) contains a value less than $6,000.

In this example, you want to list those employees for which *both* conditions are true. The employee's title field value must be Programmer and their salary field value must be less than $6,000. The SQL will use the AND operator in the WHERE clause to select only those records where both conditions are true. It is common practice to place the AND condition on a separate line and indent it for readability as shown in Figure 3-14.

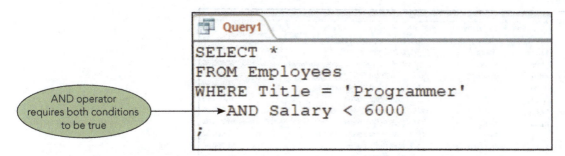

FIGURE 3-14 SQL with AND criteria

The query results appear in Figure 3-15. Note that *both* conditions need to evaluate true for each record that is selected with AND criteria.

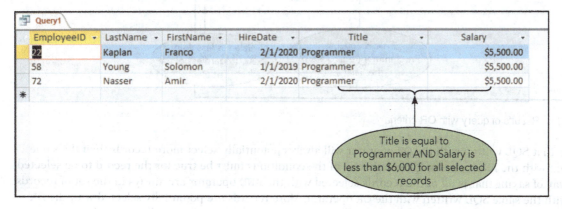

FIGURE 3-15 Results of query with AND criteria

USING COMPOUND CONDITIONS: OR CRITERIA

When you connect simple conditions using the **OR operator**, only one condition must be true for a particular record to be selected.

YOUR TURN 3-5

List all of the fields in the Employees table where the Title field contains Programmer or the Salary field (a monthly value) contains a value less than $6,000.

In this query, you want to list those employees for which *either* condition is true. The employee's title field value must be Programmer *or* their salary field value must be less than $6,000. The SQL will use the OR operator in the WHERE clause to select only those records where both conditions are true. It is common practice to place the OR condition on a separate line and indent it for readability as shown in Figure 3-16.

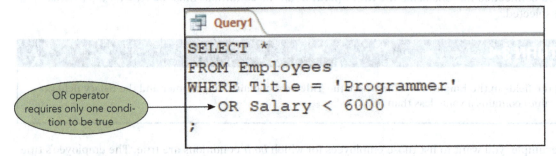

FIGURE 3-16 SQL with OR criteria

The query results appear in Figure 3-17.

EmployeeID	LastName	FirstName	HireDate	Title	Salary
19	Kohn	Ali	1/1/2020	Project Leader	$5,000.00
22	Kaplan	Franco	2/1/2020	Programmer	$5,500.00
35	Prohm	Nada	2/29/2020	Customer Support Specialist	$4,000.00
47	Alvarez	Benito	3/31/2020	Front End Developer	$5,200.00
53	Anad	Sergei	1/1/2019	Front End Developer	$5,300.00
54	Allen	Sasha	1/1/2019	Programmer	$7,000.00
55	Winter	Wendy	12/31/2020	Front End Developer	$4,300.00
56	Reddy	Kamal	9/1/2019	Programmer	$6,200.00
57	Yang	Tam	4/30/2021	Front End Developer	$5,000.00
58	Young	Solomon	1/1/2019	Programmer	$5,500.00
59	Santana	Carmen	1/1/2019	Front End Developer	$4,800.00
61	Smirnov	Tovah	10/1/2019	Programmer	$6,000.00
64	Lopez	Miguel	1/1/2019	Programmer	$6,200.00
68	Patel	Tatiana	4/1/2019	Programmer	$6,500.00
69	Jordan	Karl	11/30/2020	Customer Support Specialist	$5,000.00
72	Nasser	Amir	2/1/2020	Programmer	$5,500.00
73	Safar	Jaleel	2/1/2019	Customer Support Specialist	$4,100.00

FIGURE 3-17 Results of query with OR criteria

Notice that SQL written with the OR operator will always potentially select more records than the same SQL written with the AND operator given only one of the conditions must be true for the record to be selected. Another way of saying that is *all* of the records selected with the AND operator are always in the set of records selected with the same SQL written with the OR operator. More records are potentially selected with the OR operator, however, given only *one* of the criteria must evaluate true for the record to be selected.

USING THE BETWEEN OPERATOR

The lesser used **BETWEEN** operator allows you to specify a range and is most commonly used to select records using date criteria.

YOUR TURN 3-6

List all of the fields in the Employees table where the HireDate field is in the year 2020.

In this query, you want to list all fields in the Employees table between and including the dates of 1/1/2020 and 12/31/2020. The SQL for this query is shown in Figure 3-18.

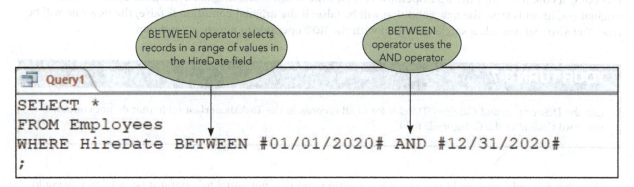

FIGURE 3-18   SQL with the BETWEEN operator

The query results appear in Figure 3-19. The BETWEEN operator includes the values at the beginning and the end of the range. Note that in Figure 3-19, one of the selected records has a HireDate value of 1/1/2020.

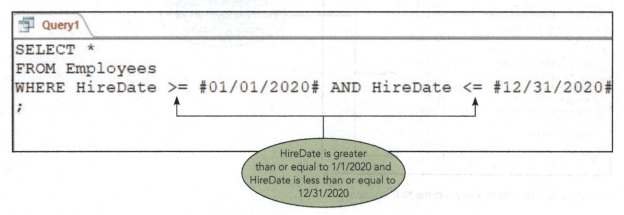

EmployeeID	LastName	FirstName	HireDate	Title	Salary
19	Kohn	Ali	1/1/2020	Project Leader	$5,000.00
22	Kaplan	Franco	2/1/2020	Programmer	$5,500.00
35	Prohm	Nada	2/29/2020	Customer Support Specialist	$4,000.00
47	Alvarez	Benito	3/31/2020	Front End Developer	$5,200.00
51	Shields	Simone	4/30/2020	Network Specialist	$7,000.00
55	Winter	Wendy	12/31/2020	Front End Developer	$4,300.00
66	Roth	Elena	10/31/2020	Network Specialist	$7,000.00
69	Jordan	Karl	11/30/2020	Customer Support Specialist	$5,000.00
72	Nasser	Amir	2/1/2020	Programmer	$5,500.00

FIGURE 3-19   Results of query with the BETWEEN operator

Note that you can create the same results as the BETWEEN operator using the >=, AND, and <= operators as shown in the SQL in Figure 3-20. The SQL is a longer because the HireDate field name must be repeated for the AND criteria, but the two statements are functionally equivalent.

```
Query1
SELECT *
FROM Employees
WHERE HireDate >= #01/01/2020# AND HireDate <= #12/31/2020#
;
```

FIGURE 3-20   SQL with >= and <= comparison operators

USING THE NOT OPERATOR

Preceding a condition with the **NOT operator** reverses the result of the original condition. That is, if the original condition is true, the new condition will be false; if the original condition is false, the new one will be true. You also can precede a single condition with the **NOT** operator to negate a condition.

YOUR TURN 3-7

List the Description and CategoryID fields for of all records in the TaskMasterList table that do not contain the word Coding in the CategoryID field.

For this example, you could use a simple condition and the "not equal to" operator (< >). Or, you could use the NOT operator to reverse the records that are selected by the SQL as shown in Figure 3-21.

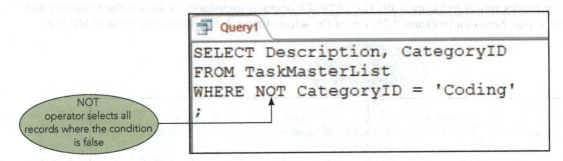

FIGURE 3-21   SQL with the NOT operator

The query results appear in Figure 3-22. None of the records selected contain "Coding" in the CategoryID field.

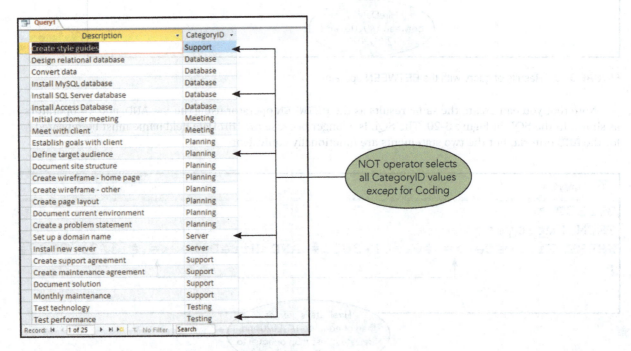

FIGURE 3-22   Results of query with the NOT operator

You can use parentheses to override or clarify the order of operations in complex WHERE statements. For example, in the following WHERE clause, parentheses clarify that the two conditions to the left and the right of the AND operator must both be true in order for the record to be selected:

WHERE (NOT CategoryID = 'Coding') AND (Per = 'Hour' OR Per = 'Hour')

Without the parentheses, the natural order of operations for logical operators is that NOT has the highest precedence, followed by AND, followed by OR with the lowest precedence. Consider the following SQL statement:

WHERE NOT CategoryID = 'Coding' AND Per = 'Hour' OR Per = 'Hour'

Without parentheses, the NOT operator would be evaluated first, followed by the AND operator, and then the OR operator. The parentheses in the following SQL statement clarify that the two conditions to the left of the OR operator are evaluated together. Either they are both true or the OR condition is true in order for the record to be selected.

WHERE ((NOT CategoryID = 'Coding') AND Per = 'Hour') OR Per = 'Hour'

CREATING CALCULATED FIELDS

Similar to QBE, you can calculate information from existing database fields using SQL. A field whose values you derive from existing fields is called a **computed field** or **calculated field**. The operators you use to create computed fields may involve addition (+), subtraction (–), multiplication (*), division (/), or **concatenation** (&) to combine information in text fields.

YOUR TURN 3-8

Select the LastName, Title, and annual salary for all employees with a Title of Programmer. The annual salary is calculated as 12 times the Salary field given the Salary field contains a monthly value.

The query design shown in Figure 3-23 creates a new field named AnnualSalary, which is computed by multiplying the Salary field by 12. By using the SQL AS keyword after the computation, followed by AnnualSalary, you can assign a name to the new, computed field. The name created using the SQL AS keyword is often called the field **alias**. You can alias any field using the AS keyword, but it is an especially common practice with computed fields.

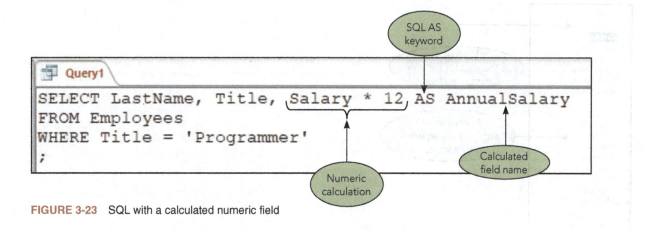

FIGURE 3-23   SQL with a calculated numeric field

The query results appear in Figure 3-24. The column heading for the computed field is the alias that you specified in the SQL command after the SQL AS keyword.

100

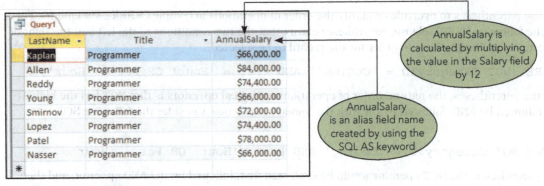

FIGURE 3-24 Results of query with a calculated numeric field

In a relational database, it is common to break out each part of a person's name into its own field so that you can easily sort, filter, find, or merge on any part of a person's name. Yet for reporting and correspondence purposes, you may want to combine the parts of a person's name for professionalism and readability. For example, you may want to combine the values in the FirstName and LastName fields into a single field. To combine the contents of two text fields, you use the **& operator** to concatenate the values together.

YOUR TURN 3-9

List the first and last names of all employees, separated by a space.

The SQL to list all employees' first and last names separated by a space is shown in Figure 3-25.

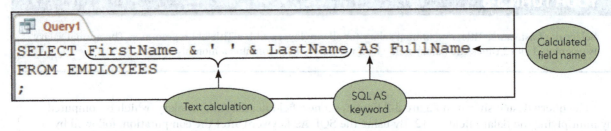

FIGURE 3-25 SQL with a calculated text field

The query results appear in Figure 3-26. The first and last name values appear to be in one field, but the FullName field is actually a computed field.

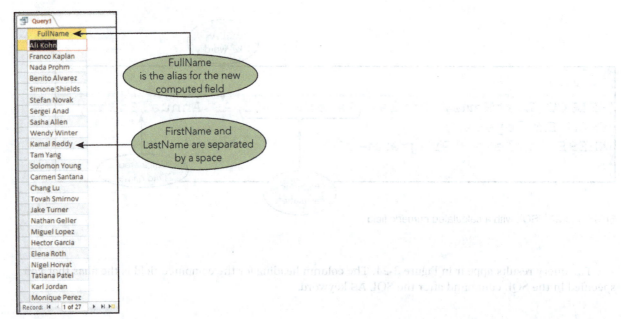

FIGURE 3-26 Results of query with a calculated text field

USING WILDCARDS AND THE LIKE OPERATOR

You might want to select records that match a pattern as opposed to an exact match. For example, you might want to find all employees with the word "Developer" anywhere in their title so you can select all employees with a Title value of Database Developer, Front End Developer, and so on.

To select a pattern, you use **wildcard characters** to represent the pattern. In Access SQL, the asterisk (*) is used to represent any number of characters. (In other versions of SQL, the percent sign (%) is often used as a wildcard.)

YOUR TURN 3-10

List all the fields from the Employees table where the Title field includes the word "Developer" anywhere in the Title value.

To use a wildcard in the criterion, use the LIKE operator in the WHERE clause. The query design shown in Figure 3-27 will retrieve the records for every employee whose Title field contains the word "Developer" somewhere in the field.

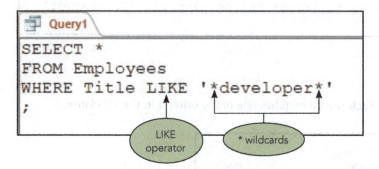

FIGURE 3-27 SQL with the * wildcard and LIKE operator

Adding the asterisk (*) wildcard both before and after the word developer ensures that no matter where the word is found in the Title field, it will be selected. The query results appear in Figure 3-28.

EmployeeID	LastName	FirstName	HireDate	Title	Salary
17	Alvarez	Benito	3/31/2020	Front End Developer	$5,200.00
53	Anad	Sergei	1/1/2019	Front End Developer	$5,300.00
55	Winter	Wendy	12/31/2020	Front End Developer	$4,300.00
57	Yang	Tam	4/30/2021	Front End Developer	$5,000.00
59	Santana	Carmen	1/1/2019	Front End Developer	$4,800.00
60	Lu	Chang	3/1/2019	Database Developer	$7,900.00
62	Turner	Jake	3/31/2021	Database Developer	$7,800.00

Each Title includes Developer

FIGURE 3-28 Results of query with the * wildcard and LIKE operator

In Access SQL, the question mark (?) is used to represent *one* character. (In other versions of SQL, the underscore (_) may be used as a wildcard.) For example, *t?m* represents the letter *T* followed by any single character, followed by the letter *m*. When used in a WHERE clause, it retrieves records that include the words *Tim, Tom,* or *T3m,* for example. Textual criteria values are not case sensitive, so t?m is the same as T?m, T?M and t?M.

USING THE IN OPERATOR

Another SQL operator, IN, provides a concise way of creating a condition to match a specific list of criteria.

YOUR TURN 3-11

List all the fields from the Employees table where the Title field is Database Developer, Front End Developer, or Programmer.

In this query, you can use the SQL IN operator to determine whether the Title field value in the Employees table is equal to Database Developer, Front End Developer, or Programmer, as shown in Figure 3-29. You could obtain the same result by using the condition WHERE Title = 'Database Developer' OR Title = 'Front End Developer' OR Title = 'Programmer'. The IN keyword contains the collection of values to match enclosed in parentheses and separated by commas.

```
Query1

SELECT *
FROM Employees
WHERE Title IN ('Database Developer', 'Front End Developer', 'Programmer')
;
```

FIGURE 3-29 SQL with the IN operator

The query results appear in Figure 3-30. Each record matches one of the criteria in the IN clause.

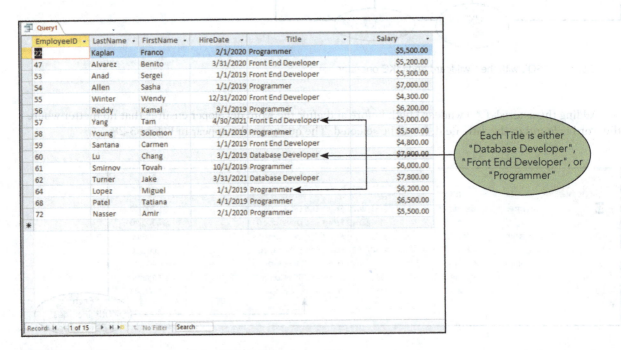

EmployeeID	LastName	FirstName	HireDate	Title	Salary
22	Kaplan	Franco	2/1/2020	Programmer	$5,500.00
47	Alvarez	Benito	3/31/2020	Front End Developer	$5,200.00
53	Anad	Sergei	1/1/2019	Front End Developer	$5,300.00
54	Allen	Sasha	1/1/2019	Programmer	$7,000.00
55	Winter	Wendy	12/31/2020	Front End Developer	$4,300.00
56	Reddy	Kamal	9/1/2019	Programmer	$6,200.00
57	Yang	Tam	4/30/2021	Front End Developer	$5,000.00
58	Young	Solomon	1/1/2019	Programmer	$5,500.00
59	Santana	Carmen	1/1/2019	Front End Developer	$4,800.00
60	Lu	Chang	3/1/2019	Database Developer	$7,900.00
61	Smirnov	Tovah	10/1/2019	Programmer	$6,000.00
62	Turner	Jake	3/31/2021	Database Developer	$7,800.00
64	Lopez	Miguel	1/1/2019	Programmer	$6,200.00
68	Patel	Tatiana	4/1/2019	Programmer	$6,500.00
72	Nasser	Amir	2/1/2020	Programmer	$5,500.00

Each Title is either "Database Developer", "Front End Developer", or "Programmer"

Record: 1 of 15 | No Filter | Search

FIGURE 3-30 Results of query with the IN operator

SORTING RECORDS

If the order in which the selected records are displayed is important, you should add a sort order in the SQL command. In SQL, you sort data using the **ORDER BY clause**. The default sort order is ascending but can be explicitly stated using the SQL ASC keyword placed after the sort key. To sort records in descending order, use the DESC keyword after the sort key.

Select all of the fields in the Clients table. Sort the selected records in ascending order by ClientName.

To sort the selected records, use the ORDER BY clause in the SQL query, followed by the sort key field, as shown in Figure 3-31.

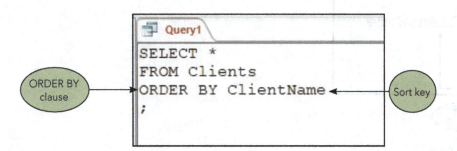

FIGURE 3-31 SQL to sort records by one field

The query results appear in Figure 3-32. All of the fields from the Clients table have been selected and are ordered in alphabetical (ascending) order on the values in the ClientName field.

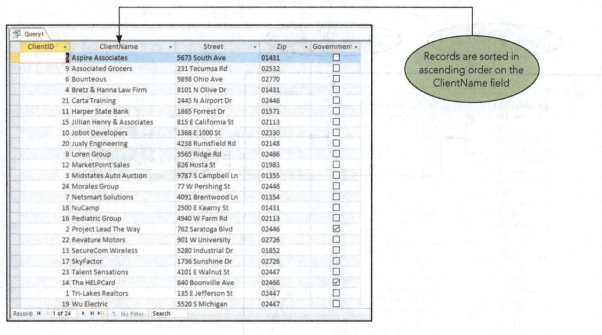

FIGURE 3-32 Results of query to sort records by one field

Sorting on Multiple Fields

When you need to sort data on more than one field, the first sort field is called the major sort key (also referred to as the primary sort key) and subsequent sort fields are called minor sort keys (also referred to as the second, third, so forth sort keys). The sort keys should be listed in the order in which you want them to be evaluated.

Select all of the fields in the Clients table. Sort the selected records by ClientName within Zip.

In this case, the Zip field is the major sort key and the ClientName field is the minor sort key. This means that the selected records will be sorted by the values in the Zip field and if two or more records have the same value in the Zip field, they will be further sorted by the values within the ClientName field as shown in Figure 3-33.

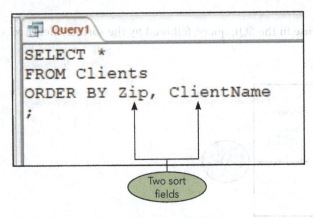

FIGURE 3-33 SQL to sort on two fields

The query results appear in Figure 3-34. Notice that when more than one record has the same value in the Zip field, the records are further sorted by the values in the ClientName field.

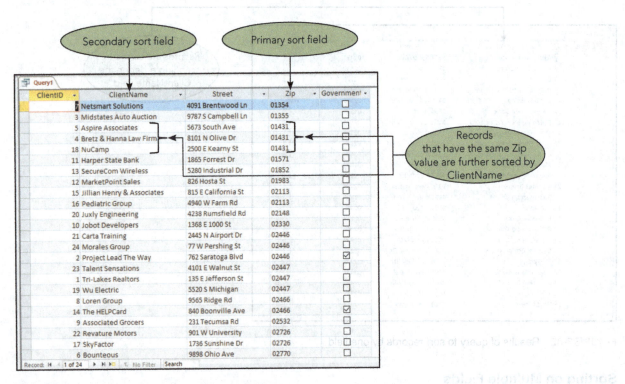

FIGURE 3-34 Results of query to sort on two fields

USING AGGREGATE FUNCTIONS

SQL **aggregate functions** (also called **built-in functions** because they are already built into the SQL language) calculate on groups of records. For example, they can subtotal or average the values in a numeric field using the SUM or AVG SQL keywords. They can also count, find the largest, or find the smallest value in a field using the COUNT, MAX, or MIN SQL keywords.

YOUR TURN 3-14

Calculate the total of the (monthly) Salary field for all employees in the Employees table, naming the field TotalSalary. Also calculate the count of all employees in the Employees table, naming the field CountOfEmployees.

This query requires the use of both the SQL COUNT and SUM keywords. Some aggregate functions such as SUM or AVG only work on data in a numeric field such as Salary. Other aggregate functions, such as COUNT, MAX, and MIN work on both numeric and textual data in Access SQL. This query will count and subtotal values for *all* of the records in the Employees table. The SQL appears in Figure 3-35.

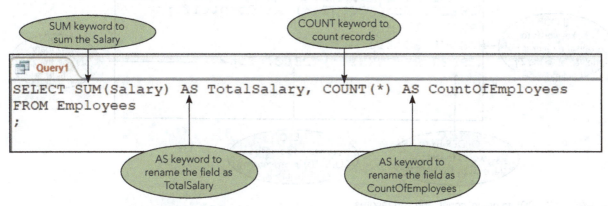

FIGURE 3-35   SQL query to SUM and COUNT all records

The query results appear in Figure 3-36. The Salary value in all of the records in the Employees table were added together for a grand total of $162,950 in the TotalSalary column. The CountOfEmployees column tells you that 27 records were included in these calculations.

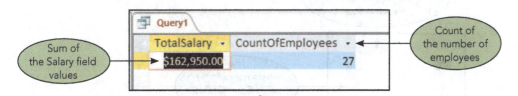

FIGURE 3-36   Results of query to SUM and COUNT all records

GROUPING RECORDS

Recall from Module 2 that you can use aggregate functions to find statistics on groups of records versus *all* of the selected records. A group of records are those that have the same value in a particular field.

YOUR TURN 3-15

For each Zip value in the Clients table, count the number of clients that have the same Zip value, naming the field CountOfZips. Order the records from the greatest count to the least. Add a secondary sort to order the records by the Zip value within each CountOfZips group.

In this query, you need to count the number of records that have the same value in the Zip field of the Clients table. To group the records based on their values in the Zip field, use the GROUP BY keywords in a **GROUP BY clause**. To count the number of records in a group, use the COUNT keyword. You could actually count any field in the Clients table given the results of counting the number of records in a group does not vary based on the field that you are counting, or use the asterisk (*) as shown in Figure 3-37. Note the DESC keyword to sort the records in descending order by CountOfZip, and also notice the secondary sort order to further order the records within each group.

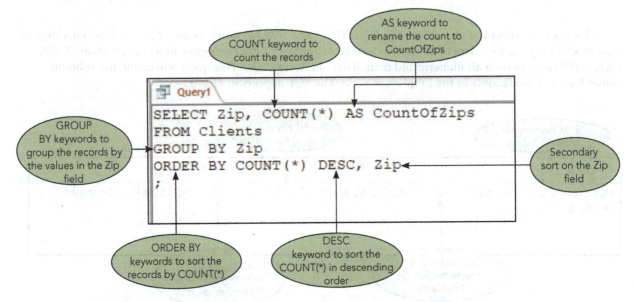

FIGURE 3-37 SQL to group, count, and sort records

The query results appear in Figure 3-38. There are 15 records, indicating that there are 15 different Zip values in the Clients table given one record is produced for each group. The records are sorted in descending order on the CountOfZips field listing those Zip values with the highest number of clients first. When more than one group of records has the same Zip value, the records are further sorted in ascending order on the Zip field.

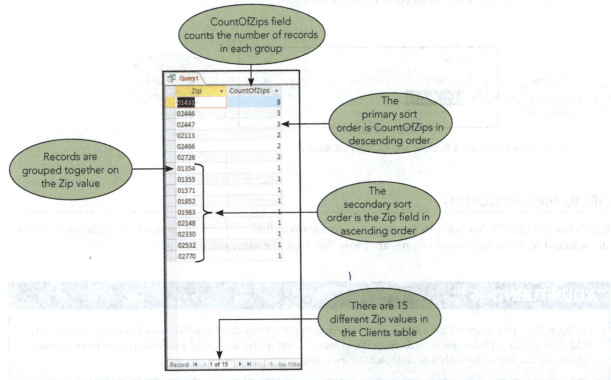

FIGURE 3-38 Results of query to group, count, and sort records

Limiting Records with the HAVING clause

If you want to include criteria to limit the number of records selected for a query that uses an aggregate function, you use the **HAVING clause**. The `HAVING` keyword for groups is analogous to the `WHERE` keyword for individual records.

YOUR TURN 3-16

Limit the number of records selected in the previous SQL statement to only those that have greater than 1 record in the group.

The SQL command is shown in Figure 3-39. Notice the addition of the `HAVING` clause to limit the final results to those groups with more than one.

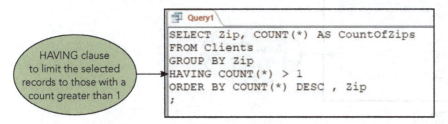

```
Query1
SELECT Zip, COUNT(*) AS CountOfZips
FROM Clients
GROUP BY Zip
HAVING COUNT(*) > 1
ORDER BY COUNT(*) DESC , Zip
;
```

HAVING clause to limit the selected records to those with a count greater than 1

FIGURE 3-39   SQL to group, count, and sort records with HAVING criteria

The query results appear in Figure 3-40. Instead of displaying a record for each group, only those groups that have more than 1 record in the CountOfZips field are shown.

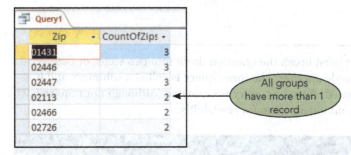

Zip	CountOfZips
01431	3
02446	3
02447	3
02113	2
02466	2
02726	2

All groups have more than 1 record

FIGURE 3-40   Results of query to group, count, and sort records with HAVING criteria

You can also include both a `WHERE` clause and a `HAVING` clause in the same query design, as shown in Figure 3-41. In this example, the Title and Salary fields are selected from the Employees table. The `AVG` function is used to find the average value in the Salary field. The `WHERE` clause selects only those records from the Employees table where the Salary field is greater than $5,000.

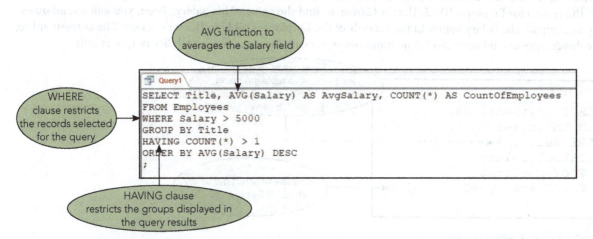

AVG function to averages the Salary field

WHERE clause restricts the records selected for the query

```
Query1
SELECT Title, AVG(Salary) AS AvgSalary, COUNT(*) AS CountOfEmployees
FROM Employees
WHERE Salary > 5000
GROUP BY Title
HAVING COUNT(*) > 1
ORDER BY AVG(Salary) DESC
;
```

HAVING clause restricts the groups displayed in the query results

FIGURE 3-41   SQL with both WHERE and HAVING clauses

The selected records are then grouped by the Title field. The HAVING clause restricts the groups to only those for which the count is greater than one. In other words, the query will not select any records where the Salary field is less than $5,000 nor will it display average Salary values for any group that does not have at least 2 employees with the same Title. Note that the WHERE clause should always come first because it selects the records that are later grouped.

Running the SQL command in Figure 3-41 produces the results shown in Figure 3-42.

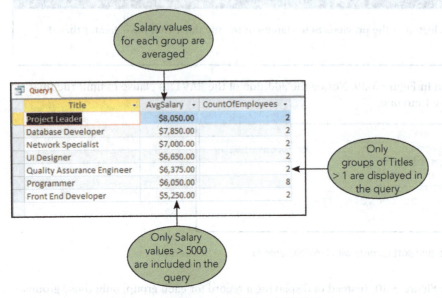

FIGURE 3-42 Results of query with both WHERE and HAVING clauses

WRITING SUBQUERIES

In some cases, to obtain the results you want, you must break the question down into two steps, or two queries. SQL handles this by placing one query inside another. The inner query is called a **subquery** and is evaluated first. After the subquery has been evaluated, the outer query is evaluated. Although not required, it is common to enclose subqueries in parentheses and indent them for readability.

YOUR TURN 3-17

Using the Employees table, find the last name and salaries of the employees who have a Salary field value greater than Hector Garcia, EmployeeID 65.

This request for information requires a subquery given it must be calculated in two steps. First you must select the record for EmployeeID 65, Hector Garcia, to find the value of his Salary. Then, you will use an outer query to compare the Salary values in the records of the Employees table to Hector's salary. The corresponding query design appears in Figure 3-43. The inner query appears indented for readability purposes only.

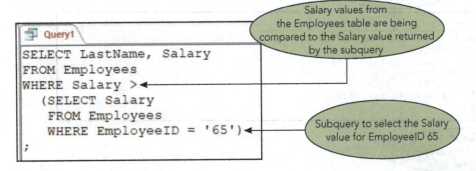

FIGURE 3-43 SQL with subquery

The query results appear in Figure 3-44. If you opened the Employees table to find EmployeeID 65, you would see that Hector's Salary value is $7,000. All of the records selected by the SQL have Salary values greater than $7,000.

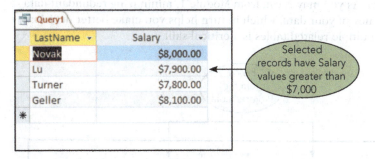

FIGURE 3-44 Results of query with subquery

JOINING TABLES WITH THE WHERE CLAUSE

Many queries require data from more than one table. In SQL, one way to accomplish this is by connecting the tables with the WHERE clause.

YOUR TURN 3-18

List the ClientID and ClientName for each client in the Clients table as well as the ProjectID and ProjectNotes for each related project in the Projects table. Order the records by ClientID, then by ProjectID.

Because you are selecting fields from both the Clients and Projects tables, you need to include both tables in your SQL query. As you may recall from Module 2, the Clients and Projects tables are connected in a one-to-many relationship based on the common ClientID field. The ClientID field is the primary key field in the Clients (parent) table and the foreign key field in the Projects (child) table. To join the tables in SQL, you could use the SQL WHERE keyword to add criteria to select records where the values in the linking fields of the two tables match as follows:

1. In the SELECT clause, list all fields from both tables you want to select.

2. In the FROM clause, list all tables involved in the query.

3. In the WHERE clause, enter the condition that joins the fields from both record into one record based on the common value in the linking fields.

While the linking field does not need to be given the same name in two tables, it is a common practice to do so to make the connection more obvious. When referencing a field name in SQL that is stored in two different tables, the field name must be qualified with the table name used as a prefix plus a period (.) such as tablename.fieldname. You may qualify all fields if desired, but doing so makes the code longer. Note that when you view the SQL generated by Query Design View, the fields will be qualified.

The query design appears in Figure 3-45.

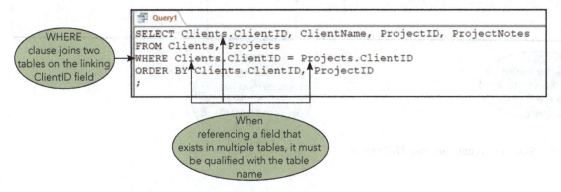

FIGURE 3-45 SQL to join two tables using WHERE

The query results appear in Figure 3-46. Note that the SQL selected 27 records showing the ClientID and ClientName for each project in the first two columns. Some clients are listed more than once given they are related to more than one project. However, each client's data is stored physically only once in the Clients table, which minimizes redundant data. As you may recall from Module 1, minimizing redundant data improves the integrity, accuracy, and consistency of your data, which in turn helps you make better decisions. Knowing how to use SQL to select data from multiple related tables is a critical skill.

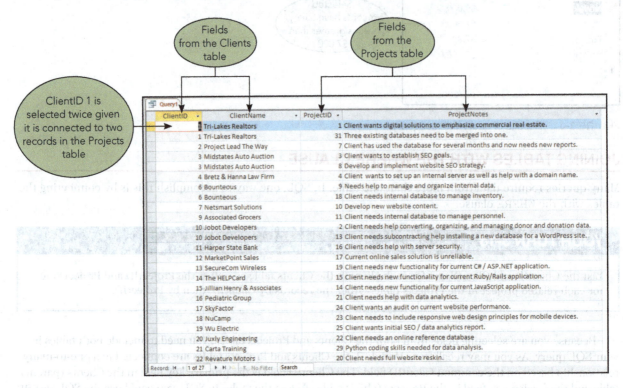

FIGURE 3-46 Results of query to join two tables using WHERE

You can add more criteria to the WHERE clause to place additional restrictions on the records that are selected. Figure 3-47, for example, shows you how to select the same records in a ProjectStartDate on or between 1/1/2020 and 3/1/2020.

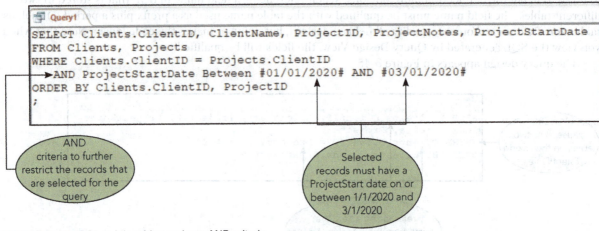

FIGURE 3-47 SQL to join tables and use AND criteria

The query results appear in Figure 3-48.

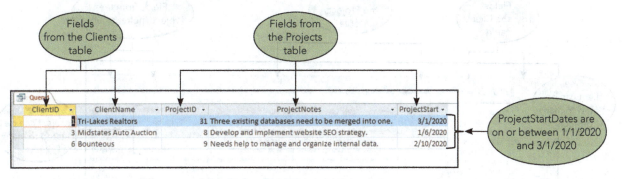

FIGURE 3-48 Results of query to join tables and use AND criteria

Remember that SQL SELECT commands do not store any data, they merely select data from the existing tables. Given the client information is stored in only one physical location, the Clients table, any update to any client in that table such as changing a client's name, would automatically update the results of every record that displayed that value in this or any other SQL command that selects that data.

Joining More Than Two Tables with the WHERE Clause

It is possible to join more than two tables with the WHERE clause. For each pair of tables to join, you must include a condition to describe how the tables are related.

YOUR TURN 3-19

Select the ClientID and ClientName fields from the Clients table, the ProjectID and ProjectNotes fields from the Projects table, and the TaskID and TaskDate fields from the ProjectLineItems table. As you may recall from Module 2, the Clients and Projects tables are connected in a one-to-many relationship based on the common ClientID field and the Projects and ProjectLineItems tables are joined in a one-to-many relationship based on the common ProjectID field.

The SQL uses the AND keyword to add the second condition that links the Projects table to the ProjectLineItems table, as shown in Figure 3-49.

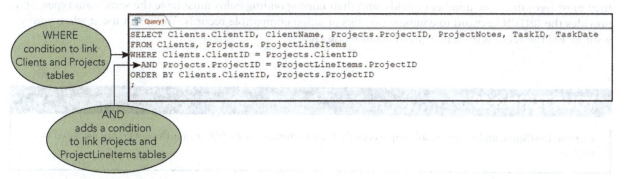

FIGURE 3-49 SQL to join three tables

The query results appear in Figure 3-50. Two fields are selected from the Clients table, two from the Projects table, and two from the ProjectLineItems table. The information from the Clients and Projects tables are selected and repeated for every record in the ProjectLineItems table even though the client information is physically stored in only one record in the Clients table and project information is stored in only one record in the Projects table.

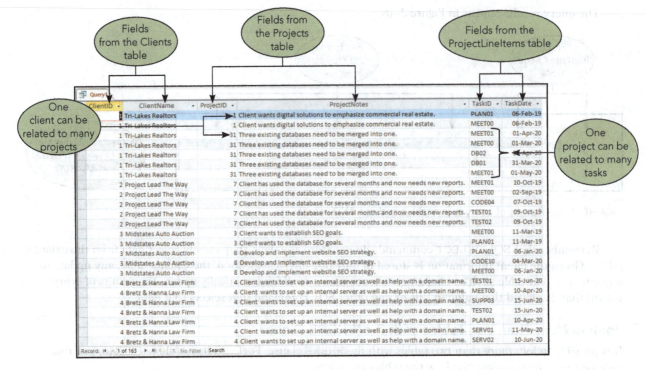

FIGURE 3-50   Results of query to join three tables

Given the client information is stored in only one physical location, the Clients table, any update to any record in that table would automatically update the results of this or any other SQL command that selects data from the Clients table. The same is true of the Projects and ProjectLineItems tables. Providing current, accurate, and consistent views of the data demonstrates the power of storing your information in a relational database and using SQL to select and define different views of the data.

USING THE UNION OPERATOR

Recall from Module 2 that the union of two sets of records contains all of the records from both sets. The two sets of records involved in a union *must* have the same structure, or be union compatible; in other words, they must have the same number of fields, and their corresponding fields must have the same data types. SQL provides the UNION keyword to combine two sets of union compatible records. You might use it when you want to add the records from two questions into one view.

YOUR TURN 3-20

List the LastName and Salary of all Employees that are earning over $7,000 a month or who are assigned to a project.

When the question contains more than one condition, and when those conditions work on different combinations of tables, you may need to separate the questions into two SELECT queries and UNION the results together as shown in Figure 3-51. The first condition queries for records from only the Employees table. The second condition queries for records that have a match in the Employees and Projects tables.

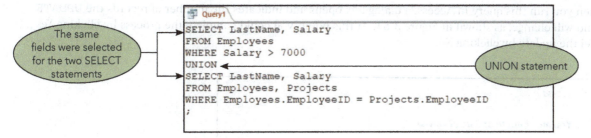

FIGURE 3-51 SQL with UNION statement

The UNION operator allows you to select the records that match each condition separately, and then combine them into a single view as shown in Figure 3-52.

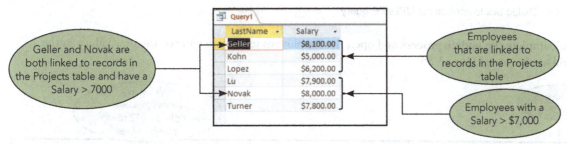

FIGURE 3-52 Results of query with UNION statement

The UNION operator generally removes duplicate rows. In this case, both Geller and Novak were selected for both conditions, but listed only once in the resulting view of the SQL command.

UPDATING VALUES WITH THE SQL UPDATE COMMAND

SQL has more uses than simply retrieving data from a database and creating tables. SQL can also be used to update and delete data.

Note that if you plan to work through the examples in this section using Access, you should use a copy of the original JCConsulting database because the version of the database used in subsequent modules does not include the updates to the data made in these queries.

You can use the SQL UPDATE and SET commands to update the values of an *existing* field. After the word UPDATE, you identify the table to be updated. After the keyword SET, you identify the field to be changed, followed by an equals sign and the new value or expression. You may also include an optional condition in the WHERE clause so that only the records that satisfy the condition will be changed. These changes update the actual data stored in the table and cannot be undone.

YOUR TURN 3-21

Update the values in the Salary field of the Employees table to display annual data versus monthly data by multiplying the existing field value by 12.

The SQL command to update the Salary field in the Employees table from monthly to annual data appears in Figure 3-53.

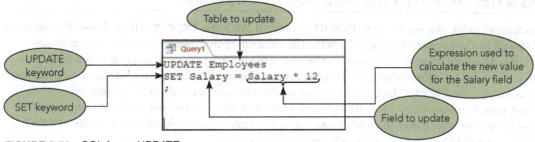

FIGURE 3-53 SQL for an UPDATE query

When you run this query in Access, a dialog box opens and indicates the number of records the UPDATE command will change, as shown in Figure 3-54. At this point, you could complete the process by clicking Yes or cancel the update by clicking No.

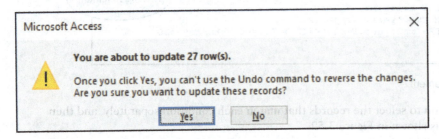

FIGURE 3-54   Dialog box to confirm the UPDATE query

If you complete the update process and open the Employees table, you can see the new values in the Salary field as shown in Figure 3-55.

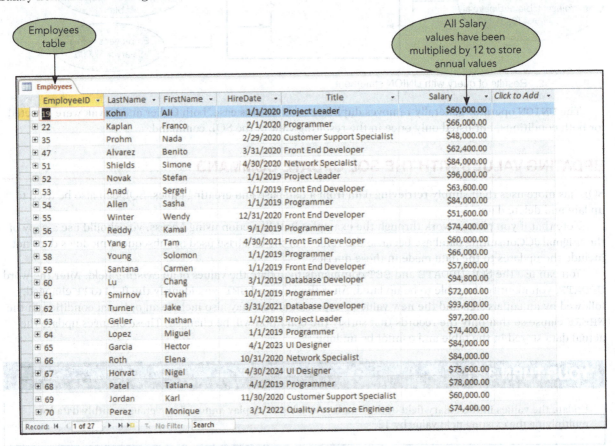

FIGURE 3-55   Updated Salary values in Employees table

INSERTING A RECORD WITH THE SQL INSERT COMMAND

To add *new* record to a table, you use the SQL **INSERT command**. After the **INSERT INTO** clause, list the name of the table, followed by the keyword **VALUES**. Then list the values in (parentheses) for each of the columns (fields) in the table. All values must be in the same order as the fields were previously defined in the table, text values must be surrounded by 'apostrophes', and date values must be surrounded by #pound signs# just like text and date criteria was specified in a SELECT query. Values for each column are separated by commas.

If you do not want to insert a new value into each field of the table, you can list the field names that you want to use in (parentheses) after the table name. After the update, any field not listed in the INSERT command will have a **null** value. Null is an intentional "nothing" value.

YOUR TURN 3-22

Insert a new record into the Employees table with the following information for each column of the table:

EmployeeID: '88',

LastName: 'Zhao',

FirstName: 'Eric',

HireDate: #01/01/2022#,

Title: 'Programmer'

Salary: 59500

Note the 'apostrophes' around the text field values, the # pound signs # around the date value for the HireDate field, and that the Salary value is numeric. The SQL command is shown in Figure 3-56.

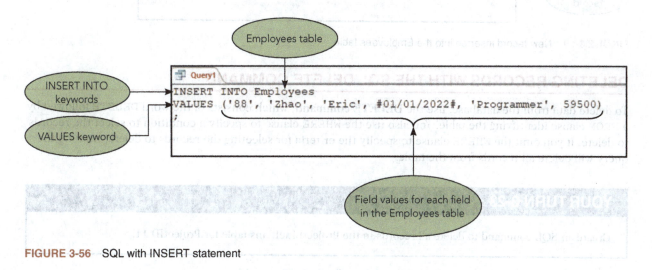

FIGURE 3-56 SQL with INSERT statement

When you run the SQL command, Access prompts you with a dialog box to confirm or cancel the process to insert (also called append) a new record, as shown in Figure 3-57.

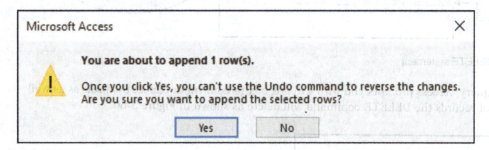

FIGURE 3-57 Dialog box to confirm INSERT query

If you confirm the update, and then open the Employees table, the Eric Zhao record, EmployeeID 88, should be in the table, which now has a total of 28 records. Given records are typically sorted by the primary key field, EmployeeID 88 is probably found near the end of the records as shown in Figure 3-58.

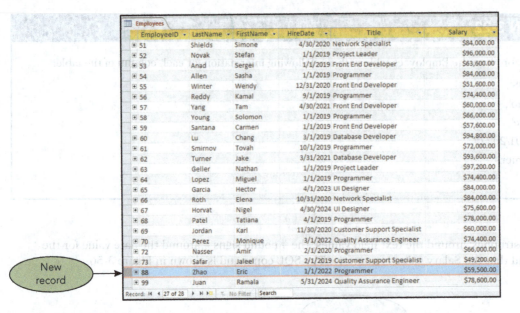

FIGURE 3-58   New record inserted into the Employees table

DELETING RECORDS WITH THE SQL DELETE COMMAND

To delete data from the database, use the **DELETE command**, which consists of the word DELETE followed by a FROM clause identifying the table. You also use the WHERE clause to specify a condition to select the records to delete. If you omit the WHERE clause to specify the criteria for selecting the records to delete, running the query will delete all records from the table.

YOUR TURN 3-23

Create an SQL command to delete all records in the ProjectLineItems table for ProjectID 11.

Use the SQL command in Figure 3-59 to delete the desired records.

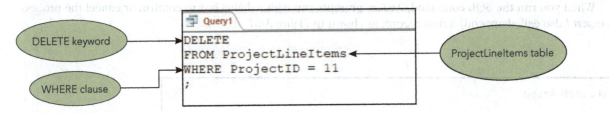

FIGURE 3-59   SQL with DELETE statement

When you run this query, Access prompts you with a dialog box to confirm or cancel the process as well as indicate the number of records the DELETE command will delete as shown in Figure 3-60.

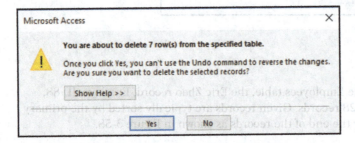

FIGURE 3-60   Dialog box to confirm DELETE query

If you confirm the process and open the ProjectLineItems table, you will not be able to find any records with a ProjectID value of 11. A portion of the remaining 156 records are shown in Figure 3-61.

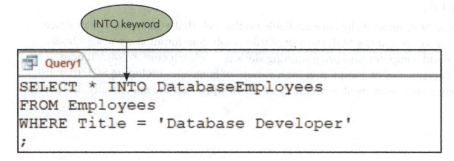

FIGURE 3-61 ProjectLineItemsTable after DELETE query

SAVING QUERY RESULTS AS A TABLE

If you need to *copy* the data from a view into a new table, you can save the results of a query as a table by including the INTO clause in the query. Use the SELECT, FROM, and WHERE commands to identify the fields, tables, and criteria to determine the selected records. Then add the INTO clause to identify the new table name.

Note, however, that you shouldn't *copy* data into another table unless it is absolutely necessary. By relating your tables and creating new views of the data using SELECT queries, you maintain only one master copy of the relational database that every query uses. As you already know, reducing data redundancy using a properly developed relational database is an extremely powerful business tool given it provides decision makers with accurate, consistent, up-to-date information that in turn helps them make better decisions.

YOUR TURN 3-24

Create a new table named DatabaseEmployees consisting of all fields from the Employees table in which the Title field value is Database Developer.

Use the SQL command in Figure 3-62 to select the desired records and copy them into the new table.

```
SELECT * INTO DatabaseEmployees
FROM Employees
WHERE Title = 'Database Developer'
;
```

FIGURE 3-62 SQL query to SELECT INTO a new table

When you run this query, Access prompts you with a dialog box to confirm or cancel the process as well as indicate the number of records you will paste as shown in Figure 3-63.

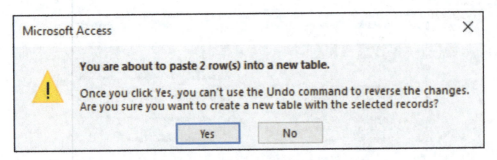

FIGURE 3-63   Dialog box to confirm the SELECT INTO query

If you confirm the process, you can open the DatabaseEmployees table as shown in Figure 3-64 to make sure that both records with a Title field value of Database Developer were successfully copied to the new table.

EmployeeID	LastName	FirstName	HireDate	Title	Salary
50	Lu	Chang	3/1/2019	Database Developer	$94,800.00
62	Turner	Jake	3/31/2021	Database Developer	$93,600.00
*					

FIGURE 3-64   New DatabaseEmployees table

DEVELOPING CAREER SKILLS: SQL

Indeed.com is a website that helps connect jobs with people. In doing so, they also accumulate data on desired skills. According to an article from codingsight.com (https://codingsight.com/structured-query-language-importance-of-learning-sql/), SQL is the most sought-after language for programmers, ahead of Java, Python, JavaScript, C++ and many others.

Perhaps this can be explained in part because SQL is a universal language for selecting and maintaining data stored in a relational database. It is also an open source language with a long history of success and large community of developers. While different relational database management systems use slightly different versions of SQL, the concepts are the same across each making it fairly easy to transfer SQL skills from one RDBMS such as Access to another such as Oracle.

Accessing Free SQL Tutorials

Many free, interactive, and robust SQL tutorial sites are available on the web that you can use to practice your SQL commands such as sqlzoo.net and the SQL portion of w3schools.com found at www.w3schools.com/sql/. Another great site to build computer and programming skills is sololearn.com. sololearn.com offers free tutorials, games, and certificates of completion for a variety of languages including SQL that are available both through a computer browser as well as a variety of phone apps that are specifically designed for smaller devices.

Summary

- **Examine Structured Query Language (SQL)**: SQL is a language that is used to create, manipulate, and select data from relational databases. See Appendix C for a list of SQL commands.

  The fundamental features of SQL and SQL concepts are the same across all relational database management systems, but systems use different versions of SQL that have slightly different syntax and keywords.

  The basic form of an SQL query that selects data from the database is SELECT-FROM-WHERE.

  SQL SELECT queries do not create copies of the data, they merely display field values and records from the specified tables. Therefore, SELECT queries are often referred to as a logical view or merely a view of the data.

  DDL, Data Definition Language, is SQL used to create table structures, indexes, and relationships.

- **Create tables and fields with SQL**: Use the CREATE TABLE SQL DDL command to describe and create a new table by defining its fields and data types.

- **Select data using criteria in SQL**: In SQL SELECT queries, fields are listed in the SELECT clause, tables are listed in the FROM clause, and conditions are listed in the WHERE clause.

  In WHERE conditions, character values must be enclosed in apostrophes (some versions of SQL also use quotation marks).

  Remember, only the tables store the data. You can create as many queries (logical views) as desired knowing that any updates to the data are automatically updated when each SELECT query is run.

- **Select data using AND, OR, BETWEEN, and NOT operators**: Compound WHERE conditions are formed by combining simple conditions using either or both of the following operators: AND and OR.

  Sorting is accomplished using the ORDER BY clause. The field on which the records are sorted is called the sort key. When the data is sorted in more than one field, the more important field is called the major sort key or primary sort key. The less important field is called the minor sort key or secondary sort key.

- **Create computed fields in SQL**: Computed fields, also called calculated fields, are created in SQL queries by including the expression, followed by the word AS, followed by the name of the computed field.

  When using the SQL AS keyword to rename a field, the new field name is called an alias.

- **Use wildcards and the LIKE and IN operators**: To select records that match a pattern, use wildcard characters such as the asterisk (*) to represent the pattern. To use a wildcard in the criterion for an SQL query, use the LIKE operator in the WHERE clause.

  Another SQL operator, IN, provides a concise way of creating a condition to match a specific list of criteria.

- **Apply built-in SQL aggregate functions**: SQL has the built-in (also called aggregate) functions such as COUNT, SUM, AVG, MAX, and MIN to calculate statistics on groups of records.

- **Group records in SQL**: Grouping is accomplished in SQL by using the GROUP BY clause.

  To restrict the rows to be displayed when they are previously grouped, use the HAVING clause.

- **Use subqueries in SQL**: An SQL query may contain an inner query is called a subquery. The subquery is evaluated first, and is generally used to limit the records that are selected by the outer query.

- **Join tables using SQL**: Joining tables can be accomplished in SQL by using a WHERE condition that identifies the common field upon which two tables in a one-to-many relationship are connected.

- **Perform union operations in SQL**: A UNION query combines the records of two separate queries. UNION queries require that the two queries have the same field names and data types.

- **Use SQL to update, insert, and delete records**: The SQL UPDATE command is used to change existing data in a field. The SQL INSERT command is used to append a new row to a table. The SQL DELETE command is used to delete existing records.

  The SQL INTO clause is used in a SELECT clause to create a new table that is a copy rather than a view of the data.

  Do not create new copies of data unless it is absolutely necessary for another application or process. Creating copies of data negates the benefits of minimizing redundant data which is the major benefit of organizing your data in a relational database.

- **Prepare for a database career by acquiring SQL skills**: As a universal language for selecting and maintaining data stored in a relational database, SQL is considered the most sought-after language for programmers.

Key Terms

& operator	HAVING clause
aggregate function	INSERT command
alias	INSERT INTO clause
American National Standards Institute (ANSI)	International Organization for Standardization (ISO)
American Standard Code for Information Interchange (ASCII)	keyword
	logical view
AND operator	monospaced
AUTOINCREMENT	NOT operator
AutoNumber	null
BETWEEN operator	OR operator
Boolean	ORDER BY clause
built-in functions	qualified field names
BYTE	reserved word
calculated field	SELECT clause
CHAR	SELECT-FROM-WHERE
compound condition	simple condition
computed field	SQL (Structured Query Language)
concatenation	subquery
CREATE TABLE	syntax
data-definition language (DDL)	VALUES
DELETE command	view
FROM clause	WHERE clause
GROUP BY clause	wildcard character

Module Review Questions

Problems

1. Which of the following is *not* an Access SQL data type?
   a. TEXT
   b. SHORT
   c. LONG
   d. DECIMAL

2. Which of the following is *not* a valid comparison operator?
   a. =
   b. <=
   c. ||
   d. < >

3. Which of the following is true?
   a. Criteria joined by OR always select fewer records than if joined by AND.
   b. Criteria joined by AND always select fewer records than if joined by OR.
   c. Criteria joined by OR criteria may select more records than if joined by AND.
   d. If a record is true for two criteria joined by an OR, it is displayed twice in the results.

4. Which of the following is *not* true about a computed or calculated field?
   a. A calculated field creates a new piece of information for each record.
   b. A calculated field starts by determining how to group the records.
   c. A calculated field may use data from numeric fields.
   d. A calculated field may use data from text fields.

5. Which SQL operator can be rewritten with >= AND <= operators?
   a. BETWEEN
   b. CONTAINS
   c. IN
   d. WITH

6. Which SQL operator provides a concise way of creating a condition to match a specific list of criteria?
   a. BETWEEN
   b. CONTAINS
   c. IN
   d. NOT

7. Which of the following is *not* an aggregate function used to calculate information on groups of records?
   a. SUM
   b. MIN
   c. COUNT
   d. SUBTOTAL

8. Which SQL clause sorts the selected records in ascending order by FirstName within LastName?
   a. ORDER BY FirstName, LastName
   b. ORDER BY FirstName, LastName ASC
   c. ORDER BY LastName, FirstName
   d. ORDER BY LastName & FirstName

9. Which SQL clause would join a Customers table with an Orders table assuming that they are related in a one-to-many relationship on a field called CustID in both tables?
   a. WHERE Customers.CustID = Orders.CustID
   b. WHERE Customers = Orders AND CustID = CustID
   c. WHERE Customers.CustID & Orders.CustID
   d. WHERE IN Customers, Orders (CustID)

10. Which SQL keyword starts an SQL statement to select fields and records from one or more related tables?
    a. LIST
    b. SELECT
    c. SORT
    d. SUM

11. Which SQL keyword(s) start an SQL statement to append a new record to a table?
    a. ADD
    b. APPEND
    c. CONCATENATE
    d. INSERT INTO

12. Which SQL keyword identifies the tables that are involved in a SELECT query?
    a. FROM
    b. HAVING
    c. TABLE
    d. WHERE

13. Which symbol is a wildcard representing any number of characters?
    a. *
    b. < >
    c. &
    d. #

14. The _____ operator allows you to select the records that match each condition separately, and then combine them into a single view.
    a. COMBINE
    b. MATCH
    c. UNION
    d. MERGE

15. What is another term for a subquery?

    a. outer query

    b. inner query

    c. union query

    d. aggregate query

16. Which of the following is the most sought-after language for programmers, according to codingsight.com?

    a. C++

    b. Java

    c. Python

    d. SQL

Critical Thinking Question

1. What would be a good Access SQL data type for a Phone Number field?

JC Consulting Case Exercises

Problems

The following exercises are based on the JCConsulting database. You may use the database to help answer these questions or refer back to the data shown in the figures of Modules 1, 2, and 3.

1. What SQL statement lists only the EmployeeID, LastName, and FirstName fields of all employees in the Employees table?

    a. `SELECT *`
       `FROM Employees;`
    b. `SELECT EmployeeID, LastName, FirstName`
       `FROM Employees;`
    c. `SELECT EmployeeID, LastName, FirstName`
       `INTO Employees;`
    d. `SELECT EmployeeID, LastName, FirstName`
       `WHERE Employees;`

2. What SQL statement lists all the fields from the records in the TaskMasterList table with a CategoryID of Database?

    a. `SELECT *`
       `FROM TaskMasterList;`
    b. `SELECT *`
       `FROM TaskMasterList`
       `WHERE Count(*) > 1;`
    c. `SELECT *`
       `FROM TaskMasterList`
       `WHERE CategoryID = 'Database';`
    d. `SELECT CategoryID`
       `FROM TaskMasterList`
       `WHERE CategoryID = 'Database';`

3. Which SQL command would be used to join the TaskMasterList and ProjectLineItems tables?

    a. `CONNECT`

    b. `COMBINE`

    c. `LINK`

    d. `WHERE`

4. Which SQL keyword would be used to find all TaskMasterList records with a CategoryID field value of Testing or Support?

    a. `AND`

    b. `ORDER`

    c. `&&`

    d. `OR`

5. Which SQL command would be used to sort all TaskMasterList records in ascending order based on the value of their TaskID within CategoryID?
   a. `ORDER BY CategoryID, TaskID`
   b. `ORDER BY TaskID, CategoryID`
   c. `SORT CategoryID, TaskID`
   d. `SORT BY TaskID IN CategoryID`

6. Which SQL keyword would be used to select all records except those with a Per field value of Hour?
   a. `WHERE NOT Per = 'Hour'`
   b. `WHERE Per = 'Hour'`
   c. `SELECT NOT Per = 'Hour'`
   d. `SELECT * EXCEPT 'Hour'`

7. What data types would you assign to the City and Zip fields when creating the Zips table?
   a. TEXT to City and SHORT to Zip
   b. LONGTEXT to City and TEXT to Zip
   c. TEXT to City and TEXT to Zip
   d. SHORT to City and SHORT to Zip

8. Which SQL statement calculates the Bonus field in the Employees table as 10 percent of Salary?
   a. `SELECT Salary * 0.1 AS Bonus`
      `FROM Employees;`
   b. `SELECT Bonus AS Salary * 0.1`
      `FROM Employees;`
   c. `SELECT *`
      `FROM Employees`
      `WHERE Bonus = Salary * 0.1;`
   d. `SELECT Salary * 0.1 = Bonus`
      `FROM Employees;`

9. Which SQL statement lists the job titles at JCC and displays the number of employees that have each title?
   a. `SELECT Title, COUNT(*) AS CountOfTitle`
      `FROM Employees`
      `GROUP BY Title;`
   b. `SELECT Title, COUNT(*) AS CountOfTitle`
      `FROM Employees;`
   c. `SELECT Title, COUNT(*) AS CountOfTitle`
      `FROM Employees`
      `HAVING Title;`
   d. `SELECT Title, COUNT(*) AS CountOfTitle`
      `FROM Employees`
      `ORDER BY Title;`

10. Which SQL statement lists the last names and salaries of employees who have a Salary field value less than Amir Nasser, EmployeeID 72?
    a. `SELECT LastName, Salary`
       `FROM Employees`
       `WHERE Salary <`
       `UNION`
       `   SELECT LastName, Salary`
       `   FROM Employees`
       `   WHERE EmployeeID = '72';`
    b. `SELECT LastName, Salary`
       `FROM Employees`
       `WHERE Salary <`
       `UPDATE`
       `SET EmployeeID = '72';`
    c. `SELECT LastName, Salary`
       `  FROM Employees`
       `  HAVING Salary < EmployeeID = '72';`

d. SELECT LastName, Salary
   FROM Employees
   WHERE Salary <
     (SELECT Salary
      FROM Employees
      WHERE EmployeeID = '72');

Critical Thinking Questions

1. What would the WHERE clause look like in a SELECT query that selects fields from the TaskMasterList, ProjectLineItems, and Projects tables?

2. Use the terms primary key field, foreign key field, one-to-many relationship, parent table and child table to describe the following WHERE clause:

   WHERE Clients.ClientID = Projects.ClientID

Pitt Fitness Case Exercises

Problems

The owner of Pitt Fitness used to work in the field of information technology and knows the importance of SQL in answering questions about the company data. Any of the queries you performed with the Access QBE, you can do in SQL. In each of the following questions, use SQL to answer them either with using the data shown in Figures 1-15 through 1-19, or by using a copy of the Pitt Fitness database. You can test the SQL statements in SQL View in Access, or write the SQL on paper.

1. Write the SQL code for the following: List the class name, room, location, day, and time for all classes.
   a. SELECT *
      FROM Classes;
   b. SELECT ClassName, Room, Location, Day, Time
      IN Classes;
   c. SELECT ClassName, Room, Location, Day, Time
      FROM Classes;
   d. SELECT ClassName, Room, Location, Day, Time
      WITHIN Classes;

2. Write the SQL code for the following: Display the last names of the customers who have registered for a class on 1/2/2021.
   a. SELECT Customers.LastName, Reservations.ClassDate
      FROM Customers
      ADD Customers.CustomerID = Reservations.CustomerID AND Reservations.ClassDate
      ='1/2/2021';
   b. SELECT Customers.LastName, Reservations.ClassDate
      FROM Customers, Reservations
      WHERE Customers.CustomerID = Reservations.CustomerID AND Reservations.ClassDate
      =#1/2/2021#;
   c. SELECT Customers.LastName, Reservations.ClassDate
      FROM Customers, Reservations
      WHERE Customers.CustomerID = Reservations.CustomerID WITH Reservations.ClassDate
      =#1/2/2021#;
   d. SELECT Customers.LastName, Reservations.ClassDate
      FROM Customers, Reservations
      WHERE Customers.CustomerID = Reservations.CustomerID INCLUDE Reservations.ClassDate
      =#1/2/2021#;

3. Write the SQL code for the following: Display the last name and street address of the customers who live on Negley.

   a. SELECT LastName, StreetAddress
      FROM Addresses
      WHERE StreetAddress LIKE "*Negley*";

   b. SELECT LastName, StreetAddress
      FROM Customers
      WHERE StreetAddress='Negley';

   c. SELECT LastName, StreetAddress
      WHERE StreetAddress LIKE "*Negley*";

   d. SELECT LastName, StreetAddress
      FROM Customers
      WHERE StreetAddress LIKE "*Negley*";

4. Write the SQL code for the following: Count the number of reservations for 1/3/2021 and display that number with a CountOfReservationID column heading.

   a. SELECT COUNT(ReservationID) AS CountOfReservationID
      FROM Reservations
      WHERE ClassDate=#1/3/2021#;

   b. SELECT CountOfReservationID
      FROM Reservations
      WHERE ClassDate=#1/3/2021#;

   c. SELECT COUNT AS CountOfReservationID
      FROM Reservations
      WHERE ClassDate=#1/3/2021#;

   d. SELECT COUNT OF ReservationID AS CountOfReservationID
      FROM Reservations
      WHERE ClassDate=#1/3/2021#;

5. Write the SQL code that answers the following question: Which instructors (showing last name only) live in zip code 15217?

   a. SELECT LastName
      FROM Instructors
      WHERE InstructorZipCode = '15217';

   b. SELECT InstructorLastName
      FROM Instructors
      WHERE InstructorZipCode = 15217;

   c. SELECT InstructorLastName
      FROM Instructors
      WHERE InstructorZipCode = "15217";

   d. SELECT InstructorLastName
      FROM Instructors
      WHERE InstructorZipCode = &15217&;

6. Write the SQL code that answers the following question: Which classes are scheduled for Wednesdays at the Downtown location? List the class name, the day, and the location.

   a. SELECT ClassName
      FROM Classes
      WHERE Day='Wednesday' AND Location='Downtown';

   b. SELECT ClassName, Day, Location
      FROM Classes
      WHERE Day='Wednesday' AND Location='Downtown';

   c. SELECT ClassName, Day, Location
      WHERE Day='Wednesday' AND Location='Downtown';

   d. SELECT *
      FROM Classes
      WHERE Day='Wednesday' AND Location='Downtown';

7. What SELECT statement would you use in a longer query to calculate the amount of money earned by each instructor based on the length of time for the class and $20 per hour? Display the instructor's last name and the amount earned.

   a. `SELECT InstructorLastName, LengthofTime*20 AS Amount Earned`

   b. `SELECT InstructorLastName, LengthofTime/60*20 AS Earnings OF Instructor`

   c. `SELECT InstructorLastName, LengthofTime/60*20 AS AmountEarned`

   d. `SELECT InstructorLastName, JOIN LengthofTime/60*20 AS Amount Earned`

8. Write the SQL code for the following: Update all class prices to reflect a 1% increase.

   a. `UPDATE Reservations`
      `SET ClassPrice = ClassPrice*1.10;`

   b. `UPDATE Reservations`
      `SET ClassPrice = ClassPrice*1%;`

   c. `UPDATE Reservations`
      `SET ClassPrice = ClassPrice*0.1;`

   d. `UPDATE Reservations`
      `SET ClassPrice = ClassPrice*1.01;`

9. How would you write the SELECT statement in a longer query if you wanted to concatenate the first and last name of the instructors and display that as InstructorFullName?

   a. `SELECT InstructorFirstName, InstructorLastName AS InstructorFullName`

   b. `SELECT InstructorFirstName & " " & InstructorLastName AS InstructorFullName`

   c. `SELECT InstructorFirstName AND InstructorLastName AS InstructorFullName`

   d. `SELECT InstructorFirstName, InstructorLastName SUBSTITUTE InstructorFullName`

10. Write the SQL code for the following: Order the reservations by class date and then by class ID. Display all fields.

    a. `SELECT *`
       `FROM Reservations`
       `ORDER BY ClassDate, ClassID;`

    b. `DISPLAY ALL FROM Reservations`
       `ORDER BY ClassDate, ClassID;`

    c. `SELECT *`
       `FROM Reservations`
       `RANK BY ClassDate, ClassID;`

    d. `SELECT *`
       `FROM Reservations`
       `BY ClassDate, ClassID;`

Critical Thinking Questions

1. Pitt Fitness is selling a line of exercise clothing at their three locations. At the beginning of this venture, they decide to sell only three types of t-shirts with the Pitt Fitness logo: two women's sizes and one men's size. How would you use SQL to create a new table in the Pitt Fitness database to capture the line of t-shirts and their retail price? This new table would be used for advertising purposes only, so no quantity-on-hand fields are necessary.

2. Write an SQL query that would ask the database to count the number of different types of t-shirts available and total their price. Your output should show only the field names: NumberOfTshirts TotalPriceOfTshirts.

Sports Physical Therapy Case Exercises

Problems

In the following exercises, you will use the data in the Sports Physical Therapy database shown in Figures 1-21 through 1-24 in Module 1. Use SQL to answer the questions, either on paper or by running the statements in Access on a copy of the Sports Physical Therapy database.

1. Write the SQL code for the following: List all the information in the patient's table sorted by city.

   a. `SELECT ALL`
      `FROM Patients`
      `ORDER BY City;`

    b. `SELECT *`
       `FROM Patients ASC City;`
    c. `SELECT *`
       `ORDER BY City;`
    d. `SELECT *`
       `FROM Patient`
       `ORDER BY City;`

2. Write the SQL code for the following: List the last names of patients whose balance is greater than $1,000.
    a. `SELECT LastName, Balance>1000`
       `FROM Patient;`
    b. `SELECT LastName, Balance`
       `FROM Patient`
       `WHERE Balance>1000;`
    c. `SELECT LastName, Balance`
       `FROM Patient`
       `WITH Balance>1000;`
    d. `SELECT LastName, Balance`
       `FROM Patient`
       `WHERE Balance<1000;`

3. Write the SQL code for the following: List the city, last name, and balance of patients who live in Waterville and have a balance greater than $1,000.
    a. `SELECT City, LastName, Balance`
       `FROM Patient`
       `WHERE 'Waterville' AND >1000;`
    b. `SELECT City, LastName, Balance`
       `WHERE City='Waterville' AND Balance>1000;`
    c. `SELECT City, LastName, Balance`
       `FROM Patient`
       `WHERE City="Waterville" AND Balance>1000;`
    d. `SELECT *`
       `FROM Patient`
       `WHERE City='Waterville' AND Balance>1000;`

4. Write the SQL code for the following: List the last name, city, and balance of patients who live in Waterville or have a balance greater than $2,000.
    a. `SELECT LastName, City, Balance`
       `FROM Patient`
       `WHERE City='Waterville' AND Balance>2000;`
    b. `SELECT LastName, City, Balance`
       `FROM Patient`
       `WHERE City='Waterville' OR Balance>=2000;`
    c. `SELECT LastName, City, Balance`
       `FROM Patient`
       `WHERE NOT City='Waterville' OR Balance>2000;`
    d. `SELECT LastName, City, Balance`
       `FROM Patient`
       `WHERE City="Waterville" OR Balance>2000;`

5. Write the SQL code for the following: Increase the balance by 2% of any patient whose balance is greater than $2,000.
    a. `UPDATE Patient`
       `SET Balance = Balance*1.2`
       `WHERE Balance>2000;`
    b. `UPDATE Patient`
       `SET Balance = Balance*1.02`
       `WHERE Balance>2000;`

128

```
c. UPDATE Patient
   SET Balance = Balance*2%
   WHERE Balance>2000;
d. SELECT Patient
   SET Balance = Balance*1.02
   WHERE Balance>2000;
```

6. Write the SQL code for the following: List the session dates and numbers for those sessions scheduled between 10/18/2021 and 10/20/2021.

```
a. SELECT SessionDate, SessionNum
   FROM Session
   WHERE SessionDate BETWEEN #10/18/2021# AND #10/20/2021#;
b. SELECT SessionDate, SessionNum
   FROM Session
   WHERE SessionDate BETWEEN '10/18/2021' AND '10/20/2021';
c. SELECT SessionDate, SessionNum
   WHERE SessionDate BETWEEN #10/18/2021# AND #10/20/2021#;
d. SELECT SessionDate, SessionNum
   FROM Session
   WHERE SessionDate  #10/18/2021# >< #10/20/2021#;
```

7. Write the SQL code for the following: List the full name of the therapist scheduled to work on 10/16/2021.

```
a. SELECT Therapist.FirstName, Therapist.LastName
   FROM Therapist
   WHERE Therapist.TherapistID = Session.TherapistID AND SessionDate = #10/16/2021#;
b. SELECT Therapist.FirstName, Therapist.LastName
   FROM Session
   WHERE Therapist.TherapistID = Session.TherapistID AND SessionDate = #10/16/2021#;
c. SELECT Therapist.FirstName, Therapist.LastName
   FROM Therapist, Session
   WHERE Therapist.TherapistID = Session.TherapistID;
d. SELECT Therapist.FirstName, Therapist.LastName
   FROM Therapist, Session
   WHERE Therapist.TherapistID = Session.TherapistID AND SessionDate = #10/16/2021#;
```

8. Write the SQL code that answers the following question: How long are the therapy sessions for the therapist whose last name is Shields? List the length of each session.

```
a. SELECT Session.LengthOfSession, Therapist.LastName='Shields'
   FROM Therapist, Session
   WHERE Therapist.TherapistID = Session.TherapistID;
b. SELECT Session.LengthOfSession
   FROM Therapist, Session
   WHERE Therapist.LastName='Shields';
c. SELECT Session.LengthOfSession
   FROM Therapist, Session
   WHERE Therapist.TherapistID = Session.TherapistID AND Therapist.
      LastName='Shields';
d. SELECT Session.LengthOfSession
   FROM Session
   WHERE Therapist.TherapistID = Session.TherapistID AND Therapist.
      LastName='Shields';
```

9. Write the SQL code that answers the following question: Which therapies have the word "movement" in their description? List the therapy description only.

```
a. SELECT Description
   FROM Therapies
   WHERE Description LIKE *movement*;
b. SELECT Description
   FROM Therapies
   WHERE Description LIKE "*movement*";
```

c. ```
SELECT Description
FROM Therapies
WHERE Description LIKE 'movement';
```

d. ```
SELECT Description
FROM Therapies
WHERE Description IS '*movement*';
```

10. Write the SQL code that answers the following question: How many therapies are offered? Answer with one number only.

a. ```
SELECT COUNT(TherapyCode) AS CountOfTherapyCode
FROM Therapies;
```

b. ```
SELECT COUNT ALL AS CountOfTherapyCode
FROM Therapies;
```

c. ```
SELECT COUNT(TherapyCode) AS "CountOfTherapyCode"
FROM Therapies;
```

d. ```
SELECT COUNT(TherapyCode) AS CountOfTherapyCode;
```

Critical Thinking Questions

1. Write an SQL query that displays the therapies and their unit of time for the therapies that include the word bath, hot, or electrical.

2. Write an SQL query to display every therapist's first name and last name as their full name, but only for those instructors not living in zip code 72511.

MODULE **4**

THE RELATIONAL MODEL: ADVANCED TOPICS

LEARNING OBJECTIVES

- Define and describe the benefits of views
- Create indexes to improve database performance
- Examine and establish security features for a relational database system
- Examine and establish entity, referential, and legal-values integrity
- Make changes to the structure of a relational database
- Create INNER, LEFT, and RIGHT joins between tables
- Define and create system information
- Explain and create stored procedures, triggers, and data macros
- Explore the essential skills for database administrators

INTRODUCTION

In this module, you will learn more about advanced relational database concepts and SQL. You will examine indexes, how to use them to improve database performance, and how to create them using SQL. You will use SQL to join tables in several ways to select information from related tables. You will investigate some of the features of a DBMS that provide system and security information, and you will learn about important rules to improve the overall integrity of the data in the database.

You will learn about using stored procedures and triggers, and you will see how Access provides the functionality of triggers using data macros. If you plan to work through the examples in this module using a computer, you should use a copy of the original JC Consulting database because the version of the database used in this module does not include the changes made in Modules 2 and 3.

CREATING AND USING VIEWS

Most DBMSs support the creation of views. In Access, when you save a query, you save SQL statements (no matter if you create the query using the QBE Query Design View tool or write the SQL statements directly into the SQL View). You execute those statements by running the query or double-clicking a query name in the Navigation Pane. Running a query in Access creates a view of the data.

A key point about views is that they are *not* a copy of the data, but rather only a window into the data that is actually stored in underlying tables. Therefore, views are often called a *logical* (as opposed to physical) representation of the data.

The views in some RDBMSs, such as those provided by basic SELECT queries in Access, also allow you to add new records or modify data directly in the view. When you are updating data in an Access query (view), you are modifying the actual data stored in the underlying table.

Views provide many important benefits and features, including the following:

- They organize the specific fields and records from one or more tables into a single object.
- They prevent the need to directly access tables with sensitive fields by unauthorized users and processes.
- They can be used to sort records.
- They can be used to create a calculation on existing fields for each record.

- They can be used to analyze groups of records.
- Some views can be used to update, delete, or add data.
- They do not duplicate data, so many views can be created using the same tables and fields, each of which displays current data.
- They display current data when run or opened.
- As many views as needed for as many purposes can be created as desired.
- In SQL, the name of a view can be used similarly to how the name of a table is used.

For example, if you want to create a view of employee first and last names from the FirstName and LastName fields of an Employees table using SQL, you use the following CREATE VIEW command to create the view and name it NameList.

```
CREATE VIEW NameList AS
    SELECT FirstName, LastName
    FROM Employees
    ;
```

Q & A 4-1

Question: Does Access support views?

Answer: Yes. Every simple SELECT query, when executed, creates a view of the data. Therefore, in Access SQL, the CREATE VIEW command used in other RDBMSs is not necessary and does not work in Access SQL.

To update a view in other DBMSs such as Oracle, you can use the SQL REPLACE command. For example, to add the EmployeeID field to the NameList view, you would write the following SQL command:

```
CREATE OR REPLACE VIEW NameList AS
    SELECT FirstName, LastName, EmployeeID
    FROM Employees
    ;
```

In SQL, you can use the name of a view in the same way that you use a table. For example, if you wanted a list of employees sorted by LastName, you could write the following SQL command:

```
SELECT *
FROM NameList
ORDER BY LastName
;
```

Notice that the view name, NameList, is used in the FROM clause instead of the actual table name of Employees. Access SQL supports using view names in place of table names in SQL View as well as using query field lists in Query Design View as opposed to table field lists.

It is also common to rename fields in custom views to make them as clear as possible for the person or process for which the view was created. In SQL, you can rename the fields of a view when you create it. In the next example, the field names of FirstName and LastName have been replaced with First and Last in the CREATE VIEW statement by specifying the new field names in parentheses immediately after specifying the view name of NameList:

```
CREATE VIEW NameList (First, Last) AS
    SELECT FirstName, LastName
    FROM Employees
    ;
```

In Access Query Design View, you can also change any existing field name by preceding the name of the field with the desired name, followed by a colon, as shown in Figure 4-1.

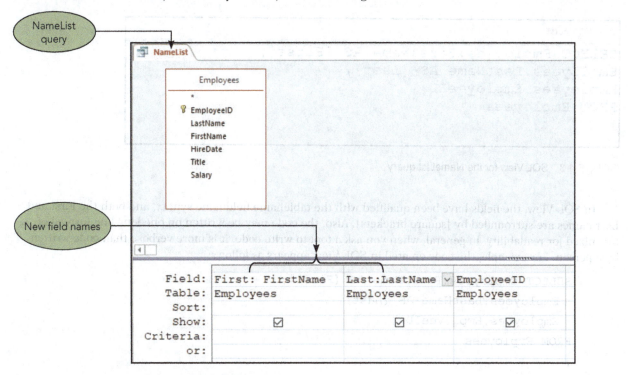

FIGURE 4-1 Renaming fields in Query Design View

The query results with the new field names are shown in Figure 4-2.

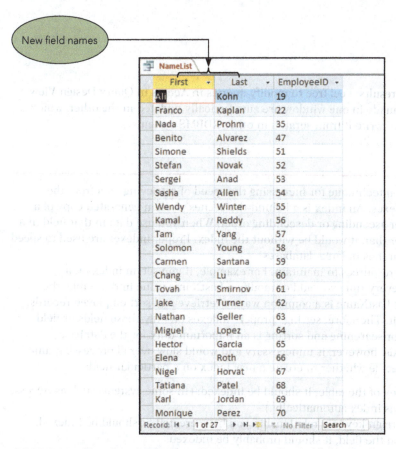

FIGURE 4-2 Datasheet for the NameList query with changed field names

You can view the SQL code created by this design in SQL View, which is shown in Figure 4-3.

```
NameList

SELECT Employees.FirstName AS [First],
Employees.LastName AS [Last],
Employees.EmployeeID
FROM Employees
;
```

FIGURE 4-3 SQL View for the NameList query

In SQL View, the fields have been qualified with the tablename.fieldname syntax, and both the First and Last names are surrounded by [square brackets]. Also, the code may be written on one long line instead of organized for readability. In general, when you ask a tool to write code, it is more verbose than code written by a person. For example, the code created in SQL View appears as follows:

```
SELECT Employees.FirstName AS [First],
  Employees.LastName AS [Last],
  Employees.EmployeeID
FROM Employees

;
```

It can be shortened to the following code:

```
SELECT FirstName AS First,
  LastName AS Last,
  EmployeeID
FROM Employees

;
```

Both sets of code produce the same results. Feel free to modify queries in Access in Query Design View and SQL in SQL View or both. Changes made in one window are automatically updated in the other, which can help you learn SQL when you have to write it from scratch in other RDBMS systems.

USING INDEXES

In relational database systems, a common technique for increasing the speed of retrieving data from the database is the proper application of indexes. An **index** is a behind-the-scenes, system-generated copy of a selected field or fields organized in either ascending or descending order. When you use data in that field in a search or sort, the process is much faster than it would be without the index. Proper indexes are used to speed up the execution time of queries and searches in large databases.

Indexes themselves take processing resources to maintain. For example, if you set an index on a LastName field in the Employees table, every time you add or modify a LastName value in that table, the index also has to be updated. Given that LastName is a common way to retrieve and sort employee records, however, the tradeoff is probably worth it. Therefore, setting "proper" indexes on only those fields or field combinations that are constantly used for searching and sorting is an important duty for the database administrator. Setting indexes on all fields, however, is unnecessary and would slow overall processing time.

The following guidelines help you decide whether to create a new index on a particular field:

- If the field is the primary key of the table, it should be indexed. (In some systems such as Access, the RDBMS might create this index automatically.)
- If the field is used as the foreign key in a relationship you have created, it should be indexed.
- If you will frequently sort on the field, it should probably be indexed.
- If you will frequently use the field to search for data, it should probably be indexed.

You can use SQL to add and delete indexes as necessary after the database is built. In very large databases, you might set up performance tests to see how long certain processes that involve large sets of data take to process a SELECT query both before and after setting an index.

The specific SQL command for creating an index varies from one RDBMS to another, but an example that works in Access SQL to create an index on the LastName field of an Employees table is shown in Figure 4-4.

```
Query1

CREATE INDEX LastNameIndex
ON Employees (LastName)
;
```

FIGURE 4-4 SQL statement to create an index

This **CREATE INDEX** SQL command creates an index named LastNameIndex on the LastName field in the Employees table. Indexes are commonly given the same name as the field that they are indexing, but LastNameIndex was used in this example for clarity.

Figure 4-5 shows how you can modify indexes in Access using Table Design View for the selected EmployeeID field. The EmployeeID field also happens to be the primary key field as indicated by the key symbol to the left of the field name.

To set an index in Access Table Design View, perform the following steps:

- Right-click the table in the Navigation Pane.
- Click Design View on the shortcut menu.
- Click the field that you want to index to select it.
- Choose the index option from the Indexed property in the lower pane of Table Design View.

As illustrated in Figure 4-5, when you click the Indexed property row, three choices appear: No, Yes (Duplicates OK), and Yes (No Duplicates).

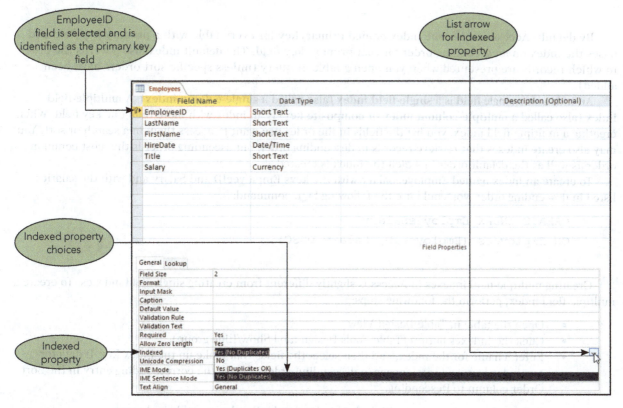

FIGURE 4-5 Using Table Design View to set an index

The first Indexed option, No, is the default for new fields. Yes (No Duplicates) is the default for the field set as the primary key field and should be used for any other field that contains only unique values such as a Social Security Number field in an Employees table. The Yes (Duplicates OK) option is used to create an index on a field that might contain duplicate field values but is not a primary key field. For example, the foreign key field or a field such as LastName that is commonly used for searching and sorting yet may have the same value across multiple records in the table are good candidates for that option.

YOUR TURN 4-1

Using the JC Consulting database, set an ascending index named LastNameIndex on the LastName field in the Employees table. The Indexes dialog box should look like Figure 4-6.

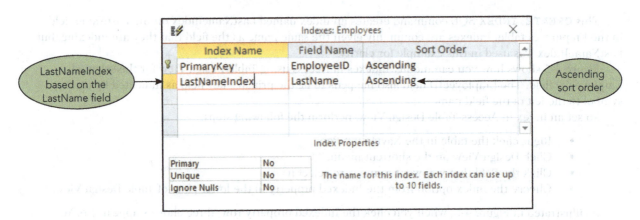

FIGURE 4-6 Creating a single-field index in Access

By default, Access creates one index named PrimaryKey for every table with a primary key field and bases the index on an ascending order for that primary key field. The default index also governs the order in which records are presented when you open a table or query (unless specific sort orders have been added).

An index on a single field is a **single-field index** (also called a **single-column index**). A **multiple-field index** (also called a **multiple-column index** or **composite key**) is an index with more than one key field. When creating a multiple-field index, you list the fields in the order you want to access them in a search or sort. You may also create indexes that retrieve records in descending order, but ascending order is the most common order as well as the default order in which the index is created.

To create an index named EmployeeSalary with the keys EmployeeID and Salary and with the salaries listed in descending order, you could use the following SQL command:

```
CREATE INDEX EmployeeSalary
ON Employees (EmployeeID, Salary DESC)
;
```

Creating multiple-field indexes in Access is slightly different from creating single-field indexes. To create a multiple-field index, perform the following steps:

- Open the table in Table Design View.
- Click the Indexes button (Table Tools Design tab | Show/Hide group).
- Enter a name for the index, and then select the fields that make up the **index key**. If data for any index key field is to appear in descending order, change the corresponding entry in the Sort Order column to Descending.

Figure 4-7 shows how to create a multiple-field index for the Employees table in Access.

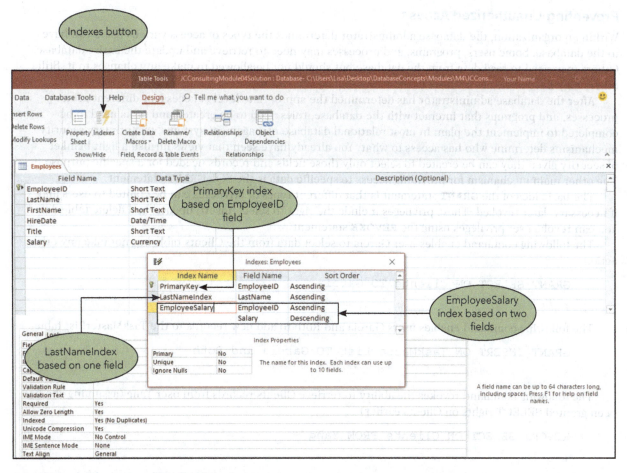

FIGURE 4-7 Creating a multiple-field index in Access

The SQL command used to drop (delete) an index is **DROP INDEX**, which consists of the words DROP INDEX followed by the name of the index to drop. To drop the EmployeeSalary index, for example, use the following command:

```
DROP INDEX EmployeeSalary
;
```

To delete an index in Access, perform the following steps:

- In Table Design View, click the Indexes button to open the Indexes dialog box.
- Click the box to the left of the index row that you want to delete.
- Press the Delete key.

Q & A 4-2

Question: When do you need to delete an index?

Answer: If an index is not improving performance, it is harming it and therefore should be deleted. Database administrators can run tests to see if indexes are being used and if they are helping or hurting performance.

EXAMINING DATABASE SECURITY FEATURES

Data security encompasses many areas, three of which are the prevention of unauthorized access to the database, the safe distribution of information, and the physical security of the hardware, software, and data.

Preventing Unauthorized Access

Within an organization, the database administrator determines the types of access various users can have to the database. Some users, programs, and processes may need to retrieve and update the entire database. Others may need to read data from the database but should not be allowed to make any changes to it. Still others may need access to a subset of the tables, fields, and records.

After the database administrator has determined the appropriate level of access for different users, processes, and programs that interact with the database, rules need to be created and tasks need to be completed to implement the plan. In most relational database management systems, two primary security mechanisms determine who has access to what. You already have seen that views furnish a light blanket of security given they can be created to select only those fields and records needed for a specific purpose. The other main mechanism for providing access to specific data is the SQL GRANT statement.

The basic idea of the **GRANT** statement is that different types of privileges can be granted to users and, if necessary, later revoked. These privileges include the right to select, insert, update, and delete table data. You can revoke user privileges using the **REVOKE** statement.

The following command enables user Garcia to select data from the Clients table but not take any other action.

```
GRANT SELECT ON Clients TO Garcia
;
```

The following command enables users Garcia and Roth to add new records to the TaskMasterList table.

```
GRANT INSERT ON TaskMasterList TO Garcia and Roth
;
```

The following command revokes the ability to retrieve Clients records from user Yang (assuming she had been granted SELECT rights on Clients earlier).

```
REVOKE SELECT ON Clients FROM Yang
;
```

Access doesn't provide user-level security. You can, however, set a password on the entire database that prevents unauthorized access to the database file. Knowing the password, however, enables the user full access to all data within the database.

To set a password on an Access database, you must open it in **exclusive mode**, which means that you are the only user currently working in the database and have locked all other users and processes from accessing it.

To set an Access database password, perform the following steps:

- Start Access without opening a database.
- Click File, and then click the Open button.
- Click Browse, and then use the Open dialog box to navigate to the folder that contains the database you want to open.
- Click the database file you want to open, click the Open arrow in the Open dialog box, and then click Open Exclusive.
- Click File, and then click the Encrypt with Password button.
- Enter the desired password in the Password dialog box and repeat the password in the Verify dialog box as shown in Figure 4-8.
- Click OK and close the database.

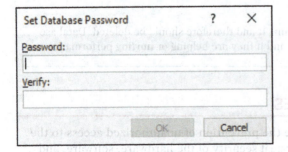

FIGURE 4-8 Set Database Password dialog box

While an overall database password doesn't apply security at the user level, it does prevent someone who should not be using the database at all from opening it or modifying the data it contains. If you need to further secure an Access database, other techniques are available within the program, such as the following:

- Setting startup options that remove the ribbon and quick keystroke combinations that give users access to unauthorized parts of the database
- Creating startup forms that provide access to only the data that users need as well as hide and prevent access to unauthorized areas
- Creating unique keystroke combinations or macros to give access to certain parts of the database that are known only to individual users or groups of users
- Creating an executable file that prevents users from modifying the design or working with any embedded code in the database

Safely Distributing Information

In Access, setting a database password also encrypts the information. **Encryption** changes the data when it is moving through a network so that if it is intercepted while being electronically distributed, it is indecipherable to the person or program that hacked into the network. **Firewalls**, software that prevents the unauthorized access to a network or server, are also used to protect against electronic attacks on a database.

Providing Physical Security

The physical security of the hardware, software, and data upon which a business depends is also a major responsibility and concern. Physical security of the data includes making regular backups of the data, storing those backups on a different server in a different physical location, and testing the backups on a regular basis. Most relational database management systems have a built-in tool for making backups, Access included. To make a backup in Access, perform the following steps:

- Click File, and then click Save As.
- Click Back Up Database, and then click the Save As button.
- The Save As dialog box opens where you can browse for the location to save the backup. It also suggests a filename that includes the current date to help identify when the backup was made.
- Click Save.

Both the password and backup options for Access are only at a **file level**, meaning the security, encryption, and backup tasks apply to the entire file, which includes all tables, queries, and other objects that the database contains. Industrial-strength database management systems such as Oracle, Db2, and MySQL can apply these tasks at an individual transaction level, meaning they can secure and roll back changes made to the database by individual users. These advanced topics will be more deeply covered in later modules.

Q & A 4-3

Question: Is it possible to set user-level or transaction-level security in Access?

Answer: Not to the same standards as large-scale relational database systems such as Oracle, given Access does not natively support user IDs and passwords to identify individual user activity, nor does it support transaction-level rollback features.

ENFORCING INTEGRITY RULES

Recall than an integrity rule is a constraint established to protect the accuracy of the data and prevent users from entering incorrect or inconsistent data into database. A relational DBMS must enforce important integrity rules including entity integrity and referential integrity, which were defined by Dr. E. F. Codd working at IBM on ways to improve relational databases in the 1970s and 1980s.

Entity Integrity

When you describe a database in some DBMSs, you can indicate that certain fields can accept a special value, called null. A **null** value is an intentional nothing or nonentry. Nulls are entered into a field when a value is intentionally not available or does not apply. Null is *not* the same as a blank or zero value, although when looking at a record, it is often impossible to visually determine if an empty field value is null or blank.

A value of zero ($0) in a Salary field for an employee may indicate that the employee is currently receiving no regular compensation; her salary is indeed set at $0. A salesperson who earns money on a 100 percent commission program is an example of an employee who might have a Salary of $0. A value of null in the Salary field might mean that the employee intentionally does not receive a salary. An unpaid position such as that of a board member fits this scenario. However, a value of blank or "" in the Salary field is probably a mistake. It neither tells you that the employee's salary is $0 or that it is intentionally empty (null).

In a text field, null also means an intentional nonentry. For example, the Employees table might have a field such as EmergencyPhoneNumber. A value of null indicates that the employee intentionally does not want to provide that information. A value of blank probably represents a mistake—either the phone number value has been unintentionally removed or entered incorrectly as a blank.

The decision about allowing nulls is generally made on a field-by-field basis. One type of field for which you should *never* allow nulls, however, is the primary key. After all, the primary key is supposed to uniquely identify each row, which would not happen if nulls were allowed. For example, how could you identify a specific client with a null ClientID value? The restriction that the primary key cannot allow null values is called **entity integrity** and is automatically built into Access when you identify the primary key field for a table.

Entity integrity guarantees that each record has a unique identity. In SQL, you can specify the primary key by entering a **PRIMARY KEY** clause in either an ALTER TABLE or CREATE TABLE command. For example, the following PRIMARY KEY clause indicates that ClientID is the primary key for the Clients table:

```
PRIMARY KEY (ClientID)
```

In general, the PRIMARY KEY clause has the form PRIMARY KEY followed, in parentheses, by the field or fields that make up the primary key. When more than one field is included, the fields are separated by commas.

To set a field as a primary key field in Access, perform the following steps:

- Open the table in Table Design View.
- Click the field you want to set as the primary key field to select it.
- Click the Primary Key button (Table Tools Design tab | Tools group).

A key symbol appears in the field's row selector to indicate that it is the primary key, as shown in Figure 4-9.

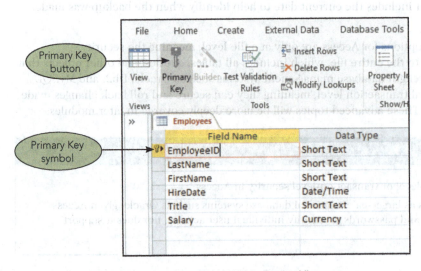

FIGURE 4-9 Setting the primary key field in Table Design View

If the primary key consists of more than one field, select the first field, press and hold the Ctrl key, and then click the other field or fields that make up the primary key.

Referential Integrity

In the relational model you have examined thus far, you have established the relationships between tables by creating a common field in the two tables that participate in the one-to-many relationship. The relationship between Employees and Projects, for example, is accomplished by including the primary key of the Employees table (EmployeeID) as the foreign key field in the Clients table.

In this relationship, the Employees table is the parent table on the "one" side of the relationship and the Projects table is the child table on the "many" side of the relationship because one record in the Employees table may be related to many records in the Projects table. The EmployeeID field in the Projects table is a foreign key field whose value must match a value in the primary key of the Employees table. This means that a project must be assigned to an employee who is already in the database. This concept is called **referential integrity**.

In SQL, you specify referential integrity using a **FOREIGN KEY clause** in either the CREATE TABLE or ALTER TABLE commands of the table that contains the foreign key.

The general form of this clause is FOREIGN KEY, followed by the foreign key field name, followed by the word REFERENCES and the name of the table containing the primary key that the foreign key is supposed to match, as in the following example:

```
FOREIGN KEY (EmployeeNo) REFERENCES Employees
```

In Access, you enforce referential integrity by first creating a one-to-many relationship between two tables. To do so, perform the following steps:

- Open the Relationships window (Database Tools tab | Relationships group).
- Drag the field that links the two tables in a one-to-many relationship from the primary key field in the "one" table to the foreign key field in the "many" table.
- Click the Enforce Referential Integrity check box as shown in Figure 4-10.
- Click OK.

If a relationship already exists, but referential integrity is not enforced, the link line between the tables does not display the "1" and infinity symbols. To set referential integrity on an existing relationship, perform the following steps:

- Open the Relationships window (Database Tools tab | Relationships group).
- Double-click a relationship line to open the Edit Relationships dialog box.
- Check the Referential Integrity check box as shown in Figure 4-10.

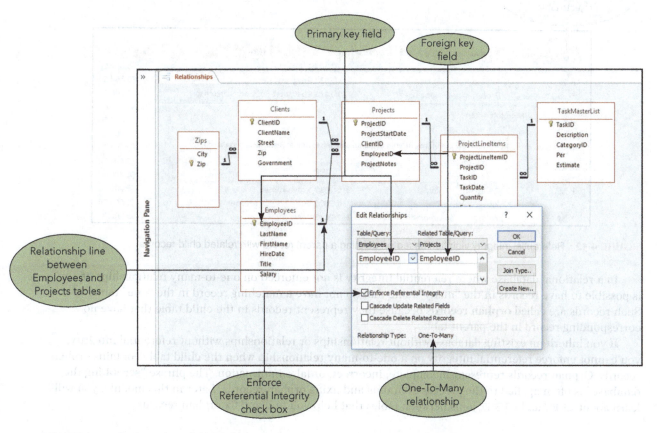

FIGURE 4-10 Setting referential integrity

With referential integrity enforced on this relationship, users cannot enter a new project and assign it to an employee that doesn't already exist. An error message, such as the one shown in Figure 4-11, appears when a user attempts to enter a nonexistent EmployeeID number into a record in the Projects table.

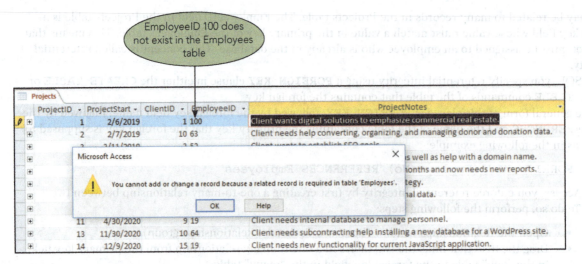

FIGURE 4-11 Referential integrity violation based on an invalid foreign key field value

Deleting an employee who is related to an existing project would also violate referential integrity because the projects with that EmployeeID value would no longer match any record in the Employees table. An error message, such as the one shown in Figure 4-12, appears if a user attempts to delete an employee record that has related records in other tables.

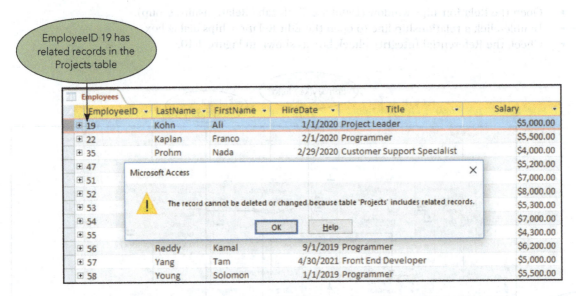

FIGURE 4-12 Referential integrity violation based on deleting a parent record with related child records

In a relational database where referential integrity is *not* enforced on one-to-many relationships, it is possible to have records in the "many" table that do not have a matching record in the "one" table. Such records are called **orphan records** because they represent records in the child table that have no corresponding record in the parent table.

If you inherit an existing database without relationships or relationships without referential integrity, you cannot enforce referential integrity on a one-to-many relationship when the child table contains orphan records. Orphan records represent incomplete, incorrect, or false information. The phrase "**scrubbing the database**" is often applied to the process of finding and fixing orphan records. Later in this module, you will learn about LEFT and RIGHT joins between tables that help you find and fix orphan records.

Cascade Options

The Edit Relationships dialog box also provides options called Cascade Update Related Fields and Cascade Delete Related Records only when the Enforce Referential Integrity box is checked. **Cascade Update Related Fields** means that if the primary key field in the table on the "one" side of the relationship changes, the foreign key field value in all related records in the table on the "many" side of the relationship also change. **Cascade Delete Related Records** means that if a record on the "one" side of a relationship is deleted, all related records in the "many" table are also deleted. Obviously, each option has serious consequences, especially the Cascade Delete Related Records option, and should be used with caution. As a general rule, these features are not automatically turned on for a relationship, but rather, are used in specific situations when scrubbing or fixing data integrity problems.

YOUR TURN 4-2

Using the JC Consulting database, check the Cascade Update Related Fields option for the relationship between the Employees and Projects table. The Edit Relationships dialog box should look like Figure 4-13.

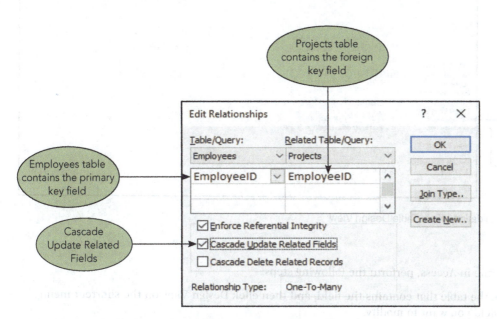

FIGURE 4-13 Setting the Cascade Update Related Fields option

If the primary key field in the Employees table, the EmployeeID field, is changed, any records that are related to that employee in the Projects table are automatically updated with the new, corresponding value in the EmployeeID foreign key field. The value in the primary key field in the parent table automatically updates all related values in the foreign key field of the child table.

In some RDBMSs, the cascade update option is accomplished by adding a constraint when you update the table and including the ON UPDATE CASCADE or ON DELETE CASCADE commands.

Legal-Values Integrity

Another type of integrity is called **legal-values integrity**. Often, only a particular set of values are allowed in a field. Legal-values integrity is the property that states that no record can exist in the database with a value in the field other than one of the legal values. For example, at JC Consulting, the legal values for CategoryID field in the TaskMasterList table are Coding, Database, Meeting, Planning, Server, Support, and Training.

In SQL, you can use the **CHECK** clause to enforce legal-values integrity. For example, to ensure that the only legal values of Hour, Month, or Project for the Per field in the TaskMasterList table are entered, use the CHECK clause in a CREATE TABLE or ALTER TABLE command as follows:

```
CHECK (Per IN ('Hour', 'Month', 'Project'));
```

The general form of the CHECK clause is the word CHECK followed by a condition. This makes the DBMS reject any update to the database that violates the condition in the CHECK clause.

In Access, you can restrict the legal values accepted by a field by entering an appropriate **validation rule** that data entered in the field must follow. Figure 4-14 shows the validation rule that restricts entries in the Per field to Hour, Month, or Project. In Access, along with the validation rule, you can enter optional **validation text** to give the user a meaningful message if the user attempts to enter data that violates the rule.

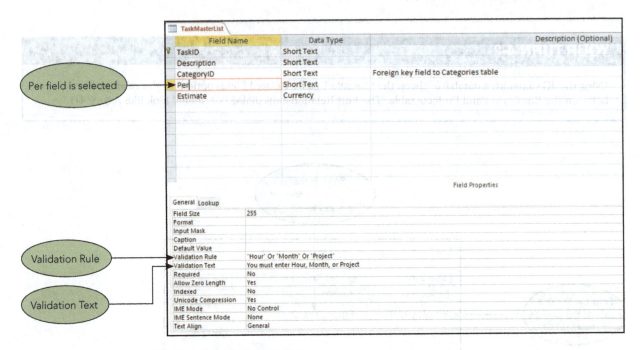

FIGURE 4-14   Setting a validation rule in Table Design View

To set a validation rule in Access, perform the following steps:

- Right-click the table that contains the field, and then click Design View on the shortcut menu.
- Click the field you want to modify.
- Click the Validation Rule property and enter the criteria.
- Click the Validation Text property and enter a meaningful message that will be presented to the user in a dialog box if the entry in the field doesn't evaluate true for the Validation Rule criteria.

CHANGING THE STRUCTURE OF A RELATIONAL DATABASE

You can change the database structure by adding and removing tables and fields, by changing the characteristics of existing fields, or by creating and dropping indexes. How you make these changes varies from one system to another, but all systems allow you to use SQL commands or built-in tools.

Adding a New Field to a Table

To change a table's structure with SQL, use the SQL **ALTER TABLE** command. For example, suppose you want to add a contact phone number to the Clients table in the JC Consulting database. To make this change using SQL, you could add a new field named ContactNumber to the Clients table as follows:

```
ALTER TABLE Clients
    ADD ContactNumber TEXT(10)
;
```

In Access, however, you don't need to use SQL. You can add a field in Table Design View at any time. Figure 4-15 shows the Clients table after adding the ContactNumber Short Text field with a Size property (length) of 10.

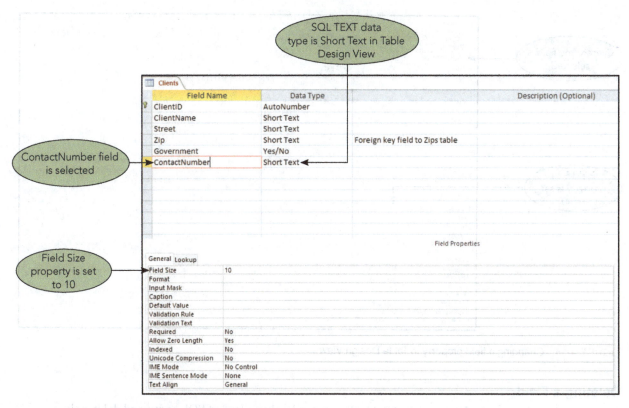

FIGURE 4-15 Adding a new field in Table Design View

For existing records in the table, ClientType automatically contains a null value, waiting for the user to enter an appropriate value.

Some systems allow you to change the properties of fields, such as increasing the length of a character field. For example, to increase the field size of a ClientName field in the Clients table from its current size to 40 characters, you could use the following SQL `ALTER TABLE` command in most systems:

```
ALTER TABLE Client
   MODIFY ClientName CHAR(40)
;
```

Modifying Field Properties

In Access, you can change **field properties**, the characteristics that define each field such as Indexed, Field Size, Validation Rule, and Validation Text, in Table Design View.

YOUR TURN 4-3

Using the JC Consulting database, change the size of the ClientName field in the Clients table to 40.

To change a property value for a field in Access such as Field Size, perform the following steps:

- Right-click the table that contains the field, and then click Design View on the shortcut menu.
- Click the field you want to modify.
- Click the property to change in the lower Field Properties pane.
- Enter the desired value for that property.

Figure 4-16 shows the ClientName field after increasing its Field Size property value to 40 characters.

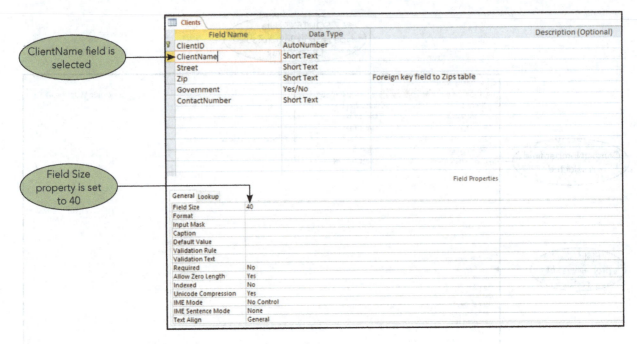

FIGURE 4-16   Changing a field property in Table Design View

Deleting a Field

Some systems allow you to delete existing fields. For example, the following SQL command deletes the ContactNumber field from the Clients table in most systems.

```
ALTER TABLE Clients
    DROP COLUMN ContactNumber
;
```

In Access, you can delete a field in Table Design View by selecting the field and pressing the Delete key. Access asks you to confirm the deletion of the field. Deleting an entire field after data has been entered, however, is rare given it permanently deletes the field and the data it stores. If a field is no longer used and you want to delete it, be sure to make a backup of your database and remove references to the field from all queries (views), expressions, and other processes or programs that use that field before deleting it.

To delete a field in an Access table, perform the following steps:

- Right-click the table that contains the field, and then click Design View on the shortcut menu.
- Click the field you want to modify.
- Click Delete Rows (Table Tools Design tab | Tools group).
- Click Yes to confirm the deletion.

Deleting a Table

You can use the SQL **DROP TABLE** command to delete a table that is no longer needed. For example, to delete the ClientProjectsPriorTo2020 table (which you may have created in Module 2) from the JC Consulting database, you could use the following command:

```
DROP TABLE ClientProjectsPriorTo2020
;
```

The DROP TABLE command deletes the table structure as well as its data, so it is a powerful command that should be executed with care. In Access, however, you can drop (delete), rename, copy, or perform other tasks with a table by right-clicking the table in the Navigation Pane as shown in Figure 4-17.

To delete, rename, or copy a table in Access, perform the following step:

- Right-click the table that contains the field, and then click the desired command on the shortcut menu.

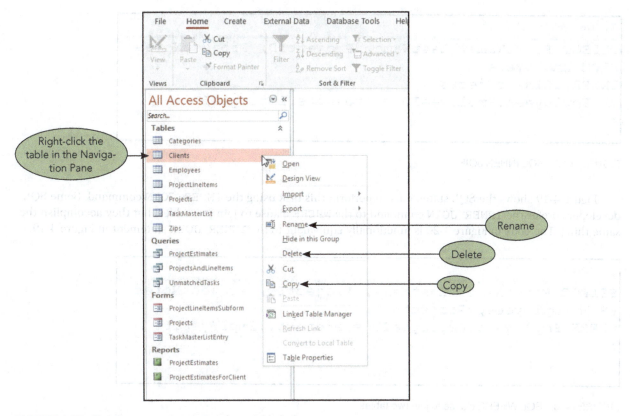

FIGURE 4-17 Deleting, renaming, or copying a table in Access

USING SQL JOIN COMMANDS

In Module 3, you learned how to write SQL statements to select fields and records from two or more tables using the SQL WHERE clause to connect the primary key field of the table on the "one" side of a one-to-many relationship with the foreign key field of the table on the "many" side of the relationship. That type of join is also called an INNER join given only those records that have a match in both tables are selected for the query. For example, if you use SQL to join the Employees and Projects tables, and if some of the records in the Employees table are not related to any records in the Projects table, they would not be selected for the view. SQL provides additional ways to join tables so that you can select records from the parent table or child table even if they do not have a match in the other. Figure 4-18 summarizes the types of join commands in SQL and the records they select.

Command	Selects
`INNER JOIN`	Records that have matching values in both tables
`LEFT JOIN`	All records in the table on the "one" side of a one-to-many relationship even if they do not have any matching records in the "many" table (recall that the "one" side is also called the parent table)
`RIGHT JOIN`	All records in the table on the "many" side of a one-to-many relationship even if they do not have any matching records in the "one" table (recall that the "many" side is also called the child table) RIGHT joins are used to find orphan records; if referential integrity is enforced on a relationship before records are entered into a table, the RIGHT and INNER joins produce the same results because the "many" table has no orphans
`FULL OUTER`	All records in both the "one" and "many" tables even if they do not have matching record in the other

FIGURE 4-18 SQL Join commands

YOUR TURN 4-4

Using the JC Consulting database, write the SQL statements to select the FirstName and LastName fields from the Employees table, and the ProjectID and ProjectNotes fields from the Projects table using an INNER JOIN command.

148

```
Query1

SELECT FirstName, LastName, ProjectID, ProjectNotes
FROM Employees
INNER JOIN Projects
ON Employees.EmployeeID = Projects.EmployeeID
;
```

FIGURE 4-19   SQL INNER JOIN

Figure 4-19 shows the SQL statements to perform this task using the INNER JOIN command. Some SQL developers prefer the INNER JOIN command to the WHERE clause to join two tables, but they accomplish the same thing. The code in Figure 4-20 is functionally equivalent to the INNER JOIN statement in Figure 4-19.

```
Query1

SELECT FirstName, LastName, ProjectID, ProjectNotes
FROM Employees, Projects
WHERE Employees.EmployeeID = Projects.EmployeeID
;
```

FIGURE 4-20   SQL WHERE clause to join two tables

The result of running the SQL statement shown in Figure 4-19 or Figure 4-20 is shown in Figure 4-21. Note that only four employee last names appear in the selected records—Novak, Geller, Kohn, and Lopez—even though the Employees table contains 27 records. Employees that are not related to any records in the Projects table are not selected for this view. To see records from the Employees table that do not have match in the Projects table, you need a different type of join command.

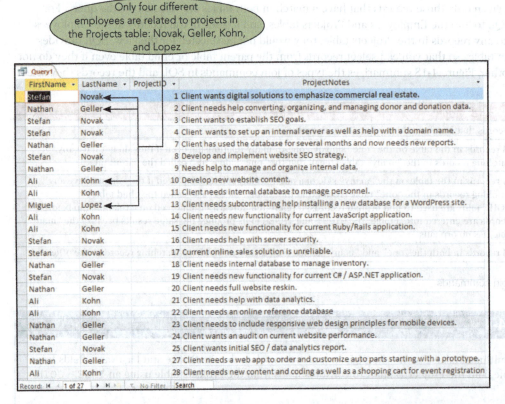

FIGURE 4-21   Results of query with joined tables

LEFT Joins

LEFT and RIGHT joins are sometimes called **OUTER joins** given the select records from either the "left" table (also called the "one" or parent table) or the "right" table (also called the "many" or child table) even if that record doesn't have a match in the other. The term "outer" contrasts this type of join to the INNER join, where there must be a matching record in both tables for the record to be selected.

For example, what if you wanted to list all employees who were not yet connected to a record in the Projects table? You would need information from the Employees and Projects tables to determine the answer to this question, but in this case, you're looking for *missing* EmployeeID field values in the Projects table. The Employees table is on the "one" side of the one-to-many relationship between the Employees and Projects tables, so you need to build an SQL statement to find all records in the Employees table that *do not have a match* in the Projects table. You need a LEFT join.

YOUR TURN 4-5

Using the JC Consulting database, write the SQL statements to select the FirstName and LastName fields from the Employees table that are *not* related to a project in the Projects table.

Figure 4-22 shows the SQL code to solve this question using the LEFT JOIN command. Figure 4-23 shows the results of running the LEFT JOIN SQL statement.

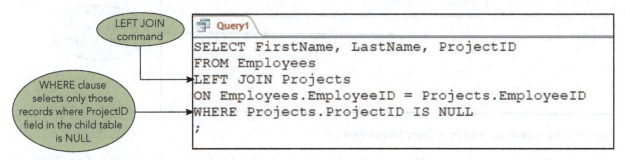

FIGURE 4-22   SQL LEFT JOIN

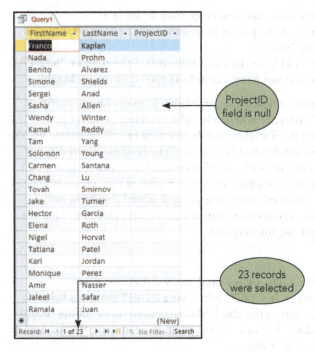

FIGURE 4-23   Results of running a SQL LEFT JOIN query

The WHERE clause in Figure 4-22 may look strange at first, but it limits the records to only those employees that do *not* have a related record in the Projects table.

In Access, you can also create a left join in Query Design View by modifying the join line and entering Is Null in the Criteria cell for a field in the child table, as shown in Figure 4-24.

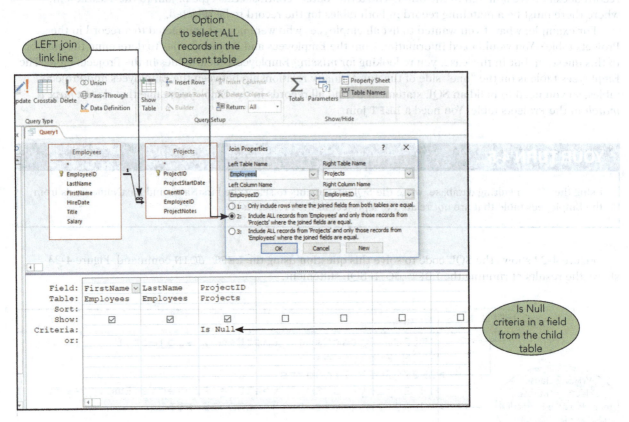

FIGURE 4-24   Creating a left join in Query Design View

The SQL statements shown in Figure 4-22 and the query designed in Figure 4-24 are equivalent. To create a left join in Query Design View, perform the following steps:

- Double-click a link line between two tables to open the Join Properties dialog box.
- Choose the option that selects ALL records from the parent (also called left or "one") table, and then click OK in the Edit Relationships dialog box.
- In the query grid, add Is Null criteria to any field from the child (also called the right or "many") table to select only those parent records that do not have a matching record in the child table.

The records returned by LEFT joins do not necessarily indicate data problems. In every one-to-many relationship between two tables, the record in the "one" (parent) side needs to be established before any records are entered in the "many" (child) table. For example, a student needs to enroll in college before he or she can register for classes and a customer needs to be established before purchasing items. However, just because a student enrolls in a college (becomes a record in the Students table) doesn't *necessarily* mean that he or she will enroll in classes (be related to record(s) in the Enrollments table). Students may enroll in the spring and not attend classes until the fall, or they may enroll in many colleges and attend classes in only one. Mining parent tables for information as to *why* those records were entered in the first place but have no related records is a business question that can reveal valuable information.

RIGHT Joins

Creating a RIGHT join, where all records from the "many" table are selected, even if they don't have a matching record in the "one" table, follows the same process as a LEFT join. Using RIGHT joins is a valuable skill if you inherit a database with orphan records, or records in the child table that have no matching record in the parent table. Often, orphan records need to be deleted because they represent a remnant of information about a transaction that was not entered correctly and has no value.

In the JC Consulting database, an orphan would be a record in the ProjectLineItems table that is not connected to a record in the Projects table, or a record in the Projects table that is not connected to a record in the Clients or Employees table. Because referential integrity has been imposed on the relationships between the tables in the JC Consulting database from the start, however, the database has no orphan records and therefore does not require you to build a view with a RIGHT join.

For reference, Figures 4-25 and 4-26 show how to write a RIGHT join as an SQL command and in Access Query Design View to apply a RIGHT join to find records in the Projects table that have no matching record in the Employees table. Note the difference in the link line between a left and right join.

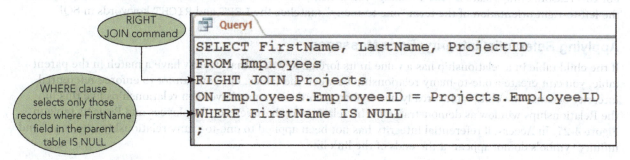

FIGURE 4-25   SQL RIGHT JOIN

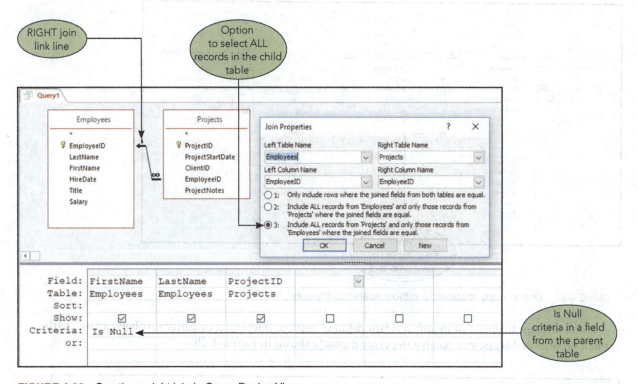

FIGURE 4-26   Creating a right join in Query Design View

This type of RIGHT join with IS NULL criteria in a field for the parent table will display the orphan records in the child table. To create a right join in Query Design View, perform the following steps:

- Double-click a link line between two tables to open the Join Properties dialog box.
- Choose the option that selects ALL records from the child (also called right or "many") table, and then click OK in the Edit Relationships dialog box.
- In the query grid, add Is Null criteria to any field from the parent (also called the left or "one") table to select only those child records that do not have a matching record in the parent table, also known as orphan records.

The decision about to how to scrub the orphan records—to either connect them to the correct parent record by editing the value in their foreign key field or to delete them altogether—depends on the situation. Scrubbing orphan records can be labor intensive, as you might need to examine each record individually to determine the best course of action. Fortunately, you now have the skills to create a temporary table of these records so you can examine them at a later time and delete them from the current child table. After orphan records are eliminated, referential integrity can be applied to a one-to-many relationship to prevent the future creation of more orphan records.

The terms `LEFT JOIN` and `RIGHT JOIN` do not have anything to do with the physical position of the tables in Query Design View. The "left" table in a `LEFT JOIN` is always the parent table, the table on the "one" side of a one-to-many relationship. The "right" table in a `RIGHT JOIN` is always the table on the "many" side of a one-to-many relationship no matter how the tables are positioned in Query Design View. For this reason, always state a "one-to-many" relationship as "one-to-many" and never "many-to-one" given the left-to-right orientation of the term "one-to-many" matches the `LEFT` and `RIGHT` keywords in SQL.

Applying Referential Integrity: Error Messages

If the child table in a relationship has a value in its foreign key field that doesn't have a match in the parent table, you *can* create a one-to-many relationship between the tables, but you *cannot* to enforce referential integrity because the child table already has orphan records. You may have seen relationships like this in the Relationships window as demonstrated in the relationship between the Employees and Projects table in Figure 4-27. In Access, if referential integrity has not been applied to one-to-many relationship, the "one" and infinity symbols do not appear at the ends of the link line.

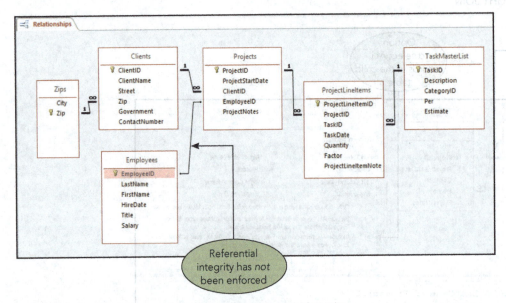

FIGURE 4-27 One-to-many relationship without referential integrity

If you attempt to create or modify a relationship to enforce referential integrity involving a table with orphan records in Access, you receive the error message shown in Figure 4-28.

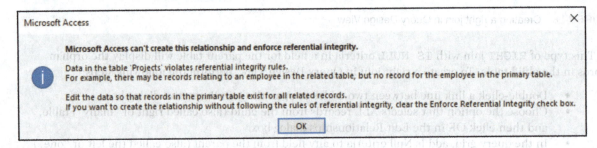

FIGURE 4-28 Error message when you cannot enforce referential integrity

This message indicates that you have orphan records, records in the child table with foreign key field values that do not match a value in the primary key field of the parent table. To address this problem, you need to create a query with a `RIGHT JOIN` to find the orphans and correct or delete them. After the orphan records are fixed, or scrubbed, you can then modify the relationship to apply referential integrity.

Applying Referential Integrity: Null Values

In some relational database management systems, you can create a relationship between two tables and enforce referential integrity even when the child table has a null value in the foreign key field. In some systems (Access included), applying referential integrity on a relationship does *not* warn you about orphan records because of null values in the foreign key field exist when the relationship is created.

To eliminate orphan records, first build queries to select all records in child tables that have null values in the foreign key field, and fix them either by entering a valid value in the foreign key field or by deleting the orphan record. Eliminating null values in all foreign key fields and using RIGHT JOIN queries as necessary to find orphan records improves management's confidence in the accuracy of the data in the database.

USING THE SYSTEM CATALOG

Information about tables and fields in the database is called **metadata** (information about information), and kept in the **system catalog** (or the **catalog**). The catalog is maintained automatically by the relational database management system. When a user adds a new table, deletes a table, or changes the fields, indexes, or relationships of an existing table, the RDBMS updates the catalog to reflect these changes.

The typical catalog contains **system tables** such as the following:

- Systables (information about the tables known to SQL), which contains the Name, Creator, and Column count for each table.
- Syscolumns (information about the columns or fields within these tables), which contains the Name, Data Type, and Table Name for each column.
- Sysindexes (information about the indexes that are defined on these tables), which contains the Name, Field(s), and Sort Orders for each index.
- Sysviews (information about the views that have been created).

An RDBMS furnishes ways of using the catalog to determine information about the structure of the database. In some cases, this means using SQL to query the tables in the catalog just as you would query any other table. For example, you could use SQL to query for all of the field names in a table if you knew the name of the system table that contained that information as well as the name of the column that stored that information.

To view or hide the system tables in Access, perform the following steps:

- Right-click the title bar in the Navigation Pane, and then click Navigation Options on the short-cut menu.
- In the Navigation Options dialog box, click the Show System Objects check box to display the system tables or clear the check box to hide them, and then click OK.

When you display the system tables in Access, they appear in the Navigation Pane, as shown in Figure 4-29.

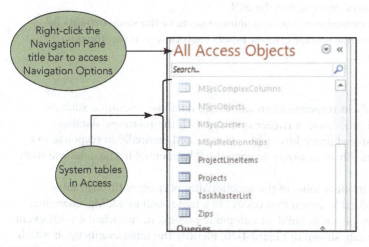

FIGURE 4-29 Displaying system tables in Access

The system tables in Access start with an MSys (Microsoft System) prefix. The MSysObjects table contains a record for every object, SQL statement, and system table in the database as well as the date it was created and last updated. The Type field identifies the type of object, 1 for tables and 5 for queries.

Q & A 4-4

Question: Why might you use the MSysObjects table in Access?

Answer: If you want to create a list of queries in the database, you could query the MSysObjects table for the Name and Type fields. The Name column stores the name of the saved queries and the Type field would be used in the WHERE clause to restrict the selection to only queries.

In some RDBMS systems, the system tables start with a DBA prefix. Each system provides basic information about the tables, columns, indexes, relationships, and views of the system. Some RDBMS systems have special tools to provide system information. For example, Access has a tool called the **Database Documenter**, which allows you to print detailed documentation about any table, query, report, form, or other object in the database. To document the objects in an Access database, perform the following steps:

- Click the Database Documenter button (Database Tools tab | Analyze group).
- Select the tables, queries, or other objects in the database that you want to study.
- Click OK in the Documenter dialog box.

A report is created with metadata about the selected objects. For a table, the report contains information on all of the table's columns (fields), properties, indexes and more.

USING STORED PROCEDURES AND TRIGGERS

In a **client/server system**, the database resides on a computer called the **server**, a centralized computer that stores the database. A user accesses the database through a **client**, a computer connected to a network that can access the server. Every time a user executes a query, the database management system must determine the best way to process the query and provide the results. For example, the database management system must determine which indexes are available and whether it can use those indexes to make the processing of the query more efficient.

If you anticipate running a particular query often, you can improve overall performance by saving the query in a special file called a **stored procedure**. The stored procedure is placed on the server, which optimizes performance as opposed to writing or initiating an SQL command from the client machine.

Stored procedures are more complex than SELECT queries. Stored procedures often combine SQL statements with programming languages such as Java, C#, or C++ to add variable inputs and logic constructs such as IF or WHILE to determine when and how often to run the SQL.

Although Access does not support stored procedures, you can achieve some of the same benefits by creating and saving parameter queries that prompt you for criteria inputs each time you run the query. Parameter queries were introduced in Module 2.

Triggers

A **trigger** is an action that occurs automatically in response to an associated database operation such as INSERT, UPDATE, or DELETE. Like a stored procedure, a trigger is stored with the relational database management system on the server. Unlike a stored procedure, which is executed manually in response to a user command, a trigger is executed automatically in response to something happening in the database such as a record being added or deleted.

Access does not use the term "trigger" but offers some of the functionality of triggers through table events and data macros. A **table event** is a definable action that occurs in a table such as adding, changing, or deleting data in a record. A **data macro** allows you to build an automatic process to run when a table event occurs. The buttons on the Table Tools Table tab, shown in Figure 4-30, identify the table events upon which you can attach data macros.

Data macros are created with macro actions, fill-in-the-blank programming functionality that allows you to perform actions such as automatically setting the value of a field or creating a message for the user. Macro actions are defined by selecting an action from the **Action Catalog**, a small window that shows you what macro actions are available, and then completing the **arguments** for that macro action, the pieces of information it needs to process.

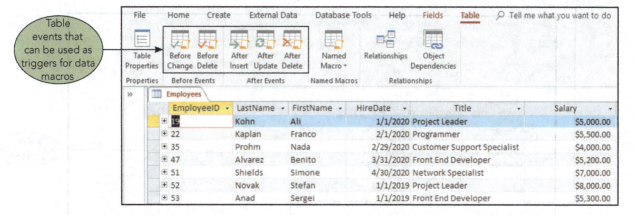

FIGURE 4-30 Table events that can trigger data macros

Notice that the table events on the Table Tools Table tab are organized into two major groups: Before Events and After Events, and are summarized in Figure 4-31.

Table Event	Runs
Before Change	Before a record is changed, to help the user validate or cancel the edits
Before Delete	Before a record is deleted, to help the user validate or cancel the deletion
After Insert	After a new record has been inserted into the table
After Update	After an existing record has been changed
After Delete	After an existing record has been deleted

FIGURE 4-31 Table events

Data macros can help build another light blanket of security by creating audit trails as data in sensitive tables or fields is changed. For example, you can use data macros to record the date and time a field was changed as well as its old value. To create a data macro in Access, perform the following steps:

- Open the table in Datasheet View.
- Click Table on the ribbon to display the Table Tools Table buttons.
- Click the table event button that represents the event on which you want to trigger the action.
- Add the data actions that describe the desired process for the data macro.

YOUR TURN 4-6

In the Employees table, create a data macro for the Before Change event so that if the Salary field is updated, the current value of the Salary field is stored in the OldSalary field and the current date and time is stored in the ChangeDate field for that record. You will have to create the two new fields in the Employees table to store this data before you can create the data macro.

Figure 4-32 shows Design View of the Employees table with the two new fields and respective data types. In Table Design View, you can use the Create Data Macros button to access the table events. This data macro should be attached to the Before Change event. Test the data macro in Table Datasheet View by changing the Salary field value from $5,000 to $6,000 for EmployeeID 19, Ali Koln.

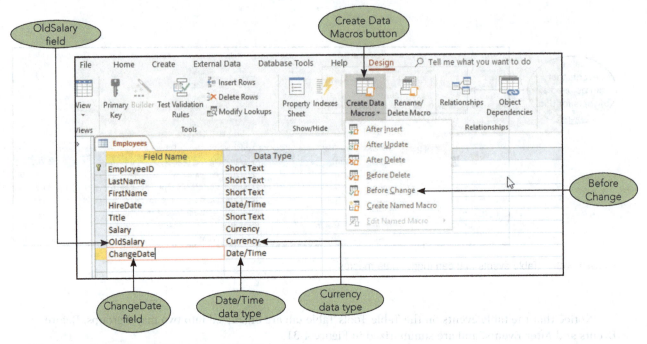

FIGURE 4-32 Design View of Employees table with new fields

Figure 4-33 shows Design View of the data macro triggered by the Before Change event. The If statement uses a built-in Updated function that checks whether the Salary field has been updated. The Salary field name must be passed to the Updated function as a string delimited by quotation marks, "Salary".

When the If statement evaluates True, the macro triggers two SetField actions that add data to the current record before it is saved. The first SetField action takes the current value of the Salary field identified in the SetField arguments as defined by the [Old].[Salary] expression and places the value in the OldSalary field you just created in Table Design View. The second SetField action uses the built-in Now() function to place the current date and time in the ChangeDate field, as shown in Figure 4-34.

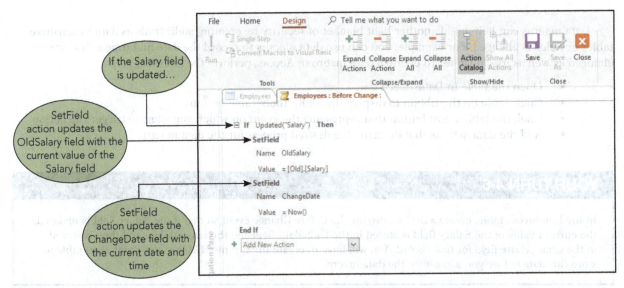

FIGURE 4-33 Data macro for the Before Change event of the Employees table

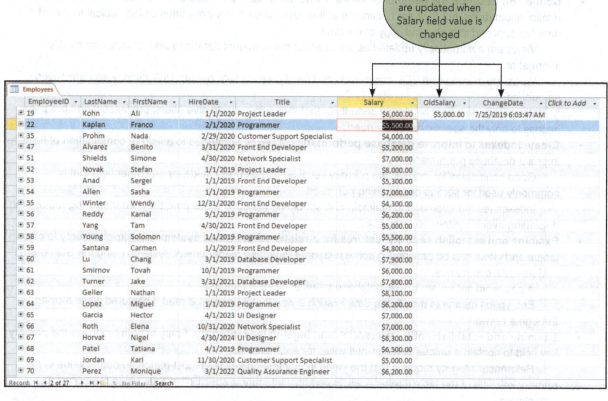

OldSalary and ChangeDate fields are updated when Salary field value is changed

FIGURE 4-34 Data macro automatically triggers two actions when Salary field is modified

While data macros attached to the five table events identified in Figure 4-31 are not as robust as the full set of triggers and processes of large-scale relational database systems such as Oracle, they demonstrate how the concept works and provide important functionality to small Access databases.

CAREER SKILLS: DATABASE ADMINISTRATORS

According to a recent *Computer Science* article (computerscience.org/careers/database-administrator/), the Bureau of Labor Statistics projects that database administration jobs will grow 11 percent through the year 2026. While the skills for database administrators vary from company to company, the article identifies fundamental technical competencies are that are common to most positions, such as the following:

- SQL: Structured Query Language, the standard language used to select data and modify the structure of a relational database
- Oracle: The popular large-scale relational database management system
- UNIX: A popular open source operating system for servers
- LINUX: A common version of UNIX
- Windows: A widespread operating system for client machines
- Microsoft Access: A popular small-scale relational database management system
- Data Analysis: A general set of skills that involves defining, dissecting, communicating, and solving problems and using data and information
- HTML: Hypertext Markup Language, the language that describes content distributed through a webpage

Summary

- **Define and describe the benefits of views**: Views are a subset of fields and records from the tables of a relational database, but they are not copies of the data. As such, they are often called "logical views" of the data (as opposed to a physical copy of the data).

  Views are automatically updated as the users of the relational database add, delete, and modify information.

  Views are created with SQL commands and can be saved with names. In Access, views are saved as queries.

  Views provide a light blanket of security in that they allow you to give users, processes, and programs access to only the specific data they need.

- **Create indexes to improve database performance**: Indexes are added to a field or combination of fields to improve database performance.

  Good candidates for indexes are primary key fields, foreign key fields, or any other field that is commonly used for sorting or searching purposes.

  Indexes require overhead to maintain and should be tested to make sure they are improving rather than degrading overall system performance.

- **Examine and establish security features for a relational database system**: User-level security to certain tables and views can be provided in some relational database management systems using the SQL GRANT and REVOKE commands.

  A password set on an Access database provides file-level security.

  Encryption means to modify the data in such a way that it cannot be read if captured while moving through a network.

- **Examine and establish entity, referential, and legal-values integrity**: Entity integrity requires the primary key field to contain a unique and non-null value for each record.

  Referential integrity requires that the value in any foreign key field must match an actual value in the primary key field of the table it references. Referential integrity is specified in SQL using the FOREIGN KEY clause.

  Referential integrity prevents the creation of orphan records, records in the "many" side of a one-to-many relationship that do not have a matching record in the "one" side of a one-to-many relationship.

  Legal-values integrity is the property that states that the value entered in a field must be one of the legal values that satisfies some particular condition. Legal-values integrity is specified in SQL using the CHECK clause. In Access, legal-values integrity is specified using the Validation Rule property.

- **Create INNER, LEFT, and RIGHT joins between tables**: The SQL INNER JOIN command joins two tables in a one-to-many relationship and is an alternative to using the WHERE clause.

  The SQL LEFT JOIN command helps you locate records on the "one" (parent) side of a one-to-many relationship that do not have related records on the "many" (child) table.

  The SQL RIGHT JOIN command helps you locate records in the "many" (child) side of a one-to-many relationship that do not have related records in the "one" (parent) table.

  Records in the "many" (child) side of a one-to-many relationship that do not have related records in the "one" (parent) table are called orphan records and need to be scrubbed (fixed or deleted) before referential integrity can be applied to a one-to-many relationship.

  You use the Relationships window in Access to create and edit relationships.

  The Cascade Update Related Records and Cascade Delete Related Fields options allow you to modify records in the "many" (child) table when an update is made to the "one" (parent) record that they are linked to.

- **Make changes to the structure of a relational database**: The SQL ALTER TABLE command allows you to add fields to a table, delete fields, or change the characteristics of fields. In Access, you can change the structure of a table by making the desired changes in Table Design View.

  The SQL DROP TABLE command lets you delete a table from a database. In Access, you can delete, rename, or copy a table by right-clicking it in the Navigation Pane and choosing the desired option.

- **Define and create system information**: The system catalog is a feature of many RDBMSs that stores information about the structure of a database such as the tables, fields, indexes, and views stored within the database. The system updates the catalog automatically.

  In Access, the system tables start with a prefix of MSys and can be viewed in the Navigation Pane.

  In Access, the Database Documenter tool provides details about each table, query, relationships, and other objects in the database.

- **Explain and create stored procedures, triggers, and data macros**: A stored procedure is program that executes programming code and SQL, and is saved on the server. Users run stored procedures to answer repetitive questions.

  A trigger is a set of actions that occur automatically in response to an associated database operation such as the insertion, deletion, or change of data in a record.

  Access provides trigger functionality through the use of data macros attached to a particular table.

- **Explore the essential skills for database administrators**: A career in database administration includes several core skills including SQL, Oracle, UNIX, LINUX, Windows, Access, Data Analysis, and HTML.

Key Terms

Action Catalog	GRANT
After Delete	index
After Insert	index key
After Update	INNER JOIN
ALTER TABLE	LEFT JOIN
argument	legal-values integrity
Before Change	metadata
Before Delete	multiple-column index
Cascade Delete Related Records	multiple-field index
Cascade Update Related Fields	null
catalog	orphan record
CHECK	OUTER join
client	PRIMARY KEY clause
client/server system	referential integrity
composite key	REVOKE
CREATE INDEX	RIGHT JOIN
data macro	scrubbing
data security	server
Database Documenter	single-column index
DROP INDEX	single-field index
DROP TABLE	stored procedure
encryption	system catalog
entity integrity	system table
exclusive mode	table event
field property	trigger
file level	validation rule
firewall	validation text
FOREIGN KEY clause	

Module Review Questions

Problems

1. Which of the following is *not* true about a view?
   a. It provides access to a subset of fields and records in one or more tables.
   b. It consists of a duplicate copy of the selected data.
   c. It provides a light blanket of security by limiting access to specific data.
   d. It automatically shows up-to-date information when it is executed.

2. Why doesn't Access SQL provide for the SQL `CREATE VIEW` statement?
   a. In Access, queries function as views.
   b. Access SQL needs to be compiled outside of the database in order to run all statements.
   c. Access is not a true relational database system.
   d. Access does not have the ability to run SQL.

3. What is the primary purpose of creating an index?
   a. documenting relationships
   b. identifying integrity issues
   c. adding event trigger functionality to tables
   d. improving the speed by which data is searched and presented

4. What best describes a null value?
   a. a zero-length string, ""
   b. a space or tab character
   c. an intentional nothing
   d. the string "null"

5. Which of the following is *not* prevented by enforcing referential integrity on a one-to-many relationship?
   a. incorrect entry into a primary key field value
   b. entry into a foreign key field that doesn't have a match in the table that contains the primary key field
   c. deleting a record in the parent table that has a matching record in a child table
   d. changing a primary key field value that has matching records in a related table

6. Which of the following is *not* true about a one-to-many relationship?
   a. The table on the "one" side is also called the parent or left table.
   b. The table on the "one" side may or may not have related records in the "many" table.
   c. The table on the "many" side may have orphan records, especially if referential integrity is not enforced.
   d. The table on the "one" side may have orphan records.

7. RIGHT JOINS in SQL are helpful to find _____.
   a. orphan records
   b. parent records with no matching child records
   c. records with AND criteria in the WHERE clause
   d. records with OR criteria in the WHERE clause

8. When two tables are joined in an Access query, the default join type is _____.
   a. `OUTER`
   b. `INNER`
   c. `LEFT`
   d. `RIGHT`

9. Which feature of Access is used to create a report on the metadata about tables and queries?
   a. data macros
   b. referential integrity
   c. cascade options
   d. Database Documenter

10. Stored procedures differ from triggers in what essential way?
    a. Stored procedures are usually run intentionally by users, whereas triggers are generally run automatically by processes.
    b. Stored procedures are stored at the server, whereas triggers are generally stored at each user's client machine.
    c. Stored procedures may include some programming commands, whereas triggers are generally pure SQL.
    d. Stored procedures can change data. Triggers do not change data.

11. Which feature of Access mimics that of relational database management system triggers?
    a. SQL View
    b. data macros
    c. referential integrity
    d. cascade options

12. Which Access field property might you use to set data integrity rules on a single field?
    a. Validation Rule
    b. Indexed?
    c. Caption
    d. Default Value

Critical Thinking Question

1. You have a table for a membership database that contains the following fields: MemberLastName, MemberFirstName, Street, City, State, ZipCode, and InitiationFee. There are 75,000 records in the table. What indexes would you create for the table, and why would you create these indexes?

JC Consulting Case Exercises

In the following exercises, you will use the data in the JC Consulting database. Don't forget to use a copy of the JC Consulting database so any changes you make will not affect future modules.

Problems

1. Which of the following is *not* a benefit of a view within the JC Consulting database?
   a. single location to store all data
   b. organizes fields and records from one or more tables
   c. shields sensitive data from unauthorized users
   d. can be used to create calculated fields

2. Which of the following fields from the Projects table is *not* a good candidate to index?
   a. ProjectID
   b. ProjectStartDate
   c. ClientID
   d. ProjectNotes

3. Which of the following security features is *not* available to the JC Consulting database given it is an Access database?
   a. encryption
   b. database password
   c. user-level security
   d. startup options

4. In the Employees table, how could you ensure that no HireDate values were entered prior to 1/1/2019?
   a. Use the Validation Rule property on the HireDate field.
   b. Set referential integrity on the HireDate field.
   c. Set the Cascade Update Related Fields option on the HireDate field.
   d. Set the HireDate field as a primary key field.

5. To query whether the Clients table has records that do not have any matching records in the Projects table, you would use a(n) _____.
   a. left join
   b. right join
   c. inner join
   d. one-to-many join

6. Which SQL command would add a new field named Region to the Clients table?
   a. `ALTER TABLE Clients ADD Region TEXT(20)`
   b. `ALTER TABLE Clients MODIFY Region TEXT(20)`
   c. `MODIFY TABLE Clients ADD Region TEXT(20)`
   d. `MODIFY TABLE Clients MODIFY Region TEXT(20)`

7. What feature could you use to create system information about the tables and fields in the JC Consulting database?
   a. Performance Analyzer
   b. Database Documenter
   c. Dependency Analyzer
   d. Table Wizard

8. Where do you create data macros in the JC Consulting Access database?
   a. as global macro objects accessed in the Navigation Pane
   b. as global module objects accessed in the Navigation Pane
   c. within the table that contains the data they work with
   d. within the system tables

9. According to the article referenced by the Bureau of Labor Statistics, knowing which of the following is *not* a fundamental competency for a job in database administration?
   a. Microsoft Access
   b. Data Analysis
   c. Oracle
   d. Java

Critical Thinking Questions

1. Using Access, open the Relationships window and identify all of the one-to-many relationships in the database as well as the field used in both tables to make the connection using the following pattern found in SQL, when connecting two tables using a WHERE or INNER JOIN clause. An example of one of the relationships is provided as a guide.

   Clients.ClientID = Projects.ClientID

2. Using Access, an employee at JC Consulting tried to delete TaskID CODE01 from the TaskMasterList table and received the following error message: "The record cannot be deleted or changed because table 'ProjectLineItems includes related records."

   Why did the employee receive this error message?

Pitt Fitness Case Exercises

In each of the following questions, use Access or SQL to answer them either with using the data shown in Figures 1-15 through 1-19, or by using a copy of the Pitt Fitness database. You can test the SQL statements in SQL View in Access.

Problems

1. Using Access, create a view for Pitt Fitness that displays all the classes held at the Downtown location. Show only the fields ClassName, Room, Day, Time, and Description. Show the ClassName field as Class Name. How many records appear in the results when you display this view?
   a. 40
   b. 10
   c. 14
   d. 0

2. Write the SQL code to create a view for Pitt Fitness that displays all the classes held at the Downtown location. Show only the fields ClassName, Room, Day, Time, and Description. Show the ClassName field as Class Name.
   a. SELECT ClassName AS [Class Name], Room, Day, Time, Description
      FROM Classes
      WHERE Location="Downtown";
   b. SELECT Class Name, Room, Day, Time, Description
      FROM Classes
      WHERE Location="Downtown";
   c. SELECT ClassName, Room, Day, Time, Description
      WHERE Location="Downtown";
   d. SELECT ClassName, Room, Day, Time, Description
      FROM Classes
      WHERE NOT Location="Downtown";

3. In the Customers table, which field would be ideal for creating an index?
   a. BirthDate
   b. PhoneNumber
   c. FirstName
   d. LastName

4. What is the SQL command to create an index on InstructorZipCode in the Instructors table?
   a. `INDEX zipindex ON Instructors (InstructorZipCode)`
   b. `CREATE INDEX zipindex ON (InstructorZipCode)`
   c. `CREATE INDEX zipindex ON Instructors (InstructorZipCode)`
   d. `CREATE INDEX ON Instructors (InstructorZipCode)`

5. What security feature can be used on the Pitt Fitness Access database?
   a. Grant a specific user rights to delete the table ClassInstructors.
   b. Grant a specific user rights to add data to the Reservations table.
   c. Set a password on the entire Pitt Fitness database.
   d. Revoke a given user's rights.

6. The Instructors table and the ClassInstructors table have a one-to-many relationship. When forming the relationship, you want to ensure that if an instructor changes his or her InstructorID in the Instructors table, the related InstructorID will change in the ClassInstructors table. What option should you select when editing the relationship?
   a. Enforce Referential Integrity
   b. Cascade Update Related Fields
   c. Cascade Delete Related Records
   d. Enforce Referential Integrity and Cascade Update Related Fields

7. Using SQL, count how many classes each customer has signed up for. Show the customer's last name, first name, and number of classes. Use an appropriate JOIN.
   a.
   ```
   SELECT LastName, FirstName, Count(ReservationID) AS [Number of Classes]
   FROM Customers INNER JOIN Reservations ON CustomerID = CustomerID
   GROUP BY LastName, FirstName;
   ```
   b.
   ```
   SELECT LastName, FirstName, Count(ReservationID) AS [Number of Classes]
   FROM Customers INNER JOIN Reservations ON Customers.CustomerID = Reservations.CustomerID
   GROUP BY LastName, FirstName;
   ```
   c.
   ```
   SELECT LastName, FirstName, Count(ReservationID) AS [Number of Classes]
   FROM Customers INNER JOIN Reservations ON Customers.CustomerID = Reservations.CustomerID;
   ```
   d.
   ```
   SELECT LastName, FirstName, Count(ReservationID) AS [Number of Classes]
   FROM Customers OUTER JOIN Reservations ON Customers.CustomerID = Reservations.CustomerID
   GROUP BY LastName, FirstName;
   ```

8. Using SQL, list the classes that do not have a reservation. Show the class name, location, and reservation ID (which will be blank).
   a.
   ```
   SELECT Classes.ClassName, Classes.Location, Reservations.ReservationID
   FROM Classes RIGHT JOIN Reservations ON Classes.ClassID = Reservations.ClassID
   WHERE Reservations.ReservationID Is Null;
   ```
   b.
   ```
   SELECT Classes.ClassName, Classes.Location, Reservations.ReservationID
   FROM Classes OUTER JOIN Reservations ON Classes.ClassID = Reservations.ClassID
   WHERE Reservations.ReservationID Is Null;
   ```
   c.
   ```
   SELECT Classes.ClassName, Classes.Location, Reservations.ReservationID
   FROM Classes LEFT JOIN Reservations ON Classes.ClassID = Reservations.ClassID
   WHERE Reservations.ReservationID Is Null;
   ```
   d.
   ```
   SELECT Classes.ClassName, Classes.Location, Reservations.ReservationID
   FROM Classes LEFT JOIN Reservations ON Classes.ClassID = Reservations.ClassID
   WHERE Reservations.ReservationID;
   ```

9. Suppose you want to create a query that displays the class name, customer's last name, instructor's last name, and class date. What tables are required to answer this query?
   a. Classes, Customers, Reservations
   b. Classes, ClassInstructors, Customers, Reservations
   c. Classes, ClassInstructors, Reservations
   d. Classes, ClassInstructors, Customers, Instructors, Reservations

10. Suppose you want to create a query that displays the class name, customer's last name, instructor's last name, and class date. What type of JOIN should you use for linking the tables together?
    a. INNER
    b. OUTER
    c. LEFT
    d. RIGHT

Critical Thinking Questions

1. Assume that the Pitt Fitness accountant has met with the owner to discuss how to handle payments and balances. They both decide to add fields to the Customers table to record any payments arriving and the subsequent balance. Add the appropriate fields to the Customers table and set up a Before data macro to check the payment and balance.

2. Discuss security issues with the Pitt Fitness database. Who should have access to the database? Can any employee change the data? What are problems with that task?

Sports Physical Therapy Case Exercises

In each of the following questions, use Access or SQL to answer them either with using the data shown in Figures 1-21 through 1-24, or by using a copy of the ports Physical Therapy database. You can test the SQL statements in SQL View in Access.

Problems

1. As the module material stated, although Access doesn't create a stored procedure, a parameter query mimics what a stored procedure might do. How would you create a parameter query in SQL to prompt for the patient's last name and display the patient's last name and their therapy?
   a. SELECT (ENTER Patient.LastName), Therapies.Description
      FROM Therapies INNER JOIN (Patient INNER JOIN [Session] ON Patient.PatientNum = Session.PatientNum) ON Therapies.TherapyCode = Session.TherapyCode;
   b. SELECT Therapies.Description
      FROM Therapies INNER JOIN (Patient INNER JOIN [Session] ON Patient.PatientNum = Session.PatientNum)
      ON Therapies.TherapyCode = Session.TherapyCode
      WHERE (((Patient.LastName)=[Enter Last Name]));
   c. SELECT Patient.LastName, Therapies.Description
      FROM Therapies
      WHERE (((Patient.LastName)=[Enter Last Name]));
   d. SELECT Patient.LastName, Therapies.Description
      FROM Therapies INNER JOIN (Patient INNER JOIN [Session] ON Patient.PatientNum = Session.PatientNum)
      ON Therapies.TherapyCode = Session.TherapyCode
      WHERE (((Patient.LastName)=[Enter Last Name]));

2. To generate a schedule list, create a view in SQL that shows the session date and the last name and first name of the therapist. Show the list in chronological order.
   a. SELECT Session.SessionDate, Therapist.LastName, Therapist.FirstName
      FROM Therapist INNER JOIN [Session] ON Therapist.TherapistID = Session.TherapistID
      ORDER BY Session.SessionDate;
   b. SELECT Session.SessionDate, Therapist.LastName, Therapist.FirstName
      FROM Therapist INNER JOIN [Session] ON Therapist.TherapistID = Session.TherapistID
      DISPLAY BY Session.SessionDate;

c. SELECT Session.SessionDate, Therapist.LastName, Therapist.FirstName
   FROM Therapist
   ORDER BY Session.SessionDate;

d. SELECT Session.SessionDate, Therapist.LastName, Therapist.FirstName
   FROM Therapist INNER JOIN [Session] ON Therapist.TherapistID = Session.
   TherapistID
   ORDER BY Date;

3. What index(es) would be appropriate to create for the Session table? Select the best answer.
   a. SessionDate
   b. PatientNum
   c. TherapistID
   d. SessionDate, PatientNum, and TherapistID

4. Assume a new patient calls to make an appointment with a therapist. The clerk recording the appointment creates a new PatientNum value for the new patient. Before entering any other data, she first enters the PatientNum value into the Session table as part of a new record. What rule does this violate?
   a. indexing
   b. cascading
   c. referential integrity
   d. This action does not violate any rule.

5. From the following views, what view would be the most appropriate for the Sports Physical Therapy accountant?
   a. PatientNum, LastName (Patient), SessionDate, SessionNum
   b. PatientNum, LastName (Patient), Address, City, State, ZipCode, Balance
   c. PatientNum, LastName (Patient), TherapistID, Description
   d. PatientNum, LastName (Patient), TherapyCode

6. If you created an SQL query to list the patient number and the session date, which tables would be joined?
   a. Session and Patient
   b. Therapies and Patient
   c. Therapist and Patient
   d. all four tables

7. If you created an SQL query to list the patient number and the session date, what type of join should you use?
   a. PLAIN JOIN
   b. OUTER JOIN
   c. INNER JOIN
   d. LEFT JOIN

8. Write the SQL code to list the session date and therapist's last name to display the upcoming schedule for the therapists.
   a. SELECT Session.SessionDate, Therapist.LastName
      FROM Therapist INNER JOIN (Therapies INNER JOIN [Session] ON Therapies.
      TherapyCode = Session.TherapyCode) ON Therapist.TherapistID = Session.
      TherapistID;
   b. SELECT Session.SessionDate, Therapist.LastName
      FROM Therapist INNER JOIN Session ON Therapist.TherapistID = Session.TherapistID;
   c. SELECT Session.SessionDate, Therapist.LastName
      FROM Therapist INNER JOIN ON Therapist.TherapistID = Session.TherapistID;
   d. SELECT LastName
      FROM Therapist INNER JOIN Session ON Therapist.TherapistID = Session.TherapistID;

9. Assume you are using two tables for an SQL query: Therapist and Session. You want to make sure that you display all the names of the therapists even if they are not yet booked into a session. What join do you need to create to ensure that all the therapists are listed?
   a. LEFT JOIN Therapist ON Therapist.TherapistID=Session.TherapistID
   b. RIGHT JOIN Therapist ON Therapist.TherapistID=Session.TherapistID
   c. INNER JOIN Therapist ON Therapist.TherapistID=Session.TherapistID
   d. OUTER JOIN Therapist ON Therapist.TherapistID=Session.TherapistID

10. If you want to send a mailing to all patients advertising a new facility, what tables would you need to generate the query that would print the mailing labels?
    a. Patient, Session, Therapies, Therapist
    b. Patient, Session, Therapies
    c. Patient, Session, Therapist
    d. Patient

Critical Thinking Questions

1. Create an SQL query that calculates how many different therapies have not yet been booked for a session.

2. Considering the information stored in the Sports Physical Therapy database, what security measures are important?

DATABASE DESIGN: NORMALIZATION

LEARNING OBJECTIVES

- Define normalization and its purpose
- Identify data modification anomalies
- Explain functional dependence and other key database terminology
- Describe the normal forms and their purpose
- Analyze data for patterns and build algorithms to convert data to atomic values
- Analyze and convert unnormalized data to 1NF
- Analyze and convert 1NF data to 2NF
- Analyze and convert 2NF data to 3NF
- Identify primary and foreign key fields
- Create lookup tables

INTRODUCTION

In previous modules, you worked with data in a relational database by selecting, analyzing, inserting, deleting, and updating data using a QBE tool and SQL commands. In this module, you will learn how to design a relational database from scratch using the normalization process and its underlying concepts. The **normalization process** is a series of progressive steps you follow to identify and correct data redundancy and integrity problems that occur when data is stored in one large table. The basic process breaks columns into smaller tables to identify entities and facts about each entity. Normalizing minimizes redundant data, which improves data consistency, reliability, and accuracy.

Normalization was invented by an English computer scientist, Dr. Edgar F. Codd, while working for IBM (International Business Machines) in the early 1970s. Dr. Codd made many contributions to computer science, such as **Codd's 12 rules**, which define what is required from a database management system in order for it to be considered relational, and his definition of **online analytical processing (OLAP)**, discussed in his paper titled "Twelve Laws of Online Analytical Processing." His work on the relational model of database management, however, is celebrated as his most significant achievement. **Codd's relational model of data**, the original normalization process, was published in 1970 and is titled "A Relational Model of Data for Large Shared Data Banks."

CASE STUDY: FACULTY/STUDENT ADVISING ASSIGNMENTS

The examples in this module come from a sample list of data about students and their faculty advisors shown in Figure 5-1, and demonstrate the steps in the normalization process. The list starts with unique student ID values in the first column. The second column identifies the student's full name. The third column contains a unique value for each professor, an attribute named ProfID. The fourth and fifth columns contain the professor's first and last names. The sixth column identifies the professor's department. The last three columns identify the majors to which each student has sequentially declared.

StudentID	Student	ProfID	ProfFirst	ProfLast	Department	Major1	Major2	Major3
003-112-224	Alexia Carnell	AKZ	Akram	Aziz	Computer Science	Programming	Web Development	
013-112-229	Savanna Sanderlin	AKZ	Akram	Aziz	Computer Science	Programming		
009-112-227	Buddy Pothier	DOM	Donnell	Meaders	Business	Accounting		
012-111-228	Verline Papadopoulos	DOM	Donnell	Meaders	Technology	Auto Technology		
002-111-223	Buddy Pothier	JJJ	James	Justus	Technology	Welding		
004-111-224	Leo Schildgen	JOF	Jose	Fred	Computer Science	Programming	Networking	
008-111-226	Dominica Clubb	KAC	Keri	Coots	Science	Biology	Nursing	
001-112-223	Monty Burse	LAF	Lisa	Fred	Computer Science	Programming	Web Development	
011-112-228	Levi Otts	LAF	Lisa	Fred	Computer Science	Programming	Web Development	
016-111-230	Soledad Mattis	LAF	Lisa	Fred	Computer Science	Web Development	Programming	Networking
000-111-222	Jami Salerno	LAR	Lisa	Ruff	Business	Finance	Accounting	
010-111-227	Li Bridgman	LAR	Lisa	Ruff	Business	Accounting		
015-112-230	Pamila Tomasek	LAR	Lisa	Ruff	Business	Marketing		
007-112-226	Davis Andry	MIM	Mckenzie	Moring	Science	Biology	Chemistry	
014-111-229	Phuong Harbison	MIM	Mckenzie	Moring	Science	Chemistry		
006-111-225	Jonna Bluhm	MEG	Monica	Gantt	Technology	Auto Technology		
005-112-225	Sanda Mines	SKK	Steve	Kime	Business	Accounting	Marketing	

FIGURE 5-1 Sample data for faculty/student advisee assignments

While Figure 5-1 shows a common way to organize data, it includes information on many subjects: students, professors, departments, majors, and faculty/student advisee assignments. Having one list store data for many topics presents several data duplication and data maintenance problems, which the relational database normalization process identifies and corrects.

Duplicated data, a problem you have studied in previous modules, unnecessarily increases storage, decreases performance, and makes it more difficult to productively maintain or accurately query the data. QBE tools and SQL commands rarely provide correct results when applied to data with redundancy problems, which in turn leads to slower and poorer decision making.

You may question the wisdom of creating multiple fields such as Major1, Major2, and Major3 to store the different majors each student may declare over a period of time. Having three fields for this purpose limits the number of times that a student can change their major to three. Furthermore, having multiple fields storing the same type of data means that to find all students who had a Programming major, for example, you would need to query all three fields that could store that data. In this case, you'd need to query the Major1, Major2, and Major3 fields to find all students involved in a particular major. The normalization process will identify and correct this type of problem.

DATA MODIFICATION ANOMALIES

Storing information about multiple topics in one list also creates problems when entering, updating, and deleting information, otherwise known as **data modification anomalies**. Data modification anomalies are of three types: insertion, update, and delete anomalies. The data in Figure 5-1 suffers from all three problems.

An **insertion anomaly** results if you cannot add data to the database due to absence of other data. For example, if a new student does not yet have a student StudentID, the new student may not be assigned to a professor, because the primary key field information for each student is required for each record, as shown in Figure 5-2.

If primary key field data is missing, the record cannot be inserted

StudentID	Student	ProfID	ProfFirst	ProfLast	Department	Major1	Major2	Major3
003-112-224	Alexia Carnell	AKZ	Akram	Aziz	Computer Science	Programming	Web Development	
013-112-229	Savanna Sanderlin	AKZ	Akram	Aziz	Computer Science	Programming		
009-112-227	Buddy Pothier	DOM	Donnell	Meaders	Business	Accounting		
012-111-228	Verline Papadopoulos	DOM	Donnell	Meaders	Technology	Auto Technology		
002-111-223	Buddy Pothier	JJJ	James	Justus	Technology	Welding		
004-111-224	Leo Schildgen	JOF	Jose	Fred	Computer Science	Programming	Networking	
008-111-226	Dominica Clubb	KAC	Keri	Coots	Science	Biology	Nursing	
001-112-223	Monty Burse	LAF	Lisa	Fred	Computer Science	Programming	Web Development	
011-112-228	Levi Otts	LAF	Lisa	Fred	Computer Science	Programming	Web Development	
016-111-230	Soledad Mattis	LAF	Lisa	Fred	Computer Science	Web Development	Programming	Networking
000-111-222	Jami Salerno	LAR	Lisa	Ruff	Business	Finance	Accounting	
010-111-227	Li Bridgman	LAR	Lisa	Ruff	Business	Accounting		
015-112-230	Pamila Tomasek	LAR	Lisa	Ruff	Business	Marketing		
007-112-226	Davis Andry	MIM	Mckenzie	Moring	Science	Biology	Chemistry	
014-111-229	Phuong Harbison	MIM	Mckenzie	Moring	Science	Chemistry		
006-111-225	Jonna Bluhm	MEG	Monica	Gantt	Technology	Auto Technology		
005-112-225	Sanda Mines	SKK	Steve	Kime	Business	Accounting	Marketing	
???	Aaron Scout	LAF	Lisa	Fred	Web Development			

FIGURE 5-2 Insertion anomaly

An **update anomaly** is marked by data inconsistencies that generally result from data redundancy, but can also occur if a record is only partially updated or if a particular field contains inappropriate null data. For example, if the department name of *Technology* changed to *Industrial Technology*, several records would need to be updated for the information to stay accurate and consistent, as shown in Figure 5-3.

One update needs to be recorded multiple times

StudentID	Student	ProfID	ProfFirst	ProfLast	Department	Major1	Major2	Major3
003-112-224	Alexia Carnell	AKZ	Akram	Aziz	Computer Science	Programming	Web Development	
013-112-229	Savanna Sanderlin	AKZ	Akram	Aziz	Computer Science	Programming		
009-112-227	Buddy Pothier	DOM	Donnell	Meaders	Business	Accounting		
012-111-228	Verline Papadopoulos	DOM	Donnell	Meaders	Industrial Technology	Auto Technology		
002-111-223	Buddy Pothier	JJJ	James	Justus	Industrial Technology	Welding		
004-111-224	Leo Schildgen	JOF	Jose	Fred	Computer Science	Programming	Networking	
008-111-226	Dominica Clubb	KAC	Keri	Coots	Science	Biology	Nursing	
001-112-223	Monty Burse	LAF	Lisa	Fred	Computer Science	Programming	Web Development	
011-112-228	Levi Otts	LAF	Lisa	Fred	Computer Science	Programming	Web Development	
016-111-230	Soledad Mattis	LAF	Lisa	Fred	Computer Science	Web Development	Programming	Networking
000-111-222	Jami Salerno	LAR	Lisa	Ruff	Business	Finance	Accounting	
010-111-227	Li Bridgman	LAR	Lisa	Ruff	Business	Accounting		
015-112-230	Pamila Tomasek	LAR	Lisa	Ruff	Business	Marketing		
007-112-226	Davis Andry	MIM	Mckenzie	Moring	Science	Biology	Chemistry	
014-111-229	Phuong Harbison	MIM	Mckenzie	Moring	Science	Chemistry		
006-111-225	Jonna Bluhm	MEG	Monica	Gantt	Industrial Technology	Auto Technology		
005-112-225	Sanda Mines	SKK	Steve	Kime	Business	Accounting	Marketing	

FIGURE 5-3 Update anomaly

A **deletion anomaly** is the unintended loss of data due to deletion of other data. For example, if James Justus retires and a record with his name is deleted, the information about what student he advised would also be deleted, as shown in Figure 5-4.

FIGURE 5-4 Deletion anomaly

To correct anomalies in a database, you convert data into multiple tables that progress through a sequence of **normal forms: first normal form (1NF)**, **second normal form (2NF)**, **third normal form (3NF)**, and **fourth normal formal (4NF)**. Each normal form possesses a certain desirable collection of properties and is a progressive step in normalization. The final result frees the data from data modification anomaly problems and provides the foundation for a healthy relational database.

Q&A 5-2

Question: How does normalization relate to the problems identified with data modification anomalies?

Answer: Normalization takes a single list and converts it into multiple tables, which frees the data from the problems associated with insertion, update, and deletion anomalies.

FUNCTIONAL DEPENDENCE

Functional dependence is a formal name given to the basic idea of how attributes depend on or relate to other attributes in a relation. Recall that relational database design often refers to each **column** as a **field** or **attribute** and refers to each **row** as a **record** or **tuple**. An entire table of rows for one subject is called an **entity** or **relation**.

For example, in Figure 5-1, given the StudentID, you could determine the student's name. In other words, the Student column (attribute) that stores the student's name is **functionally dependent** on the StudentID column. In Figure 5-1, if you knew the StudentID value of 000-111-222, you could find a *single* student (Jami Salerno), even if two students happened to have the same name.

Functional dependence is often diagrammed as X → Y, where attribute Y is dependent on X. In Figure 5-1, the functional dependence on the StudentID field is notated as:

```
StudentID → Student Name, Major1, Major2, Major3
```

The concept of functional dependence underscores why names are usually poor candidates for primary key fields. Two or more students could have the same name, making it impossible to uniquely identify each student using only their name. If you cannot uniquely identify each student, functional dependence breaks down as well. For example, if two students have the same name, it is impossible to determine which student declared which major(s).

Q&A 5-3

Question: Why are numbers such as StudentID, EmployeeID, or ProductID generally good candidates for primary key fields, and how does that relate to functional dependence?

Answer: Numbers that identify students, employees, or products are good candidates for primary key fields because they contain unique information for each record (a record is also called a row or tuple). Given an attribute (also called a column or field) with a unique value, other attributes in the record may be functionally dependent on that attribute.

KEYS

As you learned in previous modules, the **primary key field** contains unique data for each record in a table and may not be left null for any record. The nonkey fields of a table should be functionally dependent on the primary key field. For example, a field that stores the student's name is functionally dependent on the primary key field of StudentID.

In Figure 5-1, not all of the other fields are functionally dependent on the primary key field. The fields of ProfID, ProfFirst, ProfLast, and Department are not functionally dependent on the primary key field of StudentID. The process of normalization will help you identify and correct that issue.

Note that the primary key field may consist of a **composite key**, a combination of two or more fields. For example, the combination of a class code and a semester code might be used to uniquely identify a particular class offered in a particular semester. However, composite keys are inherently more difficult to query and process than single-field primary key fields. Therefore, it is common to add a field to each table to uniquely identify each new record using an automatically generated sequential number when no obvious primary key field for a that table exists.

Occasionally, more than one field contains unique information per record and thus could serve as the single-field primary key. For example, if the list in Figure 5-1 included a column to store student Social Security numbers, either the StudentID or the Social Security number could serve as a primary key field, as they both contain unique data per student. In that case, both columns are called **candidate keys**.

The choice of a primary key field from a list of candidate keys depends on other factors such as privacy and security concerns. In this example, considering the number of people and processes that read the data in the primary key field to uniquely identify a student, the choice of the StudentID data is the preferable primary key field for a table of student data. While StudentID data is valuable, a hacked list of student Social Security numbers exposes students to greater potential harm than a hacked list of StudentID numbers. Minimizing the people and processes that have access to sensitive data is one step toward protecting it.

Q&A 5-4

Question: What are two essential characteristics of a good primary key field?

Answer: First, a primary key field must contain unique data for each record. A second important consideration is that a good primary key field should not expose critical information to people and processes that do not need that data. For example, although a Social Security number is unique for each person and therefore a candidate for the primary key field, the sensitivity of the data should be protected and not used in any internal process or provided to anyone on a screen or report that doesn't need access to that specific data. Employees can be identified with a much less sensitive but unique attributes such as a Username, EmployeeID, or EmployeeNumber field.

FIRST NORMAL FORM

A table (relation) is in **first normal form (1NF)** when it does not contain repeating groups (more than one value in an attribute), each column contains atomic values, and there are no duplicate records. A relation (table) that contains a **repeating group** (or multiple entries for a single record) is called an **unnormalized relation**. A repeating group is a field that contains multiple entries. Removing repeating groups is the starting point to move an unnormalized relation to the tabular data format of 1NF, the starting point of a relational database.

Consider the example in Figure 5-5. In this case, the Professors table has one record for each professor. The first record for professor Akram Aziz shows a repeating group problem in the fields that contain student data, StudentID and Student. The StudentID and Student fields have more than one value (as do the Major1, Major2, and Major3 fields), which represent data for the two students he advises. Therefore, the list in Figure 5-5 is considered **unnormalized**, a description of data that doesn't meet the standards of 1NF.

172

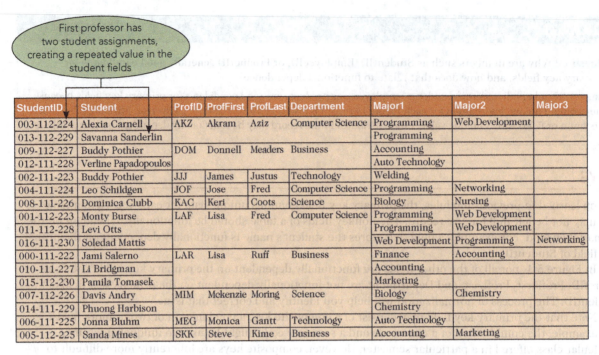

First professor has two student assignments, creating a repeated value in the student fields

StudentID	Student	ProfID	ProfFirst	ProfLast	Department	Major1	Major2	Major3
003-112-224	Alexia Carnell	AKZ	Akram	Aziz	Computer Science	Programming	Web Development	
013-112-229	Savanna Sanderlin					Programming		
009-112-227	Buddy Pothier	DOM	Donnell	Meaders	Business	Accounting		
012-111-228	Verline Papadopoulos					Auto Technology		
002-111-223	Buddy Pothier	JJJ	James	Justus	Technology	Welding		
004-111-224	Leo Schildgen	JOF	Jose	Fred	Computer Science	Programming	Networking	
008-111-226	Dominica Clubb	KAC	Keri	Coots	Science	Biology	Nursing	
001-112-223	Monty Burse	LAF	Lisa	Fred	Computer Science	Programming	Web Development	
011-112-228	Levi Otts					Programming	Web Development	
016-111-230	Soledad Mattis					Web Development	Programming	Networking
000-111-222	Jami Salerno	LAR	Lisa	Ruff	Business	Finance	Accounting	
010-112-227	Li Bridgman					Accounting		
015-112-230	Pamila Tomasek					Marketing		
007-112-226	Davis Andry	MIM	Mckenzie	Moring	Science	Biology	Chemistry	
014-111-229	Phuong Harbison					Chemistry		
006-111-225	Jonna Bluhm	MEG	Monica	Gantt	Technology	Auto Technology		
005-112-225	Sanda Mines	SKK	Steve	Kime	Business	Accounting	Marketing	

FIGURE 5-5 Professors table of data with repeating groups

A different type of repeating group problem occurs in the Major1, Major2, and Major3 fields. While each field has only one piece of data, together, the three fields represent a repeating group of data for the Major attribute for each student. As noted earlier, this organization of data limits a student's ability to change majors to the three fields that have been created to store the data. It also makes it difficult to find which students are currently Web Development majors, for example. You must query data in three fields and make sure that Web Development is the last entry in the Major1, Major2, and Major3 fields for that student.

To convert Figure 5-5 to 1NF, you need to make sure that there are no repeating groups in any single attribute, and also no repeating groups created by multiple occurrences of the same attribute (e.g., eliminate fields such as Major1, Major2, Major3) by creating more records as shown in Figure 5-6. The data in Figure 5-6 is close to 1NF because it meets one part of the 1NF definition: *the list does not contain repeating data in any attribute*. Unfortunately, it still doesn't meet the second requirement: *each column contains atomic values*.

StudentID	Student	ProfID	ProfFirst	ProfLast	Department	Major
003-112-224	Alexia Carnell	AKZ	Akram	Aziz	Computer Science	Programming
003-112-224	Alexia Carnell	AKZ	Akram	Aziz	Computer Science	Web Development
013-112-229	Savanna Sanderlin	AKZ	Akram	Aziz	Computer Science	Programming
009-112-227	Buddy Pothier	DOM	Donnell	Meaders	Business	Accounting
012-111-228	Verline Papadopoulos	DOM	Donnell	Meaders	Business	Auto Technology
002-111-223	Buddy Pothier	JJJ	James	Justus	Technology	Welding
004-111-224	Leo Schildgen	JOF	Jose	Fred	Computer Science	Programming
004-111-224	Leo Schildgen	JOF	Jose	Fred	Computer Science	Networking
008-111-226	Dominica Clubb	KAC	Keri	Coots	Science	Biology
008-111-226	Dominica Clubb	KAC	Keri	Coots	Science	Nursing
001-112-223	Monty Burse	LAF	Lisa	Fred	Computer Science	Programming
001-112-223	Monty Burse	LAF	Lisa	Fred	Computer Science	Web Development
011-112-228	Levi Otts	LAF	Lisa	Fred	Computer Science	Programming
011-112-228	Levi Otts	LAF	Lisa	Fred	Computer Science	Web Development
016-111-230	Soledad Mattis	LAF	Lisa	Fred	Computer Science	Web Development
016-111-230	Soledad Mattis	LAF	Lisa	Fred	Computer Science	Programming
016-111-230	Soledad Mattis	LAF	Lisa	Fred	Computer Science	Networking
000-111-222	Jami Salerno	LAR	Lisa	Ruff	Business	Finance
000-111-222	Jami Salerno	LAR	Lisa	Ruff	Business	Accounting
010-111-227	Li Bridgman	LAR	Lisa	Ruff	Business	Accounting
015-112-230	Pamila Tomasek	LAR	Lisa	Ruff	Business	Marketing
007-112-226	Davis Andry	MIM	Mckenzie	Moring	Science	Biology
007-112-226	Davis Andry	MIM	Mckenzie	Moring	Science	Chemistry
014-111-229	Phuong Harbison	MIM	Mckenzie	Moring	Science	Chemistry

FIGURE 5-6 Converting Figure 5-1 to eliminate repeating groups of Major data

ATOMIC VALUES

An **atomic value** is a piece of data that cannot be meaningfully divided. The term atomic comes from the word atom, the smallest division of an element that can exist on its own. While removing repeating groups is a major step to reaching 1NF, you also need to examine each column to make sure it contains only one consistent piece of data for each record.

Although the data in Figure 5-6 appears to be in 1NF, examine the Student field. Currently, the Student field contains two pieces of information, a student's first and last name. Entering full names into one attribute is a common database design mistake that breaks the rules of 1NF and the need to create atomic values for each field. Some database designers divide the names of people into several additional fields to individually store title, first, middle, last, suffix, maiden, and nicknames in separate attributes. The decision of how many attributes are needed to store name information depends on the needs of the processes and people that use that data, but at a minimum, a person's name should be stored in at least two atomic attributes: first name and last name.

Making sure that each attribute contains one and only one piece of data makes the data much easier to sort, search, and filter. Think about the difficulties of sorting the students in Figure 5-6 by last name, for example. Your sorting process would have to identify the characters that follow the last space. How would you sort names that consisted of multiple words such as Mary Lou Retton or Nazareth Mitrou Long? Combining more than one attribute into a single field limits the flexibility of the data. This problem commonly occurs in name and address fields.

To fix this problem, you have several choices, many of which depend on how much data you have to correct and how consistently the data follows a particular pattern. If you can determine a pattern that applies to the majority of the data, and if you can build a programming algorithm to separate the data based on that pattern, then you can reduce the time and improve the accuracy of separating two or more atomic values from a single piece of data.

In programming, an **algorithm** is a defined set of steps to solve a problem. The algorithm can be applied to a problem as complex as the steps needed to launch a rocket to as simple as the calculation to compute a sales tax value. In this case, the problem is to separate a single string of characters currently stored in one field into two separate fields of data. The data follows a consistent pattern, which helps build the steps of the algorithm: the two atomic values are separated by a single space character.

If you cannot define a consistent pattern to use with a programming algorithm to solve the problem, you're faced with the drudgery of manually updating the data. Sometimes this approach works for small sets of data, but you should programmatically update as much information as possible, leaving time-consuming and error-prone manual updates as the last resort. Strive to manually update the smallest amount of data as possible, only that data that contains exceptions to the patterns you have previously identified and can programmatically modify.

Breaking Out Atomic Values Using Query Design View

To break out atomic values using Query Design View, perform the following steps:

- Import the data as a new table into an empty Access database.
- Determine the pattern that defines the atomic values.
- Define an algorithm to separate the values.
- Create fields to store each atomic value you have identified.
- Use Query Design View to create and run an update query that uses the algorithm to update the new fields with the atomic values.

The data from Figure 5-6 is stored as an Excel spreadsheet named student-advisor-assignments.xls, and is provided in the Data Files for this module. In the upcoming exercises, you will use Access to accomplish the normalization steps to convert this list to 1NF by dividing the Student data into two atomic values for the student first name and the student last name.

YOUR TURN 5-1

Create a new database in Access named student-advisor-assignments, and then import the data shown in Figure 5-6 into a new table named rawdata. The data shown in Figure 5-6 is stored as an Excel spreadsheet named student-advisor-assignments.xlsx.

Creating a Blank Database with Access

To create a blank database, perform the following steps:

- Start Access.
- Click the Blank database icon.
- Navigate to the desired folder location.
- Name the new database with the desired name.
- If a new, blank table object opens, close it without saving it.

Importing Excel Data into an Access Database

To import Excel data into an Access database, perform the following steps:

- Click the External Data tab on the ribbon.
- Click the New Data Source button (External Data tab | Import & Link group), point to From File, and then click Excel.
- Click the Browse button, and then navigate to and select the desired Excel file.
- In the Get External Data – Excel Spreadsheet dialog box, choose the Import (vs. Link) option button, and then click OK.
- In the Import Spreadsheet Wizard, click the First Row Contains Headings check box (if the data contains attribute names in the first row), and then click Next.
- Click Next to accept that Access will add a primary key field (if none currently exists), or select the primary key field from the existing data.
- Enter the desired table name, click Finish, and then click Close to finish the import process.

Double-click a table in Access to open it in Datasheet View to view the records. The imported data should look like Figure 5-7.

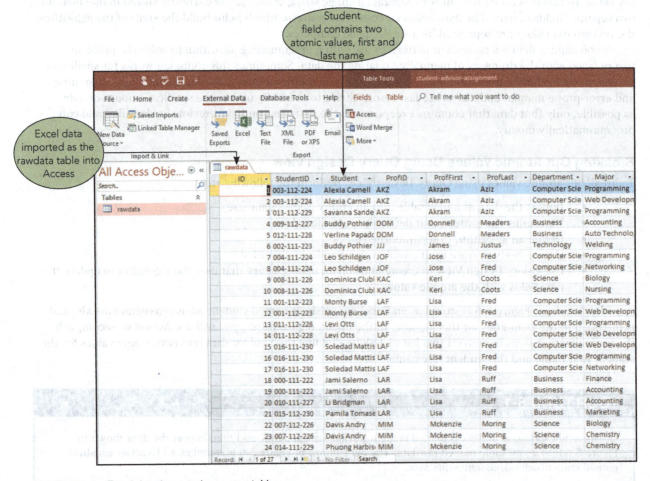

FIGURE 5-7 Excel data imported as a new table

ALGORITHMS

As noted earlier, an algorithm is a defined set of steps to solve a problem. Algorithms to separate atomic values from a single piece of data generally require a pattern that determines the start and stopping points for each atomic value. The pattern that describes the student first and last name is determined by the space character between the two atomic values. Knowing that the data in the Student field is consistently described by this pattern allows you to create the algorithm or formula to separate the atomic values.

The algorithm to define the first name can be described in words as follows:

1. Determine the location of the space character in the Student field.

2. All characters to the left of the space character constitute the student's first name.

The algorithm to define the last name can be described in words as follows:

1. Determine the location of the space character in the Student field.

2. All characters to the right of the space character constitute the student's last name.

To implement the algorithm to separate the first name data from the Student field in Access, you use the built-in Access function of **InStr** to identify the location of the space character in the current Student field and you use the built-in Access function of **Left** to extract leftmost characters with a length of one character less than the location of the space character.

YOUR TURN 5-2

Use Query Design View to create calculated fields to implement the algorithm needed to separate the student *first* name from the Student field.

Query Design View shown in Figure 5-8 uses the built-in Access function of **InStr** to first determine the numeric location of the space character in the current Student field and is identified as a new calculated field named *Space*. The third column uses the built-in Access function of **Left** to extract a number of characters from the left side of the Student field. The second argument of the Left function identifies the number of characters to extract from the Student field, and is set at *Space – 1* which precisely identifies the length of the first name for each student in each record.

For example, in the name *Edgar Codd*, the space character is at position 6, the *Space – 1* expression would return the value of 5, and the overall expression would return the five leftmost characters of *Edgar*.

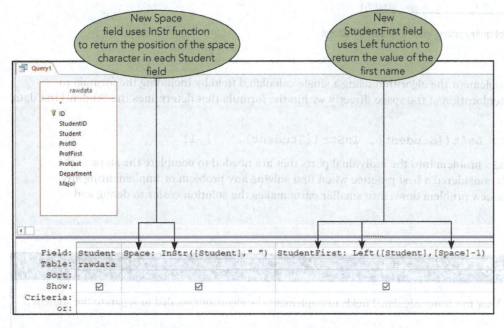

FIGURE 5-8 Implementing the algorithm to break out the first name data in Query Design View

Run the query to display the results in Datasheet View as shown in Figure 5-9.

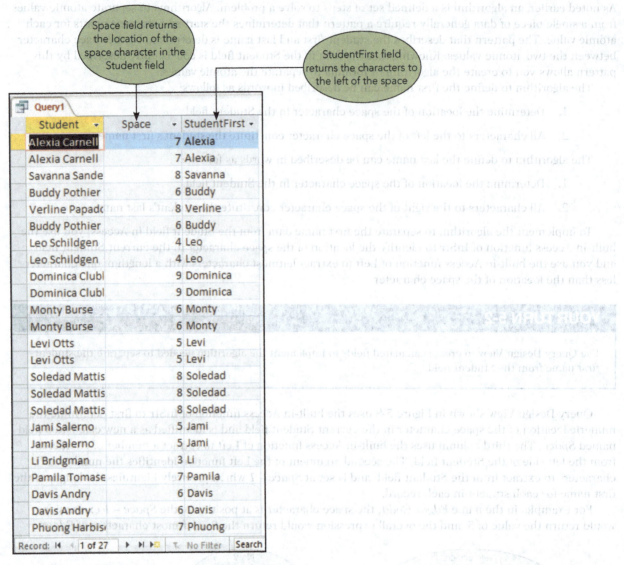

FIGURE 5-9 Results of query using InStr and Left functions

You could also implement the algorithm using a single calculated field by including the formula to calculate the character location of the space directly within the formula that determines the StudentFirst data as follows:

```
StudentFirst: Left([Student], InStr([Student]," ")-1)
```

However, dividing a problem into the individual parts that are needed to complete the steps of the algorithm is generally considered a best practice when first solving any problem or implementing any algorithm. Breaking a new problem down into smaller parts makes the solution easier to debug and understand.

YOUR TURN 5-3

Use Query Design View to create calculated fields to implement the algorithm needed to separate the student *last* name.

Query Design View shown in Figure 5-10 uses the built-in Access function of **Len** to determine the total number of characters in the Student field and is identified as a new calculated field named *Length*. The fourth column uses the built-in Access function of **Right** to extract a number of characters from the right side of the Student field. The second argument in the Right function determines the number of characters to return from the right side of the Student field and is set at *Length - Space* which precisely identifies the length of the characters after the space, the characters that represent the last name for each student.

For example, in the name *Edgar Codd*, the space character is at position 6, the overall length of the string is 10, the *Length – Space* expression would return the value of 4 and the overall expression would return the four rightmost characters of *Codd*.

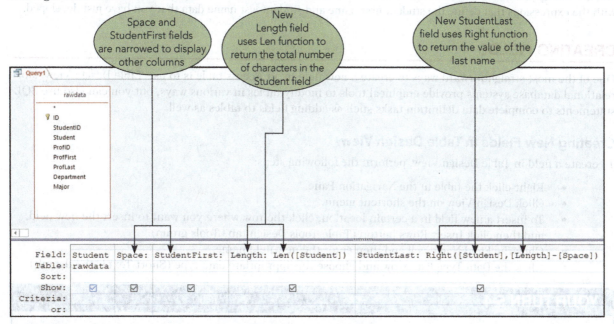

FIGURE 5-10 Implementing the algorithm to break out the last name data in Query Design View

Save the query with the name of StudentNames, and run it to display the data as shown in Figure 5-11.

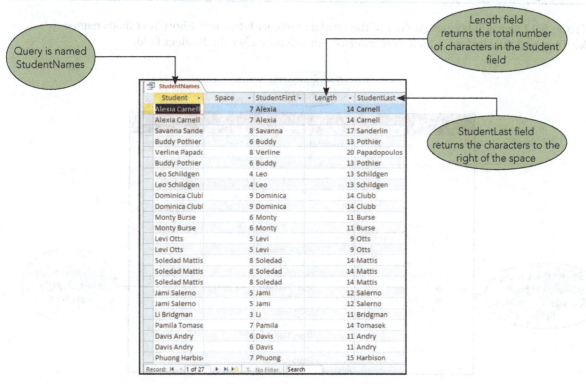

FIGURE 5-11 Results of query using Len and Right functions

You could also implement the algorithm to extract the last name characters from the Student field as follows:

```
StudentLast:Right([Student],Len([Student])-InStr([Student]," "))
```

If you prefer writing SQL statements, you can switch to SQL View in any Access query to view or modify the SQL stored in the StudentNames query.

At this point, the StudentNames query is a select query that creates calculated fields to separate the first and last names for each record. To actually update the rawdata table so that it stores atomic values for the student first and last name, you will need to create two new columns in the rawdata table, and then update the rawdata table with the expressions that define the student first name and student last name data that you have just developed.

CREATING FIELDS

One of the most straightforward ways to create a new field in an Access table is to use Table Design View. Most relational database systems provide graphical tools to modify tables in various ways, but you can also use SQL statements to complete data definition tasks such as adding fields to tables as well.

Creating New Fields in Table Design View

To create a field in Table Design View, perform the following steps:

- Right-click the table in the Navigation Pane.
- Click Design View on the shortcut menu.
- To insert a new field in a certain location, click the row where you want to insert the new field, and then click Insert Rows button (Table Tools Design tab | Tools group).
- Click the Field Name cell and then enter the new field name.
- Click the Data Type list arrow and choose the appropriate data type (Short Text is the default).

YOUR TURN 5-4

Use Table Design View of the rawdata table to create two new fields named StudentFirst and StudentLast, each with the Short Text data type, immediately after the Student field.

Figure 5-12 shows Table Design View of the rawdata table with two new Short Text fields named StudentFirst and StudentLast, which were inserted immediately after the Student field.

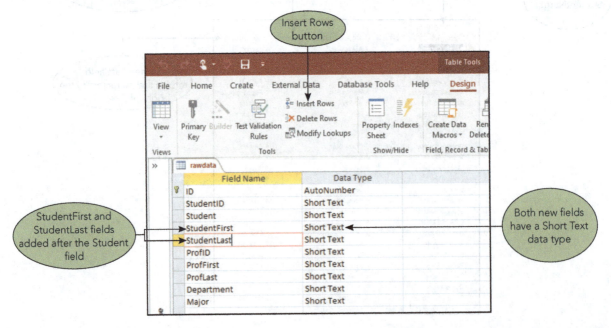

FIGURE 5-12 Adding fields in Table Design View

Figure 5-13 shows the rawdata table in Table Datasheet View with the two new empty columns.

New StudentFirst and StudentLast columns

ID	StudentID	Student	StudentFirst	StudentLast	ProfID	ProfFirst	ProfLast	Department	Major
1	003-112-224	Alexia Carnell			AKZ	Akram	Aziz	Computer Scie	Programming
2	003-112-224	Alexia Carnell			AKZ	Akram	Aziz	Computer Scie	Web Developm
3	013-112-229	Savanna Sande			AKZ	Akram	Aziz	Computer Scie	Programming
4	009-112-227	Buddy Pothier			DOM	Donnell	Meaders	Business	Accounting
5	012-111-228	Verline Papadc			DOM	Donnell	Meaders	Business	Auto Technolo
6	002-111-223	Buddy Pothier			JJJ	James	Justus	Technology	Welding
7	004-111-224	Leo Schildgen			JOF	Jose	Fred	Computer Scie	Programming
8	004-111-224	Leo Schildgen			JOF	Jose	Fred	Computer Scie	Networking
9	008-111-226	Dominica Clubl			KAC	Keri	Coots	Science	Biology
10	008-111-226	Dominica Clubl			KAC	Keri	Coots	Science	Nursing
11	001-112-223	Monty Burse			LAF	Lisa	Fred	Computer Scie	Programming
12	001-112-223	Monty Burse			LAF	Lisa	Fred	Computer Scie	Web Developm
13	011-112-228	Levi Otts			LAF	Lisa	Fred	Computer Scie	Programming
14	011-112-228	Levi Otts			LAF	Lisa	Fred	Computer Scie	Web Developm
15	016-111-230	Soledad Mattis			LAF	Lisa	Fred	Computer Scie	Web Developm
16	016-111-230	Soledad Mattis			LAF	Lisa	Fred	Computer Scie	Programming
17	016-111-230	Soledad Mattis			LAF	Lisa	Fred	Computer Scie	Networking
18	000-111-222	Jami Salerno			LAR	Lisa	Ruff	Business	Finance
19	000-111-222	Jami Salerno			LAR	Lisa	Ruff	Business	Accounting
20	010-111-227	Li Bridgman			LAR	Lisa	Ruff	Business	Accounting
21	015-112-230	Pamila Tomase			LAR	Lisa	Ruff	Business	Marketing
22	007-112-226	Davis Andry			MIM	Mckenzie	Moring	Science	Biology
23	007-112-226	Davis Andry			MIM	Mckenzie	Moring	Science	Chemistry
24	014-111-229	Phuong Harbis			MIM	Mckenzie	Moring	Science	Chemistry

Record: I◄ ◄ 1 of 27 ► ►I ►❑ No Filter Search

FIGURE 5-13 Two new empty columns in Table Datasheet View

Technically, it wouldn't matter where you inserted the new columns into the table, but placing them immediately to the right of the Student column will help you visually determine if your updates are successful.

UPDATING FIELDS

With the new columns created in the rawdata table, you are ready to use the formulas you constructed in the StudentNames query to create the new atomic values for the StudentFirst and StudentLast fields.

Updating Field Values Using Query Design View

To update field values using Query Design View, perform the following steps:

- Start a new query in Query Design View.
- Add the table that contains the fields that need to be updated to the upper pane of Query Design View.
- Add the fields that you want to update to the query grid.
- Click the Update button (Query Tools Design tab | Query Type group) to change the query into an update query.
- Enter an expression that identifies how to update each field in the Update To cell for that specific field.
- Click the Run button (Query Tools Design tab | Results group) to complete the update.

YOUR TURN 5-5

Use Query Design View and the knowledge you documented when creating the StudentNames query to update the StudentFirst and StudentLast fields with the appropriate atomic data for each column.

Figure 5-14 shows Query Design View with the expressions needed to update the StudentFirst and StudentLast fields in the Update To row of the query grid. The expressions shown are the single-expression versions of the work you completed in the StudentNames query when implementing the algorithms that identified each atomic value.

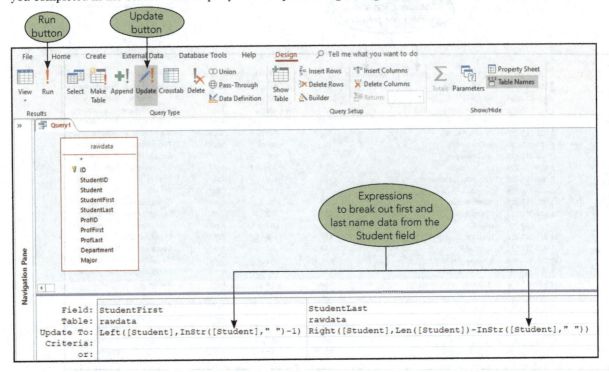

FIGURE 5-14 Updating the StudentFirst and StudentLast fields

Running the query updates all 27 rows. Often, update queries are run only once and therefore are not saved when they are closed. The result of running this update query on the rawdata table is shown in Figure 5-15, which displays the rawdata table in Table Datasheet View. Note the atomic values in the updated StudentFirst and StudentLast values.

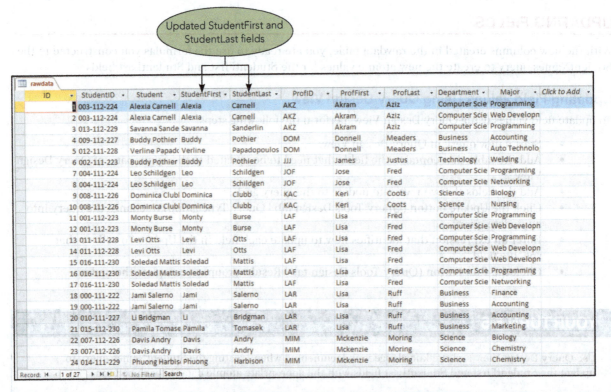

FIGURE 5-15 Rawdata table with updated StudentFirst and StudentLast fields

In a real situation, any time you run an update query that changes data, you also need to run a test to make sure the update was done correctly. For example, you could create a calculated field in an Access query based on the rawdata table with an expression using the built-in Access **IIF** function to evaluate an expression such as the following. (*Note*: The built-in Access IIF function uses two "I" characters to distinguish it from the programming keyword of *If*.) The expression is:

```
[Student] = [StudentFirst]& " " &[StudentLast]
```

The expression returns a value of true or false to test whether the values in the Student field are equal to the value of the StudentFirst field value concatenated to a space concatenated to the StudentLast field value.

If the expression evaluates true, the IIF function will return "match". If the test evaluates false, the IIF function will return "problem".

```
TEST: IIF([Student] = [StudentFirst]& " " &[StudentLast], "match", "problem")
```

For this small example, all values in the Student field match the pattern described earlier, meaning that the algorithm to separate the atomic student first and student last values works successfully on all records. In the real world, however, you'd want to run a test to make sure each step of your normalization process was accurate and successful as you move through the process of modifying your unnormalized data.

CREATING THE 1NF TABLE

Now that each column of the rawdata table contains atomic values (except for the redundant Student field), the rawdata table is basically in 1NF with the exception of the Student field. Instead of deleting the Student field from the rawdata table, however, it is safer to build a new 1NF table from the rawdata table so that you can return to the rawdata table to see what was originally imported.

Creating a New Table in Query Design View

To create a table in Query Design View, perform the following steps:

- Start a new query in Query Design View.
- Add the table that contains the fields to be used in the new table.
- Add the fields that you want to update to the query grid.
- Click the Make Table button (Query Tools Design tab I Query Type group) to change the query into a make-table query.
- Enter the new table name in the Make Table dialog box and then click OK.
- Click the Run button (Query Tools Design tab I Results group) to complete the update.

YOUR TURN 5-6

Use Query Design View and the rawdata table to make a new table named 1NF (for first normal form) using all of the fields of the rawdata table *except* for the Student field.

Query Design View should look like Figure 5-16, which shows the Make Table dialog box with the new table name as well as all fields from the rawdata table in the query grid except for the Student field.

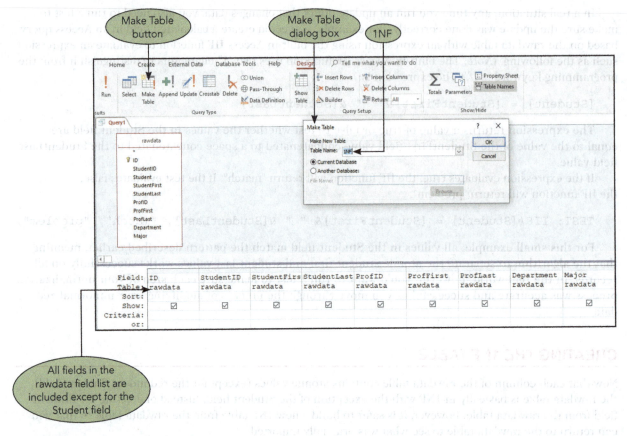

FIGURE 5-16 Making the 1NF table

Often, you run make-table queries only once when you use them to move through the normalization process, and therefore do not need to save them when you close the query. The result of running this make-table query to create the 1NF table is shown in Figure 5-17, which displays the 1NF table in Table Datasheet View.

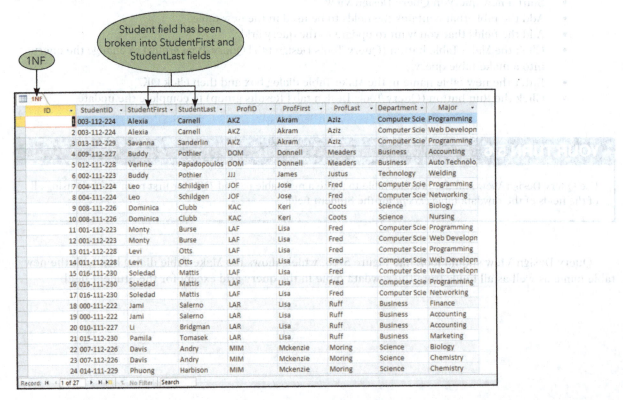

FIGURE 5-17 Initial 1NF table

The 1NF table now appears to be in first normal form because it contains no repeating groups in any attribute and each column contains atomic values. The notation for describing the 1NF table in Figure 5-17 is as follows:

1NF (StudentID, StudentFirst, StudentLast, ProfID, ProfFirst, ProfLast, Department, Major)

The benefit of having atomic values in each column is that the data is now much easier to sort, find, and filter based on either part of the name. It is also easier and more accurate to enter as the field names are clearer and represent a single piece of data.

To combine the first and last name into a single expression, you can use your relational database management system's QBE such as Query Design View for Access or write SQL statements to create a calculated field that combines the atomic values into one expression. If a record contained a StudentFirst value of *Kelsey* and a StudentLast value of *Wintersteen*, two common full-name expressions to combine that data are shown in Figure 5-18.

Expression	Result
[StudentFirst] & " " & [StudentLast]	Kelsey Wintersteen
[StudentLast] & ", " & [StudentFirst]	Wintersteen, Kelsey

FIGURE 5-18 Common expressions to combine first and last name field values

USING ATOMIC VALUES FOR QUANTITIES

When creating a field for a quantity value, strive to create clear attribute names that clarify the atomic value of the field. In other words, a field that stores quantity information should contain only the numeric portion of that data. This will preserve your ability to sort, find, and calculate the numbers in the field. For example, you might need to store a value such as *60 minutes* to record a duration, *15 millimeters* to record length, or *5 stars* to measure satisfaction on a scale of 1 to 5 stars. Strive to enter all quantities as numbers only, using a common unit of measure for all records in the table.

Another tip is to identify the unit of measure in the attribute name for clarity. For example, a field that measures duration might be named *DurationInMinutes* to prevent entries of both 60 (for 60 minutes) and 1.5 (for 90 minutes). A field that stores a length measurement might be named *LengthInMM* to clarify the unit of measure as millimeters for each record. A field that measures satisfaction on a scale of 1 to 5 might be named *Stars*, *SatisfactionRating*, or whatever helps those who use the data clarify that attribute's purpose. Storing quantities as consistent numeric data in all records of a table will vastly improve your ability to sort, filter, find, and analyze that data. Figure 5-19 illustrates the difference between unclear attribute names and problematic attribute values as compared to clear attribute names for fields that store quantities as well as consistent numeric attribute values:

Unclear Attribute Name	Problematic Attribute Values (combination of numeric and string data)	Improved Attribute Name	Improved Attribute Value (numeric data only)
Length	15 miles	LengthInMiles	15
LengthInTime	1.5 minutes	LengthInSeconds	90
Weight	4 kilograms	WeightInKilos	4
Rating	3 stars	StarRating	3
Packaging	6 per box	PerBox	6
Gas Mileage	35 mpg	MPG	35
Sugar	6 grams	SugarInGrams	6

FIGURE 5-19 Correcting unclear attribute names to store atomic numeric values

Q&A 5-5

Question: What might happen if the numbers in a Length column sometimes represented inches and other time represented centimeters? Also, how would you fix that data problem?

Answer: Data measured in inconsistent units of measurement means that the data is less clear, consistent, and reliable to the people and processes that use it. At best, unclear data leads to slower decisions given more time and effort is needed to correctly understand and process it. At worst, unclear data is evaluated in an inaccurate way leading to costly or even disastrous results.

To correct the problem, all values in a column would have to be evaluated and entered for the same and consistent unit of measurement. If a new unit of measurement was needed for all or a subset of the records, a conversion calculation could be quickly and easily created with a calculated field in a query.

FINDING DUPLICATE RECORDS

In addition to eliminating repeating groups and separating data into atomic values, a final characteristic of 1NF is that the table contains no duplicate records. Given the values in the ID field of the 1NF table are unique, the current 1NF table technically satisfies the requirements of 1NF. The ID value, however, was automatically added when you imported the data from the Excel spreadsheet. To meet the spirit of 1NF, you need to determine whether the other attributes happen to contain duplicate entries between two or more records. Access can help complete that task.

Finding Duplicate Records in Query Design View

To find duplicate records in Query Design View, perform the following steps:

- Start a new query in Query Design View.
- Add the table that contains the data to analyze.
- Add all of the fields you want to analyze for duplication to the query grid.
- Click the Totals button (Query Tools Design tab | Show/Hide group) to add the Total row to the query grid.
- Choose the Group By option for all fields that you want to analyze for duplicate records.
- If you have an AutoNumber field, choose the Count aggregate function. If you do not have an AutoNumber field, add any grouped field to the query grid again and use the Count aggregate function to count it.
- Sort the records in descending order on the Count field to place duplicate records at the top of the list.

YOUR TURN 5-7

Use Query Design View and the 1NF table to check for duplicate records. Use the Totals button to Count the ID field and Group By all the other fields in the 1NF table. Sort the records in descending order on the count of the ID field.

Query Design View to find duplicate records should look like Figure 5-20. Note that all of the fields in the table are grouped together except for the ID field, which is used to count the number of records in each group.

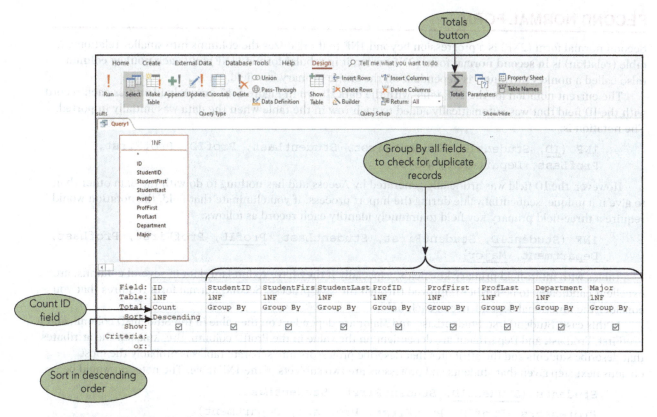

FIGURE 5-20 Checking for duplicate records

Running the query yields the datasheet shown in Figure 5-21. The records are grouped together on each field in the 1NF table (except for the ID field), and each group contains only one record. You now know that the 1NF table contains no duplicate records and meets all of the requirements of 1NF: no groups of values in any attribute(s), each attribute contains atomic values, and no duplicate records.

CountOfID	StudentID	StudentFirst	StudentLast	ProfID	ProfFirst	ProfLast	Department	Major
1	008-111-226	Dominica	Clubb	KAC	Keri	Coots	Science	Biology
1	000-111-222	Jami	Salerno	LAR	Lisa	Ruff	Business	Finance
1	001-112-223	Monty	Burse	LAF	Lisa	Fred	Computer Scie	Programming
1	001-112-223	Monty	Burse	LAF	Lisa	Fred	Computer Scie	Web Developn
1	002-111-223	Buddy	Pothier	JJJ	James	Justus	Technology	Welding
1	003-112-224	Alexia	Carnell	AKZ	Akram	Aziz	Computer Scie	Programming
1	003-112-224	Alexia	Carnell	AKZ	Akram	Aziz	Computer Scie	Web Developn
1	004-111-224	Leo	Schildgen	JOF	Jose	Fred	Computer Scie	Networking
1	004-111-224	Leo	Schildgen	JOF	Jose	Fred	Computer Scie	Programming
1	005-112-225	Sanda	Mines	SKK	Steve	Kime	Business	Accounting
1	005-112-225	Sanda	Mines	SKK	Steve	Kime	Business	Marketing
1	006-111-225	Jonna	Bluhm	MEG	Monica	Gantt	Technology	Auto Technolo
1	000-111-222	Jami	Salerno	LAR	Lisa	Ruff	Business	Accounting
1	007-112-226	Davis	Andry	MIM	Mckenzie	Moring	Science	Chemistry
1	016-111-230	Soledad	Mattis	LAF	Lisa	Fred	Computer Scie	Web Developn
1	008-111-226	Dominica	Clubb	KAC	Keri	Coots	Science	Nursing
1	009-112-227	Buddy	Pothier	DOM	Donnell	Meaders	Business	Accounting
1	010-111-227	Li	Bridgman	LAR	Lisa	Ruff	Business	Accounting
1	011-112-228	Levi	Otts	LAF	Lisa	Fred	Computer Scie	Programming
1	011-112-228	Levi	Otts	LAF	Lisa	Fred	Computer Scie	Web Developn
1	012-111-228	Verline	Papadopoulos	DOM	Donnell	Meaders	Business	Auto Technolo
1	013-112-229	Savanna	Sanderlin	AKZ	Akram	Aziz	Computer Scie	Programming
1	014-111-229	Phuong	Harbison	MIM	Mckenzie	Moring	Science	Chemistry
1	015-112-230	Pamila	Tomasek	LAR	Lisa	Ruff	Business	Marketing

Record: 1 of 27   No Filter   Search

FIGURE 5-21 Count of one record within each group reveals that no duplicate records were found

SECOND NORMAL FORM

Second normal form (2NF) is a progression beyond 1NF that organizes the columns into smaller relations. A table (relation) is in **second normal form (2NF)** when it in tabular format (1NF) *and* each **nonkey column** (also called a **nonkey attribute**) is dependent on the entire primary key field.

The current notation for the 1NF table with the data shown in Figure 5-17 uniquely identifies each record with the ID field that was automatically added to each row in the table when the data was initially imported. The notation is:

```
1NF (ID, StudentID, StudentFirst, StudentLast, ProfID, ProfFirst,
ProfLast, Department, Major)
```

However, the ID field was artificially generated by Access and has nothing to do with the data other than to give it a unique, sequential value during the import process. If you eliminate that field, the notation would require a three-field primary key field to uniquely identify each record as follows:

```
1NF (StudentID, StudentFirst, StudentLast, ProfID, ProfFirst, ProfLast,
Department, Major)
```

Tables with multi-field primary key fields, especially if they have redundant data in several columns, are excellent candidates to be further improved through the 2NF process. Second normal form requires that you consider the functional dependence of each field.

In this case, StudentFirst, StudentLast, and Major are dependent on the value in the StudentID column, and ProfFirst, ProfLast, and Department are dependent on the value in the ProfID column. Breaking out the attributes that describe students and the attributes that describe professors into separate tables is probably the most obvious next step given that students and professors are two subjects of the 1NF table. The notation would be:

```
Students (StudentID, StudentFirst, StudentLast)
```

```
Professors (ProfID, ProfFirst, ProfLast, Department)
```

The choice of Students and Professors as the table names is not a strict requirement, although many professionals use a plural form of a singular record in a particular table as a straightforward and common table-naming convention.

YOUR TURN 5-8

Use Query Design View and the 1NF table to make a new table named Students using the StudentID, StudentFirst, and StudentLast fields of the 1NF table. Use query grouping skills to create only one record per student.

Query Design View should look like Figure 5-22, which shows the Make Table dialog box with the new table name of Students as well as all fields from the 1NF table in the query grid that belong to the Students table. You use the Totals button to group the records so only one record will be created for each group of records that has the same value in the StudentID, StudentFirst, and StudentLast fields. In other words, one record for each student will be created.

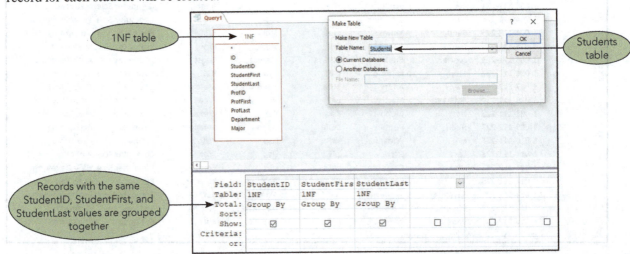

FIGURE 5-22 Creating the Students table

After running the query, the Students table should look like Figure 5-23, with 17 records, each representing a different student.

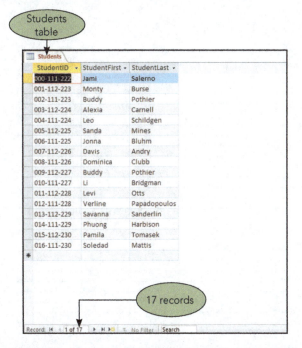

FIGURE 5-23 Students table with 17 records in Table Datasheet View

YOUR TURN 5-9

Use Query Design View and the 1NF table to make a new table named Professors using the ProfID, ProfFirst, ProfLast, and Department fields of the 1NF table. Use query grouping skills to create only one record per professor.

Query Design View should look like Figure 5-24, which shows the Make Table dialog box with the new table name of Professors, and the fields from the 1NF table in the query grid for the Professors table. You use the Totals button to group the records so only one record will be created for each group of records that has the same values in the ProfID, ProfFirst, ProfLast, and Department fields. In other words, one record for each professor will be created.

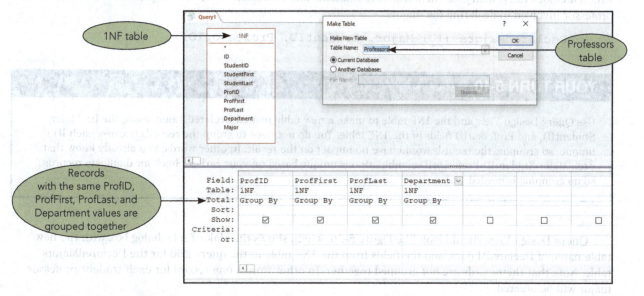

FIGURE 5-24 Creating the Professors table

After running the query, the Professors table should look like Figure 5-25, with 10 records, each representing a single professor. The data in this table displays no redundant professor names.

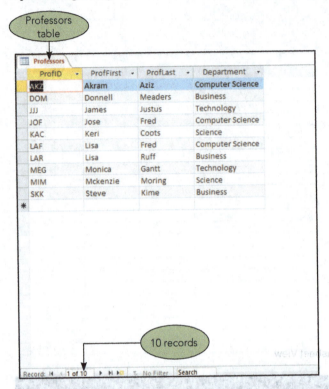

FIGURE 5-25 Professors table with 10 records in Table Datasheet View

After separating the attributes for the Students and Professors tables, the only other fields from the 1NF table are the ID field and the Major field. The notation for a table with only the ID and Major fields would be:

DeclaredMajors (ID, Major)

However, simply separating the initial 1NF data into multiple tables breaks the connections between the students, professors, and process of declaring new majors. This means that you also need to consider the relationships between the tables while you are working through the normal forms. In this case, each unique ID represents a specific student and a specific professor that were linked together when the student declared a new major. To connect the Students and Professors tables to this event, the following table must be created, which includes the primary key field from the Students and Professors tables to uniquely tie the student and professor involved in declaring the major:

DeclaredMajors (ID, Major, StudentID, ProfessorID)

YOUR TURN 5-10

Use Query Design View and the 1NF table to make a new table named DeclaredMajors using the ID, Major, StudentID, and ProfessorID fields of the 1NF table. You do not need to group the records because each ID is unique, so grouping the records would have no impact on the result. In other words, you already know that each Major-StudentID-ProfessorID combination is unique based on your earlier check for duplicate records, so no grouping is needed.

Query Design View should look like Figure 5-26, which shows the Make Table dialog box with the new table name of DeclaredMajors, and the fields from the 1NF table in the query grid for the DeclaredMajors table. Note that the records are *not* grouped together. In other words, one record for each student-professor-major will be created.

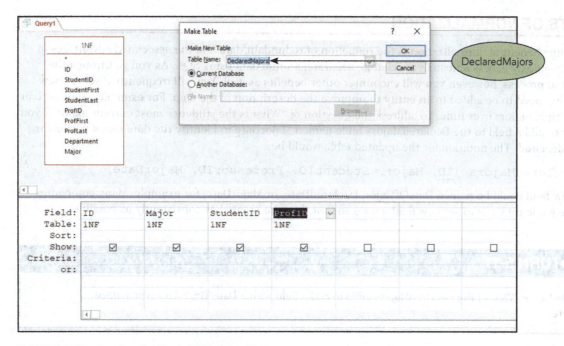

FIGURE 5-26 Creating the DeclaredMajors table

After running the query, the DeclaredMajors table should look like Figure 5-27, with 27 records, each representing a unique occurrence of a student declaring a new major and being assigned to a professor.

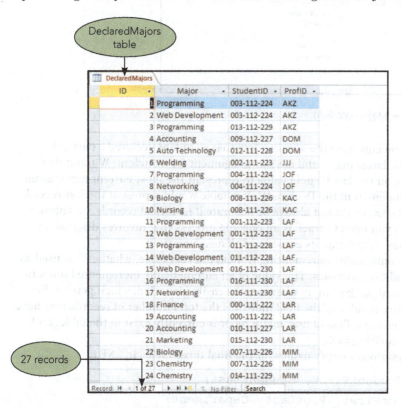

FIGURE 5-27 DeclaredMajors table with 27 records in Table Datasheet View

Each of the tables—Students, Professors, and DeclaredMajors—now conforms to 2NF because they conform to 1NF *plus* every nonkey attribute of each table is entirely dependent on only the single-field primary key of that table. Furthermore, the tables can be connected through the DeclaredMajors table to recreate the information about which individual student and which individual professor were involved each time a major was declared.

BENEFITS OF NORMALIZATION

The overriding benefit of normalization is the reduction of redundant data and the associated advantages of being able to quickly access and analyze reliable, accurate, atomic data using SQL. As you go through the normalization process, however, you will encounter other benefits as well. You will frequently discover new attributes that need to be added to an entity to improve the description of the data. For example, students can declare multiple majors over time. To address the question of "What is the student's most current major?" you might want to add a field to the DeclaredMajors table named MajorDate to identify the date that a particular major was declared. The notation for the updated table would be:

DeclaredMajors (ID, Major, StudentID, ProfessorID, MajorDate)

The new field could be named DateOfMajor, DeclaredDate, or MajorDate, for example. Many companies have a style guide they use to set new field names so that they are created as consistently as possible.

YOUR TURN 5-11

Use Table Design View of the DeclaredMajors table to add a field with a Date/Time data type named MajorDate.

Figure 5-28 shows the updated DeclaredMajors table in Table Design View with the new MajorDate field.

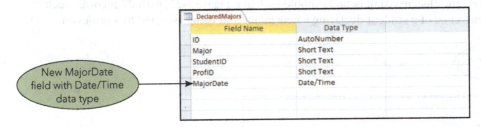

FIGURE 5-28 DeclaredMajors table with new MajorDate field

With the MajorDate field in place, you can store the specific date that a student declared a particular major, which in turn helps determine the latest major and advisor assignment for a student. Without this information, you'd probably have to rely on the last ID field value to represent the most current major given the last ID field value for a particular StudentID in the DeclaredMajors table would represent the last record that was entered. That assumption, however, might not always be accurate if historical records are entered retroactively. The decision on what data you need to track is an ongoing process that involves discussions with all who are using the data as business requirements constantly change over time.

Some database designers add an automatically incrementing ID field to every table, whether it is used as the primary key field or not, for light auditing purposes. The value of an automatically incremented numeric field cannot be reused if a record is deleted, so gaps in numbers can be easily identified, which potentially points to foul play. Furthermore, the current value of the field indicates the total number of records that have been added to a particular table over time regardless of how many records currently exist in the table, and that information can also be a valuable auditing tool.

The final notation with the most descriptive entity names for the final three tables in 2NF is:

Students (StudentID, StudentFirst, StudentLast)
Professors (ProfID, ProfFirst, ProfLast, Department)
DeclaredMajors (ID, Major, StudentID, ProfID, MajorDate)

THIRD NORMAL FORM

Tables in **3NF** conform to all of the requirements of 2NF but also exclude transitive dependencies. A **transitive dependency** occurs if a nonkey attribute determines another nonkey attribute. Third normal form is sometimes also referred to as **Boyce–Codd normal form (BCNF)**.

An example of a transitive dependency is if the Professors table has a DepartmentID field and a Department field, as shown in Figure 5-29 and described with the following notation:

Professors (ProfID, ProfFirst, ProfLast, DeptID, Department)

Both fields are nonkey attributes, and the DepartmentID field value determines the Department field value, a transitive dependency.

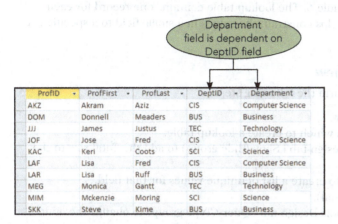

FIGURE 5-29 Transitive dependency

To address the transitive dependency in Figure 5-29, a new smaller Departments table would be created with the following notation:

Departments (DeptID, Department)

To connect the department information to the Professors table, the primary key field from the Departments table, DeptID, would remain in the Professors table to connect the data in the Department field of the Departments table to the original Professors table.

Professors (ProfID, ProfFirst, ProfLast, DeptID)

Any time attributes are removed from a particular table to eliminate transitive dependencies, the connection to the original table needs to be considered so the entire original record can be reconstructed as needed using **foreign key fields**, as you experienced when creating the DeclaredMajors table. These connecting fields create the link, or one-to-many relationship, between the tables of a relational database and will be further studied and implemented in Module 6.

The current Students, Professors, and DeclaredMajors tables have no transitive dependencies, so the tables are already in 3NF, but this example is a small set of data with only a handful of entities to describe. In larger sets of data, all tables passing through 2NF need to be evaluated and reevaluated for transitive dependencies.

Q&A 5-6

Question: Why is it important to remove transitive dependencies?

Answer: Transitive dependencies create unnecessary redundant data that can be minimized by further decomposing a table in 2NF with transitive dependencies into two or more tables in 3NF.

Although the official normalization process includes several more normal forms, relational databases are most often implemented on tables in 3NF.

FOURTH NORMAL FORM

Tables in **4NF** conform to all of the requirements of 3NF with additional requirements that further remove data redundancies and eliminate data modification anomalies. Recall that an update anomaly occurs when a change to one value in the attribute of an entity needs to be made in multiple records in order to accurately update that fact.

The Department field in the Professors table and the Major field in the DeclaredMajors table suffer from potential update anomalies such as changing the name of a department from Technology to Industrial Tech or the name of a major from Welding to Welding Tech. Should either of those changes occur, multiple updates would need to be made to multiple records.

To address that problem, the unique values in the Department field in the Professors table and the Major field in the DeclaredMajors table can be separated into one-field tables, often called **lookup tables**, a subject that will be discussed more and implemented in Module 6. The lookup table contains one record for each possible value for a particular field. A lookup table helps constrain the values in a single field to a specific list, which in turn eliminates update anomalies.

Creating Lookup Tables in Query Design View

To create a lookup table in Query Design View, perform the following steps:

- Start a new query in Query Design View.
- Add the table that contains the field on which to create a lookup table.
- Click the Totals button (Query Tools Design tab | Show/Hide group) to add the Total row to the query grid.
- Choose the Group By option in a field to create a list of unique values for that field.
- Sort the field in ascending order (optional).
- Click the Make Table button (Query Tools Design tab | Query Type group) to change the query into a make-table query.
- Enter the new table name in the Make Table dialog box and then click OK.
- Click the Run button (Query Tools Design tab | Results group) to complete the update.

> ### YOUR TURN 5-12
>
> Use Query Design View of the Professors table to create a lookup table for the Department field values.

Figure 5-30 shows the Query Design View to create a lookup table named Departments with unique Department field values in ascending order.

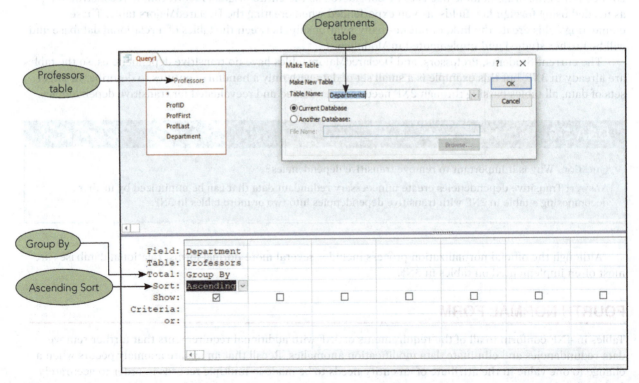

FIGURE 5-30 Creating a lookup table for Department values

Figure 5-31 shows the new Departments table with the four unique Department values.

FIGURE 5-31 Departments lookup table

YOUR TURN 5-13

Use Query Design View of the DeclaredMajors table to create a lookup table for the Major field values.

Figure 5-32 shows the Query Design View to create a lookup table named Majors with unique Major field values in ascending order.

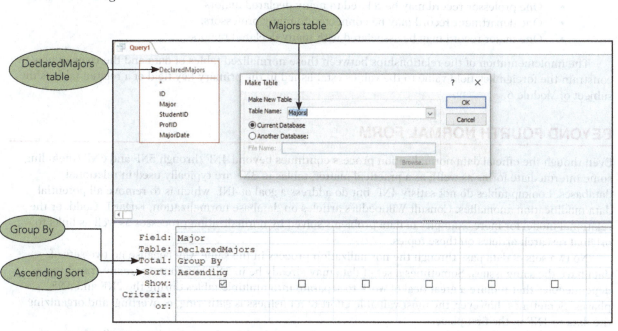

FIGURE 5-32 Creating a lookup table for Major values

Figure 5-33 shows the new Majors table with the 11 unique Major values.

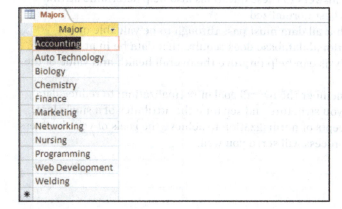

FIGURE 5-33 Majors lookup table

The final notation for the five normalized tables is shown below:

```
Students (StudentID, StudentFirst, StudentLast)
Professors (ProfID, ProfFirst, ProfLast, Department)
DeclaredMajors (ID, Major, StudentID, ProfID, MajorDate)
Departments (Department)
Majors (Major)
```

Neither the Department nor the Major fields were removed from the Professors or the DeclaredMajors tables. Instead, they have become foreign key fields that will tie that data back to the Departments and Majors tables. The newly created Departments and Majors tables will be used to constrain the potential values in the Department field of Professors table and the Major field of the DeclaredMajors table to the unique list of values provided by the records in the Departments and Majors tables. This will make the values in the Department field of Professors table and the Major field of the DeclaredMajors table more productive, consistent, and accurate and will eliminate future update data anomalies for these fields.

To implement these tables in a relational database, they must be joined together in one-to-many relationships using the primary key field of one table connected to the foreign key field of another table. For this set of data, the following statements are true:

- One student record may be connected to many declared majors.
- One professor record may be related to many declared majors.
- One department record may be connected to many professors.
- One major record may be associated with many declared majors.

The implementation of the relationships between these normalized tables of data and the issue of how to constrain the foreign key field value to the values established in the primary key field of a related table is the subject of Module 6.

BEYOND FOURTH NORMAL FORM

Even though the official data normalization process continues beyond 4NF through 5NF and 6NF (including some intermediate forms as well), as a practical matter, tables in 3NF are typically used in relational databases. Lookup tables do not satisfy 4NF, but do address a goal of 4NF, which is to remove all potential data modification anomalies. Consult Wikipedia's articles on database normalization, Edgar F. Codd, or the relational model for more examples of data problems solved by normalization processes as well as links to original research articles on these topics.

No two sets of data pass through the normalization process in the same way because no two sets of data have the same issues. Sometimes a set of data may already be in 1NF but contains many transitive dependencies that require a great deal of work to separate into multiple tables during the 2NF and 3NF phases. Sometimes, however, the most valuable effort to a business is gathering, converting, and organizing the data to 1NF in the first place.

In addition, business rules must be questioned and understood for the data to be normalized properly. For example, does a student's major require that their faculty advisor be from the department that offers that major? Or, may a student retain the same professor as their advisor even if their newly declared major is not offered by their current advisor's department? Answers to these questions also help determine attribute dependencies, which in turn determine how data is best normalized.

In the end, normalization isn't a rigid recipe that all data must pass through to be valuable or implemented through a relational database. A relational database does require that data be in at least 1NF, but now you know how further normalization analysis can help improve the overall health and value of the data.

Figure 5-34 summarizes the normal forms. Remember the overall goal of normalization: to reduce data redundancy and improve data integrity by helping you structure and separate the attributes of a single large list of data into smaller, related tables. Use the concepts of normalization to achieve the goals of your business rather than satisfy an academic standard, and the process will serve you well.

Normal Form	Description
Unnormalized	A random list of information with many potential data redundancy problems.
1NF	Each column may contain only one value (no repeating values in either in one column or in multiple columns). Entries in each column are atomic values and entries in each column are consistent (no inconsistent units of measurement). No duplicate records.
2NF	All records meet the requirements of 1NF. Each nonkey attribute is fully dependent on the primary key. (If 2NF tables have a single field primary key field, they are probably already in 3NF.)
3NF	All records meet the requirements of 2NF. No transitive dependencies exist. (3NF tables typically have a single field primary key field.) (Relational databases are often implemented on 3NF tables.)
4NF	All records meet the requirements of 3NF. Further data integrity rules have been applied to remove all potential data modification anomalies

FIGURE 5-34   Summary of the normal forms

Summary

- **Define normalization and its purpose**: The normalization process is a series of progressive steps that enable you to identify and correct data redundancy and integrity problems that occur when data is stored in one large table.
- **Identify data modification anomalies**: Data modification anomalies are of three types: insertion, update, and delete anomalies. An insertion anomaly results if you cannot add data to the database due to absence of other data. An update anomaly is marked by data inconsistencies that generally result from data redundancy. A delete anomaly is the unintended loss of data due to deletion of other data
- **Explain functional dependence and other key database terminology**: Functional dependence is a formal name given to the basic idea how of attributes depend on or relate to other attributes in a relation.
- **Describe the normal forms and their purpose**: To correct anomalies in a database, you convert data into multiple tables that progress through a series of sequential normal forms, from first normal form (1NF), second normal form (2NF), third normal form (3NF), and beyond. Each normal form possesses a certain desirable collection of properties and is a progressive step in the normalization process.
- **Analyze data for patterns and build algorithms to convert data to atomic values**: If a field contains more than one atomic value, it is not in 1NF, and that data must be separated into multiple atomic values. Recognizing a pattern to describe the atomic values in a field and building an algorithm to process and separate the data is an important skill. SQL or a relational database QBE tool such as Access Query Design View can help you analyze and separate data into atomic values.
- **Analyze and convert unnormalized data to 1NF**: 1NF requires data to be stored in a single tabular arrangement, that a column may contain only one value, that entries in each column are atomic values, that entries in each column are consistent (no inconsistent units of measurement), and that there are no duplicate rows. SQL or a relational database QBE tool such as Access Query Design View can help you analyze and update your data to 1NF.
- **Analyze and convert 1NF data to 2NF**: The process of moving from 1NF to 2NF revolves around separating attributes into multiple, smaller tables that are functionally dependent on only the primary key field of a given table.
- **Analyze and convert 2NF data to 3NF**: The process of moving from 2NF to 3NF removes all transitive dependencies which typically means that all tables have a single-field primary key field. The process of moving from 2NF to 3NF is an iterative process by which all tables are analyzed for transitive dependencies until none exist.
- **Identify primary and foreign key fields**: When smaller tables are created in the 2NF and 3NF processes, a foreign key field that corresponds to the primary key field of the new table is used in the original table to link the data together.
- **Create lookup tables**: Lookup tables are typically small, one- or two-field tables used to constrain the values in a particular field of another table. The primary key field in the lookup table connects to the foreign key field of the original table.

Key Terms

1NF	composite key
2NF	data modification anomalies
3NF	deletion anomaly
4NF	field
algorithm	first normal form (1NF)
atomic value	foreign key field
attribute	fourth normal form (4NF)
Boyce–Codd normal form (BCNF)	functional dependence
candidate key	functionally dependent
Codd's 12 rules	IIF (Access built-in function)
Codd's relational model of data	insertion anomaly
column	InStr (Access built-in function)

Left (Access built-in function)

Len (Access built-in function)

lookup table

nonkey attribute

nonkey column

normal forms

normalization process

online analytical processing (OLAP)

primary key field

record

relation

repeating group

Right (Access built-in function)

row

second normal form (2NF)

third normal form (3NF)

transitive dependency

tuple

unnormalized

unnormalized relation

update anomaly

Module Review Questions

Problems

1. Which of the following is *not* a benefit of the database normalization process?
   a. Redundant data is minimized.
   b. Data is simplified into only the important attributes.
   c. Data is more accurate.
   d. Data is more consistent.

2. Which of the following is *not* a type of data modification anomaly?
   a. entry
   b. update
   c. deletion
   d. insertion

3. Which of the following best describes functional dependence?
   a. It describes the relationship of attributes in an entity.
   b. It describes the relationship of tuples in an entity.
   c. It describes the relationship of entities as compared to other entities.
   d. It describes the relationship of unnormalized data to 1NF.

4. Which of the following is *not* a characteristic of 1NF?
   a. Data is stored in a single tabular arrangement.
   b. A column may contain only one value.
   c. Each column contains an atomic value.
   d. An entity is related to another entity through the use of the foreign key field.

5. Which of the following is *not* an atomic value?
   a. 15
   b. Oklahoma City
   c. IBM Corporation
   d. Bill Gates

6. Transitive dependencies are removed in which normal form?
   a. 1NF
   b. 2NF
   c. 3NF
   d. 4NF

7. Repeating values in attributes are removed in which normal form?
   a. 1NF
   b. 2NF
   c. 3NF
   d. 4NF

8. Smaller tables are first removed from a single large list in which normal form?
   a. 1NF
   b. 2NF
   c. 3NF
   d. 4NF

9. Which of the following is *not* true of the primary key field of a table?
   a. It may not include nulls.
   b. It must contain unique data for every record.
   c. It must contain numeric data.
   d. It may be used in a relationship with another table.

10. What is the purpose of a foreign key field?
    a. to link a record to data in another table
    b. to shorten the normalization process
    c. to uniquely identify each record
    d. to prevent unauthorized access to a table

11. Who invented normalization?
    a. Thomas John Watson
    b. Edgar F. Codd
    c. Larry Ellison
    d. Grace Hopper

12. Which of the following is least likely to be described as an algorithm?
    a. a recipe
    b. the Rosetta stone
    c. the process of normalization
    d. a mathematical formula

Critical Thinking Questions

1. Using your knowledge of the college environment, convert a table with the following notation to an equivalent collection of tables that are in third normal form:

   `Student (StudentNum, StudentName, (CourseNum, Description, Term, Grade))`

2. Again, using your knowledge of the college environment, convert the following data about student activities (Chess Club, Marching Band, Ski Club, and so forth) into third normal form:

   `Student (StudentID, StudentName, ActivityNum, ActivityName, Advisor)`

JC Consulting Case Exercises

The following exercises are based on the JC Consulting database.

Problems

1. What is the primary key field for the Employees table?
   a. EmployeeID
   b. HireDate
   c. Salary
   d. LastName

2. Open the Employees table. What field contains redundant data that most likely could be moved into a lookup table?
   a. EmployeeID
   b. LastName
   c. Title
   d. Salary

3. Which normal form do these tables adhere to?
   a. unnormalized
   b. 1NF
   c. 2NF
   d. 3NF

4. What foreign key fields does the ProjectLineItems table contain?
   a. ProjectID and TaskID
   b. ProjectLineItemID and ProjectID
   c. ProjectLineItemID and TaskID
   d. ProjectLineItemID, ProjectID, and TaskID

5. What foreign key fields does the Projects table contain?
   a. ClientID and EmployeeID
   b. ProjectID and ClientID
   c. ProjectID and EmployeeID
   d. ProjectID, ClientID, and EmployeeID

6. What foreign key fields does the Clients table contain?
   a. ClientID
   b. Zip
   c. ClientID and Zip
   d. The Clients table does not contain any foreign key fields.

7. The Categories table contains one field, Category. Which table will most be used with it to help constrain the values in a particular field?
   a. Employees
   b. Clients
   c. Projects
   d. TaskMasterList

8. Open the Relationships window and examine the field lists. What does the key symbol to the left of certain field names represent?
   a. the foreign key field for each table
   b. the primary key field for each table
   c. the composite key field for each table
   d. the combination key field for each table

9. Open the TaskMasterList table in Datasheet View. What field contains redundant data that most likely could be pulled into a lookup table?
   a. Per
   b. Description
   c. TaskID
   d. CategoryID or Per

Critical Thinking Questions

1. What is the notation for each of the seven current tables in the JC Consulting database?

2. Examine the Employees table. Note that the data in the Title field contains redundant values and therefore is a candidate for a one-field lookup table. Use your Access Query Design View or SQL skills to create a lookup table named Titles with the unique values in the Title field of the Employees table. List the steps you performed to create the lookup table.

Pitt Fitness Case Exercises

Problems

1. Suppose Pitt Fitness offered personal fitness training and the Customers table were designed as follows:

   Customers (CustomerID, LastName, FirstName, StreetAddress, City, State, ZipCode, EmailAddress, PhoneNumber, BirthDate, InstructorID)

   This design reflects that instructors also work as personal trainers. Which of the following fields is functionally dependent on InstructorID?

   a. LastName

   b. EmailAddress

   c. BirthDate

   d. None of the fields in the table is functionally dependent on InstructorID.

2. Is InstructorLastName a candidate key along with InstructorID in the Instructors table?

   a. Yes, InstructorLastName could be used as a key field because no one instructor has the same last name.

   b. No, InstructorLastName could not be a key field because an instructor might join the team with the same last name as another instructor, such as a sibling.

   c. Yes, InstructorLastName could be used as a key field as long as it was spelled correctly.

   d. Yes, InstructorLastName could be used along with InstructorFirstName as a compound key field.

3. Pitt Fitness is starting to sell its own line of clothing. The following Orders table has been created in the database to record the clothing orders, but the table may not be designed properly. The potential problem may be corrected in which normal form?

OrderID	OrderDate	CustomerID	ItemID	Quantity
2501	10/1/2021	107	S-61	1
2502	10/1/2021	108	S-59	1
			P-25	1
			T-19	3
2503	10/1/2021	105	S-45	1
			T-91	4
2504	10/1/2021	109	P-24	1

   a. first normal form

   b. second normal form

   c. third normal form

   d. It is correctly designed.

4. Pitt Fitness modified the Orders table as follows, but it may still not be designed properly. The potential problem may be corrected in which normal form?

OrderID (key)	OrderDate	CustomerID	ItemID (key)	Description	Price
2501	10/1/2021	107	S-61	T-shirt L	$25
2502	10/1/2021	108	S-59	T-shirt M	$25
2502	10/1/2021	108	P-25	Yoga Pants M	$50
2502	10/1/2021	108	T-19	Tank L	$18
2503	10/1/2021	105	S-45	T-shirt S	$25
2503	10/1/2021	105	T-91	Tank S	$18
2504	10/1/2021	109	P-24	Yoga Pants L	$50

   a. first normal form

   b. second normal form

   c. third normal form

   d. It is correctly designed.

5. Pitt Fitness modified the Reservations table as follows, but it may have an improper design. The potential problem may be corrected in which normal form?

Reservation (key)	Date	CustomerID	ClassID	Instructor	LastName	FirstName
2100001	1/5/2021	107	39	RS02	Sisto	Robert
2100002	1/8/2021	108	24	VP01	Pegues	Vicki
2100003	1/10/2021	108	10	RS02	Sisto	Robert
2100004	1/10/2021	108	10	NT01	Tahan	Neda
2100005	1/12/2021	105	8	NT01	Tahan	Neda
2100006	1/13/2021	105	35	VP01	Pegues	Vicki
2100007	1/13/2021	109	33	MS01	Said	Memo

a. first normal form
b. second normal form
c. third normal form
d. It is correctly designed.

6. Pitt Fitness asks you to create a query using the following table to find any repeating values of customer and date. What query function in Access should you use when you design this query?

Reservation (key)	Date	CustomerID	ClassID	InstructorID	LastName	FirstName
2100001	1/5/2021	107	39	RS02	Sisto	Robert
2100002	1/8/2021	108	24	VP01	Pegues	Vicki
2100003	1/10/2021	108	10	RS02	Sisto	Robert
2100004	1/10/2021	108	10	NT01	Tahan	Neda
2100005	1/12/2021	105	8	NT01	Tahan	Neda
2100006	1/13/2021	105	35	VP01	Pegues	Vicki
2100007	1/13/2021	109	33	MS01	Said	Memo

a. Totals – Group by
b. Parameters
c. Append
d. This cannot be accomplished in an Access query.

7. The Reservations table is organized as follows:
`Reservations (ReservationID, ClassID, ClassInstructors, ClassPrice, OtherFees, CustomerID)`
Knowing about normalization, what superior way could you use to organize the data?

a. Create two tables: `Reservations (ReservationID, ClassID, ClassInstructors, CustomerID); ClassPrice (ClassID, ClassPrice, OtherFees)`
b. Create three tables: `Reservations (ReservationID, ClassID, ClassInstructors, CustomerID); ClassPrice (ClassID, ClassPrice); ClassOtherFees (ClassID, OtherFees)`
c. Add a new field to the table: `Reservations (ReservationID, ClassID, ClassInstructors, PriceID, ClassPrice, OtherFees, CustomerID)`
d. The data is organized in the best possible way.

8. The table `ClassInstructors (ClassID, InstructorID)` could be considered what type of table?
a. make table
b. Codd table
c. lookup table
d. anomaly table

9. In the following table, which field does *not* contain an atomic value?

Reservation (key)	Date	CustomerID	ClassID	InstructorID	Name
2100001	1/5/2021	107	39	RS02	Robert Sisto
2100002	1/8/2021	108	24	VP01	Vicki Pegues
2100003	1/10/2021	108	10	RS02	Robert Sisto
2100004	1/10/2021	108	10	NT01	Neda Tahan
2100005	1/12/2021	105	8	NT01	Neda Tahan
2100006	1/13/2021	105	35	VP01	Vicki Pegues
2100007	1/13/2021	109	33	MS01	Memo Said

a. Reservation
b. Date
c. InstructorID
d. Name

10. What is the notation for the following new table?

OrderID (key)	OrderDate	CustomerID
2501	10/1/2021	107
2502	10/1/2021	108
2502	10/1/2021	108
2502	10/1/2021	108
2503	10/1/2021	105
2503	10/1/2021	105
2504	10/1/2021	109

a. `Orders (OrderID, OrderDate, CustomerID, ItemID)`
b. `Orders (OrderID, OrderDate, CustomerID)`
c. `Orders (OrderID, OrderDate, CustomerID)`
d. `Orders (OrderID, OrderDate, CustomerID)`

Critical Thinking Questions

1. Assume that you designed the field LengthOfTime in the Classes table in the Pitt Fitness database. The LengthOfTime field has data such as 60 minutes, 30 minutes, 1 hour, and 15 minutes. Is this the correct way to record this data? If not, what would be a better method?

2. Originally, Pitt Fitness had all their data in one large Excel spreadsheet. Suppose you were hired to help Pitt Fitness create a database to replace the spreadsheet. Outline the major steps you would perform to create a normalized database from the data in the spreadsheet.

Sports Physical Therapy Case Exercises

Problems

1. How do you diagram the functional dependence on TherapyCode in the Therapies table?
   a. TherapyCode + Description, UnitOfTime
   b. TherapyCode (Description, UnitOfTime)
   c. TherapyCode → Description, UnitOfTime
   d. TherapyCode = Description, UnitOfTime

2. What would be a candidate key for the Session table, besides the current key field of SessionNum? The design of the Session table is Session (<u>SessionNum</u>, SessionDate, PatientNum, LengthOfSession, TherapistID, TherapyCode).
   a. SessionDate
   b. PatientNum and TherapistID (compound key)
   c. TherapyCode and PatientNum (compound key)
   d. SessionNum is the only appropriate key field.

3. What foreign key(s) does the Session table contain? `Session (`<u>`SessionNum`</u>`, SessionDate, PatientNum, LengthOfSession, TherapistID, TherapyCode).`
   a. PatientNum, TherapistID, TherapyCode
   b. PatientNum only
   c. PatientNum and TherapistID only
   d. This table does not have any foreign keys.

4. What field is the link between the Therapist and Session tables?
   a. PatientNum
   b. TherapistID
   c. SessionNum
   d. TherapyCode

5. Suppose the Session table is set up as follows. Is this design correct? If not, in which normal form would you correct it?

Session							
SessionNum	SessionDate	PatientNum	LengthOfSession	TherapistID	Last	First	TherapyCode
27	10/10/2021	1011	45	JR085	Risk	Jonathan	92507
28	10/11/2021	1016	30	AS648	Shields	Anthony	97010
29	10/11/2021	1014	60	SW124	Wilder	Steven	97014
30	10/12/2021	1013	30	BM273	McClain	Bridgette	97033
31	10/15/2021	1016	90	AS648	Shields	Anthony	98960
32	10/16/2021	1018	15	JR085	Risk	Jonathan	97035
33	10/17/2021	1017	60	SN852	Nair	Saritha	97039
34	10/17/2021	1015	45	BM273	McClain	Bridgette	97112
35	10/18/2021	1010	30	SW124	Wilder	Steven	97113
36	10/18/2021	1019	75	SN852	Nair	Saritha	97116
37	10/19/2021	1020	30	BM273	McClain	Bridgette	97124
38	10/19/2021	1021	60	AS648	Shields	Anthony	97535

   a. first normal form
   b. second normal form
   c. third normal form
   d. It is correctly designed; it does not violate any form.

204

6. Patient Number 1014 is receiving three treatments in one session. Is the following design correct for the Session table?

SessionNum	SessionDate	PatientNum	LengthOfSession	TherapistID	TherapyCode
					Session
27	10/10/2021	1011	45	JR085	92507
28	10/11/2021	1016	30	AS648	97010
29	10/11/2021	1014	60	SW124	97014
			15		97016
			15		97018
30	10/12/2021	1013	30	BM273	97033
31	10/15/2021	1016	90	AS648	98960
32	10/16/2021	1018	15	JR085	97035
33	10/17/2021	1017	60	SN852	97039
34	10/17/2021	1015	45	BM273	97112
35	10/18/2021	1010	30	SW124	97113
36	10/18/2021	1019	75	SN852	97116
37	10/19/2021	1020	30	BM273	97124
38	10/19/2021	1021	60	AS648	97535

a. Yes, this is a good way to record multiple sessions.
b. Yes, but the two additional sessions do not need to be recorded. The time for the original session can just be increased.
c. No, it is not in first normal form (1NF).
d. No, the TherapyCode field is not necessary.

7. Suppose the Therapist table is set up as follows. Why is this table not in 1NF?

TherapistID	LastName	Street	City	State	ZipCode
AS648	Anthony Shields	5222 Eagle Court	Palm Rivers	TX	72511
BM273	Bridgette McClain	385 West Mill St.	Waterville	TX	76658
JR085	Jonathan Risk	1010 650 North	Palm Rivers	TX	72511
SN852	Saritha Nair	25 North Elm St.	Livewood	TX	72512
SW124	Steven Wilder	7354 Rockville Road	San Vista	TX	72510

a. The table contains repeating groups.
b. A field does not contain atomic values.
c. The table includes duplicate records.
d. The table is in 1NF.

8. When a patient comes into the Sports Physical Therapy, they often have insurance to cover some or all of the cost of the therapy sessions. Assuming that a few patients might use two insurance companies (e.g., a spouse's insurance might supplement the patient's insurance), how would you record the insurance information ensuring that the table is normalized?

a. Add two fields to the Patient table: InsuranceCompany and PolicyNumber. For patients with two policies, enter an additional record.
b. Create a new table that includes all the data from the Patient table and the new fields, InsuranceCompany and PolicyNumber.
c. Create a new Insurance table that includes the PatientNum, InsuranceCompany, and PolicyNumber fields. The Insurance table could have an autoincrementing key field or a compound key, PatientNum and PolicyNumber.
d. Add two fields to the Session table: InsuranceCompany and PolicyNumber. For patients with two policies, enter an additional record.

9. A new table needs to be added to the Sports Physical Therapy database to track which sports the patients are playing. This data will be used to analyze the results of the therapies. Assuming that many patients play multiple sports, how would you design the table?

   a. `SportsPlayed (PatientNum, SportName)`

   b. `SportsPlayed (PatientNum, SportName)`

   c. `SportsPlayed (SportsPlayedID, PatientNum, SportName)`

   d. `SportsPlayed (PatientNum, SportName1, SportName2, SportName3)`

10. The Sports Physical Therapy clinic uses supplies when conducting therapies on patients. The database administrator is creating a table that lists all the possible supplies that the clinic orders. The design of this table is `Supplies (SupplyID, Description, Price, SupplierID, SupplierName, SupplierAddress, SupplierPhone)`. Is this table designed correctly? If not, what normal form would correct it?

    a. no; first normal form

    b. no; second normal form

    c. no; third normal form

    d. yes, it is correctly designed.

Critical Thinking Questions

1. When the Sports Physical Therapy database was created, the database designers identified PatientNum and PatientSocialSecurityNumber as candidate keys for the Patient table. Why was PatientSocialSecurityNumber not chosen to be the key field of that table?

2. What is the notation for each table in the Sports Physical Therapy database?

DATABASE DESIGN: RELATIONSHIPS

INTRODUCTION

Normalizing and converting a single list of data into third normal form (3NF) or beyond is an important step toward implementing a healthy relational database. As you normalize data, a second major step in creating a relational database requires that you connect the entities into correct one-to-many relationships. Often, you perform the tasks of data normalization and defining relationships between tables in a back-and-forth process. As you isolate entities and their attributes to create tables, you are also thinking about and discussing the relationships between an entity and the rest of the database.

A database designer works with business analysts and other key users to make sure that business rules describing the operational decisions of the business are considered in the relational design. For example, the business rule for how a company's sales force interacts with its customers would affect the implementation of a relational database with SalesRep, Customers, and Orders tables. In both cases, the Customers table would no doubt be linked to the Orders table in a one-to-many relationship. But the connection to the SalesRep table could change based on how the business functioned. If a sales representative was assigned to an exclusive territory with specific customers, the SalesRep and the Customers tables would have a one-to-many relationship. However, if a sales representative could work with *any* customer, then those two tables would have no direct relationship. In that case, the SalesRep table would be linked to the Orders table in a one-to-many relationship.

Describing the attributes needed for each entity as well as the relationships between the entities based on business rules is known as **information-level design**, or conceptual design, and is independent of the particular relational database management system that the organization ultimately uses. This process typically involves creating an entity-relationship (E-R) diagram to visually represent the database design. Implementing the entities, attributes, constraints, and relationships in a particular RDBMS is called the **physical-level design**.

The database design process can be recursive such as when a new business rule is detected or management requests new information, which often changes how the relational database system should be designed. These revelations require modifying relational database entities and relationships. After discussing what data the company wants to analyze with management, business analysts, or users, it's not uncommon for new insights and requirements to emerge that require modifications to entities or relationships.

In this module, you will continue studying the process of database design. You will document and build the relationships between tables that clearly define the current relational database as well as allow it to change and adapt to new requirements. In addition, you will learn how to successfully address many table relationship issues including one-to-one, one-to-many, and many-to-many relationships. Several Your Turn activities use the professor-student-assignment.accdb database, which contains the data converted into five tables from Module 5, to reinforce the concepts.

USER VIEWS

As discussed in previous modules, a **view** of data is a particular collection of fields and records from one or more entities. You can create a view of data from a relational database with SQL SELECT FROM WHERE commands or by using a QBE tool such as Access Query Design View. A **user view** of the data is the specific data needed by a person or process for a particular task.

For example, an employee may need a particular user view of data to enter or report on a certain business issue. When you build a relational database, collecting current company forms and reports helps identify all of the current user views and attributes you need to consider in the database design. Perhaps the attributes from each user view have already been identified and converted in a previous normalization process. If not, however, reviewing all of the user views gives the database designer an opportunity to confirm the data requirements of the business as well as learn more about business rules that affect the relationships between the tables.

YOUR TURN 6-1

After reviewing current reports that show professor-student advisee information, you notice that several user views include the professor's office number and email address. Neither piece of data was provided in the original list of data at the beginning of the normalization process in Module 5. Given these attributes are functionally dependent on the ProfID data, add these fields to the Professors table.

As you learned in previous modules, you can add the new fields to the Professors table using SQL commands or define them directly in Table Design View. After adding the new fields, the Professors table should look like Figure 6-1 in Table Design View.

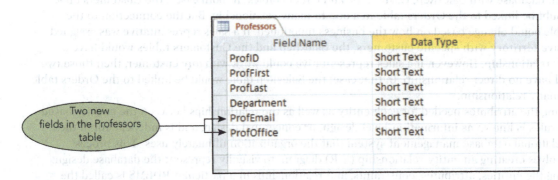

FIGURE 6-1   Updated Professors table in Table Design View

The Professors table now contains the two new fields, but neither new field contains any data yet, as shown in Figure 6-2. The Professors table contains only 10 records, so it would not be time-consuming to manually enter the ProfEmail and ProfOffice values for the 10 records. But what if you had a hundred, a thousand, or even tens of thousands of records in this table? Later in this module (Your Turn 6-8), you'll learn how to programmatically update the values of new ProfEmail and ProfOffice fields based on a connection to the unique ProfID field.

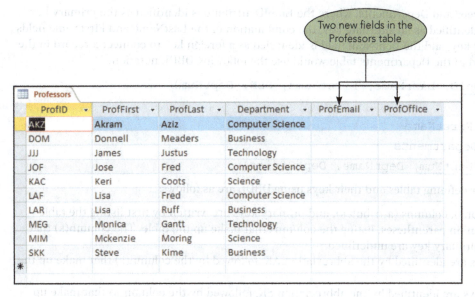

Two new fields in the Professors table

Professors					
ProfID	ProfFirst	ProfLast	Department	ProfEmail	ProfOffice
AKZ	Akram	Aziz	Computer Science		
DOM	Donnell	Meaders	Business		
JJJ	James	Justus	Technology		
JOF	Jose	Fred	Computer Science		
KAC	Keri	Coots	Science		
LAF	Lisa	Fred	Computer Science		
LAR	Lisa	Ruff	Business		
MEG	Monica	Gantt	Technology		
MIM	Mckenzie	Moring	Science		
SKK	Steve	Kime	Business		

FIGURE 6-2 Updated Professors table in Table Datasheet View

DOCUMENTING A RELATIONAL DATABASE DESIGN

After you review all of the current user views, ask about new requirements, inquire about business rules, and understand the relationships between the entities, you're ready to start documenting the relational database design.

Relational database design documentation generally identifies the following items:

1. The attributes needed for each normalized entity

2. The primary key field for each entity

3. The indexes and other properties needed to describe each attribute and entity

4. The proper one-to-many relationships between the entities

Updating the Professors table with the new ProfEmail and ProfOffice attributes gives you the following notation for the five entities in the student-advisor-assignment database:

```
Students (StudentID, StudentFirst, StudentLast)
Professors (ProfID, ProfFirst, ProfLast, Department, ProfEmail, ProfOffice)
DeclaredMajors (ID, Major, StudentID, ProfID, MajorDate)
Departments (Department)
Majors (Major)
```

Database Design Language (DBDL)

The notation used so far does a good job of identifying the entities and primary key field for each table, but it doesn't clearly identify the indexes needed for each entity nor the relationships between tables. One approach for expanding the definition of each table uses an extended notation called **Database Design Language (DBDL)**.

DBDL expands the definition of an entity by specifying different types of key fields. As a reminder, the **primary key field** is a field that contains unique data for each record and is underlined in the notation. An **alternate key** is a field that contains unique data for each record in the table but is not used as the primary key field for security or other reasons. An alternate key is identified the abbreviation as **AK**. A **secondary key** represents a field or combination of fields that may not be unique, but is commonly used for retrieval and thus should be indexed. A secondary key is identified by the abbreviation **SK**. A **foreign key field** is identified as **FK** and is used to connect a record in one table to more information in another table.

The two tables Employees and Departments, where the EmpID attribute is identified as the primary key field, the SSN attribute is identified as an alternate key, the combination of the LastName and FirstName fields is identified as a secondary key, and the DeptNum field is identified as a foreign key to connect a record in the Employees table to a record in the Departments table would use the following DBDL notation:

Employees (EmpID, LastName, FirstName, SSN, DeptNum)

AK SSN

SK LastName, FirstName

FK DeptNum → Departments

Departments (DeptNum, DeptName, DeptOffice)

The expanded rules for defining tables and their keys using DBDL are as follows:

- Tables (relations), columns (attributes), and primary keys are written by first listing the table name and then, in parentheses, listing the columns that make up the table. The column(s) that make up the primary key are underlined.
- Alternate keys are identified by the abbreviation AK, followed by the column(s) that make up the alternate key.
- Secondary keys are identified by the abbreviation SK, followed by the column(s) that make up the secondary key.
- Foreign keys are identified by the abbreviation FK, followed by the column(s) that make up the foreign key. Foreign keys are followed by an arrow pointing to the table identified by the foreign key.

Q & A 6-1

Question: How would you write the DBDL for the five tables in the student-advisor-assignments.accdb Access database?

Answer: The DBDL for the five tables in the student-advisor-assignments database is shown in Figure 6-3.

The DBDL for the five tables in the student-advisor-assignments.accdb Access database shown in Figure 6-3 is based on these business assumptions:

- The records in the Students table are commonly sorted by the combination of the StudentLast and StudentFirst fields.
- The records in the Professors table are commonly sorted by the combination of the ProfLast and ProfFirst fields and contain one foreign key field, Department, that links to the Departments table.
- The records in the DeclaredMajors table contains three foreign key fields—Major, StudentID, and ProfID—that link back to the Majors, Students, and Professors tables.

Students (StudentID, StudentFirst, StudentLast)
    SK StudentLast, StudentFirst
Professors (ProfID, ProfFirst, ProfLast, Department, ProfEmail, ProfOffice)
    SK ProfLast, ProfFirst
    FK Department → Departments
DeclaredMajors (ID, Major, StudentID, ProfID, MajorDate)
    FK Major → Majors
    FK StudentID → Students
    FK ProfID → Professors
Departments (Department)
Majors (Major)

FIGURE 6-3   DBDL for the tables in the student-advisor-assignment database

SETTING KEYS AND INDEXES

Every relational database management system has a different interface for identifying the primary key field for a table. Recall from Module 4 that you can also programmatically set a primary key field or an index using SQL.

Also recall from earlier modules that an **index** is a separate file that keeps track of the alphabetical order of the values in a particular field. Indexes are created to improve overall database performance when queries request a sort order for records. Because some overhead is required to create and maintain an index, not every field should be indexed. Only those fields that are commonly used for sorting should be indexed. Primary key fields are automatically indexed, but as a database developer, the DBDL notation helps you determine other fields in each table that should be indexed.

YOUR TURN 6-2

Set the primary key fields and indexes on the secondary keys as identified in the DBDL for the five tables in the student-advisor-assignments database in Access. Use Access Table Design View or SQL as desired.

Table Design View showing the primary key field and indexes for the five tables of the student-advisor-assignments database is shown in Figures 6-4 through 6-8.

Figure 6-4 shows Table Design View for the Professors table. The ProfID field is set as the primary key field and is automatically indexed in the Indexes dialog box with the index name of PrimaryKey. The ProfName index was created with an ascending (default) sort order on the ProfLast and ProfFirst fields. The **Unique** property for the ProfName index is set to No, which allows for the rare but potential situation where you have more than one professor in the Professors table with the same first and last names.

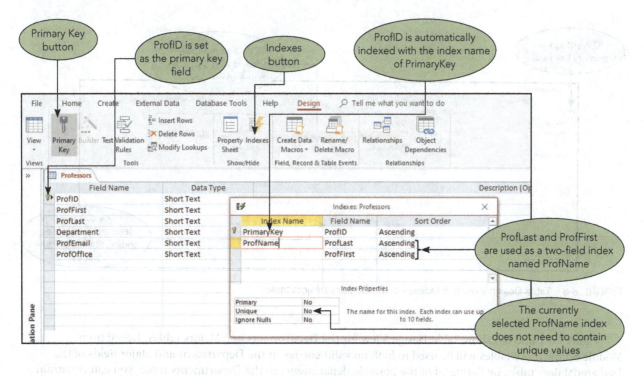

FIGURE 6-4 Table Design View and indexes of the Professors table

Figure 6-5 shows Table Design View for the Students table. The StudentID field is set as the primary key field and is automatically indexed in the Indexes dialog box with the index name of PrimaryKey. The StudentName index was created with an ascending (default) sort order on the StudentLast and StudentFirst fields. The Unique property for the StudentName index is set to No, which allows for the potential situation where you have more than one student in the Students table with the same first and last names.

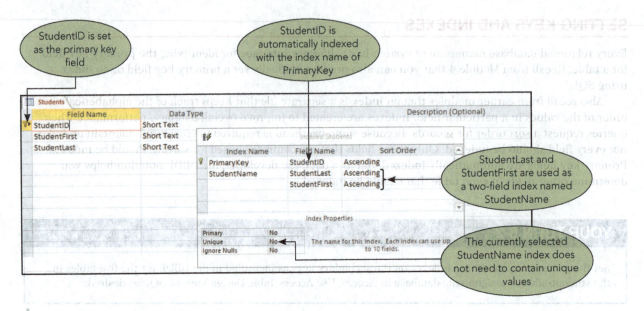

FIGURE 6-5 Table Design View and indexes of the Students table

Figure 6-6 shows Table Design View for the DeclaredMajors table. It currently has only one index named PrimaryKey, which was automatically added to the ID field when the ID field was established as the primary key field for the table. The foreign key fields of StudentID, ProfID, and Major are also candidates for indexing, but in this case, you decide to not set any more indexes on this table until you have more experience on how the application performs when the database is fully implemented.

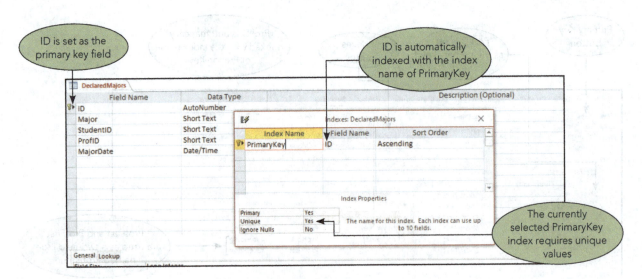

FIGURE 6-6 Table Design View and indexes of the DeclaredMajors table

Figures 6-7 and 6-8 show Table Design View for the Departments and Majors tables. Recall from Module 5 how these tables will be used to look up valid entries in the Department and Major fields of the DeclaredMajors table. By listing all of the possible departments in the Departments table, you can constrain the values in the Departments field in the DeclaredMajors table, a foreign key field, to only those values in the list. Constraining the possible foreign key field Department values to the specific list in the Departments table improves data entry accuracy and consistency of the values of the Department field in the DeclaredMajors table. Doing so also helps prevent update anomalies as the same department cannot be entered in two or more ways. The same benefits apply to the Major foreign key field in the DeclaredMajors table. This foreign key field will also be constrained to the list of valid entries stored in the Majors table.

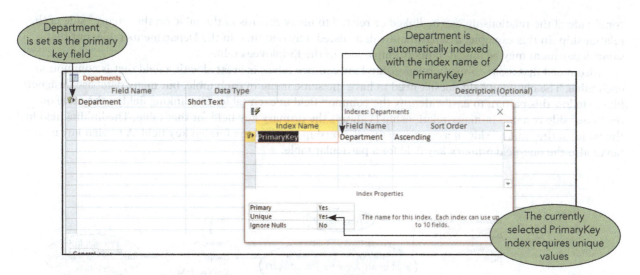

FIGURE 6-7 Table Design View of the Departments table and indexes

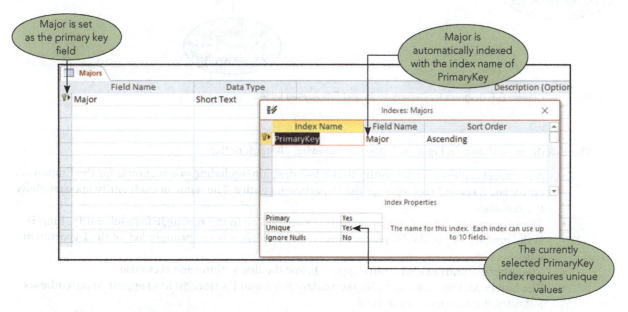

FIGURE 6-8 Table Design View and indexes of the Majors table

ENTITY-RELATIONSHIP (E-R) DIAGRAMS

Another popular way to diagram the fields and relationships between tables is to create an **entity-relationship (E-R) diagram**. An **E-R diagram** uses rectangles to represent the entities (tables) and lines to represent the relationships between the tables. As such, it provides a more visual representation of the entities, attributes, and relationships between the entities than DBDL notation.

Recall the DBDL definition for the two related tables, Employees and Departments.

```
Employees (EmpID, LastName, FirstName, SSN, DeptNum)

AK SSN

SK LastName, FirstName

FK DeptNum → Departments

Departments (DeptNum, DeptName, DeptOffice)
```

The corresponding E-R diagram is shown in Figure 6-9 with a one-to-many relationship between the Departments and Employees table. A **one-to-many relationship** means that one record in the table on the "one" side of the relationship can be linked or related to many records in the table on the "many" side of the relationship. In this example, a department will be listed only one time in the Departments table, but that same department may be linked to many employees in the Employees table.

Also recall that a one-to-many relationship between two tables is created with a field that is common to each table. The common field doesn't need to have the same name in each table, but many database designers like to follow this pattern to easily identify the common field in each table. The linking field in the table on the "one" side of a one-to-many relationship is always the primary key field for that table. The linking field in the table on the "many" side of a one-to-many relationship is called the foreign key field. A foreign key field is never also the one-field primary key field for a particular table.

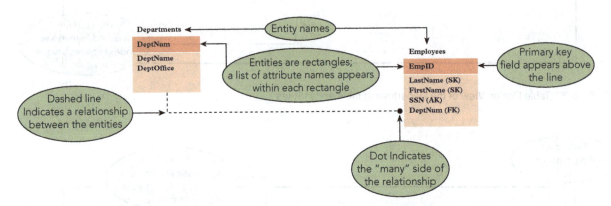

FIGURE 6-9 Classic E-R diagram for Departments and Employees tables

The E-R diagram shown in Figure 6-9 has the following characteristics:

- A rectangle represents each entity in the E-R diagram, including one rectangle for the Employees entity and a second rectangle for the Departments entity. The name of each entity appears above the rectangle.
- The primary key for each entity appears above the line in the rectangle for each entity. EmpID is the primary key of the Employees entity, and DeptNum is the primary key of the Departments entity.
- The other columns in each entity appear below the line within each rectangle.
- The letters AK (alternate key), SK (secondary key), and FK (foreign key) appear in parentheses following the field name as needed.
- For each foreign key, a dotted line leads from the rectangle that corresponds to the table being identified to the rectangle that corresponds to the table containing the foreign key. The dot at the end of the line indicates the "many" part of the one-to-many relationship between the Departments and Employees entities.
- While it's not required to place the Departments table on the left side of the diagram, the English language is read from left to right, and a LEFT join in SQL always refers to the table on the "one" side of the relationship, so placing the "one" or "parent" table on the left side of diagram when possible improves readability.

There are several variations of E-R diagram notation, but they almost always include a rectangle to represent the entity as well as some degree of information about the attributes of an entity positioned within the rectangle. The relationship line between entities varies among different notations.

Crow's Foot Notation

Another popular E-R diagram implementation is called **crow's foot notation**, which uses a symbol on the side of the "many" entity that resembles a crow's foot as shown in Figure 6-10. The diagram can be read as "one and only one" record in the Departments table contains zero, one, or many records in the Employees table. In crow's foot notation, specific attributes for each entity are not listed within each entity rectangle.

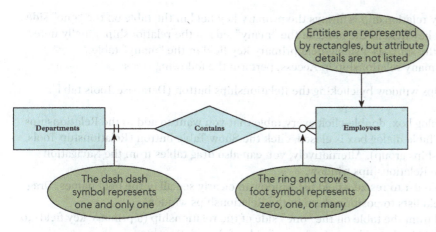

FIGURE 6-10   Crow's foot notation

Microsoft Access E-R Diagram in the Relationships window

Another popular representation of an E-R diagram is the one used by Microsoft Access, which displays the number 1 and the infinity symbol at the ends of the link line to identify the two sides of a one-to-many relationship, as shown in Figure 6-11.

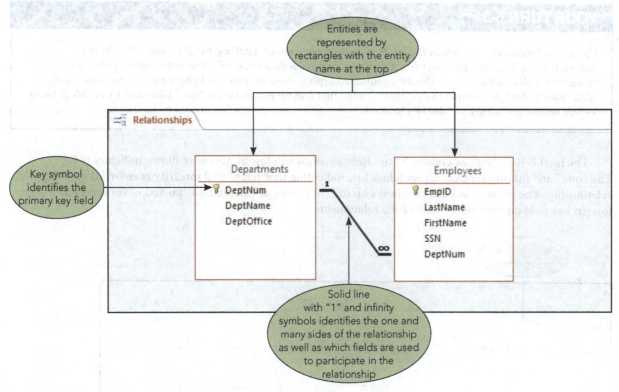

FIGURE 6-11   Access representation of an E-R diagram

In Access, the 1 and infinity symbols are only displayed on one-to-many relationships that enforce referential integrity, an important concept covered in Module 1 and reinforced throughout other modules. For one-to-many relationships that do not enforce referential integrity, no symbols are shown at either end of the link line.

Recall that **referential integrity** prevents the creation of **orphan records**, records in the "many" side of a relationship that do not have a matching value in the "one" side of the relationship. In this case, enforcing referential integrity means that you could not enter a record in the Employees table with a DeptNum value that didn't first exist in the Departments table.

In Access, the link line specifically points to the fields that create the relationship instead of pointing to the edge of the entity's rectangle in general. For example, in Figure 6-11 note that the relationship line is specifically joining the tables by pointing to the common DeptNum field in each table. Also note that the field to link two tables in a one-to-many relationship is always the primary key field in the table on the "one" side of the relationship and the foreign key field in the table on the "many" side of the relationship. Finally note that the foreign key field is never the same as a single-field primary key field in the "many" table.

To link two tables in a one-to-many relationship in Access, perform the following steps:

- Open the Relationships window by clicking the Relationships button (Database Tools tab | Relationships group).
- In the Show Table dialog box, double-click every table that you want to add to the Relationships window. If the Show Table dialog box is closed, click the Show Table button (Relationship Tools Design tab | Relationships group). Alternatively, you can also drag tables from the Navigation Pane directly into the Relationships window.
- Drag the edge of a field list to resize a field list window to clearly see all of the field names. Drag the title bar of the field lists to position them in the Relationships window.
- Drag the linking field from the table on the "one" side of the relationship (a primary key field) to the specific linking field in the table on the "many" side of the relationship.
- Review the information in the Edit Relationships dialog box to make sure you have selected the correct linking fields, and then click Enforce Referential Integrity in the Edit Relationships dialog box if desired. (Note that you can only enforce referential integrity if the table on the "many" side of the relationship currently contains no orphan records).
- Click OK in the Edit Relationships dialog box.

YOUR TURN 6-3

Use the Relationships window in the student-advisor-assignment database to relate the tables in the associated E-R diagram. This data contains no orphan records, so you will be able to enforce referential integrity on all relationships. If the data contained orphan records, you would first have to use your query or SQL skills to find the records in the "many" table that had no match in the "one" table and fix or delete them before referential integrity could be enforced.

The final E-R diagram as created by the Relationships window in Access is shown in Figure 6-12. The "one" and infinity symbols on each link line indicating that referential integrity is enforced on every relationship. The primary key field is always on the "one" side of the relationship and never serves as a foreign key field on the "many" side of the relationship.

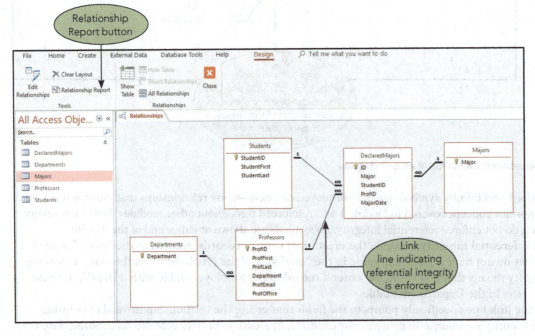

FIGURE 6-12 Access representation of an E-R diagram

The Relationships window is effectively the E-R diagram, or blueprint, for a relational database in Access, so if you are working with a relational database in Access, you should also be able to complete the following tasks.

To quickly create a report showing the relationships in the Relationships window, perform the following step:

- Click the Relationship Report button (Relationship Tools Design tab | Tools group).

To delete a relationship in the Relationships window, perform the following step:

- Right-click the link line, and then click Delete on the shortcut menu.

To modify a relationship in the Relationships window, perform the following steps:

- Right-click the link line, and then click Edit Relationship on the shortcut menu.
- Make the desired changes in the Edit Relationships dialog box, and then click OK.

Another term that describes relational databases is cardinality. In general, cardinality refers to the number of items in a set. In the context of a database, **cardinality** refers to the uniqueness of data values contained in a single field.

High cardinality means that a field contains many unique or uncommon values, and low cardinality means that a field contains only a few unique values. You could also say that low cardinality refers to many repeating values. For example, a LastName field would have a normal to high cardinality in that it would contain some repeating values, but on the whole, most of the values would be unique. A primary key field has high cardinality because all values in the field are, by definition, unique.

Foreign key fields have low cardinality given they are specifically created to allow for repeating values. The fields of Department in the Professors table and Major in the DeclaredMajors table both have low cardinality given the values in each field are constrained to a specific list, so those fields contain no unique values.

The term cardinality also sometimes refers to the actual relationships between tables. For example, some database designers refer to the relationships between tables as a one-to-one, one-to-many, or many-to-many cardinality.

THE ENTITY-RELATIONSHIP MODEL (ERM)

You have examined E-R diagrams that document entities, attributes, keys, and relationships. Another way to document a relational database is the **entity-relationship model**. The **E-R model** (also called **ERM**) uses rectangles for entities and diamonds for relationships. The lines that connect the entities contain notation to identify whether they are on the "one" or "many" side of a relationship, as shown in Figure 6-13 for the Departments and Employees example.

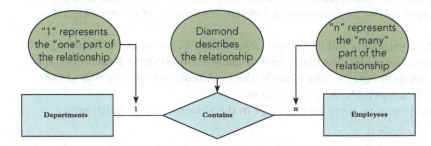

FIGURE 6-13   ERM for one-to-many relationship

In Figure 6-13, the Departments table is on the "1" side of the relationship, and the Employees table is on the "many" or "m" side of the relationship because one department can contain many employees.

An ERM can also be used to identify a "many-to-many" relationship between two tables as shown in Figure 6-14. A **many-to-many relationship** exists when one record in one entity can be related to many records in another entity. Figure 6-14 documents that one student can have many declared majors over time and one professor can also advise many students.

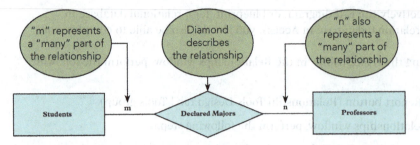

FIGURE 6-14 ERM for many-to-many relationship

Practically all relational databases have many-to-many relationships, but many-to-many relationships cannot be *directly* created between two tables in a relational database management system. To implement a many-to-many relationship in a relational database, you must insert a physical entity between the two tables to link them together. In the ERM, the middle entity is called a **composite entity**, as diagrammed in Figure 6-15.

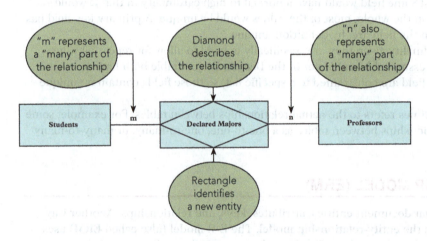

FIGURE 6-15 ERM for many-to-many relationship with a composite entity

In a physical implementation of the relational database, the composite entity is called a **junction table**. The junction table serves on the "many" side of a one-to-many relationship with each of the two original tables, as shown in Figure 6-12.

Figure 6-12 also shows that both the Students and Professors tables have a one-to-many relationship with the DeclaredMajors table. By definition, two tables that have a one-to-many relationship with the same table have a many-to-many relationship with each other. In other words, the DeclaredMajors table serves as the composite entity in an ERM and as a junction table in an E-R diagram.

Figure 6-12 identifies the following many-to-many relationships in the student-advisor-assignment database:

- Students and Professors: One student can be assigned to many professors (over time) and one professor can advise many students.
- Students and Majors: One student can declare many majors (over time) and one major can be declared by many students.
- Professors and Majors: One professor can advise many majors and one major can be advised by many professors.

If desired, you also can indicate attributes in the ERM by placing them in ovals and attaching them to the corresponding rectangles (entities), as shown in Figure 6-16. As in other notations, primary key fields are underlined.

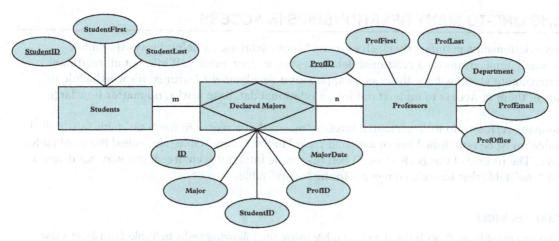

FIGURE 6-16 ERM for many-to-many relationship with attributes

Q & A 6-2

Question: How would you create the ERM for the five tables in the student-advisor-assignments.accdb Access database without including the attributes?

Answer: The ERM for the five tables in the student-advisor-assignments.accdb database is shown in Figure 6-17.

Figure 6-17 represents a basic ERM for the five tables in the student-advisor-assignments.accdb database.

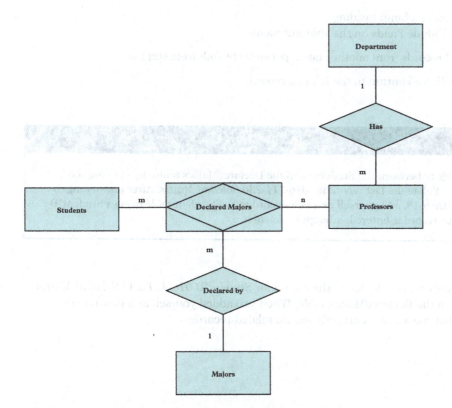

FIGURE 6-17 ERM for the five tables in the student-advisor-assignments database

EXPLORING ONE-TO-MANY RELATIONSHIPS IN ACCESS

One-to-many relationships manifest themselves in an Access database in helpful ways that allow you to build small applications on a relational database system very quickly. While not all relational database management systems have these same application development features, it's worthwhile to explore a few of them in Access to understand how a relational database works, no matter how large or small.

A one-to-many relationship with referential integrity means that a record in the "one" table (also called the parent table) must be established before a related record in the "many" table (also called the child table) can be entered. The reverse of this is also true. When referential integrity is enforced, you may not delete a record in the "one" table that has related records in the "many" table.

Table Datasheet View

In Access, you can quickly work with the data in a table using the following tasks in Table Datasheet View. To open a table in Table Datasheet View, perform the following step:

- Double-click the table in the Navigation Pane.

To add a new record, perform the following step:

- Click the New button (Home tab | Records group). New records are always entered at the bottom of the table.

To delete a record, perform the following steps:

- Click the blank record selector button to the left of the record.
- Click the Delete button (Home tab | Records group).

To edit a record, perform the following step:

- Click the cell that contains the field value you want to edit, and then use the Backspace, Delete, and other character keys on the keyboard to make the desired change.

To hide or unhide columns in Table Datasheet View, perform the following steps:

- Right-click a field name (column heading).
- Click Hide Fields or Unhide Fields on the shortcut menu.

To display or hide the related records from another table, perform the following step:

- Click the expand (collapse) button to the left of a record.

YOUR TURN 6-4

Test the rules of referential integrity between the Students and the DeclaredMajors tables by opening the Students table and attempting to delete the last record for *016-111-230 Soledad Mattis*. After responding to the error message shown in Figure 6-18, add yourself as a new record to the Student table using a StudentID value of *111-222-333*. Once your record is entered, attempt to delete it.

As shown in Figure 6-18, Access refused to delete the record for StudentID *016-111-230 Soledad Mattis* because it found related records in the DeclaredMajors table. When you added yourself as a new record, however, you could also delete that record as it currently has no related records.

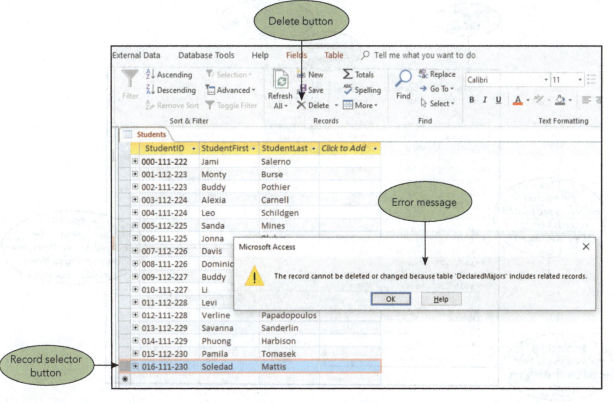

FIGURE 6-18 Attempting to delete a record in the Students table that has related records in the DeclaredMajors table

Subdatasheets

In Table Datasheet View, you can display the records from a related table by clicking the expand button to the left of the record. The related records appear in a **subdatasheet** below that record. In other words, in Table Datasheet View, you can view the records of a table on the "one" side of a one-to-many relationship in addition to the specific records it is related to on the "many" side of the relationship.

YOUR TURN 6-5

Review the related records for *016-111-230 Soledad Mattis* and unhide the foreign key field in the subdatasheet.

Soledad Mattis has declared a major three times as shown in the related records in the subdatasheet in Figure 6-19. By right-clicking a field name in the subdatasheet, choosing Unhide, and selecting the StudentID column in the Unhide Columns dialog box, you can also expose the linking foreign key field in the subdatasheet that makes the connection between the records in the DeclaredMajors table and the Students table.

The foreign key field value of *016-111-230* for *Soledad Mattis* is already included in the last record of the subdatasheet shown in Figure 6-19. The foreign key field value is ready to connect a new record to this specific student. Access automatically enters the foreign key field value in the subdatasheet, which helps you protect the integrity of your data and simplifies the process of entering and connecting new records in the "many" table.

222

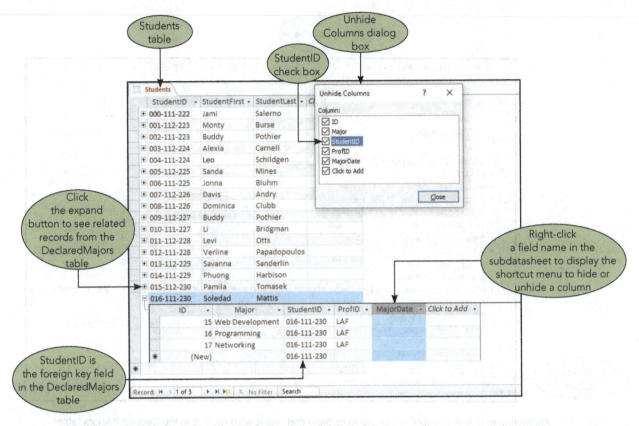

FIGURE 6-19   Working with related records in the DeclaredMajors table

Lookup Properties

Access also provides for field **Lookup properties**, which are especially useful for foreign key fields because they provide a drop-down list of possible values when you enter or update data in that field. The drop-down list helps you productively and consistently enter accurate data into the field. Lookup properties are appropriate with fields that contain a discrete set of values for listing in small lookup tables.

Figure 6-20 shows the Lookup properties for the Department field in the Professors table as established in Table Design View. Recall that the Department field in the Professors table is the foreign key field to the one-field Departments table.

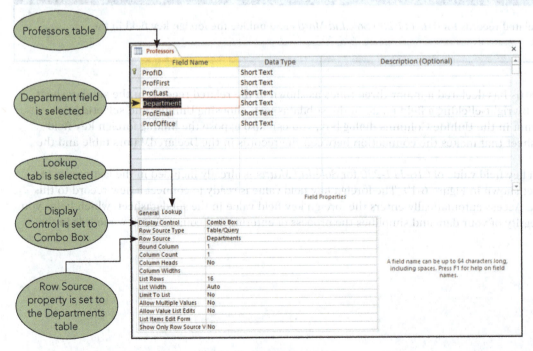

FIGURE 6-20   Setting Lookup properties for the Department field

With the Lookup properties for the Department field connected to the one-field Departments table, a distinct list of drop-down list values is now provided for the Department field in the Professors table, as shown in Figure 6-21. The only values you can choose for the Department field in the Professors table are the values that are first entered in the Department field of the Departments table. This update helps improve data entry productivity and accuracy, and eliminates potential update anomalies given all Department values in the Professors table will be entered accurately and consistently as they are constrained to the values in the Department field of the Departments table.

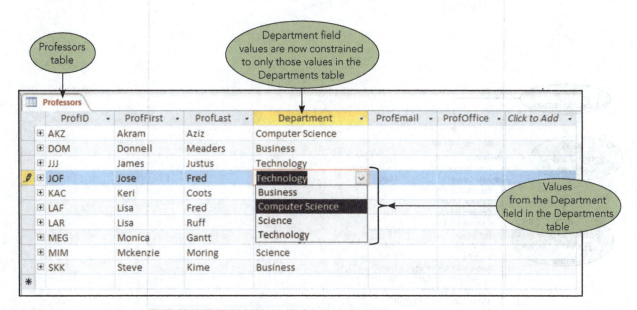

FIGURE 6-21 Constraining values to the drop-down list for the Department field

To add Lookup properties to a foreign key field, perform the following steps:

- Open the table that contains the foreign key field in Table Design View.
- Click the foreign key field to select it.
- Click the Lookup tab in the Field Properties pane.
- Modify the Display Control property to Combo Box.
- Modify the Row Source property to identify the table on the "one" side of the relationship.
- Modify other Lookup properties as needed or desired.
- Save and close the table.

YOUR TURN 6-6

Add Lookup properties to the Major field in the DeclaredMajors table to create a drop-down list of values from the one-field Majors table.

Figure 6-22 shows Table Design View of the DeclaredMajors table with the Lookup properties set on the Major field to create the drop-down list of values. Using the drop-down list in Table Datasheet View to change the value of the Major field for the third record ID 3 to Web Development is shown in Figure 6-23.

224

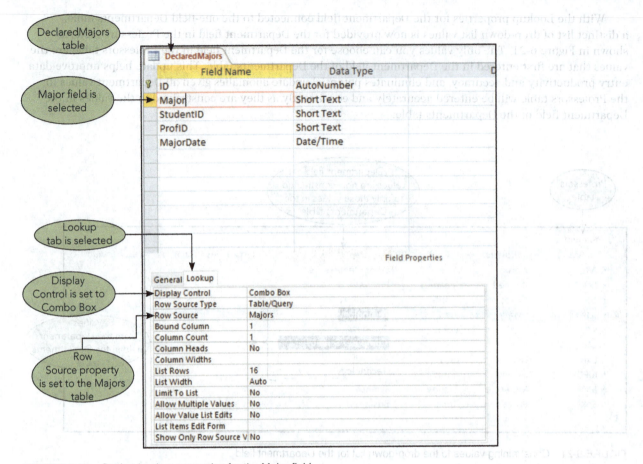

DeclaredMajors table

Major field is selected

Lookup tab is selected

Display Control is set to Combo Box

Row Source property is set to the Majors table

FIGURE 6-22 Setting Lookup properties for the Major field

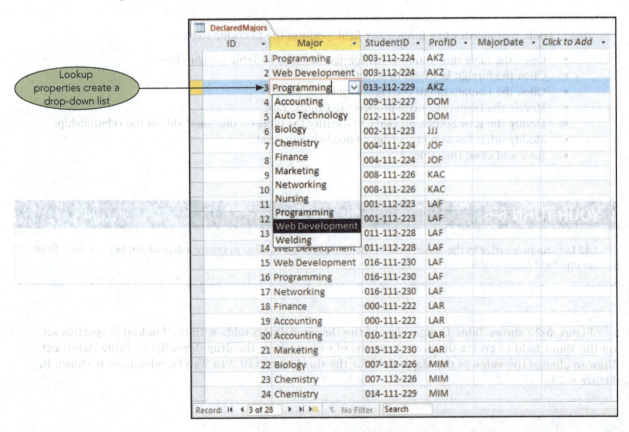

Lookup properties create a drop-down list

FIGURE 6-23 Using the Major field's drop-down list to edit data

Subforms

If you develop **forms** (data entry screens) in Access that include **subforms**, fields from records in tables with one-to-many relationships can be automatically selected and updated, similar to how a subdatasheet works to show related records in Table Datasheet View. The foreign key field value in the table used on the "many" side of the one-to-many relationship is used to display related records in the subform. When a new record is entered in the subform, the foreign key field value is added to the record whether or not it is displayed in the subform. For example, consider the new record in the subform in Figure 6-24 for student *016-111-230, Soledad Mattis.*

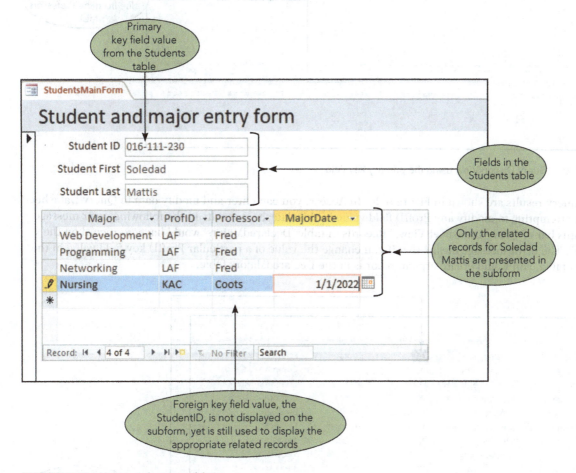

FIGURE 6-24 Using an Access subform

When using a properly constructed form/subform for data entry in Access, the "many" records in the subform *automatically* connect to the correct "one" record in the main form even though the foreign key field for the records in the subform is not even displayed on the subform.

Understanding the role of foreign key field in connecting a record in the "many" table to a preexisting record in the "one" table, as well as understanding and controlling what data is entered and edited in the foreign key field through features such as Lookup properties and form/subforms, is essential to maintaining a healthy relational database in Access. While larger relational database management systems do not have the same application development tools as Access such as subdatasheets, Lookup properties, and subforms, the role of the primary and foreign key fields as well as the rules by which either can be updated are ubiquitous in relational database management systems.

WORKING WITH ONE-TO-MANY RELATIONSHIPS IN QUERY DATASHEET VIEW

Another impressive way to experience the power of one-to-many relationships in Access is illustrated the Query Datasheet View of a SELECT query that uses fields from two related tables. Consider the Query Design View displayed in Figure 6-25. The ProfID field, the primary key field from the Professors table, was selected for the query along with other fields.

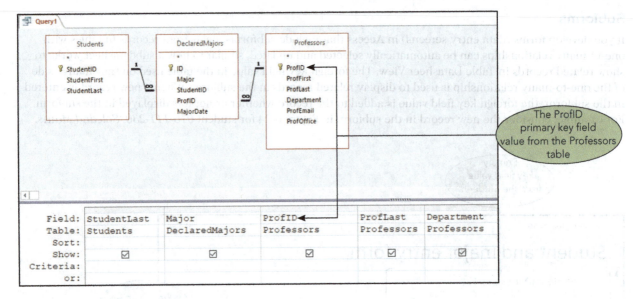

FIGURE 6-25 Query Design View using the primary key field

The query results are shown in Figure 6-26. In Access, you can enter and modify data in Query Datasheet View, but attempting to modify any ProfID field value in this datasheet results in the following error message in the status bar of Query Datasheet View: "Records in table 'DeclaredMajors' would have no record on the 'one' side". The error message means that if you change the value of a particular ProfID key field value in the Professors table, you would create orphan records in the DeclaredMajors table.

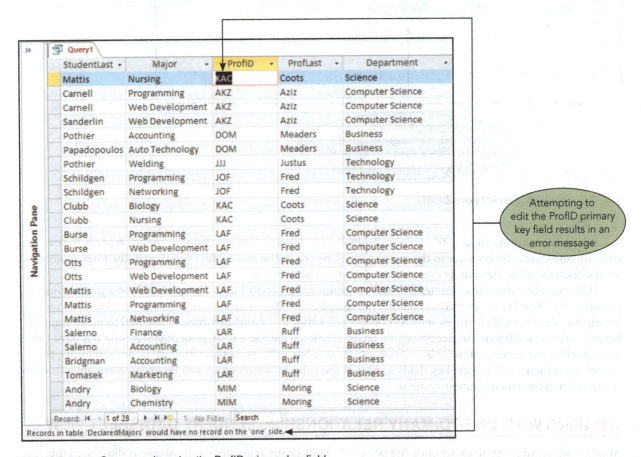

FIGURE 6-26 Query results using the ProfID primary key field

However, if you modify the query to use the ProfID field from the DeclaredMajors table, where it serves as a foreign key field as shown in Figure 6-27, you can edit that field value in Query Datasheet View with no trouble.

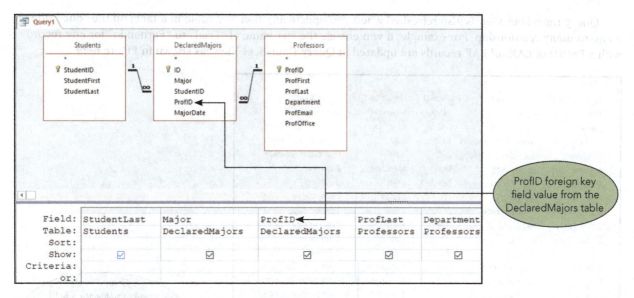

FIGURE 6-27 Query Design View using the foreign key field

Although the data selected for the datasheet *looks* the same given the same ProfID values are stored in both the primary key field in the Professors table and the foreign key field in the DeclaredMajors table, there is a difference when you attempt to modify the ProfID value.

For example, in Figure 6-28, a new ProfID value of DOM was entered for the first record. You are now using the ProfID *foreign key field,* so instead of receiving an error message, Access accepts the edit and then refreshes the entire record with new information. The one-to-many relationship between the Professors table and the DeclaredMajors table is used to select the correct ProfLast and Department field values for that new ProfID. Updating a foreign key field value in Query Datasheet View not only triggers an update to the data, but also refreshes the data in the select query.

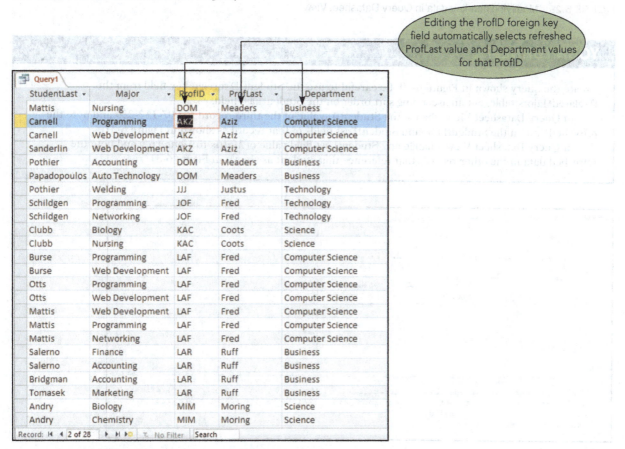

FIGURE 6-28 Automatically refreshing data when using the ProfID foreign key field

Query Datasheet View is also refreshed when you update any non-key value in a table on the "one" side of a one-to-many relationship. For example, if you change the last name of "Fred" to "Fernando" for any record with a ProfID of LAF, *all* LAF records are updated in Query Datasheet View, as shown in Figure 6-29.

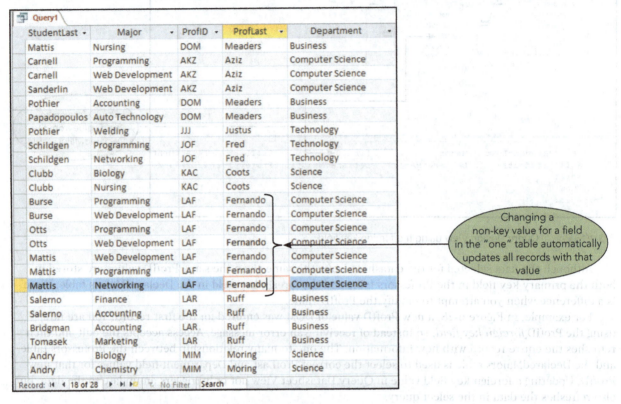

FIGURE 6-29 Modifying non-key data in Query Datasheet View

YOUR TURN 6-7

Create the query shown in Figure 6-30. Be careful to use the StudentID foreign key field from the DeclaredMajors table. Set an ascending sort order on the StudentLast field.

In Query Datasheet View, change the StudentID value of the third record to *007-112-226* and note the refreshed data in the StudentFirst and StudentLast fields of that record as shown in Figure 6-31.

In Query Datasheet View, change any StudentLast field value of *Mattis* to *Monterrey* and note the refreshed data in the other records that reference that student as shown in Figure 6-31.

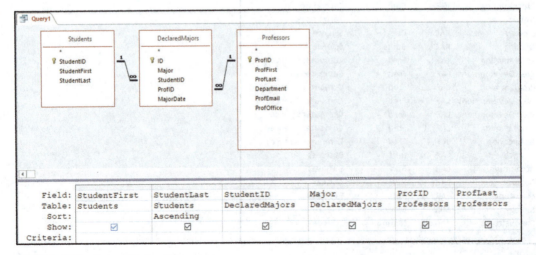

FIGURE 6-30 Query Design View

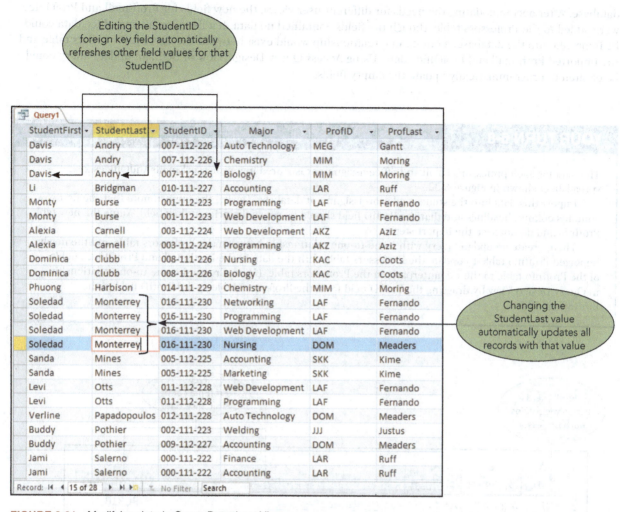

FIGURE 6-31 Modifying data in Query Datasheet View

OTHER RELATIONSHIP TYPES

Normalizing data in Module 5 and relating the normalized tables in one-to-many relationships for the student-advisor-assignments database may be a small example, but it represents the majority of relationships in a relational database. However, two other relationship types are worth exploring: the one-to-one relationship and the many-to-many relationship.

One-to-One Relationships

A **one-to-one relationship** exists between two tables when one record in the first table relates to one and only one record in another. Two tables have a one-to-one relationship when the primary key fields of each table match.

If you encounter a one-to-one relationship, ask yourself whether the two tables could be combined into one table for simplicity's sake. If so, the fields from each table should be merged into one table.

However, sometimes there are valid reasons for maintaining two separate tables that have a one-to-one relationship. For example, a different external process might be used to import each table, and this import might occur in an arbitrary frequency that prevents the data from being imported, refreshed, or stored as a single table. Some fields in one table might be sensitive and need to be separated and secured in a special manner. In general, the additional complexity of maintaining two tables, each with the same primary key field, should be avoided if possible.

Temporary one-to-one relationships can be useful, however, when connecting, converting, and updating data from two separate sources. Consider the current Professors table in the student-advisor-assignment database. After accommodating the needs for different user views, the new fields for ProfEmail and ProfOffice were added to the Professors table, though the fields contained no data. If a list of email and office data could be imported into the database, a one-to-one relationship would exist between the current Professors table and the imported ProfEmail and ProfOffice data. Using Access Query Design View or SQL, an update query could be created to programmatically update the empty fields.

YOUR TURN 6-8

The data for each professor's email and office assignment is stored in a professorEmailsAndOffices.xlsx spreadsheet shown in Figure 6-32.

Import this data into the student-advisor-assignment database. During the import, note that the first row contains column headings and that the ProfID field should be set as the primary key field. Name the new table ProfInfo and do not save the import steps.

Then, create an update query with a one-to-one relationship between the Professors table and the newly imported ProfInfo table to update the Professors table with the data in the ProfEmail and ProfOffices fields of the ProfInfo table to their counterparts in the Professors table. (*Hint*: Create the one-to-one relationship in Query Design View by dragging the ProfID field from the Professors table to the ProfID field of the ProfInfo table.)

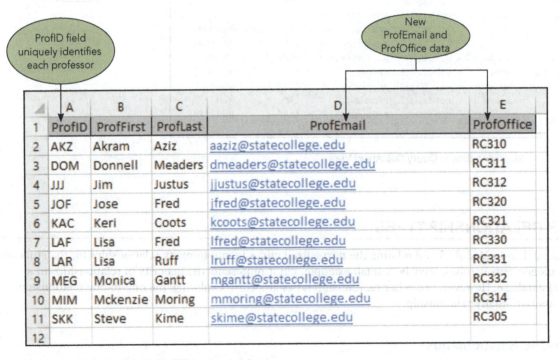

FIGURE 6-32 professorEmailsAndOffices spreadsheet

Query Design View for the update query is shown in Figure 6-33. Note the one-to-one relationship line between the two tables using the ProfID primary key field in each table. Be sure to select the fields from the *Professors* table for the update and to fully qualify the fields in the Update To row of the query grid to select the fields from the *ProfInfo* table.

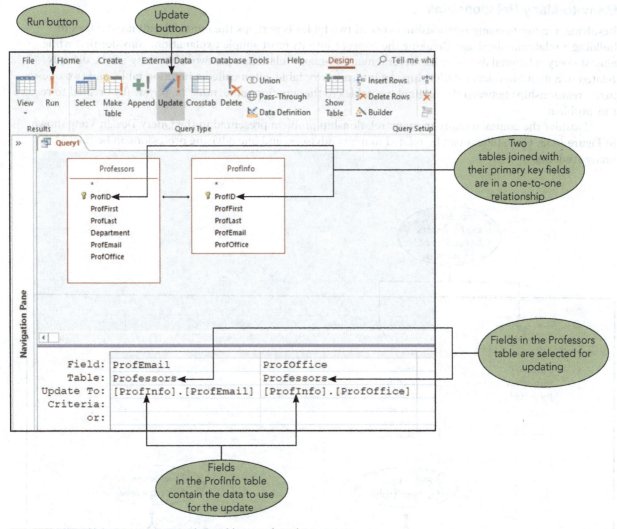

FIGURE 6-33 Using a one-to-one relationship to update data

Running the query in Figure 6-33 updates all 10 records in the Professors table. The final Professors table in Table Datasheet View is shown in Figure 6-34.

ProfID	ProfFirst	ProfLast	Department	ProfEmail	ProfOffice
⊞ AKZ	Akram	Aziz	Computer Science	aaziz@statecollege.edu	RC310
⊞ DOM	Donnell	Meaders	Business	dmeaders@statecollege.edu	RC311
⊞ JJJ	James	Justus	Technology	jjustus@statecollege.edu	RC312
⊞ JOF	Jose	Fred	Technology	jfred@statecollege.edu	RC320
⊞ KAC	Keri	Coots	Science	kcoots@statecollege.edu	RC321
⊞ LAF	Lisa	Fernando	Computer Science	lfred@statecollege.edu	RC330
⊞ LAR	Lisa	Ruff	Business	lruff@statecollege.edu	RC331
⊞ MEG	Monica	Gantt	Technology	mgantt@statecollege.edu	RC332
⊞ MIM	Mckenzie	Moring	Science	mmoring@statecollege.edu	RC314
⊞ SKK	Steve	Kime	Business	skime@statecollege.edu	RC305

FIGURE 6-34 Final Professors table with updated data

Many-to-Many Relationships

Resolving a many-to-many relationship between two tables is perhaps the most difficult mental task in building a relational database. Breaking the concept into its most simple explanation, consider that while almost every relational database has several many-to-many relationships, two tables may *not* be directly related in a many-to-many relationship. An intermediary table, often called a junction table, and two one-to-many relationships between the original two tables to the junction table, *must* be physically created to resolve this problem.

Consider the common many-to-many relationship problem presented in the Query Design View shown in Figure 6-35. One student can be related to many advisors, and one advising professor can be related to many students.

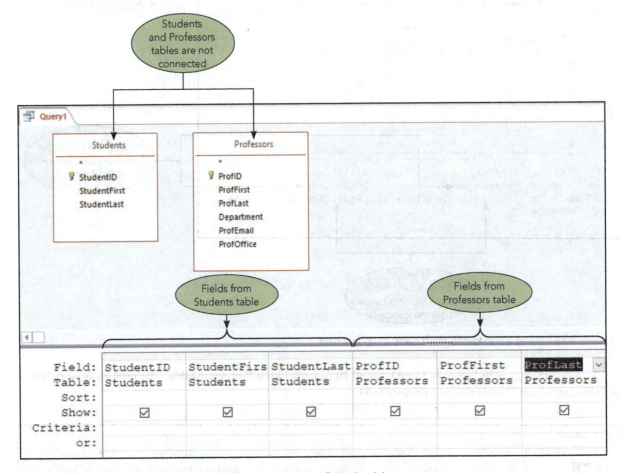

FIGURE 6-35 Tables in a many-to-many relationship create a Cartesian join

The query shown in Figure 6-35 involves two tables without a relationship, and none can be directly created in Query Design View given they do not share any common fields. When two tables in a query have no instructions about how to connect their records, *each* record in one table connects with *each record* in the other table, otherwise known as a **Cartesian join**. In some rare instances, a Cartesian join is useful. However, in many other cases, it represents an unintentional mistake. The resulting datasheet of 170 records (17 students each connected to 10 different professors) is shown in Figure 6-36.

StudentID	StudentFirst	StudentLast	ProfID	ProfFirst	ProfLast
000-111-222	Jami	Salerno	AKZ	Akram	Aziz
000-111-222	Jami	Salerno	DOM	Donnell	Meaders
000-111-222	Jami	Salerno	JJJ	James	Justus
000-111-222	Jami	Salerno	JOF	Jose	Fred
000-111-222	Jami	Salerno	KAC	Keri	Coots
000-111-222	Jami	Salerno	LAF	Lisa	Fernando
000-111-222	Jami	Salerno	LAR	Lisa	Ruff
000-111-222	Jami	Salerno	MEG	Monica	Gantt
000-111-222	Jami	Salerno	MIM	Mckenzie	Moring
000-111-222	Jami	Salerno	SKK	Steve	Kime
001-112-223	Monty	Burse	AKZ	Akram	Aziz
001-112-223	Monty	Burse	DOM	Donnell	Meaders
001-112-223	Monty	Burse	JJJ	James	Justus
001-112-223	Monty	Burse	JOF	Jose	Fred
001-112-223	Monty	Burse	KAC	Keri	Coots
001-112-223	Monty	Burse	LAF	Lisa	Fernando
001-112-223	Monty	Burse	LAR	Lisa	Ruff
001-112-223	Monty	Burse	MEG	Monica	Gantt
001-112-223	Monty	Burse	MIM	Mckenzie	Moring
001-112-223	Monty	Burse	SKK	Steve	Kime
002-111-223	Buddy	Pothier	AKZ	Akram	Aziz
002-111-223	Buddy	Pothier	DOM	Donnell	Meaders
002-111-223	Buddy	Pothier	JJJ	James	Justus
002-111-223	Buddy	Pothier	JOF	Jose	Fred

Record: ◄ ◄ 1 of 170 ► ►I ►☐ 🗐 No Filter Search

170 records are created when each record in the Students table (17) is connected to each record in the Professors table (10)

FIGURE 6-36 Incorrect query results for fields from tables in a many-to-many relationship

To resolve an unintentional Cartesian join, make sure that *all* tables in Query Design View (used in SQL) are explicitly joined, as shown in Figure 6-37. Adding the DeclaredMajors table, the junction table between the Students and Professors tables, to Query Design View clarifies how the records from the Students and Professors tables are joined in a many-to-many relationship.

DeclaredMajors junction table properly connects the Students and Professors tables

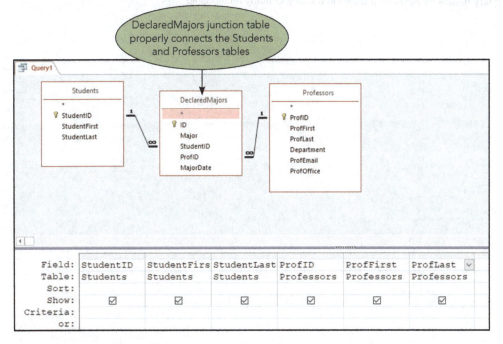

FIGURE 6-37 Using the junction table to resolve a many-to-many relationship

The result is shown in Figure 6-38. Even though no fields were selected from the DeclaredMajors table for the query, the table is still necessary to resolve the many-to-many relationship between the Students and Professors tables. The datasheet in Figure 6-38 shows the correct amount of records selected when running the query.

StudentID	StudentFirst	StudentLast	ProfID	ProfFirst	ProfLast
016-111-230	Soledad	Monterrey	DOM	Donnell	Meaders
003-112-224	Alexia	Carnell	AKZ	Akram	Aziz
003-112-224	Alexia	Carnell	AKZ	Akram	Aziz
013-112-229	Savanna	Sanderlin	AKZ	Akram	Aziz
009-112-227	Buddy	Pothier	DOM	Donnell	Meaders
012-111-228	Verline	Papadopoulos	DOM	Donnell	Meaders
002-111-223	Buddy	Pothier	JJJ	James	Justus
004-111-224	Leo	Schildgen	JOF	Jose	Fred
004-111-224	Leo	Schildgen	JOF	Jose	Fred
008-111-226	Dominica	Clubb	KAC	Keri	Coots
008-111-226	Dominica	Clubb	KAC	Keri	Coots
001-112-223	Monty	Burse	LAF	Lisa	Fernando
001-112-223	Monty	Burse	LAF	Lisa	Fernando
011-112-228	Levi	Otts	LAF	Lisa	Fernando
011-112-228	Levi	Otts	LAF	Lisa	Fernando
016-111-230	Soledad	Monterrey	LAF	Lisa	Fernando
016-111-230	Soledad	Monterrey	LAF	Lisa	Fernando
016-111-230	Soledad	Monterrey	LAF	Lisa	Fernando
000-111-222	Jami	Salerno	LAR	Lisa	Ruff
000-111-222	Jami	Salerno	LAR	Lisa	Ruff
010-111-227	Li	Bridgman	LAR	Lisa	Ruff
015-112-230	Pamila	Tomasek	LAR	Lisa	Ruff
007-112-226	Davis	Andry	MIM	Mckenzie	Moring
007-112-226	Davis	Andry	MIM	Mckenzie	Moring

Record: 1 of 28   No Filter   Search

28 records are selected when the relationship between the Students and Professors tables is properly defined using the DeclaredMajors junction table

FIGURE 6-38   Correct query results for fields from tables in a many-to-many relationship

Summary

- **Define the process and goals of database design:** The process of database design involves normalizing data into distinct entities as well as defining relationships between the entities. The process requires constant review as existing and new needs for data as well as existing and desired business rules are understood. The overall goal of database design is to organize data in a healthy relational database that meets the current and desired data analysis needs of the people and processes of an organization.
- **Describe the data using Database Design Language (DBDL):** The DBDL notation is a way to define the entity and field names, as well as the primary, alternate, secondary, and foreign key fields for an entity.
- **Determine relationships and set primary and foreign key fields:** Relationships in a relational database consist of one-to-many relationships between the entities. While many-to-many relationships exist, they are physically implemented using a junction table with two one-to-many relationships to the original two tables. One-to-one relationships can also exist but should be examined to determine if the two tables can be combined into one table.

  A primary key field has two functions. First and foremost, it uniquely identifies each record. Secondly, a primary key is necessary to link tables in one-to-many relationships. The primary key field is always on the "one" side of the relationship. The foreign key field is always on the "many" side of the relationship.
- **Create entity-relationship (E-R) diagrams to visually represent a database design:** An E-R diagram is a visual representation of the entities and relationships between entities in a relational database. An E-R diagram uses squares for entities and lines for relationships. It may or may not include details on attributes. Several versions of the E-R diagram are popular including one called crow's foot notation given the "many" symbol represents a crow's foot.
- **Create entity-relationship models (ERMs) to visually represent a database design:** An ERM is another type of visual representation of the entities and relationships between entities in a relational database, and focuses more on the relationships between entities than a typical E-R diagram. An ERM uses rectangles to represent entities and diamonds to represent relationships.
- **Implement one-to-many relationships and relationship constraints:** One-to-many relationships are implemented in Access using the Relationships window. The most important relationship constraint is called referential integrity and prevents the creation of orphan records in the table on the "many" side of the relationship.
- **Explore ways that one-to-many relationships work in Access:** Access provides many application development features that exploit the power of one-to-many relationships, including the ability to show related records in subdatasheets, the ability to create drop-down lists using field Lookup properties, the ability to connect related records in subforms, and the ability of Query Datasheet View to automatically update and refresh related data.
- **Discuss special issues related to one-to-one and many-to-many and relationships:** One-to-one relationships are rare, begging the question of why the fields in two tables in a one-to-one relationship are not combined into a single table. Many-to-many relationships exist in almost every relational database management system and are implemented with a third table and a one-to-many relationship from each of the original tables to the junction table.

Key Terms

alternate key (AK)	Lookup properties (field properties in Table Design View)
cardinality	many-to-many relationship
Cartesian join	one-to-many relationship
composite entity	one-to-one relationship
crow's foot notation	orphan record
Database Design Language (DBDL)	physical-level design
entity-relationship (E-R) diagram	primary key field
entity-relationship model (ERM)	referential integrity
E-R diagram	secondary key (SK)
E-R model	subdatasheet (Access)
foreign key field (FK)	subform
form	Unique property (field property in Table Design View)
index	user view
information-level design	view
junction table	

Module Review Questions

Problems

1. Which of the following is *not* a technique that would be used in the process of developing a relational database?
   a. Normalize the data.
   b. Review existing data forms and reports.
   c. Interview those who use the data to understand business rules.
   d. Combine all attributes into one large table.

2. Which of the following relational database tools does *not* help you document the relationships between tables?
   a. SQL
   b. DBDL
   c. E-R diagram
   d. Entity relationship model

3. How do you identify the primary key field in DBDL notation?
   a. with a circle
   b. with an underline as well as the abbreviation PK
   c. with a double underline
   d. with a key symbol

4. Which of the following is *not* considered a type of E-R diagram?
   a. DBDL
   b. ERM
   c. crow's foot notation
   d. Access Relationship window

5. The ERM emphasizes what part of a relational database?
   a. attributes
   b. relationships
   c. primary key fields
   d. foreign key fields

6. Which of the following statements is true about a one-to-many relationship?
   a. Every primary key field participates on the "one" side.
   b. Every foreign key field participates on the "one" side.
   c. Every primary key field participates on the "many" side.
   d. Every foreign key field participates on the "many" side.

7. Why might you not be able to enforce referential integrity on a one-to-many relationship?
   a. The table on the "one" side doesn't have a matching record(s) in the table on the "many" side.
   b. The table on the "many" side doesn't have primary key field.
   c. The table on the "many" side has values in the foreign key field with no matching value in the primary key field of the table on the "one" side.
   d. The table on the "many" side has many values in the foreign key field with one matching value in the primary key field of the table on the "one" side.

8. Which of the following is *not* a feature that Access uses to demonstrate and leverage the power of one-to-many relationships?
   a. subdatasheets
   b. Lookup properties
   c. automatically refreshing related data in Query Datasheet View
   d. Import wizards

9. Which of the following is true about a one-to-one relationship?
   a. They are almost always a mistake.
   b. They create Cartesian joins in queries.
   c. They relate two tables using the primary key field in both tables.
   d. They are only used to import and update data.

Critical Thinking Questions

1. What is the relationship between a table of Movies and a table of ActorsActresses and how might it be implemented in a relational database?

2. What types of business rules might determine the relationship between a table of Volunteers and a table of Activities at a nonprofit?

JC Consulting Case Exercises

The following exercises are based on the JC Consulting database used throughout Modules 1-5.

Problems

1. If management wanted to start tracking the date the entire project was closed, which table should the field be added to?
   a. Clients
   b. Projects
   c. ProjectLineItems
   d. TaskMasterList

2. Which field in the TaskMasterList table is a good candidate for Lookup properties that constrain it with a one-to-many relationship to a one-field table?
   a. Description
   b. Per
   c. Estimate
   d. TaskID

3. Which of the following best describes the Zips table in DBDL if City is often used for sorting?
   a. Zips (City, Zip)
      PK Zip
      SK City
   b. Zips (City, Zip)
      PK Zip
   c. Zips (City, Zip)
      PK Zip
      FK City
   d. Zips (City, Zip)
      FK Zip
      FK City

4. In the Relationships window of the JC Consulting database, which primary key field does *not* participate in a one-to-many relationship?
   a. ProjectLineItemID
   b. ProjectID
   c. TaskID
   d. All primary key fields participate in one-to-many relationships.

5. What can you assume based on the existence of the "one" and infinity symbols on all relationships in the Relationships window of the JC Consulting database?
   a. Referential integrity is applied.
   b. Referential integrity with the cascade update and cascade delete constraints is applied.
   c. The database has no many-to-many relationships.
   d. There will never be a need for a one-to-one relationship in this database.

6. What is the benefit of using the same names for the primary and foreign key fields?
   a. It allows you to enforce referential integrity on the relationship.
   b. It allows you to create one-to-one relationships.
   c. It clarifies the linking field between the tables.
   d. It clarifies where Lookup properties have been applied.

7. What is true about the relationship link line in the Access Relationships window that isn't true about generic E-R diagrams?
   a. The link line can be curved.
   b. The link line indicates where records in the "one" table exist that do not have matching records in the "many" table.
   c. The link line uses crow's foot notation.
   d. The link line points specifically to the primary key field and foreign field.

8. Which value ties the records in the "many" table to the proper record in the "one" table?
   a. the value of the surrogate key
   b. the value of the primary key field in the "many" table
   c. the value of the foreign key field in the "one" table
   d. the value of the foreign key field in the "many" table

9. Many-to-many relationships _____.
   a. are common in almost all relational databases
   b. represent unnormalized data
   c. create orphan records
   d. can be directly implemented using two link lines in most relational database management systems

Critical Thinking Questions

1. Identify the steps you would take to create a one-field table named Titles that could be used to constrain the values in the Title field of the Employees table to the existing values in that field.

2. The ProjectsAndLineItems query currently uses the ProjectID field from the Projects table. Explain why that field cannot be edited in Query Datasheet View.

Pitt Fitness Case Exercises

Problems

1. For the table Customers (CustomerID, LastName, FirstName, StreetAddress, City, State, ZipCode, EmailAddress, PhoneNumber, BirthDate), which field is the primary key field?
   a. LastName
   b. BirthDate
   c. PhoneNumber
   d. CustomerID

2. For the table Customers (CustomerID, LastName, FirstName, StreetAddress, City, State, ZipCode, EmailAddress, PhoneNumber, BirthDate), which field is a foreign key?
   a. LastName
   b. CustomerID
   c. There isn't a foreign key.
   d. PhoneNumber

3. For the table Customers (CustomerID, LastName, FirstName, StreetAddress, City, State, ZipCode, EmailAddress, PhoneNumber, BirthDate), which of the following is a secondary key?
   a. LastName, FirstName
   b. BirthDate
   c. PhoneNumber
   d. CustomerID

4. What field(s) in the Customers table would be the most appropriate for a CustomerName index?
   a. LastName
   b. LastName and FirstName
   c. LastName, FirstName, and BirthDate
   d. CustomerID

5. What is the relationship between the tables Classes and Reservations?
   a. One to one
   b. One to many
   c. Many to many
   d. The tables aren't related.

6. What is the relationship between the tables Instructors and Classes?
   a. One to one
   b. One to many
   c. Many to many
   d. The tables aren't related.

7. What is the relationship between the tables Classes and Customers?
   a. One to one
   b. One to many
   c. Many to many
   d. The tables aren't related.

8. Which of the following tables could be considered a composite entity in an ERM and a junction table in an E-R diagram?
   a. Classes
   b. Instructors
   c. Reservations
   d. Customers

9. Which of the following tables could be considered a composite entity in an ERM and a junction table in an E-R diagram?
   a. ClassInstructors
   b. Instructors
   c. Customers
   d. Classes

10. The Pitt Fitness program director wants to list customer last names and first names along with the classes they are taking. He creates a query using the Customers and Classes tables. In the query grid, he adds the LastName and FirstName fields from the Customers table and the ClassName field from the Classes table. What is most likely wrong with this query?
   a. You need the Reservations table to join the Customers and Classes tables together.
   b. The relationship between Customers and Classes is one to many.
   c. The relationship between the fields LastName and FirstName is one to one.
   d. There is nothing wrong with this query.

Critical Thinking Questions

1. Write the Pitt Fitness database in DBDL notation.
2. What prevents a user from entering a reservation for a customer who has not yet been registered in the Customers table?

Sports Physical Therapy Case Exercises

Problems

1. What would be a possible alternative key field for the Session table?
   a. There isn't a good choice for an alternative key field.
   b. SessionDate
   c. PatientNum
   d. TherapyCode

2. What is a good choice for a secondary key in the Therapist table?
   a. Street
   b. LastName, FirstName
   c. FirstName
   d. City

3. Identify the foreign key(s) in the Session table.
   a. SessionDate
   b. PatientNum, TherapyCode
   c. PatientNum, TherapistID
   d. PatientNum, TherapyCode, TherapistID

4. What is the relationship between the tables Patient and Session?
   a. One to one
   b. One to many
   c. Many to many
   d. There isn't a relationship.

5. What is the relationship between the tables Patient and Therapies?
   a. One to one
   b. One to many
   c. Many to many
   d. There isn't a relationship.

6. What is the relationship between the tables Therapist and Therapies?
   a. One to one
   b. One to many
   c. Many to many
   d. There isn't a relationship.

7. What is the relationship between the tables Therapist and Session?
   a. One to one
   b. One to many
   c. Many to many
   d. There isn't a relationship.

8. Which of the following tables is a junction table?
   a. Patient
   b. Therapies
   c. Session
   d. Therapist

9. Which of the following fields in the Therapist table would have the highest cardinality?
   a. TherapistID
   b. LastName
   c. FirstName
   d. Street

10. Assume that PatientNum 1021 is entered into a record in the table Session. However, PatientNum 1021 does not appear in the Patient table. What type of record would this be (in the Session table)?
    a. Hanging record
    b. Nonfield record
    c. Orphan record
    d. Distinct record

Critical Thinking Questions

1. Create a query in Access that uses two tables, the Patient table and the Session table. Add the LastName, FirstName, and SessionDate fields to the query grid. Run the query. How many records are displayed? Delete the join line between the field lists in Query Design View. Rerun the query. How many records are now displayed? Why are the results different? You do not need to save the queries.

2. Enter an additional record in the Session table with the PatientNum 1022. What happens when you try to move onto another record? What is the error message? Why?

DATABASE MANAGEMENT SYSTEMS PROCESSES AND SERVICES

LEARNING OBJECTIVES

- Identify the services provided by a database management system
- Examine the catalog feature in a DBMS
- Describe the concurrent update problem
- Explain the data recovery process in a database environment
- Describe security services
- Examine data integrity features
- Discuss data independence
- Define and describe data replication

INTRODUCTION

In this module, you will learn about several processes and services performed by a database management system. Key processes and services include the following:

- *Update and retrieve data.* Provide users with the ability to update and retrieve data in a database.
- *Provide catalog services.* Store data about the data (**metadata**) and make it accessible to users.
- *Support concurrent update.* Ensure that the database is updated correctly among multiple, concurrent users.
- *Recover data.* Provide methods to recover a database that has been corrupted or otherwise compromised.
- *Provide security services.* Ensure that the database requires proper user authorization.
- *Provide data integrity features.* Follow rules so that the DBMS updates data accurately and consistently.
- *Support data independence.* Separate the database services from the programs that use it.
- *Support data replication.* Manage multiple copies of the same data at multiple locations, sometimes called distributed databases.

All relational database management systems from those with the smallest amount of data managed by Microsoft Access through the largest relational database management systems such as IBM Db2, Oracle, and Microsoft SQL Server share many characteristics such as the way data should be normalized, how tables should be related, and how SQL may be used to retrieve and update data. Some advanced features, however, such as user-level security and replication, are only provided by the larger systems.

Remember that while Microsoft Access illustrates many features of a relational database, it should only be implemented in a local environment with a handful of trusted users. Oracle, MySQL, Db2, SQL Server, and other large-scale database management systems can support thousands of simultaneous users across the world and are often referred to as **enterprise-level systems**.

In addition, **database-as-a-service** products such as **Amazon Relational Database Service** and **Microsoft Azure SQL Database** are becoming more popular because they provide high-performance, reliable, scalable, and secure products for large-scale applications without requiring a company to locally manage the infrastructure and personnel needed to support the database. Database-as-a-service solutions are managed by the company from which you are buying the service. They are typically purchased for a monthly fee determined by the volume of data or traffic that is managed by the service.

CREATE, READ, UPDATE, AND DELETE DATA

A relational database system allows users to **create**, **read**, **update**, and **delete** data in a database. These processes are required in all database management systems no matter how large or small. They are sometimes referred to with the acronym **CRUD** and map to the SQL keywords and common HTTP methods shown in Figure 7-1.

Operation	SQL Keyword	Common HTTP Method	Other Common Terms
Create	`INSERT`	POST	Add
Read	`SELECT`	GET	Retrieve
Update	`UPDATE`	PATCH	Edit, modify
Delete	`DELETE`	DELETE	Destroy

FIGURE 7-1   Create read update delete (CRUD) keyword map

HTTP (Hypertext Transfer Protocol) is a protocol for passing webpages, resources, and data through the web. HTTP **methods** do not communicate directly with a database but rather, identify the action to perform on a particular resource and help pass data to that resource. The resource is typically a file or procedure, which in turn connects to the database and executes SQL to retrieve or update data.

Q & A 7-1

Question: What is the main difference between the SQL keywords and HTTP methods shown in Figure 7-1?

Answer: You use the SQL keywords in statements that work directly with the relational database to insert, select, update, or delete data.

   HTTP methods are actions that are performed on resources or files at the server, often at the request of a user working in a webpage. For example, the GET method can be used to complete a search process.

   You enter a word or phrase that describes what you are looking for on a webpage and click a Search button. The click initiates the GET method, which passes the data entered into the search box to another file at the server.

   The file at the server might be a PHP, Java, C#, Python, or Ruby file that can connect to a database and use the search terms passed to it through the GET method as criteria in an SQL statement. The SQL statement selects the relevant data from a database and passes it back to another program, which inserts that data in a webpage that is then sent back to the user.

Theoretically, any relational database program can work with any modern programming language to read or modify data in the database. Realistically, however, developer communities gravitate together to create **solution stacks**, a set of software components, that are well documented and have a proven track record of working well together.

   A few of the current popular server-side web app development software stacks, including their preferred relational database software management system, are shown in Figure 7-2.

Solution Stack Acronym	Server Operating System	Web Server	Database Management System	Server-side Programming Language
LAMP	Linux	Apache	MySQL	PHP*
LAPP	Linux	Apache	PostgreSQL	PHP*
WAMP	Windows	Apache	MySQL	PHP*
WIMP	Windows	Internet Information Services	MySQL	PHP*
WINS	Windows	Internet Information Services	SQL Server	.NET (C#)

*The "P" most commonly refers to PHP, but may also refer to Perl (although currently declining in popularity) and Python (currently increasing in popularity).

FIGURE 7-2   Current popular server-side web app development software stacks

PROVIDE CATALOG SERVICES

As described in Module 4, a database **catalog** is maintained automatically by the relational database system, and contains table and field **metadata**, data about the data. Metadata includes information about table relationships, views, indexes, and properties. In large systems with user-level security, the catalog contains information about users, user groups, and privileges.

The catalogs for many database management systems consist of a set of special tables included in the database. They are typically hidden tables, but in some cases, the **DBA** (**database administrator**) may want to access them to see or create documentation about the database to answer a variety of questions such as the following:

- What tables and fields are included in the database?
- What are the properties such as descriptions, default values, captions, and other restrictions of the fields?
- What relationships between the tables exist in the database?
- What are the properties of the relationships such as referential integrity and cascade options?
- Which fields are indexed?
- What groups, users, and programs have which types of access to each table and view in the database?

Catalog Services in Microsoft Access

For Microsoft Access, the **Database Documenter** feature creates a catalog report of the information about the tables, fields, relationships, and other objects in the database, and was discussed in Module 4.

In addition, the Relationships window has a self-documenting feature called the Relationship report. The **Relationship report** creates a compact report showing the table names, field names, and relationships between the tables. The report can be printed or shared for handy reference by those who need to know table and field names so they can productively write SQL. The information in the Relationship report is often called the **database schema**, a model or blueprint of the tables and relationships between the tables.

YOUR TURN 7-1

Create a Relationship report for the JCConsulting database.

The Relationship report for the JCConsulting database in Figure 7-3 is shown in landscape orientation so that all of the field lists and relationship lines fit on one page.

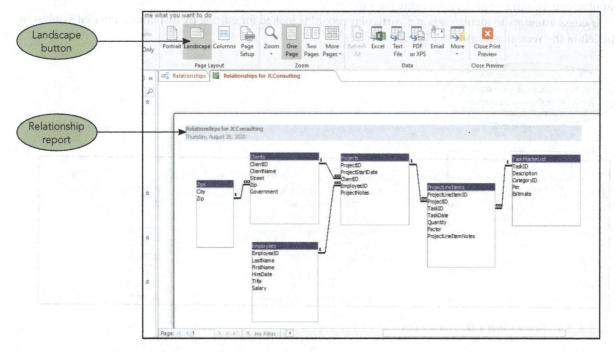

FIGURE 7-3 Database schema for the JCConsulting database

Catalog Services in Enterprise Database Management Systems

Some enterprise-level systems as Oracle and Db2 refer to the catalog as the **data dictionary**. The data dictionary is a read-only set of tables that provides the following types of information about the database:

- Definitions of all objects in the database including tables and views
- Amount of current and allocated space for each object
- Default values for each column
- Integrity constraint information
- Name of each database user
- All privileges and roles granted to each user
- Auditing information, such as who has accessed or updated various schema objects and when
- Other general database information

The data dictionary is a critical communication tool for database analysts, application developers, and database administrators. You use SQL statements to access the data in the data dictionary, just as you would any other table or view the database. Because the data dictionary contains read-only data, you can use the SQL SELECT statement, but not any update commands.

SUPPORT CONCURRENT UPDATES

Concurrent update occurs when multiple users make updates to the same database at the same time. Even Microsoft Access allows for multiple users to retrieve, enter, and update data in the same database file at the same time. This sometimes comes as a surprise to users because the other applications in the Microsoft Office suite such as Word, Excel, and PowerPoint do not allow concurrent updates.

For example, if an Excel spreadsheet is stored on a server that multiple people can work with, and you open it in Excel on your computer, you can obviously enter and update the spreadsheet. If a second person attempts to open the same Excel file, however, he or she receives a read-only version of the file. A **read-only** version allows that person to display (read) the data, but doesn't allow that person to edit or modify it. Only the first person that opens a Microsoft Office Excel file has the ability to edit it. Any other users are locked out of updating the file until the first person closes it, which in turn allows someone else to open it with full privileges to modify the data.

Concurrent Updates in Microsoft Access

In Microsoft Access, however, data is not locked at the file level, but rather, at the record level. **Record-level locking** means that two or more users can simultaneously work in the same database file, but they cannot simultaneously enter or update the same *record*.

Access attempts to identify when a particular record is locked for editing by displaying a **pencil symbol** to the left of the record as shown in Figure 7-4.

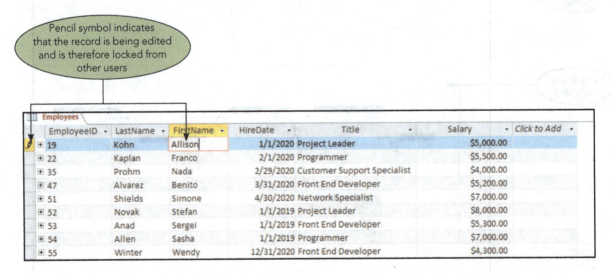

FIGURE 7-4 Record-level locking in Access

In Access, the pencil symbol means that you are currently editing that record and therefore no other user can currently edit the same record. If you attempt to edit a record that is currently locked, you receive an error message such as *"Cannot update. Currently locked because you and another user are attempting to update the same data at the same time."* In Access, moving to a new record or closing the current window saves the edits to the current record, unlocks the record for use by others, and removes the pencil symbol indicator to the left of the record. Access is designed to handle a small number of concurrent users, so the times that two or more users want to update the same record are somewhat rare, but the main thing to note is that Access can manage concurrent updates.

Concurrent Updates in Enterprise Database Management Systems

Enterprise database management systems that have many users across wide area networks must deal with the issue of concurrent updates in large volumes. Private networks are sometimes established to secure internal database applications, but if the application is used on the web or communicates with outside users and processes, additional complexities arise due to the **stateless** nature of the web, where a continuous connection between the server and client is not maintained.

For a deep dive into the concurrent update issue or any aspect of using enterprise-level relational database management systems, check the free documentation for each product as referenced in Figure 7-5.

Database Management System	Free Documentation
Oracle	docs.oracle.com
Microsoft SQL Server Microsoft Azure	docs.microsoft.com
Db2	ibm.com – search for Db2 database product documentation
MySQL	dev.mysql.com/doc/
Amazon Web Services	docs.aws.amazon.com/

FIGURE 7-5 Free, official, online documentation for enterprise-level relational database management systems

For example, you can go to docs.oracle.com and search for "Data Concurrency and Consistency" to find an article about those features as implemented by Oracle.

Some of the key issues surrounding the management of concurrent updates in large-scale systems include data concurrency and data consistency for all transactions. **Data concurrency** means that many users can access data at the same time. **Data consistency** means that each user sees a consistent view of the data, including real-time changes made by others.

Each task that a user completes, such as selecting a product for an order, is called a **transaction**. A transaction triggers a number of steps the database management system needs to complete so the data remains consistent for each user. According to the Oracle's documentation, Oracle processes transactions in a series of steps that maintain data consistency by *preventing* the following three types of database concurrency problems:

- **Dirty reads**: A transaction that reads data that has been written by another transaction but has not been committed yet.
- **Nonrepeatable (fuzzy) reads**: A transaction rereads data it has previously read and finds that another committed transaction has modified or deleted that data.
- **Phantom reads (or phantoms)**: A transaction reruns a query, returning a set of rows that satisfies a search condition, and finds that another committed transaction has inserted additional rows that satisfy the condition.

Another important concept that governs the definition of a successful transaction is expressed in the acronym **ACID (atomicity, consistency, isolation, durability)**. ACID defines a set of properties for a transaction that guarantees its success even in the event of a problem or interruption in the process. **Atomicity** means that the transaction is an atomic transaction—it is indivisible or irreducible to the point that either the entire transaction occurs—or nothing occurs. **Consistency** refers to the requirement that a transaction may change data in only predetermined, allowed ways. **Isolation** refers to the rules that govern when other users can see the updates made by the transaction. **Durability** guarantees that committed transactions are permanent.

Consider your personal experiences in placing an order using a web application. For example, have you ever ordered tickets to a concert with assigned seating? If so, you have first-hand experience with the difficult issues of managing data concurrency and data consistency. When ordering tickets for a concert, you need to see which seats are available, yet anyone else who is interested in the concert also needs to see the same information at the same time. To complete a purchase, you need to pick your specific seats. Ordering tickets to a concert can take several minutes, yet you don't want to get to the end of the transaction only to find that the seats you've chosen have just been purchased by another person. Moreover, you don't want the system to sell the same seats to more than one person.

Two common techniques for maintaining concurrency control are two-phase locking and timestamping. **Two-phase locking** blocks other transactions from accessing the same data during the transaction's life. **Timestamping** is a technique that determines the order for processing records based on an automatic timestamp applied to a record and avoids the need to lock rows in the database. Enterprise-level relational database systems such as Oracle consider all of these issues to accurately and reliably process transactions within a database to maintain data consistency and data concurrency while providing successful concurrent updates.

Q & A 7-2

Question: How do modern online shopping carts help maintain data concurrency?

Answer: Modern online shopping carts reserve and remove a product from available inventory as soon as it is selected for a shopping cart so another user cannot inadvertently purchase the same item. Modern online shopping carts typically give a user an obvious, specific amount of time to complete a transaction before items in a shopping cart are returned to inventory for other potential customers to see.

RECOVER DATA

Recovery is the process of returning a database that has encountered some sort of problem to a state known to be correct. Periodic **backups**, an entire copy of the database created at a specific point in time, help an organization recover. Unfortunately, any updates made to the database since the backup was made are lost. For example, if the backup was created at midnight, and the database was compromised to the point that a backup had to be implemented at 3:00 that afternoon, all entries from midnight to 3:00 pm would be lost. Still, offsite backups are an important part of an overall emergency recovery plan. A good **offsite** backup is stored on a server in a different physical location from the production server.

Enterprise-level database management systems have more detailed techniques of recovering lost data than restoring a complete backup. For example, large-scale databases make several incremental backups throughout the day. They also have sophisticated tools to analyze and repair corrupted data, and can often fix a database without resorting to a complete overwrite of the physical data from a backup.

Recovering Data in Microsoft Access

Microsoft Access provides two features to help recover data: a backup tool and a repair tool. The backup tool in Access creates a complete backup of the entire database including all objects. To create a backup in Access, perform the following steps:

- All users (except the one creating the backup) must close the database.
- Click the File tab on the ribbon.
- Click Save As.
- Double-click Back Up Database.
- Navigate to the folder where you want to save the database, and then click Save in the Save As dialog box.

By default, an Access backup file has the name of the database file followed by an underscore (_) and the current date in a yyyy-mm-dd format, such as JCConsulting_2020-08-29. That way, the backup file is automatically identified with the date the backup was made. Backups do not need to be saved forever, but it is wise to save a backup at key business milestones such as the first (or last) day of each quarter and each day of the previous week.

Microsoft Access provides a compact and repair tool that helps you find and fix corrupt data within a database. To repair corrupt data in an existing Microsoft Access database, perform the following steps:

- All users (except the one compacting and repairing the database) must close the database.
- Click the Database Tools tab on the ribbon.
- Click the Compact & Repair Database button (Database Tools tab | Tools group).

The Microsoft Access compact and repair tool not only finds and fixes many data corruption issues that creep into the database after a long period of continued use, it also reorganizes the database file to remove unused space caused by deleted data or deleted objects. An Access database can significantly shrink in size if it has not been compacted for a long period of time. Most Access developers recommend compacting and repairing databases that are used on a daily basis at least once a month if not at the end of every day.

To automatically compact and repair an Access database when the last person closes it at the end of every working day, perform the following steps:

- Click the File tab on the ribbon.
- Click Options.
- Click the Current Database option.
- Click the Compact on Close check box.
- Click OK in the Access Options dialog box.

Access databases have a physical size limitation of 2 GB. Increasing the size of an Access database beyond that limit causes corruption. The type of data a database manages influences the total size of the database. Traditional data, including text and numbers, does not take much space, and even Access databases can store hundreds of thousands of records in multiple tables of traditional data.

Nontraditional or multimedia data such as photos, external files, and video require much more space and can increase the size of a database quickly. Various approaches to managing nontraditional data are explored further in Module 9.

YOUR TURN 7-2

Compact and repair the JCConsulting database, and then create a backup of the database.

Recovering Data in Enterprise Database Management Systems

As you might expect, enterprise systems provide sophisticated features to avoid the costly and time-consuming task of having users redo their work. These features include **journaling**, which involves maintaining a **journal** or **log** of all updates to the database. The log is a separate file from the database, so the log is still available if a catastrophe destroys the database.

Several types of information are typically kept in the log for each transaction. This information includes the transaction ID and the date and time of each individual update. The log also includes a record of what the data in the row looked like before the update (called a **before image**) and a record of what the data in the row looked like after the update (called an **after image**). In addition, the log may contain an entry to indicate the start of a transaction and the successful completion (**commit**) of a transaction.

To illustrate the use of a log, consider the four sample transactions shown in Figure 7-6. Three transactions—1, 3, and 4—require a single update to the database. The second transaction, adding client, project, and project line item records, requires four updates to the database.

TransactionID	Transaction Description
1	1. In the Employees table, change the Title value for EmployeeID 22 to Project Leader.
2	1. Add a new record to the Clients table: ClientID of 25, ClientName of KC Solutions, Street of 12345 College Blvd, Zip of 02446, and No for Government. 2. Add a new record to the Projects table: ProjectID of 32, ProjectStart of 7/1/2022, ClientID of 25, EmployeeID of 52, and ProjectNotes of Evaluate relational database. 3. Add a record to the ProjectLineItems table: ProjectLineItemID of 211, ProjectID of 32, TaskID of MEET00, TaskDate of 7/1/2022, Quantity of 1, Factor of 1. 4. Add another record to the ProjectLineItems table: ProjectLineItemID of 212, ProjectID of 32, TaskID of MEET01, TaskDate of 8/1/2022, Quantity of 1, Factor of 1.
3	1. In the Employees table, change the Salary value for EmployeeID 22 to $6000.
4	1. In the TaskMasterList table, delete the record for TaskID TEST04.

FIGURE 7-6 Four sample transactions

Suppose these four transactions are the first transactions in a day, immediately following a backup of the database, and they are all completed successfully. In this case, the log might look like the sample log shown in Figure 7-7.

TransactionID	Time	Action	Record Updated	Before Image	After Image
1	8:00	Start			
2	8:01	Start			
2	8:02	Insert	Clients table, ClientID 25		(new values)
1	8:03	Update	Employees table, EmployeeID 22	(old value)	(new value)
2	8:04	Insert	Projects table ProjectID 32		(new values)
1	8:05	Commit			
3	8:06	Start			
2	8:07	Insert	ProjectLineItems table ProjectLineItemID 211		(new values)
2	8:08	Insert	ProjectLineItems table ProjectLineItemID 212		(new values)
4	8:09	Start			
2	8:10	Commit			
3	8:11	Update	Employees table EmployeeID 22	(old value)	(new value)
3	8:12	Commit			
4	8:13	Delete	TaskMasterList table TaskID TEST04	(old values)	
4	8:14	Commit			

FIGURE 7-7 Sample log in which all four transactions commit normally

Each record in the log includes the ID of the transaction, as well as the time the particular action occurred. For simplicity in this example, each action occurs one minute after the preceding action. In a real log, the timestamp would be more precise.

The actions are *Start* to indicate the start of a transaction, *Commit* to indicate that the transaction completed successfully, *Insert* to identify the addition of a record to the database, *Update* to identify the change of a record, and *Delete* to identify the deletion of a record. For an Insert action, no before image appears in the log because the data did not exist prior to the action. Similarly, for a Delete action, no after image appears in the log.

The sample log shows, for example, the following for transaction 2. It began at 8:01. A database change occurred at 8:02 (Client 25 inserted). Other database changes occurred at 8:04 (the Projects record inserted), 8:07 (the first ProjectLineItems record inserted), and 8:08 (the second ProjectLineItems record inserted). At 8:10, transaction 2 was committed. During the time span from 8:00 to 8:14, the other three transactions were executed and committed.

Forward Recovery

How do you use the log in the recovery process? Suppose a catastrophe destroys the database just after 8:11. In this case, recovering the database begins with the most recent database backup from the previous evening at 10:00. As shown in Figure 7-8, the DBA copies the backup over the live database. Because the database is no longer current, the DBA executes a DBMS recovery program that applies the after images of committed transactions from the log to bring the database up to date. This method of recovery is called **forward recovery**.

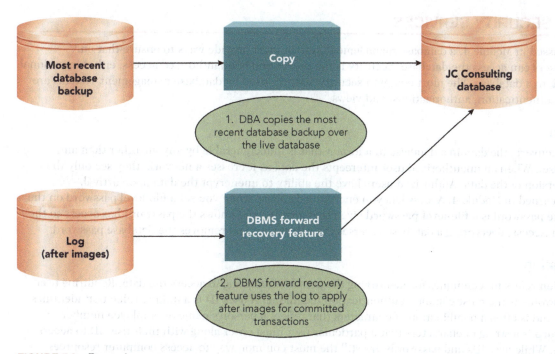

FIGURE 7-8 Forward recovery

The recovery program copies the after image of each record in the log over the actual record in the database in chronological order. You can improve the recovery process by realizing that if a specific record was updated 10 times since the last backup, the recovery program only needs to apply the last after image.

Backward Recovery

If the database has not been destroyed, the problem might involve transactions that were either incorrect or, more likely, stopped in midstream. In either case, the database is currently not in a valid state. You can use **backward recovery**, or **rollback**, to recover the database to a valid state by undoing the problem transactions. The DBMS accomplishes the backward recovery by reading the log for the problem transactions and applying the before images to undo their updates, as shown in Figure 7-9.

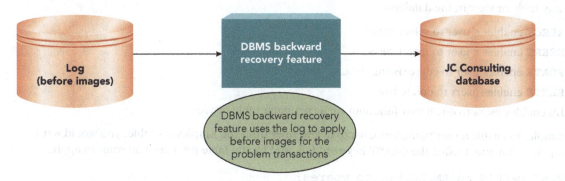

FIGURE 7-9 Backward recovery

Q & A 7-3

Question: How do you back up an online service such as a cloud-based database?

Answer: A key characteristics of a valid backup is that the backup should be stored in a different location than the production database. If the database is located in the cloud, consider storing the backup locally. If the database is stored on a local server, consider storing the backup in the cloud.

PROVIDE SECURITY SERVICES

As first discussed in Module 4, a database management system must provide ways to ensure that only authorized users can access the database. Security is the prevention of unauthorized access, either intentional or accidental, to a database. The most common security features used by database management systems are encryption, authentication, authorizations, and views.

Encryption

Encryption converts the data in a database to a format that is indecipherable by anyone other than an authorized user. When an unauthorized user intercepts the data as it crosses a network, they see only the encrypted version of the data. Authorized users have the ability to unencrypt the data upon arrival.

As you learned in Module 4, Access lets you encrypt a database when you set a file-level password on the database. The password is a **file-level password** given that anyone who knows the password has access to the entire file. In Access, **decrypting** a database reverses the encryption and removes the database password.

Authentication

Authentication refers to techniques for identifying the person attempting to access the data. Requiring user IDs and passwords is the most common authentication technique. A **user ID** is a unique value that identifies each person and is often a combination of characters that reflect a person's name or employee number.

A **password** is a string of characters that a particular user must enter along with their user ID to access the database. While user IDs and passwords are still the most common way to access computer resources, biometric identification techniques and smart cards are increasing in use as an alternative to password authentication.

Biometric identification techniques recognize users by physical or behavioral characteristics such as fingerprints, voiceprints, retina scans, handwritten signatures, and facial characteristics. **Smart cards** or **smart fobs** have processing logic that can be programmed to periodically change and synchronize with passwords stored on the database so that only the person who has physical possession of the card or fob can successfully access the system.

Authorization

Enterprise-level database systems provide **user-level** security, which means that each user and process has specific privileges to select, insert, update, and delete data for different tables and views. The following SQL keywords can be used across all large-scale relational database systems to set **table privileges**, which can be applied to any table or view in the database.

> **SELECT** enables a user to select data.
>
> **INSERT** enables a user to insert rows.
>
> **UPDATE** enables user to edit existing data.
>
> **DELETE** enables users to delete rows.
>
> **ALL** enables users to do all four functions on a particular table or view.

For example, to enable a user named *mperez* to delete rows from the Employees table, you would write the following SQL statement using the GRANT keyword followed by the table privilege you want to apply.

```
GRANT DELETE on EMPLOYEES to mperez;
```

Views

Recall from Module 4 that a view is a named subset of fields and records from one or more tables in the database. As such, views can be used to give users and processes access to only the specific data needed for their job responsibilities. Data not in a particular view is effectively hidden from that user.

Privacy

No discussion of security is complete without at least a brief mention of privacy. Security and privacy are separate but related concepts. **Privacy** refers to the right of individuals to have certain information about them kept confidential. Privacy and security are related because appropriate *security* measures protect *privacy*.

Laws and regulations dictate some privacy rules. For example, **HIPAA**, the Health Insurance Portability and Accountability Act, passed in 1996, is a federal law and sets a national standard to protect medical records and other personal health information that identifies an individual and is maintained or exchanged electronically or in hard copy. **FERPA**, the Family Educational Rights and Privacy Act, protects the rights of students and parents regarding educational records.

Confidential information varies widely among organizations. For example, salaries at governmental and many service organizations are public information, but salaries at many private enterprises are confidential.

Q & A 7-4

Question: How do you create a strong password (one that can't be easily hacked)?

Answer: A strong password has the following characteristics:

- It contains 12 characters, minimum
- It includes numbers, symbols, and both upper and lowercase characters
- It isn't an obvious word and doesn't contain an obvious substitution such as 0 (zero) for O (capital letter o).
- It includes a memorable phrase of random words and symbols such as 4321SillyCount-down4Me! Or $Money$=*Happiness*?

PROVIDE DATA INTEGRITY FEATURES

Data integrity constraints have been discussed in previous modules and are categorized as either key integrity constraints or data integrity constraints.

Key integrity constraints consist of primary key constraints and foreign key constraints. Primary keys are, by definition, constrained to a unique value for each record. Foreign key fields are constrained to values previously entered in the primary key field of the table on the "one" side of a relationship when referential integrity is enforced on a relationship.

Data integrity constraints help to ensure the accuracy and consistency of individual field values and include the following:

- *Data type.* The value entered for any field should be consistent with the data type for that field. For example, only numbers should be allowed in a numeric field. If the field is a date, only a legitimate date is permitted.
- *Legal values.* For some fields, not every possible value of the assigned data type is legitimate. For example, you could constrain a CreditLimit field to specific predetermined values of 5000, 10000, or 20000. In Access, you can set legal values with the Validation Rule property.
- *Format (Input Mask in Access).* Some fields require a special entry or display format. For example, you might want to require users to enter four digits for the year portion of a date field to distinguish dates in the 1900s from those in the 2000s.
- *Validation Rule and Validation Text.* Some fields allow you to use the Validation Rule property to define the valid entries by entering a logical expression that evaluates true or false. You use the Validation Text property to display a useful message when the Validation Rule is broken.

The trick is to apply all data integrity constraints that are necessary and appropriate, but none that hamstring the user from being able to enter new or unexpected data into the database. For example, you wouldn't want to constrain a CreditLimit field to values less than 5000 if an exceptional customer could have a higher credit limit.

To set data integrity constraints in Access, perform the following steps:

- Open the table that contains the fields on which you want to set constraints in Table Design View.
- Click the field on which you want to set the constraints.
- Click the property in the Field Properties pane that you want to modify and enter the property value.

SUPPORT DATA INDEPENDENCE

One advantage of working with a data stored in a database management system is **data independence**, a property that lets you change the database structure without requiring you to change all of the programs that access the database. For example, you may need to add a new field, change a field property, change the name of a field, table, or view, create an index, or modify a relationship. The following sections describe the data independence considerations for each type of change.

Adding a Field

If you add a new field to a database, it does not affect any programs except those that will use the new field. However, if you use the SQL SELECT * FROM command to select all the fields from a table, you are presented with all fields including the newly added field. To prevent this from happening, you need to change the program to restrict the output to only the desired fields. Therefore, it's generally better to explicitly list all the required fields in an SQL SELECT command instead of using the * (asterisk) wildcard to represent all fields.

Changing the Property of a Field

In general, you do not need to change associated programs because you have changed a property such as the size or length of a field. However, you may need to alter the width of some input boxes or report columns to accommodate larger sizes or different formats.

Managing Indexes

You can create a new index using an SQL command as covered in previous modules. New indexes should be carefully monitored to make sure they improve the performance of the processes that use the new index. Deleting unneeded indexes and adding needed indexes is a common task to fine-tune overall database performance.

Changing the Name of a Field, Table, or View

Changing the name of a field, table, or view can affect all SQL statements and processes that reference the field, table, or view later. Fortunately, many relational database programs have tools that help you identify dependencies between the tables and views in your database.

Microsoft Access has a tool called **Object Dependencies** that helps you identify all objects dependent on a particular table, query, form, or report, as well as vice versa—the objects that the particular table or query depends on. For example, several other queries, forms, and reports might be dependent on a particular query which in turn is dependent on three tables.

To view the object dependencies for a particular object in Microsoft Access, perform the following steps:

- Click the object in the Navigation Pane to select it.
- Click Database Tools on the ribbon, and then click the Object Dependencies button (Database Tools tab | Relationships group).

Adding or Changing a Relationship

Adding or changing a relationship can have a major impact on the queries and processes of a relational database management system depending on how many other tables are connected to the relationship. Thoughtful database normalization prior to relational database implementation helps avoid the rework required to add or change a relationship. In general, though, if you need to add or change a relationship, the sooner you fix it, no matter how much rework is involved, the better.

Improperly related tables cause confusion and errors in application development, which undermines the confidence of everyone who uses the database throughout the rest of its life. Improperly related tables are the primary reason relational database applications fail. While the work of adding or changing a relationship can seem daunting at first, the effort is almost always necessary and worth it in the long run.

YOUR TURN 7-4

Display the object dependencies for the ProjectEstimates query. Identify the objects that depend on the query. Identify the objects that the query depends on.

SUPPORT DATA REPLICATION

Database replication means that a copy of the database is distributed to other computers or locations. The early reasons for replicating a database involved network limitations. For example, sales reps needed to have the entire catalog of products from a database on their laptops to show customers in locations that didn't have a network connection to the main office. These early versions included **master-slave** configurations, in which the headquarters location contained the master copy of the database, and the copy, also called the **replica**, was refreshed when it was reconnected to the master.

Over time, technology improved to allow the replica copies to be more functional, even giving users the ability to enter and edit new data. This created a need for **synchronization**, a process to apply and reconcile updates and changes from the various copies of the database with the master.

Now, with the ubiquitous nature of the web, traditional "master-slave" models of distributed databases are not as common. Users connected to the web have programs and applications that allow them to access database information from the centralized database whenever and wherever they need it.

Still, the concept of **distributed databases** is thriving with technologies such as **Git**, a free and open source distributed version control system that allows multiple developers to work on the same code base using distributed copies of the code. Git can also be described as a version control system language that provides the commands to create, compare, and merge changes between files.

With Git, each developer checks out their own repository or copy of the code base, often called a **branch**. After they work on their own branch to accomplish a single task, they **stage** and then **commit** the changes they've made back to the main repository and issue a **pull** request to alert others that it's time to review and accept or reject their changes. The owner of each branch can **merge** or ignore changes into their branch. There can be as many branches, and branches of branches, as desired.

Git uses **snapshots** to compare code statements, and knows how to apply or roll back the change sets between two snapshots to merge (or not merge) code from one branch into its parent branch and vice versa. **GitHub** and **BitBucket** are two popular websites for hosting projects that use the Git language for version control.

Q & A 7-5

Question: What is the main difference between reconciling the copies of data involved in traditional database replication as compared to the copies created in the distributed database model used by Git?

Answer: Traditional database replication relies on centralized control that determines when replicas may be created and how they are synchronized with the master copy.

The distributed database model used by Git allows users to create a new branch (copy of the code base) as well as commit or merge changes from a parent branch at any time.

Summary

- **Introduce the services provided by a database management system**. The primary job of a relational database management system is to provide access to and maintain data. A popular acronym for these activities is to CRUD (Create, Read, Update, and Delete) data.
- **Examine the catalog feature**. The catalog, also called the data dictionary in some systems, contains metadata, data about the data. For example, all table names, field names, field properties, and relationships between the tables are stored in the catalog.
- **Study the concurrent update problem**. The concurrent update problem refers to the issue of two or more people wanting to update the same data at the same time, and how that conflict is resolved. It includes the concepts of data concurrency, giving all users access to the same data at the same time, and data consistency, making sure all updates to data are presented to all users at the same time. Database management systems have sophisticated features to address and resolve this issue, including features such as two-phase locking and timestamps.
- **Explain the data recovery process in a database environment**. Recovering from an attack or outage on a database starts with a reliable backup that allows a company to reset from a specific point in time. Incremental backups throughout the day, journaling, and snapshots are features that help update a backup to a specific point in time.
- **Describe the security services**. Security is the prevention of unauthorized access, either intentional or accidental, to a database. It involves encryption of data as well as the implementation of user IDs and passwords, which grant specific access to database tables and views.
- **Examine the data integrity features**. Data integrity features refer to rules set on fields and relationships in a database to prevent or at least minimize the entry of incorrect data. Enforcing referential integrity on a one-to-many relationship prevents the entry of orphan records in the "many" table. Paying careful attention to setting appropriate properties on individual fields starting with the best data type as well as considering the Validation Rule, Validation Text, Format, and Size properties helps constrain the data entered into a field to valid entries.
- **Discuss data independence**. Data independence refers to the concept that changes can be made to the database without affecting each program and process that uses the database. This is achieved because the data is controlled and managed by the relational database management system itself, not the program that selects or modifies it. Not all changes to a relational database are independent from programs. Changes to relationships and field names require rework in the processes and programs that use that data.
- **Define and describe data replication**. Data replication means making a copy of data for use in a distributed environment. Traditional data replication schemes included a master-slave arrangement where all changes were dictated to the replica by the master. Today's distributed databases such as those used by Git version control software systems focus on users and let users decide when to make copies and when to merge changes into parent branches.

Key Terms

ACID	consistency
after image	CRUD (create, read, update, delete)
Amazon Relational Database Service	data concurrency
atomicity	data consistency
authentication	data dictionary
backup	data independence
backward recovery	data integrity constraint
before image	data type
biometric	database-as-a-service
BitBucket	Database Documenter (Access cataloging feature)
branch (Git term)	database replication
catalog	database schema
commit (Git command)	DBA (database administrator)
concurrent update	decrypting

dirty read	password
distributed database	pencil symbol (Access icon)
durability	phantom read (phantom)
encryption	privacy
enterprise-level system	pull (Git command)
FERPA (Family Educational Rights and Privacy Act)	read-only
file-level	record-level locking
Format (Access field property)	recovery
forward recovery	Relationship report (Access database schema report)
Git	replica
GitHub	rollback
HIPAA (Health Insurance Portability and Accountability Act)	smart card
	smart fob
HTTP (HyperText Transfer Protocol)	snapshot
Input Mask (Access field property)	solution stack
isolation	SQL keywords (INSERT, SELECT, UPDATE, DELETE)
journal	stage (Git term)
journaling	stateless
key integrity constraint	synchronization
LAMP (Linux, Apache, MySQL, PHP)	table privilege
LAPP (Linux, Apache, PostgreSQL, PHP)	timestamping
legal value	transaction
log	two-phase locking
master-slave configuration (database)	user ID
merge (Git command)	user-level
metadata	Validation Rule (Access field property)
methods (HTTP: POST, GET, PATCH, DELETE)	Validation Text (Access field property)
Microsoft Azure SQL Database	WAMP (Windows, Apache, MySQL, PHP)
nonrepeatable (fuzzy) read	WIMP (Windows, Internet Information Services, MySQL, PHP)
Object Dependencies (Access tool)	
offsite	WINS (Windows, Internet Information Services, SQL Server, .NET (C#))

Module Review Questions

Problems

1. Which of the following programming languages does the "P" in modern software solution stacks such as the LAMP, LAPP, and WAMP stacks *not* stand for:
   a. PHP
   b. Python
   c. Perl
   d. Pascal

2. Which of the following would *not* be an example of metadata found in a database catalog?
   a. values in a primary key field
   b. table and view names
   c. relationship descriptions
   d. index definitions

3. Data consistency means _____.
   a. allowing two or more users to access the database at the same time
   b. giving each user a consistent view of the data including changes
   c. using properties such as the Validation Rule property to improve data entry accuracy
   d. implementing offsite backups

4. Which feature potentially helps you recover data in an Access database?
   a. journaling
   b. incremental backups
   c. two-step locking
   d. compact and repair

5. Which SQL statement would give user cyclone1 the ability to select, insert, update, or delete records from the Students table?
   a. `GRANT SELECT, INSERT on STUDENTS to cyclone1`
   b. `GRANT ALL on STUDENTS to cyclone1`
   c. `GRANT GLOBAL on STUDENTS to cyclone1`
   d. `GRANT cyclone1 TO STUDENTS`

6. Which of the following is *not* a constraint on the primary key field for a table?
   a. There may be no null values.
   b. All values must be unique.
   c. All values must have a matching value in the foreign key field of the table in which it has a one-to-many relationship.
   d. All values must contain data within the data type assigned to that field.

7. Which of the following changes to a database would most likely require the most rework to existing programs and queries?
   a. adding a new field to a table
   b. creating a new index
   c. changing relationships between tables
   d. adding a new view

8. GitHub and BitBucket are popular websites for _____.
   a. hosting projects that use the Git language for version control
   b. completing full-stack web app projects
   c. posting technical questions and receiving answers
   d. reading about trends in the digital development industry

Critical Thinking Questions

1. Create a list of five practical and free precautions you can take to protect your Social Security number.

2. Use Figure 7-5 to research a database service for an enterprise-level relational database and document three new key terms based on how that particular vendor handles that particular service. (Examples: Data security by Oracle, Data integrity by MySQL, Backups by SQL Server).

JC Consulting Case Exercises

For the following exercises, you address problems and answer questions for management at JC Consulting. Open and use the JCConsulting.accdb database to answer your questions.

Problems

1. Which of the following types of Access objects may *not* be used for data entry?
   a. ProjectEstimates report
   b. Projects form
   c. ProjectEstimates query
   d. Projects table

2. Which of the following represents information that the Database Documenter feature *cannot* supply?
   a. property information for tables
   b. list of current unique values for fields
   c. index information for tables
   d. relationship information

3. What symbol does Access use to the left of a record when it is currently being edited and is therefore locked so that other users cannot currently update it?
   a. lock
   b. black right arrow
   c. plus sign
   d. pencil

4. Which Access tool helps you recover data in the current database?
   a. Analyze Performance
   b. Database Documenter
   c. Compact and Repair Database
   d. Backup Database

5. A database password in Access works at the _____ level.
   a. record
   b. user
   c. file
   d. group

6. What does Access automatically add to backup files?
   a. current user's name
   b. current date
   c. current time of day
   d. backup sequential value

7. Which SQL statement would add a new field in the Employees table to a query?
   a. `SELECT ALL FROM EMPLOYEES`
   b. `SELECT * FROM EMPLOYEES`
   c. `SELECT EACH FROM EMPLOYEES`
   d. `SELECT FROM EMPLOYEES`

8. Which process can you set to automatically occur when a database is closed?
   a. compact
   b. backup
   c. document
   d. analyze

Critical Thinking Questions

1. What type of backup schedule and process would you recommend for JC Consulting?
2. What type of compact and repair schedule would you recommend for JC Consulting?

Pitt Fitness Case Exercises

Problems

1. The new DBA at Pitt Fitness is working on catalog services in Microsoft Access. This employee has published an internal report on the database schema, but the managers receiving this report are confused by the term "database schema." What does the report contain?
   a. a model of the tables and relationships between the tables
   b. a new type of query output
   c. a newsletter on the status of the database
   d. the disk space the database consumes

2. The new IT person hired by Pitt Fitness is becoming familiar with the database and requests the database schema. How can you generate the schema from the current Access database?
    a. Click the All Relationships button (Database Tools tab | Relationships group).
    b. Click the Direct Relationships button (Database Tools tab | Relationships group).
    c. Click the Relationships button (Database Tools tab | Relationships group), and then click the Clear Layout button (Relationship Tools Design tab | Tools group).
    d. Click the Relationships button (Database Tools tab | Relationships group), and then click the Relationship Report button (Relationship Tools Design tab | Tools group).

3. Two clerks at Pitt Fitness need to update an address in the Access database for the customer Min Jee Choi. One clerk sees a note about updating the address and begins to edit Min Jee's record. At the same time, another clerk receives a phone call from Min Jee about changing the address and opens the Customers table. She sees a pencil symbol next to the record for Min Jee Choi and cannot change the address. What is happening with the database?
    a. Min Jee's record cannot be changed. Once you enter an address in the Customers table, it can never be altered or deleted.
    b. The record is locked from editing by any user except the first clerk. Only one person can edit a record at one time.
    c. The entire database is read-only because the first clerk is working on changing the record.
    d. The database has been corrupted because two people are working on the record at the same time.

4. Popular classes at Pitt Fitness fill up almost immediately. What database technique would work well to determine which people should be admitted into a popular class based on when they requested entry?
    a. two-phase locking
    b. timestamping
    c. phantom locking
    d. concurrent locking

5. Pitt Fitness's IT person backs up the database every day at the end of business hours. After completing their evening classes, customers register for classes for the upcoming week. Assume that a thunderstorm made Pitt Fitness lose power 12 hours starting at midnight. What state would the database be in when the power was restored?
    a. All class registrations after business hours would be lost.
    b. All class registrations after business hours would be recorded.
    c. The database would be entirely corrupted.
    d. The database would become fragmented.

6. Suppose Pitt Fitness were using an enterprise-level DBMS when a thunderstorm caused a brief power loss to the database, stopping a class registration entry in midstream. When the power was fully restored, the database would not be in a valid state. What type of recovery is needed to undo the problem transaction?
    a. forward recovery
    b. backward recovery
    c. instant recovery
    d. timed recovery

7. The IT manager at Pitt Fitness is creating a backup of the company database. What is the best location for storing the backup?
    a. at the Downtown location
    b. next to the current database for easy access
    c. in the cloud
    d. Pitt Fitness is too small to have a backup.

8. Which of the following data integrity constraints would ensure Pitt Fitness has a consistent method to record customer phone numbers?
    a. format (Input Mask)
    b. legal values
    c. data type
    d. Validation Rule

9. Pitt Fitness is now routinely creating backups of their database. They store them on a server and have a number of backup files that need to be deleted. Which of the following files is the correct backup and should *not* be deleted?
   a. PittFitness_2021-08-12
   b. PittFitness_2021-09-30
   c. PittFitness_2021-10-31
   d. PittFitness_2021-11-27

10. The IT manager at Pitt Fitness wants to secure the database using a method that includes processing logic to periodically change and synchronize with passwords stored on the database. Which of the following choices would fit that requirement?
    a. fingerprint
    b. smart card
    c. facial recognition
    d. voice recognition

Critical Thinking Questions

1. Pitt Fitness would like to analyze their options for an in-house database versus a cloud database-as-a-service. What are the benefits to moving their database to the cloud?

2. Create a data integrity constraint for the Pitt Fitness database that only allows a user to enter one of the three fitness locations into the Classes table.

Sports Physical Therapy Case Exercises

Problems

1. If Sports Physical Therapy had an enterprise DBMS, the IT manager might look at the journal log if a record seemed wrong. Which log entry would indicate that a transaction was completed successfully?
   a. Start
   b. Commit
   c. Insert
   d. Update

2. If Sports Physical Therapy had an enterprise DBMS and the IT manager looked at the journal log, which log entry would indicate a change of a record?
   a. Start
   b. Commit
   c. Insert
   d. Update

3. Security is especially important for Sports Physical Therapy because the medical information stored on the database must be kept private by law. What is the federal law that protects medical records and other personal health information?
   a. FERPA
   b. FDA
   c. HIPAA
   d. FDIC

4. The IT manager at Sports Physical Therapy would like to secure the database with an authentication method that identifies users by physical or behavioral characteristics. What type of authentication fits that requirement?
   a. password
   b. biometric
   c. smart card
   d. key fob

5. The IT manager at Sports Physical Therapy would like to incorporate a data integrity constraint to ensure accuracy and consistency to the database. Specifically, the manager wants to consider a legal value for the UnitOfTime field in the Therapies table. What is a reasonable legal value constraint for this field?
   a. >15
   b. <15
   c. <=60
   d. >=0

6. Which of the following fields in the Patient table in the Sports Physical Therapy database would be appropriate for an Access input mask?
   a. LastName
   b. FirstName
   c. Address
   d. State

7. How can Sports Physical Therapy ensure that if an unauthorized user attempts to gain access to the database, they see only an indecipherable version of the database?
   a. Set a strong password.
   b. Encrypt the database.
   c. Authenticate the database.
   d. Ensure the server room has a good lock on the door.

8. What type of concurrent update occurs when two physical therapists are trying to update the record of the same patient at the same time?
   a. record-level locking
   b. read-only locking
   c. stateless locking
   d. data concurrent locking

9. What is the property of the Sports Physical Therapy database that lets the users change the database structure without requiring changes to all the programs that might access that database?
   a. clean data
   b. updated data
   c. data independence
   d. separated data

10. The IT manager at Sports Physical Therapy finds it useful to identify all objects that depend on a particular table, query, form, or report. How can that be accomplished in Access?
    a. Double-click the object, and then click the Database Documenter button (Database Tools tab | Analyze group).
    b. Click the object, and then click the Analyze Table button (Database Tools tab | Analyze group).
    c. Click the object, and then click the Object Dependencies button (Database Tools tab | Relationships group).
    d. Click the object, and then click the Relationships button (Database Tools tab | Relationships group).

Critical Thinking Questions

1. The IT manager at Sports Physical Therapy finds it useful to identify all objects that are dependent on a particular table, query, form, or report. List the tables that the Session table depends on.

2. The IT manager at Sports Physical Therapy needs to know all the relationships in the database. Use Access to create a Relationship report for the Sports Physical Therapy database for your own reference. Use Database Design Language to identify the relationships in the database.

MODULE **8**

DATABASE INDUSTRY CAREERS

LEARNING OBJECTIVES

- Explore and describe jobs and careers in the database industry
- Summarize the policy-making, technical, and administrative responsibilities of a database administrator (DBA)
- Define the job titles and responsibilities for employees who may report to the DBA
- Describe the responsibilities of a data analyst
- Explain the responsibilities of a data scientist
- Explore the educational credentials and industry certifications that support a career in the database industry

INTRODUCTION

In this module, you will learn about careers in the database industry. You will study the responsibilities of the **database administrator** (**DBA**), whose primary task is to ensure that a database is available as needed and is protected and secured from unauthorized users and activities. You will learn about the DBA's role in setting data policies as well as the DBA's technical and administrative duties.

In addition, you will explore the expanding list of job titles for those who analyze data to help organizations make faster and better decisions. These job titles include data analyst, research analyst, and data scientist. You will also study the educational credentials and technical certifications that support these important and rewarding job titles and career paths.

CAREERS IN THE DATABASE INDUSTRY

Careers in the database industry that lead to the prominent position of database administrator (DBA) have traditionally been strong and financially rewarding given the importance of healthy, secure data to practically every traditional operation within a business. "Traditional" operations of a business include the internal processes of billing, inventory control, accounts receivable, sales analysis, general ledger, accounts payable, and payroll, historically identified with the acronyms **BICARSA** and **GLAPPR**.

Today, however, new careers on the data analysis side of the database industry have emerged to address the desire for modern businesses to make faster and better data-driven business decisions. Data analysts, professionals whose focus is to analyze internal data and relationships among data as well as data scientists, people employed to interpret complex and very large sets of data, are in high demand.

Today's business leaders want quick and reliable access to internal data, but also have an unquenchable appetite for relevant external information. External information might include:

- News about competitors
- Industry trends
- Technology shifts
- Scientific discoveries
- Government mandates
- Weather patterns
- Worldwide political events

Executives have traditionally gleaned news from sources such as the *Wall Street Journal, Business Week,* or online websites and news feeds for anything happening outside of the internal operations of the organization that might have a significant impact on their business.

Now, however, external data can be collected digitally, including **big data**, which may be defined as an extremely large set of nontraditional data that can be used to gain meaningful business insights or predict significant business events. Big data includes the following information sources:

- Blog postings
- Images
- Reviews
- Clicks
- Tweets
- Connections
- Voice commands
- Search keywords
- Other Internet-driven processes

This data also has relevance to business decisions, but it is often not stored in a company's internal, centralized relational database that was originally set up to handle the traditional business processes of the organization. Big data typically is too large, is too varied, and changes too quickly to be managed by a traditional relational database system. The characteristics of big data, as well as other current database issues and trends, are further studied in Module 9.

A rewarding career in any technical area relies on a combination of relevant educational credentials, industry certifications, and a track record of successful experience. The same is true of the database industry no matter whether you seek a career in traditional database management as a DBA or in the new and evolving area of data science.

Q & A 8-1

Question: What is the main difference between traditional and emerging careers in the database industry?

Answer: While all careers in the database industry are currently strong, a "traditional" career that leads to a position of database administrator (DBA) focuses on the management and security of internal, transactional data.

Modern emerging careers focus on the analysis of data: internal, external, and big data. The goal of data analysis is to help an organization make better and faster business decisions.

ROLE OF A DATABASE ADMINISTRATOR

The **database administrator (DBA)** is the person responsible for organizing, managing, and securing an existing database. A DBA typically reports to the **CIO (chief information officer)** in a large organization and to the president in a small company. According to the U.S. Bureau of Labor Statistics, the 2018 the median annual pay for a database administrator was $90,070, and the job outlook for 2018–2028 was 9 percent growth (faster than average).

Duties and Responsibilities of a DBA

The responsibilities of the database administrator vary depending on the size and nature of the business. In larger organizations, the role is more administrative, given that the DBA manages several employees who in turn handle specific skills and responsibilities. In smaller companies, the DBA may do everything from database design to data analysis. In large organizations or companies that handle sensitive data such as the medical industry, the DBA must have extensive experience in security, disaster recovery planning, and government compliance. Sometimes the responsibilities of data security, disaster recovery, and compliance issues are shared with a **CSO (chief security officer)**.

In general, DBAs help define and model data requirements, business rules, and database policies. They also work closely with software application developers to write SQL and grant appropriate access to data and metadata. DBAs are also involved with installing, configuring, and testing database hardware and software. They are typically responsible for the security of the database and the data disaster recovery plan.

Figure 8-1 summarizes the responsibilities of a DBA within three major categories: database policy formation and enforcement, database technical functions, and other database administrative functions.

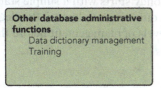

Database policy formation and enforcement
Access privileges
Security
Disaster planning
Archiving

Database technical functions
Database design
SQL and views
Testing
Performance tuning
Database maintenance

Other database administrative functions
Data dictionary management
Training

FIGURE 8-1   Responsibilities of a DBA

Q & A 8-2

Question: What are the major areas of responsibility for a DBA?

Answer: Data policy formation and enforcement, technical activities as they relate to creating and maintaining the database, and administrative duties such as documentation and training.

DATABASE POLICY FORMULATION AND ENFORCEMENT

No matter how large or small the organization, the DBA is responsible for developing, communicating, and enforcing database policies. Important database policies include granting access privileges, setting up proper database security, creating and testing a disaster recovery plan, and implementing a backup and archiving system.

Access Privileges

The DBA ultimately determines the access privileges for all users and enters the appropriate authorization rules in the database management system catalog to ensure that users access the database only in ways to which they are entitled. As you learned in Module 7, the SQL GRANT statement defines access privileges. Figure 8-2 lists SQL GRANT and REVOKE database privilege keywords for a table or view:

Privilege	Description
SELECT	Ability to perform SELECT statements
INSERT	Ability to perform INSERT statements
UPDATE	Ability to perform UPDATE statements
DELETE	Ability to perform DELETE statements
REFERENCES	Ability to create a constraint
ALTER	Ability to perform ALTER TABLE statements to change the table definition
ALL	ALL grants the permissions of SELECT, INSERT, UPDATE, DELETE, and REFERENCES

FIGURE 8-2   Basic SQL GRANT and REVOKE privileges

For example, if a new employee with the username *bbtoma7* needs to maintain the Employees table, the DBA might write the following SQL code:

```
GRANT ALL ON Employees TO bbtoma7;
```

The REVOKE statement rescinds privileges in a similar manner. For example, if the same employee should not be able to delete records or change the constraints on the Employees table, the DBA might issue the following SQL command:

```
REVOKE REFERENCES, DELETE ON Employees TO bbtoma7;
```

Note that multiple privileges are delineated with commas.

The DBA should document the access privilege policy for approval by top-level management as well as communicate the policy to all users. Typically, the access privilege policy starts with a simple statement that grants privileges to only those users and processes with a "need or requirement to know." Privileges should be dated and documented, and are generally approved by multiple levels of management before they are implemented by the DBA.

Security

Recall that security is the prevention of unauthorized access, either intentional or accidental, to a database. Granting only the minimum amount of privileges needed by each user and process to complete their responsibilities helps prevent intentional or accidental modification of data.

To implement and enforce security, many companies start by installing **spyware/malware detection software** on all computers to detect and stop cyberattack threats at the first point of entry. **Malware** refers to malicious software of any sort that exploits system vulnerabilities such as a bug in an operating system that allows an unauthorized user access to that computer. **Spyware** refers to software that enables an intruder to covertly obtain information about a computer's activities such as the keystrokes made on the keyboard. The DBA also uses the security features within the relational database system, such as the following:

- **Encryption**: The process of scrambling data—that is, moving it through a network so that if intercepted, it is unintelligible to the intruder
- **Authentication**: The process of verifying the identity of the person or process accessing the data
- **Authorization**: The process of granting specific rights and privileges to a user, program, or process.
- **Views**: Using SQL to create a subset of fields and records for a particular user, programs, or purpose.

Securing data has become such a major issue for most companies, an entirely new career area that focuses on data security has emerged. The term **cybersecurity** refers to the process of protecting networks, devices, and data from any type of digital attack or **cyberattack**. Cybersecurity experts are typically well skilled in the technical aspects of how networks operate and work closely with the DBA to protect company data from cyberattacks. A partial list of job titles within the greater field of cybersecurity includes the following:

- Security software developer
- Information security analyst
- Ethical hacker
- Penetration tester
- Computer forensic analyst
- Security systems administrator

Disaster Planning

Disaster recovery planning involves documenting and practicing a step-by-step plan of instructions to minimize the effects of a natural disaster on the mission-critical operations of a business. **Mission critical** refers to those systems that are essential to the survival of the business, and the central relational database system that manages the traditional business processes of an organization is typically central to many mission critical processes.

A **disaster recovery plan** specifies the ongoing and emergency actions and procedures required to ensure data availability if a disaster occurs. For example, a disaster recovery plan includes steps for protecting an organization's data against a successful cyberattack or physical failures that might include hardware failures, power loss, or even a complete loss of a data center due to a natural disaster. Key elements of a successful disaster recovery plan include the following:

- Define a recovery time objective and a recovery point objective.
  A **recovery time objective (RTO)** is the length of time it takes a company to resume mission-critical services after a disaster. A **recovery point objective (RPO)** is the maximum amount of data you are willing to lose in a disaster. The RTO and RPO decisions help drive many of the other tasks necessary to support the disaster recovery plan.

- Define and communicate protocols, roles, and responsibilities.
  Disasters create chaos. All employees should know and practice personal safety protocols such as knowing the location of safety equipment and shelters well before a disaster occurs. The disaster recovery plan should include documentation such as employee contact lists, emergency telephone numbers, and all task assignments for as many types of disasters as possible to predict (fire, flood, hurricane, power outage, cyberattack, hardware failure, and medical emergency, for example).

- Inventory all assets.
  The disaster recovery plan should list all inventory, both physical and digital, as well as vendor contact information.

- Back up data and systems.
  The disaster recovery plan should identify the backup and recovery procedures at the offsite backup locations necessary to support the RTO and RPO decisions. **Cloud backup** is a scalable strategy for backing up data to an offsite server **"in the cloud"** (a metaphor for data and processes run through the Internet). Fees are based on capacity, bandwidth, or the number of users. Alternatively, a backup might be kept locally if the production system runs in the cloud.

  To protect against local hard drive failures, organizations often use a **redundant array of inexpensive/independent drives (RAID)**, in which database updates are replicated to multiple hard drives so that an organization can continue to process the updates after losing one of its hard drives. To protect against local electrical power interruptions and outages, organizations use an **uninterruptible power supply (UPS)**, which is a power source such as a battery or fuel cell for short interruptions and a power generator for longer outages.

  Some transactions are extremely time sensitive such as credit card processing, stock exchanges, and airline reservations. In these situations, RPO is zero. Data must be continuous. A **hot site** is a backup site that an organization can switch to within minutes because the site is completely equipped with duplicate hardware, software, and data and may even run in parallel to the production system. A less expensive **warm site** (also sometimes called a **cold site**) is a backup site that is equipped with duplicate hardware and software but for which current data would need to be loaded to function.

- Test the disaster recovery plan.
  A disaster recovery plan should be tested against various scenarios. Simulating realistic disasters helps uncover where the plan needs to be improved and provides invaluable experience in the event of an actual disaster.

Archiving

Data archiving is the process of moving data that is not needed on a regular basis by the functions of the organization to a separate storage device for long-term retention. Archiving unneeded data can have a positive impact on the performance of daily processes. However, the DBA needs to understand their current legal responsibilities regarding both the retention and destruction of old data. Examples of laws that govern data access, retention, and destruction include the following:

- The **Sarbanes–Oxley (SOX) Act** of 2002, a federal law that specifies data retention and verification requirements for public companies, requires CEOs and CFOs to certify financial statements and makes it a crime to destroy or tamper with financial records. Congress passed this law in response to major accounting scandals involving Enron, WorldCom, and Tyco.

- The **Patriot Act** of 2001 is a federal law that specifies data retention requirements for the identification of clients opening accounts at financial institutions, allows law enforcement agencies to search companies' and individuals' records and communications, and expands the government's authority to regulate financial transactions. President George W. Bush signed the Patriot Act into law 45 days after the September 11, 2001, terrorist attacks against the United States.
- The Security and Exchange Commission's Rule 17a-4 (**SEC Rule 17a-4**) specifies the retention requirements of all electronic communications and records for financial and investment entities.
- The **Department of Defense (DOD) 5015.2 Standard** of 1997 provides data management requirements for the DOD and for companies supplying or dealing with the DOD.
- The **Health Insurance Portability and Accountability Act (HIPAA)** of 1996 is a federal law that specifies the rules for storing, handling, and protecting healthcare transaction data.
- The **Family Educational Rights and Privacy Act (FERPA)** of 1974 and subsequent amendments is a federal law that affords parents the right to access their children's education records, the right to seek to have the records amended, and the right to have some control over the disclosure of personally identifiable information from the education records. When a student turns 18 years old, or enters a postsecondary institution at any age, the rights under FERPA transfer from the parents to the student.
- The **Presidential Records Act** of 1978 is a federal law that regulates the data retention requirements for all communications, including electronic communications, of U.S. presidents and vice presidents. Congress passed this law after the scandals during the Nixon administration.

If a company does business internationally, additional laws govern the use, retention, storage, and destruction of data. For example, in 2015 Australia passed a law requiring all companies doing business in Australia to keep customer data, including telephony, Internet, and email metadata, for a period of two years.

Q & A 8-3

Question: What has been one of the most recent significant cyberattacks?

Answer: In May of 2019, according to *Wired* magazine, a surveillance contractor for the U.S. Customs and Border Protection, Perceptics, suffered a breach in which hackers stole photos of travelers and license plates for about 100,000 people. Your answer should reflect cyberattacks in the year 2020 or beyond.

DATABASE TECHNICAL FUNCTIONS

The DBA is responsible for database technical functionality, including relational database design, testing, performance tuning, and maintenance.

Database Design

The DBA makes sure that the current database is clearly and accurately created using normalization techniques discussed in Module 5, as well as implemented and documented using the database models discussed in Module 6. Often, the database management system itself has a feature that provides documentation about the tables, views, and relationships, but the DBA may want to provide a simplified overall data schema to different users of the database. For clarity and simplicity, the DBA may want to provide information on only the views that a particular user or process has access to rather than a description of the entire database.

The DBA oversees all of the changes in the design of the database. The DBA also controls all documentation that describes the tables, views, columns, and constraints of the database and verifies that programmers modify all programs and documentation affected by any changes.

SQL and Views

Typically, the DBA is very skilled at SQL and creating views for the various users, programs, and needs of the business. The creation of views and SQL is the primary subject of Modules 3, 4, and 5. Often, entry-level jobs in the database industry involve excellent SQL skills within job titles such as data analyst, research analyst, and business analyst.

Testing

The combination of hardware, software, and database that the users and regular applications of the company use is called the **production system**, or **live system**. For testing and application development, the DBA can create a separate system, called the **test system**, or **sandbox**, that programmers use to develop new programs and modify existing programs. After programmers complete the testing of their programs in the test system, a separate quality assurance group can perform further tests. After testing and approving any new features, the DBA can transfer the programs to the production system and make any required database changes, as shown in Figure 8-3.

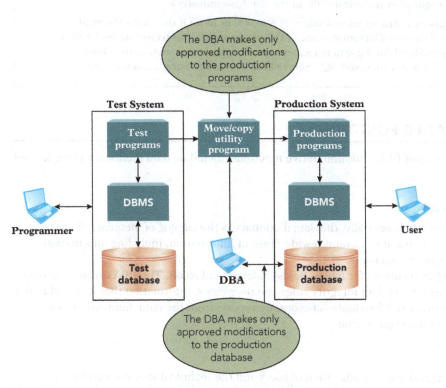

FIGURE 8-3 DBA controls the interaction between the test and production systems

Performance Tuning

Database performance deals with the ability of the production system to serve users in a timely and responsive manner. Faster computers with faster storage media, faster network connections, faster software, and other production system expenditures help improve performance, but the DBA can also take other measures to improve performance as well. This process is called **tuning** the design and includes creating and deleting indexes, minimizing the complexity of each view to only what is needed, and changing the table design.

Although you design database tables in third normal form to prevent the anomaly problems discussed in Module 5, the DBA occasionally denormalizes tables to improve performance. **Denormalizing** converts a table in third normal form to a table with redundant data. Occasionally this makes sense to improve performance, but because it creates redundant data, the performance benefits must be carefully weighed against the offsetting inherent problems associated with redundant data.

Another performance consideration that a DBA may evaluate is to run multiple instances of a single, shared database, called a **parallel database system**. A parallel database system can balance the workload among CPUs to improve overall throughput.

DBMS Maintenance

Like all software programs, database management systems are improved over time and offer new **software releases**, the distribution of a final version, to their users. Software releases may include new features or bug fixes. Often, vendors encourage their customers to install new software releases in an effort to patch known problems, which makes it faster and easier for the vendor to support the customer and address any issues. The DBA is typically responsible for evaluating, scheduling, and applying all new database management system software releases.

A **run-book** is a log of all database maintenance, with dates, license keys, issues or updates, involved personnel, and resolutions. It also may contain a record of where backups and **archives** are located and list other database maintenance activities.

Q & A 8-4

Question: What are the most sought-after technical skills in the database industry?

Answer: Database administrators can earn an annual salary of $90,000 or more if they have the right credentials and a successful track record. Currently, some of the most sought-after technical credentials are those offered by the enterprise-level database management system companies such as the Oracle Administrator Certified Professional and Microsoft SQL Server Database Administration certificates.

DATABASE ADMINISTRATIVE FUNCTIONS

The DBA is also responsible for several DBMS administrative functions, including data dictionary management and training.

Data Dictionary Management

The DBA manages the data dictionary. Essentially, the data dictionary is the catalog of metadata about the database mentioned in Module 7 and usually contains a wide range of information, including information about tables, fields, indexes, programs, and users.

The DBA establishes naming conventions for tables, fields, indexes, and so on. The DBA creates the data definitions for all tables, as well as for any data integrity rules and user views, information that is stored in the data dictionary. The DBA also creates and distributes appropriate reports from the data dictionary to users, programmers, and other people in the organization.

Training

The DBA coordinates the training and ongoing education of users and the technical staff responsible for developing and maintaining database applications. Successful organizations commit to excellent training because they know that without knowledgeable and confident users, resources are wasted, expensive mistakes occur, and profitable business opportunities are lost.

Q & A 8-5

Question: How long does it take to become a DBA?

Answer: The specific answer to this question depends on the size of the employer's business, but in general, the job of a DBA requires a broad spectrum of technical knowledge, business knowledge, communication skills, and management experience. It can easily take 10–15 years of experience in the data industry before a person has the credentials and experience necessary to apply for a position as a DBA for a medium to large business, and typically that path goes through a job with a title similar to database operations manager. On the other hand, a small business might add DBA responsibilities to a responsible programmer, data analyst, or systems analyst in a short period of time.

PROFESSIONALS REPORTING TO THE DBA

Given the widespread activities and responsibilities of a DBA, in large organizations, these tasks are handled by several employees who often report to the DBA. Those employees have a variety of job titles and responsibilities such as the following:

- **Application DBA:** Focuses on database design and the ongoing support and administration of databases for a specific application or set of applications within a business.

- **System DBA:** Focuses on technical rather than business issues, primarily in the system administration area such as the installation, performance, and maintenance of the database management system.
- **Task-oriented DBA or database operations manager:** Centers on a specific, important DBA task such as backup-and-recovery, security, or government regulations and compliance.
- **Performance analyst:** Concentrates on database performance. Has very detailed technical knowledge of the database management system, indexes, and SQL so that improvements can be made in speed and response times. A performance analyst will typically report to a system DBA.
- **Database architect:** Focuses on database design. Helps determine new information requirements, builds logical views for users and processes, and helps convert research into better products.
- **Data modeler:** Performs data modeling for a particular business area by collecting and analyzing data requirements. Data modelers typically report to the company's database architect.
- **Database analyst:** Creates logical views of the data to respond to user and application requests. Summarizes and analyzes data to extract trends, insights, and knowledge. Has deep SQL skills. Database analysts typically report to the database architect or perhaps an application DBA.
- **Research analyst:** Works as a database analyst when the job responsibilities focus on the analysis of specific research data. Research analysts may report up through the information systems department or the internal operations areas of a business.
- **Business analyst:** Works as a database analyst when the job responsibilities focus on bridging the gap between the information and data needs of the business in general and the technical requirements of extracting and analyzing that data. Business analysts typically report up through the business departments to which they serve. For example, a company might have a different business analyst in the personnel, inventory, logistics, and finance departments.
- **Product manager:** Directs the activities specific to a product or technical service such as access to a database. The title is used in many different ways across different organizations, but in a technical company, often acts a liaison between departmental and user needs and technical teams.
- **Data warehouse administrator:** Requires traditional DBA skills plus knowledge of any data warehousing technologies in place such as **BI (business intelligence)** tools, **ETL (extract, transform, load)** technologies, and **OLAP (Online Analytical Processing)** tools.
- **Data scientist:** Analyzes massive sets of data, typically in a stand-alone department versus reporting to the DBA. A senior data scientist often has an entire department of data scientists that know how to model, interpret, and present insights from volumes of internal, external, and "big" data. In technology businesses, data scientists often conduct infrastructure testing to plan for future optimization of hardware, software, datasets, and networks.
- **Data visualization expert:** Works with data to visually present patterns, trends, anomalies, and other significant information in the form of a chart, diagram, picture, infographic, map, or other graphical or pictorial format. Data visualization experts help others quickly understand patterns in data that traditional descriptions of data such as lists, summarized reports, or other statistical presentations cannot. Other terms for data visualization include information graphics, statistical graphics, and information visualization.

Q & A 8-6

Question: What is the best career path to becoming a DBA?

Answer: There is no single best career path to becoming a DBA, but the data analyst position is probably the most identifiable entry-level position that typically reports directly to the DBA. Other common entry points for a career in the data industry include entry-level jobs in either programming or networking or any job title with the word "analyst" such as business analyst, operations analyst, financial analyst, or research analyst. A DBA requires a broad understanding of all technical aspects of the company's computer operations as well as a deep understanding of the business operations.

RESPONSIBILITIES OF A DATA ANALYST

A **data analyst** is a data professional who has the skills to complete the statistical and graphical analysis of internal data such as sales figures, cost of goods and services, transportation expenses, and other operational expenses to help an organization make faster and better decisions. Typically, a data analyst focuses on the analysis of internal transactions as well as research conducted by the company. A data analyst is also skilled at creating **data visualizations**, the representation of information in the form of an easy-to-understand chart, diagram, or picture using tools such as Microsoft Excel charts, Microsoft Visio flowcharting software, Microsoft Power BI (Business Intelligence) tools, or **Tableau**, a software program dedicated to helping create meaningful data visualizations.

According to glassdoor.com, almost 8,000 job postings for "data analyst" were available in 2019. The average base pay was $67,377. Related job titles included the following:

- Entry-level data analyst, $64,000
- Data analyst intern, $68,000
- Analytics, $72,000

Q & A 8-7

Question: What are typical qualifications for a data analyst?

Answer:

- Bachelor's degree in Computer Science, Statistics, Operations Research, or Math.
- Strong data analysis and programming skills. (Some of the programming languages and tools most commonly used by data analysts include Excel, Access, Power BI, SQL, Tableau, and SQL Server.)
- Two or more years of success working in any general business or technical field.

RESPONSIBILITIES OF A DATA SCIENTIST

A **data scientist** is a data professional who has the skills, experience, and insights to analyze massive sets of internal, external, and big data to help an organization make faster and better decisions. Most data scientists have spent a considerable amount of time being a data analyst or statistician, and are skilled with programming algorithms and the application of statistics to analyze large sets of data. Data scientists look for patterns and trends to discover new opportunities and solutions. Some are focused on internal processes such as how large-scale research produces better products. Others are more focused on strategies and scalable technologies that allow the company to improve and grow.

According to glassdoor.com, more than 4,000 job postings for "data scientist" were available in 2019. The average base pay was $117,345. Related job titles included the following:

- Data scientist intern, $97,000
- Quantitative analyst, $116,000
- Senior data scientist, $137,000

Q & A 8-8

Question: What are typical qualifications for a data scientist?

Answer:

- Master's or Ph.D. degree in Computer Science, Statistics, Operations Research, or Math.
- Strong data modeling, statistical modeling, programming, and other analytical skills. (Some of the programming languages most commonly used by data scientists include R, Python, SQL, and C#.)
- Experience with big data and current big data technologies such as Hadoop, which is an open source distributed processing framework for managing and processing massive sets of data.

DATABASE INDUSTRY CERTIFICATIONS

According to an article by *Business News Daily*, the top five database certifications for 2019 include those shown in alphabetical order in Figure 8-4, based on job postings from four popular online job sites: SimplyHired, Indeed, LinkedIn, and LinkUp.

Certification	SimplyHired	Indeed	LinkedIn Jobs	LinkUp	Total
IBM Certified Database Administrator—DB2	428	475	284	221	1,408
Microsoft SQL Server database certifications	5,447	6,525	8,984	3,522	24,478
Oracle Certified Professional, MySQL Database Administrator	432	534	50	200	1,216
Oracle Database 12c Administrator	217	241	33	176	667
SAP HANA	88	82	12	43	225

FIGURE 8-4 Top five database certifications of 2019 according to Business News Daily

Source: businessnewsdaily.com/10734-database-certifications.html

In addition the article states the following:

"If the sheer number of available database-related positions isn't enough motivation to pursue a certification, consider average salaries for database administrators. SimplyHired reports $86,861 as the national average in the U.S., in a range from $59,696 to over $126,000. Glassdoor's average is somewhat higher—$93,164—with a top rung right around $123,000."

Microsoft offers many certifications from Access through SQL Server. Figure 8-5 provides information for current Microsoft Access database MOS (Microsoft Office Specialist) certifications.

Certification Name	Exams
Access 2019/365	Coming soon
Access 2016: Core Database Management, Manipulation, and Query Skills	77-730
Access 2013	77-422
Access 2010	77-885
Current cost per exam	Approximately $75/exam, but varies by location. Often provided free of charge at community colleges and other educational institutions
Website	www.microsoft.com/learning

FIGURE 8-5 Microsoft Access database certifications

Microsoft SQL Server credentials fall into three major categories:

- MTA, Microsoft Technology Associate
- MCSA, Microsoft Certified Solutions Associate
- MCSE, Microsoft Certified Solutions Expert

Figure 8-6 identifies information for Microsoft SQL Server database certifications.

Certification Name	Exams
MTA Database	One exam: • Database Fundamentals (98-364)
MCSA: SQL Server 2012/2014	Three exams: • Querying Microsoft SQL Server 2012/2014 (70-461) • Administering Microsoft SQL Server 2012/2014 Databases (70-462) • Implementing a Data Warehouse with Microsoft SQL Server 2012/2014 (70-463)
MCSA: SQL 2016 BI Development	Two exams: • Implementing a SQL Data Warehouse (70-767) • Developing SQL Data Models (70-768)
MCSA: SQL 2016 Database Administration	Two exams: • Administering a SQL Database Infrastructure (70-764) • Provisioning SQL Databases (70-765)
MCSA: SQL 2016 Database Development	Two exams: • Querying Data with Transact-SQL (70-761) • Developing SQL Databases (70-762)
MCSE: Data Management and Analytics	Pick one exam from the following: • Designing and Implementing Cloud Data Platform Solutions (70-473) • Designing and Implementing Big Data Analytics Solutions (70-475) • Developing Microsoft SQL Server Databases (70-464) • Designing Database Solutions for Microsoft SQL Server (70-465) • Implementing Data Models and Reports with Microsoft SQL Server (70-466) • Designing Business Intelligence Solutions with Microsoft SQL Server (70-467) • Developing SQL Databases (70-762) • Implementing a Data Warehouse Using SQL (70-767) • Developing SQL Data Models (70-768) • Analyzing Big Data with Microsoft R (70-773) • Perform Cloud Data Science with Azure Machine Learning (70-774) • Perform Data Engineering on Microsoft Azure HDInsight (70-775) • Implementing Microsoft Azure Cosmos DB Solutions (70-777)
Current cost per exam	MTA: $127 MCSA/MCSE: $165
Website	www.microsoft.com/learning

FIGURE 8-6   Microsoft SQL Server database certifications

Figure 8-7 identifies information for IBM DB2 database certification.

Certification Name	Exams
IBM Certified Database Administrator—DB2	Two exams: • IBM DB2 11.1 DBA for LUW (C2090-600) • DB2 10.5 Fundamentals for LUW (C2090-615) OR one exam: • DB2 11.1 Fundamentals for LUW (C2090-616)
Current cost per exam	$200
Website	www.ibm.com/certify/

FIGURE 8-7   IBM DB2 database certification

Figure 8-8 identifies information for Oracle Certified Professional MySQL database certification.

Certification Name	Exams
Oracle Certified Professional, MySQL 5.7 Database Administrator	One exam: • MySQL 5.7 Database Administrator (1Z0-888)
Cost per exam	$245
Website	education.oracle.com

FIGURE 8-8 Oracle Certified Professional MySQL database certification

Figure 8-9 identifies information for Oracle Database Administrator database certifications.

Certification Name	Exams
Oracle Database 12c Administrator Certified Associate (OCA 12c)	Two exams: Choose one exam from the following: • Oracle Database 12c SQL (1Z0-071) • Oracle Database 12c: SQL Fundamentals (1Z0-061) Plus the following exam: • Oracle Database 12c: Installation and Administration (1Z0-062)
Oracle Database 12c Administrator Certified Professional (OCP 12c)	One exam: • Oracle Database 12c: Advanced Administration (1Z0-063)
Oracle Database 12c Administrator Certified Master Certification (OCM 12c)	One exam: • Oracle Database 12c Certified Master (12COCM)
Oracle Database 12c Maximum Availability Certified Master	No exam
Oracle Database 12c R2 Administration Certified Associate (OCA 12c R2)	One exam: • Oracle Database 12cR2 Administration (1Z0-072)
Oracle Database 12c R2 Administration Certified Professional (OCP 12c R2) upgrade	One exam: • Oracle DBA 12cR2 Advanced Administration (1Z0-073)
Current cost per exam	Prices vary from $125 to $245 by test and by geography
Website	education.oracle.com

FIGURE 8-9 Oracle Database Administrator database certifications

Additional database industry certifications from other vendors such as SAP and PostgreSQL are also available. New certifications on emerging database technologies to help employees prove skills and help employers find and vet database talent are constantly being developed and improved.

The database industry offers tremendous career potential for the lifelong learner. Practically every job outlook article and study predicts that the database industry will continue with a high-growth and financially rewarding trajectory no matter whether you prefer the traditional data management or the expanding data analysis side of this exciting field.

Q & A 8-9

Question: What should someone considering a career in the database industry keep in mind?

Answer: Database professionals at candidcareers.com offer these final pieces of advice for anyone considering a career in the database industry:

- It doesn't matter exactly where you start. The main thing is to grab an opportunity that comes along and do well with that opportunity. Think serendipity.
- Develop a constant curiosity about all things.
- Practice being detail- and process-oriented.
- The job changes every single day. It's never the same, but it also provides rewarding, tangible results.
- Look for a mentor and attend meetups in your area to learn and make friends.

Summary

- **Explore and describe jobs and careers in the database industry**. Job and career growth in the database industry is strong and predicted to remain strong over the next decade. Traditional database industry jobs terminate in the position of DBA (database administrator) or even CIO (chief information officer). Jobs in the data analysis side of the business are also emerging and growing, particularly with the new emphasis on the analysis of external and big data.
- **Summarize the policy-making, technical, and administrative responsibilities of a database administrator (DBA)**. The traditional responsibilities of a DBA span from policy-making decisions such as data retention, destruction, and compliance through deep technical skills in data design, SQL, testing, and maintenance, through management and administrative responsibilities such as documentation and training.
- **Define the job titles and responsibilities for employees who may report to the DBA**. The job responsibilities of employees who often report to the DBA vary from those who maintain and monitor internal databases to those who work on the data analysis side of both internal and external data. Job titles include various types of DBAs such as application and system DBAs through various types of data analysts and data scientists.
- **Describe the responsibilities of a data analyst**. A data analyst's primary responsibility is to analyze internal data and transactions to identify and communicate important relationships, trends, and issues in order for organizations to make faster and better decisions.
- **Explain the responsibilities of a data scientist**. A data scientist's primary responsibility is to analyze both internal, external, and big data to identify and communicate important relationships, trends, and issues in order for organizations to make faster and better decisions.
- **Explore the educational credentials and industry certifications that support a career in the database industry**. All of the major database management vendors including IBM, Microsoft, and Oracle have a number of industry certifications that help employees prove their skills and help employers identify talent. New industry certifications are emerging all the time as the database industry grows and changes.

Key Terms

application DBA	database administrator (DBA)
archive	database analyst
authentication	database architect
authorization	database operations manager
BI (business intelligence)	database performance
BICARSA	denormalizing
big data	Department of Defense (DOD) 5015.2 Standard
business analyst	disaster recovery plan
chief information officer (CIO)	disaster recovery planning
chief security officer (CSO)	encryption
cloud backup	ETL (extract, transform, load)
cold site	Family Educational Rights and Privacy Act (FERPA)
cyberattack	GLAPPR
cybersecurity	Health Insurance Portability and Accountability Act (HIPAA)
data analyst	hot site
data archiving	"in the cloud"
data modeler	live system
data scientist	malware
data visualization	mission critical
data visualization expert	Online Analytical Processing (OLAP)
data warehouse administrator	

parallel database system

Patriot Act

performance analyst

Presidential Records Act

product manager

production system

RAID (redundant array of inexpensive/independent drives)

recovery point objective (RPO)

recovery time objective (RTO)

research analyst

run-book

sandbox

Sarbanes–Oxley (SOX) Act

SEC Rule 17a-4

software release

spyware

spyware/malware detection software

system DBA

Tableau

task-oriented DBA

test system

tuning

uninterruptible power supply (UPS)

view

warm site

Module Review Questions

Problems

1. Which of the following is a common job responsibility for someone in the database industry?
   a. network security
   b. data security
   c. application programming
   d. web app development

2. Which of the following would generally *not* be a typical responsibility of the DBA?
   a. data security
   b. data entry
   c. data disaster planning
   d. data dictionary maintenance

3. Which of the following technical job titles typically does *not* report to the DBA?
   a. data analyst
   b. data operations manager
   c. application programmer
   d. system DBA

4. Which of the following is typically *not* a responsibility of a data analyst?
   a. data visualization
   b. writing SQL
   c. big data analysis
   d. transaction data analysis

5. Which of the following is typically *not* a primary responsibility of a data scientist?
   a. data security
   b. statistical analysis
   c. big data analysis
   d. data visualization

6. Which of the following is *not* a currently popular database industry credential?
   a. Microsoft Access MOS
   b. Microsoft Technology Associate
   c. Oracle Certified Professional, MySQL
   d. Universal Relational Database Designer

Critical Thinking Questions

1. What policies have you seen your school or college take to protect your privacy?
2. What mission-critical applications must your college or university protect?

JC Consulting Case Exercises

For the following exercises, you do not use the JCConsulting database.

Problems

1. Which of the following types of external data might be valuable to JC Consulting, but is not currently stored in their internal Access database?
   a. clicks on their home page
   b. hashtag references in tweets
   c. company name references in blog postings
   d. Each of these types of external data might be helpful for JC Consulting to analyze.

2. JC Consulting is a small business without a dedicated DBA. An employee with which of the following skills would probably be the best candidate to train for the position?
   a. marketing background and excellent management skills
   b. computer information systems background and excellent written skills
   c. construction background and excellent mechanical skills
   d. sales background and excellent speaking skills

3. JC Consulting is a small business without a dedicated DBA. An employee with which job title is most likely to be in charge of the database?
   a. operations manager
   b. sales manager
   c. personnel manager
   d. construction manager

4. What skills would someone need at JC Consulting to analyze the potential revenue by ZipCode?
   a. how to build summary queries
   b. how table relationships are set up
   c. how fields are organized within each table
   d. An employee would need all of these skills to successfully analyze potential revenue by ZipCode for JC Consulting.

5. JC Consulting just hired a new summer intern in his first year of college to gather social media information about the company. The intern wants to be called a "data scientist." Is this an appropriate title for the intern?
   a. Yes. Data scientists deal with big data from social media feeds so anyone who is working with social media is also a data scientist.
   b. No. Data scientists typically have post-graduate degrees in statistics or math.
   c. Yes. The title of data scientist can be appropriately applied to anyone who works in the data industry.
   d. No. You must be skilled in Hadoop to be appropriately given the title of "data scientist."

6. Which of the following would be the most appropriate industry credential to earn for the person responsible for the JCConsulting database?
   a. Microsoft Access MOS
   b. Microsoft Technology Associate
   c. Oracle Certified Professional, MySQL
   d. IBM Certified Database Administrator—DB2

Critical Thinking Questions

1. Is it as important for a small business like JC Consulting to have a disaster recovery plan as it is for a large corporation? Please cite three different examples to support your position.
2. How might JC Consulting use the cloud?

Pitt Fitness Case Exercises

Problems

1. Pitt Fitness realizes that the company needs to be on top of all trends in fitness centers to keep up with the competition. To ensure they stay on the cutting edge, the company would like to employ a person who could help the business make faster and better data-driven decisions. What position should they advertise for?
   a. CSO
   b. data analyst
   c. SQL programmer
   d. CIO

2. Pitt Fitness employs a person who defines and models data requirements, business rules, and database policies. This employee installs, configures, and tests database hardware and software. What is this employee's title?
   a. chief security officer
   b. chief information officer
   c. database administrator
   d. big data administrator

3. Who at Pitt Fitness determines access privileges for users and enters the appropriate authorization rules in the DBMS?
   a. chief security officer
   b. chief information officer
   c. database administrator
   d. big data administrator

4. Pitt Fitness suspects their system contains software that enables someone to surreptitiously record keystrokes. What might their system be infected with?
   a. spyware
   b. keyware
   c. recorders
   d. keystroke crackers

5. Pitt Fitness requires that all employees come into the main office (Shadyside) on a Saturday to practice a step-by-step plan to minimize the effects of a natural disaster. For example, if a freak tornado hit the city of Pittsburgh, Pitt Fitness's computer systems might be incapacitated. What type of planning is this practice?
   a. tornado watch
   b. natural disaster
   c. disaster recovery
   d. crisis mitigation

6. Assume that a destructive storm hit the city of Pittsburgh and it took 20 hours for Pitt Fitness's computer specialists to return the system to normal working operation. Twenty hours, the length of time this would normally take in a disaster situation, would be considered the _____.
   a. recovery time objective (RTO)
   b. recovery point objective (RPO)
   c. recovery computer objective (RCO)
   d. recovery system objective (RSO)

7. As a backup system, Pitt Fitness replicates their DBMS to multiple hard drives that can process reservations if another hard drive fails. What is this system for backup called?
   a. HD
   b. RAID
   c. REPLICATE
   d. multiplicity

8. In the summer months, Pitt Fitness often suffers from power outages due to thunderstorms. What would be a good investment to prevent losing data during power outages?
   a. a dedicated electrical line
   b. a lightning rod
   c. an uninterruptible power supply
   d. moving their computers outside the city

9. Considering Pitt Fitness is a privately held company, which of the following data archiving laws must they comply with?
   a. Sarbanes–Oxley
   b. Patriot Act
   c. FERPA
   d. None of the choices is required of the company.

10. What is the repository at Pitt Fitness that contains the log of database maintenance, license keys, and updates to the system?
    a. DB Diary
    b. check list register
    c. run-book
    d. captain notes

Critical Thinking Questions

1. The database administrator at Pitt Fitness wants to develop and test new applications. What is the safest way to do this, considering the company has customers reserving classes frequently?

2. Considering that Pitt Fitness is a small company, what type of backup site would be appropriate for their smaller budget?

Sports Physical Therapy Case Exercises

Problems

1. The Sports Physical Therapy group has hired a student intern who is an expert in using the software Tableau. What position should that intern fill?
   a. data analyst
   b. database administrator
   c. SQL programmer
   d. Python programmer

2. Sports Physical Therapy is looking to hire an employee that is certified in Microsoft Office to help run the Access database, analyze data with Excel, and use other Office tools. What certification should the Human Resources Department look for?
   a. OCA
   b. SQL
   c. MOS
   d. HANA

3. If you consider that Sports Physical Therapy is a large organization employing many computer personnel, who is the employee that the database administrator most likely reports to?
   a. chief executive officer
   b. chief information officer
   c. chief personnel officer
   d. chief data analyst

4. An employee at Sports Physical Therapy who had access to the database management system has been fired for inappropriate conduct. Immediately, their database privileges must be rescinded. What is the SQL command that will accomplish this?
   a. REVOKE
   b. RESCIND
   c. REMOVE
   d. REPLACE

5. Because Sports Physical Therapy deals with sensitive health data, only certain employees should be able to access the sensitive data. What is the process of granting specific rights and privileges to a user?
   a. encryption
   b. authentication
   c. authorization
   d. views

6. The database at Sports Physical Therapy that contains the health records of the patients is essential to the survival of the business and all the business processes. In terms of disaster planning, this would be considered a system that is _____.
   a. highly critical
   b. unbelievably critical
   c. mission critical
   d. critical

7. Which of the following laws most likely governs the data archiving of the database at Sports Physical Therapy, considering it is a privately held company?
   a. HIPAA
   b. FERPA
   c. SOX
   d. Patriot Act

8. Sports Physical Therapy regularly uses hardware, software, and databases in a _____ system and tests and develops applications in a _____ system.
   a. test, live
   b. test, sandbox
   c. production, test
   d. production, live

9. Sports Physical Therapy is always striving to improve their database systems. What do you call the process of creating and deleting indexes, minimizing the complexity of each view to only what is needed, and changing the table design?
   a. tuning the design
   b. upgrading the design
   c. cleansing the design
   d. perfecting performance

10. Employees at Sports Physical Therapy are concerned about protecting their networks, devices, and data from digital attacks. What is the process of this protection called?
   a. cybersecurity
   b. stealth bombarding
   c. computer wrapping
   d. malware repulsion

Critical Thinking Questions

1. Considering that Sports Physical Therapy constantly deals with health information, who would be the best person to hire to handle the government regulations and compliance? This person would report to the DBA.

2. What sorts of big data might be important for Sports Physical Therapy? Research physical therapy clinics online to find out more information about what they might find vital to be competitive.

MODULE 9

DATABASE INDUSTRY TRENDS

LEARNING OBJECTIVES

- Compare and contrast database architectures, including centralized, client/server, data warehouse, and distributed systems
- Explore online analytical processing (OLAP) and business-intelligence (BI) tools used in data warehousing
- Define a distributed database
- Compare and contrast how database management systems are selected from a historical and modern perspective
- Explore alternatives to relational database management systems, including NoSQL document systems and object-oriented database management systems
- Explain the current issues and trends in big data
- Describe data stored in XML and JSON formats
- Explore data visualization concepts and tools

INTRODUCTION

Like every technology-related area, the database industry is also constantly changing and evolving. Some of the trends are in response to breakthroughs in technology such as high-speed networks, the expansion of cloud-based services, and the proliferation of mobile devices. Other trends, such as the increased focus on database security discussed in Module 7, are in response to modern problems such as sophisticated cyberattacks. The massive amount of big data such as clicks, page loads, pictures, voice clips, emails, text messages, search keywords, shopping data, and financial transactions create opportunities to both serve and exploit.

This module will touch upon some of the most important trends in the database industry by comparing and contrasting historical milestones with the current state of various database architectures and emerging technologies. It will also explore trends in new database management systems, data formats, and data analysis tools.

DATABASE ARCHITECTURES

Database architecture refers to how hardware and software are organized, implemented, and operated to process data. Database architectures include centralized, client/server, data warehouse, and distributed systems.

Centralized Approach

The **centralized approach** refers to a single, centrally located computer system that processes all data. The centralized approach to database processing ruled the database industry during the 1960s with the introduction of the first widely installed commercial computer system, the **IBM System/360 mainframe**, shown in Figure 9-1. Some thought that the number "360" represented 360 degrees of a circle, a "complete" system.

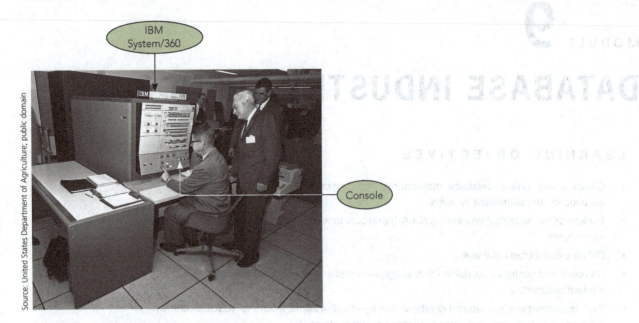

282

FIGURE 9-1   IBM System/360 mainframe

Early mainframes were physically very large pieces of hardware controlled by punched cards or paper tapes that were fed into "readers." Cards were used for input, and paper printouts were used for output, which is still called **hard copy** today. The IBM System/360 mainframe shown in Figure 9-1 had a **console**, a panel of lights, switches, and knobs that controlled its operation. Depending on the model, some mainframes created so much heat that they were considered to be "**water-cooled**" mainframes. Cold water ran through pipes installed under the floor, inside, or around the hardware cabinetry to dissipate the heat created by the electronic components. (Some supercomputers are still "liquid-cooled" today.)

Later, **monitors** or **terminals** were installed to communicate with the mainframe. Terminals are screens that have no processing power themselves, hence they were sometimes called **dumb terminals**. However, they were a major improvement given commands from a keyboard could be used as input, and the screen itself could be used for output or **soft copy**, as shown in Figure 9-2.

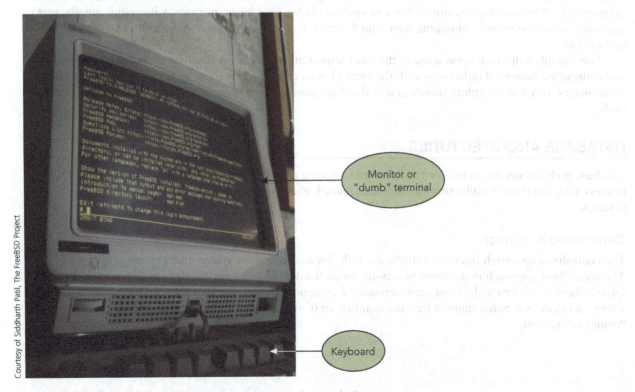

FIGURE 9-2   Monitor or "dumb" terminal electronic input/output device

The 1960s and 1970s were decades when many large businesses were busy installing mainframes and considering relational database management systems for the first time. As new software applications such as billing, accounts receivable, and payroll were developed and installed, the pressure for bigger, better, and faster database management systems grew quickly as well. Couple the explosion in technological breakthroughs in the computer industry with Edgar F. Codd's profound work on the relational model as well as the SQL language developed at IBM, the mainframe became an indispensable business tool for all medium-to-large organizations. In the mainframe industry, the market share of the IBM System/360 in the 1960s and the replacement **IBM System/370** in the 1970s was greater than the next five competitors grouped together, which were nicknamed the **BUNCH** (Burroughs, UNIVAC, NCR, Control Data, and Honeywell).

Historically, centralized architecture conceptually followed a straightforward model as shown in Figure 9-3.

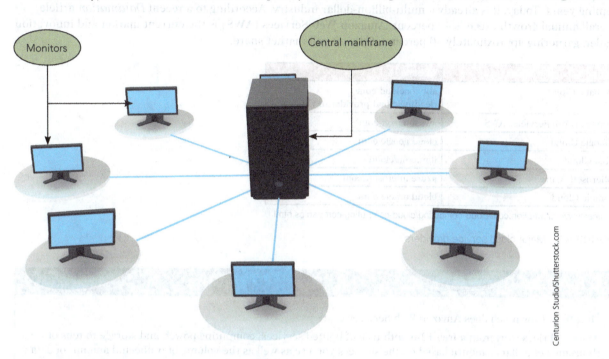

Centurion Studio/Shutterstock.com

FIGURE 9-3   Early schematic of centralized architecture

Cloud Computing

Today, centralized architecture is back in vogue but is implemented in a different way. Many companies are disbanding some internal traditional data centers and moving their processes to the **cloud. Cloud computing** means that programs and services are accessed via the Internet versus through a traditional network managed within the walls of the company. The internal mainframe of the past is being replaced with stacks of servers "in the cloud." A modern cloud computing data center is shown in Figure 9-4.

kwarkot/Shutterstock.com

FIGURE 9-4   Modern cloud computing data center

The cloud infrastructure is maintained by the **cloud provider** who builds and connects the infrastructure of large pools of systems that include servers, storage devices, and high-speed networks to serve many clients. The hardware in the cloud infrastructure is sometimes called a **data center** or **server farm**. Virtualization techniques are used to maximize the power and efficiency of the resources for each client.

Virtualization means to create a **virtual**, or not real, version of a resource. So while many clients share the same resources, a company's systems operate as if they were running on their own dedicated system. Virtualization can be as simple as partitioning a large hard drive to create two separate drives, or it can combine physical storage devices to create what appears to the client to be one massive hard drive.

Many of the major cloud service providers are summarized in Figure 9-5. Considering that cloud computing is still a young and growing movement, it is certain to spawn new competition and services in the coming years. Today, it is already a multi-billion-dollar industry. According to a recent *Datamation* article, overall annual growth exceeds 40 percent. **Amazon Web Services (AWS)** is the current market and innovation leader, garnering approximately 30 percent of the overall market share.

Cloud Service Provider	Website
Alibaba Cloud	alibabacloud.com (leading cloud provider in China)
Amazon Web Services, AWS	aws.amazon.com
Google Cloud	cloud.google.com
IBM Cloud	ibm.com/cloud
Microsoft Azure	azure.microsoft.com
Oracle Cloud	cloud.oracle.com

Source: www.datamation.com/cloud-computing/cloud-computing-companies.html

FIGURE 9-5 Major cloud service providers

Q & A 9-1

Question: How much does Amazon Web Services cost?

Answer: Prices start from a free 12-month trial of limited services, computing power, and storage to tens of thousands of dollars a month based on the services you use as well as the volume of traffic and amount of data you store.

PERSONAL COMPUTER REVOLUTION

By the late 1970s, technological breakthroughs in microchip manufacturing meant that many companies were racing to introduce successful **personal computers**, computers with memory and hard drives, and intended to be used by a single person. The Apple II, Commodore PET 2001, and TRS-80 Model 1 were all announced in 1977.

IBM was late to the microprocessor industry, releasing the IBM PC in 1981. In a rush to enter the market, the IBM PC was based on an open architecture, not a proprietary one. **Open architecture** meant that IBM provided enough details on the hardware and operating system of the IBM PC so that other vendors could build additional hardware components and write software applications for the computer. Even the first operating system for the IBM PC, **DOS (Disk Operating System)**, was subcontracted to Microsoft.

A **proprietary architecture** approach was used by Apple and the others. **Proprietary** meant that the company did not divulge the details of how the system worked so that other companies could not build complimentary components or software. The proprietary approach was eventually unsustainable for any microcomputer vendor except for Apple who continued to innovate and offer outstanding products. The open architecture approach eventually proved unsustainable for IBM, too. In 2005, IBM sold what was left of their microcomputer business to Lenovo. The open architecture strategy was successful, however, for other vendors who specialized in different areas of the system and software such as Dell, Intel, and Microsoft. Figure 9-6 displays a 1980s-vintage Apple Macintosh beside an IBM personal computer.

The open architecture approach meant that many hardware and software developers quickly rushed to build products for the new IBM microcomputer platform. "**Killer applications**," software that is so necessary or desirable, it justifies the expense of whatever hardware platform is required to run it, hit the scenes such as the **Visicalc** spreadsheet program, **WordStar** for word processing, and later, **dBase** for relational database management.

Apple Macintosh

IBM PC

5¼" floppy disk drives, A: and B:

3½" disk drive

iStockphoto.com/mikkelwilliam

FIGURE 9-6 Early Apple Macintosh and IBM personal computer

Clones or **compatibles**, computers that could do everything the IBM PC could do, as well as the eventual dominance of the Microsoft Windows operating system, were big factors ending IBM's influence in the microcomputer industry. However, because the popularity of personal computing now meant that a personal computer was located on the desktop of every white collar worker, a new database architecture emerged to cooperatively harness the power of the both mainframe and the local microcomputer: client/server.

Advancements in chip technology continued at a phenomenal pace sometimes referred to as Moore's Law. **Moore's Law** is attributed to Gordon Moore, who, as a co-founder of Intel, predicted in 1975 that the number of transistors on a chip would likely double every two years. While not precisely accurate, the overall point of the prediction held true, and an explosion of smaller and faster computers including laptops, tablets, and smartphones followed.

Today, according to an article from Northwestern University, an average smartphone has more computing power than all of NASA when it put the first men on the moon in 1969! It further states that the number of smartphones is set to rise to 6 billion in 2020. This substantial amount of new data and processing power gives rise to new computing strategies, including distributed computing and crowdsourced processing power. According to an article by AI Impacts, "computing power available per dollar has probably increased by a factor of ten roughly every four years over the last quarter of a century."

Crowdsourced processing power is an innovative implementation of client/server computing that allows your device to share its processing power when it's not being used. Crowdsourcing computing projects are sometimes referred to as distributed computing projects and typically involve the analysis of very large sets of data.

Berkeley Open Infrastructure for Network Computing (BOINC) is an open-source platform that many crowdsourced computing projects use. Current projects that run on the BOINC-based platform include climate prediction models, image processing, stock market prediction, cancer research, universe modeling, earthquake detection, and many more.

Q & A 9-2

Question: What competitors dominate the operating systems for mobile devices today?

Answer: Open source Google/Android and proprietary Apple iOS technologies account for the majority of operating systems on mobile smartphone devices today. The Microsoft mobile Windows operating system made a valiant run, but currently has about 0.2 percent worldwide market share.

CLIENT/SERVER ARCHITECTURE

Traditionally, **client/server architecture** was a computing model where a central computer (the **server**, which may be mainframe computer or a large personal computer), delivered and managed centralized resources working cooperatively with a **client** computer to run an entire application. A server was also called a **back-end processor** or a **back-end machine**, and a client was also called a **front-end processor** or a **front-end machine**. For example, an early client/server application might have downloaded a subset of data, such as past sales by a particular customer, from a large centralized relational database to an individual employee's computer. The employee could then analyze the data in a spreadsheet when working with a customer during a sales process or customer service inquiry.

Access and Client/Server Architecture

If you store an Access database on a centralized file server for usage by three or four trusted colleagues in a local department, you are also running a client/server application. The server stores and controls access to the central database file, but each workstation must also have storage and processing power in order to work with the database. Each client must have the Access application loaded on its local hard drive. To work with the database, the client computer starts Access and then accesses the database stored on the server. The server manages the centralized data, record-locking issues between users, and the communication of new or updated data between each client computer. The client computer handles the queries and data updates from that local user and also communicates those requests back to the server.

To further minimize traffic on the network, you could split an Access database into a front-end and back-end database. The **back-end database** contains only the tables, the actual data, and is stored on the server. The **front-end database** contains all of the queries, data entry forms, reports, and other objects. The front-end has no physical tables, but rather, contains links to the tables physically stored in the back-end database. Front-end databases can be copied and tailored to contain only those queries, forms, and reports needed by a particular user, which can provide a thin layer of security to protect sensitive information.

Moreover, however, by splitting a database into a back-end copy stored at the server, and front-end copies stored at each client, you can greatly improve overall database performance. The arrangement provides interface components such as data entry screens and reports directly on the user's computer and minimizes the amount of traffic that moves through the network. Figure 9-7 presents a conceptual description of client/server architecture using front-end and back-end Access database files.

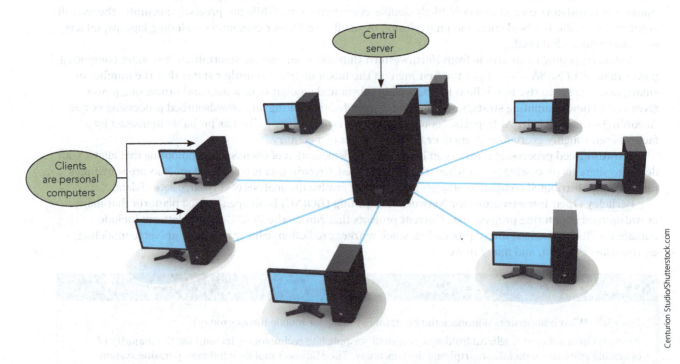

FIGURE 9-7 Schematic of early client/server architecture

To create front-end and back-end Access databases from a single database for use in a client/server implementation, perform the following steps:

- Close all open objects.
- Click the Database Tools tab on the ribbon.
- Click the Access Database button (Database Tools tab | Move Data group).
- Click Split Database.
- Select the location and enter the name for the back-end database.
- Click Split in the Create Back-end Database dialog box as shown in Figure 9-8.

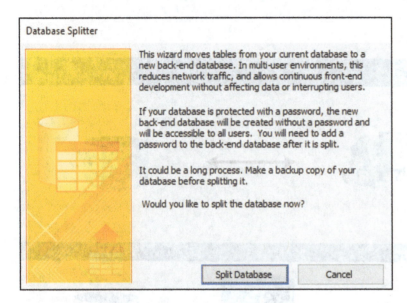

Database Splitter

This wizard moves tables from your current database to a new back-end database. In multi-user environments, this reduces network traffic, and allows continuous front-end development without affecting data or interrupting users.

If your database is protected with a password, the new back-end database will be created without a password and will be accessible to all users. You will need to add a password to the back-end database after it is split.

It could be a long process. Make a backup copy of your database before splitting it.

Would you like to split the database now?

Split Database   Cancel

FIGURE 9-8   Access Database Splitter dialog box

Splitting an Access database in this way creates a **two-tier architecture** where the server performs database functions and the clients perform the **presentation functions** (or **user interface functions**), such as determining which form to display on the screen and how to format the form's data. Given that the front-end copies of the database also run the queries that execute the business rules for selecting and calculating data, each client in this situation is called a **fat client** (as opposed to a **thin client**, which doesn't do as much processing).

Although performance is excellent when implementing a split Access database because much of the processing is handled by each client's front-end database and network traffic is minimized, this arrangement has a significant shortcoming. If several clients are involved, whenever a developer changes a form, report, or a calculation in a query, each client front-end database has to be updated as well.

For this reason, while it's common to split an Access database into its respective front-end and back-end copies, the front-end database is rarely copied to each user's computer unless very little future application development is anticipated.

Rather, most Access developers recommend storing both the front-end and back-end databases on the server. Although this practice does not improve performance, it does protect the back-end copy with the tables should the front end become so corrupted it cannot be opened. In that case, the developer only needs to restore the application by deleting the corrupted front end and replace it with a backup. Corruption of an unsplit database, however, could potentially lock developers out of the entire file, forcing them to restore the data from the latest backup. If backups are made on a daily basis, corruption of an unsplit database could cost a company an entire day's work.

Three-Tier Client/Server Architecture

Three-tier architecture is a type of client/server architecture where the clients perform the presentation functions, a **database server** performs the database functions, and separate centralized computers (called **application servers**) perform the business functions as well as serve as an interface between clients and the database server. A three-tier architecture distributes the processing functions so that you eliminate the fat client maintenance problem and improve the application's **scalability**, the ease and capacity to grow. As the number of users increases, you can upgrade the application and database servers by adding faster processors, disks, and other components without changing any client computers. A three-tier architecture is sometimes referred to as an **n-tier architecture** because application servers can be added for scalability without affecting the design for the client or the database server.

Figure 9-9 shows 2-, 3- and n-tier client/server architecture. Two-tier architecture refers to a client merely requesting shared files from the hard drive of a centralized file server. Three-tier architecture means that the centralized server also completes some of the business processes of the application. N-tier means that files, data, businesses processes, and other activities are being cooperatively processed by multiple computers.

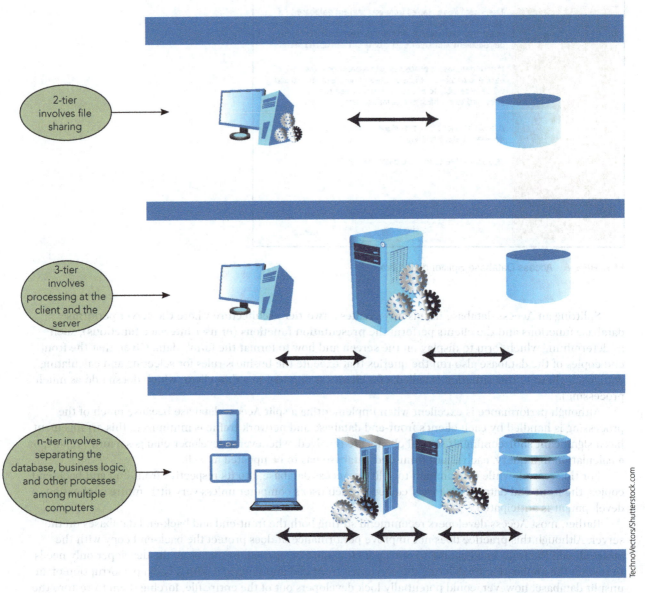

FIGURE 9-9   Two, three, and n-tier client/server architecture

Many n-tier client/server applications are used today. For example, when you use a browser to open a webpage or run a web app from any device, including a smartphone, you are running some sort of client/server application. Client/server technology encompasses any application that requires processing power at both the server and the client to complete the process.

Q & A 9-3

Question: How does a browser and the web represent an application of client/server computing?

Answer: When you click a link or enter a webpage address into the address bar of a browser, the browser sends a request to a web server for that webpage file. The file (and any associated files such as style sheets, JavaScript files, images, or other files) are downloaded to the browser, which processes the code in those files and presents the results to the user in the browser. Using a browser to surf the web is an excellent example of modern-day client/server computing.

DATA WAREHOUSES

The term data warehouse has different meanings depending on the organization, but the basic concept grew from the problem of what happens when you try to run a production system and a data analysis system out of the same database management system at the same time. DBAs found that allowing users to make large queries on their relational database management system could cause severe performance issues with the day-to-day transaction operational processing systems. The term **data warehouse architecture** refers to the hardware and software an organization needs to address the analytical requirements of users without detracting from traditional operations.

A more formal definition for a data warehouse is credited to W. H. Inmon (Inmon, W. H. *Building the Data Warehouse*. QED, 1990), who originally coined the phrase. Inmon defined a **data warehouse** as a subject-oriented, integrated, time-variant, nonvolatile collection of data in support of management's decision-making process. **Subject-oriented** means that data is organized by topic rather than by the application that uses the data. **Integrated** means that data is stored in one place in the data warehouse even though the data may originate from a variety of external sources. The data can come from recently developed applications or from legacy systems developed many years ago. **Time-variant** means that data in a data warehouse represents snapshots of data at various points in time in the past, such as at the end of each month. This is unlike an operational application, which has data that is accurate as of the moment. Data warehouses may also retain historical data for long periods or data summarized to specific time periods, such as daily, weekly, monthly, or annual subtotals. **Nonvolatile** means that data is read-only. Data is loaded into a data warehouse periodically, but users cannot update a data warehouse directly.

A data warehouse contains **read-only snapshots** of highly consolidated and summarized data from multiple internal and external sources that users periodically refresh as needed. **Read-only** means that the data cannot be edited, added to, deleted, or otherwise modified by the users. **Snapshot** means that the data is current as of a particular moment such as the previous day, week, or month.

The hardware for a data warehouse can be as small as a single personal computer or as large as a mainframe, depending on the amount of data, number of users, and other organizational requirements. Companies use data warehouses to support their decision-making processes, which includes many **ad hoc** (unpredictable and as needed) requests as well as **data mining** efforts, which is the practice of uncovering new knowledge, patterns, trends, and rules from data.

Because the data warehouse system is updated at regularly scheduled intervals from real-time data in the production system (also called the **OLTP, online transaction processing system**), the two systems can be separately managed, secured, and tuned for maximum performance.

Online Analytical Processing (OLAP)

The data in a traditional data warehouse is often made available to users through the use of **online analytical processing (OLAP)** software. OLAP is a database technology that optimizes data for querying, *analyzing*, and reporting (as opposed **OLTP**, online *transaction* processing).

Data processed through OLAP software is organized in hierarchies, which are stored in conceptual "cubes" (as opposed to data in an OLTP system, which is stored in relational database tables). This organization lends itself to analysis of large amounts of data through PivotTable or PivotChart tools, which can display high-level summaries.

A **PivotTable** is a crosstabular organization of summarized data. A PivotTable typically uses three fields to organize and summarize the data. Two fields group the data, and data from a third field is summarized within the intersection of each column and row. Figure 9-10 displays 163 records of data selected from four related tables in the Access JCConsulting database, and provides information about clients, projects, and tasks assigned to each project.

ProjectEstimates						
ClientID	ClientName	ProjectID	ProjectStartDate	TaskID	Description	Estimate
1	Tri-Lakes Realtors	1	2/6/2019	PLAN01	Establish goals with client	200.00
1	Tri-Lakes Realtors	1	2/6/2019	MEET00	Initial customer meeting	0.00
1	Tri-Lakes Realtors	31	3/1/2020	MEET00	Initial customer meeting	0.00
1	Tri-Lakes Realtors	31	3/1/2020	DB01	Design relational database	1,000.00
1	Tri-Lakes Realtors	31	3/1/2020	MEET01	Meet with client	100.00
1	Tri-Lakes Realtors	31	3/1/2020	DB02	Convert data	5,000.00
1	Tri-Lakes Realtors	31	3/1/2020	MEET01	Meet with client	100.00
2	Project Lead The Way	7	9/2/2019	MEET00	Initial customer meeting	0.00
2	Project Lead The Way	7	9/2/2019	CODE04	Code SQL	750.00
2	Project Lead The Way	7	9/2/2019	TEST02	Test performance	300.00
2	Project Lead The Way	7	9/2/2019	TEST01	Test technology	300.00
2	Project Lead The Way	7	9/2/2019	MEET01	Meet with client	200.00
3	Midstates Auto Auction	3	3/11/2019	MEET00	Initial customer meeting	0.00
3	Midstates Auto Auction	3	3/11/2019	PLAN01	Establish goals with client	240.00
3	Midstates Auto Auction	8	1/6/2020	PLAN01	Establish goals with client	200.00
3	Midstates Auto Auction	8	1/6/2020	MEET00	Initial customer meeting	0.00
3	Midstates Auto Auction	8	1/6/2020	CODE10	Apply SEO	1,500.00
4	Bretz & Hanna Law Firm	4	4/10/2020	PLAN01	Establish goals with client	240.00
4	Bretz & Hanna Law Firm	4	4/10/2020	MEET00	Initial customer meeting	0.00
4	Bretz & Hanna Law Firm	4	4/10/2020	SERV01	Set up a domain name	200.00
4	Bretz & Hanna Law Firm	4	4/10/2020	SERV02	Install new server	650.00
4	Bretz & Hanna Law Firm	4	4/10/2020	TEST02	Test performance	2,400.00
4	Bretz & Hanna Law Firm	4	4/10/2020	SUPP03	Document solution	400.00
4	Bretz & Hanna Law Firm	4	4/10/2020	TEST01	Test technology	2,400.00

Record: 1 of 163   No Filter   Search

FIGURE 9-10 Selected records

Figure 9-11 shows one arrangement of that data exported to Excel and then organized in a basic Excel PivotTable. Note that only three fields are used in the PivotTable: ClientName, TaskID, and Estimate. ClientName is used as row headings, TaskID is used as column headings, and the Estimate field is subtotaled for each client and task at the intersecting cell for that client and task. Both the ClientName and TaskID fields are filtered to show only certain clients and certain tasks.

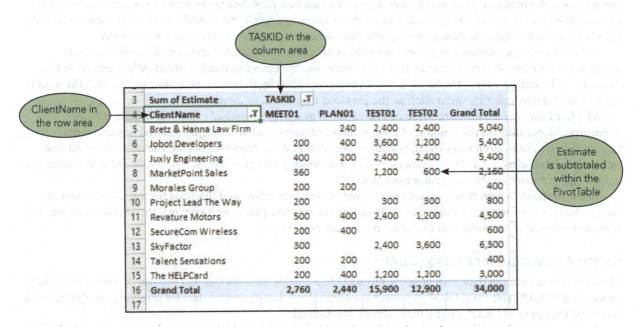

		TASKID				
3	Sum of Estimate					
4	ClientName	MEET01	PLAN01	TEST01	TEST02	Grand Total
5	Bretz & Hanna Law Firm		240	2,400	2,400	5,040
6	Jobot Developers	200	400	3,600	1,200	5,400
7	Juxly Engineering	400	200	2,400	2,400	5,400
8	MarketPoint Sales	360		1,200	600	2,160
9	Morales Group	200	200			400
10	Project Lead The Way	200		300	300	800
11	Revature Motors	500	400	2,400	1,200	4,500
12	SecureCom Wireless	200	400			600
13	SkyFactor	300		2,400	3,600	6,300
14	Talent Sensations	200	200			400
15	The HELPCard	200	400	1,200	1,200	3,000
16	Grand Total	2,760	2,440	15,900	12,900	34,000
17						

ClientName in the row area — TASKID in the column area — Estimate is subtotaled within the PivotTable

FIGURE 9-11 PivotTable that summarizes three fields of data from the selected records

A **PivotChart** is a graphical representation of the data in a PivotTable. Figure 9-12 shows an Excel PivotChart based on the PivotTable shown in Figure 9-11.

Although the objects in Figure 9-11 and Figure 9-12 are created using Microsoft Excel PivotTable and PivotChart features, the underlying concept of summarizing data in a crosstabular fashion based on two or more fields holds true for all PivotTables, no matter the source or size of the data.

290

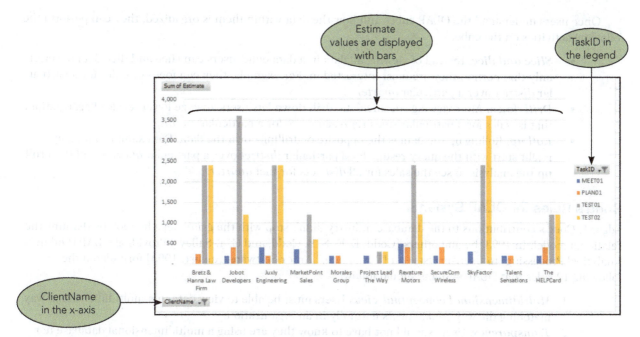

FIGURE 9-12 PivotChart to graphically present information in a PivotTable

In OLAP, a **cube** is a data structure that aggregates data by hierarchies for each dimension you want to analyze. A **hierarchy** is a tree structure for data where every piece of data is a child of the next **level** in the hierarchy. For example, a hierarchy for *location* data might have three levels: states within regions within countries. A hierarchy for *sales representative* data might have only two levels: individual sales representatives within districts. A hierarchy for *time* data may have four levels: weeks within months within quarters within years. All the levels of the hierarchy are referred to as a single **dimension**. The dimensions that you want to analyze together create a cube. As such, a "cube" is not a physical six-sided block, but rather a metaphor for the multiple hierarchies within each dimension that identify or describe a business process and for which you want to use for ad hoc analysis.

Figure 9-13 illustrates the relationship between raw information sources, the concept of the data warehouse, the transformation of the data into OLAP cubes, and the eventual use of the data by the clients as a Business Intelligence Architecture.

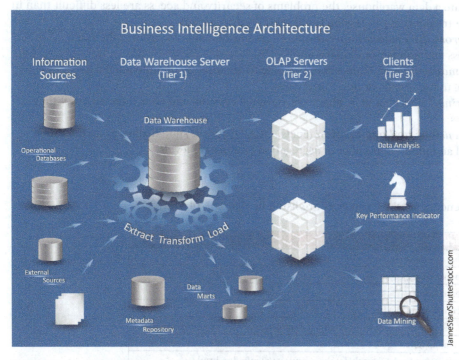

FIGURE 9-13 Data warehouse and OLAP technologies

Once users understand the OLAP cubes and how the data within them is organized, they can perform the following activities on the cube:

- *Slice and dice.* Instead of viewing all data in a data cube, users can **slice and dice** data to select only that portion they are most interested in. For example, they can focus on sales for a particular *district* over a particular *quarter*.
- *Drill down.* After viewing specific data, **drill down** lets users analyze lower levels of aggregation; that is, sales for a particular *sales representative* for a particular *month*.
- *Roll up.* Rolling up the data is the opposite of drilling down the data. For example, an analyst might start with the query results for a particular *district* over a particular *quarter* and then **roll up** the analysis to see the sales for all *districts* for that *quarter*.

Codd's Rules for OLAP Systems

Edgar F. Codd's contributions to the database industry didn't stop with the giant steps he took by defining the relational model. In 1993, he and others [Codd, E. F., S. B. Codd, and C. T. Salley. "Providing OLAP (Online Analytical Processing) to UserAnalysts: An IT Mandate." Arbor Software, August, 1993] formulated the following 12 rules that OLAP systems should follow:

1. *Multidimensional conceptual view.* Users must be able to view data in a multidimensional way, matching the way data appears naturally in an organization.
2. *Transparency.* Users should not have to know they are using a multidimensional database nor need to learn special software tools to access data.
3. *Accessibility.* Users should perceive data as a single user view even though the data may be physically located in several heterogeneous locations and in different forms, such as relational databases or flat files.
4. *Consistent reporting performance.* Retrieval performance should not significantly degrade as the number of dimensions and the size of the warehouse grow.
5. *Client/server architecture.* The server component of OLAP software must be intelligent enough that a variety of clients can be connected with minimal effort.
6. *Generic dimensionality.* Every dimension must be equivalent in both its structural and operational capabilities.
7. *Dynamic sparse matrix handling.* Missing data should be handled correctly and efficiently and not affect the accuracy or speed of data retrieval.
8. *Multiuser support.* OLAP software must provide secure, concurrent retrieval of data. Because you do not update a data warehouse, the problems of security and access are less difficult than in an **OLTP online transaction processing** (production) environment.
9. *Unrestricted, cross-dimensional operations.* Users must be able to perform the same operations across any number of dimensions.
10. *Intuitive data manipulation.* Users should be able to act directly on individual data values without needing to use menus or other interfaces.
11. *Flexible reporting.* Users should be able to retrieve data results and view them any way they want for analysis.
12. *Unlimited dimensions and aggregation levels.* OLAP software should allow at least 15 data dimensions and an unlimited number of aggregation (summary) levels.

Current OLAP Vendors

Some of the many current vendors of OLAP products are listed in Figure 9-14.

Vendor	Website
IBM Cognos	ibm.com/cognos
MicroStrategy	microstrategy.com
Jedox	jedox.com
icCube	iccube.com
Microsoft Analysis Services	docs.microsoft.com/en-us/analysis-services/analysis-services-overview
Apache Kylin	kylin.apache.org
Oracle OLAP	oracle.com/technetwork/database/options/olap/index.html

FIGURE 9-14 Current vendors of OLAP products

DISTRIBUTED DATABASES

A **distributed database** is a single logical database that is physically divided among computers at several sites on a network. As discussed in Module 7, distributed databases occur in traditional "master-slave" configurations as well as in new "snapshot" models such as those used by Git and GitHub. Recall that **Git** is a free and open source distributed version control system (see git-scm.com), and **GitHub** (see github.com) and **Bitbucket** (see bitbucket.org) are popular code-hosting websites to help manage software development projects created using Git.

Rules for Distributed Databases

In a *ComputerWorld* article titled "Twelve Rules for a Distributed Database," C. J. Date formulated 12 rules that traditional distributed databases should aspire to. The overarching goal of a distributed database is that it should feel and work like a single database to the users.

1. *Local autonomy.* No site should depend on another site to perform its database functions.
2. *No reliance on a central site.* The database should not rely on a single central site to control database functions such as data dictionary management, query processing, update management, database recovery, and concurrent update.
3. *Continuous operation.* Database maintenance functions such as adding sites, creating backups, and upgrading hardware should not require planned shutdowns of the entire distributed database.
4. *Location transparency.* Users should not be concerned with the location of any specific data in the database. Users should feel as if the entire database is stored at their location.
5. *Fragmentation transparency.* Users should not be aware of any data fragmentation. Users should feel as if they are using a single central database.
6. *Replication transparency.* Users should not be aware of any data replication.
7. *Distributed query processing.* The database must process queries as rapidly as possible.
8. *Distributed transaction management.* The database must effectively manage transaction updates at multiple sites.
9. *Hardware independence.* The database should be able to run on different types of hardware.
10. *Operating system independence.* The database should be able to run using different operating systems.
11. *Network independence.* The database should not be restricted to a single type of network.
12. *DBMS independence.* The distributed databases must "speak" the common language of SQL.

Summary of Current Database Architecture Implementations

Most large businesses deploy each of the four common database architectures discussed in this module—centralized, client/server, data warehouse, and distributed databases—in both their traditional and modern forms to some degree or another. Each architecture has its particular strengths and weaknesses as applied to different data management challenges.

Problems such as generating monthly electronic utility bills by a large utility company or writing monthly Social Security checks by the federal government still rely on a strong, traditional centralized database architecture. However, modern-day implementations of centralized processing using "as-a-service" cloud computing rely on centralized racks of fast servers that can be scaled, shared, and optimized to meet and balance the performance demands of growing businesses.

Sharing files in a local area network is still a common use of client/server architecture. Collaborating with a small, local, trusted group of users who share an Access relational database stored at a centralized a file server is another common use of client/server architecture. All web apps run from a smartphone also rely on collaborative client/server processing.

Data warehouses use many technologies, depending on the size of the organization and the location and format of the raw data, but the benefits of separating operational processes from analytical processes that execute in the data warehouse are acknowledged across most medium to large organizations.

The use of distributed databases also varies depending on the age of the technology and the problem being addressed. Implemented correctly, distributed databases can revolutionize performance in situations where version control and security issues are well understood.

Q & A 9-5

Question: Why might distributed databases work extremely well for software version control projects but not so well for traditional transaction systems?

Answer: Traditional transactional systems rely on current data about inventories, orders, payments, and receivables. It is difficult to separate those traditional business systems and still maintain concurrency. Software updates, on the other hand, are not as time sensitive. Days, weeks, or even months can occur before software updates are thoroughly vetted and merged into master branches without causing chaos in terms of clear and accurate communication with customers and financial transactions.

SELECTING A RELATIONAL DATABASE SYSTEM

Just as database architectures have evolved and changed over the years, so has the manner in which **MIS (Management Information Systems)** Departments, DBAs, and other data industry professionals select relational database system software. Figure 9-15 shows a sample "DBMS Evaluation and Selection" checklist, probably created during the 1980s when early mainframe programming languages such as **COBOL (Common Business-Oriented Language)** and Microsoft's **Visual Basic (Beginner's All-purpose Symbolic Instruction Code)** still dominated legacy software programs, though high-level, object-oriented languages based on the C language such as C++ and Java were growing quickly.

```
1. Data Definition
   a. Data types
      (1) Numeric
      (2) Character
      (3) Date
      (4) Logical (T/F)
      (5) Memo
      (6) Currency
      (7) Binary object (pictures, drawings, sounds, and so on)
      (8) Link to an Internet, Web, or other address
      (9) User-defined data types
      (10) Other
   b. Support for nulls
   c. Support for primary keys
   d. Support for foreign keys
   e. Unique indexes
   f. Views
2. Data Restructuring
   a. Possible restructuring
      (1) Add new tables
      (2) Delete existing tables
      (3) Add new columns
      (4) Change the layout of existing columns
      (5) Delete columns
      (6) Add new indexes
      (7) Delete existing indexes
   b. Ease of restructuring
3. Nonprocedural Languages
   a. Nonprocedural languages supported
      (1) SQL
      (2) QBE
      (3) Natural language
      (4) Language unique to the DBMS. Award points based on
          ease of use as well as the types of operations (joining,
          sorting, grouping, calculating various statistics, and
          so on) that are available in the language. You can use
          SQL as a standard against which you can judge the language.
   b. Optimization done by one of the following:
      (1) User (in formulating the query)
      (2) DBMS (through built-in optimizer)
      (3) No optimization possible; system does only sequential
          searches.
```

FIGURE 9-15 DBMS evaluation checklist *(continued)*

4. Procedural Languages
   a. Procedural languages supported
      (1) Language unique to the DBMS. Award points based on
          the quality of this language in terms of both the types of
          statements and control structures available, and the database
          manipulation statements included in the language.
      (2) Java
      (3) C or C++
      (4) GUI language such as Visual Basic
      (5) COBOL
      (6) Other
   b. Can a nonprocedural language be used in conjunction with
      the procedural language (for example, could SQL be
      embedded in a COBOL program)?
5. Data Dictionary
   a. Type of entries
      (1) Tables
      (2) Columns
      (3) Indexes
      (4) Relationships
      (5) Users
      (6) Programs
      (7) Other
   b. Integration of data dictionary with other components of
      the system
6. Concurrent Update
   a. Level of locking
      (1) Field value
      (2) Row
      (3) Page
      (4) Table
      (5) Database
   b. Type of locking
      (1) Shared
      (2) Exclusive
      (3) Both
   c. Responsibility for handling deadlock
      (1) Programs
      (2) DBMS (automatic rollback of transaction causing
          deadlock)
7. Backup and Recovery
   a. Backup services
   b. Journaling services
   c. Recovery services
      (1) Recover from backup copy only
      (2) Recover using backup copy and journal
   d. Rollback of individual transactions
   e. Incremental backup
8. Security
   a. Encryption
   b. Passwords
   c. Authorization rules
      (1) Access to database only
      (2) Access/update access to any column or combination of
          columns
   d. Views
   e. Difficulty in bypassing security controls
9. Integrity
   a. Support for entity integrity
   b. Support for referential integrity
   c. Support for data integrity
   d. Support for other types of integrity constraints
10. Replication and Distributed Databases
   a. Partial replicas
   b. Handling of duplicate updates in replicas
   c. Data distribution
   d. Procedure support
      (1) Language used
      (2) Procedures stored in database
      (3) Support for remote stored procedures
      (4) Trigger support
11. Limitations
   a. Number of tables
   b. Number of columns
   c. Length of individual columns
   d. Total length of all columns in a table
   e. Number of rows per table
   f. Number of files that can be open at the same time
   g. Sizes of database, tables, and other objects
   h. Types of hardware supported
   i. Types of LANs supported
   j. Other

FIGURE 9-15 DBMS evaluation checklist *(continued)*

12. Documentation and Training
    a. Clearly written manuals
    b. Tutorial
       (1) Online
       (2) Printed
    c. Online help available
       (1) General help
       (2) Context-sensitive help
    d. Training
       (1) Vendor or other company
       (2) Location
       (3) Types (DBA, programmers, users, others)
       (4) Cost
13. Vendor Support
    a. Type of support available
    b. Quality of support available
    c. Cost of support
    d. Reputation of support
14. Performance
    a. External benchmarking done by various organizations
    b. Internal benchmarking
    c. Includes a performance monitor
15. Portability
    a. Operating systems
       (1) Unix
       (2) Microsoft Windows
       (3) Linux
       (4) Other
    b. Import/export/linking file support
       (1) Other databases
       (2) Other applications (for example, spreadsheets and
           graphics)
    c. Internet and intranet support
16. Cost
    a. Cost of DBMS
    b. Cost of any additional components
    c. Cost of any additional hardware that is required
    d. Cost of network version (if required)
    e. Cost and types of support
17. Future Plans
    a. What does the vendor plan for the future of the system?
    b. What is the history of the vendor in terms of keeping the
       system up to date?
    c. When changes are made in the system, what is involved in
       converting to the new version?
       (1) How easy is the conversion?
       (2) What will it cost?
18. Other Considerations (Fill in your own special requirements.)
    a. ?
    b. ?
    c. ?
    d. ?

FIGURE 9-15 DBMS evaluation checklist *(continued)*

Figure 9-16 shows Grace Hopper, the inventor of COBOL, who is also credited with coining the word "bug" when she pulled a moth out of a computer cabinet, referring to it as a "bug."

Source: Used with permission from Unisys Corporation

FIGURE 9-16 Grace Hopper, computer pioneer and inventor of COBOL, with associates

A **legacy program** is software that at one time was valuable to a business, but is now out of date. Sometimes legacy programs must be maintained for several years depending on the amount of time and effort it takes to convert the program to modern languages and technologies. A **high-level programming language** is closer to human language. C is often considered to be the first high-level programming language, and its keywords and object-oriented constructs have influenced most modern languages today, including C++, an extension of the C language, as well as C#, Java, JavaScript, PHP, and Python. **Object-oriented languages** use a pattern of programming where data and **methods** (tasks an object can complete) are organized in objects that collaborate with one another. Much application software today such as the Microsoft Office products as well as Windows were written in C++.

Software Solution Stacks

Today, conducting an independent analysis to compare relational database systems is far less common than it once was. Large-scale relational database-processing software such as Oracle and IBM Db2 are both mature and solid products with loyal followings. Most large businesses have significant investments in their database management software, making the switch from Oracle to IBM Db2 (or vice versa) highly unlikely for legacy programs and existing applications that use the data.

New application development projects, such as one creating a new web app or forming a startup business, do have more flexibility in terms of choosing database management software. Often, however, other technologies such as the programming tools used to build the app or services of the business highly influence the choice of database management software. Certain software stacks have emerged that help developers identify which database management systems have widespread documentation, support, and a track record of success.

As discussed in Module 7, a **software stack**, also called a **solution stack** or **technology stack**, is a group of programs and technologies that commonly work together to build a digital solution. The term "stack" became popular in the context of web development. Not all stacks contain parallel technologies. For example, several common web application solution stacks are shown in Figure 9-17.

Stack Name	Products	Description
Front-end stack	**HTML (HyperText Markup Language)** **CSS (Cascading Style Sheets)** **JavaScript** (scripting language)	HTML is the standard markup language to describe content on a webpage. CSS is the standard language to style and position content on a webpage. JavaScript is currently the de facto (by fact) standard front-end scripting language used to respond to user interactivity such as clicks and entries on a webpage.
LAMP	Linux (server operating system) Apache (web server) MySQL (relational database) Perl, PHP or Python (back-end programming language)	LAMP is considered the most popular back-end stack (especially with PHP), appreciated for its scalability, security, and long-term track record of success.
WINS	Windows Server (server operating system) Internet Information Services (web server) .NET (framework) SQL Server (relational database)	WINS is the all-Microsoft version of LAMP. WINS adds the .NET application development framework to the stack, making application development faster and more consistent across programmers. The programming language most commonly used in the .NET framework is C#.
MEAN/MERN	MongoDB (document database) Express.js (framework) AngularJS (framework) or React.js (framework) Node.js (web server)	MEAN and MERN use JavaScript as the primary programming language for both the front-end, its traditional role, and the back-end programming requirements at the server through JavaScript development frameworks. AngularJS is a JavaScript web app development framework managed by Google. React.js is a competing JavaScript web app development framework managed by Facebook. Node.js is an open source JavaScript environment that allows JavaScript to run on a server.
Ruby on Rails	Ruby (programming language) Rails (framework) **SQLite** (relational database)	Ruby on Rails is an open source web app development stack that comes embedded with open source SQLite as the relational database, but larger Ruby/Rails projects use MySQL.

FIGURE 9-17 Popular software stacks

Note in Figure 9-17, the term "front end" is used in yet another context, that of a web application. Within a web application, the front-end refers to the processes and technologies that execute at the client machine in a browser. For example, the front-end languages of HTML, CSS, and JavaScript are all processed by browser software located on a user's device. When the browser processes HTML and CSS, it is sometimes called **parsing** the code to **render** the webpage's content. When a browser processes JavaScript, it does so with functionality built directly into the browser called the **JavaScript engine**.

In contrast, the other stacks in Figure 9-17 are referred to as "back-end" technologies within the context of a web app because they execute on the server. Back-end technologies must read and write files as well as communicate with a centralized database, so they must run on a server, not an individual user's client machine. Java, C#, Ruby, PHP, and C++ are back-end programming languages. When a centralized application server executes code written in those languages for a web app, the result is the creation of files that contain data (such as the result of a database query) and HTML, CSS, and JavaScript—the three technologies that browsers understand and can further processing. Knowing how the front-end and back-end technologies fit together is referred to as the **full-stack**.

Of particular note is a clarification of one of the most common and unfortunate misunderstandings in computer science today—Java versus JavaScript. While both are object-oriented programming languages, they typically work in different environments. JavaScript has traditionally been used as a front-end scripting language that responds to user interactivity on a webpage. A **scripting language** refers to a language designed to create small, specific programs as opposed to complete, large applications.

For example, JavaScript has often been used to give the user messages, change or display content, or total prices in a shopping cart while a user is interacting with a webpage in their browser. Java has traditionally been used as a back-end application development language that interacts well with a centralized database. (Current exceptions to these traditional roles are the JavaScript frameworks, which allow JavaScript to run on the server, as well as Java applets, which can be downloaded and run in browsers that have enabled Java.) The fact that Java and JavaScript start with the first same four letters has been described as having the same relationship between the words "ham" and "hamster." Just because they start with the same first four characters does not mean that one is a subset of the other but rather, was a marketing decision to create more interest in JavaScript during its early life; a decision that continues to cause much confusion.

A **software framework**, or **framework** for short, is a set of standards, development tools, and software libraries that help programmers develop software solutions faster and with more consistency across programmers. Not all frameworks include the same pieces, but one of the most popular software frameworks, **Microsoft ASP.NET** (also referred to as **ASP.NET** or just **.NET**) specifies Microsoft Visual Studio as the **integrated development environment (IDE)** in which the programmer codes, C# (or Visual Basic, though VB is currently declining in popularity and therefore rarely used for new projects) as the programming language, and SQL Server as the relational database. Within the ASP.NET framework, menus, toolbars, commands, and libraries are easily accessible to support the work of application development.

Each current programming language has more than one popular framework, each competing to be the best. Popular programming languages and some of their frameworks are shown in Figure 9-18.

Language	Popular Frameworks
JavaScript	Node.js Meteor Express Angular.js ReactJS Vue.js
Ruby	Rails
Python	Django Flask
PHP	Laravel WordPress Symfony CakePHP
C#	ASP.NET
Java	Spring

FIGURE 9-18 Popular programming language frameworks

WordPress is considered a **CMS, content management system**, rather than a software framework. The focus of a CMS is not creating new web apps, but rather, managing existing digital content within a predeveloped structure. However, it's worth mentioning WordPress in the discussion of how to select a database management system given WordPress uses MySQL (and to a lesser degree MariaDB and SQLite), thus giving MySQL a major influence and presence in the database operations of the web.

Considering the power and advantages of programming within frameworks used in a common solution stack, the choice of a database management product today is highly influenced by those decisions as opposed to the features of the individual database management system itself.

Q & A 9-6

Question: What makes Access a **RAD (rapid application development)** framework, and when is it appropriate to choose Microsoft Access as the relational database system for a new application?

Answer: Microsoft Access is a RAD framework because it includes relational database management functionality along with other application development tools such as a QBE to write SQL (queries), Form Design View to develop input forms, Report Design View to write reports, and other application development tools such as macros and **VBA (Visual Basic for Applications)** modules.

Access works well as a relational database management system for a handful of local, trusted users working within the application across a **local area network (LAN)**. Access does not scale well across more than a handful of concurrent users nor does it integrate well with open Internet communications technologies.

NOSQL DATABASE MANAGEMENT SYSTEMS

An important distinction between the traditional LAMP and WINS web application development stacks and the up-and-coming MEAN/MERN stacks is the type of database management system each stack uses. The LAMP and WINS stacks use open source MySQL and Microsoft SQL Server, respectively. Both MySQL and Microsoft SQL Server are traditional, large-scale relational database management systems.

The MEAN and MERN stacks both specify MongoDB as the database of choice. **NoSQL database system** refers to "not only SQL." The following are types of NoSQL database systems:

- *Document database management system*: Stores data in a set of descriptive documents rather than the specific columns, rows, tables, and relationships of a relational database. Commonly used in web apps.
- *Graph databases*: A **graph database** emphasizes connections between data elements, which accelerates queries. Commonly used in recommendation engines and **AI (artificial intelligence)** applications.
- *Key-value databases*: A **key-value database** stores simple key/value pairs of data.
- *Wide column stores*: Stores data in tables with a very many columns.

MongoDB is a **document database management system**. A NoSQL database therefore doesn't use SQL to select or update the data, so "no SQL" is written to interact with it. Data in NoSQL databases may be written and read with object-oriented languages such as JavaScript, Java, and C# that iterate over the documents to read, write, update, or delete the desired data.

NoSQL databases do not require you to predetermine the name or type of the data you want to store, as do relational databases. Therefore, NoSQL databases are often used to store and manage inconsistent, unpredictable, and nontraditional data such as images, videos, postings, and social media data. Due to their ability to store "messy" data, NoSQL databases are typically faster and easier to scale up than relational databases.

If you have the opportunity to develop a new application from scratch and the power and desire to develop with a proven software solution stack, use the guidelines in the following decision tree to select a database management system for a new software application:

1. Will the application be using data from existing database management systems? If the answer is yes, use that system.

2. If the answer to #1 is no, has a particular software development stack and programming framework already been selected? If the answer is yes, use the database management system most closely aligned with that stack and framework.

3. If the answer to #2 is no, is the data highly predictable and structured? If the answer is yes, lean toward a development stack using a relational database product. Or, is the data unpredictable, inconsistent, or non-traditional? If the answer is yes, lean toward a development stack using a NoSQL database.

Q & A 9-7

Question: What primary limitation of relational database management systems do NoSQL database management systems address?

Answer: Relational database management systems are designed to ensure database consistency across all users. However, relational database management systems have limitations related to maximizing availability across a wide or distributed network. NoSQL databases do a better job of distributing themselves across a wide area, but are not always immediately consistent for all users. NoSQL databases often aim for eventual consistency. Depending on your application, you may prefer the speed of a NoSQL database over the data consistency of a relational database.

OBJECT-ORIENTED DATABASE MANAGEMENT SYSTEMS

Another category of NoSQL databases has also emerged called **object-oriented database management system (OODBMS)**. In an OODBMS, the database encapsulates all data in the form of an object. An **object** is a set of related attributes along with the actions that are associated with the set of attributes. A client object, for example, consists of the attributes associated with clients (number, name, contact information) together with the actions that are associated with client data (add, edit, delete client data).

While relational databases may be able to store complex data such graphics, drawings, photographs, video, sound, voice mails, and spreadsheets using special data types, called **binary large objects (BLOBs)**, OODBMS systems are especially useful for these types of data. Because the primary focus of certain applications is storing and managing complex objects such as **computer-aided design and manufacturing (CAD/CAM)** and **geographic information systems (GISs)**, these applications typically use object-oriented database management systems.

OODBMs are closely aligned with specific object-oriented programming languages. Figure 9-19 provides data on some of the current object-oriented database companies and the object-oriented programming language to which they are most directly connected.

Vendor	Language	Website
ObjectDatabase++	C++	dbdb.io/db/objectdatabase
ObjectStore	C++	ignitetech.com/objectstore/
Perst	Java, C#	mcobject.com/perst/
ZODB	Python	zodb.org/en/latest/
Wakanda	JavaScript	wakanda.io/
ObjectDB	Java	objectdb.com/

FIGURE 9-19 Object-oriented database vendors

To work with and document an OODBMS, the object-oriented terminology summarized in Figure 9-20 is helpful.

Object-Oriented Term	Definition
Object	A container for properties and methods. Sometimes referred to as an instance of a class.
Class	An object that is a blueprint for more objects. A class defines what properties and methods a new object may contain.
Property	A characteristic of an object. A property may store a single value or another object.
Method	Something that an object can do.
Encapsulation	A concept that helps hide and protect data by restricting access only to public methods.
Abstraction	A concept that allows programmers to create classes, objects, and variables, and to reuse those things as needed for more specificity. Abstraction allows programmers to avoid writing duplicate code.
Inheritance	A concept that gives new classes and objects all of the properties and methods of the parent class. Sometimes inheritance is defined as the "is/a" or "has/a" relationship between two objects.
Polymorphism	A concept that allows a particular method to work in different ways based on how it is used.
Unified Modeling Language (UML)	A standardized modeling approach used to model all the various aspects of software development for object-oriented systems. UML includes a way to represent database designs.

FIGURE 9-20 Object-oriented terminology

Rules for Object-Oriented Database Management Systems

As in the early days of distributed and OLAP database systems, a set of desired characteristics for object-oriented database systems was developed when they were introduced. Most of the following principles are the same general principles that guide object-oriented programming languages.

1. *Complex objects.* Must support the creation of complex objects from simple objects such as integers and characters.
2. *Object identity.* Must provide a way to distinguish between one object and another.
3. *Encapsulation.* Must encapsulate data and associated methods together in the database.
4. *Information hiding.* Must hide the details concerning the way data is stored and the actual implementation of the methods from the user.
5. *Types or classes.* Must support either abstract types or classes (it does not matter which).
6. *Inheritance.* Must support inheritance.
7. *Late binding.* Must allow for **late binding**, the association of an operation to actual program code when the code is run.
8. *Computational completeness.* Must be able to use functions to perform various computations.
9. *Extensibility.* Must be **extensible**, meaning that it is possible to define new data types.
10. *Persistence.* Must have **persistence**, the ability to have a program *remember* its data from one execution to the next.
11. *Performance.* Must have sufficient performance capabilities to manage very large databases effectively.
12. *Concurrent update support.* Must support concurrent update.
13. *Recovery support.* Must provide recovery services.
14. *Query facility.* Must provide query facilities.

Q & A 9-8

Question: Object-oriented database management systems are most appropriate for what types of data, and in what applications are they commonly implemented?

Answer: OODBMS are most appropriate for unstructured or complex data types such as graphics, drawings, photographs, video, sound, and voice mail. OODBMS are commonly implemented in CAD/CAM and GIS applications given they typically involve the storage and relationships between many drawings and images.

BIG DATA

Big data can be defined as an extremely large set of nontraditional data that can be used to gain meaningful business insights or predict significant business events. Big data is often characterized by what has become known as the "3Vs": volume, variety, and velocity.

Volume refers to the amount of data from many sources. **Variety** involves the types of data: traditional text and numbers plus pictures, video, sound, and behavioral data such as clicks and pauses. **Velocity** refers to the speed at which the data is created.

Big data includes, but it not limited to, the following type of information:

- Blog postings
- Images
- Reviews
- Clicks on a webpage
- Tweets
- Connections
- Voice commands
- Search keywords
- Other Internet-driven processes

Almost every business in every industry can imagine positive outcomes to the analysis of big data. For example, companies that interact directly with you and other consumers such Amazon and Facebook analyze big data to make individualized news, ad, and content suggestions based on your past behavior. Banking and securities companies analyze big data to better detect and predict fraud. The healthcare industry uses big data to track the spread of chronic disease. The energy industry uses big data to improve energy exploration as well as environmental protection. Technology companies use big data to analyze traffic and demand on their resources.

Big data is typically too large and varied, and changes too quickly to be managed internally by any of the database management models discussed so far. Big data analysis is often left to expensive data scientists and data engineers within a large companies who work with big data vendors such as Cloudera, Amazon Web Services, Microsoft, and IBM and use Hadoop systems delivered through the cloud "as-a-service." **Hadoop** is a set of open source modules released by the Apache Software Foundation that provides the infrastructure for big data analytics. Even companies with smaller budgets can benefit from a subset of big data analysis using free or moderately priced services such as Google Analytics to start mining data from traffic on their website.

Google Analytics

Google Analytics is a service provided by Google that tracks and reports website information such as **session duration** (the length of time a user is at the website), the number of pages accessed per session, the **bounce rate** (the percentage of visitors who enter the site and then leave, or "bounce," rather than continuing to view other pages), and the geographical location of your users.

Google Analytics is considered an entry-level digital marketing tool that helps monitor important facts that lead to positive outcomes for your business, such as direct sales or requests for information, also called **conversions**. Google Analytics can also tell you the types of devices people are using, which helps you determine whether you need to invest in more **mobile-friendly** website improvements, those designed for quick access to common functionality on small screens, as well as what **channels** are directing traffic to your website. Channels include the following types of searches:

- Organic search from Google: A user enters keywords into the Google home page and finds your site.
- Paid search: A user clicks a paid ad to reach your site.
- Social media: A user finds your site from a Facebook posting.
- Referrals and backlinks: A user finds your site from another site.
- Direct traffic: A user types your URL directly into the browser.

Answers to these questions help a business focus valuable resources to solve problems and seize valuable opportunities.

Q & A 9-9

Question: How do you start using Google Analytics at a website?

Answer: Go to google.com/analytics, create a free account, and follow the instructions to add the tracking functionality to the pages of your website.

DATA FORMATS

Sometimes you need to export data to share with another application in a particular database format. Historically, **ASCII (American Standard Code for Information Interchange)** text files were used to do the job. ASCII is a character encoding standard for electronic communication. Today, most database management systems can export data to common data file formats such as **CSV (comma-separated text files)**, Excel, and **ODBC (Open Database Connectivity)** to share with other databases that have ODBC drivers such as Oracle, MySQL and SQL Server.

303

Each database management system has specific tools and options for exporting data. For example, using the tools on the External Data tab of the ribbon shown in Figure 9-21, Microsoft Access lets you export data in the following ways:

- As an Excel spreadsheet file
- As a comma-delimited or fixed-width text file
- To an XML file
- As a PDF or XPS file
- As an Outlook email attachment
- To another Access database
- To a Word document for use in a Word mail merge
- To a Word document as a rich text file
- To a SharePoint list
- To another database with an ODBC driver
- As an HTML document
- As a dBASE file

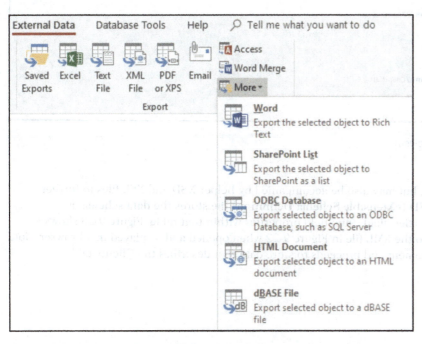

FIGURE 9-21 Microsoft Access data file format export options

Two of today's most notable file formats include **XML (eXtensible Markup Language)** and **JSON (JavaScript Object Notation)**. XML is a web-related specification managed by the W3C (w3.org). **W3C, the World Wide Web Consortium**, is an international community that develops and maintains web standards, including those that define HTML (HyperText Markup Language), CSS (Cascading Style Sheets), XML (Extensible Markup Language), and related web technologies.

XML

Extensible Markup Language (XML) is designed for the exchange of data on the web. It is closely related to HTML, HyperText Markup Language, in that both fall under the standards defined for **markup languages** that use **elements** (commonly called **tags**) to identify content and data. The term "markup" comes from the fact that the content is identified or "marked up" in a manner that meaningfully describes what it is. **Semantic markup** means that the language meaningfully describes the data within it.

Figure 9-22 shows an XML file created by exporting the Clients table in the JCConsulting database to an XML file, and then opened and displayed in a browser. Note how the XML elements define each record and the field data within each record.

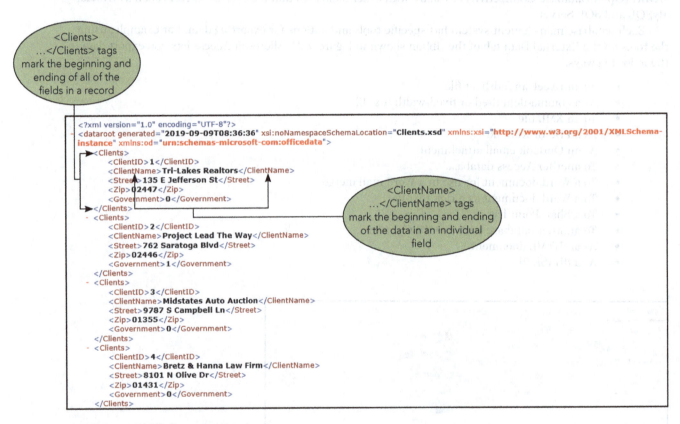

FIGURE 9-22 XML file opened in a browser

XML files store the actual data, but may also be accompanied by helper XSD and XSL files to further describe and style the data. The **XSD (eXtensible Schema Definition)** file stores the **data schema**, a description of the table, table properties, fields, and field properties within that table. Figure 9-23 shows a portion of the XSD file connected to the XML file in Figure 9-22 when opened and displayed in a browser. Note that the file starts with an <xsd> element and proceeds to store data that describes the Clients table.

304

FIGURE 9-23 XSD file opened in a browser

The **XSL (eXtensible Stylesheet Language)** file determines the styling and layout of the data. XSL is a standard W3C language for creating stylesheets for XML documents. A **stylesheet** is a document that specifies how to process the data contained in another document and present the data in a web browser, in a printed report, on a mobile device, in a sound device, or in other presentation media. Figure 9-24 shows a portion of an XSL file connected to the XML file in Figure 9-22 when opened and displayed in a browser. Note that the file starts with an <?xsl> element and proceeds to define styles and a table layout for the data.

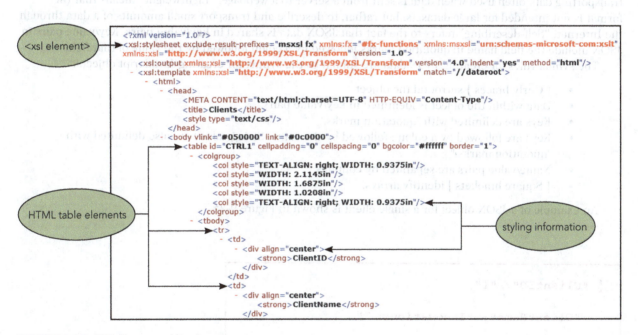

FIGURE 9-24 XSL file opened in a browser

A related W3C standard language is **XSL Transformations (XSLT)**, which defines the rules to process an XML document and change it into another type of document, such as an HTML or XHTML document. As more data is being stored, exchanged, and presented using XML, the W3C has also developed **XQuery**, which is a language for querying web-based documents and similarly structured data repositories.

Starting with the Office 2007 suite, Microsoft switched from its native file formats to a new file format that it calls Office Open XML for the Excel, PowerPoint, and Word programs as noted by the native four-character .xlsx, .pptx, and .docx file extensions. The **Office Open XML** file format is a compressed version of XML.

To open and examine the XML files stored within a current Word document, Excel spreadsheet, or PowerPoint file, perform the following steps:

- Change the file extension of .docx, .xlsx, or .pptx to .zip.
- Double-click the zip file to view the XML folders and files within it or right-click it and choose Extract from the shortcut menu to extract the files from the compressed .zip file.

Q & A 9-10

Question: Why might it be helpful to export data from an Access database to an HTML file?

Answer: You may want to distribute information from an Access database such as the information in a query or report on a regular basis as an HTML file so that the data can be shared in a read-only fashion across the web when accessed by a web browser.

JSON

JSON stands for **JavaScript Object Notation**, a lightweight and self-describing format for storing and transporting data often used when data is sent from a server to a webpage. "Lightweight" means that the format is not intended for large datasets, but rather, to describe and transport small amounts of a data through the Internet. "Self-describing" refers to the fact that JSON data is shared in **key/value pairs**. Key/value pairs in JSON include the field name in quotation marks followed by a colon followed by the value of that field.

The syntax rules for creating JSON data are similar to the syntax for creating JavaScript objects:

- { Curly braces } surround the object.
- Data within the object is identified in key/value pairs.
- Keys are delimited with "quotation marks."
- Keys are followed by a colon : followed by the value. String values are also delimited with "quotation marks."
- Name/value pairs are separated by commas.
- [Square brackets] identify arrays.

An example of a JSON object for a single client is shown in Figure 9-25.

```
{ "ClientID": "1",

  "ClientName": "InnovationsKC",

  "Street": "12345 College Blvd",

  "Zip": "66222"

}
```

FIGURE 9-25 Sample JSON object

An **array** (a programming variable that contains a list) of three JSON objects is shown in Figure 9-26. An array of JSON objects is a common way to share small amounts of data across the web.

```
"clientlist": [{ "ClientID": "1",

    "ClientName": "InnovationsKC",

    "Street": "12345 College Blvd",

    "Zip": "66222"

},

{ "ClientID": "2",

    "ClientName": "Perez Enterprises",

    "Street": "400 Switzer St",

    "Zip": "66221"

},

{ "ClientID": "3",

    "ClientName": "MSTS and Associates",

    "Street": "505 Quivira Rd",

    "Zip": "66220"

}]
```

FIGURE 9-26   Sample array of JSON objects

Because JSON data is pure text, it is a data format that can be read and manipulated by any programming language. However, considering the similarities between JSON syntax and JavaScript syntax, data stored in JSON files is most commonly and easily used by JavaScript applications.

DATA VISUALIZATION TOOLS

Perhaps one of the most exciting trends in the database industry is the use of data visualization tools such as the Microsoft Excel charting tools, Microsoft Power BI, and Tableau. As the old saying goes, "a picture is worth a thousand words," which also means that an effective chart or graph can often communicate information more quickly and effectively than a report of columns of numbers.

Visualization Tools in Microsoft Excel

Microsoft Excel is perhaps the most common data visualization tool given most every organization of all sizes uses Excel. Most database management systems can export data directly to an Excel file or to a generic text format that can be opened by Excel.

Excel also natively supports live connections to certain database management systems including Microsoft Access, Microsoft SQL Server, Microsoft Azure, any database that participates with ODBC drivers such as SQL Server, Oracle, and PostgreSQL, Hadoop databases, and several specific online services such as Facebook, SalesForce, and SharePoint services. Excel offers the standard business charting tools shown in Figure 9-27.

Chart Type	Typical Use	Sample Data Visualization Problem	Excel Icon
Column	To compare vertical bars	To compare the total sales across several sales representatives for a given year	
Line	To show trends over time	To track the trends in sales for several products across several months.	
Pie	To compare values of a whole as slices of a pie	To compare the total sales between several regions for a given year.	
Bar	To compare horizontal bars	To compare the total sales for different products over several months	
Area	To show trends over time based on a cumulative group	To show the accumulation of total sales for different products over several months	
X Y (Scatter)	Shows the relationship between two variables	To identify the relationship between advertising expenses and sales	
Map	To compare values across geographical locations.	To geographically show sales by country	
Stock	To show stock prices over time including high/low bars	To show high-low-close information for a particular stock over time	
Surface	To show trends over time based on a cumulative group (area) in a 3D landscape	To find the highest or lowest overall sales when comparing sales over time by product	
Radar	To show the relationship between three or more variables of the same thing	To plot the performance of a product using several different metrics	
Treemap	To show data as proportionally-sized rectangles	To compare the relative amount of sales between different categories of products	
Sunburst	To show data as proportionally-sized rings for one or more categories	To compare the relative amount of sales between different categories of products within different regions	
Histogram	To show distributions of numerical data.	To compare the frequency of the total dollar amount per sale	
Box & Whisker	To display the distribution of data through quartiles (a simplified histogram)	To compare the distribution of the total dollar amount per sale	
Waterfall	To display how a value's starting position either increases or decreases through a period of time to reach its ending value.	To display how a budget line item's actual expenses are consumed to the final actual expense	
Funnel	To present data in a series of centered, horizontal bars to show a shrinking progression data through time	To display how many website visitors eventually convert to customers after visiting your website	
Combo	To present data in a combination of ways, for example as both bars and a line	To display how sales compare to an economic indicator such as the stock marker over time	

FIGURE 9-27 Excel chart types

In addition to these major Excel chart types, many chart types have common subtypes to help illustrate a specific point such as stacked and 3-D versions of the column chart. The "3-D" refers to three dimensions and requires three axes for the chart. You can use many high-quality websites, images, and textbooks such as *Microsoft Excel 2019 Illustrated* published by Cengage to help you understand and pick the best chart type for your data and the message you are trying to convey. Excel also offers sophisticated PivotTable and PivotChart tools, previously displayed in Figures 9-11 and 9-12.

Microsoft Power BI

Microsoft Power BI is a business analytics solution that lets you visualize data and share that visualization with others or embed it in a webpage. Power BI has all of the capabilities of Excel to chart data, plus the power to allow the employees of an organization to collaboratively share, build, and create data visualizations.

Power BI is also often used to create a **dashboard**, a one-page grouping of **key performance indicators (KPIs)** that allow decision makers to quickly evaluate and act on important data. A sample dashboard is shown in Figure 9-28.

Each chart monitors a different key performance indicator

Singular Fact/Shutterstock.com

FIGURE 9-28 Sample Power BI dashboard

Tableau

No discussion of data visualization would be complete without mentioning one of the premiere data visualization companies, **Tableau**. Tableau software is a competitor to Microsoft Excel and Power BI. Tableau promotes **embedded analytics**, which it defines as "the integration of your data with external facing applications," in an effort to create meaningful collaborative evaluations of data with a company's business partners such as customers or suppliers.

Tableau also claims to have a superior approach to discovering insights to data with built-in drill-down and intuitive visualization suggestions. Many data analysts and data scientists also prefer Tableau's professionally styled visualizations and user interactivity features. Two sample Tableau visualizations are shown in Figures 9-29 and 9-30. Figure 9-29 shows the path of pain pills that enter the state of Arizona from manufacturer to pharmacy around the United States.

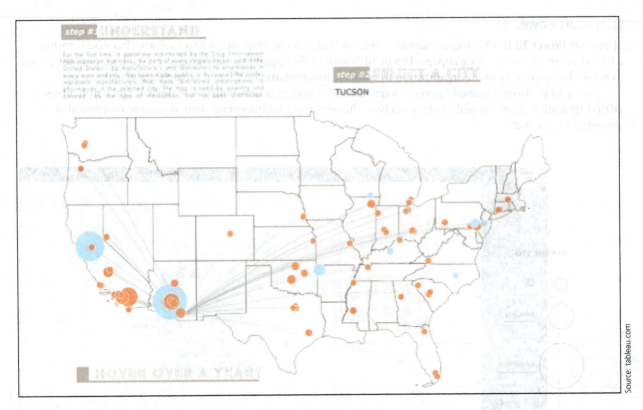

FIGURE 9-29   Sample Tableau visualization to trace the spread of opioids

Figure 9-30 shows a matrix indicating how often each pair of Supreme Court justices agreed with one another during a recent term.

FIGURE 9-30   Sample Tableau visualization of Supreme Court decisions

Q & A 9-11

Question: Where can you find more examples of data visualizations?

Answer: Visit the Tableau website (tableau.com) and explore the Tableau Viz Gallery (tableau.com/solutions/gallery). The website also features Tableau visualizations from the public at public.tableau.com/en-us/gallery.

Summary

- **Compare and contrast database architectures, including centralized, client/server, data warehouse, and distributed systems**. A centralized database architecture refers to a single, centrally located computer system that processes all data. In a client/server architecture, a central server delivers and manages resources and works cooperatively with a client computer to run an entire application. A data warehouse architecture refers to the hardware and software an organization needs to address the analytical requirements of users without disrupting traditional operations. A distributed system is physically divided among several network sites.

- **Explore online analytical processing (OLAP) and business-intelligence (BI) tools used in data warehousing**. OLAP is a database technology that optimizes data for querying, analyzing, and reporting. It organizes the data in hierarchies, which are stored in conceptual cubes and often analyzed through PivotTable or PivotChart tools to display high-level summaries of large amounts of data.

- **Define a distributed database**. A distributed database is a single logical database that is physically divided among computers at several sites on a network.

- **Compare and contrast how database management systems are selected from a historical and modern perspective**. Traditionally, a DBMS was evaluated based on features such as ease of restructuring data, support of procedural and nonprocedural programming languages, cost, and ease of use. New application development projects often choose a DBMS based on other technologies in its solution stack, such as the programming tools used to build the app or services of the business as opposed to the features of the individual database management system itself.

- **Explore alternatives to relational database management systems, including NoSQL document systems and object-oriented database management systems**. A NoSQL database system refers to "not only SQL," meaning it can store data in a set of descriptive documents rather than the specific columns, rows, tables, and relationships of a relational database. Web and artificial intelligence apps often use a NoSQL document system. Another alternative to a relational DBMS is an OODBMS, which encapsulates all data in the form of an object, a set of related attributes along with their actions.

- **Explain the current issues and trends in big data**. Big data is an extremely large set of nontraditional data that can be used to gain meaningful business insights or predict significant business events. Big data is often characterized by the "3Vs": volume, variety, and velocity. Most businesses can benefit from analyzing big data from blogs, reviews, social media comments, and other web-based information. However, big data is typically too large and varied, and changes too quickly to be managed internally by many database management models.

- **Describe data stored in XML and JSON formats**. Extensible Markup Language (XML) is a data file format designed for the exchange of data on the web. XML files store the actual data, but may also be accompanied by helper XSD and XSL files to further describe and style the data.

  JSON stands for JavaScript Object Notation, a lightweight and self-describing format for storing and transporting data often used when data is sent from a server to a webpage. "Lightweight" means that the format is intended to describe and transport small amounts of a data through the Internet. "Self-describing" indicates that JSON data is shared in key/value pairs, which include the field name in quotation marks, followed by a colon, followed by the value of that field.

- **Explore data visualization concepts and tools**. You use a data visualization tool to display data in graphical form as a chart or graph, which can be two-dimensional or three-dimensional and may offer interactive features. A dashboard is a one-page grouping of key performance indicators (KPIs) that allow decision makers to quickly evaluate and act on important data.

Key Terms

.NET

3Vs

abstraction

ad hoc

AI (artificial intelligence)

Amazon Web Services (AWS)

application server

array

ASCII (American Standard Code for Information Interchange)

ASP.NET

back-end database

back-end machine

back-end processor

Berkeley Open Infrastructure for Network Computing (BOINC)

big data

binary large object (BLOB)

Bitbucket

bounce rate

BUNCH (Burroughs, UNIVAC, NCR, Control Data, Honeywell)

centralized approach

channel

class

client

client/server architecture

clone

cloud

cloud computing

cloud provider

CMS (content management system)

COBOL (Common Business-Oriented Language)

compatible

computer-aided design and manufacturing (CAD/CAM)

console

conversion

crowdsourced processing power

CSS (Cascading Style Sheets)

CSV (comma-separated text file)

cube (OLAP term)

dashboard

data center

data mining

data schema

data warehouse

data warehouse architecture

database architecture

database server

dBase

dimension (OLAP term)

distributed database

document database management system

DOS (Disk Operating System)

drill down (OLAP term)

dumb terminal

element (as it relates to a markup language)

embedded analytics

encapsulation

extensible

Extensible Data Schema (XSD)

Extensible Markup Language (XML)

Extensible Stylesheet Language (XSL)

fat client

framework

front-end database

front-end machine

front-end processor

full-stack

geographic information systems (GIS)

Git

GitHub

Google Analytics

Graph database

Hadoop

hard copy

hierarchy (OLAP term)

high-level programming language

Hypertext Markup Language (HTML)

IBM System/360 mainframe

IBM System/370 mainframe

inheritance

integrated

integrated development environment (IDE)

JavaScript

JavaScript engine

JSON (JavaScript Object Notation)

key performance indicator (KPI)

key/value pair

key-value database

killer application

LAMP (Linux, Apache, MySQL, PHP)

late binding

legacy program

level (OLAP term)

local area network (LAN)

markup language

MEAN (MongoDB, Express.js, AngularJS, Node.js)

MERN (MongoDB, Express.js, React.js, Node.js)

method

Microsoft ASP.NET

Microsoft Power BI

MIS (Management Information Systems)

mobile-friendly

MongoDB

monitor

Moore's Law

nonvolatile

NoSQL database system

n-tier architecture

object

object-oriented database management system (OODBMS)

object-oriented language

ODBC (Open Database Connectivity)

Office Open XML

online analytical processing (OLAP)

online transaction processing (OLTP)

open architecture

parsing

persistence

personal computer

PivotChart

PivotTable

polymorphism

presentation functions

property

proprietary

proprietary architecture

RAD (rapid application development)

read-only data

read-only snapshot

render

roll up (OLAP term)

Ruby on Rails

scalability

scripting language

semantic markup

server

server farm

session duration

slice and dice (OLAP term)

snapshot

soft copy

software framework

software stack

solution stack

SQLite

stylesheet

subject-oriented

Tableau

tag

technology stack

terminal

thin client

three-tier architecture

time-variant

two-tier architecture

Unified Modeling Language (UML)

user interface function

variety (as it relates to big data)

VBA (Visual Basic for Applications)

velocity (as it relates to big data)

virtual

virtualization

Visicalc

Visual Basic (Beginner's All-purpose Symbolic Instruction Code)

volume (as it relates to big data)

wide column stores

WINS (Window Server, Internet Information Services, .NET, SQL Server)

WordPress

WordStar

World Wide Web Consortium (W3C)

XML (Extensible Markup Language)

XQuery

XSD (Extensible Schema Definition)

XSL (Extensible Style Language)

XSL Transformations (XSLT)

Module Review Questions

Problems

1. Which of the following database architectures is most closely aligned with traditional, enterprise-level relational databases?
   a. centralized
   b. client/server
   c. data warehouse
   d. distributed

2. Which of the following best describes the concept of an OLAP cube?
   a. Selected columns and rows from one or more tables.
   b. A read-only snapshot of data organized in levels and hierarchies of categories.
   c. An object-oriented key/value pair description of data.
   d. A BLOB.

3. Big data typically does *not* include which of the following?
   a. Clicks on webpages
   b. Images
   c. Billing information
   d. Keyword search data

4. Which of the following databases would probably be considered for a web app if your company had a significant commitment to JavaScript?
   a. IBM Db2
   b. Microsoft Access
   c. Microsoft SQL Server
   d. MongoDB

5. Which of the following types of databases would most likely be used for tracking connections between people?
   a. document
   b. relational
   c. graph
   d. flat file

6. Which file extension is a type of XML file?
   a. xlsx
   b. json
   c. txt
   d. dbf

7. Line charts are best used for which type of visualization?
   a. comparing values
   b. identifying relationships
   c. showing trends over time
   d. displaying cumulative totals

Critical Thinking Questions

1. Identify the characteristics of a new application that lends itself to the MEAN or MERN stack.

2. The term "big data" is trendy and means different things to different businesses. Ask five people in the Computer Science Department within your college what the term means to them, and organize the results.

JC Consulting Case Exercises

For the following exercises, you will answer problems and questions from management at JC Consulting. You do not need to use the JCConsulting database for any of these exercises.

Problems

1. Which of the following database architectures best describes how Access works when the database is stored on a file server and accessed by many users with personal computers?
   a. centralized
   b. client/server
   c. data warehouse
   d. distributed

2. If you wanted to evaluate Access data using Excel PivotTables and PivotCharts, what would be the first step?
   a. Select the data you want to evaluate with a query.
   b. Export all of your tables to text files.
   c. Create OLAP cubes in Access.
   d. Use the Database Business Intelligence Wizard in Access.

3. If JC Consulting used Google Analytics, what type of information might they learn?
   a. What areas of the country had the most potential for their services
   b. Which employees were most productive
   c. Which customers were most profitable
   d. How long users were interacting with their website

4. JC Consulting wants to upgrade some Access data to a larger, enterprise-scale database management system. Which is the most likely candidate?
   a. MongoDB
   b. Oracle
   c. IBM Db2
   d. SQL Server

5. Which of the following is a NoSQL database?
   a. IBM Db2
   b. Microsoft Access
   c. Microsoft SQL Server
   d. MongoDB

6. Which menu option on the More button of the External Data tab of the ribbon in Access do you use to export data to SQL Server?
   a. ODBC Database
   b. dBASE File
   c. SQL Server
   d. Relational

7. When creating a query in Access for data that you later want to analyze as a PivotTable or PivotChart in Excel, how many fields do you typically use in the visualizations?
   a. 1
   b. 2
   c. 3
   d. At least 4 or more

Critical Thinking

1. Identify the characteristics of the business problem that lends itself to an Access solution.
2. As JC Consulting grows, they may need to convert their Access application into technologies that can handle more users and locations. What solution stacks would you recommend they consider?

Pitt Fitness Case Exercises

Problems

1. Pitt Fitness, having transitioned to a larger database system to accommodate their recent growth, is now considering moving their database to the cloud. However, management is concerned that they will be sharing the resources with other cloud clients. The cloud provider assures Pitt Fitness that they can maintain maximum power and efficiency for Pitt. How can the cloud provider do this?
   a. by creating a server farm
   b. by building a data center
   c. through a technique called virtualization
   d. as long as the provider is AWS, they can do this

2. Pitt Fitness stores their Access database on a centralized file server for usage by a few employees. What type of architecture are they using?
   a. client/server
   b. cloud-based
   c. LAN-based
   d. front end

3. Pitt Fitness has hired summer interns for data analysis. The interns are running complex queries that take enormous processing power. The clerks at Pitt Fitness have found that registering customers and classes has slowed to an unacceptable pace. What type of system does Pitt Fitness need to correct this slow registration problem?

   a. a cloud-based system

   b. a data warehouse

   c. an integrated system

   d. a split form

4. The summer interns at Pitt Fitness explain to management that they will be initially summarizing data in a crosstabular organization. What type of tool are the interns using to create these cubes of data?

   a. OLTPs

   b. scalables

   c. thin clients

   d. PivotTables

5. Considering that Pitt Fitness is a relatively new company, what types of computer programs does Pitt Fitness *not* have?

   a. legacy

   b. dinosaur

   c. JavaScript

   d. object-oriented

6. Managers at Pitt Fitness want developers to write back-end applications that interact with the centralized database. Which computer language should they use?

   a. Java Lite

   b. JavaScript

   c. Java

   d. JavaVB

7. Pitt Fitness has decided to employ Google Analytics to analyze traffic on their website. The first report has come in with a recording of the bounce rate. What does the bounce rate measure?

   a. a site visitor that views many pages on the site

   b. a site visitor from a mobile device

   c. a site visitor that posts the site on social media

   d. a site visitor that leaves the site

8. Pitt Fitness has hired a full-time data analyst to produce various data visualizations to help management better serve their customers. Which of the following tools could the new employee use for data visualization?

   a. Excel

   b. Power BI

   c. Tableau

   d. Excel, Power BI, and Tableau

9. The new data analyst at Pitt Fitness wants to create a chart that compares the monthly class registrations by displaying them in horizontal lines. What type of chart would be appropriate?

   a. Column

   b. Line

   c. Pie

   d. Bar

10. The data analyst at Pitt Fitness is creating a chart that displays the relationship between advertising expenses and new customers. What type of chart is she using?

    a. Bar

    b. Area

    c. XY Scatter

    d. Map

Critical Thinking Questions

1. Pitt Fitness would like to enhance their web presence and enable the exchange of data on the web. What type of markup language should they use and why?

2. Describe some of the big data that Pitt Fitness might collect and find useful.

Sports Physical Therapy Case Exercises

Problems

1. When physical therapists are scheduled to see a patient, they ask the clerk for a "hard copy" to view what is needed for that day's session with the specific treatments. What are the physical therapists referring to when they request a hard copy?
   a. a poster board with the daily schedule
   b. a printed paper
   c. a tablet with the session information
   d. an electronic hard screen

2. The Sports Physical Therapy clinic is considering moving their database to the cloud. Which of the following is the current market leader in cloud storage, and therefore would be a safe bet for the organization?
   a. IBM
   b. Oracle
   c. Microsoft
   d. AWS

3. The Sports Physical Therapy clinic's Access database is stored on a centralized computer for usage by a few trusted colleagues. They are therefore running a _____ application.
   a. client/server
   b. back/end
   c. front/end
   d. crowdsourced

4. As the Sports Physical Therapy clinic grows, management is considering moving to a larger database management system, where the clients perform the presentation functions, a database server performs the database functions, and separate centralized computers perform the business functions as well as serve as an interface between clients and the database server. What type of architecture is management considering?
   a. Oracle
   b. nonvolatile
   c. three-tier
   d. thin client

5. The Sports Physical Therapy clinic has an Access database for patients, therapists, and appointments. The clinic also has other systems that record information such as insurance details, accounting of payments, and miscellaneous employee data. The IT manager at the organization wants to consolidate and summarize the data from these systems to produce management reports. What type of system is needed to accomplish this?
   a. data warehouse
   b. PivotTables
   c. client/server
   d. split database

6. The IT manager at the Sports Physical Therapy clinic created a system to consolidate and summarize data from its Access database and other insurance, accounting, and employee systems to produces management reports. What database technology optimizes data for querying, analyzing, and reporting?
   a. online analytical processing (OLAP)
   b. online transaction processing (OLTP)
   c. online database processing (OLDP)
   d. online integrated processing (OLIP)

7. The summer intern at Sports Physical Therapy clinic has been using Excel to analyze some data. The intern is displaying a crosstabular organization of the data with the session date as the row heading, the therapist ID as the column heading, and the session number as a counted value. What Excel tool is this summer intern using?
   a. Scenario Manager
   b. Solver
   c. PivotTable
   d. regression

8. The Sports Physical Therapy clinic is not a large business, but management still would like to analyze their "big data" using a moderately priced service. Which of the following would be appropriate for this task?
   a. Hadoop
   b. Amazon Web Services
   c. IBM
   d. Google Analytics

9. The summer intern at Sports Physical Therapy clinic would like to do data visualizations that are more sophisticated than the software Excel can provide. Which of the following solutions would be the best to use?
   a. Microsoft Access
   b. Microsoft Power BI
   c. Microsoft Project
   d. Microsoft OneNote

318

10. The summer intern at Sports Physical Therapy clinic is using Excel to create some interesting charts of the activities at the clinic. The intern would like to show trends over time based on a cumulative group of sessions. Which of the following chart types would be appropriate?
    a. XY Scatter
    b. Map
    c. Pie
    d. Area

Critical Thinking Questions

1. The Sports Physical Therapy clinic is considering centralizing their database operations. What are their options for this centralized computing?

2. The Sports Physical Therapy clinic is having trouble with the performance of their Access database. They would like to split the database between front end and back end to improve performance. How would they do this?

COMPREHENSIVE DESIGN EXAMPLE: DOUGLAS COLLEGE

Douglas College has decided to computerize its operations. In this appendix, you will design a database that satisfies many user requirements by applying the design techniques you learned in Modules 5 and 6 to a significant set of requirements.

DOUGLAS COLLEGE REQUIREMENTS

Douglas College has provided you with the following requirements that its new system must satisfy. You will use these requirements to design a new database.

General Description

Douglas College is organized by department (Mathematics, Physics, English, and so on). Most departments offer more than one major; for example, the Mathematics department might offer majors in calculus, applied mathematics, and statistics. Each major, however, is offered by only one department. Each faculty member is assigned to a single department. Students can have more than one major, but most students have only one. Each student is assigned a faculty member as an advisor for his or her major; students who have more than one major are assigned a faculty advisor for each major. The faculty member may or may not be assigned to the department offering the major.

A code that has up to three characters (CS for Computer Science, MTH for Mathematics, PHY for Physics, ENG for English, and so on) identifies each department. The combination of the department code and a three-digit number (CS 162 for Programming I, MTH 201 for Calculus I, ENG 102 for Creative Writing, and so on) identifies each course. The number of credits offered by a particular course does not vary; that is, all students who pass the same course receive the same number of credits.

A two-character code identifies the semester in which a course is taught (FA for fall, SP for spring, and SU for summer). The code is combined with two digits that designate the year (for example, FA21 represents the fall semester of 2021). For a given semester, a department assigns each section of each course a four-digit schedule code (schedule code 1295 for section A of MTH 201, code 1297 for section B of MTH 201, code 1302 for section C of MTH 201, and so on). The schedule codes might vary from semester to semester. The schedule codes are listed in the school's time schedule, and students use them to indicate the sections in which they want to enroll. (You will learn more about the enrollment process later in this section.)

After all students have completed the enrollment process for a given semester, each faculty member receives a class list for each section he or she will be teaching. In addition to listing the students in each section, the class list provides space to record the grade each student earns in the course. At the end of the semester, the faculty member enters the students' grades in this list and sends a copy of the list to the records office, where the grades are entered into the database. (In the future, the college plans to automate this part of the process.)

After an employee of the records office posts the grades (by entering them into the database), the DBMS generates a report card for each student; the report cards are then mailed to the addresses printed on the report card. The grades earned by a student become part of his or her permanent record and will appear on the student's transcript.

REPORT REQUIREMENTS

Employees at Douglas College require several reports to manage students, classes, schedules, and faculty members; these reports have the following requirements.

Report card: At the end of each semester, the system must produce a report card for each student. A sample report card is shown in Figure A-1.

DOUGLAS COLLEGE

Department	Course Number	Course Description	Grade	Credits Taken	Credits Earned	Grade Points
Computer Science	CS 162	Programming I	A	4	4	16.0
Mathematics	MTH 201	Calculus I	B+	3	3	9.9

Current Semester Totals

7	7	3.70	25.9
Credits Taken	Credits Earned	GPA	Total Points

Semester: FA21

Cumulative Totals

44	44	3.39	149.2
Credits Taken	Credits Earned	GPA	Total Points

Student Number: 381124188

Student Name & Address	Local Address (IF DIFFERENT)
Fredrick Starks 8006 Howard Ave. Baring, ID 83224	1605b College Park Douglas, ID 83260

FIGURE A-1 Sample report card for Douglas College

Class list: The system must produce a class list for each section of each course (for the faculty member); a sample class list is shown in Figure A-2. Note that space is provided for the grades. At the end of the semester, the instructor enters each student's grade and sends a copy of the class list to the records office.

CLASS LIST

Department: CS   Computer Science   Term: FA21
Course: 162   Programming I   (4 CREDITS)
Section: B
Schedule Code: 2366

Time: 1:00 - 1:50 M, T, W, F
PLACE: 118 SCR

Instructor: 462   Diane Johnson

Student Number	Student Name	Class Standing	Grade
381124188	Fredrick Starks	2	
.	.	.	.
.	.	.	.
.	.	.	.

FIGURE A-2 Sample class list for Douglas College

Grade verification report: After the records office processes the class list, it returns the class list to the instructor with the grades entered in the report. The instructor uses the report to verify that the records office entered the students' grades correctly.

Time schedule: The time schedule shown in Figure A-3 lists all sections of all courses offered during a given semester. Each section has a unique four-digit schedule code. The time schedule lists the schedule code; the department offering the course; the course's number, section letter, and title; the instructor teaching the course; the time the course meets; the room in which the course meets; the number of credits generated by the course; and the prerequisites for the course. In addition to the information shown in Figure A-3, the time schedule includes the dates the semester begins and ends, the dates final exams begin and end, and the last withdrawal date (the last date on which students may withdraw from a course for a refund and without academic penalty).

```
                    TIME SCHEDULE        Term: FA21


  Course #   Code #  Sect  Time              Room      Faculty
  ‾‾‾‾‾‾‾     ‾‾‾‾‾   ‾‾‾‾  ‾‾‾‾              ‾‾‾‾      ‾‾‾‾‾‾‾
      .         .      .     .                .          .
      .         .      .     .                .          .
  ⌐
  CHEMISTRY (CHM) Office: 341 NSB

    111  Chemistry I                         4 CREDITS
             1740    A    10:00-10:50 M, T, W, F   102 WRN   Johnson
             1745    B    12:00-12:50 M, T, W, F   102 WRN   Lawrence
                .    .         .                   .
                .    .         .                   .

                .    .         .                   .
             Prerequisite:  MTH 110
    112  Chemistry II                        4 CREDITS
             1790    A    10:00-11:50 M, W        109 WRN   Chang
             1795    B    12:00-1:50 T, R         102 WRN   Nelson
                .    .         .                   .
                .    .         .                   .

                .    .         .                   .
             Prerequisite:  CHM 111
    114  ....
```

Sample time schedule for Douglas College

Registration request form: A sample registration request form is shown in Figure A-4. A student uses this form to request classes for the upcoming semester. Students indicate the sections for which they want to register by entering each section's schedule code; for each of these sections, students may also enter a code for an alternative section in case the first requested section is full.

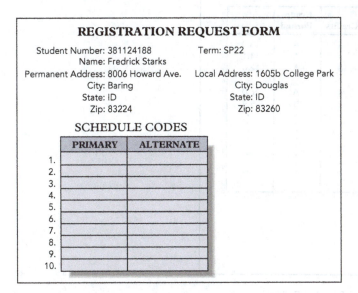

REGISTRATION REQUEST FORM

Student Number: 381124188   Term: SP22
        Name: Fredrick Starks
Permanent Address: 8006 Howard Ave.   Local Address: 1605b College Park
        City: Baring   City: Douglas
        State: ID   State: ID
        Zip: 83224   Zip: 83260

SCHEDULE CODES

	PRIMARY	ALTERNATE
1.		
2.		
3.		
4.		
5.		
6.		
7.		
8.		
9.		
10.		

FIGURE A-4   Sample registration request form for Douglas College

Student schedule: After all students have been assigned to sections, the system produces a student schedule form, which is mailed to students so that they know the classes in which they have been enrolled. A sample student schedule form is shown in Figure A-5. This form shows the schedule for an individual student for the indicated semester.

STUDENT SCHEDULE

Student Number: 381124188
Name: Fredrick Starks
Permanent Address: 8006 Howard Ave.
City: Baring
State: ID
Zip: 83224

Term: SP22

Local Address: 1605b College Park
City: Douglas
State: ID
Zip: 83260

Schedule Code	Course Number	Course Description	Section	Credits	Time	Room
2366	CS 253	Programming II	B	4	1:00–1:50 M, T, W, F	118 SCR
.	.	.		.		
.	.	.		.		
.	.	.		.		
		Total Credits:		16		

FIGURE A-5 Sample student schedule for Douglas College

Full student information report: This report lists complete information about a student, including his or her major(s) and all grades received to date. A sample of a full student information report is shown in Figure A-6.

FULL STUDENT INFORMATION

Student Number: 381124188
Name: Fredrick Starks
Current Address: 8006 Howard Ave.
City: Baring
State: ID
Zip: 83224

Term: FA21

Local Address: 1605b College Park
City: Douglas
State: ID
Zip: 83260

Major 1: Information Sys. Department: Computer Science Advisor: Mark Lawerence
Major 2: Accounting Department: Business Advisor: Jill Thomas
Major 3: Department: Advisor:

Term	Course Number		Credits	Grade Earned	
SP21	MTH 123	Trigonometry	4	A	16.0
	HST 201	Western Civilization	3	A-	11.1
	ENG 101	American Literature	3	A	12.0
FA21	CS 162	Programming I	4	A	16.0
	MTH 201	Calculus I	4	B+	9.9
.	.	.	.	.	.
.	.	.	.	.	.
.	.	.	.	.	.
.	.	.	.	.	.
.	.	.	.	.	.
.	.	.	.	.	.

Credits Attempted: 44
Credits Earned: 44
Grade Points: 149.2
Grade Point Avg: 3.39
Class Standing: 2

FIGURE A-6 Sample full student information report for Douglas College

Faculty information report: This report lists all faculty by department and contains each faculty member's ID number, name, address, office location, phone number, current rank (Instructor, Assistant Professor, Associate Professor, or Professor), and starting date of employment. It also lists the number, name, and local and permanent addresses of each faculty member's advisees; the code number and description of the major in which the faculty member is advising each advisee; and the code number and description of the department to which this major is assigned. (Remember that this department need not be the one to which the faculty member is assigned.)

Work version of the time schedule: Although this report is similar to the original time schedule (see Figure A-3), it is designed for the college's internal use. It shows the current enrollments in each section of each course, as well as the maximum enrollment permitted per section. It is more current than the time schedule. (When students register for courses, enrollment figures are updated on the work version of the time schedule. When room or faculty assignments are changed, this information also is updated. A new version of this report that reflects the revised figures is printed after being updated.)

Course report: For each course, this report lists the code and name of the department that is offering the course, the course number, the description of the course, and the number of credits awarded. This report also includes the department and course number for each prerequisite course.

UPDATE (TRANSACTION) REQUIREMENTS

In addition to being able to add, change, and delete any information in the report requirements, the system must be able to accomplish the following update requirements:

Enrollment: When a student attempts to register for a section of a course, the system must determine whether the student has received credit for all prerequisites to the course. If the student is eligible to enroll in the course and the number of students currently enrolled in the section is less than the maximum enrollment, enroll the student.

Post grades: For each section of each course, the system must post the grades that are indicated on the class list submitted by the instructor and produce a grade verification report. (*Posting the grades* is the formal term for the process of entering the grades permanently in the students' computerized records.)

Purge: Douglas College retains section information, including grades earned by the students in each section, for two semesters following the end of the semester, then the system removes this information. (Grades assigned to students are retained by course but not by section.)

DOUGLAS COLLEGE INFORMATION-LEVEL DESIGN

You should consider the overall requirements before you apply the method to the individual user requirements. For example, by examining the documents shown in Figures A-1 through A-6, you may have identified the following entities: department, major, faculty member, student, course, and semester.

NOTE: Your list might include the section and grade entities. On the other hand, you might not have included the semester entity. In the end, as long as the list is reasonable, what you include will not make much difference. In fact, you may remember that this step is not even necessary. The better you do your job now, however, the simpler the process will be later.

After identifying the entities, you assign a primary key to each one. In general, this step will require some type of consultation with users. You may need to ask users directly for the required information, or you may be able to obtain it from some type of survey form. Assume that having had such a consultation, you created a relation for each of these entities and assigned them the following primary keys:

```
Department (DepartmentCode,
Major (MajorNum,
Faculty (FacultyNum,
Student (StudentNum,
Course (DepartmentCode, CourseNum,
Semester (SemesterCode,
```

Note that the primary key for the Course table consists of two attributes, DepartmentCode (such as CS) and CourseNum (such as 153), both of which are required. The database could contain, for example, CS 153 and CS 353. Thus, the department code alone cannot be the primary key. Similarly, the database could contain ART 101 and MUS 101, two courses with the same course number but with different department codes. Thus, the course number alone cannot be the primary key either.

Now you can begin examining the individual user views as stated in the requirements. You can create relations for these user views, represent any keys, and merge the new user views into the cumulative design. Your first task is to determine the individual user views. The term *user view* never appeared in the list of requirements. Instead, Douglas College provided a general description of the system, together with a collection of report requirements and another collection of update requirements. How do these requirements relate to user views?

Certainly, you can think of each report requirement and each update requirement as a user view, but what do you do with the general description? Do you think of each paragraph (or perhaps each sentence) in the report as representing a user view, or do you use each paragraph or sentence to furnish additional information about the report and update requirements? Both approaches are acceptable. Because the second approach is often easier, you will follow the approach in this text. Think of the report and update requirements as user views and when needed, use the statements in the general description as additional information about these user views. You will also consider the general description during the review process to ensure that your final design satisfies all the functionality it describes.

First, consider one of the simpler user views, the course report. (Technically, you can examine user views in any order. Sometimes you take them in the order in which they are listed. In other cases, you may be able to come up with a better order. Often, examining some of the simpler user views first is a reasonable approach.)

Before you proceed with the design, consider the following method. First, with some of the user views, you will attempt to determine the relations involved by carefully determining the entities and relationships between them and using this information when creating the relations. This process means that from the outset, the collection of tables created will be in or close to third normal form. With other user views, you will create a single relation that may contain some number of repeating groups. In these cases, as you will see, the normalization process still produces a correct design, but it also involves more work. In practice, the more experience a designer has, the more likely he or she is to create third normal form relations immediately.

Second, the name of an entity or attribute may vary from one user view to another, and this difference requires resolution. You will attempt to use names that are the same.

User View 1—Course report: For each course, list the code and name of the department that is offering the course, the course number, the course title, and the number of credits awarded. This report also includes the department and course number for each prerequisite course. Forgetting for the moment the requirement to list prerequisite courses, the basic relation necessary to support this report is as follows:

Course (<u>DepartmentCode</u>, DepartmentName, <u>CourseNum</u>, CourseTitle, NumCredits)

The combination of DepartmentCode and CourseNum uniquely determines all the other attributes. In this relation, DepartmentCode determines DepartmentName; thus, the table is not in second normal form. (An attribute depends on only a portion of the key.) To correct this situation, the table is split into the following two tables:

Course (<u>DepartmentCode</u>, <u>CourseNum</u>, CourseTitle, NumCredits)

Department (<u>DepartmentCode</u>, DepartmentName)

The DepartmentCode attribute in the first relation is a foreign key identifying the second relation. To maintain prerequisite information, you need to create the relation Prereq:

Prereq (<u>DepartmentCode</u>, <u>CourseNum</u>, <u>DepartmentCode/1</u>, <u>CourseNum/1</u>)

In this table, the attributes DepartmentCode and CourseNum refer to the course and the attributes DepartmentCode/1 and CourseNum/1 refer to the prerequisite course. If CS 362 has a prerequisite of MTH 345, for example, there will be a row in the Prereq table in which the DepartmentCode is CS, the CourseNum is 362, the DepartmentCode/1 is MTH, and the CourseNum/1 is 345.

NOTE: Because the Prereq relation contains two attributes named DepartmentCode and two attributes named CourseNum, you must be able to distinguish between them. The software used to produce these diagrams makes the distinction by appending the characters /1 to one of the names, which is why these names appear in the Prereq table. In this example, the DepartmentCode/1 and CourseNum/1 attributes represent the department code and course number of the prerequisite course, respectively. When it is time to implement the design, you typically assign them names that are more descriptive. For instance, you might name them PrereqDepartmentCode and PrereqCourseNum, respectively.

The DBDL version of these tables is shown in Figure A-7.

```
Department (DepartmentCode, DepartmentName)

Course (DepartmentCode, CourseNum, CourseTitle, NumCredits)
    FK DepartmentCode → Department

Prereq (DepartmentCode, CourseNum, DepartmentCode/1,
    CourseNum/1)
    FK DepartmentCode, CourseNum → Course
    FK DepartmentCode/1, CourseNum/1 → Course
```

FIGURE A-7 DBDL for User View 1

The result of merging these relations into the cumulative design appears in the E-R diagram shown in Figure A-8. Notice that the Department and Course tables have been merged with the existing Department and Course tables in the cumulative design. In the process, the attribute DepartmentName was added to the Department table and the attributes CourseTitle and NumCredits were added to the Course table. In addition, the attribute DepartmentCode in the Course table is a foreign key. Because the Prereq table is new, it was added to the cumulative design in its entirety. Notice also that you do not yet have any relationships among the entities Student, Major, Faculty, and Semester.

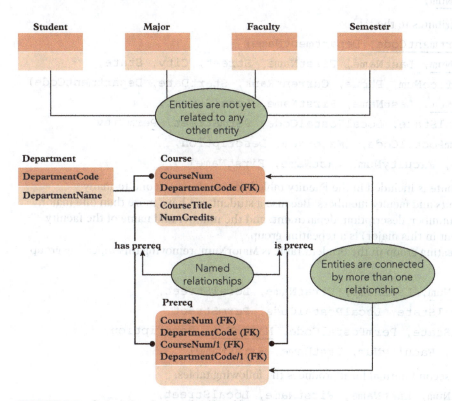

FIGURE A-8 Cumulative design after User View 1

Figure A-8 shows two relationships between Course and Prereq. To distinguish between them, it is necessary to name the relationships. In the figure, the name for the first relationship is "has prereq" and the name for the second relationship is "is prereq."

NOTE: When using a software tool to produce E-R diagrams, the software might reverse the order of the fields that make up the primary key. For example, the E-R diagram in Figure A-8 indicates that the primary key for the Course table is CourseNum and then DepartmentCode, even though you intended it to be DepartmentCode and then CourseNum. This difference is not a problem. Indicating the fields that make up the primary key is significant, not the order in which they appear.

User View 2—Faculty information report: List all faculty by department and each faculty member's ID number, name, address, office location, phone number, current rank (Instructor, Assistant Professor, Associate Professor, or Full Professor), and starting date of employment. In addition, list the number, name, and local and permanent addresses of each faculty member's advisees; the code number and description of the major in which the faculty member is advising each advisee; and the code number and description of the department to which this major is assigned. This user view involves three entities (departments, faculty, and advisees), so you can create the following three tables:

```
Department (
Faculty (
Advisee (
```

The next step is to assign a primary key to each table. Before doing so, however, you should briefly examine the tables in the cumulative design and use the same names for any existing tables or attributes. In this case, you would use DepartmentCode as the primary key for the Department table and FacultyNum as the primary key for the Faculty table. There is no Advisee table in the cumulative collection, but there is a Student table. Because advisees and students are the same, rename the Advisee entity to Student and use the StudentNum attribute as the primary key rather than AdvisorNum. Your efforts yield the following tables and primary keys:

```
Department (DepartmentCode,
Faculty (FacultyNum,
Student (StudentNum,
```

Next, add the remaining attributes to the tables:

```
Department (DepartmentCode, DepartmentName)
Faculty (FacultyNum, LastName, FirstName, Street, City, State,
    PostalCode, OfficeNum, Phone, CurrentRank, StartDate, DepartmentCode)
Student (StudentNum, LastName, FirstName, LocalStreet,
    LocalCity, LocalState, LocalPostalCode, PermStreet, PermCity,
    PermState, PermPostalCode, (MajorNum, Description,
    DepartmentCode, FacultyNum, LastName, FirstName) )
```

The DepartmentCode attribute is included in the Faculty table because there is a one-to-many relationship between departments and faculty members. Because a student can have more than one major, the information about majors (number, description, department, and the number and name of the faculty member who advises this student in this major) is a repeating group.

Because the key to the repeating group in the Student table is MajorNum, removing this repeating group yields the following:

```
Student (StudentNum, LastName, FirstName, LocalStreet,
    LocalCity, LocalState, LocalPostalCode, PermStreet,
    PermCity, PermState, PermPostalCode, MajorNum, Description,
    DepartmentCode, FacultyNum, LastName, FirstName)
```

Converting this relation to second normal form produces the following tables:

```
Student (StudentNum, LastName, FirstName, LocalStreet,
    LocalCity, LocalState, LocalPostalCode, PermStreet,
    PermCity, PermState, PermPostalCode)
Major (MajorNum, Description, DepartmentCode, DepartmentName)
Advisees (StudentNum, MajorNum, FacultyNum)
```

In this case, you must remove the following dependencies to create third normal form tables: OfficeNum determines Phone in the Faculty table, and DepartmentCode determines DepartmentName in the Major table. Removing these dependencies produces the following collection of tables:

Department (DepartmentCode, DepartmentName)

Faculty (FacultyNum, LastName, FirstName, Street, City, State, PostalCode, OfficeNum, CurrentRank, StartDate, DepartmentCode)

Student (StudentNum, LastName, FirstName, LocalStreet, LocalCity, LocalState, LocalPostalCode, PermStreet, PermCity, PermState, PermPostalCode)

Advisees (StudentNum, MajorNum, FacultyNum)

Office (OfficeNum, Phone)

Major (MajorNum, Description, DepartmentCode)

The DBDL representation is shown in Figure A-9.

```
Department (DepartmentCode, DepartmentName)

Student (StudentNum, LastName, FirstName, LocalStreet, LocalCity,
     LocalState, LocalPostalCode, PermStreet, PermCity, PermState, PermPostalCode)

Office (OfficeNum, Phone)

Faculty (FacultyNum, LastName, FirstName, Street, City, State, PostalCode,
        OfficeNum, CurrentRank, StartDate, DepartmentCode)
     FK OfficeNum → Office
     FK DepartmentCode → Department

Major (MajorNum, Description, DepartmentCode)
     FK DepartmentCode → Department

Advisees (StudentNum, MajorNum, FacultyNum)
     FK StudentNum → Student
     FK FacultyNum → Faculty
     FK MajorNum → Major
```

FIGURE A-9   DBDL for User View 2

The result of merging these tables into the cumulative design is shown in Figure A-10. The tables Student, Faculty, Major, and Department are merged with the existing tables with the same primary keys and with the same names. Nothing new is added to the Department table in the process, but the other tables receive additional attributes. In addition, the Faculty table also receives two foreign keys, OfficeNum and DepartmentCode. The Major table receives one foreign key, DepartmentCode. The Advisees and Office tables are new and thus are added directly to the cumulative design.

User View 3—Report card: At the end of each semester, the system must produce a report card for each student. Report cards are fairly complicated documents in which the appropriate underlying relations are not immediately apparent. In such a case, it is a good idea to first list all the attributes in the report card and assign them appropriate names, as shown in Figure A-11. After identifying the attributes, you should list the functional dependencies that exist between these attributes. The information necessary to determine functional dependencies must ultimately come from the user, although you can often guess most of them accurately.

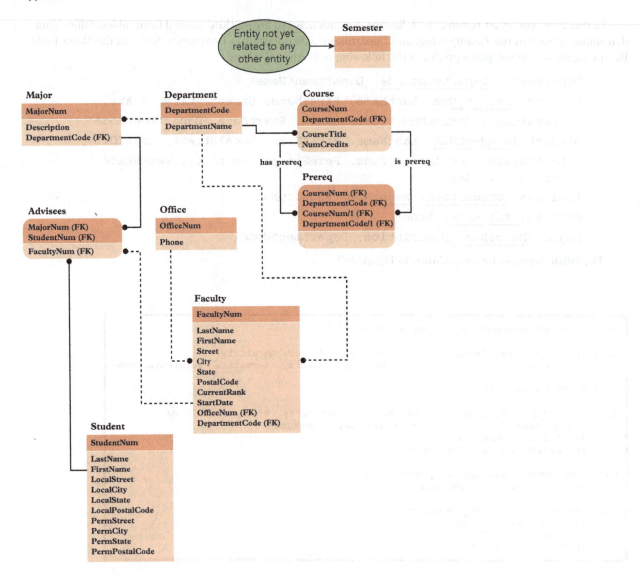

FIGURE A-10 Cumulative design after User View 2

NOTE: Notice that there are duplicate names in the list. CreditsEarned, for example, appears three times: once for the course, once for the semester, and once for the cumulative number of credits earned by the student. You could assign these columns different names at this point. The names could be CreditsEarnedCourse, CreditsEarnedSemester, and CreditsEarnedCumulative. Alternatively, you could assign them the same name with an explanation of the purpose of each one in parentheses, as shown in Figure A-11. Of course, after you have determined all the tables and assigned columns to them, you must ensure that the column names within a single table are unique.

```
Department
CourseNum
CourseTitle
Grade
CreditsTaken        (Course)
CreditsEarned       (Course)
GradePoints         (Course)
CreditsTaken        (Semester)
CreditsEarned       (Semester)
GPA                 (Semester)
TotalPoints         (Semester)
CreditsTaken        (Cumulative)
CreditsEarned       (Cumulative)
GPA                 (Cumulative)
TotalPoints         (Cumulative)
SemesterCode
StudentNum
LastName
FirstName
Address
City
State
PostalCode
LocalAddress
LocalCity
LocalState
LocalPostalCode
```

FIGURE A-11   Attributes on a report card from Douglas College

Assume the system's users have verified the attributes listed in Figure A-11 and your work is correct. Figure A-12 shows the functional dependencies among the attributes you identified on the report card. The student number alone determines many of the other attributes.

```
StudentNum→
    CreditsTaken        (Cumulative)
    CreditsEarned       (Cumulative)
    GPA                 (Cumulative)
    TotalPoints         (Cumulative)
    LastName
    FirstName
    Address
    City
    State
    PostalCode
    LocalAddress
    LocalCity
    LocalState
    LocalPostalCode

StudentNum, SemesterCode →
    CreditsTaken        (Semester)
    CreditsEarned       (Semester)
    GPA                 (Semester)
    TotalPoints         (Semester)

DepartmentName, CourseNum→
    CourseTitle
    CreditsTaken        (Course) (Same as NumCredits)

StudentNum, SemesterCode, DepartmentName, CourseNum →
    Grade
    CreditsEarned       (Course)
    GradePoints         (Course)
```

FIGURE A-12   Functional dependencies among the attributes on a report card

In addition to the student number, the semester must be identified to determine credits taken and earned, grade point average (GPA), and total points each semester. The combination of a department name (such as Computer Science) and a course number (such as 153) determines a course title and the number of credits.

Finally, the student number, the semester (semester and year), the department, and the course (department and course number) are required to determine an individual grade in a course, the credits earned from the course, and the grade points in a course. (The semester is required because the same course might be offered during more than one semester at Douglas College.)

NOTE: There is a parenthetical comment after CreditsTaken in the section determined by DepartmentName and CourseNum. It indicates that CreditsTaken is the same as NumCredits, which is a column already in the cumulative design. Documenting that the name you have chosen is a synonym for a name already in the cumulative design is a good practice.

The next step is to create a collection of tables that will support this user view. A variety of approaches will work. You could combine all the attributes into a single table, which you then would convert to third normal form. (In such a table, the combination of department, course number, course title, grade, and so on, would be a repeating group.) Alternatively, you could use the functional dependencies to determine the following collection of relations:

Student (StudentNum, LastName, FirstName, PermStreet, PermCity, PermState, PermPostalCode, LocalStreet, LocalCity, LocalState, LocalPostalCode, CreditsTaken, CreditsEarned, GPA, TotalPoints)

StudentSemester (StudentNum, SemesterCode, CreditsTaken, CreditsEarned, GPA, TotalPoints)

Course (DepartmentCode, CourseNum, CourseTitle, NumCredits)

StudentGrade (StudentNum, SemesterCode, DepartmentName, CourseNum, Grade, CreditsEarned, GradePoints)

All these relations are in third normal form. The only change you should make involves the DepartmentName attribute in the StudentGrade table. In general, if you encounter an attribute for which there exists a determinant that is not in the table, you should add the determinant. In this case, DepartmentCode is a determinant for DepartmentName, but it is not in the table, so you should add DepartmentCode. In the normalization process, DepartmentName will then be removed and placed in another table whose key is DepartmentCode. This other table will be merged with the Department table without the addition of any new attributes. The resulting StudentGrade table is as follows:

StudentGrade (StudentNum, SemesterCode, DepartmentCode, CourseNum, Grade, CreditsEarned, GradePoints)

Before representing this design in DBDL, examine the StudentSemester entity. Some of the attributes it contains (CreditsTaken, CreditsEarned, GPA, and TotalPoints) refer to the current semester, and all appear on a report card. Assume after further checking that you find that all these attributes are easily calculated from other fields on the report card. Rather than storing these attributes in the database, you can ensure that the program that produces the report cards performs the necessary calculations. For this reason, you will remove the StudentSemester table from the collection of tables to be documented and merged. (If these attributes are also required by some other user view in which the same computations are not as practical, they might find their way into the database when that user view is analyzed.) Figure A-13 shows the design after User View 3.

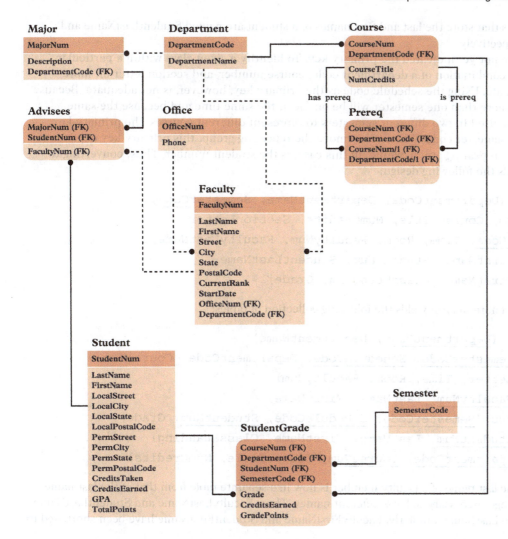

FIGURE A-13 Cumulative design after User View 3

User View 4—Class list: The system must produce a class list for each section of each course. Space is provided for the grades. At the end of the semester, the instructor enters each student's grade and sends a copy of the class list to the records office. Assume that, after examining the sample class list report (see Figure A-2), you decide to create a single table (actually an unnormalized table) that contains all the attributes on the class list, with the student information (number, name, class standing, and grade) as a repeating group. (Applying the tips for determining the relations to support a given user view would lead more directly to the result, but for the sake of developing the example, assume you have not done that yet.) The unnormalized table created by this method would be as follows:

```
ClassList (DepartmentCode, DepartmentName, SemesterCode,
     CourseNum, CourseTitle, NumCredits, SectionLetter,
     ScheduleCode, Time, Room, FacultyNum, FacultyLastName,
     FacultyFirstName, (StudentNum, StudentLastName,
          StudentFirstName, ClassStanding, Grade) )
```

NOTE: Because attribute names within a single table must be unique, it is not permissible to assign the attribute name LastName to both the faculty and student last names. Thus, the attributes that store the last and first names of a faculty member are named FacultyLastName and FacultyFirstName, respectively.

Similarly, the attributes that store the last and first names of a student are named StudentLastName and StudentFirstName, respectively.

Note that you have not yet indicated the primary key. To identify a given class within a particular semester requires the combination of a department code, course number, and section letter or, more simply, the schedule code. Using the schedule code as the primary key, however, is not adequate. Because the information from more than one semester will be on file at the same time and because the same schedule code could be used in two different semesters to represent different courses, the primary key must also contain the semester code. When you remove the repeating group, this primary key expands to contain the key for the repeating group, which, in this case, is the student number. Thus, converting to first normal form yields the following design:

ClassList (DepartmentCode, DepartmentName, <u>SemesterCode</u>,
   CourseNum, CourseTitle, NumCredits, SectionLetter,
   <u>ScheduleCode</u>, Time, Room, FacultyNum, FacultyLastName,
   FacultyFirstName, <u>StudentNum</u>, StudentLastName,
   StudentFirstName, ClassStanding, Grade)

Converting to third normal form yields the following collection of tables:

Department (<u>DepartmentCode</u>, DepartmentName)
Section (<u>SemesterCode</u>, <u>ScheduleCode</u>, DepartmentCode, CourseNum,
   SectionLetter, Time, Room, FacultyNum)
Faculty (<u>FacultyNum</u>, LastName, FirstName)
StudentClass (<u>SemesterCode</u>, <u>ScheduleCode</u>, <u>StudentNum</u>, Grade)
Student (<u>StudentNum</u>, LastName, FirstName, ClassStanding)
Course (<u>DepartmentCode</u>, <u>CourseNum</u>, CourseTitle, NumCredits)

NOTE: Because the last name of a faculty member is now in a separate table from that of the last name of a student, it is no longer necessary to have different names. Thus, FacultyLastName and StudentLastName have been shortened to LastName. Similarly, FacultyFirstName and StudentFirstName have been shortened to FirstName.

Figure A-14 shows the design after User View 4.

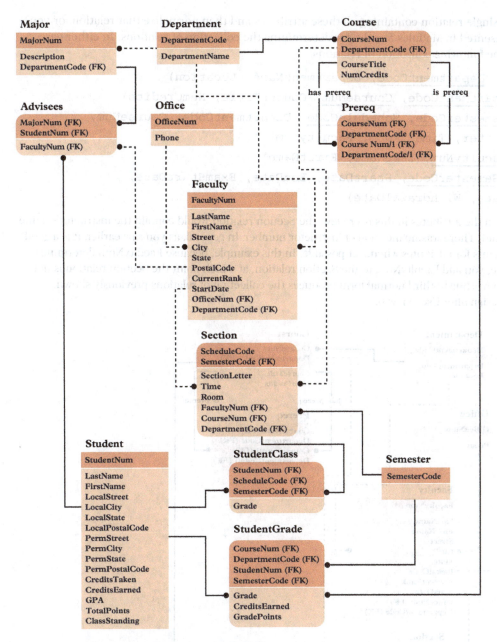

FIGURE A-14 Cumulative design after User View 4

User View 5—Grade verification report: After the records office processes the class list, it returns the class list to the instructor with the grades entered in the report. The instructor uses the report to verify that the records office entered the students' grades correctly. Because the only difference between the class list and the grade verification report is that the grades are printed on the grade verification report, the user views will be quite similar. In fact, because you made a provision for the grade when treating the class list, the views are identical, and no further treatment of this user view is required.

User View 6—Time schedule: List all sections of all courses offered during a given semester. Each section has a unique four-digit schedule code. The time schedule lists the schedule code; the department offering the course; the course's number, section letter, and title; the instructor teaching the course; the time the course meets; the room in which the course meets; the number of credits generated by the course; and the prerequisites for the course. In addition to the information shown in the figure, the time schedule includes the date the semester begins and ends, the date final exams begin and end, and the last withdrawal date. The attributes on the time schedule are as follows: term (which is a synonym for semester), department code, department name, location, course number, course title, number of credits, schedule code, section letter, meeting time, meeting place, and instructor name.

You could create a single relation containing all these attributes and then normalize that relation, or you could apply the tips presented in Modules 5 and 6 for determining the collection of relations. In either case, you ultimately create the following collection of relations:

Department (<u>DepartmentCode</u>, DepartmentName, Location)

Course (<u>DepartmentCode</u>, <u>CourseNum</u>, CourseTitle, NumCredits)

Section (<u>SemesterCode</u>, <u>ScheduleCode</u>, DepartmentCode, CourseNum, SectionLetter, Time, Room, FacultyNum)

Faculty (<u>FacultyNum</u>, LastName, FirstName)

Semester (<u>SemesterCode</u>, StartDate, EndDate, ExamStartDate, ExamEndDate, WithdrawalDate)

NOTE: Actually, given the attributes in this user view, the Section relation would contain the instructor's name (LastName and FirstName). There was no mention of instructor number. In general, as you saw earlier, it is a good idea to include determinants for attributes whenever possible. In this example, because FacultyNum determines LastName and FirstName, you add FacultyNum to the Section relation, at which point the Section relation is not in third normal form. Converting to third normal form produces the collection of relations previously shown. Figure A-15 shows the design after User View 6.

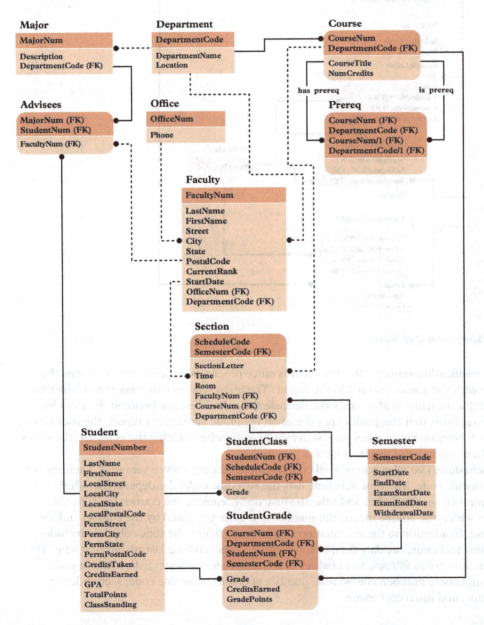

FIGURE A-15 Cumulative design after User View 6

User View 7—Registration request form: A student uses this form to request classes for the upcoming semester. Students indicate the sections for which they want to register by entering the sections' schedule codes; for each section, students may also enter a code for an alternate section in case the requested primary section is full. The collection of tables to support this user view includes a Student table that consists of the primary key, StudentNum, and all the attributes that depend only on StudentNum. These attributes include LastName, FirstName, and LocalStreet. Because all attributes in this table are already in the Student table in the cumulative design, this user view will not add anything new and there is no need for further discussion of it here.

The portion of this user view that is not already present in the cumulative design concerns the primary and alternate schedule codes that students request. A table to support this portion of the user view must contain both a primary and an alternate schedule code. The table must also contain the number of the student making the request. Finally, to allow the flexibility of retaining this information for more than a single semester (to allow registration for more than a semester at a time), the table must also include the semester in which the request is made. This leads to the following relation:

RegistrationRequest (<u>StudentNum</u>, <u>PrimaryCode</u>, AlternateCode, SemesterCode)

For example, if student 381124188 were to request the section with schedule code 2345 and then request the section with schedule code 2396 as an alternate for the FA21 semester, the row (381124188, 2345, 2396, "FA21") would be stored. The student number, the primary schedule code, the alternate schedule code, and the semester code are required to uniquely identify a particular row.

Figure A-16 shows the design after User View 7.

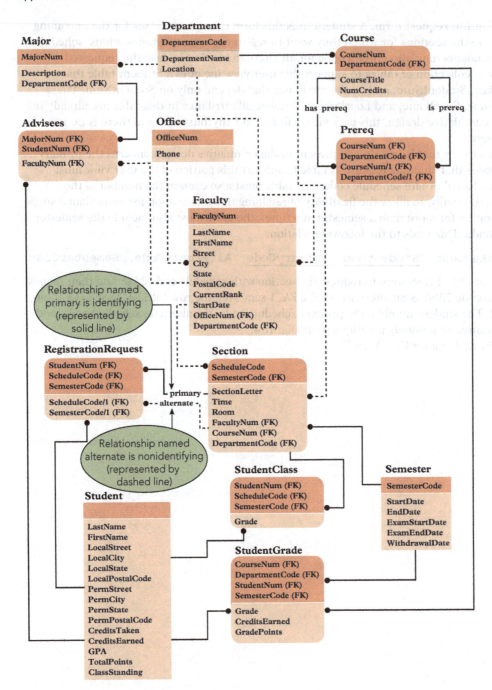

FIGURE A-16 Cumulative design after User View 7

NOTE: The foreign keys are the combination of PrimaryCode and SemesterCode as well as the combination of AlternateCode and SemesterCode. Because PrimaryCode and AlternateCode are portions of the foreign keys that must match the ScheduleCode in the Section table, they have been renamed ScheduleCode and ScheduleCode/1, respectively. Likewise, the second SemesterCode has been renamed SemesterCode/1.

User View 8—Student schedule: After all students are assigned to sections, the system produces a student schedule form, which is mailed to students to inform them of the classes in which they have been enrolled. Suppose you had created a single unnormalized relation to support the student schedule. This unnormalized relation would contain a repeating group representing the lines in the body of the schedule as follows:

```
StudentSchedule (StudentNum, SemesterCode, LastName, FirstName,
    LocalStreet, LocalCity, LocalState, LocalPostalCode, PermStreet,
    PermCity, PermState, PermPostalCode, (ScheduleCode,
    DepartmentName, CourseNum, CourseTitle, SectionLetter,
    NumCredits, Time, Room) )
```

At this point, you remove the repeating group to convert to first normal form, yielding the following:

```
StudentSchedule (StudentNum, SemesterCode, LastName, FirstName,
    LocalStreet, LocalCity, LocalState, LocalPostalCode, PermStreet,
    PermCity, PermState, PermPostalCode, ScheduleCode,
    DepartmentCode, CourseNum, CourseTitle, SectionLetter,
    NumCredits, Time, Room)
```

Note that the primary key expands to include ScheduleCode, which is the key to the repeating group. Converting this table to second normal form produces the following:

```
Student (StudentNum, LastName, FirstName, LocalStreet, LocalCity,
    LocalState, LocalPostalCode, PermStreet, PermCity,
    PermState, PermPostalCode)
StudentSchedule (StudentNum, SemesterCode, ScheduleCode)
Section (SemesterCode, ScheduleCode, DepartmentCode, CourseNum,
    CourseTitle, SectionLetter, NumCredits, Time, Room)
Course (DepartmentCode, CourseNum, CourseTitle, NumCredits)
```

Removing the attributes that depend on the determinant of DepartmentCode and CourseNum from the Section table and converting this collection of tables to third normal form produces the following tables:

```
Student (StudentNum, LastName, FirstName, LocalStreet,
    LocalCity, LocalState, LocalPostalCode, PermStreet,
    PermCity, PermState, PermPostalCode)
StudentSchedule (StudentNum, SemesterCode, ScheduleCode)
Section (SemesterCode, ScheduleCode, DepartmentCode, CourseNum,
    SectionLetter, Time, Room)
Course (DepartmentCode, CourseNum, CourseTitle, NumCredits)
```

Merging this collection into the cumulative design does not add anything new. In the process, you can merge the StudentSchedule table with the StudentClass table.

User View 9—Full student information report: List complete information about a student, including his or her majors and all grades received to date. Suppose you attempted to place all the attributes on the full student information report into a single unnormalized relation. The table has two separate repeating groups: one for the different majors a student might have and the other for all the courses the student has taken.

NOTE: Several attributes, such as name and address, would not be in the repeating groups. All these attributes are already in the cumulative design, however, and are not addressed here.

The table with repeating groups is as follows:

```
Student (StudentNum, (MajorNum, DepartmentCode, LastName,
    FirstName), (SemesterCode, DepartmentCode, CourseNum,
    CourseTitle, NumCredits, Grade, GradePoints) )
```

Recall from Module 5 that you should separate repeating groups when a relation has more than one. If you do not, you will typically have problems with fourth normal form. Separating the repeating groups in this example produces the following:

```
StudentMajor (StudentNum, (MajorNum, DepartmentCode, LastName,
   FirstName))
StudentCourse (StudentNum, (SemesterCode, DepartmentCode,
   CourseNum, CourseTitle, NumCredits, Grade, GradePoints))
```

Converting these tables to first normal form and including FacultyNum, which is a determinant for LastName and FirstName, produces the following:

```
StudentMajor (StudentNum, MajorNum, DepartmentCode, FacultyNum,
   LastName, FirstName)
StudentCourse (StudentNum, SemesterCode, DepartmentCode,
   CourseNum, CourseTitle, NumCredits, Grade, Grade Points)
```

The StudentCourse table is not in second normal form because CourseTitle and NumCredits depend only on the DepartmentCode, CourseNum combination. The StudentMajor table is not in second normal form either because DepartmentCode depends on MajorNum. Removing these dependencies produces the following tables:

```
StudentMajor (StudentNum, MajorNum, FacultyNum, LastName, FirstName)
Major (MajorNum, DepartmentCode)
StudentCourse (StudentNum, SemesterCode, DepartmentCode,
   CourseNum, Grade, GradePoints)
Course (DepartmentCode, CourseNum, CourseTitle, NumCredits)
```

Other than the StudentMajor table, all these relations are in third normal form. Converting the StudentMajor table to third normal form produces the following tables:

```
StudentMajor (StudentNum, MajorNum, FacultyNum)
Faculty (FacultyNum, LastName, FirstName)
```

Merging this collection into the cumulative design does not add anything new. (You can merge the StudentMajor table with the Advises table without adding any new attributes.)

User View 10—Work version of the time schedule: This report is similar to the original time schedule (see Figure A-3), but it is designed for the college's internal use. It shows the current enrollments in each section of each course, as well as each section's maximum enrollment. The only difference between the work version of the time schedule and the time schedule itself (see User View 6) is the addition of two attributes for each section: current enrollment and maximum enrollment. Because these two attributes depend only on the combination of the semester code and the schedule code, you would place them in the Section table of User View 6, and after the merge, they would be in the Section table in the cumulative design. The cumulative design thus far is shown in Figure A-17.

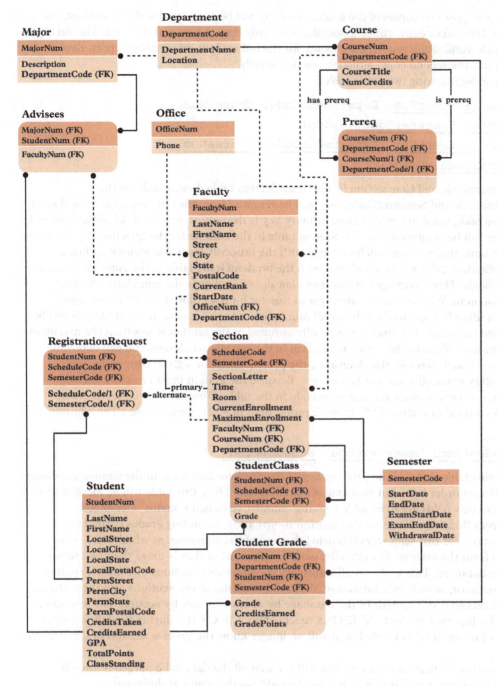

FIGURE A-17 Cumulative design after User View 10

Because the process of determining whether a student has had the prerequisites for a given course involves examining the grades (if any) received in these prior courses, it makes sense to analyze the user view that involves grades before treating the user view that involves enrollment.

User View 11—Post grades: For each section of each course, the system must post the grades that are indicated on the class list submitted by the instructor and produce a grade verification report. There is a slight problem with posting grades—grades must be posted by section to produce the grade report (in other words, you must record the fact that student 381124188 received an A in the section of CS 162 whose schedule code was 2366 during the fall 2021 semester). On the other hand, for the full student information report, there is no need to have any of the grades related to an actual section of a course. Further, because section information, including these grades, is kept for only two semesters, grades would be lost after two semesters if they were kept only by section because section information would be purged at that time.

A viable alternative is to post two copies of the grade: one copy will be associated with the student, the term, and the section, and the other copy will be associated with only the student and the term. The first copy would be used for the grade verification report; the second, for the full student information report. Report cards would probably utilize the second copy, although not necessarily.

Thus, you would have the following two grade tables:

GradeSection (<u>StudentNum</u>, DepartmentCode, CourseNum, <u>ScheduleCode</u>, <u>SemesterCode</u>, Grade)

GradeStudent (<u>StudentNum</u>, <u>DepartmentCode</u>, <u>CourseNum</u>, <u>SemesterCode</u>, Grade)

Because the DepartmentCode and CourseNum in the GradeSection table depend only on the concatenation of ScheduleCode and SemesterCode, they will be removed from the GradeSection table during the normalization process and placed in a table whose primary key is the concatenation of ScheduleCode and SemesterCode. This table will be combined with the Section table in the cumulative design without adding new fields. The GradeSection table that remains will be merged with the StudentClass table without adding new fields. Finally, the GradeStudent table will be combined with the StudentGrade table in the cumulative design without adding any new fields. Thus, treatment of this user view does not change the cumulative design.

User View 12—Enrollment: When a student attempts to register for a section of a course, you must determine whether the student has received credit for all prerequisites to the course. If the student is eligible to enroll in the course and the number of students currently enrolled in the section is less than the maximum enrollment, enroll the student. With the data already in place in the cumulative design, you can determine what courses a student has taken. You can also determine the prerequisites for a given course. The only remaining issue is the ability to enroll a student in a course. Because the system must retain information for more than one semester, you must include the semester code in the table. (You must have the information that student 381124188 enrolled in section 2345 in SP22 rather than in FA21, for example.) The additional table is as follows:

Enroll (<u>StudentNum</u>, <u>SemesterCode</u>, <u>ScheduleCode</u>)

The primary key of this table matches the primary key of the StudentClass table in the cumulative design. The fields occur in a different order here, but that makes no difference. Thus, this table will be merged with the StudentClass table. No new fields are to be added, so the cumulative design remains unchanged.

User View 13—Purge: Douglas College retains section information, including grades earned by the students in each section, for two semesters following the end of the semester, at which time this information is removed from the system. Periodically, certain information that is more than two terms old is removed from the database. This includes all information concerning sections of courses, such as the time, room, and instructor, as well as information about the students in the sections and their grades. The grade each student received will remain in the database by course but not by section. For example, you will always retain the fact that student 381124188 received an A in CS 162 during the fall semester of 2021, but once the data for that term is purged, you will no longer know the precise section of CS 162 that awarded this grade.

If you examine the current collection of tables, you will see that all the data to be purged is already included in the cumulative design and that you do not need to add anything new at this point.

FINAL INFORMATION-LEVEL DESIGN

Now that you are finished examining the user views, Douglas College can review the cumulative design to ensure that all user views have been met. You should conduct this review on your own to make certain that you understand how the requirements of each user can be satisfied. You will assume that this review has taken place and that no changes have been made. Therefore, Figure A-17 represents the final information-level design.

At this point, Douglas College is ready to move on to the physical-level design process. In this process, the appropriate team members will use the information-level design you produced to create the design for the specific DBMS that Douglas College selects. After it has done so, it will be able to create the database, load the data, and create the forms, reports, queries, and programs necessary to satisfy its requirements.

EXERCISES

1. Discuss the effect of the following changes on the design for the Douglas College requirements:

   a. More than one instructor might teach a given section of a course, and each instructor must be listed on the time schedule.

   b. Each department offers only a single major.

   c. Each department offers only a single major, and each faculty member can advise students only in the major that is offered by the department to which the faculty member is assigned.

   d. Each department offers only a single major, and each faculty member can advise students only in the major that is offered by the department to which the faculty member is assigned. In addition, a student can have only one major.

   e. There is an additional transaction requirement: given a student's name, find the student's number.

   f. More than one faculty member can be assigned to one office.

   g. The number of credits earned in a particular course cannot vary from student to student or from semester to semester.

   h. Instead of a course number, course codes are used to uniquely identify courses. (In other words, department numbers are no longer required for this purpose.) However, it is still important to know which courses are offered by which departments.

   i. On the registration request form, a student may designate a number of alternates along with his or her primary choice. These alternates are listed in priority order, with the first one being the most desired and the last one being the least desired.

2. Complete an information-level design for Holt Distributors.

   General description. Holt Distributors buys products from its vendors and sells those products to its customers. The Holt Distributors operation is divided into territories. Each customer is represented by a single sales rep, who must be assigned to the territory in which the customer is located. Although each sales rep is assigned to a single territory, more than one sales rep can be assigned to the same territory.

   When a customer places an order, the computer assigns the order the next available order number. The data entry clerk enters the customer number, the customer purchase order (PO) number, and the date. (Customers can place orders by submitting a PO, in which case, a PO number is recorded.) For each part that is ordered, the clerk enters the part number, quantity, and quoted price. (When it is time for the clerk to enter the quoted price, the computer displays the price from the master price list. If the quoted price is the same as the actual price, the clerk takes no special action. If not, the clerk enters the quoted price.)

   When the clerk completes the order, the system prints the order acknowledgment/picking list form shown in Figure A-18 on the next page and sends it to the customer for confirmation and payment. When Holt Distributors is ready to ship the customer's order, this same form is used to "pick" the merchandise in the warehouse and prepare it for delivery.

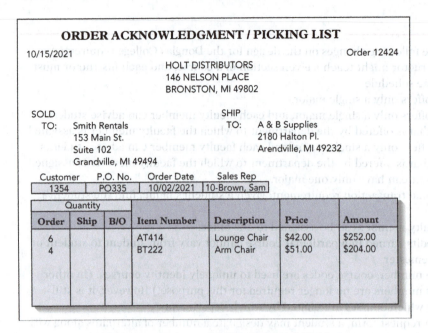

ORDER ACKNOWLEDGMENT / PICKING LIST

10/15/2021

HOLT DISTRIBUTORS
146 NELSON PLACE
BRONSTON, MI 49802

Order 12424

SOLD
TO: Smith Rentals
153 Main St.
Suite 102
Grandville, MI 49494

SHIP
TO: A & B Supplies
2180 Halton Pl.
Arendville, MI 49232

Customer	P.O. No.	Order Date	Sales Rep
1354	PO335	10/02/2021	10-Brown, Sam

Quantity						
Order	Ship	B/O	Item Number	Description	Price	Amount
6			AT414	Lounge Chair	$42.00	$252.00
4			BT222	Arm Chair	$51.00	$204.00

FIGURE A-18 Order acknowledgment/picking list for Holt Distributors

An order that has not been shipped (filled) is called an open order; an order that has been shipped is called a released order. When orders are released, the system prints an invoice, sends it to the customer, and then increases the customer's balance by the invoice amount. Some orders are completely filled; others are only partially filled, meaning that only part of the customer's order was shipped. In either case, when an entire order or a partial order has been shipped, the order is considered to have been filled and is no longer considered an open order. (Another possibility is to allow back orders when the order cannot be completely filled. In this case, the order remains open, but only for the back-ordered portion.) When the system generates an invoice, it removes the order from the open orders file. The system stores summary information about the invoice (number, date, customer, invoice total, and freight) until the end of the month. A sample invoice is shown in Figure A-19.

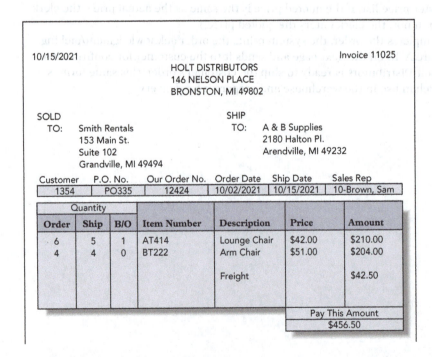

10/15/2021

HOLT DISTRIBUTORS
146 NELSON PLACE
BRONSTON, MI 49802

Invoice 11025

SOLD
TO: Smith Rentals
153 Main St.
Suite 102
Grandville, MI 49494

SHIP
TO: A & B Supplies
2180 Halton Pl.
Arendville, MI 49232

Customer	P.O. No.	Our Order No.	Order Date	Ship Date	Sales Rep
1354	PO335	12424	10/02/2021	10/15/2021	10-Brown, Sam

Quantity						
Order	Ship	B/O	Item Number	Description	Price	Amount
6	5	1	AT414	Lounge Chair	$42.00	$210.00
4	4	0	BT222	Arm Chair	$51.00	$204.00
				Freight		$42.50

Pay This Amount
$456.50

FIGURE A-19 Invoice for Holt Distributors

Most companies use one of two methods to accept payments from customers: open items and balance forward. In the open-item method, customers make payments on specific invoices. An invoice remains on file until the customer pays it in full. In the balance-forward method, customers have balances. When the system generates an invoice, the customer's balance is increased by the amount of the invoice. When a customer makes a payment, the system decreases the customer's balance by the payment amount. Holt Distributors uses the balance-forward method.

At the end of each month, the system updates and ages customers' accounts. (You will learn about month-end processing requirements and the update and aging processes in the following sections.) The system prints customer statements, an aged trial balance (described in the report requirements section), a monthly cash receipts journal, a monthly invoice register, and a sales rep commission report. The system then removes cash receipts and invoice summary records from the database and sets month-to-date (MTD) fields to zero. When the system processes the monthly data for December, it also sets the year-to-date (YTD) fields to zero.

Transaction requirements. Holt Distributors has the following transaction requirements:

a. Enter and edit territories (territory number and name).

b. Enter and edit sales reps (sales rep number, name, address, city, state, postal code, MTD sales, YTD sales, MTD commission, YTD commission, and commission rate). Each sales rep represents a single territory.

c. Enter and edit customers (customer number, name, first line of address, second line of address, city, state, postal code, MTD sales, YTD sales, current balance, and credit limit). A customer can have a different name and address to which goods are shipped (called the "ship-to" address). Each customer has a single sales rep who is located in a single territory. The sales rep must represent the territory in which the customer is located.

d. Enter and edit parts (part number, description, price, MTD and YTD sales, units on hand, units allocated, and reorder point). The Units allocated field is the number of units that are currently present on some open orders. The reorder point is the lowest value acceptable for units on hand without the product being reordered. On the stock status report, which will be described later, an asterisk indicates any part for which the number of units on hand is less than the reorder point.

e. Enter and edit vendors (vendor number, name, address, city, state, and postal code). In addition, for each part supplied by the vendor, enter and edit the part number, the price the vendor charges for the part, the minimum order quantity that the vendor will accept for this part, and the expected lead time for delivery of this part from this vendor.

f. Order entry (order number, date, customer, customer PO number, and order detail lines). An order detail line consists of a part number, a description, the number ordered, and the quoted price. Each order detail line includes a sequence number that is entered by the user. Detail lines on an order must print in the order of this sequence number. The system should calculate and display the order total. After all orders for the day have been entered, the system prints order acknowledgment/picking list reports (see Figure A-18). In addition, for each part ordered, the system must increase the units allocated for the part by the number of units that the customer ordered.

g. The invoicing system has the following requirements:
    1. Enter the numbers of the orders to be released. For each order, enter the ship date for invoicing and the freight amount. Indicate whether the order is to be shipped in full or in part. If an order is to be partially shipped, enter the number shipped for each order detail line. The system will generate a unique invoice number for this invoice.
    2. Print invoices for each of the released orders. (A sample invoice is shown in Figure A-19.)
    3. Update files with information from the printed invoices. For each invoice, the system adds the invoice total to the current invoice total. It also adds the current balance and the MTD and YTD sales for the customer that placed the order. The system also adds the total to the MTD and YTD sales for the sales rep who represents the customer. In addition, the system multiplies the total by the sales rep's commission rate and adds this amount to the MTD commission earned and the YTD commission earned. For each part shipped, the system decreases units on hand and units allocated by the number of units of the part or parts that were shipped. The system also increases the MTD and YTD sales of the part by the amount of the number of units shipped multiplied by the quoted price.

4. Create an invoice summary record for each invoice printed. These records contain the invoice number, date, customer, sales rep, invoice total, and freight.

5. Delete the released orders.

h. Receive payments on account (customer number, date, and amount). The system assigns each payment a number, adds the payment amount to the total of current payments for the customer, and subtracts the payment amount from the current balance of the customer.

Report requirements. The following is a list of the reports required by Holt Distributors:

a. **Territory List:** For each territory, list the number and name of the territory; the number, name, and address of each sales rep in the territory; and the number, name, and address of each customer represented by these sales reps.

b. **Customer Master List:** For each customer, list the customer number, the bill-to address, and the ship-to address. Also list the number, name, address, city, state, and postal code of the sales rep who represents the customer and the number and name of the territory in which the customer is located.

c. **Customer Open Order Report:** This report lists open orders organized by customer. It is shown in Figure A-20.

10/16/2021   **HOLT DISTRIBUTORS**   PAGE 1
CUSTOMER OPEN ORDER REPORT

Order Number	Item Number	Item Description	Order Date	Order Qty	Quoted Price
Customer 1354 - Smith Rentals					
12424	AT414	Lounge Chair	10/12/2021	1	$42.00
Customer 1358 - · · · · · · · ·					

FIGURE A-20   Open order report (by customer)

d. **Item Open Order Report:** This report lists open orders organized by item and is shown in Figure A-21.

10/16/2021   **HOLT DISTRIBUTORS**   PAGE 1
ITEM OPEN ORDER REPORT

Item Number	Item Description	Customer Number	Customer Name	Order Number	Order Date	Order Qty	Quoted Price
AT414	Lounge Chair	1354	Smith Rentals	12424	10/02/2021	1	$42.00
		1358	Kayland Enterprises	12489	10/03/2021	8	$42.00
					Total on order -	9	
BT222	Arm Chair	1358	Kayland Enterprises	12424	10/03/2021	3	$51.00

FIGURE A-21   Open order report (by item)

e. **Daily Invoice Register:** For each invoice produced on a given day, list the invoice number, invoice date, customer number, customer name, sales amount, freight, and invoice total. A sample of this report is shown in Figure A-22.

Invoice Number	Invoice Date	Customer Number	Customer Name	Sales Amount	Freight	Invoice Amount
11025	10/15/2021	1354	Smith Rentals	$414.00	$42.50	$456.50
·	·	·	·	·	·	·
·	·	·	·	·	·	·
·	·	·	·	·	·	·
·	·	·	·			
·	·	·	·	$2,840.50	$238.20	$3,078.70

10/16/2021 — HOLT DISTRIBUTORS — DAILY INVOICE REGISTER FOR 10/15/2018 — PAGE 1

FIGURE A-22   Daily invoice register

f. **Monthly Invoice Register:** The monthly invoice register has the same format as the daily invoice register, but it includes data for all invoices that occurred during the selected month.

g. **Stock Status Report:** For each part, list the part number, description, price, MTD and YTD sales, units on hand, units allocated, and reorder point. For each part for which the number of units on hand is less than the reorder point, an asterisk should appear at the far right of the report.

h. **Reorder Point List:** This report has the same format as the stock status report. Other than the title, the only difference is that parts for which the number of units on hand is greater than or equal to the reorder point will not appear on this report.

i. **Vendor Report:** For each vendor, list the vendor number, name, address, city, state, and postal code. In addition, for each part supplied by the vendor, list the part number, the description, the price the vendor charges for the part, the minimum order quantity that the vendor will accept for this part, and the expected lead time for delivery of this part from the vendor.

j. **Daily Cash Receipts Journal:** For each payment received on a given day, list the number and name of the customer that made the payment and the payment amount. A sample report is shown in Figure A-23.

Payment Number	Customer Number	Customer Name	Payment Amount
·	·	·	·
·	·	·	·
5807	1354	Smith Rentals	$1,000.00
·	·	·	·
·	·	·	$12,235.50

10/05/2021 — HOLT DISTRIBUTORS — DAILY CASH RECEIPTS JOURNAL — PAGE 1

FIGURE A-23   Daily cash receipts journal

k. **Monthly Cash Receipts Journal:** The monthly cash receipts journal has the same format as the daily cash receipts journal, but it includes all cash receipts for the month.

l. **Customer Mailing Labels:** A sample of the three-across mailing labels printed by the system is shown in Figure A-24.

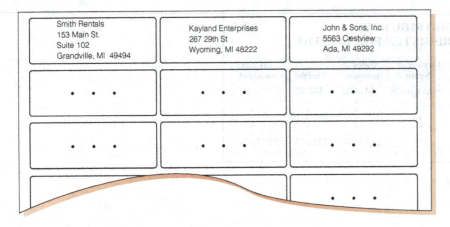

FIGURE A-24 Customer mailing labels

m. **Statements:** The system must produce a monthly statement for each active customer. A sample statement is shown in Figure A-25.

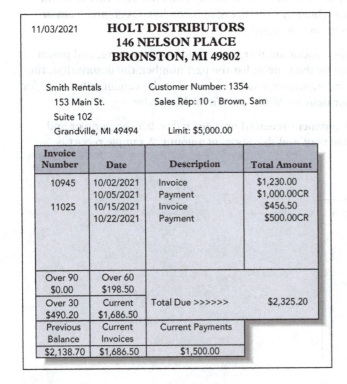

11/03/2021	**HOLT DISTRIBUTORS**
	146 NELSON PLACE
	BRONSTON, MI 49802

Smith Rentals — Customer Number: 1354
153 Main St. — Sales Rep: 10 - Brown, Sam
Suite 102
Grandville, MI 49494 — Limit: $5,000.00

Invoice Number	Date	Description	Total Amount
10945	10/02/2021	Invoice	$1,230.00
	10/05/2021	Payment	$1,000.00CR
11025	10/15/2021	Invoice	$456.50
	10/22/2021	Payment	$500.00CR

Over 90	Over 60		
$0.00	$198.50		
Over 30	Current	Total Due >>>>>>	$2,325.20
$490.20	$1,686.50		
Previous Balance	Current Invoices	Current Payments	
$2,138.70	$1,686.50	$1,500.00	

FIGURE A-25 Statement for Holt Distributors

n. **Monthly Sales Rep Commission Report:** For each sales rep, list his or her number, name, address, MTD sales, YTD sales, MTD commission earned, YTD commission earned, and commission rate.

o. **Aged Trial Balance:** The aged trial balance report contains the same information that is printed on each customer's statement.

Month-end processing. Month-end processing consists of the following actions that occur at the end of each month:

a. Update customer account information. In addition to the customer's actual balance, the system must maintain the following records: current debt, debt incurred within the last 30 days, debt that is more than 30 days past due but less than 60 days past due, debt that is 60 or more days past due but less than 90 days past due, and debt that is 90 or more days past due.

The system updates the actual balance, the current invoice total, and the current payment total when it produces a new invoice or receives a payment; however, the system updates these aging figures only at the end of the month. The actual update process is as follows:

1. The system processes payments received within the last month and credits these payments to the past due amount for 90 or more days. The system then credits any additional payment to the 60 or more days past due amount, then to the more than 30 days past due amount, and then to the current debt amount (less than 30 days).

2. The system "rolls" the amounts by adding the 60 or more days past due amount to the 90 or more days past due amount and by adding the more than 30 days past due amount to the 60 or more days past due amount. The current amount becomes the new more than 30 days past due amount. Finally, the current month's invoice total becomes the new current amount.

3. The system prints the statements and the aged trial balances.

4. The system sets the current invoice total to zero, sets the current payment total to zero, and sets the previous balance to the current balance in preparation for the next month. To illustrate, assume before the update begins that the amounts for customer 1354 are as follows:

```
Current Balance:  $2,375.20      Previous Balance: $2,138.70
Current Invoices: $1,686.50             Current:  $490.20
Current Payments: $1,500.00             Over 30:  $298.50
                                        Over 60:  $710.00
                                        Over 90:  $690.00
```

The system subtracts the current payments ($1,500.00) from the over 90 amount ($690.00), reduces the over 90 amount to zero, and calculates an excess payment of $810.00. The system subtracts this excess payment from the over 60 amount ($710.00), reduces the over 60 amount to zero, and calculates an excess payment of $100.00. The system then subtracts the excess payment from the over 30 amount ($298.50) and reduces this amount to $198.50. At this point, the system rolls the amounts and sets the current amount to the current invoice total, producing the following:

```
Current Balance:  $2,375.20      Previous Balance: $2,138.70
Current Invoices: $1,686.50             Current: $1,686.50
Current Payments: $1,500.00             Over 30:  $490.20
                                        Over 60:  $198.50
                                        Over 90:    $0.00
```

The system then produces statements and the aged trial balance and updates the Previous Balance, Current Invoices, and Current Payments amounts, yielding the following:

```
Current Balance:  $2,375.20      Previous Balance: $2,375.20
Current Invoices: $0.00                 Current: $1,686.50
Current Payments: $0.00                 Over 30:  $490.20
                                        Over 60:  $198.50
                                        Over 90:    $0.00
```

a. Print the monthly invoice register and the monthly cash receipts journal.

b. Print a monthly sales rep commission report.

c. Set all MTD fields to zero. If necessary, set all YTD fields to zero.

d. Remove all cash receipts and invoice summary records. (In practice, such records would be moved to a historical type of database for future reference. For the purposes of this assignment, you will omit this step.)

SQL REFERENCE

You can use this appendix to review important SQL commands. Items are arranged alphabetically. Each item contains a description and, where appropriate, both an example and a description of the query results. Some SQL commands also include a description of the clauses associated with them. For each clause, there is a brief description and an indication of whether the clause is required or optional.

ALTER TABLE

Use the ALTER TABLE command to change a table's structure. As shown in Figure B-1, you type the ALTER TABLE command, followed by the table name, and then the alteration to perform. (*Note*: In Access, you usually make these changes to a table in Design view rather than using ALTER TABLE.)

Clause	Description	Required?
ALTER TABLE *table name*	Indicates the name of the table to be altered.	Yes
alteration	Indicates the type of alteration to be performed.	Yes

FIGURE B-1 ALTER TABLE command

The following command alters the Customer table by adding a new column named CustType:

```
ALTER TABLE Customer
ADD CustType CHAR(1)
;
```

The following command alters the Customer table by changing the length of the CustomerName column:

```
ALTER TABLE Customer
CHANGE COLUMN CustomerName TO CHAR(50)
;
```

The following command alters the Item table by deleting the Storehouse column:

```
ALTER TABLE Item
DELETE Storehouse
;
```

COLUMN OR EXPRESSION LIST (SELECT CLAUSE)

To select columns, use a SELECT clause with the list of columns separated by commas. The following SELECT clause selects the CustomerNum, CustomerName, and Balance columns:

```
SELECT CustomerNum, CustomerName, Balance
```

Use an asterisk in a SELECT clause to select all columns in the table. The following SELECT command selects all columns in the Item table:

```
SELECT *
FROM Item
;
```

Computed Fields

You can use a computation in place of a field by typing the computation. For readability, you can type the computation in parentheses, although it is not necessary to do so.

The following SELECT clause selects the CustomerNum and CustomerName columns as well as the results of subtracting the Balance column from the CreditLimit column:

```
SELECT CustomerNum, CustomerName, CreditLimit-Balance
```

Functions

You can use aggregate functions in a SELECT clause. The most commonly used functions are AVG (to calculate an average), COUNT (to count the number of rows), MAX (to determine the maximum value), MIN (to determine the minimum value), and SUM (to calculate a total).

The following SELECT clause calculates the average balance:

```
SELECT AVG(Balance)
```

CONDITIONS

A condition is an expression that can be evaluated as either true or false. When you use a condition in a WHERE clause, the results of the query contain those rows for which the condition is true. You can create simple conditions and compound conditions using the BETWEEN, LIKE, and IN operators, as described in the following sections.

Simple Conditions

A simple condition includes the field name, a comparison operator, and another field name or a value. The available comparison operators are = (equal to), < (less than), > (greater than), <= (less than or equal to), >= (greater than or equal to), and < > (not equal to).

The following WHERE clause uses a condition to select rows on which the balance is greater than the credit limit:

```
WHERE Balance>CreditLimit
```

Compound Conditions

Compound conditions are formed by connecting two or more simple conditions using one or both of the following operators: AND and OR. You can also precede a single condition with the NOT operator to negate a condition. When you connect simple conditions using the AND operator, all the simple conditions must be true for the compound condition to be true. When you connect simple conditions using the OR operator, the compound condition will be true whenever any of the simple conditions are true. Preceding a condition with the NOT operator reverses the result of the original condition. That is, if the original condition is true, the new condition will be false; if the original condition is false, the new one will be true.

The following WHERE clause is true if those items for which the Storehouse number is equal to 3 *or* the number of units on hand is greater than 20:

```
WHERE Storehouse='3'
OR OnHand>20
```

The following WHERE clause is true if those items for which *both* the Storehouse number is equal to 3 *and* the number of units on hand is greater than 20:

```
WHERE Storehouse='3'
AND OnHand>20
```

The following WHERE clause is true if the Storehouse number is not equal to 3:

```
WHERE NOT (Storehouse='3')
```

BETWEEN Conditions

You can use the BETWEEN operator to determine whether a value is within a range of values. The following WHERE clause is true if the balance is between 1,000 and 5,000:

```
WHERE Balance BETWEEN 1000 AND 5000
```

LIKE Conditions

LIKE conditions use wildcards to select rows. Use the percent sign (%) to represent any collection of characters. The condition LIKE '%Oxford%' will be true for data consisting of any character or characters followed by the letters "Oxford" followed by any other character or characters. Another wildcard is the underscore character (_), which represents any individual character. For example, 'T_m' represents the letter *T* followed by any single character followed by the letter *m* and would be true for a collection of characters such as *Tim*, *Tom*, or *T3m*.

NOTE: In Access SQL, the asterisk (*) is used as a wildcard to represent any collection of characters. Another wildcard in Access SQL is the question mark (?), which represents any individual character. Many versions of SQL use the underscore (_) instead of the question mark to represent any individual character.

The following WHERE clause is true if the value in the Street column is Oxford Rd., Oxford, or any other value that contains "Oxford":

```
WHERE Street LIKE '%Oxford%'
```

Access version:

```
WHERE Street LIKE '*Oxford*'
```

IN Conditions

You can use the IN operator to determine whether a value is in some specific collection of values. The following WHERE clause is true if the credit limit is 7,500, 10,000, or 15,000:

```
WHERE CreditLimit IN (7500, 10000, 15000)
```

The following WHERE clause is true if the item number is in the collection of item numbers located in Storehouse 3:

```
WHERE ItemNum IN
(SELECT ItemNum
FROM Item
WHERE Storehouse='3')
```

CREATE INDEX

Use the CREATE INDEX command to create an index for a table. Figure B-2 describes the CREATE INDEX command.

Clause	Description	Required?
CREATE INDEX *index name*	Indicates the name of the index.	Yes
ON *table name*	Indicates the table for which the index is to be created.	Yes
column list	Indicates the column or columns on which the index is to be tested.	Yes

FIGURE B-2   CREATE INDEX command

The following CREATE INDEX command creates an index named RepBal for the Customer table on the combination of the RepNum and Balance columns:

```
CREATE INDEX RepBal
ON Customer (RepNum, Balance)
;
```

CREATE TABLE

Use the CREATE TABLE command to create a table by describing its layout. Figure B-3 describes the CREATE TABLE command.

Clause	Description	Required?
CREATE TABLE *table name*	Indicates the name of the table to be created.	Yes
(column and data type list)	Indicates the columns that make up the table along with their corresponding data types (see the "Data Types" section).	Yes

FIGURE B-3 CREATE TABLE command

The following CREATE TABLE command creates the Rep table and its associated columns and data types:

```
CREATE TABLE Rep
(RepNum CHAR(2),
LastName CHAR(15),
FirstName CHAR(15),
Street CHAR(15),
City CHAR(15),
State CHAR(2),
PostalCode CHAR(5),
Commission DECIMAL(7,2),
Rate DECIMAL(3,2) )
;
```

Access version:

```
CREATE TABLE Rep
(RepNum CHAR(2),
LastName CHAR(15),
FirstName CHAR(15),
Street CHAR(15),
City CHAR(15),
State CHAR(2),
PostalCode CHAR(5),
Commission CURRENCY,
Rate NUMBER )
;
```

NOTE: Unlike other SQL implementations, Access doesn't have a DECIMAL data type. To create numbers with decimals, you must use either the CURRENCY or NUMBER data type. Use the CURRENCY data type for fields that will contain currency values; use the NUMBER data type for all other numeric fields.

CREATE VIEW

Use the CREATE VIEW command to create a view. Figure B-4 describes the CREATE VIEW command.

Clause	Description	Required?
CREATE VIEW *view name* AS	Indicates the name of the view to be created.	Yes
query	Indicates the defining query for the view.	Yes

FIGURE B-4 CREATE VIEW command

The following CREATE VIEW command creates a view named Games, which consists of the item number, description, units on hand, and unit price for all rows in the Item table on which the category is GME:

```
CREATE VIEW Games AS
SELECT ItemNum, Description, OnHand, Price
FROM Item
WHERE Category='GME'
;
```

DATA TYPES

Figure B-5 describes the data types that you can use in a CREATE TABLE command.

Data Type	Description
INTEGER	Stores integers, which are numbers without a decimal part. The valid data range is –2147483648 to 2147483647. You can use the contents of INTEGER fields for calculations.
SMALLINT	Stores integers but uses less space than the INTEGER data type. The valid data range is –32768 to 32767. SMALLINT is a better choice than INTEGER when you are certain that the field will store numbers within the indicated range. You can use the contents of SMALLINT fields for calculations.
DECIMAL(p,q)	Stores a decimal number p digits long with q of these digits being decimal places. For example, DECIMAL(5,2) represents a number with three places to the left and two places to the right of the decimal. You can use the contents of DECIMAL fields for calculations.
CHAR(n)	Stores a character string n characters long. You use the CHAR type for fields that contain letters and other special characters and for fields that contain numbers that will not be used in calculations. Because neither sales rep numbers nor customer numbers will be used in any calculations, for example, both of them are assigned CHAR as the data type. (Some DBMSs, such as Access, use SHORT TEXT rather than CHAR, but the two data types mean the same thing.)
DATE	Stores dates in the form DD-MON-YYYY or MM/DD/YYYY. For example, May 12, 2021, could be stored as 12-MAY-2021 or 5/12/2021.

FIGURE B-5 Data types

DELETE ROWS

Use the DELETE command to delete one or more rows from a table. Figure B-6 describes the DELETE command.

Clause	Description	Required?
DELETE FROM *table name*	Indicates the name of the table from which the row or rows are to be deleted.	Yes
WHERE *condition*	Indicates a condition. Those rows for which the condition is true will be retrieved and deleted.	No (If you omit the WHERE clause, all rows will be deleted.)

FIGURE B-6 DELETE command

The following DELETE command deletes any row from the OrderLine table on which the item number is DL51:

```
DELETE
FROM OrderLine
WHERE ItemNum='DL51'
;
```

DROP INDEX

Use the DROP INDEX command to delete an index, as shown in Figure B-7.

Clause	Description	Required?
DROP INDEX *index name*	Indicates the name of the index to be dropped.	Yes

FIGURE B-7   DROP INDEX command

The following DROP INDEX command deletes the index named RepBal:

```
DROP INDEX RepBal
;
```

DROP TABLE

Use the DROP TABLE command to delete a table, as shown in Figure B-8.

Clause	Description	Required?
DROP TABLE *table name*	Indicates the name of the table to be dropped.	Yes

FIGURE B-8   DROP TABLE command

The following DROP TABLE command deletes the table named SmallCust:

```
DROP TABLE SmallCust
;
```

GRANT

Use the GRANT statement to grant privileges to a user. Figure B-9 describes the GRANT statement.

Clause	Description	Required?
GRANT *privilege*	Indicates the type of privilege(s) to be granted.	Yes
ON *database object*	Indicates the database object(s) to which the privilege(s) pertain.	Yes
TO *user name*	Indicates the user(s) to whom the privilege(s) are to be granted.	Yes

FIGURE B-9   GRANT statement

The following GRANT statement grants the user named Jones the privilege of selecting rows from the Customer table:

```
GRANT SELECT ON Customer TO Jones
;
```

INSERT

Use the INSERT command and the VALUES clause to insert a row into a table by specifying the values for each of the columns. As shown in Figure B-10, you must indicate the table into which to insert the values and then list the values to insert in parentheses.

Clause	Description	Required?
INSERT INTO *table name*	Indicates the name of the table into which the row will be inserted.	Yes
VALUES *(values list)*	Indicates the values for each of the columns on the new row.	Yes

FIGURE B-10 INSERT command

The following INSERT command inserts the values shown in parentheses as a new row in the Rep table:

```
INSERT INTO Rep VALUES
('75','Argy','Dorothy','424 Bournemouth','Grove',
'CA','90092',0.00,0.06)
;
```

INTEGRITY

You can use the ALTER TABLE command with an appropriate CHECK, PRIMARY KEY, or FOREIGN KEY clause to specify integrity. Figure B-11 describes the ALTER TABLE command for specifying integrity.

Clause	Description	Required?
ALTER TABLE *table name*	Indicates the name of the table for which integrity is being specified.	Yes
integrity clause	CHECK, PRIMARY KEY, or FOREIGN KEY	Yes

FIGURE B-11 Integrity options

The following ALTER TABLE command changes the Customer table so that the only legal values for credit limits are 5,000, 7,500, 10,000, and 15,000:

```
ALTER TABLE Customer
CHECK (CreditLimit IN (5000, 7500, 10000, 15000))
;
```

The following ALTER TABLE command changes the Rep table so that the RepNum column is the table's primary key:

```
ALTER TABLE Rep
ADD PRIMARY KEY(RepNum)
;
```

The following ALTER TABLE command changes the Customer table so that the RepNum column in the Customer table is a foreign key referencing the primary key of the Rep table:

```
ALTER TABLE Customer
ADD FOREIGN KEY (RepNum) REFERENCES Rep
;
```

JOIN

To join tables, use a SELECT command in which both tables appear in the FROM clause, and the WHERE clause contains a condition to relate the rows in the two tables. The following SELECT statement lists the customer number, customer name, rep number, first name, and last name by joining the Rep and Customer tables using the RepNum fields in both tables:

```
SELECT CustomerNum, CustomerName, Customer.RepNum, FirstName, LastName
FROM Rep, Customer
WHERE Rep.RepNum=Customer.RepNum
;
```

NOTE: Many implementations of SQL also allow a special JOIN operator to join tables. The following command uses the JOIN operator to produce the same result as the previous query:

```
SELECT CustomerNum, CustomerName, Customer.RepNum, FirstName, LastName
FROM Rep
INNER JOIN Customer
ON Rep.RepNum=Customer.RepNum
;
```

REVOKE

Use the REVOKE statement to revoke privileges from a user. Figure B-12 describes the REVOKE statement.

Clause	Description	Required?
REVOKE *privilege*	Indicates the type of privilege(s) to be revoked.	Yes
ON *database object*	Indicates the database object(s) to which the privilege pertains.	Yes
FROM *user name*	Indicates the user name(s) from whom the privilege(s) are to be revoked.	Yes

FIGURE B-12   REVOKE statement

The following REVOKE statement revokes the SELECT privilege for the Customer table from the user named Jones:

```
REVOKE SELECT ON Customer FROM Jones
;
```

SELECT

Use the SELECT command to retrieve data from a table or from multiple tables. Figure B-13 describes the SELECT command.

Clause	Description	Required?
SELECT *column or expression list*	Indicates the column(s) and/or expression(s) to be retrieved.	Yes
FROM *table list*	Indicates the table(s) required for the query.	Yes
WHERE *condition*	Indicates one or more conditions. Only the rows for which the condition(s) are true will be retrieved.	No (If you omit the WHERE clause, all rows will be retrieved.)
GROUP BY *column list*	Indicates the column(s) on which rows are to be grouped.	No (If you omit the GROUP BY clause, no grouping will occur.)
HAVING *condition involving groups*	Indicates a condition for groups. Only groups for which the condition is true will be included in query results. Use the HAVING clause only if the query output is grouped.	No (If you omit the HAVING clause, all groups will be included.)
ORDER BY *column or expression list*	Indicates the column(s) on which the query output is to be sorted.	No (If you omit the ORDER BY clause, no sorting will occur.)

FIGURE B-13   SELECT command

The following SELECT command groups and orders rows by rep number. It displays the rep number, the count of the number of customers having this rep, and the average balance of these customers. It renames the count as NumCustomers and the average balance as AverageBalance. The HAVING clause restricts the reps to be displayed to only those whose customers' average balance is less than $2,000.

```
SELECT RepNum, COUNT(*) AS NumCustomers, AVG(Balance) AS AverageBalance
FROM Customer
GROUP BY RepNum
HAVING AVG(Balance)<2000
ORDER BY RepNum
;
```

SELECT INTO

Use the SELECT command with an INTO clause to insert the rows retrieved by a query into a table. As shown in Figure B-14, you must indicate the name of the table into which the row(s) will be inserted and the query whose results will be inserted into the named table.

Clause	Description	Required?
SELECT field list	Indicates the list of fields to be selected.	Yes
INTO *table name*	Indicates the name of the table into which the row(s) will be inserted.	Yes
remainder of query	Indicates the remainder of the query (for example, FROM clause and WHERE clause) whose results will be inserted into the table.	Yes

FIGURE B-14   SELECT command with INTO clause

The following SELECT command with an INTO clause inserts rows selected by a query into the SmallCust table:

```
SELECT *
INTO SmallCust
FROM Customer
WHERE CreditLimit<=7500
;
```

SUBQUERIES

In some cases, it is useful to obtain the results you want in two stages. You can do so by placing one query inside another. The inner query is called a subquery and is evaluated first. After the subquery has been evaluated, the outer query can be evaluated.

The following command contains a subquery that produces a list of item numbers located in storehouse 3. The outer query then produces those order numbers in the OrderLine table that are on any rows containing an item number in the list.

```
SELECT OrderNum
FROM OrderLine
WHERE ItemNum IN
(SELECT ItemNum
FROM Item
WHERE Storehouse='3')
;
```

UNION

Connecting two SELECT commands with the UNION operator produces all the rows that would be in the results of the first command, the second command, or both.

The following query displays the customer number and customer name of all customers that are represented by sales rep 15 *or* that have orders *or* both:

```
SELECT Customer.CustomerNum, CustomerName
FROM Customer
WHERE RepNum='15'
UNION
SELECT Customer.CustomerNum, CustomerName
FROM Customer, Orders
WHERE Customer.CustomerNum=Orders.CustomerNum
;
```

UPDATE

Use the UPDATE command to change the contents of one or more rows in a table. Figure B-15 describes the UPDATE command.

Clause	Description	Required?
UPDATE *table name*	Indicates the name of the table whose contents will be changed.	Yes
SET *column = expression*	Indicates the column to be changed, along with an expression that provides the new value.	Yes
WHERE *condition*	Indicates a condition. The change will occur only on those rows for which the condition is true.	No (If you omit the WHERE clause, all rows will be updated.)

FIGURE B-15 UPDATE command

The following UPDATE command changes the street address on the row in the Customer table on which the customer number is 502 to 1445 Rivard:

```
UPDATE Customer
SET Street='1445 Rivard'
WHERE CustomerNum='502'
;
```

FAQ REFERENCE

This appendix answers frequently asked questions about how to accomplish a variety of tasks using SQL. Use the second column to locate the correct section in Appendix B that answers your question.

How do I?	Review the Named Section(s) in Appendix B
Add columns to an existing table?	ALTER TABLE
Add rows?	INSERT
Calculate a statistic (sum, average, maximum, minimum, or count)?	1. SELECT 2. Column or Expression List (SELECT clause) (Use the appropriate function in the query.)
Change rows?	UPDATE
Create a data type for a column?	1. Data Types 2. CREATE TABLE
Create a table?	CREATE TABLE
Create a view?	CREATE VIEW
Create an index?	CREATE INDEX
Delete a table?	DROP TABLE
Delete an index?	DROP INDEX
Delete rows?	DELETE Rows
Drop a table?	DROP TABLE
Drop an index?	DROP INDEX
Grant a privilege?	GRANT
Group data in a query?	SELECT (Use a GROUP BY clause.)
Insert rows using a query?	SELECT INTO
Insert rows?	INSERT
Join tables?	Conditions (Include a WHERE clause to relate the tables.)
Order query results?	SELECT (Use an ORDER BY clause.)
Remove a privilege?	REVOKE
Remove rows?	DELETE Rows
Retrieve all columns?	1. SELECT 2. Column or Expression List (SELECT clause) (Type * in the SELECT clause.)
Retrieve all rows?	SELECT (Omit the WHERE clause.)

FIGURE C-1 FAQ reference *(continued)*

How do I?	Review the Named Section(s) in Appendix B
Retrieve only certain columns?	1. SELECT 2. Column or Expression List (SELECT clause) (Type the list of columns in the SELECT clause.)
Revoke a privilege?	REVOKE
Select all columns?	1. SELECT 2. Column or Expression List (SELECT clause) (Type * in the SELECT clause.)
Select all rows?	SELECT (Omit the WHERE clause.)
Select only certain columns?	1. SELECT 2. Column or Expression List (SELECT clause) (Type the list of columns in the SELECT clause.)
Select only certain rows?	1. SELECT 2. Conditions (Use a WHERE clause.)
Sort query results?	SELECT (Use an ORDER BY clause.)
Specify a foreign key?	Integrity (Use a FOREIGN KEY clause in an ALTER TABLE command.)
Specify a primary key?	Integrity (Use a PRIMARY KEY clause in an ALTER TABLE command.)
Specify a privilege?	GRANT
Specify integrity?	Integrity (Use a CHECK clause in an ALTER TABLE command.)
Specify legal values?	Integrity (Use a CHECK clause in an ALTER TABLE command.)
Update rows?	UPDATE
Use a computed field?	1. SELECT 2. Column or Expression List (SELECT clause) (Enter a calculation in the query.)
Use a compound condition in a query?	Conditions
Use a compound condition?	1. SELECT 2. Conditions (Use simple conditions connected by AND, OR, or NOT in a WHERE clause.)
Use a condition in a query?	1. SELECT 2. Conditions (Use a WHERE clause.)
Use a subquery?	Subqueries
Use a wildcard?	1. SELECT 2. Conditions (Use LIKE and a wildcard in a WHERE clause.)
Use UNION operation?	UNION (Connect two SELECT commands with UNION.)

FIGURE C-1   FAQ reference

APPENDIX **D**

INTRODUCTION TO MYSQL

INTRODUCTION

MySQL is a free, open source relational database management system (RDBMS) from Oracle. **Open source** means that the software and its original code may be modified and redistributed freely. MySQL is one of the most popular RDMBS's, especially with database administrators, programmers, and web developers who use MySQL to create web, cloud, mobile, and embedded applications using other open source programming languages such as PHP. MySQL has both commercial and "community" versions available. The community version allows you to freely use the software.

MySQL has the following important features:

- It is widely available and can be installed on many different platforms.
- It comes standard with most web-hosting setups.
- It is fast, reliable, and flexible.
- Setting up and working with MySQL databases is straightforward.
- It works well with web programming languages.

This appendix will introduce you to MySQL and the graphical MySQL client interface called MySQL Workbench on a Windows machine. You will learn how to complete the following tasks:

- Complete a basic installation of MySQL and MySQL Workbench on your Windows computer.
- Use MySQL Workbench to open and execute a previously created SQL file that creates the tables, data, and views of the JC Consulting database.
- Use MySQL Workbench to refresh schemas.
- Use MySQL Workbench to display database data.
- Use MySQL Workbench to write and execute SQL statements.

DOWNLOADING AND INSTALLING MYSQL

In this section, you will download and install MySQL and the client graphical interface, MySQL Workbench, on your local Windows machine. (The figures shown in this appendix are based on MySQL Server version 8.0.17, but your version may be newer, and of course download and installation options change over time. As with any new installation, work through the steps in this appendix slowly and carefully to read and understand the process at hand. If presented with options that you are unsure of, the default options are generally the best choice.)

MySQL is a relational database server that manages your relational database as well as connections to the database. To communicate with a relational database managed by MySQL, you have a couple of choices. One of the most popular is **MySQL Workbench**, an integrated visual tool that helps you manage MySQL databases on Windows-based machines. Another way to communicate with a MySQL database is to use a command line interface software product called **MySQL Shell**. This appendix will use MySQL Workbench.

There are several places on the web to obtain MySQL and MySQL Workbench software. For example, open a browser and navigate to https://dev.mysql.com/downloads/installer, as shown in Figure D-1.

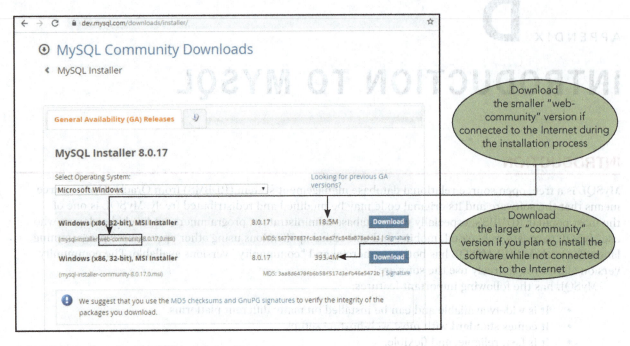

FIGURE D-1   Download MySQL Installer webpage

If you have an online connection while installing the software, download the smaller "web" version. If you do not have an online connection while running the installer, choose the larger download file. The download is free. You do not have to create or log in to an Oracle account to download MySQL Server software if you click the download you want to use, and then choose the "No thanks, just start my download" link.

The download includes an .msi file. An **MSI file** is a Microsoft installer package file format used by Windows for installation, storage, and removal of programs. Download the file and proceed with the installation of the MySQL Server. After a few prompts, the opening screen of the MySQL Installer appears (see Figure D-2). If you are familiar with MySQL, you can customize your installation. If not, choose the Developer Default option and click Next.

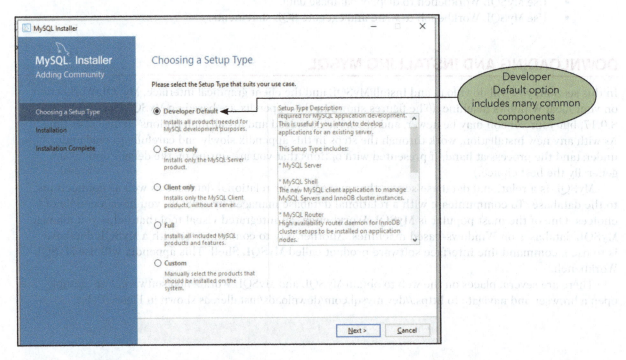

FIGURE D-2   MySQL Installer: Choosing a Setup Type

At a minimum you should install the MySQL Server and the MySQL Workbench client. The MySQL Documentation as well as the Samples and Examples are also highly recommended. The other options help you connect to languages or tools that you may or may not need. Depending on your connection and system, you may have to click the "Try again" link a few times to install all components in the Developer Default package. If you are unable to install every component, but do not have a current need for a particular component, you can continue without it. As long as you have MySQL Server and the MySQL Workbench client, you can continue.

After continuing through a few informational screens, the installer will ask you to configure the MySQL Server. Choose the Standalone MySQL Server/Classic MySQL Replication option shown in Figure D-3, and the default options in the other categories: Type and Networking and Authentication Method.

FIGURE D-3 MySQL Installer: Walking through installer options

When you reach the Accounts and Roles area, the installer will ask you to create a password for your system. After entering an appropriate password in both the MySQL Root Password and Repeat Password boxes, click the Next button to accept the default values in the Windows Service and Apply Configuration areas. Be sure to record your password in a secure location. Click the Execute button to apply the configuration, and the Finish button to complete the process as shown in Figure D-4.

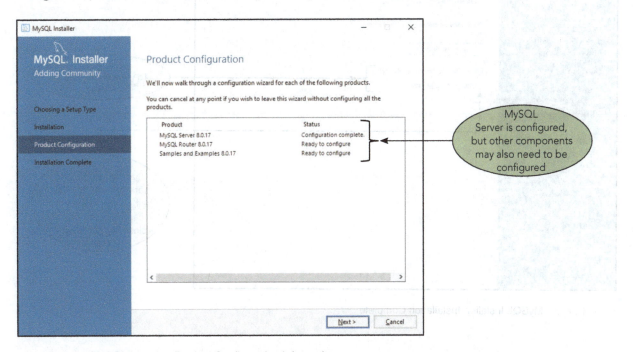

FIGURE D-4 MySQL Installer: Product Configuration information

If you have selected other MySQL components that need to be configured, continue through the dialog boxes clicking Next to accept the default options.

When you are prompted to Connect To Server, enter the password and click the Check button to check the connection as shown in Figure D-5.

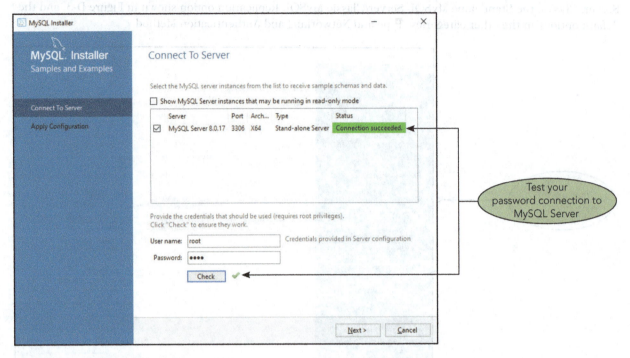

FIGURE D-5 MySQL Installer: Connect To Server

Continue through the installation steps accepting default options until you reach the Installation Complete dialog box as shown in Figure D-6.

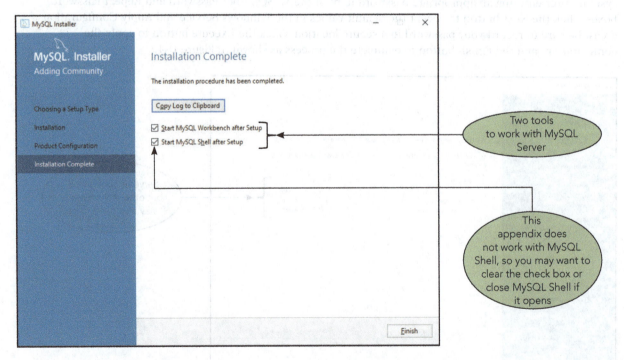

FIGURE D-6 MySQL Installer: Installation Complete

The MySQL Shell program is a command-driven way to work with MySQL, so clear the check box to start the MySQL Shell program as shown in Figure D-6, or merely close the MySQL Shell program if it automatically opens. Some developers find the command prompt approach to be a faster way to manipulate data stored in MySQL, but in this appendix, you will use MySQL Workbench. MySQL Workbench is more graphical and therefore generally considered easier to use for those new to MySQL.

RUNNING MYSQL WORKBENCH AND CONNECTING TO MYSQL SERVER

If MySQL Workbench does not automatically open, you can open it from your Windows Start button or by typing MySQL Workbench into the search box like any other program installed on your computer. The first time you open MySQL Workbench, a screen similar to Figure D-7 will be displayed, prompting you to connect to an existing database or start a new connection.

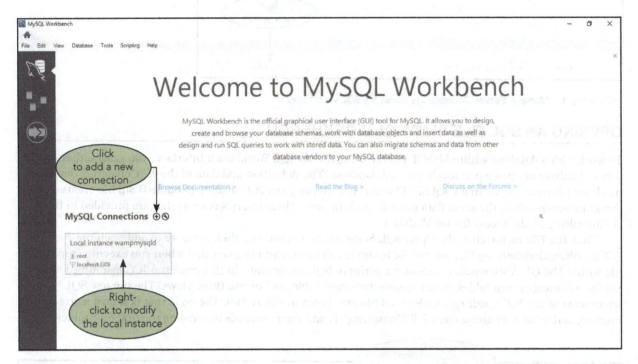

FIGURE D-7 Welcome to MySQL Workbench

Right-click the connection named "Local instance…", click Edit Connection on the shortcut menu, change the Connection Name to something like *LocalTestSystem* as shown in Figure D-8, click the Test Connection button, and then enter your password. (Note that in this situation, the SQL Server software is stored on your *local* Windows computer, in effect, turning your local machine into a database server. Any valid connection name can be used, but the name *LocalTestSystem* clarifies that this particular connection represents a test system installed on your local machine rather than a production system stored on a centralized server.)

Now that you have established a valid connection between MySQL Workbench and your local installation of MySQL, you will not be prompted for this information again when you start MySQL Workbench.

Click *LocalTestSystem* to start that instance of SQL Server within the MySQL Workbench interface. If you have already closed MySQL Workbench, start it, click *LocalTestSystem*, and enter your password to start the connection.

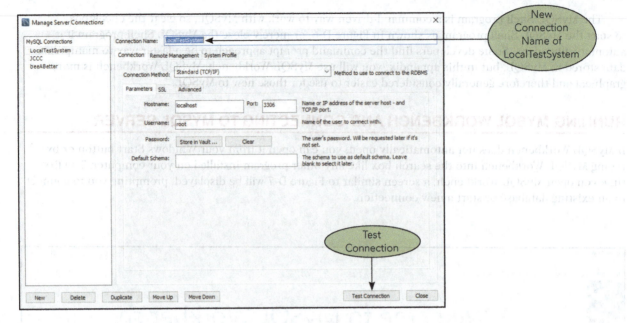

FIGURE D-8 Manage Server Connections within MySQL Workbench

OPENING AN SQL FILE IN MYSQL WORKBENCH

To work with a database within MySQL Server using the MySQL Workbench interface, you must either create a new database or open a previously created database. The definition and data of the JC Consulting database has been provided to you in an .sql file. Opening and running the JCConsultingModule01.sql file creates the same seven tables, the same data records, and the same three queries (views) that are provided in the JCConsulting.accdb Access file for Module 1.

Click the File menu, click the Open SQL Script menu option, and then navigate to and open the JCConsultingModule01.sql file. An .sql file is also is called a **script** file given that when you execute (run) the file within MySQL Workbench, it executes a series of SQL commands. In this case, the JCConsultingModule01.sql file will create seven tables, insert records into each table, and create three views. The top few SQL statements of the JCConsultingModule01.sql file are shown in Figure D-9. The code that is shown starts by creating and using a database named JCConsulting01, and then proceeds to creating the first four tables.

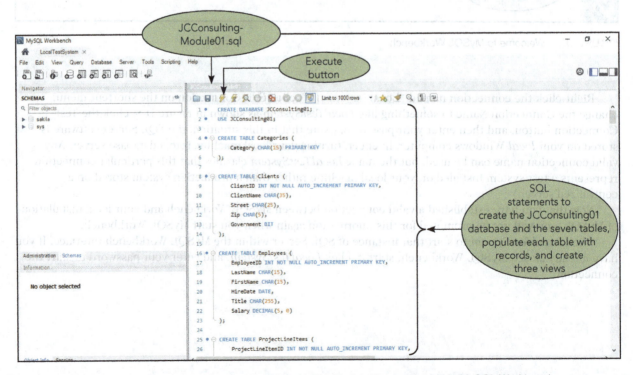

FIGURE D-9 Opening, viewing, and executing the JCConsultingModule01.sql script within MySQL Workbench

RUNNING AN SQL SCRIPT IN MYSQL WORKBENCH

At this point, you could scroll through the JCConsultingModule01.sql file to read the statements that create the tables, insert records into the tables, and create three views. You could also modify the SQL to add or change the statements as desired. To run the existing JCConsultingModule01.sql file, click the **Execute button**, identified in Figure D-9.

REFRESHING SCHEMAS IN MYSQL WORKBENCH

After running an .sql file that creates a database or modifies tables or views within a database, you need to refresh the schemas in order to see the results. In MySQL, a **schema** represents all of the tables of data, views, stored procedures, and functions that are associated with that database.

If the Schemas pane is not displayed, click the Schemas tab in the Navigator panel. Click the Refresh button in the Navigator panel identified in D-10, and then click the expand button to the left of the Tables and Views to make sure that all seven tables and all three views were created as shown in Figure D-10. Click the Close button for the JCConsultingModule01.sql window given that you have already run the script and therefore no longer need it.

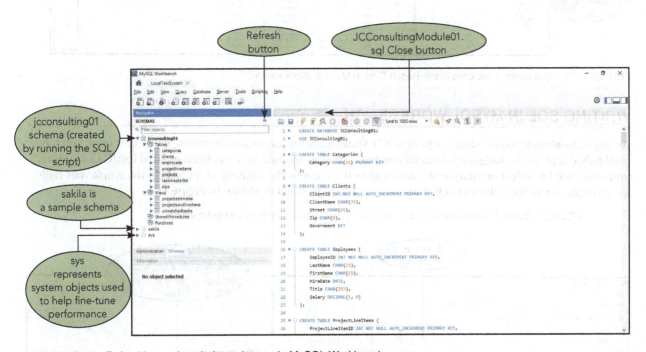

FIGURE D-10 Refreshing and exploring schemas in MySQL Workbench

VIEWING TABLE DATA IN MYSQL WORKBENCH

To view table data in MySQL, click the table you want to view in the Navigator panel, and then click the Result Grid button as shown in Figure D-11.

The **Result Grid** shows the result of running the SQL statements in the upper **SQL panel**. The Result Grid provides a number of commands that you can execute through the Result Grid toolbars, or you can write and execute your commands in SQL in the SQL panel and execute (run) them with the Execute button.

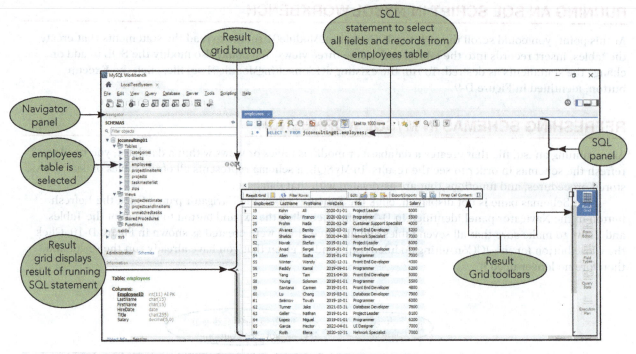

FIGURE D-11 Displaying table data in the Result Grid in MySQL Workbench

WRITING SQL IN MYSQL WORKBENCH

As you have already experienced, SQL SELECT statements are extremely common, given that once you have established a properly designed relational database, such as the one that has been created for JC Consulting, you often need to select or analyze the data within it. To count the number of records in the employees table, for example, write the following SQL statement in the SQL panel as shown in Figure D-12.

```
SELECT Count(EmployeeID) FROM jcconsulting01.employees;
```

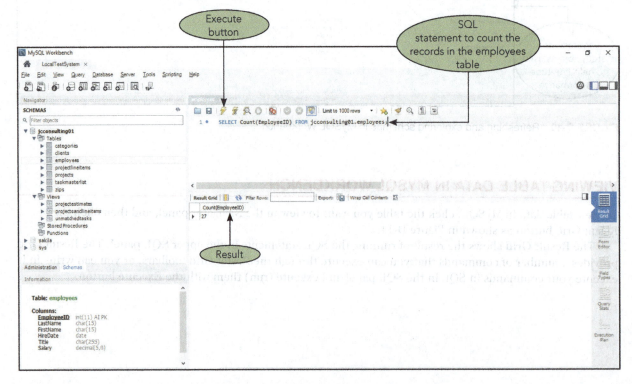

FIGURE D-12 Writing and executing SQL statements in MySQL Workbench

As before, click the Execute button to execute the SQL statement you've written. The Results Grid displays the result of running the SQL statement, also as shown in Figure D-12. Click File on the menu bar, and then click Save Script As if you want to save the statements in the current SQL panel as an external .sql file for later use.

PRACTICING WITH MYSQL WORKBENCH

For further practice with MySQL Workbench using the jcconsulting01 database, refer to Module 3, which provides SQL statements to select, sort, create, and analyze data. Module 3 also covers SQL that joins tables, updates, deletes, and inserts data. Also refer to Module 4, which provides SQL statements to build indexes, perform advanced joins on tables, and change table structures. Click the File menu, and then click Exit to close MySQL Workbench.

Summary

- MySQL is a free, open source relational database management system from Oracle.
- Open source means that the software and its original code may be modified and redistributed freely.

- MySQL is one of the most popular RDMBS's with database administrators, programmers, and web developers who use MySQL to create web, cloud, mobile, and embedded applications.
- Advantages of MySQL include multi-platform availability, standard web-hosting setups, reliability, flexibility, and the ease of use with several different web programming languages including PHP, C#, and Java.
- You can install MySQL on your own local Windows machine, in effect making your machine work as if it is a database server.
- MySQL Workbench has a graphic user interface used to manage MySQL databases.
- You can use MySQL Workbench to execute stored SQL files or write new SQL.

Key Terms

Execute button (MySQL)

MSI file

MySQL

MySQL Shell

MySQL Workbench

open source

Result Grid

schema

script

SQL panel

E

A SYSTEMS ANALYSIS APPROACH TO INFORMATION-LEVEL REQUIREMENTS

INTRODUCTION

In this appendix, you will study **information systems analysis**, the process of collecting and interpreting facts, identifying problems, and documenting the components of a system in order to define what a new information system should do. The traditional approach to information systems analysis starts with the identification of specific **user views**—the specific information that the users of the system need to be able to access quickly using a screen or report.

This appendix will separate the different elements and considerations that are involved in information systems analysis starting with big picture of an information system. It will also drill down into many of the specific questions that need to be considered when completing an information systems analysis.

INFORMATION SYSTEMS

As illustrated in Figure E-1, an **information system** is the collection of data, people, procedures, stored data, software, hardware, and information required to support a specific set of related functions. Examples of information systems include billing, payroll, reservations, point of sale, government tax collections and assessments, online registries, or insurance premium processing. The JC Consulting, Pitt Fitness, and the Sports Physical Therapy cases are also examples of information systems, although this book has primarily focused on the database components of these information systems.

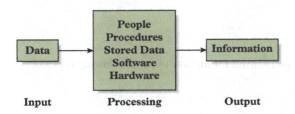

FIGURE E-1   Information system components

The primary goal of an information system is to turn data (recorded facts) into information (the knowledge gained by processing those facts). *Data* is input to an information system, and the information system outputs *information*. Data can be input to an information system manually with keyboards or mobile devices, or with automated systems such as point-of-sale scanners, credit or debit card readers, or external files and databases. Information can be output from an information system as printed reports, screen displays, external files, databases, specialized devices, or webpages.

Information systems exist within a wide range of organizations from multinational businesses to government agencies to local small businesses. Information systems have goals that should be consistent with the goals and objectives of the organization. If a goal of JC Consulting, for example, is to minimize the amount of time needed to process an estimate, then the estimate processing information system should be designed to meet that goal.

Each organization also has its own organizational structure and culture. **Organizational structure** refers to the hierarchical arrangement of lines of authority (who reports to whom), communication, rights, and duties. **Culture** includes the organization's values, beliefs, norms, and habits. Organizational culture influences the way people and groups interact with each other. Understanding of the organization's business, structure, and culture is helpful before designing any information system.

An information system is a success only when the *people* interacting with it and obtaining information from it consider it to be successful. The people component of an information system include the **users** (those directly interacting with the information system), management, auditing and other support staff groups, as well as people in outside entities such as government agencies, suppliers, and financial institutions. The people component also includes those who develop and maintain the information system and who support the operating environment for the information system.

A **procedure** is a series of steps followed in a regular, specified order to accomplish one end result. Examples of procedures in information systems are signing up a new customer, auditing a payroll's direct deposits, or adding items to an online shopping cart. Procedures are often in written the form of manuals, webpages, or other system documentation.

The data input to an information system must be retained for future processing and legal reasons. This data is retained as *stored data* on hard drives and other storage media. The stored data is a critical information system component because all information either is produced directly from stored data or is derived from stored data in the form of calculated fields.

The *software* component consists of system software and application software. **System software** consists of the programs that control the hardware and software environment. These programs include the operating system, network managers, device drivers, and utility programs such as backup systems. **Application software** consists of the programs that directly support the information system in processing the data to produce the required information.

The *hardware* component consists of all the physical equipment used within the information system. This equipment includes computer hardware, such as computers, servers, printers, and any IoT (Internet of Things) device that connects to the corporate network to interact with company programs and data.

It's important to consider the broad range of components of an information system in order to effectively analyze, design, develop, and implement a successful information system.

SYSTEM REQUIREMENT CATEGORIES

To create the user views for an information system, you determine all of its system requirements. A **system requirement** is a feature that must be included in an information system to fulfill business, legal, or user needs. Using the definition of an information system, system requirements can be classified into output, input, and processing categories.

Output Requirements

To determine an information system's output requirements, you search for answers to the following types of questions about each output:

- What data is needed to include in the output?
- How should the data be sorted and formatted?
- What subtotals, totals, or other calculations are needed in the output?
- How will the data be accessed? Via the web, a computer screen, a printout, or another special device?
- Who should receive each view?
- What are the intervals and/or conditions under which the output should be created?
- What is the physical size of the output, and how can it best be presented?
- What are the security restrictions on the output, both in general, and by user?

Input Requirements

To determine an information system's input requirements, you find answers to the following types of questions about each input:

- How is the input originated and what types of devices are used for that input?
- Are source documents such as forms used in the process?
- What is the format of the input data, and how is it best entered into the system?

- What are the attributes of each field in the input?
- What formatting and validation requirements should be used for each field's data?
- Is there a natural primary key field for each transaction?
- When is the data created, how often, and in what volume?

Processing Requirements

To determine an information system's processing requirements, you find answers to the following types of questions:

- Which input data must be retained as stored data to provide the required outputs? How long must data be retained?
- What calculations must be performed to create desired outputs?
- Are there special cycle processing requirements that occur daily, weekly, monthly, quarterly, annually, or on some other frequency?
- Are there any special legal or auditing requirements for the data in the information system?
- Which stored data has special security requirements that permit only authorized users access or update privileges?
- What is the sequence and relationship between procedures?
- Which users should be able to access which procedures?

Technical and Constraining Requirements

To determine an information system's technical and constraining requirements, you find answers to the following types of questions:

- Must the information system operate with a specific operating system or with multiple operating systems?
- Which DBMS will be used to store retained data?
- Does the hardware—entry, storage, output, and other devices—impose any restrictions or provide special capabilities?
- Which programming languages will be used for creating the application programs for the information system?
- How many users must the information system support concurrently, and what response time is expected for online processing?
- Which portions of the information system must be available to users at all times?
- Does the company plan to use big data?

In addition to constraining requirements, you also determine the business rules for the organization. A business rule is a statement that defines or constrains some aspect of the business. A **business rule** for JC Consulting could be: "JC Consulting will not process an estimate until a project manager is assigned to the project." Business rules must be captured and documented to ensure that the information system works correctly, and that users understand the purpose and reasons for these constraints.

DETERMINING SYSTEM REQUIREMENTS

Many tools and methods have been developed to help analyze and document the system requirements, but to determine the system requirements, you work as a detective to collect the facts about the information system. The most commonly used techniques for determining the facts about an information system are interviews, document collection, observation, and research.

Interviews

An **interview** is a planned meeting during which you obtain system requirements from other people. You conduct these interviews with the individuals who represent the people component of the information system, each of whom has a personal perspective about what the information system should do. You conduct individual and group interviews, during which you determine how the information system operates now, how it should operate in the future, and what requirements need to be included in the new information system.

Include both open-ended and closed questions in your interview to gather as much information as possible. An **open-ended question** is one that requires a general response, such as "How do you currently create estimates for new projects?" A **closed question** is a question that can be answered with a simple "yes," "no," or single-fact response.

Questionnaires

In large organizations with hundreds of users and other people who have system requirements, you may want to use questionnaires to allow as many people to participate and contribute to system requirements as possible. Questionnaires can include both open-ended and closed questions. It's helpful to test your questionnaire on a small group and use the feedback from that pilot to refine the questionnaire before disseminating it to a larger audience.

Document Collection

Every information system has existing paper forms, online forms, reports, manuals, written procedures, and other documents that contain valuable system requirements. You should review these documents and then confirm their validity with users. Documents are a rich source for the data content of an information system, although you need to verify the documents' accuracy with users and revise them for currency as needed.

Observation

Observing current operating processing provides insight into how users interact with the system and how the interaction can be improved. Observation verifies what you learn during interviews and what is documented in procedure manuals. Observation can also identify undocumented processing and uncover exceptions and processes that differ from standard practice.

Research

You can also research journals, periodicals, books, other businesses, and information provided on the web to obtain examples and requirements related to your information system. You can attend professional seminars and work with vendors and other companies to gain insight from others who have been through similar processes.

TRANSITIONING FROM SYSTEMS ANALYSIS TO SYSTEMS DESIGN

To document the requirements, you may employ the Unified Modeling Language, briefly discussed in Module 9, and other diagrams and modeling tools to model an information system. Another popular approach uses data flow diagrams to model the transformations of data into information, a data dictionary for data and table documentation, and various process description tools and techniques. Completing the documentation and systems model marks the transition from systems analysis to systems design.

Key Terms

application software

business rule

closed question

culture

user

information system

information systems analysis

interview

IoT (Internet of Things)

open-ended question

organizational structure

procedure

system requirement

system software

user view

Critical Thinking Questions

1. Use books, the Internet, and/or other sources to investigate "best practices" in conducting interviews to determine system requirements. Prepare a one-page, double-spaced document report that summarizes your findings. Include links or citations for your source documents.

2. Use books, the Internet, and/or other sources to investigate "best practices" in creating questionnaires to determine system requirements. Prepare a one-page, double-spaced document report that summarizes your findings. Include links or citations for your source documents.

3. Use books, the Internet, or other sources to investigate modeling tools such as use cases and data flow diagram tools. Prepare a one-page, double-spaced document report that summarizes the features and benefits of use cases versus data flow diagram tools. Include a sample of each, as well as links or citations for your source documents.

& operator An operator used to combine the contents of two text fields.

.NET A popular software framework that includes Microsoft Visual Studio, C#, and SQL Server. Also called *Microsoft ASP.NET* and *ASP.NET*.

1NF A table (relation) is in first normal form when it does not contain repeating groups (more than one value in an attribute), each column contains atomic values, and it has no duplicate records.

2NF A relation is in second normal form if it is in first normal form and no nonkey attribute depends on only a portion of the primary key.

3NF A table is in third normal form if it is in second normal form and the only determinants it contains are candidate keys.

3Vs Refers to the characteristics of big data, including volume (amount of data from different sources), variety (types of data such as traditional text and numbers plus pictures, video, sound, and behavioral data such as clicks and pauses), and velocity (the speed at which the data is created).

4NF A table is in fourth normal form if it is in third normal form and contains no multivalued dependencies.

Abstraction A concept that allows programmers to create classes, objects, and variables, and to reuse those things as needed for more specificity. Abstraction allows programmers to avoid writing duplicate code.

ACID (Atomicity, Consistency, Isolation, Durability) A set of properties for a transaction that guarantees its success even in the event of a problem or interruption in the process.

Action Catalog In Access, a small window that displays available macro actions.

Action query A query that changes data in a batch process.

Ad hoc Unpredictable and as needed.

After Delete An Access table event that runs after an existing record has been deleted.

After image A record of what the data in a row looked like after an update.

After Insert An Access table event that runs after a new record has been inserted into the table.

After Update An Access table event that runs after an existing record has been changed.

Aggregate function Part of an expression used to calculate the number of entries, the sum or average of all the entries in a given column, or the largest or smallest of the entries in a given column; also called *function*.

AI (artificial intelligence) The simulation of human intelligence processes by machines, especially computer systems.

Algorithm A defined set of steps to solve a problem.

Alias A field name created using the SQL AS keyword.

ALL The SQL keyword that enables users to select and update data and insert and delete rows in a table or view.

Alternate key (AK) A field that contains unique data for each record in the table but is not used as the primary key field for security or other reasons.

ALTER TABLE The SQL command used to change the structure of a table.

Amazon Relational Database Service A popular database-as-a-service product.

Amazon Web Services (AWS) The current market and innovation leader among cloud service providers.

American National Standards Institute (ANSI) An organization that oversees the development of voluntary consensus standards for products, services, processes, systems, and personnel in the United States.

American Standard Code for Information Interchange (ASCII) A standardized system for representing characters in numeric form.

AND criteria Combination of criteria in which each criterion must be true.

AND operator An operator that connects conditions when all the conditions must be true to select for a particular record.

Application DBA A role that focuses on database design and the ongoing support and administration of databases for a specific application or set of applications within a business.

Application server In a three-tier client/server architecture, a centralized server that performs business functions and serves as an interface between clients and the database server.

Application software Programs that directly support an information system in processing the data to produce the required information.

Archive A place where a record of certain corporate data is kept. Data that is no longer needed in a corporate database but must be retained for future reference is removed from the database and placed in the archive. Also called a *data archive*.

Argument Information a macro action needs to complete processing; also, specific information provided to a function so it can operate.

Array A programming variable that contains a list.

ASCII (American Standard Code for Information Interchange) A character encoding standard for electronic communication.

ASP.NET A popular software framework that includes Microsoft Visual Studio, C#, and SQL Server. Also called *Microsoft ASP.NET* and *.NET*.

Atomicity A transaction property indicating that a transaction is indivisible or irreducible to the point that either the entire transaction occurs, or nothing occurs.

Atomic value A piece of data that cannot be meaningfully divided.

Attribute A characteristic or property of an entity; also called a column or a field.

Authentication The process of verifying the identity of the person or process accessing data.

Authorization The process of granting specific rights and privileges to a user, program, or process.

AUTOINCREMENT A field whose values automatically increment by 1 as new records are added.

AutoNumber The Access data type for a field whose values automatically increment by 1 as new records are added.

Back-end database A database that contains only the tables, the actual data, and is stored on the server.

Back-end machine A historical term for "server." Also called a *back-end processor*.

Back-end processor A historical term for "server." Also called a *back-end machine*.

Backup An entire copy of a database created at a specific point in time.

Backward recovery A DBMS recovery method that restores a database to a valid state by reading the log for problem trans-actions and applying the before images to undo their updates. Also called a *rollback*.

Batch update To modify several records in a single process.

Before Change An Access table event that runs before a record is changed to help the user validate or cancel the edits.

Before Delete An Access table event that runs before a record is deleted to help the user validate or cancel the deletion.

Before image A record of what the data in a row looked like before an update.

Berkeley Open Infrastructure for Network Computing (BOINC) An open-source platform for implementing crowd-sourced computing projects.

BETWEEN operator An operator that allows you to specify a range of values for the criteria, including the lower number, the higher number, and all numbers in between.

BI (business intelligence) Application software that can collect and process large amounts of unstructured data from internal and external systems, including books, journals, doc-uments, health records, images, files, email, video, and other business sources.

BICARSA "Traditional" operations of a business that include the internal processes of billing, inventory control, accounts receivable, and sales analysis.

Big data The large volume of data produced by every digital process, system, sensor, mobile device, and even social media exchange.

Binary large object (BLOB) A collection of binary data stored as a single entity in a database management system.

Biometric An identification technique that identifies users by physical or behavioral characteristics such as fingerprints, voiceprints, retina scans, handwritten signatures, and facial characteristics.

BitBucket A popular website for hosting projects that use the Git language for version control. See also GitHub.

Boolean A data type for fields that store only Yes or No (On or Off, True or False) values.

Bounce rate The percentage of visitors who enter a website and then leave ('bounce") rather than continuing to view other pages.

Boyce–Codd normal form (BCNF) A relation is in Boyce-Codd normal form if it is in second normal form and the only determinants it contains are candidate keys; also called *third normal form* in this text.

Branch (Git term) A repository or copy of a code base.

Built-in function A function such as SUM built into the SQL language.

BUNCH (Burroughs, UNIVAC, NCR, Control Data, and Honeywell) The five major competitors to IBM in the 1970s.

Business analyst A role that performs the tasks of a database analyst when the job responsibilities focus on bridging the gap between the information and data needs of the business in

general and the technical requirements of extracting and ana-lyzing that data.

Business rule A statement that defines or constrains some aspect of the business.

BYTE Microsoft Access data type used in the CREATE TABLE statement for a number field of BYTE size (0-255).

Calculated field A field whose value is calculated from other fields in the database; also called a *computed field*.

Candidate key A column (or field) in a table that can uniquely identify a database record without referring to any other data.

Cardinality The uniqueness of data values contained in a single field. Also sometimes used to refer to the actual relation-ships between tables.

Cartesian join When two tables in a query have no instruc-tions about how to connect their records, each record in one table connects with each record in the other table.

Cartesian product The table obtained by concatenating every row in the first table with every row in the second table.

Cascade Delete Related Records An Access setting specifying that if a record on the "one" side of a relationship is deleted, all related records in the "many" table are also deleted.

Cascade Update Related Fields An Access setting specifying that if the primary key field in the table on the "one" side of the relationship changes, the foreign key field value in all related records in the table on the "many" side of the relation-ship will also change.

Catalog A structure that contains information about the objects (tables, columns, indexes, views, and so on) in a database. Also called the *system catalog*.

Centralized approach A database architecture consisting of a single, centrally-located computer system that processes all data.

Channel Sources of traffic to a website.

CHAR A data type for a fixed-length string field, often expressed as CHAR(n), where (n) identifies the length.

CHECK The SQL clause used to enforce legal-values integrity.

Chief information officer (CIO) The most senior executive in an organization who works with information technology and computer systems to support enterprise goals.

Chief security officer (CSO) The most senior executive in an organization who develops and oversees policies and pro-grams related to security, especially information technology security.

Child table The table on the "many" side of a "one-to-many" relationship.

Class An object that is a blueprint for more objects. A class defines what properties and methods a new object may contain.

Client A computer that is connected to a network and has access to the server in a client/server system; also, hardware or software that accesses a service made available by a server.

Client/server architecture A computing model where a central computer (the server, which may be mainframe computer or a large personal computer) delivers and manages centralized resources working cooperatively with a client computer to run an entire application.

Client/server system A networked system in which a special site on the network, called the server, provides services to the other sites, called the clients. Clients send requests for the specific services they need. Software, often including a DBMS, running on the server then processes the requests and sends only the appropriate data and other results back to the clients.

Clone A computer that could do everything the IBM PC could do. Also called a *compatible*.

Closed question A question that can be answered with a simple "yes," "no," or single-fact response.

Cloud A global network of servers.

Cloud backup A scalable strategy for backing up data to an off-site server.

Cloud computing Programs and services that are accessed via the Internet as opposed to a traditional network managed within the walls of the company.

Cloud provider An organization that builds and connects the infrastructure of large pools of systems including servers, storage devices, and high-speed networks to serve many clients.

CMS (content management system) A software tool for managing existing digital content within a pre-developed structure.

COBOL (Common Business-Oriented Language) An early mainframe programming language for business applications.

Codd's 12 rules Rules that define what is required from a database management system in order for it to be considered relational.

Codd's relational model of data The original relational model, which represents data in the form of relations or tables.

Cold site A backup site that is equipped with duplicate hardware and software but for which current data would need to be loaded in order to function. Also called a *warm site*.

Column A characteristic or property of an entity; also called an *attribute* or a *field*.

Commit A successful completion of a transaction. As a Git term, to save changes in the main repository.

Comparison operator An operator used to compare values. Valid operators are =, <, >, <=, >=, < >, and !=. Also called a *relational operator*.

Compatible A computer that could do everything the IBM PC could do. Also called a *clone*.

Composite entity An entity in the entity-relationship model used to implement a many-to-many relationship.

Composite key An identifier consisting of a combination of two or more fields that is used when more than one column is necessary to make a row unique in a table; also, an index with more than one key field.

Composite primary key An identifier used when more than one column is necessary to make a row unique in a table. See also *primary key*.

Compound condition Two simple conditions (criteria) in a query that are combined with the AND or OR operators.

Compound criterion Two simple criteria (conditions) in a query that are combined with the AND or OR operators.

Computed field A field whose value is computed from other fields in the database; also called a *calculated field*.

Computer-aided design and manufacturing (CAD/CAM) A system used to design and manufacture prototypes, finished products, and production runs.

Concatenation The combination of two or more rows in an operation, such as a join, or the combination of two or more columns for a primary key field to uniquely identify a given row in the table; also, joining two or more strings of textual data into one piece of data.

Concurrent update When multiple users make updates to the same database at the same time.

Consistency A transaction property requiring that a transaction may change data in only predetermined, allowable ways.

Console A panel of lights, switches, and knobs that controlled various aspects of a mainframe computer's operation.

Conversion When a visitor to a website completes a desired action, such as making a purchase or requesting information.

CREATE INDEX The SQL command that creates an index in a table.

Create, read, update, and delete (CRUD) Operations required by and performed in all database management systems.

CREATE TABLE The SQL command used to describe the layout of a table. The word TABLE is followed by the name of the table to be created and then by the names and data types of the columns (fields) that comprise the table.

Criteria More than one criterion or condition.

Criterion A statement that can be either true or false. In queries, only records for which the statement is true will be included; also called a *condition*. The plural is *criteria*.

Crowdsourced processing power An implementation of client/server computing that allows a device to share its processing power when it's not being used.

Crow's foot notation An E-R diagram implementation that uses a symbol on the side of the "many" entity resembling a crow's foot.

CRUD (create, read, update, and delete) Operations required by and performed in all database management systems.

CSS (Cascading Style Sheets) The standard language to style and position content on a webpage.

CSV (comma-separated text file) A delimited text file that uses a comma to separate values.

Cube In OLAP, a data structure that aggregates data by hierarchies for each of the dimensions you want to analyze.

Culture An organization's values, beliefs, norms, and habits.

Cyberattack An attempt by unauthorized users to damage or destroy a computer network or system.

Cybersecurity The process of protecting networks, devices, and data from any type of digital attack or cyberattack.

Dashboard A one-page grouping of key performance indicators (KPIs) that allow decision makers to quickly evaluate and act on important data.

Data-definition language (DDL) The part of SQL used for creating and altering database objects.

Data analyst A job title for a person who uses tools and algorithms to mine a database for answers, information, trends, and insights in internal organization data.

Data archiving The process of moving data that is not needed on a regular basis by the functions of the organization to a separate storage device for long-term retention.

Database-as-a-service A database hosted online that typically provides access for a monthly fee; a service provider manages and maintains the database so that the subscribing company does not need to locally manage the infrastructure and personnel that support the database.

Database A collection of data organized in a manner that allows access, retrieval, and use of that data.

Database administrator (DBA) The person or group in charge of a database. Also called *database administration (DBA)*.

Database analyst A role that creates logical views of the data to respond to user and application requests, and summarizes and analyzes data to extract trends, insights, and knowledge.

Database architect A role that focuses on database design in helping to determine new information requirements, building logical views for users and processes, and helping to convert research into better products.

Database architecture How hardware and software are organized, implemented, and operated to process data. Types include centralized, client/server, data warehouse, and distributed systems.

Database design The process of creating the entities, attributes, and relationships between tables of data.

Database Design Language (DBDL) A relational-like language that is used to represent the result of the database design process.

Database Documenter An Access tool that allows you to print detailed documentation about any table, query, report, form, or other object in the database.

Database management system (DBMS) A program through which users interact with the data stored in a database.

Database operations manager A role that focuses on a specific, important DBA task such as backup-and-recovery, security, or government regulations and compliance. Also called the *task-oriented DBA*.

Database performance The ability of the production system to serve users in a timely and responsive manner.

Database replication Distributing a copy of a database to many computers or locations.

Database schema A model or blueprint of the tables and relationships between the tables in a database.

Database server In a three-tier client/server architecture, a server that performs database functions.

Data center The hardware in the cloud infrastructure, including servers, storage devices, and high-speed networks. Also called a *server farm*.

Data concurrency A characteristic of a system that allows many users to access data at the same time.

Data consistency A characteristic of a system that allows each user to see a consistent view of the data, including real-time changes made by others.

Data dictionary A read-only set of tables that provides information about the objects in a database, including default values and database user names.

Data file A file that stores data about a single entity in one table or list.

Data independence A quality that allows you to change the structure of a database without requiring you to make major changes to the programs that access the database.

Data integrity constraint A requirement that helps to ensure the accuracy and consistency of individual field values.

Data macro An automatic process that runs when a table event occurs.

Data mining The practice of uncovering new knowledge, patterns, trends, and rules from data.

Data modeler A role that performs data modeling for a particular business area by collecting and analyzing data requirements.

Data modification anomaly A problem generated when entering, updating, and deleting data in a database table.

Data redundancy The duplication of data, or the storing of the same data in more than one place.

Data schema A description of the table, table properties, fields, and field properties within that table.

Data scientist A data professional that analyzes massive sets of data, typically in a stand-alone department, to model, interpret, and present insights from internal, external, and big data.

Data security Protection of data from threats including the prevention of unauthorized access to the database, encryption of data as it travels through a network, protection against data corruption, and protection against all other electronic and physical attacks to the data.

Datasheet View An Access view that shows a table as a collection of rows and columns, similar to a spreadsheet.

Data type The field property that determines what field values you can enter for the field and what other properties the field will have.

Data visualization The representation of information in the form of an easy-to-understand chart, diagram, or picture.

Data visualization expert A role that works with data to visually present patterns, trends, anomalies, and other significant information in the form of a chart, diagram, picture, infographic, map, or other graphical or pictorial format.

Data warehouse A subject-oriented, integrated, time-variant, nonvolatile collection of data in support of management's decision-making process.

Data warehouse administrator A role that requires traditional DBA skills plus knowledge of data warehousing technologies.

Data warehouse architecture The hardware and software an organization needs to address the analytical requirements of users without disrupting traditional operations.

DBA (database administrator) The person or group in charge of a database.

dBase One of the first popular database programs.

Decrypting Reversing the encryption on a database and removing the password.

DELETE SQL keyword to delete records in a relational database.

DELETE command The SQL command used to delete a table. The word DELETE is followed by a FROM clause identifying the table. Use a WHERE clause to specify a condition. Any records satisfying the condition will be deleted.

Delete query A query that permanently deletes all the records satisfying the criteria entered in the query.

Deletion anomaly The unintended loss of data due to deletion of other data.

Denormalizing To convert a table in third normal form to a table with redundant data.

Department of Defense (DOD) 5015.2 Standard Data management requirements for the DOD and for companies supplying or dealing with the DOD.

Design grid In Access, the area in which you specify the fields to include in the query results, a sort order for the query results, any criteria, and other instructions.

Design View An Access view in which the structure of an object can be manipulated.

Difference When comparing tables, the set of all rows that are in the first table but that are not in the second table.

Dimension All of the levels of a hierarchy.

Dirty read A transaction that reads data that has been written by another transaction but has not been committed yet.

Disaster recovery plan A set of documents that specifies the ongoing and emergency actions and procedures required to ensure data availability if a disaster occurs.

Disaster recovery planning The process of documenting and practicing a step-by-step plan of instructions to minimize the effects of a natural disaster on the mission-critical operations of a business.

Distributed database A single logical database that is physically divided among computers at several sites on a computer network.

Division The relational algebra command that combines tables and searches for rows in the first table that match all rows in the second table.

Document database management system A database that stores data in a set of descriptive documents rather than the specific columns, rows, tables, and relationships of a relational database.

DOS (Disk Operating System) The first operating system for the IBM PC.

Drill down To analyze lower levels of aggregation, such as sales for a particular sales representative for a particular month.

DROP INDEX The SQL command that drops (deletes) an index.

DROP TABLE The SQL command that drops (deletes) a table from a database.

Dumb terminal A computer screen that has no processing power itself. Also called a *monitor* or *terminal*.

Durability A transaction property guaranteeing that committed transactions are permanent.

Element A sequence of characters or other symbols that indicates how the file should look when it is printed or displayed or to describe the document's logical structure. Also called a *tag*.

Embedded analytics Integrating data with external facing applications to create meaningful collaborative evaluations of data with a company's business partners such as their customers or suppliers.

Encapsulation A concept that helps hide and protect data by restricting access only to public methods.

Encryption Converting the data in a database to a format that is indecipherable by anyone other than an authorized user.

End user A person directly interacting with an information system.

Enterprise-level system A large-scale database management system that can support thousands of simultaneous users across the world.

Entity-relationship (E-R) diagram A graphic model for database design in which entities are represented as rectangles and relationships are represented as either arrows or diamonds connected to the entities they relate. Also called an *ERD*.

Entity A person, place, event, item, or other transaction for which you want to store and process data. Also called a *table*.

Entity integrity The rule that no column (attribute) that is part of the primary key may accept null values.

Entity-relationship model (ERM) An approach to representing data in a database that uses E-R diagrams exclusively as the tool for representing entities, attributes, and relationships.

E-R model An approach to representing data in a database that uses E-R diagrams exclusively as the tool for representing entities, attributes, and relationships.

E-R diagram A graphic model for database design in which entities are represented as rectangles and relationships are represented as either arrows or diamonds connected to the entities they relate.

ETL (extract, transform, load) Three database functions that are combined into one tool to retrieve data from one database and place it into another database.

Exclusive mode A way of opening a database so that you are the only user currently working in the database and have also locked all other users and processes from accessing it.

Execute button In MySQL, the button you use to run SQL statements.

Expression A combination of data and operators that results in a single value.

Extensible The quality of a system that allows it to define new data types.

Extensible Data Schema (XSD) A file type that stores the data schema, which is a description of the table, table properties, fields, and field properties within that table.

Extensible Markup Language (XML) A web-related specification managed by the W3C (w3.org) and designed for the exchange of data on the web.

Extensible Stylesheet Language (XSL) A file type that determines the styling and layout of the data. XSL is a standard W3C language for creating stylesheets for XML documents.

Family Educational Rights and Privacy Act (FERPA) A federal law that affords parents the right to have access to their children's education records, the right to seek to have the records amended, and the right to have some control over the disclosure of personally identifiable information from the education records.

Fat client In a client/server architecture or network, a client computer that typically provides rich functionality independent of the central server.

FERPA (Family Educational Rights and Privacy Act) The Family Educational Rights and Privacy Act, a federal law that protects the rights of students and parents regarding educational records.

Field A characteristic or property of an entity; also called an *attribute* or a *column*.

Field property A characteristic that defines each field such as Indexed, Field Size, Validation Rule, and Validation Text.

File-level password A password that allows access to an entire file.

File level Tasks such as those for security, encryption, and backup are applied to the entire database file, including all tables, queries, and other objects that the database may contain.

Firewall Software that prevents the unauthorized access to a network or server, and can protect against electronic attacks on a database.

First normal form (1NF) A table (relation) is in first normal form when it does not contain repeating groups (more than one value in an attribute), each column contains atomic values, and it has no duplicate records.

Flat file A file that stores data in lists that have no relationship to other lists.

FOREIGN KEY clause The clause in an SQL CREATE TABLE or ALTER TABLE command that specifies referential integrity.

Foreign key field (FK) In a one-to-many relationship between two tables, the field in the "many" table that links the table to the primary key field in the "one" table.

Form A screen object used to maintain and view data from a database.

Format An Access field property that controls how information is displayed and printed.

Forward recovery A DBMS recovery method that applies the after images of committed transactions from the log to a backup to bring the database up to date.

Fourth normal form (4NF) A table is in fourth normal form if it is in third normal form and contains no multivalued dependencies.

Framework A set of standards, development tools, and software libraries that help programmers develop software solutions faster and with more consistency across programmers. Also called a *software framework*.

FROM clause The part of an SQL SELECT command that indicates the tables in the query.

Front-end database A database that contains all of the queries, data entry forms, reports, and other objects. Instead of physical tables, it contains links to the tables physically stored in the back-end database.

Front-end machine A historical term for "client." Also called a *front-end processor*.

Front-end processor A historical term for "client." Also called a *front-end machine*.

Full stack A set of front-end and back-end web technologies.

Function Part of an expression used to calculate the number of entries, the sum or average of all the entries in a given column, or the largest or smallest of the entries in a given column; also called *aggregate function*.

Functional dependence Attributes depending on or relating to other attributes in a relation.

Functionally dependent Column B is functionally dependent on column A (or on a collection of columns) if a value for column A determines a single value for column B at any one time.

Geographic information system (GIS) A computer system that analyzes and displays geographically referenced information.

Git A free and open source distributed version control system that allows multiple developers to work on the same code base using distributed copies of the code.

GitHub A popular website for hosting projects that use the Git language for version control. See also *BitBucket*.

GLAPPR "Traditional" operations of a business that include the internal processes of general ledger, accounts payable, and payroll.

Google Analytics A service provided by Google that tracks and reports website information such as session duration, the number of pages accessed per session, the bounce rate, and the geographical location of visitors.

GRANT The SQL command that provides privileges to users, including the right to select, insert, update, and delete table data.

Graph database A database that emphasizes connections between data elements, which accelerates queries. Commonly used in recommendation engines and AI applications.

Graphical user interface (GUI) A visual way of interacting with a computer using items such as icons and menus instead of textual commands.

Group To create collections of records that share a common characteristic.

GROUP BY clause The SQL keywords to group records together in order to count, sum, or do other statistics on groups of records.

Grouping field The field that divides records into groups based on the values in the specified field.

Hadoop A set of open source modules released by the Apache Software Foundation that provide the infrastructure for big data analytics.

Hard copy A physical printout of computer data.

HAVING clause The part of an SQL SELECT command that restricts the groups to be displayed.

Health Insurance Portability and Accountability Act (HIPAA) A federal law that specifies the rules for storing, handling, and protecting healthcare transaction data.

Hierarchy A tree structure for data where every piece of data is a child of the next level in the hierarchy.

High-level programming language A programming language that uses commands and other keywords that are similar to human language.

Hot site A backup site that an organization can switch to within minutes because the site is completely equipped with duplicate hardware, software, and data and may even run in parallel to the production system.

HTTP (HyperText Transfer Protocol) The data communication method used by web clients and web servers to exchange data on the Internet.

HyperText Markup Language (HTML) The standard markup language to describe content on a webpage.

IBM System/360 mainframe The first widely installed commercial mainframe computer system.

IBM System/370 mainframe An improvement upon the IBM System/360 mainframe sold in the 1970s.

IIF An Access function that returns one value if a specified condition evaluates to true, or another value if it evaluates to false

Index A behind-the-scenes, system-generated copy of a selected field or fields organized in ascending or descending order so that when data in that field is used in a search or sorted, the process is much faster than it would be without the predeveloped index.

Index key The field or fields on which an index is built.

Information-level design Describing the attributes needed for each entity as well as the relationships between the entities based on business rules.

Information system A collection of data, people, procedures, stored data, software, hardware, and information required to support a specific set of related functions.

Information systems analysis The process of collecting and interpreting facts, identifying problems, and documenting the components of an system in order to define what a new information system should do.

Inheritance A concept that gives new classes and objects all of the properties and methods of the parent class. Sometimes inheritance is defined as the "is/a" or "has/a" relationship between two objects.

INNER JOIN The SQL command that selects records that have matching values in both tables.

Input Mask An Access field property that provides a visual guide for users as they enter data.

INSERT SQL keyword to insert records in a relational database.

INSERT command The SQL command to add new data to a table. After the words INSERT INTO, you list the name of the table, followed by the word VALUES. Then you list the values for each of the columns in parentheses.

INSERT INTO clause The SQL keywords for adding a new record to a table.

Insertion anomaly Being unable to add data to the database due to absence of other data.

InStr An Access function that returns the position of a character within a string (one or more characters).

Integrated In a data warehouse, to store data in one place even if the data may originates from many external sources.

Integrated development environment (IDE) A software suite that provides basic tools required to write and test software.

Integrity A database has integrity if the data in it satisfies all established integrity constraints.

Integrity constraint A rule that must be followed by data in a database.

International Organization for Standardization (ISO) An international standard-setting body composed of representatives from various national standards organizations.

INTERSECT The relational algebra command for performing the intersection of two tables.

Intersection When comparing tables, an intersection is a new table containing all rows that are in both original tables.

Interview A planned meeting during which you obtain system requirements from other people.

In the cloud A metaphor for data and processes run through the Internet.

IoT (Internet of Things) Everyday objects connected via the Internet, enabling them to send and receive data.

Isolation A transaction property that determines when other users can see the updates made by the transaction.

JavaScript The standard front-end scripting language used to respond to user interactivity such as clicks and entries on a webpage.

JavaScript engine Browser technology that process JavaScript code.

JOIN The relational algebra command that connects two tables on the basis of common data.

Join To connect two tables based on common data.

Join column The column on which two tables are joined. Also see *join*.

Join line In an Access query, the line drawn between tables to indicate how they are related.

Journal A record of all the updates made to a database and stored separately from the database. Also called a *log*.

Journaling To maintain a journal, or log, of all updates to the database.

JSON (JavaScript Object Notation) A lightweight and self-describing format for storing and transporting data often used when data is sent from a server to a webpage.

Junction table The table that serves on the "many" side of a one-to-many relationship with each of the two original tables in a many-to-many relationship.

Key-value database A database that stores simple key/value pairs of data.

Key/value pair An abstract data type that includes a group of key identifiers and a set of associated values.

Key integrity constraint A primary key or foreign key restriction. Primary keys are constrained to a unique value for each

record. Foreign key fields are constrained to values previously entered in the primary key field value of the table on the "one" side of a relationship when referential integrity is enforced on a relationship.

Key performance indicator (KPI) A critical indicator of progress toward an intended result.

Key symbol In Access, the symbol that identifies the primary key field in each table.

Keyword A word that SQL uses for defining, manipulating, and accessing databases. Also called a *reserved word*.

Killer application Software that is so necessary or desirable, it justifies the expense of whatever hardware platform is required to run it.

LAMP (Linux, Apache, MySQL, PHP) A popular server-side web app development software stack that includes Linux, Apache, MySQL, and PHP.

LAPP (Linux, Apache, PostgreSQL, PHP) A popular server-side web app development software stack that includes Linux, Apache, PostgreSQL, and PHP.

Late binding The association of an operation to actual program code when the code is run.

Left An Access function that returns the position of a character within a string (one or more characters).

LEFT JOIN The SQL command that selects all records in the table on the "one" side of a one-to-many relationship even if they do not have any matching records in the "many" table.

Legacy program Software that at one time was valuable to a business, but is now out of date.

Legal-values integrity The property that no record can exist in the database with a value in a field other than a legal value.

Legal value An acceptable, valid value in a field.

Len An Access function that determines the total number of characters in a specified field.

Level In a hierarchy, a category or subcategory of data.

Live system The combination of hardware, software, and database that the users and regular applications of the company use. Also called a *production system*.

Local area network (LAN) A computer network that spans a relatively small geographic area.

Log A record of all the updates made to a database and stored separately from the database. Also called a *journal*.

Logical view Refers to the result of a query because it is not a copy of the data, but rather, a selected view of data from the underlying tables.

Lookup properties Field properties that allow you to supply a drop-down list of values for a field.

Lookup table A table that contains one record for each possible value for a particular field.

Major sort key When sorting on two fields, the more important field; also called a *primary* sort key.

Make-table query A query that creates a new table in the current or another database with the records selected by the query.

Malware Malicious software of any sort that exploits system vulnerabilities such as a bug in an operating system that allows an unauthorized user access to a computer.

Many-to-many relationship A relationship between three entities in which each occurrence of each entity can be related to many occurrences of each of the other entities.

Markup language A system for annotating a document for the processing, definition, and presentation of text.

Master-slave configuration A database configuration where one location contains the master copy of the database, and another copy, also called the replica, is refreshed when it is reconnected to the master.

MEAN (MongoDB, Express.js, AngularJS, Node.js) A popular server-side web app development software stack that includes MongoDB, Express.js, AngularJS, and Node.js.

Merge (Git command) To integrate independent lines of development into a single branch.

MERN (MongoDB, Express.js, React.js, Node.js) A popular server-side web app development software stack that includes MongoDB, Express.js, React.js, and Node.js.

Metadata Information about information; also descriptive data stored with input sources.

Method An HTTP action performed on resources or files at the server, often at the request of a user working in a webpage. HTTP methods include POST, GET, PATCH, and DELETE; also, in an object-oriented programming language, a task an object can complete.

Microsoft ASP.NET A popular software framework that includes Microsoft Visual Studio, C#, and SQL Server. Also called *ASP.NET* and *.NET*.

Microsoft Azure SQL Database A popular database-as-a-service product.

Microsoft Power BI A business analytics solution that lets you visualize data and easily share that visualization with others or embed it in a webpage.

Minor sort key When sorting on two fields, the less important field; also called *secondary* sort key.

MIS (Management Information Systems) A department that oversees the installation and maintenance of hardware and software to support processes, operations, and information technology in an organization.

Mission critical A system that is essential to the survival of a business, including the central relational database system that manages the traditional business processes of an organization.

Mobile-friendly A website designed for quick access to common functionality on small screens.

MongoDB A popular document database management system that stores data in a set of descriptive documents.

Monitor A computer screen that has no processing power itself. Also called a *terminal* or *dumb terminal*.

Monospaced A font face that gives each character the same horizontal width.

Moore's Law An observation attributed to Gordon Moore, who, as a co-founder of Intel, predicted in 1975 that the number of transistors on a chip would likely double every two years.

MSI file A Microsoft installer package file format used by Windows for installation, storage, and removal of programs.

Multiple-column index An index with more than one key field.

Multiple-field index An index with more than one key field.

MySQL A free, open source relational database management system (RDBMS) from Oracle.

MySQL Shell Command-line interface software that allows you to communicate with a MySQL database.

MySQL Workbench An integrated visual tool that helps you manage MySQL databases on Windows-based machines.

N-tier architecture Another term for three-tier architecture that emphasizes adding application servers for scalability without affecting the design for the client or the database server.

Natural join The most common form of a join.

Nonkey attribute An attribute (column) that is not part of the primary key.

Nonkey column An attribute (column) that is not part of the primary key.

Nonrepeatable (fuzzy) read A type of transaction that rereads data it has previously read and finds that another committed transaction has modified or deleted that data.

Nonvolatile In a data warehouse, read-only data.

Normal form A defined standard structure for relational databases in which a relation may not be nested within another relation.

Normalization process A series of progressive steps that enable you to identify and correct data redundancy and integrity problems that occur when data is stored in one large table.

NoSQL A database management system such as MongoDB that uses a document model made up of collections and documents to store data.

NoSQL database system A database that does not use a table-oriented, relational model, but a more flexible system that can accommodate structured, semi-structured, and unstructured data. NoSQL means "not only SQL."

NOT operator An operator that reverses the result of the original condition.

Null An intentional "nothing" value meaning "unknown" or "not applicable."

Object-oriented database management system (OODBMS) A database that encapsulates all data in the form of an object.

Object-oriented language A programming language that organizes data and methods in objects that collaborate with one another.

Object A set of related attributes along with the actions that are associated with the attributes. In object-oriented terminology, a container for properties and methods. Sometimes referred to as an instance of a class.

Object Dependencies An Access tool that helps you identify all objects dependent on a particular table, query, form, or report as well as the objects that the particular table or query depends on.

ODBC (Open Database Connectivity) A standard application programming interface (API) for accessing DBMSs designed to be independent of database systems and operating systems.

Office Open XML A compressed version of XML used in Microsoft Excel, PowerPoint, and Word.

Offsite A location separate from where the database is used for normal processing, such as a server in a different physical location from the production server.

One-to-many relationship A relationship between two entities in which each occurrence of the first entity is related to many occurrences of the second entity, and each occurrence of the second entity is related to at most one occurrence of the first entity.

One-to-one relationship A relationship between two entities in which each occurrence of the first entity is related to one occurrence of the second entity, and each occurrence of the second entity is related to at most one occurrence of the first entity.

Online analytical processing (OLAP) A database technology that optimizes data for querying, analyzing, and reporting, especially in multidimensional databases in a data warehouse environment.

Online transaction processing (OLTP) Database software designed to support transaction-related applications.

Open-ended question A question that requires a general response, such as "How do you currently create estimates for new projects?"

Open architecture A computer for which enough hardware and operating system details are provided so that other vendors can build additional hardware components and write software applications for the computer.

Open source Software, including its original code, that may be modified and redistributed freely.

Operator A mathematical symbol used in an expression to combine different values, resulting in a single value.

OR criteria Combination of criteria in which only one criterion must be true.

ORDER BY clause The part of an SQL SELECT command that indicates a sort order.

Organizational structure The hierarchical arrangement of lines of authority (who reports to whom), communication, rights, and duties.

OR operator An operator that connects conditions when only one condition must be true to select a particular record.

Orphan record A record in the "many" (child) table that has no match in the "one" (parent) table in a one-to-many relationship.

OUTER join The form of a join in which all records appear, even if they don't match.

Parallel database system A single, shared database that can balance the workload among CPUs to improve overall throughput.

Parameter query A query that allows you to enter criterion when you run the query, as opposed to placing it in the Access design grid.

Parent table The table on the "one" side of a "one-to-many" relationship.

Parsing To process code and translate it into content on a webpage.

Password A string of characters that a user must enter along with a user ID to access a database.

Patriot Act A federal law that specifies data retention requirements for the identification of clients opening accounts at financial institutions, allows law enforcement agencies to search companies' and individuals' records and communications, and expands the government's authority to regulate financial transactions.

Pencil symbol A visual identifier that indicates when a record is locked for editing.

Performance analyst A role that concentrates on database performance, requiring detailed technical knowledge of the database management system, indexes, and SQL so that improvements can be made in speed and response times.

Persistence The quality of a system that allows it to remember its data from one execution to the next.

Personal computer A computer with memory and a hard drive, intended to be used by a single person.

Phantom read A type of transaction that reruns a query returning a set of rows that satisfies a search condition, and finds that another committed transaction has inserted additional rows that satisfy the condition. Also called a *phantom*.

Physical-level design Implementing the entities, attributes, constraints, and relationships in an RDBMS.

PivotChart A graphical representation of the data in a PivotTable.

PivotTable A crosstabular organization of summarized data.

Polymorphism A concept that allows a particular method to work in different ways based on how it is used.

Presentation function A database service that manages data presented to users, such as determining which form to display and how to format the form's data. Also called a *user interface function*.

Presidential Records Act A federal law that regulates the data retention requirements for all communications, including electronic communications, of U.S. presidents and vice presidents.

Primary key The column or columns that uniquely identify a row in a table.

PRIMARY KEY clause The SQL clause that is used in a CREATE TABLE or ALTER TABLE command to set a table's primary key field(s).

Primary key field A field that contains unique information for each record. A primary key field cannot contain a null entry.

Primary sort key When sorting on two fields, the more important field; also called a *major sort key*.

Privacy The right of individuals to have certain information about them kept confidential.

Procedure A series of steps followed in a regular, specified order to accomplish an end result.

Production system The combination of hardware, software, and database that the users and regular applications of the company use. Also called a *live system*.

Product The table obtained by concatenating every row in the first table with every row in the second table.

Product manager A role that directs the activities specific to a product or technical service such as access to a database.

PROJECT The relational algebra command used to select columns from a table.

Property A characteristic of an object. A property may store a single value or another object.

Proprietary architecture A computer for which system details are divulged only within the company that manufactures the machine so that other companies could not build complimentary components or software.

Proprietary Owning or holding exclusive right to something.

Pull (Git command) To fetch and download content from a remote repository and update the local repository to match that content.

Qualified field name A convention that identifies a field name by adding the table name followed by a period, followed by the field name.

Qualify To indicate the table (relation) of which a given column (attribute) is a part by preceding the column name with the table name. For example, Clients.Street indicates the column named Street in the table named Clients.

Query A question structured in a way that the DBMS can recognize and process.

Query-By-Example (QBE) A visual interface that helps you retrieve data from relational databases.

Query Design View The Access window in which you develop queries by specifying the fields, sort order, and limiting criteria that determine which fields and records are displayed in the resulting datasheet.

Query optimizer A DBMS component that analyzes a query and attempts to determine the most efficient way to execute it.

RAD (rapid application development) An agile software development methodology that emphasizes working software and user feedback over strict planning and requirements recording.

RAID (redundant array of inexpensive/independent drives) A system in which database updates are replicated to multiple hard drives so that an organization can continue to process database updates after losing one of its hard drives.

Read-only A version of a file allows you to display (read) the data, but not to edit or modify it.

Read-only data Data that cannot be edited, added to, deleted, or otherwise modified by users.

Read-only snapshot Highly consolidated and summ*arized data* from multiple internal and external sources that are refreshed periodically as needed by users.

Record-level locking Rights that allow two or more users to simultaneously work in the same database file, but not simultaneously enter or update the same record.

Record A collection of related fields that describe one item in a table; can be thought of as a row in a table. Also called a *row* or *tuple*.

Recovery point objective (RPO) The maximum amount of data you are willing to lose in a disaster.

Recovery Returning a database that has encountered a problem to a state that is known to be correct.

Recovery time objective (RTO) The length of time it takes a company to resume mission-critical services after a disaster.

Redundancy The duplication of data, or the storing of the same data in more than one place.

Referential integrity A relational database concept that sets rules called integrity constraints on table relationships primarily to prevent the creation of orphan records.

Relational algebra A query language that takes instances of relations as input and yields instances of relations as output.

Relational database A collection of related tables of data.

Relational operator An operator used to compare values. Valid operators are =, <, >, <=, >=, < >, and !=. Also called a *comparison operator*.

Relation A two-dimensional table-style collection of data in which all entries are single-valued, each column has a distinct name, all the values in a column are values of the attribute that is identified by the *column name*, the order of columns is immaterial, each row is distinct, and the order of rows is immaterial. Also called a *table*.

Relationship An association between entities.

Relationship report An Access report that shows the table names, field names, and relationships between the tables in the database.

Render To generate content, typically from computer code.

Repeating group Multiple entries for a single record in a table.

Replica A copy of a database stored separate from the master copy.

Report A database object that creates a professional printout of data.

Research analyst A role that performs the tasks of a database analyst when the job responsibilities focus on the analysis of specific research data.

Reserved word A word that SQL uses for defining, manipulating, and accessing databases. Also called a *keyword*.

Result Grid Shows the result of running the SQL statements in the upper SQL panel of the MySQL Workbench window.

Return value The data a function returns when it completes its task.

REVOKE The SQL command that removes privileges granted to users.

Right An Access function that returns a string (one or more characters) containing a specified number of characters from the right side of a string.

RIGHT JOIN The SQL command that *selects* all records in the table on the "many" side of a one-to-many relationship even if they do not have any matching records in the "one" table.

Rollback A DBMS recovery method that restores a database to a valid state by reading the log for problem transactions and applying the before images to undo their updates. Also called a *backward recovery*.

Roll up To analyze higher levels of aggregation, such as sales for all districts for a particular quarter.

Row A collection of related fields. Also called a *record* or *tuple*.

Ruby on Rails An open source web app development stack that comes embedded with open source SQLite as the relational database, though larger Ruby/Rails projects use MySQL.

Run-book A log of all database maintenance, with dates, license keys, issues or updates, involved personnel, and resolutions.

Sandbox A system separate from the production system that programmers use to develop new programs and modify existing programs. Also called a *test system*.

Sarbanes–Oxley (SOX) Act A federal law that specifies data retention and verification requirements for public companies.

Scalability The ease and capacity to grow.

Schema In MySQL, represents all of the tables of data, views, stored procedures, and functions that are associated with that database.

Script A type of file that executes a series of commands when run.

Scripting language A programming language designed to create small, specific programs as opposed to complete, large applications.

Scrub To remove and fix orphan records in a relational database.

Secondary key (SK) A field or combination of fields that may not be unique, but which is commonly used for retrieval and thus should be indexed.

Secondary sort key When sorting on two fields, the less important field; also called *minor* sort key.

Second normal form (2NF) A relation is in second normal form if it is in first normal form and no nonkey attribute is depends on only a portion of the primary key.

SEC Rule 17a-4 A Security and Exchange Commission rule that specifies the retention requirements of all electronic communications and records for financial and investment entities.

SELECT-FROM-WHERE The basic form of an SQL data-retrieval command.

SELECT SQL keyword to select fields and records from a relational database; also, the relational algebra command to select rows from a table.

SELECT clause The part of an SQL SELECT command that indicates the columns to include in the query results.

Select query A query that selects fields and records from the database. Also called a *simple query*.

Semantic markup An element or tag using language that meaningfully describes the data within it.

Server A centralized computer that stores the database and provides services to the clients in a client/server system; also a computer or program that provides functionality for other programs or devices and access to resources, especially network resources.

Server farm The hardware in the cloud infrastructure, including servers, storage devices, and high-speed networks. Also called a *data center*.

Session duration The length of time a visitor spends at a website.

Simple condition A condition that involves only a single field and a single value.

Simple query A query that selects fields and records from the database. Also called a *Select query*.

Single-column index An index built on a single field (column).

Single-field index An index built on a single field (column).

Slice and dice To select only a portion of data in a cube, such as sales for a particular district rather than a particular quarter.

Smart card A card with built-in processing logic that can be programmed to periodically change and synchronize with passwords so that only the person who has physical possession of the card can successfully access the system. Also called a *smart fob*.

Smart fob A card with built-in processing logic that can be programmed to periodically change and synchronize with passwords so that only the person who has physical possession of the card can successfully access the system. Also called a *smart card*.

Snapshot A collection of data that is current as of a particular moment in time such as the previous day, week or month; also, the contents (files and folders) of a repository at a particular point in time.

Soft copy Computer output displayed on a screen.

Software framework A set of standards, development tools, and software libraries that help programmers develop software solutions faster and with more consistency across programmers. Also called a *framework*.

Software release The distribution of a final version of software that may include new features or bug fixes.

Software stack A group of programs and technologies that commonly work together to build a digital solution. Also called a *solution stack* or *technology stack*.

Solution stack A group of programs and technologies that commonly work together to build a digital solution. Also called a *software stack* or *technology stack*.

Sort key The field on which records are sorted.

Sort To arrange rows in a table or results of a query in a particular order.

Spyware/malware detection software Programs that can detect and stop cyberattack threats at the first point of entry.

Spyware Software that enables an intruder to covertly obtain information about a computer's activities such as the keystrokes made on the keyboard.

SQL See *Structured Query Language (SQL)*.

SQLite An open source relational database.

SQL keywords (INSERT, SELECT, UPDATE, DELETE) SQL commands that enable users to select data, insert rows, edit data, and delete rows.

SQL panel The area of the MySQL Workbench window where you enter SQL commands.

Stage (Git term) To continue making changes to a working directory or code base.

Stateless A type of communications in which no connection or session information is retained by the receiver, usually a server.

Stored procedure A file containing a collection of compiled and optimized SQL statements that are available for future use.

String Text data, including spaces, symbols, and punctuation marks.

Structured data Data that is traditional in its retrieval and storage in database management systems.

Structured Query Language (SQL) A very popular relational data definition and manipulation language that is used in many relational DBMSs.

Stylesheet A document that specifies how to process the data contained in another document and present the data in a web browser, in a printed report, on a mobile device, in a sound device, or in other presentation media.

Subdatasheet A datasheet that is nested within another datasheet to show related records; the subdatasheet shows the records on the "many" side of a one-to-many relationship.

Subform A form placed within a form that shows related records from another table or query; generally displays many records at a time in a datasheet arrangement.

Subject-oriented In a data warehouse, to organize data by topic rather than by the application that uses the data.

Subquery An SQL SELECT statement placed inside another SELECT statement and contained within parentheses so it will be evaluated first.

SUBTRACT The relational algebra command for performing the difference of two tables.

Synchronization A process to apply and reconcile updates and changes from various copies of a database with the master.

Syntax The rules by which statements in a language such as SQL must be written.

System catalog A structure that contains information about the objects (tables, columns, indexes, views, and so on) in a database. Also called the *catalog*.

System DBA A role that focuses on technical rather than business issues, primarily in the system administration area such as the installation, performance, and maintenance of the database management system.

System requirement A feature that must be included in an information system to fulfill business, legal, or user needs.

System software Programs that control the hardware and software environment.

System table A table containing metadata about the database.

Table A person, place, event, item, or other transaction for which you want to store and process data. Also called an *entity*.

Tableau A data visualization company and product.

Table event A definable action that occurs in a database table such as adding, changing, or deleting data in a record.

Table privilege An access right that can be applied to any table or view in the database.

Tag A sequence of characters or other symbols that indicates how the file should look when it is printed or displayed or to describe the document's logical structure. Also called an *element*.

Task-oriented DBA A role that focuses on a specific, important DBA task such as backup-and-recovery, security, or government regulations and compliance. Also called the *database operations manager*.

Technology stack A group of programs and technologies that commonly work together to build a digital solution. Also called a *software stack* or *solution stack*.

Terminal A computer screen that has no processing power itself. Also called a *monitor* or *dumb terminal*.

Test system A system separate from the production system that programmers use to develop new programs and modify existing programs. Also called a *sandbox*.

Thin client In a client/server architecture or network, a computer that runs from resources stored on a central server instead of a local hard drive.

Third normal form (3NF) A table is in third normal form if it is in second normal form and the only determinants it contains are candidate keys.

Three-tier architecture A computer architecture in which the clients perform the presentation functions, a database server performs the database functions, and separate centralized computers called application servers perform the business functions and serve as an interface between clients and the database server.

Time-variant In a data warehouse, data that represents snapshots of data at various points in time in the past, such as at the end of each month.

Timestamping A technique that determines the order in which records should be processed based on an automatic timestamp applied to a record; it avoids the need to lock rows in the database.

Transaction A task a user completes in a DBMS.

Transitive dependency A nonkey attribute determining another nonkey attribute.

Trigger An action that occurs automatically in response to an associated database operation such as INSERT, UPDATE, or DELETE.

Tuning Database administrations tasks that include creating and deleting indexes, minimizing the complexity of each view to only what is needed, and changing the table design.

Tuple A collection of related fields; can be thought of as a row in a table. Also called a *record* or *row*.

Two-phase locking To block other transactions from accessing the same data during the transaction's life.

Two-tier architecture A client/server arrangement where the server performs database functions and the clients perform presentation functions (or user interface functions).

Unified Modeling Language (UML) A standardized modeling approach used to model all the various aspects of software development for object-oriented systems. UML includes a way to represent database designs.

Uninterruptible power supply (UPS) A power source such as a battery or fuel cell for short interruptions and a power generator for longer outages.

Union A combination of two tables consisting of all records that are in either table.

UNION The relational algebra command that combines two tables consisting of all records that are in either table.

Union compatible Two tables are union compatible if they have the same number of fields and if their corresponding fields have identical data types.

Unique An Access index property that when set to Yes, requires every value in the index to be unique.

Unnormalized Data that doesn't meet the standards of 1NF.

Unnormalized relation A relation (table) that contains a repeating group (or multiple entries for a single record).

Unstructured data Data not organized or easily interpreted by traditional databases or data models, which may involve a lot of text and metadata.

UPDATE SQL keyword to edit existing data in a relational database.

Update anomaly A data inconsistency that results from data redundancy, but can also occur if a record is only partially updated or if a particular field contains inappropriate null data.

Update query A query that makes a specified change to all records satisfying the criteria in the query.

User-level security A type of security where users and processes are assigned different privileges to select, insert, update, and delete data for different tables and views.

User ID A unique value that identifies each person and is often a combination of characters such as a person's name or employee number.

User interface function A database service that manages data presented to users, such as determining which form to display and how to format the form's data. Also called a *presentation function*.

User view The specific data needed by a person or process for a particular task.

Validation Rule In Access, a field property that helps eliminate unreasonable entries by establishing criteria for an entry before it is accepted into the database.

Validation Text In Access, a field property that is displayed in a dialog box if a user enters an invalid value for the field.

VALUES The SQL keyword for listing the values in parentheses and separated by commas for each of the columns (fields) in a new record being added to the table.

Variety In reference to big data, the amount of data from different sources.

VBA (Visual Basic for Applications) A programming language developed by Microsoft and provided in Office applications such as Access.

Velocity The speed at which big data is created.

View A particular collection of fields and records from one or more entities created for a particular user, program, or purpose; also called a *query*.

Virtualization To create a virtual, or not real, version of a resource.

Virtual Not physically existing but made by software to appear as real.

Visicalc The original spreadsheet program.

Visual Basic (Beginner's All-purpose Symbolic Instruction Code) A programming language introduced by Microsoft to be relatively easy to learn and use.

Volume Refers to the types of big data: traditional text and numbers plus pictures, video, sound, and behavioral data such as clicks and pauses.

W3C (World Wide Web Consortium) An international community that develops and maintains web standards including those that define HTML (HyperText Markup Language), CSS (Cascading Style Sheets), XML (Extensible Markup Language), and related web technologies.

WAMP (Windows, Apache, MySQL, PHP) A popular server-side web app development software stack that includes Windows, Apache, MySQL, and PHP.

Warm site A backup site that is equipped with duplicate hardware and software but for which current data would need to be loaded in order to function. Also called a *cold site*.

Water-cooled mainframe A computer that required cold water running through pipes installed under the floor, inside, or around the hardware cabinetry to dissipate the heat created by the electronic components.

WHERE clause The part of an SQL SELECT command that indicates the condition rows must satisfy to be displayed in the query results.

Wide column stores A database that stores data in tables with many columns.

Wildcard character In Access SQL, the asterisk (*) is used as a wildcard to represent any collection of characters, and the question mark (?) is used to represent one character.

WIMP (Windows, Internet Information Services, MySQL, PHP) A popular server-side web app development software stack that includes Windows, Internet Information Services, MySQL, and PHP.

WINS (Windows, Internet Information Services, SQL Server, .NET (C#)) A popular server-side web app development software stack that includes Windows, Internet Information Services, SQL Server, and .NET (C#).

WordPress An online, open source website creation tool written in PHP.

WordStar One of the first popular word-processing programs.

World Wide Web Consortium (W3C) An international community that develops and maintains web standards including those that define HTML (HyperText Markup Language), CSS (Cascading Style Sheets), XML (Extensible Markup Language), and related web technologies.

XML (Extensible Markup Language) A web-related specification managed by the W3C (w3.org) and designed for the exchange of data on the web.

XQuery A language for querying web-based documents and similarly structured data repositories.

XSD (Extensible Schema Definition) A file type that stores the data schema, which is a description of the table, table properties, fields, and field properties within that table.

XSL (Extensible Stylesheet Language) A file type that determines the styling and layout of the data. XSL is a standard W3C language for creating stylesheets for XML documents.

XSL Transformations (XSLT) A standard W3C language that defines the rules to process an XML document and change it into another document, such as an HTML or XHTML document.

Note: Page numbers in boldface indicate key terms.

SYMBOLS